HISTORIANS and HISTORICAL SOCIETIES IN THE PUBLIC LIFE of IMPERIAL RUSSIA

HISTORIANS AND HISTORICAL SOCIETIES IN THE PUBLIC LIFE OF IMPERIAL RUSSIA

Vera Kaplan

Indiana University Press

Bloomington and Indianapolis

This book is a publication of

Indiana University Press
Office of Scholarly Publishing
Herman B Wells Library 350
1320 East 10th Street
Bloomington, Indiana 47405 USA

iupress.indiana.edu

Manufactured in the United States of America

Cataloging information is available from the Library of Congress.

ISBN 978-0-253-02398-8 (cloth)
ISBN 978-0-253-02406-0 (ebook)

1 2 3 4 5 22 21 20 19 18 17

For my father,
and in fond memory of my mother

Contents

Acknowledgments

It is a distinct pleasure to begin this book with words of thanks to all those people and institutions who have advised, assisted, and supported me in the course of the research for this book, and during its writing.

My research was supported by the Israel Science Foundation (grant no. 134/09). Its generous funding enabled me to undertake extensive archival research, which constitutes the most fascinating part of the historian's labor. Yet, anyone who has ever visited the Russian archives knows how complicated their structure and methods of operation are. However, my work there was made pleasant and effective thanks to the assistance of my colleague from the Cummings Center of Russian and East European Studies at Tel Aviv University, Boris Morozov. As a renowned expert on Russian archives, he helped me to collect documents from the Moscow archives. Furthermore, I would never have been able to discover and explore the treasures of St. Petersburg's archives without the invaluable aid and advice of Viktor Efimovich Kelner, who shared with me his extraordinary erudition and experience. I am also deeply grateful to the staff of the Russian state and municipal archives, whose names usually remain unknown, but whose everyday efforts to fulfill researchers' requests deserve much greater appreciation. I am especially grateful to the personnel of the Department of Manuscripts of the Russian National Library, who were so kind and helpful. Special thanks are due to this Department and its head, Aleksei Ivanovich Alekseev, for permission to reproduce some photographs from its rich collection of visual sources.

I was privileged to be able to discuss the idea for this book with the late Michael Confino, from whom so many of us learned so much. My colleagues and, in various ways, academic mentors, Gabriel Gorodetsky and Avner Ben-Amos, read the first version of a project proposal in which the plan for the study was outlined; their thoughtful criticism helped me to turn my vague aspirations into a "flesh and blood" research program. The study has also benefited a great deal from my conversations and correspondence with Boris Kolonitsky, Pavel Tribunskii, Vitalii Tikhonov, Wladimir Bérélowitch, Frances Nethercott, Larry Holmes, and Ben Eklof. The members of Tel Aviv University's Department of History were very attentive and encouraging when I presented them the intermediary results of the research; their questions and suggestions made a valuable contribution to its further progress. Mark Gamsa, Igal Halfin, Yaacov Ro'i, and Oded Rabinovitch read various portions of the manuscript; their critical comments were constructive and extremely beneficial for me. Iris Rachamimov, Dina Moyal, Inna Shtakser, and Deena Leventer, with whom I have worked closely in the Cummings Center in different periods of time, were always ready to offer comfort at moments of distress and advice when necessary; their friendship has been and remains my most precious achievement. I discussed some of my ideas with my seminar students at Tel Aviv University. Their responses—frequently challenging but never indifferent—were refreshing and stimulating. Throughout the preparation of this book my devoted research assistant, Stas Tarasov, and my wonderful style editor, Philippa Shimrat, bore with me all the ups and downs of the writing. Their help and empathy made this (sometimes exhausting) process much more effective and enjoyable.

Some aspects of this study were presented in the article "From *Soslovie* to Voluntary Associations: New Patterns of Collective Identities in Late Imperial Russia," which appeared in *Cahiers du Monde russe* in 2010; I am delighted to acknowledge this journal's part in advancing my research.

I was most fortunate that Indiana University Press selected my manuscript among the plethora of submissions that this renowned publishing house regularly receives. Its editor-in-chief, Robert Sloan, found time to read the manuscript critically but carefully. His insightful recommendations, together with the thought-provoking comments of the anonymous readers, helped me to make some important finishing touches and to place my findings in a broader historical context. I appreciate their knowledge and contribution. During the final stage of the manuscript's transformation into a book, Janice Elizabeth Frish, Darja Malcolm-Clarke, and Melissa Dalton guided me through the strains and pressures of the publishing process.

Nonetheless, I would hardly have been able to complete this almost decade-long project without the support and care of my family. My uncle and aunt, Vladimir and Raisa Lebedev, cordially received me in their hospitable home in St. Petersburg, where I stayed for weeks during my archival trips there. My cousins, Lucy and Michael Rudin, welcomed me in Moscow and New York where they used to live, and where I used to visit them in search of more materials for my research. My sisters, Anna and Helena, who know the secret of how to combine raising children with a career without losing their natural joy and sense of humor, always appeared just at the moment when the problems of everyday life seemed insoluble, and resolved them by taking the difficulties upon their shoulders. My husband, Boris, whose interests lie in the spheres of music and mathematics, so different in their precision from the spontaneity and unpredictability of history, still never doubted that there is (bewildering) significance in my occupation as well. My daughter and son, Ksana and Kosta, who managed to become adult, independent, and extremely creative individuals while this book was taking shape, continue to impress me with their vigorous aspirations for new experiences and discoveries. And I owe most of all to my beloved parents, Lev and Liudmila, who have ever been the major source of light, tenderness, and inspiration for me.

Note on Transliteration

I HAVE APPLIED THE system of transliteration that is widely used in the historical scholarship and is based on ALA-LC system. In particular, the Russian vowels have been transliterated as follows:

"ю" as "iu," "я" as "ia," "ё" as "ë," "э" as "e," "ы" as "y," and "й" as "i."

The consonants are transliterated in following way:

"ж" as "zh," "х" as "kh," "ц" as "ts" and "щ" as "shch."

Apostrophe ' stands for "ь."

List of Abbreviations

AHA—the American Historical Association

ASpbII RAN—Arkhiv Sankt-Peterburgskogo instituta istorii Rossiiskoi Akademii Nauk

GARF—Gosudarstvennyi arkhiv Rossiiskoi Federatsii

IOR—*Izvestiia Obshchestva Revnitelei russkogo istoricheskogo prosveshcheniia v pamiat' imperatora Aleksandra III*

MHS—Massachusetts Historical Society

MGH—*Monumenta Germaniae Historica*

OIDR—Obshchestvo istorii i drevnostei rossiiskikh

OR RNB—Otdel rukopisei Rossiiskoi natsional'noi biblioteki

OR GTG—Otdel rukopisei Gosudarstvennoi Tret'iakovskoi galerei

ORTZ—Obshchestvo rasprostraneniia tekhnicheskikh znanii

RTO—Russkoe tekhnicheskoe obshchestvo

RGALI—Rossiiskii gosudarstvennyi arkhiv literatury i iskusstva

RGADA—Rossiiskii gosudarstvennyi arkhiv drevnikh aktov

RGIA—Rossiiskii gosudarstvennyi istoricheskii arkhiv

RIO—Russkoe istoricheskoe obshchestvo

TsGIA Spb—Tsentral'nyi gosudarstvennyi istoricheskii arkhiv Sankt-Peterburga

TsMAM LS—Tsentral'nyi moskovskii arkhiv-muzei lichnykh sobranii

ZhMNP—*Zhurnal Ministerstva Narodnogo Prosveshcheniia*

HISTORIANS AND HISTORICAL SOCIETIES IN THE PUBLIC LIFE OF IMPERIAL RUSSIA

Introduction

IT ALL BEGAN with an archival discovery. While in Russia in 2005 for the purpose of finalizing my previous research project, I was astonished to find a rich collection of practically untouched documents belonging to the formerly unknown Society of Zealots of Russian Historical Education in Memory of Alexander III, which was established in 1895 and remained active until 1918. These archival materials revealed a surprising picture. Well-known personages of the Russian past—the aristocrat Count Sergei Sheremetev, the poet Arsenii Golenishchev-Kutuzov, the former revolutionary Lev Tikhomirov, the historian Sergei Platonov, the conservative politician Dmitrii Sipiagin and the renowned orientalist Esper Ukhtomskii, as well as many other familiar figures—appeared there in unexpected roles and situations. Sheremetev turned out to be a devoted historian and the authoritarian head of this historical society; the refined lyricist Golenishchev-Kutuzov demonstrated the ability of an experienced politician as he skillfully pulled strings at the Imperial court in order to bring the society into existence, while the former *narodovolets* Tikhomirov acted as his unofficial adviser. University professors participated in an endeavor that was initiated and controlled by amateur historians; future Minister of Interior Sipiagin wrote the rules for the society's free public libraries, and the ideologist of Russian imperialist policy in the Far East, Ukhtomskii, came into conflict with other members of the society because he criticized Russification of the empire's Western regions. It was not only the personal composition of this voluntary body that aroused my curiosity. The documents revealed an intricate matrix of interconnections between state and society, far more complex than the one portrayed by the stereotypical top-down version of domination and oppression. Yet the same sources also indicated that the activity of the Society of Zealots did not bear out the assumption (generally accepted in contemporary historiography) regarding the emancipatory impulse purportedly inherent in voluntary associations per se. Its founders' worldview was essentially conservative, geared to defending Russia's type of autocracy, which, they believed, was embodied in the person and politics of Alexander III. Still, the Society of Zealots championed the principle of voluntarism, promoted the importance of associational activity, and refused to impose estate, occupation, or gender limits on its membership.

A further search in the archives and libraries of St. Petersburg and Moscow made the riddle of conservative activism even more fascinating. I found the traces of the Zealots' activity in various, sometimes unpredictable, places. While the main corpus of their documents was housed in the Russian State Historical Archive, a range of the Zealots' materials was located in a variety of places. Some were housed in the Sheremetev family collection in the Russian State Archive of Ancient Acts. A history of the society's conception was found among documents that were still waiting to be explored by researchers in the Russian State Archive of Literature and Art. Other valuable information about the society's internal life was scattered throughout collections of correspondence kept in the Pushkin House and the State Tret'iakovskaia Gallery.[1] These documents indicated that the Society of Zealots was part and parcel of the broader network of historical societies whose number continued to grow in the course of the long nineteenth century. Some of them, such as the Society for Russian History and Antiquities and numerous archeological societies, had already been in existence since the first decades of the century. A number of others, including the historical circles and societies at St. Petersburg and Moscow universities, appeared only in the 1880s. All of them, however, provided a meeting place for people belonging to different social strata and with different levels of education and ways of life but with a shared interest in history. Altogether, they constituted the focal points of a rich and dynamic historical community and served as flexible frameworks for negotiating and challenging the notion of history as a discipline: the very format of a voluntary association made it possible to discuss, interpret, and reinterpret various approaches to historical writing. Moreover, Russian historical societies were aware of and critically utilized the models and modes of functioning of various European voluntary bodies. This made them part of the broader phenomenon of the "age of associations."[2]

My quest for information about the members of the historical circles and societies led me to another kind of discovery: since the 1990s valuable documentary sources and biographical studies on prerevolutionary Russian historians have appeared in a variety of professional publications in Russia. The veteran historical journal *Voprosy istorii* (*Questions of History*) started this trend in 1991, when it launched a new section entitled "Istoriki o vremeni i o sebe" (Historians on the times and on themselves), which published diaries of prominent, but virtually forgotten historians of previous generations.[3] About a decade later new periodicals such as *Dialog so vremenem* (*Dialogue with Time*) and the annual *Istoriia i istoriki: istoriograficheskii vestnik* (*History and Historians: Historiographical News*) expanded the scope by including not only documentary materials but also research papers of a historiographic and anthropological nature.[4] In addition, an impressive number of monographs and collections of articles dealing with prerevolutionary Russian historians' scholarly heritage also appeared during these same two decades. In their endeavor to restore the scholarly reputation of history, which had been placed in doubt in the late Soviet years, post-Soviet historians paid serious attention to their predecessors' works and lives.[5] Although the issue of historians' voluntary associations was only rarely addressed in these publications—and even then, mainly in passing—they nonetheless provided prosopographic context for a study of nineteenth-century historical societies.

Further exploration of these societies' modus operandi revealed the organizational patterns and core values of educated sociability that had been inherited from the eighteenth-century societies of the educated. The attempt to answer the most basic questions—when and how the first societies of the educated emerged in Russia—led to semi-apocryphal stories about the secret Neptune Society at the court of Peter the Great and the literary and philosophical circle known as the Brotherhood of Learning, which supposedly existed in the 1720s–early 1730s and included one of the first Russian historians, Vasilii Tatishchev. The logic of this quest then required an understanding of the role of the body that was later defined as "the primary learned society of the Empire"—the Academy of Sciences. Although the Academy was established on the initiative of Peter I and continued to be both supported and controlled by all subsequent rulers of Russia, it embodied the ideal of a free association of scholars open "to new people, new ideas, and new modes of intellectual expression" that underlay the phenomenon of the early modern European academies.[6] Functioning as a state-sponsored learned society, the St. Petersburg Academy of Sciences contributed to the emergence of less formal circles of the educated that were connected to it in various ways. Moreover, it became clear that the structure and the planned (albeit never implemented) mode of functioning of its historical department served as a model for future governmental and voluntary bodies involved in historical studies. An inquiry into the various circles connected with the Academy revealed the first attempt to found a historical society, which was undertaken by educated merchants in Archangelsk in 1759, and the appearance of "free societies" (*vol'nye obshchestva*) with a general educational agenda acting under the aegis of Empress Catherine II. These were followed by the establishment of "friendly circles" of a more private nature (including the Masonic ones) dedicated to the self-cultivation of their members. Eighteenth-century historians took an active part in both kinds of voluntary bodies, which served as a venue where a new perception of knowledge in general and historical knowledge in particular was developed. Moreover, participation in such educational societies became part and parcel of an educated lifestyle and thus prepared the ground for the emergence of specialized learned societies in the nineteenth century.

Research into the eighteenth-century origins of the Russian associational movement made it possible to explore the dynamic process eventually leading to the emergence of voluntary historical societies. However, deeper examination was needed in order to understand these societies' role in the public life of their time, and, for this purpose, appropriate concepts, able to serve as analytical instruments for studying the Russian associational world, were necessary. The choice of such concepts, it became clear, was not without its own complexity.

* * *

Joseph Bradley, the author of the first monograph devoted specifically to voluntary associations in Tsarist Russia, wrote: "By the beginning of the twentieth century, Russia, not known as a nation of joiners, had by rough estimate, ten thousand voluntary associations. Private associations, sanctioned by the government, entered the public realm with a breathtaking number and variety of missions and projects. Societies were everywhere—St. Petersburg and Moscow, the capitals of non-Russian regions of the empire, the major provincial centers and even small towns."[7] Yet he also noted the paradoxical discrepancy between the "startling ubiquity of associations" and the lack of studies of this phenomenon. Indeed, for years numerous voluntary associations remained "invisible" to historical research. Until the 1990s, the very notion of voluntary associations as forms of a collective based on fellowship or comradeship that an individual joins out of choice and as "networks of people in similar situations solving similar problems and fulfilling like needs" was absent from the Russian scholars' repertoire of concepts.[8] Moreover, the majority of Western Russianists still remained under the influence of the conventional assumption that "in Russia the state was everything; civil society was primordial and gelatinous."[9] An exploration of voluntary associations as significant elements of the Russian social landscape started only in the 1990s when Russianists began to employ new methodological tools such as the concepts of the public and the public sphere. Douglas Smith's and Rafaela Faggionato's writings on Russian Masonry, Adele Lindenmeyr's works on charitable societies and her more recent research on People's Houses, A. S. Tumanova's and Lutz Häfner's publications on local voluntary associations, and I. S. Rosental's study on clubs all created an impressive picture of lively associational life.[10] The next major contribution to the subject was made by Bradley, whose study was a pioneering attempt to contextualize the topic of voluntary associations as part of a theoretical discussion on civil society in Imperial Russia.[11] There were also efforts to correlate the emerging research on associational life with the more traditional scholarship on social structures and social identities in Imperial Russia.[12]

Indeed, voluntary societies appeared in eighteenth-century Russia at a time when the system of ranks and estates (*sosloviia*) was under construction, and their emergence was closely connected with the formation of that system.[13] Free societies and assemblies (*vol'nye obshchestva i sobraniia*), followed by friendly societies (*druzheskie obshchestva*), clubs, and later, *soiuzy and kruzhki* began to proliferate from the 1780s, precisely when the estate institutions such as the district and provincial nobles' assemblies and urban corporations (*gil'dii, tsekhi, gorodskie obshchestva*) were being shaped.[14] Although encompassing only the small educated elite, these voluntary associations played a significant role in fashioning the *modus vivendi* of the new estate institutions, in particular those of the noble estate. Regardless of their particular goals, the voluntary societies became a kind of greenhouse for promoting and refining the norms of educated sociability, which became essential for the nobles. As Marc Raeff wrote, "No one who lacked a Western-type general education could in truth be considered a member of good society or (in fact if not in law) claim all the privileges of noble status."[15] Furthermore, appropriation of this type of education and the corollary mode of behavior served those who officially belonged to non-noble *sosloviia* (or fell into the interstices between legal definitions, being considered *raznochintsy*) as a ticket for entering the elite group—a cultural phenomenon that has been analyzed in particular in Catriona Kelly's study of Russia's polite culture.[16] Yet, as Marc Raeff, Iurii Lotman and Douglas Smith have demonstrated in different ways, these earlier voluntary associations' internal structures were influenced by the existing rank system.[17] Moreover, their everyday practices were based on the patronage mode of relationships, which crossed the boundaries of legally defined estates and correlated not only to the ladder of ranks but also to the patriarchal hierarchy characteristic of another powerful institution of Russian imperial society—the peasant community or *obshchina*.[18] While constituting a kind of complementary framework for legally defined estates until the mid-nineteenth century, voluntary associations became much more significant—and numerous—from the period of the Great Reforms, when Russia embarked on its transition to modernity. At this stage they became the focus of public life, providing a variety of alternatives to increasingly outdated estate institutions.

The existence of the expanding network of voluntary associations alongside legally defined estate structures might explain the flexibility, dynamism, and cultural richness of social life in Imperial Russia. The latter was described by Elise Kimerling Wirtschafter as a "society where social groupings can be understood as contiguous relationships in specific contexts and where the shifting, changeable boundaries between such groupings represented contingent moments of cohesion in response to concrete conditions and events."[19] Voluntary associations appeared to be the most dynamic element of Russia's social body and served as essential frameworks for shaping and reshaping these social groupings. But, focusing on voluntary associations in order to inquire how people changed, invented and confirmed their identities via participation in voluntary activity or, as Wirtschafter formulated it, how they "reconciled the idea of society with the reality of social experience,"[20] historians were confronted with the necessity of reconciling their theoretical concepts with the terms that the historical actors themselves used for describing their own activity—*obshchestvo* and *obshchest-vennost'*. Whilst the former was conventionally translated as "society," the latter was more difficult to interpret and was at first explained rather than translated, according to the meanings it was given in late nineteenth-century historical discourse. It was defined both as the qualities of social engagement (or, as Ben Eklof and Christine Ruane put it, "civil consciousness") and as the sector of society most likely to manifest such qualities—the intelligentsia.[21] That meaning of *obshchestvennost'* implied liberal and antistatist inclinations, as well as certain leftist and oppositionist overtones. Yet eventually the status of the term *obshchestvennost'* was changed: instead of being explained, it started to be used as an explanatory construct and, in this capacity, was employed as a suitable interpretative equivalent to the public and the public sphere. This tendency to equate "the public" and "the public sphere" with *obshchestvennost'* has become manifest since the early 2000s.[22] The sociologist Vadim Volkov was among the first scholars to write about the theoretical potential of the notion of *obshchestvennost'*, while Stefan-Ludwig Hoffmann claimed that "Russian society at the end of the tsar's empire possessed a public sphere of societal relations, described by the contemporary term *obshchestvennost'*."[23] The meaning of "the public," however, is broader than that of *obshchestvennost'*, and its semantic structure is different.

As scholarly concepts, the terms "public" and "public sphere" were introduced into English in the late 1980s with the translation of works by Reinhardt Koselleck and Jürgen Habermas.[24] The term public, which was used to translate the German "Öffentlichkeit," signified private persons, the addressees of public authorities, who eventually managed to make their concern for private interests publicly relevant. In so doing, they were transformed from being an abstract counterpart to "public authority" to being an opposition to that authority. The very ability to make private concerns publicly relevant was attributed by both authors to a distinctive social body—the bourgeoisie, although they defined the latter in different ways.[25] Therefore, Habermas described "a sphere constituted of private persons who assembled to form a public" as "the bourgeois public sphere."[26] That new public sphere, in contrast to the sphere governed by the state, issued from and belonged to the private realm. Habermas subsequently introduced the notion of "institutions of the public sphere," which referred to such voluntary associations as clubs, societies, salons, and coffee houses, and formulated their "common institutional criteria." He noted, first and foremost, the nature of their social intercourse, which, "far from presupposing the equality of status, disregarded status altogether." Second, discussions that took place in the institutions of the public sphere presupposed the public's intervention in those discursive areas that had heretofore been regarded as the preserve of the church and the state. By this process, culture (which, in the particular context of Habermas's doctrine, meant products of "high culture" such as philosophical, literary, and artistic works) was turned into a commodity available for consumption by private persons. The same process, Habermas claimed, "established the public as in principle inclusive." Such inclusivity constituted the third common feature of the new public sphere's institutions, which functioned as forums for discussions in which public opinion took shape. Eventually, he argued, it led to the appropria-tion of the state-governed public sphere "by the public of private people making use of their reason" and to the evolution of a public sphere in the political realm, where public opinion became the principal instrument of influence.[27]

A wave of criticism followed the appearance of Habermas's work in English. Paradoxically, while challenging Habermas's basic assumptions, his critics will-ingly appropriated his terminology. Geoff Eley, Anthony J. La Vopa, Dena Good-man, and Frank Trentmann pointed to the existence of "competing publics" alongside the bourgeoisie and argued that the values of civil society, attributed to the bourgeoisie, were articulated through voluntary associations by a wide spec-trum of liberal landowners, professionals, and government officials.[28] Gabriele B. Clemens revealed the cooperation between noble and bourgeois "publics" in the framework of historical societies active in nineteenth-century Germany and Italy.[29] As a result, the bourgeois character of the public sphere and its institutions was reinterpreted—through the prism of the practice of voluntary associations— as "hostility" to older principles of corporate organization, which had ascribed social place according to hereditary and legal estate.[30] Questions were raised regarding the role of the state in initiating new forms of social communication, which then laid the ground for a further consolidation of the public sphere as distinct from the state. Eventually the emphasis was shifted from rational to rela-tional aspects of the public sphere, from "disinterested reasoning" to emotional exchange and longing for moral approval. The latter, Trentmann claimed, was the primary motivation governing social relations as they took shape in clubs, societies, and lodges, whose participants were concerned "with pleasing others and being admired, not with universal principles."[31] Feminist scholarship has further expanded the study of these associations through a gendered approach, underlining the male domination of the "public sphere."[32] Postcolonial studies have drawn attention to the part played by voluntary associations in the modern-ization process and in the emergence of modern culture in non-European societ-ies and countries.[33] All these stimulating methodological arguments contributed to the eventual appropriation of "the public" and "the public sphere" as flexible general concepts—which Koselleck defined as "collective singulars," represent-ing a multitude of possible variations and concrete forms of social phenomena.[34] This development, however, makes it necessary to ask what are the consequences of reinterpreting *obshchestvennost'* as the public.

The history of the notions of *obshchestvo* and *obshchestvennost'* indi-cated a certain (albeit limited) "genetic" affinity to the concept of the public in its post-Habermasian meaning. The term *obshchestvo* gradually emerged as a definition of voluntary public activity in the course of the eighteenth cen-tury. There did not seem to be an appropriate word in Russian in the 1720s to describe this phenomenon. The awkward expression *sotsietet person* was used in the "Plan for the Establishment of the Russian Academy of Sciences" (1724) in order to describe the academy as a learned society. The word *obshchestvo* had already appeared in the lexicon of Trediakovskii and Sumarokov in 1740s,[35] but a decade later the members of the first Russian historical society were still referring to their association interchangeably as an assembly (*sobranie*), a society (*obshchestvo*), or a *klevretstvo* (derived from the word *klevret*, or adherent).[36] It was Catherine II's *Instruction* (*Nakaz*) to the Legislative Commission established in 1767 for composing a new code of laws that defined the conceptual status of the terms society (*obshchestvo*) and civil society (*grazhdanskoe obshchestvo*) through their juxtaposition to the notion of the state (*gosudarstvo*).[37] The Empress described the state as a "gathering of people who live as a society," thus relying on the classical conflation of state and society (*civitas sive societas civilis sive res publica*), but, at the same time, she consistently distinguished between the state and civic spheres and between social and political issues.[38] The *Nakaz* recognized civic and state freedom (*obshchestvennaia i gosudarstvennaia vol'nost'*), state and civic administration (*pravlenie gosudarstvennoe i grazhdanskoe*), state and civic order (*poriadok gosudarstvennyi i grazhdanskii*), and civil and state law (*pravo grazhdanskoe i gosudarstvennoe*).[39] According to the Empress's vision, an autocrat was a legislator whose persona represented both state and society and whose power was to be used to protect society, first and foremost from criminal acts. Catherine employed the term "civic" (*grazhdanskii*) to delineate the social sphere, where she located the citizen. Assigning a special role to education as the means for preventing crime and improving human nature, the Empress identified a citizen's honesty with his ability to become a useful member of society.

A more detailed explanation of the concept of society was provided by the first Russian dictionary produced by the Russian Academy in the 1790s. The dictionary suggested two definitions of the word "*obshchestvo*": first, "people, who live together under the same laws and certain rules and regulations" and second, "an estate (*soslovie*) of people; an assembly of many persons having the same intention and object." To illustrate the first meaning, it cited such phrases as "to live in society," "a man is born for society" and "a man should be useful to society," while examples of the second meaning included "a society of learned men" and "a society of merchants, industrialists, craftsmen."[40] By using the more traditional term "*soslovie*" to render one of the meanings of "*obshchestvo*," the dictionary included "society" in the set of concepts used to classify Russia's social body.

In the same years when the Russian Academy was preparing its dictionary, future historiographer Nikolai Karamzin coined the word *obshchestvennost'*, which first appeared in his *Pis'ma russkogo puteshestvennika* (*Letters of the Russian Traveler*). The *Letters*, which were written in the wake of his journey to Europe in 1789–1790, were published in installments in the *Moscow Journal* in

1791–1792 and then as a series of books in 1797–1801.[41] The new word did not stand alone; it was part of two different expressions. In the first instance it appeared in the phrase "the spirit of *obshchestvennost'*" (*dukh obshchestvennosti*), which was used with reference to Frankfurt's Jewish community and signified the solidarity and close connections among European Jews that helped them to withstand their harsh fate:

> It has long been noted that common calamity creates the tightest bonds between people. Hence the Jews too, who are persecuted by fate and oppressed by other people, are bound more tightly together than we triumphant Christians. What I mean is that there is a greater spirit of *obshchestvennost'* among Jews than among any other people.[42]

In the second instance the word appeared in a different phrase, "the wise connection of *obshchestvennost'*" (*mudraia sviaz' obshchestvennosti*), signifying a kind of network of civilization that enabled Karamzin to enjoy his stay in different countries:

> And the wise connection of *obshchestvennost'*, thanks to which I find in every land all possible comforts of life as if they had been invented specially for me; thanks to which the citizens of all countries offer me the fruits of their work, their industry and call on me to participate in their amusements and merriment.[43]

Obshchestvennost', therefore, was first used to denote various kinds of informal social connections. Karamzin may have been inspired to invent this term not only by his impressions during the journey but also as a result of his experience as a member of the Masonic Friendly Learned Society (*Druzheskoe Uchenoe Obshchestvo*) in the previous four years (1785–1789), which had made him aware of the phenomenon of such relations.

It was also during the reign of Catherine II that the term *obshchestvo*, implying in this case a private association (*chastnoe obshchestvo*), appeared as a key concept in an act of legislation. This was the Police Code (*Ustav Blagochiniia ili Politseiskii*), issued in 1782, which Marc Raeff described as a "well-known, but still inadequately studied" document of Russia's legislative thought.[44] The Code stipulated that a Police Department (*Uprava Blagochiniia*) had to protect any society (*obshchestvo*), association (*tovarishchestvo*), fraternity (*bratstvo*), or any assembly that was approved by law but would not recognize any such bodies that were not approved by law (*zakonom ne utverzhdennoe*). It also laid down that any society, association, or fraternity that caused any loss or damage to the common weal, or "was useless," would be prohibited.[45] The document referred to only one form of legal approval, namely permission by the *Uprava Blagochiniia*. The early twentieth-century scholar N. P. Anufriev assumed that Catherine envisioned two forms of authorization for voluntary associations: approval of their statutes by the monarch, which was intended for more important societies, and registration of the society in the *Uprava Blagochiniia*, which was appropriate for smaller local associations that were not obliged to submit their statutes for approval, but consequently could not enjoy the rights of a juridical body. However, the latter procedure was not implemented at that time; a similar method of authorization was introduced only in 1906 by the Temporary Rules on Societies and Associations.[46] Indeed, in the entire period from the 1782 Police Code to the 1906 Temporary Rules, there was no legislation that dealt with voluntary societies in general.[47] Nonetheless, the concept of voluntary society was employed and further developed in the legislative practice of the nineteenth century.[48]

At the same time, both *obshchestvo* and *obshestvennost'* gradually changed their meaning. Abbott Gleason has shown that in the early nineteenth century the notion of *obshchestvo* denoted a binary opposition to *narod* (the common people) and was initially characterized by a mixture of aristocratic and elitist traits, together with elements of meritocracy, devotion to enlightenment values, and a commitment to service. By the end of the nineteenth century, *obshchestvo* had undergone a process of modification and bifurcation. While it continued to refer to enlightened high society, its aristocratic component "lost its central shaping power." The new version of *obshchestvo* came to signify an intellectual rather than a social elite, one with liberal ideological inclinations.[49] Nathaniel Knight and Denis Sdvizhkov in their later studies emphasized the *obshchestvo*'s claim to represent the *narod* and suggested it prepared the ground for the later appearance of the concept of *intelligentsia*.[50] Meanwhile, in the 1830s–50s *obshchestvennost'* entered the language of literary critics and publicists in the sense of social awareness, sometimes appearing in conjunction with the new term *narodnost'*.[51] Gradually, it became used as a synonym for public opinion and from the period of the Great Reforms came to denote both the liberal oppositional stance and the intelligentsia as its bearer.[52] This concept of *obshchestvennost'* merged with a modernized version of *obshchestvo*, which became endowed with certain antistatist connotations. It also introduced a novel element of political and social activism into the notion of service, the object of which was now the people rather than the state.

This liberal paradigm of *obshchestvo* became predominant in the late nineteenth-century discourse and eventually was appropriated by the scholars who perceived Russian prerevolutionary *obshchestvo* as synonymous with the liberal intelligentsia and identified conservative social bodies with the "governmental camp."[53] Nonetheless, a careful study of the contemporary historical documents reveals that various visions of society coexisted with and challenged its liberal paradigm.[54] Furthermore, these different meanings of *obshchestvo* had a common denominator, namely a shared sense of agency in regards to the enlightenment of the Russian people.[55] Recognizing that the notion of cultural agency is implicit in the rival concepts of *obshchestvo* can serve as a starting point for exploring the societal norms that underlay the proliferation of educational (including historical) societies in the late nineteenth century and the shared context within which voluntary bodies of distinct ideological orientations operated. Hence, employing the theoretical concepts of "the public" and "the public sphere" *alongside* the "historical" perspective of *obshchestvo* seemed to be most conducive to grasping these elusive developments. The situation, however, became more complicated when it was not the concept of the public, but the notion of *obshchestvennost'*, refashioned and reinterpreted as "the public," that was applied to the study of Russian history. As a result, the new, theoretically laden *obshchestvennost'* clashed with that particularistic, "historical" perception of *obshchestvennost'* that existed in Russian nineteenth-century discourse. The results were ambivalent.

On the one hand, constructing *obshchestvennost'* as "the public" makes it possible to explore those facets of this notion that have not been conceptualized in a more "historically authentic" context. The new perspective enables us to examine the structures of *obshchestvennost'* as frameworks in which new discourses were shaped, new social experience was gained, and new norms of behavior were formed at a time when old hierarchical rules and values were undergoing serious crises and losing their relevance. The usefulness of this methodological approach is demonstrated by a collective volume *The Self-Organization of the Russian Obshchestvennost' in the Last Third of the Eighteenth–Early Twentieth Century*, whose basic postulate is that "the self-organization of the Russian *obshchestvennost'* took place in the *obshchestvennye organizatsii*—voluntary, self-governing and properly registered associations involved in socially useful (*obshchestvenno-poleznyi*) activity in such spheres as charity, scholarship, art, the transmission of cultural values (*kulturtregerstvo*), professional and social mutual aid, agriculture etc."[56] Yet, on the other hand, such an expanded interpretation of *obshchestvennost'* leads to a radical reconfiguration of its frame of reference. Considering voluntary associations as a whole, in all their multifarious forms and modes, as institutions of *obshchestvennost'* means that this notion becomes applicable to those charitable societies or leisure clubs that in fact never identified themselves as the liberal *obshchestvennost'*. The problem becomes even more acute when we deal with those politically engaged voluntary associations that satisfied the modified criteria of *obshchestvennost'* but, like the Society of Zealots, had an aggressively antiliberal agenda. The results could have been profoundly misleading. It therefore seems necessary to reconsider the conceptual overlap between *obshchestvennost'* and "the public," to restore to the former its original particularistic status, but also to retain, as far as possible, the stimulating effect of the cross-fertilization of both sets of notions.

* * *

When examined from the dual conceptual and historical perspectives, voluntary historical societies, which were involved in both scholarly and educational activity, are seen to be important institutions of the expanded public sphere. In accordance with the tradition of Russian literati since the eighteenth century, nineteenth-century historians continued to see their mission as enlightening the country. The novelty of their approach lay in the fact that taking part in voluntary educational projects now implied fulfillment of the scholar's public, rather than state, duty. When joining educational initiatives, liberal-minded scholars acted as representatives of *obshchestvennost'*, not as agents of the state. Yet the antistatist and oppositionist overtones of the notion of *obshchestvennost'* led to a reaction by those members of the "cultured class" who shared the ethos of enlightening the people but did not identify with the liberal ideals implied by that notion. The foundation of the Society of Zealots thus heralded the appearance of historical societies of a distinct nationalist and monarchist ideological profile, which strove to shape a cohesive historical narrative that would advance their ideology in response to the increasing influence of the liberal *Weltanschauung*. While resolutely distancing themselves from the group that was consensually perceived as the main bearer of *obshchestvennost'*—the liberal intelligentsia—these societies nevertheless emphasized the importance of public educational activity. A close analysis of the Society of Zealots' everyday life and its relations with governmental bodies exposed a still understudied current of voluntary activity characterized by a conservative rather than a liberal or emancipatory thrust. It also pointed to processes in which voluntary associations helped to build a pro-state, rather than an antistate, civil society. The Society of Zealots embodied this tendency of collaboration and interdependence vis-à-vis the state, which calls into question the general assumption regarding the growing gap between the ruling authorities and society in late imperial Russia. Furthermore, paradoxically, it was the conservative Society of Zealots that embodied in its activity some significant elements of modernity.

As David L. Hoffmann has suggested, modernity can be characterized—along with a belief in progress, faith in reason, the veneration of science, and the disparagement of religion and tradition—as a "rationalist ethos of progressive social intervention." Consequently, scientism, or "an effort to organize all political, social and economic relations according to scientifically determined norms," becomes its most universal trait.[57] He argues that the emergence of science as a source of political legitimization, together with the growing political influence of experts perceived as "arbiters of the public good," developed hand in hand with the rise of mass politics. This combination led to an ambiguous situation: "At the very moment when modern rationalism was destroying traditions, the demands of mass politics led to the creation of invented traditions."[58] In the case of the Zealots, while working vigorously to strengthen the image of the Russian monarchy as a traditional institution capable of facing the challenges of modernity, they tried to find a balance between scholarship and politics and experimented with different ways of creating popular history that would be accessible to the people. In so doing, they modernized contemporaneous historical discourse and contributed to inventing a tradition of monarchy based on the "Russian principles" that they sought to preserve.

Another aspect of modernity manifested in the activity of the historical societies in general was their contribution to the development of history as a profession. The role of voluntary associations as frameworks "where activists within an expanding number of occupational groups aspired to the corporal identity, social status, and, frequently, the autonomy of free professions" has already been examined by scholars of modern Russian history.[59] The studies by Nathaniel Knight, Vera Tolz, and Wladimir Bérélowitch revealed the impact of the learned societies on establishing oriental studies, ethnography, and historiography as scholarly disciplines.[60] A closer investigation of the actual membership of the historical societies and the patterns of communication between their members reveals a complex network of contacts between experts and laymen and between academic and non-academic historians, as well as the role of patronage relationships in the societies' everyday life.

Despite the different tasks that they undertook, the conflicts among them, and the fierce internal quarrels that frequently plagued them, the various voluntary historical societies constituted an important element of the developing professional community. Moreover, a detailed analysis of their practices reveals the norms and the codes of behavior that characterized the associational world of modernizing Russia as a whole. The members of these societies made a large contribution to publishing historical documents and writing books on the Russian past; they deserve that their collective life be "read" now as a meaningful source for the history of Imperial Russia.

The study of Russian historical societies in the broader context of the contemporary associational world provides an opportunity to reevaluate some longstanding but misleading tropes about the absence of civil society in Russia. It also suggests a new perspective on the process of Russian educated society's "historical awakening," which began in the eighteenth-century societies of the educated and ultimately led to the institutionalization of the historical community and to the transformation of the study of the national past into a sphere of public activity.

Notes

1. Rossiiskii gosudarstvennyi istoricheskii arkhiv (RGIA), f. 747, Obshchestvo revnitelei russkogo istoricheskogo prosveshcheniia; f. 878, S. S. Tatishchev; f. 1072, E. E. Ukhtomskii; Rossiiskii gosudarstvennyi arkhiv drevnikh aktov (RGADA), f. 1287, Sheremetevy, Lichnyi arkhiv S. D. Sheremeteva; Rossiiskii gosudarstvennyi arkhiv literatury i iskusstva (RGALI),

f. 143, Golenishchev-Kutuzov Arsenii Arkad'evich, graf (1848–1913); Otdel rukopisei Gosudarstvennoi Tret'iakovskoi galerei (OR GTG), f. 66, V. M. Vasnetsov; Rukopisnyi otdel Instituta russkoi literatury (Pushkinskii Dom) Akademii nauk (RO IRLI), f. 463, K. A. Gubastov;
Otdel rukopisei Rossiiskoi natsional'noi biblioteki (OR RNB), f. 585, S. F.Platonov.

2. The definition belongs to Karl Preusker, who wrote in 1839: "One calls the current era
the 'age of associations [*Vereine*],'" *Über öffentliche, Vereins- und Privat-Bibliottheken, so wie
andere Summlungen, Lesezirkel und verwandte Gesenstände*, 2 vols. (Leipzig, 1839–40), 2: 80;
quoted in Susan A. Crane, *Collecting and Historical Consciousness in Early Nineteenth-Century
Germany* (Ithaca and London: Cornell University Press, 2000), 81. On the development of
voluntary associations as a pan-European phenomenon, see Robert T. Anderson, "Voluntary
Associations in History," *American Anthropologist*, n.s., 73, no. 1 (Feb. 1971): 209–222; Frank
Trentmann, "Paradoxes of Civil Society," in idem, ed., *Paradoxes of Civil Society: New Perspectives on Modern German and British History* (New York and Oxford: Berghahn Books, 2000),
3–46. Stefan-Ludwig Hoffmann, "Democracy and Associations in the Long Nineteenth Century: Toward a Transnational Perspective," *Journal of Modern History* 75, no. 2 (June 2003):
269–299. For voluntary associations in different national contexts see: R. J. Morris, "Voluntary
Societies and British Urban Elites, 1780–1850," *Historical Journal* 26, no. 1 (Mar. 1983): 95–119;
idem, "Clubs, Societies and Associations" in F. M. L. Thompson, ed., *The Cambridge Social
History of Britain, 1750–1950* (Cambridge: Cambridge University Press, 1990), 3: 403–443; Peter
Clark, *British Clubs and Societies, 1580–1800: The Origins of an Associational World* (Oxford:
Clarendon, 2000); David Blackbourn, "The Discreet Charm of the Bourgeoisie," in idem and
Geoff Eley, eds., *The Peculiarities of German History* (Oxford: Oxford University Press, 1984),
159–292; James Van Horn Melton, "The Emergence of 'Society' in Eighteenth- and Nineteenth-
Century Germany" in Penelope J. Corfield, ed., *Language, History and Class* (Cambridge, MA:
Basil Blackwell, 1991), 132–149; Gerald Gamm and Robert D. Putnam, "The Growth of Volun-
tary Associations in America, 1840–1940," *Journal of Interdisciplinary History* 29, no. 4 (Spring
1999): 511–537.

3. Iu. V. Got'e, "Moi zametki," *Voprosy istorii*, no. 6: 150–175; no. 7–8: 164–190; no. 9–10:
160–185; no. 11: 150–177; no. 12: 137–164 (1991); no. 1: 119–138; no. 2–3: 146–161; no. 4–5: 107–118;
no. 11–12: 124–160 (1992); no. 1: 72–87; no. 2: 139–155; no. 3: 157–176; no. 4: 78–99; 5: no. 151–167
(1993); A. A. Kornilov, "Vospominaniia," ibid., no. 2: 143–159; no. 3: 120–139; no. 4: 136–149; no.
5: 106–124; no. 7: 126–152; no. 8; 108–128; no. 9: 112–122; no. 10: 122–134 (1994); S. B. Veselovskii,
"Dnevniki 1915–1923, 1944," ibid., no. 2: 69–83; no. 3, 84–110; no. 6: 93–11; no. 8: 86–109; no. 9:
114–133; no. 10: 113–140; no. 11–12: 59–77 (2000); no. 2 (2001): 69–83. In addition, the journal
published excerpts from the memoirs of Georgii (George) Vernadskii. See G. V. Vernadskii,
"Iz vospominanii," *Voprosy istorii*, no. 3 (1995): 79–103.

4. *Istoriia i istoriki: istoriographicheskii vestnik* has been issued annually since 2001; *Dialog so vremenem* was established in 1999 and in 2001 became an organ of the Russian Society
of Intellectual History (ROII). The society, which operates in thirty-six regions of the Russian
Federation, launched a series of conferences devoted to history as a profession that have been
held in various provincial universities. For example, in 2009 a conference on "The Community
of Historians of Russia's Institutions for Higher Education: Scholarly Practice and Educational
Mission," took place at Kazan' University. See *Soobshchestvo istorikov vysshei shkoly Rossii:
Nauchnaia praktika i obrazovatel'naia missiia: Vserossiiskaia nauchnaia konferentsiia*: Programma i priglashenie (Kazan': ROII - Institut vseobshchei istorii RAN - Kazanskii gosudarstvennyi universitet et al., 2009). In 2011 a conference on "History and Historians in the Space
of National and World Culture of the Eighteenth-Early Twenty-First Centuries" was held by
Cheliabinsk University. In 2012 a conference "Historical Scholarship and Education in Russia
and at the West: The Fates of Historians and Scientific Schools: on the 175th Anniversary of

the Birth of Vladimir Ivanovich Ger'e" took place in Moscow. The material associated with these conferences was published in *Dialog so vremenem* and issued as collections of articles. See L. P. Repina (ed.), *Soobshchestvo istorikov vysshei shkoly Rossii: Nauchnaia praktika i obrazovatel'naia missiia* (Moscow: IVI RAN, 2009); N. N. Alevras, N. V. Grishina and Iu. V. Krasnova (eds.), *Istoriia i istoriki v prostranstve natsional'noi i mirovoi kul'tury XVIII–XIX vekov* (Cheliabinsk: Entsiklopediia, 2011); L. P. Repina (ed.), *Istoricheskaia nauka i obrazovanie v Rossii i na Zapade: Sud'by istorikov i nauchnykh shkol* (Moscow: IVI RAN, 2012).

5. B. B. Kobrin, K. A. Aver'ianov, *S. B. Veselovskii: Zhizn', Deiatel'nost', Lichnost'* (Moscow: Nauka, 1989); A. M. Dubrovskii, *S. V. Bakhrushin i ego vremia* (Moscow: Izdatel'stvo Rossiiskogo Universiteta Druzhby Narodov, 1992); A. N. Sakharov, ed., *Istoriki Rossii XVIII-nachalo XX veka* (Moscow: Skriptorii, 1996); S. N. Pogodin, *Russkaia shkola istorikov: N. I. Kareev, I. V. Luchitskii, M. M. Kovalevskii* (St. Petersburg: SPbGTU, 1997); G. N. Sevast'ianov, L. P. Marinovich and L. T. Mil'skaia, eds., *Portrety istorikov: Vremia i sud'by*, in two volumes (Moscow-Jerusalem: Universitetskaia kniga-Gesharim, 2000); V. M. Paneiakh, *Tvorchestvo i sud'ba istorika: Boris Aleksandrovich Romanov* (St. Petersburg: Dmitrii Bulanin, 2000); A. A. Preobrazhenskii, *Istorik ob istorikakh Rossii XX stoletiia* (Moscow: Russkoe slovo, 2000); G. P. Miagkov, *Nauchnoe soobshchestvo v istoricheskoi nauke: Opyt "Russkoi istoricheskoi shkoly"* (Kazan': Izdatel'stvo Kazanskogo Universiteta, 2000); A. V. Malinov, S. N. Pogodin, *Aleksandr Lappo-Danilevskii: istorik i filosof* (St. Petersburg: Iskusstvo-Spb, 2001); S. O. Shmidt, ed. *Akademik S. F. Platonov: perepiska s istorikami* (Moscow: Nauka, 2003); A. N. Shakhanov, *Russkaia istoricheskaia nauka vtoroi poloviny XIX- nachala XX veka: Moskovskii i Peterburgskii Universitety* (Moscow: Nauka, 2003); V. A. Berdinskikh, *Uezdnye istoriki: Russkaia provintsial'naia istoriografiia* (Moscow: Novoe literaturnoe obozrenie, 2003); A. V. Sveshnikov, V. P. Korzun, M. A. Mamontova, eds., *Pis'ma russkikh istorikov: S. F. Platonov, P. N. Miliukov* (Omsk: Poligrafist, 2003); E. A. Rostovtsev, *A. S. Lappo-Danilevskii i peterburgskaia istoricheskaia shkola* (Riazan': NRIID, 2004); O. B. Vakhromeeva, *Chelovek s otkrytym serdtsem: Avtobiograficheskoe i epistoliarnoe nasledie I. M. Grevsa* (St. Petersburg, ID SPbGU, 2004); A. N. Tsamutali, ed., *Aleksandr Evgen'evich Presniakov: Pis'ma i dnevniki, 1889–1927* (St. Petersburg: IISPb RAN and Dmitrii Bulanin, 2005); V. V. Boiarchenkov, *Istoriki-federalisty: Kontseptsiia mestnoi istorii v russkoi mysli 20kh-70kh godov XIX veka* (St. Petersburg: Dmitrii Bulanin, 2005); B.S. Kaganovich, *Russkie medievisty pervoi poloviny XX veka* (St. Petersburg: Giperion, 2007); P. A. Tribunskii, "Perepiska A. S. Lappo-Danilevskogo i P. N. Miliukova," *Journal of Modern Russian History and Historiography*, no. 3 (2010): 77–160; D. A. Tsygankov, *Professor V. I. Ger'e i ego ucheniki* (Moscow: ROSSPEN, 2010); A. Iu. Dvornichenko and S. O. Shmidt, eds., *Pamiati akademika Sergeia Fedorovicha Platonova: Issledovaniia i materialy* (St. Petersburg: St. Petersburg State University and OIFN RAN, 2011); A. V. Makushin, P. A. Tribunskii, eds., *Perepiska P. N. Miliukova i S.F. Platonova, 1886–1901* (Moscow: Feoriia, 2011); O. M. Beliaeva, *Ervin Davidovich Grimm v Peterburgskom universitete: akademicheskoe soobshchestvo pozdneimperskogo perioda* (PhD diss., Institute of History of the Russian Academy of Sciences, St. Petersburg, 2011); V. V. Tikhonov, *Moskovskaia istoricheskaia shkola v pervoi polovine dvadtsatogo veka: Nauchnoe tvorchestvo Iu. V. Got'e, S. B. Veselovskogo, A. I. Iakovleva, S. V. Bakhrushina* (Moscow-St. Petersburg: Nestor-Istoriia, 2012). A significant contribution has been made by historians from the universities of Voronezh (V. I. Chesnokov, *Pravitel'stvennaia politika i istoricheskaia nauka Rossii 60kh-70kh godov XIX v.: Issledovatel'skie ocherki* [Voronezh: Voronezhskii gosudarstvennyi universitet, 1989]), Riazan' (A. V. Makushin, P. A. Tribunskii, *Pavel Nikolaevich Miliukov: Trudy i dni (1859–1904)* [Riazan', 2001]) and, especially, Omsk. Here V. P. Korzun, A. V. Sveshnikov and their students not only write extensively on phenomenological aspects of historians' professional life (especially interesting are V. P. Korzun, *Obrazy istoricheskoi nauki na rubezhe XIX–XX vv.: analiz otechestvennykh istoriograficheskikh*

kontseptsii [Ekaterinburg-Omsk: Omskii gosudarstvennyi universitet, 2000], and A. V. Sveshnikov, *Peterburgskaia shkola medievistov nachala XX veka: Popytka antropologicheskogo analiza nauchnogo soobshchestva* [Omsk: Omskii gosudarstvennyi universitet, 2010]), but also, since 2005, have been issuing their own annual historiographic anthology, *The World of the Historian* (*Mir istorika*). In addition both central and provincial universities have organized "biographical" conferences focused on a particular historian while exploring different aspects of his activity; one of the most significant of such events was devoted to Alexander Lappo-Danilevskii ("Akademik A. S. Lappo-Danilevskii v istorii nauki i kul'tury [k 150-iu so dnia rozhdeniia: mezhdunarodnaiia nauchnaia konferentsiia]") and was held by St. Petersburg University (in cooperation with a number of the Academy of Sciences' research centers) in October 2013. Frances Nethercott's review essay "Reevaluating Russian Historical Culture," *Kritika: Explorations in Russian and Eurasian History* 15, no. 2 (Spring 2014): 421–439, offers an insightful analysis of the study of historical scholarship in early twenty-first century Russia.

    6. Ian F. McNeely, "The Renaissance Academies between Science and the Humanities," *Configurations*, 17, no. 3 (Fall 2009): 227–258, here 228. On early modern academies see also Frances Yates, *The French Academies of the Sixteenth Century* (London: Warburg Institute, 1947); Steven Shapin, "The House of Experiment in Seventeenth-Century England," *Isis* 79, no. 3 (special issue on *Artifact and Experiment*): 373–404; David Chambers and François Quiviger, eds., *Italian Academies of the Sixteenth Century* (London: Warburg Institute, 1995), 1–14; Mario Biagioli, "Etiquette, Interdependence, and Sociability in Seventeenth-Century Science," *Critical Inquiry* 22 (1996): 193–238; Lorraine Daston, "The Academies and the Unity of Knowledge: The Disciplining of the Disciplines," *Differences* 10, no. 2 (1999): 67–86 and Stephen Gaukroger, "The Académie des Sciences and the Republic of Letters: Fontenelle's Role in the Shaping of a New Natural-Philosophical Persona, 1699–1734," *Intellectual History Review* 18 no. 3, Special Issue: *The Persona of the Philosopher in the Eighteenth Century* (2008): 385–402.

    7. Joseph Bradley, *Voluntary Associations in Tsarist Russia: Science, Patriotism and Civil Society* (Cambridge, MA: Harvard University Press, 2009), 2.

    8. R. J. Morris, "Clubs, Societies and Associations," in *The Cambridge Social History of Britain, 1750–1950*, edited by F. M. L. Thompson, vol. 3: *Social Agencies and Institutions* (Cambridge: Cambridge University Press, 1990), 403–443, here 414. For a sociological definition of voluntary associations see David L. Sills, "Voluntary Associations: Sociological Aspects" in *International Encyclopedia of the Social Sciences*, vol. 16 (New York, Macmillan and Free Press, 1968), 363–379; Constance Smith and Anne Freedman, *Voluntary Associations: Perspective on the Literature* (Cambridge, MA: Harvard University Press, 1972). In the early 1980s a Soviet historian, A. D. Stepanskii, made an attempt to conceptualize the phenomenon of "voluntary organizations" (*obshchestvennye organizatsii*), defining them as "voluntary, self-governing, and officially registered associations of citizens that act on a regular basis in order to achieve certain political, socio-economic, and cultural goals of a non-commercial nature." See his *Obshchestvennye organizatsii v Rossii na rubezhe XIX–XX vv.* (Moscow: Moskovskii gosudarstvennyi istoriko-arkhivnyi institut, 1982), 5. However, Stepanskii and his successors, prominent historians of the next generation, I. N. Il'ina and A. S. Tumanova (in her early works), placed an emphasis on the state legislation and state policy towards voluntary organizations, while largely neglecting the internal life and dynamics of such organizations. See I. N. Il'ina, *Obshchestvennye organizatsii Rossii v 1920-e gody* (Moscow: Rossiiskaia Akademiia Nauk, Institut rossiiskoi istorii, 2001); A. S. Tumanova, *Samoderzhavie i obshchestvennye organizatsii v Rossii: 1905–1917* (Tambov: Tambovskii gosudarstvennyi universitet imeni G. R. Derzhavina, 2002).

    9. This catch-phrase was coined by Antonio Gramsci in 1920s in his *Prison Notebooks* and has been quoted widely in the works devoted to the problem of civil society in Tsarist Russia.

See Adele Lindenmeyr, "'Primordial and Gelatinous?': Civil Society in Imperial Russia," *Kritika: Explorations in Russian and Eurasian History*, 12, no. 3 (Summer 2011): 705–720, here 707.

10. Douglas Smith, *Working the Rough Stone: Freemasonry and Society in Eighteenth-Century Russia* (DeKalb: Northern Illinois University Press, 1999); Douglas Smith, "Freemasonry and the Public in Eighteenth-Century Russia," in Jane Burbank and David L. Ransel eds., *Imperial Russia: New Histories for the Empire* (Bloomington: Indiana University Press, 1998), 281–304; Raffaella Faggionato, *A Rosicrucian Utopia in Eighteenth-Century Russia: The Masonic Circle of N. I. Novikov* (Springer, 2005); Adele Lindenmeyr, "Voluntary Associations and the Russian Autocracy: The Case of Private Charity," *The Carl Beck Papers in Russian and East European Studies*, no. 807 (1990); idem, "The Rise of Voluntary Associations During the Great Reforms: The Case of Charity," in Ben Eklof, John Bushnell, and Larissa Zakharova, eds., *Russia's Great Reforms, 1855–1881* (Bloomington: Indiana University Press, 1994), 264–279; idem, *Poverty Is Not a Vice: Charity, Society and the State in Imperial Russia* (Princeton: Princeton University Press, 1996); idem., "Building Civil Society One Brick at a Time: People's Houses and Worker Enlightenment in Late Imperial Russia," *Journal of Modern History* 84, no. 1 (Mar. 2012): 1–39; A. S. Tumanova, *Obshchestvennye organizatsii g. Tambova na rubezhe XIX-XX vekov (1900–1917 gg.)* (Tambov: Tambovskii gosudarstvennyi universitet imeni G. R. Derzhavina, 1999); Lutz Häfner, "'The Temple of Idleness': Associations and the Public Sphere in Provincial Russia," in Susan P. McCaffray and Michael Melancon, eds., *Russia in the European Context 1789–1914: A Member of the Family* (Palgrave: Macmillan, 2005), 141–160; I. S. Rozental', *"I vot obshchestvennoe mnenie!" Kluby v istorii rossiiskoi obshchestvennosti, konets XVIII-nachalo XX vv.* (Moscow: Novyi khronograf, 2007).

11. Bradley, *Voluntary Associations in Tsarist Russia*. See also his earlier articles: "Subjects into Citizens: Societies, Civil Society and Autocracy in Tsarist Russia," *American Historical Review* 107, no. 4 (Oct. 2002): 1094–1123; "Voluntary Associations, Civic Culture and *Obshchestvennost'* in Moscow," in Edith W. Clowes, Samuel D. Kassow and James L. West, eds., *Educated Society and the Quest for Public Identity* (Princeton: Princeton University Press, 1991), 131–148; "Merchant Moscow after Hours: Voluntary Associations and Leisure," in James L. West and Iurii A. Petrov, eds., *Merchant Moscow: Images of Russia's Vanished Bourgeoisie* (Princeton: Princeton University Press, 1998), 133–143; "Russia's Parliament of Public Opinion: Association, Assembly, and the Autocracy, 1906–1914," in Theodore Taranovski, ed., *Reform in Modern Russian History: Progress or Cycle?* (Cambridge: Woodrow Wilson Center Press and Cambridge University Press: 1995), 212–236. For a useful survey of the notion of civil society and its application to Russian imperial history, see David Wartenweiler, *Civil Society and Academic Debate in Russia, 1905–1914* (Oxford: Clarendon, 1999); Christopher Ely, "The Question of Civil Society in Late Imperial Russia," in Abbott Gleason, ed., *A Companion to Russian History* (Chichester, U.K.; Malden, MA: Wiley Blackwell, 2009), 225–242; Wayne Dowler, *Russia in 1913* (DeKalb: Northern Illinois University Press: 2010), 90–140; and Lindenmeyr, "'Primordial and Gelatinous?,'" 705–720.

12. E. Iu. Kazakova-Apkarimova, *Formirovanie grazhdanskogo obshchestva: Gorodskie soslovnye korporatsii i obshchestvennye organizatsii na Srednem Urale* (Ekaterinburg: RAN, Ural'skoe otdelenie, Institut istorii i arkheologii, 2008); Vera Kaplan, "From *Soslovie* to Voluntary Associations: New Patterns of Collective Identities in Late Imperial Russia," *Cahiers du Monde russe*, 51, no. 2–3 (2010): 369–396; V. Ia. Grosul, "Rossiiskaia obshchestvennost' XVIII-XX vv. Osnovnye etapy stanovleniia i uchrezhdeniia," in A. S. Tumanova, ed., *Samoorganizatsiia rossiiskoi obshchestvennosti v poslednei treti XVIII- nachale XX vv.* (Moscow: ROSSPEN, 2011), 28–165; S. V. Liubichankovskii, *Formation and Development of Informal Associations of the Ural's Provincial Officials at the End of the 19th Century and the Beginning of the 20th Century* (Lewiston-New York: Edwin Mellen, 2014).

13. The literature on *sosloviia* is extensive, but there are a number of important works devoted mainly to the concept. A fundamental work is V. O. Kliuchevskii's "Istoriia soslovii v Rossii," in idem, *Sochineniia*, vol. 6: *Spetsial'nye kursy* (Moscow: Izdatel'stvo sotsial'no-ekonomicheskoi literatury, 1959), 276–466. In the 1980s the discussion on *soslovie* as a paradigm of historical research was begun by Gregory L. Freeze, "The Soslovie (Estate) Paradigm and Russian Social History," *American Historical Review* 91, no. 1 (February 1986): 11–36; it was developed further by Abbott Gleason, "The Terms of Russian Social History," and Alfred J. Riber, "The Sedimentary Society," in Clowes, Kassow and West, eds., *Between Tsar and People*, 15–27 and 343–366; by Boris Mironov, *A Social History of Imperial Russia, 1700–1917*, vol. 2 (Boulder, Colorado: Westview, 2000), especially the chapter "Social Structure and Social Mobility," 197–285; and, more thoroughly, in the works of Elise Kimerling Wirtschafter: *Structures of Society: Imperial Russia's "People of Various Ranks"* (Dekalb: Northern Illinois University Press, 1994); *Social Identity in Imperial Russia* (Dekalb: Northern Illinois University Press, 1997); "The Groups between: Raznochintsy, Intelligentsia, Professionals," in *The Cambridge History of Russia*, vol. 2 (Cambridge: Cambridge University Press, 2006), 245–263; and Alison K. Smith, *For the Common Good and Their Own Well-Being: Social Estates in Imperial Russia* (Oxford: Oxford University Press, 2014). A new stage in the discussion was stimulated by Michael Confino, "The Soslovie (Estate) Paradigm: Reflections on Some Open Questions," *Cahiers du Monde russe* 49, no. 4 (Oct.–Dec. 2008): 681–700, followed by Wirtschafter's article in the next issue of the same journal, "Social Categories in Russian Imperial History," *Cahiers du Monde russe* 50, no. 1 (Jan.–Mar. 2009): 231–250, and by a special issue devoted to "Social and Legal Classifications in the Russian Empire," *Cahiers du Monde russe*, 51, no. 2–3 (Apr.–Sept. 2010).

14. Mironov, *A Social History of Imperial Russia, 1700–1917*, 2: 206, 234.

15. Marc Raeff, *Origins of the Russian Intelligentsia: The Eighteenth-Century Nobility* (New York: Harcourt, Brace & World, 1966), 145.

16. Catriona Kelly, *Refining Russia: Advice Literature, Polite Culture, and Gender from Catherine to Yeltsin* (Oxford: Oxford University Press, 2001).

17. Raeff, *Origins of the Russian Intelligentsia*; idem, "At the Origins of a Russian National Consciousness: Eighteenth Century Roots and Napoleonic Wars," *The History Teacher* 25, no. 1 (Nov. 1991): 7–18; Iu. M. Lotman, "Ocherki po istorii russkoi kul'tury XVIII-nachala XIX veka," in A. D. Koshelev, ed., *Iz istorii russkoi kul'tury*, vol. 4, *XVIII-nachalo XIX veka* (Moscow: Iazyki russkoi kul'tury, 2000), 13–346; Smith, *Working the Rough Stone*.

18. Geoffrey A. Hosking, "Patronage and the Russian State," *Slavonic and East European Review* 78 (Apr. 2000): 301–320; Colum Leckey, "Patronage and Public Culture in the Russian Free Economic Society, 1765–1796," *Slavic Review* 64, no. 2 (Summer 2005): 355–379; David L. Ransel, "Character and Style of Patron-Client Relations in Russia," in Antoni Maczak and Elisabeth Mueller-Leuckner, eds., *Klientelsysteme im Europa der Frühen Neuzeit* (Munich: R. Oldenbourg Verlag, 1988), 214–224; György Péteri, ed. *Patronage, Personal Networks and the Party-State: Everyday Life in the Cultural Sphere in Communist Russia and East Central Europe*, special issue of *Contemporary European History* 11, no. 1 (Feb. 2002).

19. Wirtschafter, *Social Identity in Imperial Russia*, 98.

20. Wirtschafter, "Social Categories in Russian Imperial History," 249.

21. Catriona Kelly and Vadim Volkov, "Obshchestvennost', Sobornost': Collective Identities," in Catriona Kelly and David Shepherd, eds., *Constructing Russian Culture in the Age of Revolution, 1881–1940* (Oxford: Oxford University Press, 1998); Abbot Gleason, "The Terms of Russian Social History," in Clowes, Kassow and West, eds., *Between Tsar and People*, 15–27; Christine Ruane and Ben Eklof, "Cultural Pioneers and Professionals: The Teachers in Society," in ibid., 199–211, here 199; Alice K. Pate, "Workers and *Obshchestvnnost'*: St Petersburg,

1906–14," *Revolutionary Russia* 15, no. 2 (Dec. 2002): 53–71; Tsuyoshi Hasegawa, "Gosudarstven-nost', Obshchestvennost', and Klassovost': Crime, the Police, and the State in Russian Revolution in Petrograd," *Canadian-American Slavic Studies* 35, nos. 2–3 (Summer-Fall 2001): 157–188.

22. Lutz Häfner, "Civil Society, Bürgertum, and 'Local Society': In Search for Analytical Categories for Studies of Public and Social Modernization in Late Imperial Russia," *Ab Imperio*, no. 3 (2002): 161–208, and M. Khil'dermaier, "Obshchestvo i obshchestvennost' na zakate tsarskoi imperii: Nekotorye razmyshleniia o novykh problemakh i metodakh" in *Stranitsy rossiiskoi istorii: Problemy, sobytiia, liudi. Sbornik statei v chest' B. V. Anan'icha* (St. Petersburg, 2003), 217–221, are especially representative of this tendency. Michael David-Fox's review of I. N. Il'ina, *Obshchestvennye organizatsii Rossii v 1920-e gody*, published in *Kritika: Explorations in Russian and Eurasian History* 3, no. 1 (2002): 173–181, is useful for analyzing the question of the translation and conceptualization of *obshchestvennost'*.

23. Vadim Volkov, "Obshchestvennost': Russia's Lost Concept of Civil Society," in Norbert Götz and Vörg Hackmann, eds., *Civil Society in the Baltic Sea Region* (Aldershot: Ashgate, 2003), 63–82; Stefan-Ludwig Hoffmann, "Democracy and Associations in the Long Nineteenth Century: Toward a Transnational Perspective," *Journal of Modern History* 75, no. 2 (June 2003): 290.

24. Reinhart Koselleck, *Critique and Crisis: Enlightenment and the Pathogenesis of Modern Society* (Cambridge, MA: MIT Press, 1988); Jürgen Habermas, *The Structural Transformation of the Public Sphere: An Inquiry into a Category of Bourgeois Society* (Cambridge, MA: MIT Press, 1989).

25. Koselleck adopted the concept of *Bürgertum* (translated into English as "bourgeoisie" or "bourgeois intelligentsia") for definition of that social class, or stratum, which constituted itself as the public by means of associations. This public was composed of groups that enjoyed social and cultural acceptance as well as economic power, though they were politically powerless vis-à-vis the state. This list included nobles who demanded autonomy from the absolutist monarchy, émigrés forced to leave their countries and move to other parts of the "European universe" (including America), merchants and financiers, and, last but not least, philosophers of the Enlightenment. It was their shared condition of political isolation that brought these highly varied groups together, Koselleck argued; see idem, *Critique and Crisis*, 72–75. When Habermas assigned the central position within the "public" to a new stratum of the "bourgeoisie," he meant, first and foremost, the "capitalists"—the merchants, bankers, entrepreneurs, and manufacturers who were associated with the process of capitalist trade and production as property owners dependent on the market and who enjoyed a private standing vis-à-vis public authority. Significantly, Habermas added education (*Bildung*) as a distinguishing characteristic of this group. The bourgeoisie, he emphasized, "from the outset was a reading public." Habermas, *The Structural Transformation of the Public Sphere*, 11–19.

26. Habermas, *The Structural Transformation of the Public Sphere*, 27.

27. Ibid., 37–43; 51.

28. Geoff Eley, "Nations, Politics, and Political Cultures: Placing Habermas in the Nineteenth Century," in Craig Calhoun, ed., *Habermas and the Public Sphere* (Cambridge, MA: MIT Press, 1992), 289–339; Anthony J. LaVopa, "Conceiving a Public: Ideas and Society in Eighteenth-Century Europe," *Journal of Modern History* 64, no. 1 (Mar. 1992): 79–116, especially 92–98; Dena Goodman, "Public Sphere and Private Life: Toward a Synthesis of Current Historiographical Approaches to the Old Regime," *History and Theory* 31, no. 1 (Feb. 1992): 1–20; Frank Trentmann, ed., *Paradoxes of Civil Society: New Perspectives on Modern German and British History*.

29. Gabriele B. Clemens, "Ancestors, Castles, Tradition: The German and Italian Nobility and the Discovery of the Middle Ages in the Nineteenth Century," *Journal of Modern Italian Studies* 8, no. 1 (2003): 1–15.

30. Eley, "Nations, Politics, and Political Cultures: Placing Habermas in the Nineteenth Century," 298.

31. Trentmann, "Paradoxes of Civil Society," 8–11, 25–27.

32. Belinda Davis, "Reconsidering Habermas, Gender and the Public Sphere: The Case of Wilhelmine Germany, " in Geoff Eley, ed., *Society, Culture, and the State in Germany, 1870–1930* (Ann Arbor: University of Michigan Press, 1996), 397–426; Elisabeth Clemens, "Securing Political Returns to Social Capital: Women's Associations in the United States, 1880s–1920s," *Journal of Interdisciplinary History* 29, no. 4 (Spring 1999): 613–638; Anna Firor Scott, *Natural Allies: Women's Associations in American History* (Urbana: University of Illinois Press, 1993); Joanne Landes, *Women and the Public Sphere in the Age of the French Revolution* (Ithaca: Cornell University Press, 1988); Morag Bell and Cheryl McEwan, "The Admission of Women Fellows to the Royal Geographical Society, 1892–1914: The Controversy and the Outcome," *Geographical Journal* 162, no. 3 (November 1996): 295–312.

33. Partha Chatterjee, "On Civil and Political Society in Post-Colonial Democracies," in Sudipta Kaviraj and Sunil Khilnani, eds., *Civil Society: History and Possibilities* (Cambridge: Cambridge University Press, 2001), 165–178.

34. Reinhart Koselleck, "Historical Criteria of the Modern Concept of Revolution," in idem, *Futures Past: On the Semantics of Historical Time* (Cambridge, MA: MIT Press, 1985), 40, 46–47.

35. D. A. Sdvizhkov, "Ot obshchestva k intelligentsii: Istoriia poniatii kak istoriia samosoznaniia" in Aleksei Miller, Denis Sdvizhkov and Ingrid Shirle, eds., *Poniatiia o Rossii: K istoricheskoi semantike imperskogo perioda*, vol. 1 (Moscow: Novoe literaturnoe obozrenie, 2012), 382–427, here 386–387.

36. V. V. Krestinin, *Kratkaia istoriia o gorode Arkhangel'skom* (St. Petersburg: pri Imperatorskoi Akademii Nauk, 1792), 155, 243, 245; A. A. Ivanova, "V. V. Krestinin, Osnovatel' pervogo chastnogo istoricheskogo obshchestva," *Nasha starina* (St. Petersburg), no. 11 (1916), 778; A. A. Kizevetter, *Istoricheskie ocherki* (Moscow: n.p., 1912), 100–118.

37. "Nakaz Komissii o sostavlenii proekta novogo Ulozheniia," clause 250, *Polnoe sobranie sochinenii imperatritsy Ekateriny II*, vol. 1 (St. Petersburg: Izdanie knizhnogo sklada "Rodina," 1893), 5–84, clauses 2, 36, 37, 41, 110, 78, 92, 110, 148, 149, 210, 228, 229, 250, 356, 574, 648. For the history of the concept of state see M. M. Krom, "Rozhdenie 'gosudarstva': Iz istorii moskovskogo politicheskogo diskursa XVI veka," in N. E. Koposov, ed., *Istoricheskie poniatiia i politicheskie idei v Rossii XVI–XX veka* (St. Petersburg: EUSP Press/Aletheia, 2006), 54–69.

38. "Nakaz," clause 37, p. 8. On theoretical approaches to the concepts of state and society that existed in the eighteenth century see Trentmann, "Paradoxes of Civil Society," 6–7, and Van Horn Melton, "The Emergence of 'Society,'" 132–149.

39. "Nakaz," clause 36, 8; clause 92, 15; clause 409, 59; clause 410, 59.

40. *Slovar' Akademii Rossiiskoi*, part IV (St. Petersburg, pri Imperatorskoi Akademii Nauk, 1793), stolbets 601.

41. N. M. Karamzin, *Pis'ma russkogo puteshestvennika*, chasti 1–3 (Moscow: Universitetskaia tipografiia Khr. Ridigera i Kh. Klaudia, 1797); chasti 4–6 (Moscow: Universitetskaia tipografiia Khr. Ridigera i Kh. Klaudia, 1801).

42. N. M. Karamzin, "Pis'ma russkogo puteshestvennika," in idem, *Izbrannye sochineniia v 2-kh tomakh* (Moscow-Leningrad: Khudozhestvennaia literatura, 1964), 1: 194.

43. Ibid., 201.

44. Marc Raeff, "The Well-Ordered Police State and the Development of Modernity in Seventeenth- and Eighteenth-Century Europe: An Attempt at a Comparative Approach," *American Historical Review* 80, no. 5 (Dec. 1975): 1236.

45. "Ustav Blagochiniia ili Politseiskii, 15.379, Aprelia 8, [1782]" in M. M. Speranskii, ed., *Polnoe sobranie zakonov Rossiiskoi Imperii*, vol. 21 (St. Petersburg: Tipografiia II Otdeleniia Sobstvennoi Ego Imperatorskogo Velichestva Kantseliarii, 1830), 461–488, here 467, clauses 64, 65. Some of these clauses are cited in K. A. Papmehl, "The Empress and 'Un Fanatique': A Review of the Circumstances Leading to the Governmental Action against Novikov in 1792," *Slavonic and East European Review* 68, no. 4 (1990): 665–691.

46. Nikolai Anufriev, "Pravitel'stvennaia reglamentatsiia obrazovaniia chastnykh obshchestv v Rossii," in A. I. Elistratov, ed., *Voprosy administrativnogo prava*, book 1 (Moscow: 1916), 15–44: 17–18; "Vremennye pravila ob obshchestvakh i soiuzakh: Vysochaishii ukaz 4 marta 1906 g," in A. S. Tumanova, *Samoderzhavie i obshchestvennye organizatsii v Rossii 1905–1917 gody* (Tambov: Tambovskii gosudarstvennyi universitet imeni G. R. Derzhavina, 2002), Appendix I, 440–447.

47. Anufriev, "Pravitel'stvennaia reglamentatsiia," 17–18; Tumanova, *Samoderzhavie i obshchestvennye organizatsii*, 13.

48. A. S. Tumanova, "Formirovanie sotsio-kul'turnykh i pravovykh osnov dlia obshchestvennoi samoorganizatsii v imperatorskoi Rossii" in idem, ed., *Samorganizatsiia rossiiskoi obshchestvennosti*, 166–217, especially 193–209.

49. Gleason, "Terms of Russian Social History," 15–27, 20.

50. Sdvizhkov, "Ot obshchestva k intelligentsii," 395–401; Nathaniel Knight, "Was the Intelligentsia Part of the Nation? Visions of Society in Post-Emancipation Russia," *Kritika: Explorations in Russian and Eurasian History* 7, no. 4 (2006): 733–758.

51. Sdvizhkov, "Ot obshchestva k intelligentsii," 404.

52. Ruane and Eklof, "Cultural Pioneers and Professionals," 199; O. Iu. Malinova, "Obshchestvo, publika, obshchestvennost' v Rossii serediny XIX-nachala XX veka: Otrazhenie v poniatiiakh praktik publichnoi kommunikatsii i obshchestvennoi samodeiatel'nosti," in Miller, Sdvizhkov and Shirle, eds., *Poniatiia o Rossii*, 1: 445–447.

53. Nicholas Riazonovsky, *A Parting of Ways: Government and the Educated Public in Russia, 1801–1855* (Oxford: Oxford University Press, 1977), might serve as an almost classical example of such an approach.

54. Christopher Ely has emphasized the importance of recognizing wider circles of the Russian society beyond the liberal intelligentsia. See Ely, "The Question of Civil Society in Late Imperial Russia," 237. See also Laura Engelstein, *Slavophile Empire: Imperial Russia's Illiberal Path* (Ithaca and London: Cornell University Press, 2009), 82, for the lack of a "clean sociological divide in nineteenth century Russia between state servitors and members of 'society,'" as well as the informative chapters by M. V. Kalashnikov, "Poniatie *liberalism* v russkom obshchestvennom soznanii XIX veka," and L. V. Bibikova, "Politicheskaia politsiia, konservatory i sotsialisty: igra liberalizmami v publichnom i nepublichnom politicheskom prostranstve Rossiiskoi imperii v kontse XIX-nachale XX veka," in Miller, Sdvizhkov and Shirle, eds., *Poniatiia o Rossii*, 1: 464–513 and 1: 514–573.

55. Jeffrey Brooks, *When Russia Learned to Read: Literacy and Popular Literature, 1861–1917* (Evanston, IL: Northwestern University Press, 2003), 295–299.

56. Tumanova, ed., *Samoorganizatsiia rossiiskoi obshchestvennosti*, 11. This definition of *obshchestvennye organizatsii* is based on the one suggested by Stepanskii in the early 1980s. See n. 8 above.

57. David L. Hoffmann, "European Modernity and Soviet Socialism," in David L. Hoffmann and Yanni Kotsonis, eds., *Russian Modernity: Politics, Knowledge, Practices* (London: Macmillan and New York: St. Martin's, 2000), 246, 247.

58. Ibid., 247.

59. Harley D. Balzer, "Introduction," in Harley D. Balzer, ed., *Russia's Missing Middle Class: The Professions in Russian History* (Armonk, New York: M.E. Sharpe, 1996), 15.

60. Nathaniel Knight, "Science, Empire, and Nationality: Ethnography in the Russian Geographical Society, 1845–1855," in Burbank and Ransel, eds., *Imperial Russia*, 108–141; Vera Tolz, "European, National and (Anti-) Imperial: the Formation of Academic Oriental Studies in Late Tsarist and Early Soviet Russia," and Wladimir Bérélowitch, "History in Russia Comes of Age: Institution-Building, Cosmopolitanism, and Theoretical Debates among Historians in Late Imperial Russia," *Kritika: Explorations in Russian and Eurasian History* 9, no. 1 (Winter 2008): 53–81, 113–134; Vera Tolz, "*Sobstvennyi Vostok Rossii*": *Politika identichnosti i vostokovedenie v posdneimperskii i rannesovetskii period* (Moscow: Novoe literaturnoe obozrenie, 2013), 14–16.

1 From Associations of the Educated to Societies for Education: Historical Background

THE EARLIEST ASSOCIATIONS of the educated emerged in Russia during the first half of the eighteenth century. These nascent voluntary organizations appeared at a stage in Russian history when voluntary activity would hardly seem to have a place in a society characterized by immobility and serfdom. Half of the country's peasantry lived as serfs who belonged to private owners. The other half were state peasants and were no freer to manage their own lives. Like private serfs, they were tied to an *obshchina*. The urban population was subject to the controls of the city administration. Even the nobility could not be called free since, until 1762, it was subjected to compulsory state service. This combination of dependence and compulsory obligation on the part of all groups in the Russian population resulted in a system of control that would not appear to offer any opportunity for voluntary initiative. "In Russia at the beginning of the eighteenth century the only free man was the tsar, and every one [*sic*] else was in bondage in one degree or another," as Boris Mironov described the country's distinctive conditions during this period.[1]

But the military and administrative reforms launched by Peter the Great at the beginning of that century, which were initially driven by the aim of strengthening the army, gradually evolved into a grand effort to create what Marc Raeff has termed a "well-ordered" state. The result was a new social dynamic. The reforms extended the obligations of the nobility and increased the burden on other groups in society, but they also stimulated a great deal of social mobility.[2] The introduction of the Table of Ranks provided commoners with the possibility of acquiring noble status. New demands and conditions for service created a system of meritocracy and the rational organization of state structures. Administrative changes based on the principles of cameralism, which sought to reform society and promote economic development, regularized the duties of officials.[3] Chancery work became specialized. Staffing and salaries were standardized, and a new element of collegiality was introduced into decision-making processes.[4] A new mode of service required a new kind of education. The establishment of secular institutions of education based on "European" (principally German) models led to the appearance of eighteenth-century Russia's first men of letters, who, at this early stage, consisted mostly of foreign specialists.[5] It also contributed to the consolidation of educated strata among the Russian population and transformed education into an important tool for climbing the social ladder. In the long run, "Western" education became one of the defining characteristics of the Russian elite.

As Raeff explained, the ideal of a well-ordered state also rested on a "shift" in the traditional concept of government from one based on "the passive duty" of maintaining law and order and defending the realm against foreign enemies to the dynamic, activist goals of "fostering the productive energies of society."[6] This new definition meant that the state began to intervene in a range of spheres of its subjects' lives that were once regulated by church, family, or the common law. Such state policy, described as social disciplining, involved a series of legislative steps by which the early modern state sought to "civilize" the behavior of its subjects.[7] In Russia's case, the state's vision of what constituted proper behavior was first of all directed toward the nobility. The newly prescribed conduct marked a sharp departure from existing norms and manners. Ranging from the notorious decrees (*ukazy*) mandating the wearing of "German" garments and the removal of beards (which radically altered the nobility's appearance) to the promotion of a "Western" mode of entertainment for the elites, this social disciplining generated new, and initially coerced, forms of sociability. These served the goal of a well-ordered state while also facilitating the rise of new conventions and values that replaced old frames of reference. The members of the elite had little choice but to accustom themselves to these new norms and codes.[8]

It was state activity, therefore, that introduced elements of mobility, rational organization, and collegiality—characteristics typical of modern voluntary associations—into Russian life. State-sponsored social activity also gave rise to new forms of interaction and communication within the country's elite. Hence it is not surprising that the ethos of voluntary initiative so essential to the formation of such associations first appeared within the educated strata consolidated in the course of the reform. Indeed, the chief reformer, Peter the Great himself, took a personal role in that initiative.

Beginnings: Did the Neptune Society and the Brotherhood of Learning (*Uchenaia Druzhina*) Ever Exist?

It seems that the first Russian quasi-learned society (which was also the very first voluntary association to appear in Russia) was the Neptune Society (*Obshchestvo Neptunovo*), about which very little is known.[9] According to the sparse information provided by the few scholarly sources that have addressed the subject, the Neptune Society operated like a secret club and was associated with the Moscow

School of Mathematics and Navigation, whose headmaster, Henry Farquharson, was among its members and on whose premises, in Sukharev Tower, it is reported to have held its meetings.[10] Little is known about the society's actual activities, and it is hard to determine even the exact period when it was active. It may be assumed that the foundation of the Moscow School of Mathematics and Navigation in 1701 marks the earliest possible date of its appearance, and there is no evidence of its existence after Peter's death in early 1725. Popular legend has connected it with black magic. Scholarly accounts have assumed that this was evidence of experiments in alchemy conducted by the society, similar to the kind then popular in England; it has also been suggested that this was a Masonic lodge.[11] All sources note that Peter himself served as the society's supervisor (*nadziratel'*) and that his close associates, Franz Lefort and Feofan Prokopovich, served as its chairman (*predsedatel'*) and orator (*vitiia*), respectively, while some of Peter's protegés, such as Alexander Menshikov, Fedor Apraksin, the astronomer Jacob Bruce, and Princes Cherkassky and Golitsyn were also members of the society.[12] Twentieth-century researchers have thus relied on the evidence provided by the nineteenth-century historian of the Navy Cadet Corps, who published this membership data.[13]

However, there is a problem with the chronology. The purported chairman of the society, Franz Lefort, died in 1699, two years before the Moscow School of Mathematics and Navigation was even established.[14] Feofan Prokopovich was still studying in Rome between 1698 and 1702, after which he began to teach in Kiev at the Ecclesiastical Academy. He was only summoned to St. Petersburg by Peter in 1715. At the same time, several sources use vague evidence to tie the Neptune Society to Jacob Bruce's studies in astronomy. The top floor of Sukharev Tower housed an astronomical observatory that was established by Bruce, who is regarded as one of the first practitioners and promoters of the study of astronomy in Russia.[15] This hypothesis is supported by the fact that scholars of education have noted the excellent quality of the scientific equipment at the Moscow School of Mathematics and Navigation.[16] Moreover, a survey of amateur astronomical studies in Russia referred to the life-long interest in astronomy shared by the alleged members of the Neptune Society, Alexander Menshikov and Feofan Prokopovich.[17] In addition, the most recent scholarship on alchemists in Russia points to Peter's personal interest in the field and emphasizes Jacob Bruce's active involvement in chemical experiments, as well as Prokopovich's favorable attitude toward scientific experimentation and alchemy in general.[18] All in all, certain apocryphal elements notwithstanding, the story of the Neptune Society suggests that this was a kind of secret association, oriented toward the acquisition of knowledge understood in both rational and esoteric terms. As such, the society stimulated a mode of interaction among its members that was distinct from both the "old" patriarchy and the new "regular" forms of sociability. Another way of interpreting the phenomenon of the Neptune Society is to see it as a form of entertainment, to be compared to such a notorious and well-studied Petrine institution as the Most Comical All-Drunken Council (*Sumasbrodneishii, Vseshuteinyi i Vsep'ianeishii Sobor*).[19] While the latter constituted a parody of traditional practices, the Neptune Society would seem to have introduced a new, educationally oriented kind of entertainment, creating a link to the European tradition of learned societies.[20]

The next association of the educated emerged in the late 1720s and was also connected to Feofan Prokopovich. This was the literary and philosophical circle known as the Brotherhood of Learning (*Uchenaia Druzhina*), in which Prokopovich played a leading role.[21] S. M. Solov'ev briefly mentioned the existence of such a group, but later historians of Russian literature have described the Brotherhood of Learning as an organized circle.[22] According to G. A. Gukovskii, this was a group of enlightened figures who subscribed to Peter's state ideology. He identified Prokopovich as one of the founders of this circle and listed Prince Antioch Kantemir, a son of the former ruler of Moldavia, and Vasilii Tatishchev, the author of the first comprehensive *History of Russia*, as members.[23] Iu. M. Lotman suggested that the Brotherhood of Learning should be considered an "early literary organization" that exemplified the notion of a "nonstate" and "nonofficial" institution. It was, he claimed, "a rather consolidated and coherent group" which, in addition to Prokopovich, Kantemir, and Tatishchev, included among its members Nikita Iurievich Trubetskoi, who was a friend of Kantemir's and to whom Kantemir dedicated some of his poetry. According to Lotman, literature served the Brotherhood of Learning as an instrument of propaganda on behalf of Peter's state ideal *after* the tsar's death, which implied an element of opposition to the actual post-Petrine state.[24]

Historians of ideas have been more cautious in defining the triumvirate of Prokopovich, Kantemir, and Tatishchev as an organized body. G. V. Plekhanov employed the phrase *Uchenaia Druzhina* to depict them as adherents of the Enlightenment within the post-Petrine Russian elite, describing them as representatives of eighteenth-century "Westernizers." He also observed that the expression *Uchenaia Druzhina* was, in fact, coined by Prokopovich in one of his poetic addresses to Kantemir.[25] Soviet historians were uncertain whether to define the Brotherhood of Learning as a formal organization with a fixed political agenda or as an expression of a vague ideological program that was shared by the "fledglings of Peter's nest."[26] A compromise was proposed by P. P. Epifanov, who argued that Prokopovich, Tatishchev, and Kantemir constituted a group of like-minded persons who were united not only by a common worldview but also by personal ties expressed in the support they gave each other in both the literary and political spheres.[27] A closer reading of the poetic dialogue between Kantemir and Prokopovich actually reveals that the latter used the term "Brotherhood of Learning" in reference to Kantemir's first satirical poem, "To those reviling learning, or to my mind" (*Na khuliashchikh ucheniia: K umu moemu*), written in 1729. This poem depicted a colorful array of ignoramuses, including one who dismissed the possibility of devoting himself to learning for fear that he would consequently lose his friends and that he would be left with "ink, pen, and paper" as his only "brotherhood" (*sodruzhestvo*).[28] Prokopovich, in support of Kantemir (who at that time was an unknown young poet), was apparently adopting the image of a brotherhood of ink and pen when he attacked "those who dislike the brotherhood of learning."[29] Kantemir and Prokopovich only became personally acquainted in 1730. A year later Kantemir was appointed ambassador to London and left Russia for good on January 1, 1732.[30] The circumstances of service to the state also framed the meetings between Kantemir and Tatishchev.[31] While Kantemir served as a young guard officer in the Preobrazhenskii regiment in the capital, subsequently moving with the court to Moscow in 1728, Tatishchev was in Sweden until 1727. Upon his return to Russia, he was assigned to the monetary office in Moscow.[32] Hence, the two could not have been personally acquainted before 1728. Actual evidence of personal cooperation between Kantemir, Tatishchev, and Prokopovich appears only in relation to the succession crisis of 1730.[33] Prokopovich was active in the political efforts to save the autocratic nature of the Russian monarchy. Tatishchev authored documents that justified this position and represented the opinions of the rank-and-file nobility.[34] When the material was ready, Tatishchev and several of his collaborators approached Kantemir and requested that he pen a declaration calling on Anna Ioannovna to assume autocratic power.[35] Some Soviet scholars interpreted this cooperation as evidence that the Brotherhood of Learning took part in the events of 1730 as a political organization.[36]

Nonetheless, this version of events is undermined by the absence of testimony regarding the active involvement of any other organized body except for the Supreme Privy Council in these events. It is more likely that there was temporary political cooperation among those who considered themselves an opposition to *verkhovniki* (members of the Supreme Privy Council). During the following two years, from 1730 to 1731, when the Russian court was in Moscow and Tatishchev served as its master of ceremonies (*ober-tseremonimeister*), the connection between Prokopovich and Kantemir, and between Prokopovich and Tatishchev, continued.[37] Kantemir's satire and poem of thanks dedicated to Prokopovich, as well as his "Epodos Consolatoria" written in response to Prokopovich's elegy "A Shepherd Weeps in the Long Period of Foul Weather" (*Plachet pastushok v dolgom nenast'i*), reveal the intense intellectual exchange that existed between them.[38] At the same time, as Tatishchev's biographers have noted, his essay "A Conversation between Two Friends on the Usefulness of Sciences and Schools," composed in 1733, was inspired by his actual conversations with Prokopovich and with members of the Academy of Sciences.[39] Tatishchev, according to his biographer, also consulted with Prokopovich while writing *Istoriia Rossiiskaia (The Russian History)*.[40] Kantemir's extensive correspondence of the 1730s included exchanges of letters with both Prokopovich and Tatishchev although neither the subject nor even the name of the Brotherhood of Learning was ever mentioned.[41] The association among Prokopovich, Kantemir, and Tatishchev therefore seems to have been based mainly on common political ideals as well as on the sense of solidarity and shared mission of an "educated minority." As such, it can be defined as a kind of embryonic Russian republic of letters.[42] The connection among these three distinguished personalities was strengthened by the patronage that Prokopovich bestowed on both Kantemir and Tatishchev.[43] It is also significant that during the same years, 1730–1731, Kantemir and Tatishchev became connected to the Russian Academy of Sciences.[44] The Academy, founded in 1725, was the focal point of the Enlightenment in Russia, making an important contribution to the institutional consolidation of the country's emerging educated strata. In fact, the Academy was the first institution in Russia to be later officially declared the "primary learned society of the Empire."[45]

The Academy of Sciences as the Primary Learned Society of the Empire

The idea of creating an Academy of Sciences in Russia took shape in the course of an exchange between Peter and Gottfried Wilhelm Leibniz, the most famous polymath of the time, who served as Peter's scientific advisor from 1711 until Leibniz's death in 1716.[46] In accordance to Leibniz's views, the academy was to function as a learned society comprising "those who are advanced in their studies and are concerned with the improvement [of knowledge]."[47] He believed that it should be at the top of the country's hierarchy of educational institutions, which were to include primary and secondary schools as well as universities. Leibniz envisioned a worldwide network of such learned societies contributing to the advancement of science and education. Russia would be an extremely important link in this proposed network. Tsarist patronage would guide the proper development of scientific institutions while the systematic "construction" of educational institutions would help prevent the errors of piecemeal, spontaneous development that plagued other European countries.[48]

Leibniz's view of the academy's goals was informed by his understanding of learned (scientific) societies as bodies designed to provide the inspiration for rationality, harmony, and order in society as a whole.[49] He was also influenced by the contemporary European experience (including his own): the leading academies of that time—the Académie Royale des Sciences in Paris and the Royal Society of London, as well as the Berlin Society of Sciences (*Kurfürstlich Brandenburgische Societät der Wissenschaften*), which had been established on

Leibniz's initiative—functioned as learned societies.[50] These institutions rather than the universities, which retained their medieval structure, played the leading role in advancing modern science in the early eighteenth century.[51] The European academies were thus distinct from the universities. The fundamental difference was described by Marie Jean P. Flourens, permanent secretary of the Académie Royale des Sciences: "The Academy is no University. The barrier which separates them should be eternal. Universities teach, the Academy discovers and improves."[52] There were certain differences between the various academies. The French Académie Royale des Sciences, for instance, was subsidized and controlled by the state. The Royal Academy of London, although chartered by the crown, presented a model of a voluntary association that "controlled its own affairs, agenda, officers and membership and which lacked the propaganda and ideological functions assigned to the French Royal Academy."[53] These two patterns—statist and voluntary—constituted the basic institutional structures of eighteenth-century academies.

The statist model apparently influenced the Russian Academy of Sciences. At the institutional level, however, the Russian Academy diverged significantly from existing European practices. In recognizing the particular Russian need for educating servants of the state, Peter the Great preferred to establish an Academy of Sciences that would incorporate both a university and a gymnasium. This constituted a clear deviation from the division between academies and universities that was prevalent in the rest of Europe, as the academy's future president, Lavrentii Blumentrost, acknowledged in his "Plan for the Establishment of the Academy of Science and Arts, 22 January 1724" (*Proekt polozheniia Akademii nauk i khudozhestv, 22 ianvaria 1724*): "It is impossible to adopt the pattern followed in other states, for we must consider the conditions existing in this country."[54] Hence, the plan proposed a learned association "consisting of the very best men of learning who would: (1) develop and perfect the sciences, but in such a way that they would at the same time (2) teach young people publicly (those who are found fit for it) and (3) give special instruction to several men who would then be able to teach the fundamentals of the sciences to young men."[55] Education therefore became the academy's basic goal. It would establish the paradigm of placing equal emphasis on scientific and educational programs that came to guide the future activities of Russian learned societies.

Despite this deviation from Leibniz's vision of the academy as a purely scientific institution, his influence on the character of the Russian Academy of Sciences was remarkable. Its goals accorded with Leibniz's ideals of rational knowledge. His impact also explains the crucial role played by German scholars in the Russian Academy during the early decades of its existence. In addition, Leibniz influenced the perception of science within Russian scholarly discourse: the term *nauka*, like the German *Wissenschaft* and in contrast to the English *science*, included history and philosophy alongside the natural and exact sciences.[56] This perspective had practical implications. The "Plan for the Establishment of the Academy" declared that one class was to be devoted to the humanities, history, and law and that one of that class's three members was to be responsible for the study and teaching of ancient and contemporary history.[57] Historical subjects featured in the academy's scholarly discussions and in articles published in the popular journal launched by the academy in 1728 as a supplement to the first Russian newspaper, the *Sankt -Peterburgskie vedomosti* (*St. Petersburg News*). The journal, the *Mesiachnye istoricheskie, genealogicheskie i geograficheskie primechaniia v vedomostiakh* (*Monthly Historical, Genealogical and Geographical Notes to Vedomosti*), was edited by the academy's vice secretary, Gerhard Friedrich Müller, who was to become Russia's first official historiographer. Müller also happened to be the author of most of the articles on historical subjects that appeared in the journal.[58] Not surprisingly, Prince Antioch Kantemir, Feofan Prokopovich, V. N. Tatishchev, and Prince N. Iu. Trubetskoi were devoted readers of the *Primechaniia*.[59] In 1732 Müller launched the academy's scholarly journal of Russian history, which was published in German under the title *Sammlung Russischer Geschichte*. Its first volume contained the program for future issues, comprising the publication of primary sources of Russian history, along with historical and geographical descriptions of various parts of the Russian Empire. This was indeed the format of the journal until 1740, when it ceased to be published, and from 1758 to 1764, when its publication was resumed. [60] The *Sammlung Russischer Geschichte* emerged as the principal source of knowledge about Russian history for "enlightened" readers in both Russia and abroad. After 1755, Müller served as the editor of another Academy journal, *Ezhemesiachnye sochineniia* (*Monthly Essays*), which appeared in Russian. Although *Monthly Essays* was conceived to be "encyclopedic" in character, and thus included material from sundry fields of scholarly activity pursued by the academy, it was especially interested in publishing works on literature and history.[61] These early academic journals played a critical role in the formation of a Russian reading public, nurturing a general interest in history among the country's educated readers.[62]

Furthermore, the Russian Academy of Sciences accorded with the conception of the academy as an association of peers. The first Russian academicians were of German or Swiss origins and started their career in the cosmopolitan European academic world. The latter was described by an educated contemporary as an assembly of free societies of scholars flourishing under the patronage of monarchs: "Here and there in Europe, especially in Germany, France, England and Italy so-called academies, colleges, gatherings, societies, orders, and brotherhoods are set up, often with imperial and royal privileges and substantial revenues, to investigate the character and effects of natural things, to practice medicine, to improve the mathematical disciplines, to study ancient and modern history, to learn about Greek and Roman numismatics, to practice eloquence, poetry and foreign languages, to search out antiquities, to develop music, sculpture, and painting."[63] Altogether, these associations formed the basis of the renowned Republic of Letters, "that transcendent intellectual domain characteristic of the age, to which advanced men of learning ascribed their allegiance irrespective of their national origins."[64] Thus, in 1714 the last Moldavian *gospodar*, Prince Dmitrii Kantemir, Antioch's father—who in 1711 had become a Russian subject—was elected a foreign member of the Berlin Society of Sciences and was commissioned to write about the history and geography of his native Moldavia.[65] Scholars' ability to participate in various academies and to move freely from one to another constituted the fundamental principle of the eighteenth-century Republic of Letters, to which the Russian Academy of Sciences eagerly subscribed. On the basis of this particular principle, the St. Petersburg Academy managed to create an impressive list of participants. A historian of the Berlin Academy lamented that the *Kurfürstlich Brandenburgische Societät der Wissenschaften* "lacked support and was never able to attract internationally distinguished members, unlike the St. Petersburg Academy, which had already risen to European prominence in the 1720s."[66]

In practice, however, eighteenth-century scholars usually participated in a number of academies and learned societies: thus, Swiss Leonhard Euler (one of the "most famous men of science of the day"), who joined the St. Petersburg Academy in 1727, left it for the Berlin Academy in 1741, stayed there until 1766, and then returned to St. Petersburg, where he continued his brilliant career up to his death in 1783.[67] This mobility was possible due to the common norms of behavior shared by scholars of different origins, and accepted by varied learned societies, which is why it was very important to maintain and cultivate these norms in the St. Petersburg Academy. Its members enjoyed a distinctive status: as Michael Gordin has demonstrated in his study on the early years of that institution, "the academy was left out of the Table of Ranks . . . and so did not qualify as official state service: generating the perception of academicians as servants of state would contradict their intended image as free intellectuals." Yet he also claimed that they not only could, but were actually *expected* to, behave in accordance with the cosmopolitan academic code of behavior since Peter the Great wanted to instill into the Russian public "a particular etiquette regime of refined manners that characterized Western natural philosophy in the eighteenth century."[68]

Accordingly, the "Plan for the Establishment of the Academy" included detailed prescriptions for how its members should communicate with each other and how they should represent their work to the outside world. With regard to internal cooperation, the plan stipulated that "since the Academy is nothing but a society of persons (*sotsietet person*) who must cooperate with one another in the development of sciences, it is highly important that they should meet together for several hours each week. Each member could then present his own opinions, benefit from the advice and opinions of others, and check in the presence of all the members [those] experiments that he had performed alone."[69] Special privileges were bestowed upon the academy as a learned society. These included the right to award an academic degree and "to govern itself (*samo sebia pravit'*)." Such self-government meant in this case the right to elect its president, while the mode of election remained undefined. But all this was at best theoretical, since the presidents of the academy were in practice appointed by Peter the Great's successors.[70] Indeed, according to the plan, self-government coexisted along with direct subordination to the emperor, who was formally recognized as the academy's protector. As such, he was to take part in the academy's public assemblies, which were to be held three times a year in order to present the academy's achievements and "show the public the manner in which science was conducted."[71] The plan's vision of these assemblies included the presence of an audience consisting of foreigners (*chuzhestrannye*) who would enjoy "a great amusement" (*velikaia zabava*). The assemblies, as outlined in the plan, assigned a significant role to the tsar. Indeed, the main event was to be an oration delivered by a member of the academy that would elaborate about "his science" and also express "praise (*pokhvaly*) of the protector [the Tsar]."[72]

The program of public assemblies was inaugurated in December 1725, ten months after Peter's death. Although held in the private home of the diplomat Petr P. Shafirov, the first assembly bore the character of an official public event. It opened with a special ceremony and the protocol recorded the various speeches, which were delivered in Latin. Approximately four hundred people attended. The size of audiences in future assemblies remained limited as long as the lectures continued to be delivered in Latin. This began to change around 1750 with the introduction of Russian lectures or Russian translations to Latin lectures. In addition to these public assemblies, the academy also held weekly lectures open to the public.[73] The academy, therefore, not only introduced the notion of a learned society into Russian culture but also promoted a paradigmatic relationship between this type of organization and the monarch, on the one hand, and a broader public, on the other. In so doing, it created and propagated the model of communication and discourse that characterized the contemporary European academies, which "constituted . . . a domain of sociability which was not exclusively defined either in terms of the old principles of privilege and particularism or in terms of the newer principles of equality and universalism, but found both combined and inflected in the common language of enlightenment."[74]

While playing a significant role in fashioning and enlightening the Russian public, the academy also stimulated the formation of new learned circles that functioned within its framework or were connected to it. The first was the Russian Conference (*Rossiiskoe sobranie*), established in 1735 as a new unit of the academy by decree of its third president, Baron von Korff. Its declared goals were improvement of the Russian language and the translation of foreign works of scholarly and general interest into Russian.[75] It was mainly composed of the academy's translators, who, according to Korff's decree, were to meet twice a week in order "to confer among themselves, bringing and reading everything which each of them had translated until that day [with the goal of] improving the quality of the prepared translations."[76] Participation in the Russian Conference was thus initially conceived as part of the translators' academic duties. And yet, the poet Vasilii Trediakovskii, who was appointed secretary of the Russian Conference, viewed its program in much broader terms than simply that of an auxiliary unit of the academy. In his speech at the opening session of the Russian Conference, Trediakovskii referred to the French and Florentine Academies, as well as to the learned society of Leipzig, as models of emulation and emphasized the role of the translator as a "medium for transmitting European culture and knowledge to Russian society."[77] It was this sense of serving a mission of enlightenment that gave the Russian Conference the character of a learned society and turned it into a venue where the Russian educated elite gathered and where Trediakovskii, Lomonosov, and Sumarokov could present their views and works on language and literature.[78]

The Plan for a Department of History and the First Voluntary Society for Historical Studies

Was Gerhard Friedrich Müller influenced by the Russian Conference when he proposed the establishment of a department of history at the academy? Müller submitted his proposal in 1744, a year after returning from a decade-long Siberian expedition and at a time when the Russian Conference had already ceased its activity.[79] According to Müller, a history department was needed to provide sources for the academy's production of a scholarly history of the Russian Empire. He argued that it should be headed by a historiographer, a post that Müller desired, promoting his candidacy by presenting himself as possessing the necessary qualifications, which included, by his own purport, the ability to interpret Russian historical documents.[80] Müller's proposal focused on the practical aspects of staffing and functions. The department, he wrote, should consist of eight people. In addition to the head of the department (a historiographer), there were to be two adjuncts. One was to assist the historiographer in writing history; the second was to travel throughout the empire to collect documentary materials. Special attention was devoted to the adjuncts' nationality. The first adjunct could be either a Russian who knew the major European languages or a foreigner who knew Russian. The second had to be a native Russian in order to effectively carry out his mission. Apparently conscious of the importance of disseminating the results of the scholarly research, Müller included a translator among the department's personnel. Following the Russian Academy's principle of combining scholarship with an educational mission, Müller then suggested that two students be affiliated with the department who would serve as copyists of German and Russian texts. These students would eventually assume the position of adjuncts. An office clerk, a copyist subordinated to the clerk, and a watchman completed the department's technical staff.[81]

Müller's department of history was conceived as a symbiosis of state service and public activity. It required, together with the appropriate education and professional skills, an awareness of the project's social significance, as indicated by the plan for a systematic search for historical documents. In accordance with the dominant spirit of the times, Müller proposed a comprehensive taxonomy of sources for writing Russian history, together with an elaborate program for collecting those documents, based on a combination of government measures and public involvement.[82] First, Müller suggested that special decrees be issued calling for those who possessed relevant materials to hand them over to *gubernia* and city chancelleries. The documents would then be transferred to the history department for copying and later returned to their owners. Significantly, Müller envisioned a system of voluntary cooperation rather than coercion. "If the strict decrees required a seizure of the chronicles," he wrote, "their owners could declare that they had no such books."[83] Müller made note of the various motivations that would lead private persons to cooperate with the academy, emphasizing the nobility's interest in the publication of information regarding their families.

While appealing to the public's cooperation in unearthing historical sources held in private hands, Müller also sought to secure special rights under government aegis for the prospective department. This entailed mobilizing governmental agencies on behalf of his proposal and winning state support for the use of both central and local government archives and for attaining church documents. He also sought to establish the status of the historiographer and the history department within the academy: the latter was to acquire whatever foreign books the historiographer requested, supplying them first to the history department and only then transferring the material to the academy's library.[84]

Müller's proposal thus conceived of the history department as a scholarly unit that not only engaged in research activity but also took part in the academy's educational efforts. The department was to enjoy a certain degree of autonomy, and its public activity was to be supported by the state. However, action on the proposal was delayed by the academy, and when a department of history was finally established four years later, in 1748, the historiographer's freedom was severely restricted by the supervisory functions lodged in the Chancellery of the academy and by the subsequent creation of a Historical Assembly (*istoricheskoe sobranie*). The members of this Assembly acted as censors of all the materials prepared for publication by Müller's department.[85] But while Müller's vision of an autonomous research body was not realized, the academy's activity in the field of history stimulated the emergence of Russia's first historical society, a voluntary body that had no institutional relationship with the academy but whose goals echoed Müller's ideas.

Surprisingly, this first Russian historical society appeared on the geographical and cultural edge of the empire, in the northern port city of Arkhangel'sk. In 1759 some local merchants and petty officials, Vasilii Krestinin, Alexander Fomin, Aleksei Sveshnikov, Vasilii Naryshkin and Nikifor Zykov, established the Free Historical Assembly for the City of Arkhangel'sk's Antiquities (*Vol'noe istoricheskoe dlia arkhangelogorodskikh drevnostei sobranie*).[86] Its membership increased steadily over the nine years of its existence. Defining their goal as the collection of ancient manuscripts to be submitted to the Academy of Sciences, and searching for "evidence on the state of the local citizenry" (*zdeshnee grazhdanstvo*) in former and recent times, the assembly's members sought to convince the local governor that these aims were compatible with the government's attempts to expand the common good through the dissemination of science and useful knowledge among the citizenry.[87] It is significant that at the same time Krestinin wrote a proposal for establishing a merchants' gymnasium where children of local citizens would be taught, inter alia, history and law.[88]

This amateur undertaking was only partly successful. While the members of the Archangel'sk historical society managed to collect such valuable documents as a copy of the ancient law code *Russkaia Pravda* (later known as Krestinin's copy), the statutes of the great princes Vladimir Sviatoslavich and Iaroslav Sviatoslavich, and several ancient letters (*gramoty*), they failed to persuade the governor to allow them access to the local archive.[89] Moreover, both the local authorities and local denizens reacted with suspicion to the *klevretstvo*'s activities. This was probably the principal cause of its demise. Nonetheless, the society's most devoted member, Krestinin, continued to work with historical documents and began to compose a local history. From the 1770s he wrote historical essays that were based on local materials, work that was recognized by the academy in 1786 when he was elected a corresponding member.[90] A recent study of Krestinin's later writings has shown that they expressed the same discourse of civic enlightenment that characterized the historical *klevretstvo* of his younger years.[91] The story of this early historical society is representative of the private initiatives that developed with the aim of serving the public good through the accumulation of knowledge. Nonetheless, the suspicion and even hostility aroused by this initiative demonstrated that in Russia's autocratic polity the monarch's personal aegis was necessary for legitimating a new social institution. It was only when the enlightened Empress Catherine II extended her support to private voluntary associations that such organizations could gain a public standing. The case of the Free Economic Society is a good example of this dynamics.

The Free Economic Society, the *Nakaz*, and Catherine's Conception of Society

The Free Economic Society was founded in order to improve Russian agriculture by promoting economic knowledge. The very idea for such a society derived from the intellectual fashion sweeping through Europe in the midcentury.[92] More tangible designs took shape among the empress's close circle during the early years of her reign. These did not originally include any plans for a voluntary association. The first proposal envisioned the founding of an additional, "agricultural" class at the Academy of Sciences. The empress's decree establishing a special commission of the academy, which was charged with preparing an outline of the proposed class, was issued in September 1763; Gerhard Müller served as one of the members of that commission.[93] Several months later, however, M. V. Lomonosov submitted an "Opinion on the Establishment of a Government College for Management of Agriculture" (*Mnenie ob uchrezhdenii Gosudarstvennoi kollegii [sel'skogo] zemskogo domostroitel'stva*), in which he proposed that an agricultural college be created as a unit of the central state administration. Although the college's president and vice president were supposed to be educated in "agricultural science," the institution was envisioned by Lomonosov to function as a governmental rather than an academic body.[94] A third plan was submitted by Jacob Sivers, who was a governor of the Novgorod gubernia and one of Catherine's most effective administrators. Sivers promoted a public association whose members would be chosen by the empress herself and which would then create a course of agricultural study, mostly by translating foreign agronomic literature. This proposal implicitly made academic activity the dominant aspect of the new body.[95] A similar public association based on an educational agenda and entirely controlled and supervised by the empress was established in St. Petersburg in 1764, at the same time that Sivers made his proposal. This was the Society for the Education of Noble Girls (*Vospitatel'noe obshchestvo blagorodnykh devits*), established by a decree of the empress and supported and administrated by the crown. This institution later became the famous Smolnyi Institute for Noble Girls.[96]

But it appears that Sivers actually drew on a different source for his ideas, borrowing, in particular, from the experience of the London Society for the Encouragement of the Arts, Manufactures and Commerce. The London Society, established in 1754 on the initiative of drawing master William Shipley, was well known throughout Europe and served as the model of an effective institution for the advancement of the economy.[97] It also constituted an exemplary voluntary association. It principally focused on awarding prizes for discoveries and inventions, and eventually included representatives of the political, social, and intellectual elites among its members.[98] Sivers himself attended the society in the 1750s, while serving at the Russian embassy in London. The success of the London Society can explain why voluntary associations for promoting economic knowledge in Russia were preferred to "statist" projects. Sivers's proposal was finally implemented with the establishment of the Free Economic Society in 1765, which was also purportedly the result of a private initiative. Significantly, this initiative came from Catherine's librarian, Ivan Ivanovich Taubert, a member of the St. Petersburg Academy of Sciences and one of the members of the earlier commission that had been assigned with planning an "agricultural class" at the academy.[99] The fifteen founding members of the society included noble courtiers (the list was headed by the empress's favorite, Count Grigorii Orlov) and academicians, as well as court-employed professional "commoners" such as a medical doctor, a chief druggist, and a court gardener.[100]

To what extent can these individuals, and their initiative, be characterized as private? All were affiliated with state bodies. All were close to the empress. Some were actively involved in previous projects for advancing economic knowledge. And though the society had no visible connections to the empress during its first stage of existence (May–October 1765), historians of the Free Economic Society have no doubt that Catherine provided support, if not the original initiative.[101] Moreover, once the society's statutes had been drawn up, the founders appealed to the empress for patronage (*pokrovitel'stvo*). Remarkably, the same document also asked that Catherine confirm the voluntary nature of the society, which was expressed in the organization's very title, the Free Economic Society (*Vol'noe ekonomicheskoe obshchestvo*).[102] The empress responded favorably to both requests. She promised the society her protection and allowed it to use her coat of arms as well as her personal emblem—a bee bringing honey to the hive, along with the single word inscription, "useful." She also awarded the society six thousand rubles for the purchase of a building and establishment of an economic library.[103] At the same time, she confirmed its status as a free society (*vol'noe obshchestvo*), which, as the society's founders stated in their appeal to Catherine, referred to the freedom inherent in the voluntary character of their association ("We join by our willing agreement") and in the right to self-government ("To govern ourselves in our works by those obligations and rules which we would impose on ourselves."). Moreover, the empress's personal protection would grant the society independence from state authorities. In practice, the Free Economic Society struck a balance between obedience to the empress, on the one hand, and persistent refusals to accede to requests from the Senate, on the other hand.[104] Apparently, both Catherine and the founders of the society saw no contradiction between monarchical patronage and the voluntary character of the society, viewing the latter as a nongovernmental, and thus private, body that enjoyed the empress's personal support.

Why, then, did Catherine and her noble collaborators prefer the model of a nongovernmental association? The explanations provided in the existing scholarship are mainly based on the cameralist interpretation of Catherine's policies. From that perspective, this was part of an effort to shape a new kind of public role for the nobility who had been liberated from mandatory state service by Peter III's Manifesto of 1762.[105] Another view has emphasized that this was the first attempt to create a type of corporate body that had heretofore been absent in Russia.[106] However, a more satisfactory explanation might be one that addresses the more profound aspects of Catherine's vision of society. The Free Economic Society was founded while Catherine was intensively engaged in writing her *Instruction* (*Nakaz*), which was designed to go beyond its immediate purpose of instructing the legislative commission and to present Catherine's political ideals, both to the cosmopolitan Republic of Letters to which Catherine aspired to belong, and to the Russian population, which she happened to rule. The *Nakaz* can thus shed light on the enigmatic aspects of the empress's efforts to create a model nongovernmental voluntary association. It was the interplay between the new concepts of society and civil society and the notion of the state that made the idea of voluntary associations viable.

The relationship between state and citizen were defined by the *Nakaz* as a "union." Catherine even began the document with the assumption that "each honest man in society" desired "to see the motherland at the highest degree of well-being, glory, felicity, and tranquility."[107] As a disciple of advanced philosophical ideas, Catherine's writings reflected the transition from the older notion of *societas civilis* as a governed body of people to the new concept of civil society as an autonomous entity existing outside the domain of state.[108] In the context of the *Nakaz*, therefore, voluntary associations (societies) were to be considered building blocks for constructing this new social domain, a venue in which the union of citizens and state could be realized.

One aspect of Catherine's civic thought was especially significant for the development of voluntary associations. The *Nakaz* constituted a program for the future. As such, the semantic structure of its central concepts was dominated by promises and expectations. Description of the past played a much less important role.[109] This, in turn, made the political ideas contained in the *Nakaz* susceptible to diverging interpretations. On the one hand, different perceptions of the future could generate distinct meanings for future-oriented concepts. On the other hand, no interpretation could, of course, delineate a future that did not yet exist. This is what made Catherine's concepts of state and society essentially modern, presuming as they did a potential conflict between them.[110] Though barely anticipated at the time, a conflict over the role of society, in general, and voluntary associations, in particular, did indeed break out several decades later. In the 1760s, however, as manifested in Krestinin's historical *klevretstvo* and the Free Economic Society, the enlightened empress and her educated subjects shared similar expectations and spoke the same conceptual language.

A different problem did, nevertheless, arise. The future-oriented enlightened discourse was not entirely compatible with contemporary Russian cultural practices, which were still prevalently paternalistic and personalistic. Though modified by Petrine reform, these older elements had an impact on the new institutions, manifest, in particular, in the mechanism of patron-client relations. Colum Leckey's study of the Free Economic Society shows that a network of internal patronage developed alongside the external patronage bestowed by the empress on the society. Strengthened by habits of deference and hierarchy, which members of the society internalized in the course of their service in state structures based on rank, these relationships served a system in which "society membership merely validated and reinforced [the members'] preexistent status."

But if that was indeed the case, to what extent did the Free Economic Society constitute a new type of enlightened sociability? Leckey's answer to this question is unequivocal. "Although a significant portion of notable members were attracted by the organization's claims to patriotism and usefulness," he argues, "there is little evidence to support the impression that the society, simply by virtue of its nongovernmental status, favored a new climate of 'sociability.'" Joseph Bradley, in contrast, maintains that the society's institutional practices and written statutes generated a new form of sociability that became paradigmatic for future voluntary associations.[111] The problem seems to lie in the discrepancy between the relations as conceived by the society's statutes and the actual interpersonal practices of the membership. The statutes formally prohibited any arguments over rank or precedence among the society's members and established a relatively egalitarian procedure for joining the society. A prospective member was required to submit an essay and be recommended by three members of the society. The statutes also decreed that new members be approved by a general vote. The society's president, treasurer, and secretary were to be elected in the same fashion.[112] The statutes thus prescribed formal equality among the members of the Free Economic Society.

Although such egalitarianism was hardly realized in practice, it did signal an ideal type that would serve as a model for future learned societies. Moreover, while patronage and personal dependence played the most significant role in the relations among the society's core group located in St. Petersburg, the promise of equality strongly appealed to the society's "distant" members in the provinces. The experience of regularly reading and occasionally writing in the society's journal, *Trudy Vol'nogo ekonomicheskogo obshchestva* (*Transactions of the Free Economic Society*), gave these provincials a sense of belonging and served, in the long run, to realize (at least in part) the egalitarian brand of sociability that was conceived by the statutes.[113] Andrei Bolotov provides the most noteworthy personal example of this dynamic: he had been a member of the society since 1766, devotedly responding to its regular questionnaires, submitting numerous essays for publication in *Trudy*, and maintaining a correspondence with the society's secretary (and later president) Andrei A. Nartov. Bolotov did all this while living on his remote estate in the Tul'skaia gubernia. Only in 1803 did Bolotov actually attend the Free Economic Society for the first time and personally participate in its meetings during an eleven-month stay in St. Petersburg.[114] *Trudy* was, thus, not only a site of common intercourse and the dissemination of useful information. It also constituted an axis around which a community of the educated could develop, a dynamic that had been unfolding since the establishment of the Academy of Sciences and the initiation of its publishing enterprises. The founding of the Free Economic Society expanded the boundaries of this discursive space in which a community had begun to take shape and added to it a physical space as well. As such, it played a pivotal role in creating a Russian public sphere, which, according to Douglas Smith, consisted of a combination of the discursive and physical spaces and functioned as "the arena inhabited by the [educated] public."[115] Being the first voluntary body to declare its specific purposes, elaborate self-imposed rules, and establish a formal procedure for the enrollment of members, the Free Economic Society emerged as a cornerstone of the eighteenth-century Russian public sphere.[116]

The Empress as a Private Patron and the State as a Guarantor of Learned Societies

The Free Economic Society was the first but not the last society to be launched by Catherine II. In 1769 she founded the Society for the Translation of Foreign Books (*Sobranie staraiushcheesia o perevode inostrannykh knig*), which was given an annual subsidy of five thousand rubles from her own purse. The funds were intended for the "benefit of the society" and for the remuneration of translators. The empress's secretary, Grigorii Kozitskii, together with Counts Vladimir G. Orlov and Andrei P. Shuvalov, were entrusted with looking after this money.[117] The society had forty-four members, who were socially less homogeneous than in the case of the Free Economic Society.[118] They included several educated courtiers and well-known writers (Yakov Kozel'skii, Grigorii Kozitskii, and Vasilii Ruban), but most of them were translators or junior employees of the academy, along with a number of guard officers.[119] Gary Marker, author of an important study on publishing and printing in Russia, noted the ambiguous status of the Translation Society, which fell somewhere between the academy and informal literary circles at court.[120] On the one hand, the head of the society, Vladimir Orlov, was also director of the Academy of Sciences, which bore the expenses of printing the translations.[121] On the other hand, Catherine served as the society's patroness, paying translators' salaries and choosing texts for translation. This list of works was dominated by French philosophy, which turned the Translation Society, as Marker has claimed, into the leading Russian voice of the French Enlightenment.

The society kept busy. During the fifteen years of its existence, until 1783, it published 154 translations and prepared another forty-seven manuscripts for publication. Ninety-five texts were still in the process of translation and an additional seventeen had already been chosen for translation.[122] However, despite its members' singular devotion to the task at hand and despite their common interests, the society could hardly be called a voluntary association. Established, staffed, and subsidized by the empress, it had no structure of self-government or any of the self-imposed rules that characterized the Free Economic Society. At the same time, the Translation Society was not a state body; the empress acted toward it in the capacity of a private patron. In that respect, the society functioned as a kind of fictitious public association, or, as Kliuchevskii described it, a "transitional entity between governmental office and private association."[123]

Two years later, in 1771, another such transitional society appeared, with a similar purpose but a different combination of voluntary and statist elements: this was the Free Russian Assembly (*Vol'noe rossiiskoe sobranie*). Founded by a curator of the Moscow University, Ivan Melissino, the Free Russian Assembly intended to contribute to the improvement and enrichment of the Russian language, thereby reviving the aims that had been declared earlier by the Russian Conference. There was, however, an important difference: while the Russian Conference had been established as an auxiliary unit of the academy, the Free Russian Assembly emerged as a voluntary society affiliated with Moscow University. Like the Russian Conference, the Free Russian Assembly was inspired by the example of the French Academy, and, like the empress's earlier publishing enterprises, the Assembly assumed the task of issuing "useful (especially for the education of youth) Russian works (*sochineniia*) and translations, both poetry and prose." While its main goal was to compile a Russian dictionary, its "Announcement to Lovers of the Russian Language" (*Ob'iavlenie liubiteliam rossiiskogo iazyka*) placed a special emphasis on working with historical documents, describing the intention to collect ancient Russian chronicles, "open the archives of public and private books and letters," and issue historical documents intended to expose the ancestors' memorable deeds "for the people's pleasure and to enhance the state of Russian historiography."[124] The Assembly's core group consisted of professors, teachers, and students of the university, but its membership was also open to literati who did not belong to the university's staff. Among the latter were Müller, who had moved to Moscow in 1765 and since 1766 had served as the director of the archives of the College of Foreign Affairs, Prince Mikhail M. Shcherbatov, who replaced Müller as the official historiographer, and Nikolai Novikov, one of the first Russian private publishers.[125]

The aim of compiling a Russian dictionary made the Free Russian Assembly an active participant in the process of forming the Russian literary language, which Hans Rogger and Mark Raeff considered to be a manifestation of a growing national consciousness.[126] The most significant result of the Assembly's activity was the *Tserkovnyi slovar'* (*Ecclesiastical Dictionary*), which demonstrated the way in which language and history were intertwined in the Assembly's work.[127] According to Rogger, it was not "a dictionary in the strict sense of the word, but a guide to the reading of Church books; it contained, in addition, explanations of archaic Slavisms and excursions into history, old Russian literature, ceremonial and customs."[128] From 1774 the Free Russian Assembly also issued a journal, *Opyt trudov vol'nogo rossiiskogo sobraniia pri Moskovskom Universitete* (*Essays of the Transactions of the Free Russian Assembly at the Moscow University*), of which six volumes were published between 1774 and 1783, when the Assembly ceased functioning. As a result of Müller's participation, a significant portion of the *Transactions'* contents consisted of historical documents.[129]

The Free Russian Assembly, therefore, provided an important venue for communication and collaboration among people engaged in historical studies. Moreover, it was ancient Russian history rather than the glorious days of Peter the Great that drew the attention of both the historiographers and laymen involved in the historical activity of the Free Russian Assembly. This signified the crucial turn in the attitude to Russian history that Raeff characterized as the transition from "the eighteenth century belief that modern Russia had its source exclusively in the reign of Peter I" to the "growing feeling that Russia's difference from Europe had to be preserved along with the conscious efforts at imitating the latter."[130] The Free Russian Assembly therefore reflected the emerging national stance of Russian early modernity.

In 1783 Catherine established another "transitional" body that dealt exclusively with Russia's national past: this was a "historical assembly" (*istoricheskoe sobranie*) intended to prepare materials for *Notes on Ancient Russian History*.[131] Count Andrei Shuvalov, who had previously participated in the Translation Society, became its supervisor.[132] The *sobranie* was composed of ten members, chosen by Shuvalov and approved by the empress; one of them, Khariton Chebotarev, was a professor of history at Moscow University. Three or four of the members, who were paid for their work, were expected to be free of all other obligations in order to focus exclusively on preparing excerpts from ancient Russian chronicles and works of foreign writers. The head of this body had to report to the empress on the results of their work, but he was not subordinated to any government office and was completely responsible for the *sobranie's* agenda and affairs. He also assumed responsibility for working procedures and expenditures. He thus functioned, Kliuchevskii observed, in a way similar to "a director of the historical department, as earlier proposed by Müller, and, at the same time, as a chair of a learned society."[133] With Catherine's approval, the prepared materials were to be published at the government's expense. Such a work, entitled *Vypis' khronologicheskaia iz istorii russkoi* (*Chronological Excerpts from Russian History*), appeared in 1787.[134]

The transitional character of the three societies described above stemmed from their nongovernmental status. Nonetheless, their members were mainly state officials of different ranks, while the Russian Assembly, which emerged as a free (*vol'noe*) society, was established in the framework of the state university and initiated by its curator. The elements of private associations that can be discerned in the structure of the Translation Society and the historical assembly derived from (and were protected by) the empress's personal patronage and financial support. Moreover, the nonstatist status of these societies could be easily changed: thus, the Translation Society and the Free Russian Assembly both stopped their activity and merged with the Russian Academy, established as a statist entity in 1783. Like its predecessors, the academy was founded in order to improve the Russian language by means of creating a standard Russian grammar and a comprehensive dictionary. It also strove to formulate rules for Russian rhetoric and prosody. In this respect, the academy was a direct successor of the Russian Conference, the Society for the Translation of Foreign Books, and the Free Russian Assembly. Indeed, it even inherited the Translation Society's unfinished projects and budget, while most of the Free Russian Assembly's members became members of the Russian Academy, and its preliminary work on the Russian Dictionary was used by the Russian Academy when preparing the first Russian academic dictionary.

The idea of a Russian Academy was proposed to Catherine II by her longtime collaborator, Princess Catherine Dashkova, whom Catherine also appointed as its president.[135] While Dashkova conceived the academy as a learned society, she believed that the stability of private learned societies was liable to be undermined by their lack of financial means or the inability of their members to reach a consensus. She therefore suggested that the academy be made dependent on a "supreme power," which would provide a secure basis for its ongoing activity.[136] The impersonal formulation, "supreme power," rather than a direct reference to the empress, reflected a shift in the very notion of a statist learned society. This change was formalized when the president of the Russian Academy was granted the standing of a state official. And though the appointment of a woman to such a post was certainly unusual for the age, it was not so extraordinary in the case of Dashkova who had already been appointed as head of the Academy of Sciences several months earlier, in January 1783.

As a statist learned society, the Russian Academy differed from its predecessors in its larger number of members (around sixty) and its more sophisticated internal structure. It was divided into grammatical, explanatory, and editorial departments, and there was a special department for the explanation of terminology used in the sciences, arts, crafts, and trades. Moreover, the Russian Academy was conceived as a national enterprise: in order to enrich the Russian language, its tasks included the study of ancient literary texts commemorating Russian historical events. Consequently, its members included, alongside writers, academicians, and educated courtiers, the leading historians of the time—the second historiographer Prince Shcherbatov and his rival Ivan N. Boltin—as well as several high-ranking Orthodox clergy.[137]

Its statist character notwithstanding, the Russian Academy also had some features that were typical of a voluntary association, in particular those that had already appeared in the Free Economic Society. First and foremost, the Russian Academy enjoyed a certain degree of autonomy. Its relative independence was protected in the same way as in the case of the earlier society: it was declared to be "under the protection of her Imperial Majesty."[138] In addition, Dashkova sought to give the members of the Russian Academy control over its finances in order to develop some elements of self-government. However, only a few members had the status of paid employees: there were two secretaries, a translator, four copyists and a treasurer. Other members of the Russian Academy were to enjoy symbolic awards, such as special tokens (*zhetony*) granted at weekly meetings and golden medals bestowed at the end of each year. The latter practice was typical of, and probably borrowed from, the Free Economic Society. Furthermore, the Russian Academy's rules, written by Dashkova, as well as her presidential policy were intended to ensure the members' formal equality. Each member of the academy had the same rights and duties, including the right to propose new candidates for open vacancies (*ubyloe mesto*), to vote at the sessions and to receive the awards bestowed by the collective decision of the academy. Indeed, the idea of formal equality (*ravenstvo*) was declared as the strongest bond uniting the members of the academy in their common labor.[139]

Hence, two main tendencies can be discerned in the practice of the learned societies established by the empress in the 1760s–1780s. On the one hand, these societies, despite their proclaimed voluntary character, were usually initiated and, to different extents, controlled by the empress as their patroness. On the other hand, the emergence of these societies served to legitimize and promote the very notion of a public society, in which private citizens come together voluntarily in order to serve the common good, thus stimulating the establishment of voluntary associations by private persons.

Private Voluntary Associations

While the aims and character of the first private voluntary associations of the literati initially resembled the associations established by the empress, they functioned outside her control and mostly without her support although with a certain level of cooperation with state bodies. Thus, in 1773–1774, the Academy of Sciences and the Translation Society cooperated with the Society for the Printing of Books (*Obshchestvo staraiushcheesia o napechatanii knig*), founded by Nikolai Novikov (some years later a member of the Free Russian Assembly) and a bookseller, Karl Müller.[140] The authors of a Russian university textbook on the *History of the Book* have defined this society as a cooperative body.[141] Its appearance, according to Gary Marker, "marked a milestone" in Russian publishing, for it was the first time that "individuals had come together on the periphery of a scholastic institution to create a separate publishing society that exercised a high degree of autonomy over manuscript procurement, fund raising and editorial decisions."[142] Although pursuing commercial interests, this society also might be defined as a kind of transitional entity—in this case, from a private profit-seeking enterprise to a private voluntary association with educational goals. During its two years of existence (1773–1774), the Society for the Printing of Books issued twenty-four books, mainly translations. Among them was Radishchev's translation of the French political thinker Gabriel Bonnot de Mably's *Reflections on the History of Greece, or The Reasons for the Prosperity and Misfortune of the Greeks* (1773), which included his famous remark on despotism "as the state of affairs most repugnant to human nature."[143] Remarkably, Radishchev translated despotism as *samoderzhavie*, using the same word which was used officially to designate the Russian monarchy. This does not mean, however, that the society assumed any kind of ideological stance: another of Radishchev's translations produced for the Translation Society and issued by the Printing Society was *The Officers' Exercises* by Friedrich II's aide-de-camp, Anthon Leopold von Oelsnitz.[144]

In the same years Novikov launched the *Drevniaia Rossiiskaia Vivliofika* (*Ancient Russian Library*)—a periodical devoted to publishing Russian historical documents in order to introduce the reading public to its national past. Novikov was supported in this enterprise by Catherine II, who gave him some rare manuscripts, granted him generous sums of money (1,000 rubles in 1773 and 200 Dutch *chervonets* in 1774), and subscribed to the *Library*.[145] W. Gareth Jones, a leading expert on Novikov, claimed that in launching both the Printing Society and the *Ancient Russian Library*, Novikov was following the empress's example: "It was the Imperial Society for the Translating of Foreign Books that Novikov's Society for the Printing of Books had seconded, and it was Catherine's historiographical enthusiasms that had led Novikov to gather and edit material for his *Ancient Russian Library*."[146] A large number of documents were transferred to Novikov by Müller from the archives of the College of Foreign Affairs. The second Russian historiographer, Shcherbatov, was also among Novikov's advisers and collaborators.[147] This cooperation with Shcherbatov, who was working on his *History of Russia from the Earliest Times* at that time, was especially meaningful for Novikov: Shcherbatov had access to archival documents and the right to copy them for the purpose of writing his *magnum opus*. Although Catherine, Müller, and Shcherbatov supplied Novikov with the most important materials, he also had some additional sources. According to G. N. Moiseeva's thorough study of Novikov's archeographic activity, he managed to solicit ancient documents from the private archives of Prince Mikhail Volkhonsky, Count Peter Sheremetev, Archpriest (*protoierei*) Peter Alekseev, Prince Sergei Kantemir, the Archbishop of Archangel'sk and Kholmogor, Antonii, and Nikolai Bantysh-Kamenskii.[148] Novikov thus partially realized Müller's earlier idea of cooperation between the historiographer and the broader public—albeit in his own distinctive way.

Among the *Vivliofika*'s subscribers (whose number reached 246 in 1773) could be found courtiers from Catherine's immediate entourage, church hierarchs, merchants, literati (including Kheraskov and Radishchev), and even a peasant from Kholmogor uezd, Aleksei Banev.[149] Yet the number of subscribers began to decline in 1774, which brought this enterprise to an end in the following year, after the appearance of the tenth volume (a second edition of these volumes was produced by Novikov in 1788). Nevertheless, the experience of the Society for the Printing of Books as a private company, working in cooperation with statist and semistatist institutions, and of the *Ancient Russian Library* as a private initiative of a publisher striving to impart an interest in history to different segments of the reading public, makes these short-lived enterprises an important preparatory phase in the development of private voluntary associations aiming to enlighten the Russian population.

Such an association was established by Novikov two years later, in 1777; this time his initiative was not supported financially by the empress. Novikov (at this stage already a Freemason) announced that a group (*sobranie*) of his ten friends would launch a new monthly philosophical journal entitled *Utrennii svet* (*Morning Light*), whose profits were to be devoted to establishing schools for poor children in St. Petersburg. For this purpose Novikov and his friends founded the Society for Establishing Schools (*Obshchestvo staraiushchimsia o spomoshchestvovanii zavedeniiu uchilishch*).[150] Although the names of Novikov's collaborators are unknown, Russian scholars of eighteenth-century Freemasonry, literature, and journalism have assumed that the journal's leading contributors included the noble literati Aleksei Kutuzov, Mikhail Murav'ev, Ivan Turgenev and Mikhail Kheraskov.[151] Murav'ev's letters to his father reveal that the most active role in founding the journal was played by Novikov and Kheraskov. It was Kheraskov who initially suggested that Murav'ev join the *sobranie* and contribute to the journal. Murav'ev, in his turn, not only wrote for the journal, but also asked his father, who, at this stage of his career, was posted in Tver' (from October 1777 as vice governor), to subscribe to the journal and to disseminate an announcement about it among his Tver' acquaintances ("mezhdu tverskikh okhotnikov," as he put it). Murav'ev defined the journal as "pertaining to ethics and history."[152]

The results of this enterprise were most impressive. Schools for day pupils and boarders were opened at St. Catherine's and St. Alexander's churches in St. Petersburg in 1777 and 1778 respectively, and so many donations were collected that in the end it was the schools that subsidized the *Morning Light*.[153] However, the schools' achievements would probably not have been possible without the publicity provided by the journal. The names of the sponsors and the sums donated were publicized by the *Morning Light*, which thus stimulated participation in this philanthropic enterprise. The journal's employees contributed their salaries; one of its subscribers, general-auditor-lieutenant P. K. Khlebnikov, donated an amount of paper that sufficed to publish the journal for an entire year, and another subscriber, *Hoffurier* Kupreianov, accommodated one of the schools in his house. Some subscribers expressed their willingness to subsidize one of the boarders (*pansioner*) or simply donated various sums of money. In response, the pupils of the schools gave up a portion of their meals in order to save money for the poorest.[154] The journal's subscribers reached 789, including those who lived in remote provincial towns such as Poltava in Ukraine or Orenburg in the Urals. The *Morning Light* was distributed in twenty-six gubernia cities, twenty-four uezd centers and seven *mestechki*, apart from Moscow and St. Petersburg.[155] While most of the subscribers belonged to the nobility, there were also merchants, shop-assistants, and members of the clergy.[156] Novikov's schools functioned successfully until 1784 when, along with other private schools, they were taken over by the new national state system of public schools.[157]

How did a private voluntary association, which existed without the empress's support and outside the safe framework of state educational bodies, manage to maintain its schools so successfully? First and foremost, the Society for Establishing Schools might be seen as a kind of sodality based on comradeship among its founders, which was strengthened by the fact that most of them were Masons. Indeed, *Morning Light* became the first Russian journal with a Masonic stance, and Masonic connections were indispensable to its dissemination. With the help of fellow Masons who were governors, army officials and clerks, some fifty-eight points of sale were created for the journal's distribution in the provinces.[158] Not all the journal's contributors, however, were Masons. Murav'ev himself acted devotedly for what he called "our journal" without taking part in Novikov's and Kheraskov's Masonic activities.[159] Moreover, Murav'ev mentioned in a letter the intention of a certain princess (Ekaterina Urusova) to provide the *Morning Light* with items translated by herself, which increased the circle of the journal's non-Masonic contributors.[160] Murav'ev's letters make it clear that not only the *Morning Light*'s philosophical and moral stance, but also the educated conviviality of Novikov's and Kheraskov's homes attracted him to their endeavor. The letters include numerous descriptions of dinners with twenty-five to thirty guests as well as more intimate meetings of friends in Novikov's house where participants celebrated, talked about poetry, and discussed the journal's matters—what more could a young poet dream of?

In addition to the inner circle of the journal's contributors, the *Morning Light*'s founders managed to build an extensive external network of benefactors for the schools, motivated by the journal's philanthropic goal and based on the principle of patronage and the adoption of certain pupils by distinguished patrons. Among the first patrons (both chronologically and financially) was Gabriel, the Archbishop of Novgorod and St. Petersburg, who supported three boarders; other clerics followed his example. The list of benefactors also included high-ranking officials, such as I. P. Osokin, Director of Copper and Iron Ore Mining, M. S. Golikov, Chief Superintendant of State Liquor Factories (both of whom, as Jones has noted, belonged to the Free Economic Society), and members of the empress's court, the most prominent being the poet V. P. Petrov, who was Catherine's librarian, and P. I. Turchaninov, the empress's cabinet secretary.[161] In one case at least the benefactor, historian Ivan Golikov, the author of *Deianiia Petra Velikogo* (*Peter the Great's Deeds*), donated money not only in order to support two pupils, but also "to engage for St. Alexander's a man capable of teaching German, and in time Geography and History," which enabled him to influence the nature of the school's curriculum.[162] It was the combination of all these factors—the egalitarian cooperation among the fellow founders, the hierarchically structured patronage relations, the wide network for disseminating the *Morning Light* and its use for publicizing the society and fundraising—that contributed to the success of the society. The Society for Establishing Schools therefore can be seen as an additional site in the landscape of the early Russian public sphere, signifying another deliberate attempt to expand the community of the educated.

Nonetheless, the society had some distinctive—and novel—features. The *Morning Light*'s philanthropic calling appealed to representatives of different social groups—not only the nobility and academicians, but also members of the clergy, nonnoble civil servants, and merchants. The society's charitable activity both reinforced its supporters' preexistent status and provided them with an opportunity to attain a new social standing. Paradoxically, while maintaining the centuries-old pattern of patronage relations, the society created not only a new form of social engagement, but also a new hierarchy. Thus, the young Mikhail Murav'ev, who was still a sergeant in the Izmailovskii regiment at that time and who had been admitted into Kheraskov's home due to the connections between their families, eventually became an equal member of the society and, as a result of his involvement in the journal, attained the informal status of being a collaborator, rather than a client, of Kheraskov and Novikov. Murav'ev, who was already a member of the Free Russian Assembly, thereby strengthened his position among the capital's literary elite.

This informal hierarchy crossed the lines not only of ranks, but also of the estate (*soslovie*) structure. Clerics, who played the leading role in providing the society with organizational and financial help, apparently occupied the highest position on the ladder of its benefactors. But it was a merchant, seemingly one of the main donors to the *Morning Light*, who received particular recognition: in order to call attention to his generous support, two pupils whom he had "adopted" were henceforth called "Pupils of Piotr Terentievich Rezvoy and His Family." Remarkably, when an anonymous sponsor sent money for the charity schools, his gift was defined as that of a "True Patriot" and pupils chosen by lot to be supported by this grant were named the "Pupils of the True Patriot."[163] Indeed, the term "patriot" played an important part in the lexicon of enlightened citizenship and duly served to commend an individual who acted for the sake of the common good. At the same time, it implied a belonging to an overarching national collective without reference to the individual's legally determined social status. Yet the Society for Establishing Schools was much less structured than the Free Economic Society and lacked its transparency. The *Morning Light* did not disclose the names of the founders of the society, and subscribers were not informed about the society's decision-making procedures. Instead, Novikov placed the emphasis on the friendly relations among the group of founders, thus creating a link between the two different modes of voluntary association that had previously emerged in the sphere of learning—the institutionalized learned societies, which sought to disseminate knowledge and functioned as "social influence" associations, and the informal friendly circles of the educated, which strove to foster the intellectual growth of their own members.[164] The Brotherhood of Learning might be seen as a predecessor of these friendly circles, which mostly took the form of societies of lovers of literature or learning. Their appearance reflected not only the social, but also the profound psychological changes that the Russian educated stratum, and especially its core element, the nobility, underwent in the eighteenth century.

"Status Anxiety" and Its Impact on the Emergence of Friendly Circles

Enforced rationalization and the new opportunity for upward mobility introduced by the Petrine reforms radically changed the perception of the noble status, which officially became regarded as an outcome of one's rank in the service hierarchy rather than of one's lineage. The consequences of this change have been extensively discussed in studies on eighteenth-century Russia, but one aspect is of particular relevance in our context. An opportunity for people of low birth or foreigners who rose above a certain rank to enter the nobility raised the question of the very nature of nobility and produced an obsessive preoccupation with its definition, which Liah Greenfeld interpreted as a sign of "status anxiety."[165]

Eventually, as Marc Raeff and Iurii Lotman have demonstrated in their seminal works, Western education became the major sign of noble status. Raeff has also shown how a combination of Western-style education and traditional service values of the Russian nobility (*dvorianstvo*) endowed service with the new meaning of vocation, whose object could be not only the monarch or state, but also society and, at a later stage, the people.[166] As a result, the demands of education and service modified the relations among the nobility's immediate social milieu, or what sociologists have termed their primary group.

The concept of primary groups was suggested in the early twentieth century by the American sociologist Charles Horton Cooley for characterizing intimate face-to-face association and cooperation within the family, a play group of children, and the neighborhood. These groups, according to Cooley, are fundamental in the formation of the social nature and ideals of the individual. Their main quality is a sense of togetherness and the fusion of individualities in the common whole. Many such relations, he claimed, are formed at school and among people brought together by their occupation.[167]

It is hard to say whether Raeff was applying Cooley's theory or simply thinking along the same lines when he wrote about the education of the eighteenth-century Russian nobility. In any event, he examined family, playmates, and school friendships as the most meaningful factors in forming the personal and collective identity of the Russian nobility at that time. The long absence of the father, whose service obligations took him away from his family, childhood on the family estate, in the company of serf children, followed by the traumatic experience of moving from home to a boarding school, all combined to forge deep emotional bonds between pupils in eighteenth-century Russian schools. The sense of togetherness led to the formation of a new primary group—a friendly circle of schoolmates who experienced a similar psychological state of loneliness. Emerging first in educational institutions, such circles also appeared among young officers or officials, fulfilling the function of psychological protection from the feelings of insecurity and instability which, according to Raeff, were the plight of the post-Petrine nobility.[168] In terms of Daniel Gordon's concept of sociability, such circles can be seen as providing protection by conceiving their own norms in a milieu where old hierarchical frames of reference were blurred and where "fixed conventions of the group allowed one to classify both oneself and others according to a consistent scale of values."[169]

In his later work, *Understanding Imperial Russia*, Raeff expanded the zone of psychological insecurity by discerning the same phenomenon among other groups of the population—such as townspeople, merchants, certain segments of the peasantry—who were drawn into the dynamics of Europeanization and consequently became "dragged out" of their primary groups and habitual social surrounding. The phenomenon of self-contained friendly circles, however, was characteristic mainly of the educated elite. Explaining this tendency, Raeff emphasized the role of educational institutions that intended to shape a "new type of man." The combination of Western pedagogical ideas and traditional Russian values of service, Raeff claimed, led to the formation in the nobility of a self-image and social ethic similar to those of the Western bourgeoisie.[170] The exclusiveness of this "new type of man" became conducive to developing a "cliquish" solidarity among the members of these informal sodalities. It was this sense of duty and orientation to action, therefore, that provided a fertile ground for the further transformation of self-contained circles of friends into associations seeking social influence, which strove to translate their members' sense of moral obligation into positive deeds. From the mid-eighteenth century onward, these circles sometimes called themselves "societies," and by the end of the century this was the usual term for that kind of association. It was the circumstances of their evolution that contributed to the educational nature of most of these societies.

Apparently, one of the first friendly circles that identified itself as a society, the Society of Lovers of Russian Literature (*Obshchestvo liubitelei rossiiskoi slovesnosti*), appeared in the Cadet Corps (*Sukhoputnyi shliakhetskii korpus*). The nineteenth-century historian of literature, Sergei Glinka, wrote that this society was formed by Alexander Sumorokov and his schoolmates and that its activity consisted of irregular meetings where participants read and discussed their writings and translations. Such an authoritative researcher of eighteenth-century Russian literature as Pavel Berkov assumed that this circle included in its ranks a future head of the Free Russian Assembly and curator of Moscow University, Ivan Melissino, and claimed that it was not Sumorokov but another cadet—one of the first (albeit completely forgotten) Russian poets—Mikhail Sobakin, who played the most active role in the society.[171] While Glinka and Berkov related the appearance of the society to the late 1730s, Gukovskii wrote more cautiously about the possible existence of such a group in the 1740s.[172] More definite information is available about another attempt to establish a literary circle, this time in 1757 at Moscow University. Organized by Ivan Melissino, this society already had an element of a formal structure such as a list of participants; among those who read their poems at its first meeting was Mikhail Kheraskov, Novikov's future collaborator. Only two meetings of that society actually took place.[173]

From the 1760s, however, literary circles became an increasing trend in the educated milieu. Due to their ephemeral and informal character, it is not easy to draw a line between these circles and more or less regular soirées such as those that took place at Shuvalov's or Kheraskov's homes.[174] Nonetheless, there were some distinctive traits that characterized the friendly literary circles/societies. The first was their masculine character, unlike the French-style salons, which were mixed-gender literary gatherings based on collective admiration for the salon's hostess.[175] Another trait was the significant role played by connections based on kinship, neighborhood, and service among the members of such circles.[176] In addition, unlike the soirée, these societies declared their goals, which, in opposition to the more formal and public-oriented learned societies, did not directly relate to the common good but concerned personal accomplishment: the members strove to be better citizens and worthy individuals. Their most distinctive feature, however, was the proclaimed bonds of friendship among the members as the basis for the society's existence. Although the exaltation of friendship has usually been ascribed to a later, *romantic* stage of Russian cultural history, the very concept of friendship as free association among individuals based on their personal choice gradually became current in late eighteenth-century circles.[177] Lacking the tension of romantic attachment, the eighteenth-century perception of friendship emphasized shared values rather than passionate feeling, and signified a union of equals rather than an intimate relationship.[178] The first friendly circles, therefore, institutionalized friendship as an egalitarian, nonhierarchical form of interpersonal relations, which may have been animated by mutual admiration or affection, but could also develop into more formal connections based on cooperation, shared interests, or awareness of their group exclusivity.

One of the most intriguing questions, however, is why such friendly circles mainly took the form of literary societies. Lotman has attributed this phenomenon to the unique status of literature (especially poetry) in the secularized culture of post-Petrine Russia, where it became a bearer of ethical authority that had previously belonged to religion, with poetry, to some extent, replacing the sacred texts. Literature thus became a kind of counterbalance to the cultural domination of the state. Yet the appearance of literary societies may also be seen as a particular mode of the "recovery of logos," which Daniel Gordon discerned in eighteenth-century France.[179] What Gordon has described as the turning of "reason and speech" toward philosophical, aesthetic, and moral concerns that were unrelated to the direct exercise of sovereign authority was developed in eighteenth-century Russia primarily in the sphere of literature. While at the beginning of that century literature was mobilized to serve an emerging absolutist state, by the end of the century it had transcended the limit of this narrow functional role. The new Russian secular literature, as Lotman argues, strove to achieve an independent status as the depository of moral values and norms of behavior. As a result, it produced simultaneously two apparently opposing ethical ideals: that of service to the state, and, that of private life independent of the state.[180] Literature thereby established a model of the private sphere in a society where state service dominated the life of the nobility and where it was still almost impossible to realize this model. Therefore, although individual literary societies were usually short-lived, they became important venues for shaping and experiencing that ideal of private life. Furthermore, if we view the same phenomenon through the prism of Habermas's theory, the emergence of circles where private persons came together in order to discuss literature and to present their own literary writings to a group of chosen friends might be seen as an important phase in the consolidation of the public sphere.

New developments in this sphere became possible after Peter III issued the *Manifesto on Granting Liberty and Freedom to the Russian Nobility* in 1762. The possibility of early retirement from state service made different styles of private life possible. Choice and leisure, which noblemen could afford at least in a certain period of their lives, provided an opportunity for an individual to engage in public activity outside state service. From this perspective, Lotman regarded Novikov as a pioneer of that new nongovernmental public activity.[181] Not surprisingly, Novikov was the first who tried to combine the two models of early Russian educational voluntary associations: the learned society acting as an extension of or in cooperation with a statist institution, and the friendly sodality of educated private persons. Novikov thus created the prototype of a new kind of educational society, defined later, in early twentieth-century practice and scholarship, as a cultural-educational society (*kul'turno-prosvetitel'noe obshchestvo*). The Society for Establishing Schools was one of the first examples of that kind of society, followed by the Friendly Learned Society (*Druzheskoe uchenoe obshchestvo*), whose foundation was also connected with the name of Novikov and whose activity had the greatest impact on the subsequent history of voluntary associations in Russia. However, the Friendly Learned Society appeared not in St. Petersburg, but in Moscow and, like the Free Russian Assembly, was affiliated with Moscow University, which from the 1770s became the center of Russia's associational life.

Moscow University as a Hothouse of Voluntary Associations: the Friendly Learned Society

Moscow University became the center for the emergence of voluntary associations of literati in the late eighteenth to early nineteenth centuries due to a number of favorable conditions that stemmed from the elements of autonomy it enjoyed. Established in 1755, the university was subordinate to the Senate, the highest organ of the state's administrative structure, while its academic and administrative staff as well as its students were placed under the jurisdiction of the university's own legal court.[182] Its curators, who were given a central role in governing the university, were appointed directly by the monarch (at that time Empress Elisabeth) in order "to supervise the whole body" (*kotorye by ves' korpus v svoem smotrenii imeli*) and to report directly to the monarch about the university's needs. The university's director, responsible for its everyday activity, was subordinated to the curators. Similar to its predecessor, the academy's University in St. Petersburg, Moscow University was open to all groups of the population except for serfs. It was not, however, estate-blind: the founding decree defined the university's future students as "nobles and people of different ranks" (*dvoriane i raznochintsy*). Yet, while referring to the estate hierarchy, it recognized only two major criteria: the distinction between freemen and serfs and between the nobility and the nonnobility, thus unifying the various kinds of free nonnoble population in the category of *raznochintsy* and declaring that "the people of different ranks would study the sciences freely."[183] The organization of the university's preparatory and core studies translated this dualism into educational practice: two different gymnasiums were established—one for scions of the nobility and another one for *raznochintsy*—in order to prepare potential university students. Graduates of both gymnasiums were, however, supposed to mix together in the university as "students of the higher sciences, in order to encourage diligent learning." Those who excelled in their studies were promised service rights, which provided an opportunity to achieve social status through academic achievement; this provision reinstated the importance of social ranking.[184]

The list of the subjects taught at the university reveals that history not only retained its place among the sciences, but also became more structured as a discipline. In comparison with the founding documents of the Academy of Sciences, which referred to two broad fields of history, ancient and contemporary, the decree on establishing Moscow University included a variety of specific subjects such as universal and Russian history, antiquities (*drevnosti*), and heraldry.[185] The document's notion of "studying the sciences freely" is particularly interesting since it was used both to justify the exclusion of serfs and to provide those who were liberated by their owners with an opportunity for higher studies. "Since the sciences cannot tolerate any coercion and are justly regarded among the most noble of human occupations, it is not permitted to admit serfs or people belonging to estate-owners either into the university or into the gymnasium." Yet, it continued, "if a nobleman has a serf's son in whom he discerns a particularly keen intelligence and desires to teach him free sciences, he [the nobleman] must in advance declare that young man to be free and renounce any right and power that he previously exercised over him."[186] The university was therefore supposed to be a zone of freedom and equality, where estate boundaries temporarily lost their relevance. Not surprisingly, the idea of "free societies" found fertile ground there. While Melissino's early attempt to create a literary circle in 1757 and his establishment of the Free Russian Assembly in 1771 constituted the first chapter in the history of the university's voluntary associations, its next and especially remarkable phase began with the appearance of the Friendly Learned Society in the early 1780s.

The Friendly Learned Society, whose establishment was officially announced in 1782, developed from a friendly circle of Masons who shared the view that education was a means to the moral perfection of individuals and society.[187] A professor of the university, Johann-Georg Schwarz, and Nikolai Novikov, who since 1779 had leased the university's publishing house, became its leading figures. The core group of the future society emerged in 1779, shortly after both Schwarz and Novikov arrived in Moscow—in different circumstances, but with the support of the same fellow mason, Mikhail Kheraskov, who since 1778 had served as the university's curator.[188] The initially informal circle included, in addition to Schwarz, Novikov, and Kheraskov, Novikov's former collaborators from the *Morning Light*'s editorial board, I. P. Turgenev, A. M. Kutuzov, and V. V. Chulkov.[189] Its next member was N. N. Trubetskoi, who had moved from St. Petersburg to Moscow in 1778 and whose home served as "a meeting place for intellectuals, noblemen, and university professors" attracted to Masonic ideas.[190] During this initial period, the core group of the future Friendly Learned Society developed along two intertwining paths, on the one hand launching new educational institutions and undertaking new publishing ventures, based on its affiliation with Moscow University and sponsored by the circle's participants, and on the other hand establishing a network of clandestine Masonic organizations.

The educational activities were based on Schwarz's ideas of how to disseminate "real" enlightenment in Russia. Schwarz's suggestions, formulated in a number of projects submitted to the university's authorities, included such measures as spreading the correct principles of education, publishing useful books, and inviting good teachers from abroad, along with training native Russian educators.[191] Some elements of this program were supported by the university: thus, a Pedagogical Seminary for training teachers was established in November 1779, and Schwarz was appointed as its inspector.[192] In order to select future students, Schwarz solicited graduates of ecclesiastical schools, whose educational background was seen as the most appropriate for this purpose. Three graduates of St. Alexander's school also studied in the seminary.[193] Special stipends were established in order to support its students: the university transferred to the seminary interest from Demidov's endowment, sufficient for maintaining six students.[194] In the following years, when the number of students reached thirty and the annual stipends were expected to rise to 3,000 rubles (about 100 rubles each), the members of the friendly circle donated additional money for stipends. Schwarz contributed 5,000 rubles to the Seminary—probably almost all that he had at that time.[195] Two years later, in March 1781, the Assembly of University Pupils (*Sobranie Universitetskikh Pitomtsev*) was established on Schwarz's initiative with the two-fold aim of "cultivating the mind and taste of the members, their moral perfection and exercise in philanthropy," on the one hand, and publishing their works in order to finance their philanthropic activity, on the other.[196] One of the university's brightest students, Mikhail Antonovskii, became the president of this assembly; according to his memoirs, he also authored its statutes (*ustav*).[197]

In the following year, 1782, a third step was taken: the establishment of a Translators' (Philological) Seminary (*Perevodcheskaia*, or *filologicheskaia seminariia*), in which the participants of the Assembly of University Pupils, graduates of the Pedagogical Seminary, and newly recruited students were given an opportunity to apply their knowledge to translating moral, religious, pedagogical, and philosophical literature. This seminary was supported by private donations only. Six of its students were maintained by the money contributed by a new associate, Petr Tatishchev. He joined the circle via Masonic ties and personal relations with Schwarz, who served as a private tutor to Tatishchev's son. Ten additional students were supported by other members of the circle. Subsequently, a house for accommodating the students of both the Pedagogical and Translators' (Philological) seminaries was purchased and registered as Schwartz's private property.[198] Translations by the seminary's members were published by Novikov in books and periodicals issued by the University Press. Furthermore, according to P. N. Miliukov, Novikov gradually transferred the editing and management of the University Press's periodicals to members of the Translators' Seminary.[199] Among the latter was Karamzin, who joined the Friendly Learned Society at a later stage, in 1785. Karamzin started to provide his translations to the University Press in the same year and in 1787 became a member of the editorial board of the journal *Detskoe chtenie dlia serdtsa i razuma (Children's Reading for the Heart and Mind)*, which was issued as a free supplement to *Moskovskie vedomosti (Moscow News)* in 1787–1789.[200]

At the same time the friendly circle expanded as a result of its members' involvement in the activity of the Freemasons. In 1780, they established their own scientists' lodge, "Harmony,"[201] mainly dedicated to what Novikov later termed the "search for the true Masonry," which meant (at least for him personally) a system that would be "consonant with Christian teaching" and "would lead us by the most direct path to spiritual self-improvement through self-knowledge and education (*prosveshchenie*)."[202] Despite the vague definition, this quest had a practical effect. In order to obtain the authentic Masonic writings, Schwarz was dispatched to Courland and Germany in June 1781–February 1782. During this trip, he succeeded in establishing the status of Russian Masons vis-à-vis European Freemasonry and in creating contacts with German Rosicrucians, who constituted the most esoteric, select, elitist, and secret branch of Masonry and occupied the highest level in its hierarchy. His ability to make such prestigious connections has led some scholars to speculate on Schwarz's previous ties with the order.[203] What is important here, however, is the consequent transformation of Harmony Lodge into a multilayered hierarchical Masonic organization subordinated to the Rosicrucian Order.

First and foremost, in the wake of Russia's recognition as an Independent Masonic Province of the European Freemasonry, the members of the expanded Schwarz/Novikov friendly circle who had made up Harmony Lodge now became officers of the newly instituted Provincial Chapter (*kapitul*). Thus, Tatishchev became Prior, Novikov—treasurer, Schwarz—Chancellor, and Kheraskov—a member of the Provincial Chapter. However, the highest post in the Provincial Chapter, that of Provincial Grandmaster, remained vacant—ostensibly in the hope that Grand Duke Paul would accept it. The Directory of the Province, which functioned as the "standing executive body responsible for day-to-day business," was headed by Novikov: he became its President. A network of new Masonic lodges was formed under the Provincial Grand Chapter, which were also organized in a certain hierarchy. In Moscow, three mother lodges, headed by Tatishchev, Novikov, and Prince N. N. Trubetskoi, supervised thirteen lesser lodges. Later, additional mother lodges were formed in St. Petersburg and the provincial towns of Orel, Vologda and Simbirsk.[204]

Nevertheless, this rigid organization was intended to serve as what In-Ho L. Ryu has termed a kind of façade or, as Rafaella Faggionato has put it, the broader base for another, inner structure, which was supposed to become a Russian branch of the Rosicrucian Order. This secret inner structure implied a different hierarchy. Thus, Schwarz, who held the modest post of Chancellor in the "façade organization," acted as the Supreme Director (*Verkhovnyi predstoiatel'*) of the Theoretical Degree of the Rosicrucian Order in the inner structure. According to the patent that the Berlin Rosicrucians granted to Schwarz, he was allowed to confer the Theoretical Degree on those "worthy of recognition."[205] Therefore, in 1782, in a highly secret ceremony, Schwarz bestowed the Theoretical Degree on Novikov, and later on some other associates. Not surprisingly, the nucleus of the secret Rosicrucian organization was made up of the members of the friendly circle, but their membership in the Order remained unknown to the uninitiated.

By 1782, therefore, a sophisticated network of open educational and clandestine Masonic bodies had developed from the nucleus of the Schwarz/Novikov friendly circle. The formal establishment of the Friendly Learned Society in November 1782 was the peak of this process. Technically, it was Tatishchev's generous endowment that enabled the society to be founded, followed by additional donations by the two Princes Trubetskie, Cherkasskii, and Turgenev. The society was open to the broader public. Its foundation was officially authorized by the Moscow Governor-General Zakhar Chernyshev and staged as a public ceremony, which took place at Tatishchev's home and was attended by the highest local officials—Governor-General Chernyshev and Moscow Archbishop Platon.[206] The official inaugural announcement declared the society's main purpose to be the promotion of learning (*uchenost'*) and emphasized the importance of making good use of leisure time (*prazdnost'*), which was described as free time that had the potential of being the most fruitful portion of one's life and which could be used to contribute to fellow citizens. Two conditions were needed to take advantage of *prazdnost'*: education and cooperation between friends based on utilizing "their examples, advice and good qualities." Consequently, the Friendly

Learned Society was presented as an association of private persons, "different in their occupations and gifts of happiness," but bound together by their willingness to put their leisure time to effective use by means of their love of scholarship and their aspiration to the common and private weal. The announcement noted that "the mutual union among them [the members], their mutual favor and mutual good qualities brought them mutual advantage, mutual service and mutual perfection."[207] It therefore conveyed the vision of the Friendly Learned Society as a private body contributing to the common good from outside the domain of the state, even though it was by no means detached from that domain.

Like Novikov's earlier educational society, patronage relations connected the Friendly Learned Society with both the secular and ecclesiastical authorities of Moscow and the university's governing figures. The names of Zakhar Chernyshev and Archbishop Platon headed the announcement's list of patrons, followed by the university's curators, Melissino and Kheraskov. The announcement also expressed hope that the society would attain the auspices of the main patroness of the sciences, the empress herself. Alongside such official figures, the scheme of patronage comprised Tatishchev and other private sponsors whose names were not disclosed in this document. The patronage network, therefore, embraced both those who were identified with governmental offices and those who assumed the role of sponsor on a private basis. Surprisingly, however, there were no references to the body that should have been closest to the society, the Free Russian Assembly, which had already been active for ten years. This omission is especially striking in view of the fact that the Friendly Learned Society's leading figures, Novikov and Kheraskov, had belonged to the assembly, and that its head, Melissino, was indeed mentioned in the announcement but only as the university's curator. In practice, Melissino offered to amalgamate the Free Russian Assembly and the Friendly Learned Society, but Schwarz turned down this suggestion. As a result, he had to resign from the university under Melissino's pressure some months later: Melissino, according to nineteenth-century scholars, saw the Friendly Learned Society as a rival to the Free Russian Assembly.[208] The founders of the Friendly Learned Society, in their turn, were apparently ready to accept Melissino as a patron but rejected collaboration with him in his public capacity. Whatever the specific reasons, their decision demonstrated that they preferred to be clients of powerful patrons rather than to cooperate with another voluntary association.

According to the announcement, the Friendly Learned Society aimed to promote the scholarly endeavors of its members, establish contacts with foreign scholars, publish educational literature, and supply books to various types of schools. The latter task, it was emphasized, was the most important for "not limiting the usefulness of learning to the narrow confines of the society." The document mentioned that a large number of books, whose cost amounted to the sum of 3,000 rubles, had already been transferred to various (mainly ecclesiastical) educational institutions. It also referred to the recently created Philological Seminary as a body that was intended to play a key role in achieving the society's goals. Students of ecclesiastical academies and seminaries were invited to take up the Philological Seminary's vacant places; after three years of study they were expected "to return to their places in order to assume teachers' posts."[209] According to I. V. Lopukhin, more than fifty students who had been chosen by diocesan archpriests were educated under the Friendly Learned Society's aegis.[210] The society also continued the practice of supporting students with the help of its wealthier members and even sent some students to study abroad. It has been suggested that among those who benefited from these educational trips was a young member who was to become the third (and the last) official historiographer of the Russian Empire, Karamzin.[211] What is probably even more important, the Friendly Learned Society included a significant number of university professors. Thus, Chebotarev, who was in charge of the education and conduct of the pupils of the university's gymnasiums, served as secretary of the society; together with Schwarz, he "maintained relations with the University and seminaries, held lessons and managed the library."[212] University professors Theodor Bauze, Yacov Shneider and Petr Strakhov were also distinguished members of the society.[213] Through its members, therefore, the society had an impact on the educational process in the university. The peak of the society's influence, according to Longinov, was in 1783. Its members felt that they belonged "to an almost official pedagogical and learned corporation," whose distinctiveness was expressed even in a self-imposed dress code: a kind of a blue uniform with golden buttons. The students of both the Pedagogical and the Philological Seminaries (among them Karamzin), supported by the Friendly Learned Society, lived together in the society's house in an atmosphere of creativity and almost monastic modesty.[214] But this was not a closed world: on the contrary, Longinov noted the open character of the society's meetings, whose format was similar to that of the other learned societies, with the presentation of financial reports, reading of correspondence, discussions on pedagogical and philanthropic projects, and the delivery of edifying addresses (*chtenie nazidatel'nykh rechei*). [215] The Friendly Learned Society, however, was more sophisticated and more effective in implementing its tasks.

Following the official establishment of the Friendly Learned Society, a Typographical Company (*Tipograficheskaia kompaniia*) was set up in 1784. The relations between these two bodies have been assessed differently in various studies: Miliukov claimed that the Friendly Learned Society actually turned into the Typographical Company; Marker described the company as an attempt by Novikov to organize a new patronage society intended to support its publishing activity; while Faggionato assumed that it functioned within the Friendly Learned Society as a kind of "executive committee in charge of publications."[216] Another question that has intrigued all researchers of the society is the correlation between the open educational and clandestine Masonic aspects of its activity. The founders of the Friendly Learned Society rejected any connections between them. Thus, Schwarz confirmed in a letter to Shuvalov that he (and some other members of the society) belonged to the Freemasons but denied that the Friendly Learned Society had any kind of Masonic character, arguing that, unlike learned societies, Masonic bodies had never been involved in translation and education.[217] Even when Novikov was arrested and interrogated in Schlüsselburg Fortress in June 1792 for affiliation with the Freemasons, he also insisted that the society's only goal was to disseminate educational literature and that there were no intentions to draw students affiliated with the society into Masonic lodges.[218]

Nonetheless, none of the scholars who have studied the issue has had any doubts about the links between the educational and the Masonic character of the Friendly Learned Society. A program of study presented in the society's inaugural document might shed light on this question. It declared that the Friendly Learned Society would focus on the advancement of those "fields of learning" or "sciences" that had previously been underdeveloped, such as Greek and Latin, antiquities, "knowledge about the qualities of things in nature," and chemistry.[219] This combination of subjects pertained to the body of knowledge adopted by the Freemasons and also corresponded both to the courses that Schwarz taught at the seminars and to the corpus of materials published by the Typographical Company. Altogether, these published and taught materials represented a new distinctive conception of knowledge. Alexander Vucinich noted that Novikov "defined 'science' as a generic term which included not only knowledge derived from Baconian induction but also 'knowledge' arrived at by a manipulation of supernatural forces."[220] Later, Kulakova explored the Masonic conception of knowledge in the broader context of the eighteenth-century notion of cognition, which was characterized by a combination of both rational and nonrational elements and demanded a specific language and means of expression.[221]

The notion of knowledge as spiritually laden science deeply interwoven with religion (or, as Marc Raeff put it, the blending of "traditional Christian spirituality with scientific insight into the working of Nature") led to the development of an approach to learning as an endless process of comprehending the eternal verities, which ascribed a special role to history.[222] In this context learning about the past was seen as a tool for obtaining universal ancient wisdom. This attitude was expressed in the program of the journal *Vecherniaia zaria* (*Evening Glow*), which was launched in 1782 and, according to Miliukov, represented the Friendly Learned Society's philosophical worldview.[223] The journal would "in the first instance present materials relating to knowledge and rational enlightenment; secondly, materials of a morally uplifting type for the improvement of our depraved will; and lastly, so that these may have the greater impact, there will be examples drawn from history."[224] These examples, as Schwarz explained in his lectures, should by no means be viewed as a mere collection of instructive facts. He warned against the superficial approach to history that saw "only appearance" without grasping the "cohesion of everything," which could turn a scholar into "a great antiquary" but without "living knowledge (*zhivye poznaniia*)."[225] Real (living) historical knowledge was moral, physical, and metaphysical. While its moral aspect related to such topics as human deeds and characters and the "rise and fall of monarchies," its metaphysical aspect concerned the knowledge of religion and law.[226]

It was this view of history as a repository of reason and civic and moral virtues that informed the Friendly Learned Society's pedagogical and publishing activities. In addition, in 1788–1791 the Typographic Company issued the second edition of the *Ancient Russian Library*, which stimulated the growing interest in the national past and contributed to shaping the fashion of collecting ancient documents that was popular among the late eighteenth-century educated elite. This fashion emerged among high-ranking courtiers who were inspired by Catherine's interest in Russian history. Following her example, such persons as the procurator (and later, member) of the Military College I. P. Boltin, the music and theater director I. P. Elagin, and ober-procurator of the Synod Count A. I. Musin-Pushkin became the most prominent collectors of ancient Russian manuscripts. In 1784–1786 they made up Musin-Pushkin's *kruzhok* of Lovers of Russian History, whose members collected and prepared for publication a number of most valuable documents, including "The Lay of Igor's Host."[227] The republication of the *Ancient Russian Library* and other publishing projects of the Typographic Company aroused the interest of a broader stratum of literati in collecting ancient documents.

It was in this particular atmosphere that there appeared such figures as Theodor Bauze, a university professor of German origin and a member of the Friendly Learned Society, who "wandered through the Moscow flea market in search of old books and manuscripts," and consequently established a unique collection of ancient Russian documents.[228] In so doing, Bauze followed the fashion characteristic not only of the Russian elite, but also of educated society in his native Germany.[229] Although Bauze's fascination with the Russian chronicles was essentially different from his German compatriots' admiration for their own national relics, it signified the development of a "historical feeling," which could be shared with other enthusiasts of history and thus transformed the collecting of ancient manuscripts and artifacts into what Susan Crane defined as a collective experience. This new attitude to collecting contributed to the emergence of historical associations that "brought together those who had experienced the historical feeling on their own and wanted to share it with others, and further promote the conditions that would allow them to repeat this experience."[230] While formally such associations appeared in Russia (as well as in German lands) some years later, the Friendly Learned Society and the circle of Lovers of Russian History had already functioned as informal institutions of "shared historical feelings." Moreover, Moiseeva has pointed that among the young people surrounding Novikov were head of the Moscow Archive of the Foreign Affairs College, N. N. Bantysh-Kamenskii, and his deputy and future successor A. F. Malinovskii, both of whom later, in 1797, joined Musin-Pushkin's *kruzhok*, thereby serving as a link between this circle and the Friendly Learned Society's young followers. [231] The interest in and awareness of the value of historical sources, which the Friendly Learned Society strove to instill in its members, were particularly significant in view of the fact that not only the most influential Russian historiographer, Karamzin, emerged from the society but also the first members of the future Society for Russian History and Antiquities.[232]

The latter was established at Moscow University at the beginning of the nineteenth century, a decade after the Friendly Learned Society had ceased its activity in the wake of Novikov's prosecution. Chebotarev became its first chairman; another former member of the Friendly Learned Society, Strakhov, became a member of the new society, while Karamzin was given an honorary membership.[233] As Kliuchevskii noted, Chebotarev, Strakhov and other early members of the Society for Russian History and Antiquities brought with them "the attitudes and opinions of Novikov's circle."[234]

Kliuchevskii's comment accords with more general assessments of the Friendly Learned Society's impact on Russian cultural life in that period. Tikhonravov emphasized its innovative pedagogical ideas and practices.[235] Lotman underlined its intellectual input and claimed that "a whole generation of the Russian intelligentsia of the late eighteenth century—writers, translators, journalists, pedagogues, teachers of the Alexandro-Nevsky Seminar and officers of the Baltic Fleet—grew up in the atmosphere of the ideas of Novikov's circle."[236] Faggionato has drawn attention to its cult of brotherhood and friendship, describing how its "discovery of an inner communion among men inspired by a similar faith gave rise to the idea that they should combine their forces in the name of a common end and share their entire existence to the point of renouncing its individual, as well as its private aspects." This combination of "inner communion" and sense of moral duty constituted the legacy of ideas that Novikov's circle "left to the Decembrist movement and the numerous societies that studded nineteenth century Russian culture."[237] Moreover, Michael Speranskii's unrealized project to reform the Russian clergy bore a striking resemblance to the Friendly Learned Society's attempts to educate prospective educators. As Andrei Zorin has shown, this 1810 project proposed that the most promising clergymen would participate in a new Masonic lodge to be established specifically for that purpose, while all previously existing lodges would be closed; the new lodge would operate under state control.[238] Although Zorin does not mention the influence of the Friendly Learned Society's ideas and experience in this context, the very similarity of the programs suggests such a possibility.

The extent and endurance of the Friendly Learned Society's influence might be explained by its syncretic nature. It was the last learned society that succeeded in pursuing a combination of scholarly, educational, and philanthropic aims; the learned societies that appeared in the early nineteenth century were much more specialized. In a sense, the Friendly Learned Society culminated the development of eighteenth-century learned societies, serving as a fertile source of ideas and as a kind of model even for those who tried to reject this heritage, as illustrated by Melissino's abortive attempt to establish the Assembly of Lovers of Russian Learning (*Sobranie liubitelei rossiiskoi uchenosti*) at Moscow University in 1789. The draft of its statutes was replete with critical remarks, apparently directed at the Friendly Learned Society's organizational principles, secrecy, and esoteric character ("vain and useless mystical or secretive philosophizing"). Nonetheless, the assembly appropriated the Friendly Learned Society's concept of transmitting universal knowledge through the translation and publication of "the best and most well-known ancient and modern writings" from various fields of knowledge.[239]

Thus emerged a kind of pattern for a learned society, whose main features constantly reappeared in the structure and practices of the various societies, reflecting a certain "normalization" of the concept of voluntary associations. This concept survived even when, according to Anufriev, "the Catherinian reaction swallowed up almost all the voluntary societies that were established in the beginning of her reign," and subsequently under Paul I when, as Bradley noted, the very use of the word *obshchestvo* was forbidden.[240] The concept and the pattern of the learned society revived in the early years of Alexander I's reign and further developed in the course of the nineteenth century when such societies became the focal points of both scholarly and associational life.

The involvement of eighteenth-century Russian historians in various circles and societies of the educated, each of which contributed in its own distinctive way to augmenting public interest in the national past, awakened the "historical perception" among the Russian educated elite.[241] This new vision of the past provided fertile ground for the development of the "historical-mindedness" characteristic of early nineteenth-century Europe. Exploring the modes of representation of history in nineteenth-century Britain and France, Stephen Bann quoted Mme de Staël's daughter, Albertine de Broglie, who in 1825 told the historian Prosper de Barante: "We are . . . the first who had understood the past."[242] This nineteenth-century fascination with the past, combined with the emergence of the historical profession that "distanced itself from the wider intellectual community of writers and readers," was eventually institutionalized in the historical societies that mushroomed throughout Europe.[243] One of the first of such societies appeared in Moscow.

Notes

1. Boris Mironov, *A Social History of Imperial Russia, 1700–1917* (Boulder: Westview, 2000), 2: 66.

2. Marc Raeff, *The Well-Ordered Police State: Social and Institutional Change through Law in the Germanies and Russia, 1600–1800* (New Haven: Yale University Press, 1983).

3. On cameralism, see Dorinda Outram, *The Enlightenment* (Cambridge: Cambridge University Press, 1995), pt. 7: "Enlightenment and Government: New Departure or Business as Usual?" 102–103; and Andre Wakefield, *The Disordered Police State: German Cameralism as Science and Practice* (Chicago: University of Chicago Press, 2009). For an example of the application of the principles of cameralism to Russian administrative practice, see Marc Raeff, "The Well-Ordered Police State and the Development of Modernity in Seventeenth- and Eighteenth-Century Europe: An Attempt at a Comparative Approach," *American Historical Review* 80, no. 5 (1975): 1221–1243; Evgenii Anisimov, *The Reforms of Peter the Great: Progress through Coercion in Russia* (Armonk, NY: M. E. Sharpe, 1993); Lindsey Hughes, *Russia in the Age of Peter the Great* (New Haven: Yale University Press, 1998).

4. Anisimov, *The Reforms of Peter the Great*, 147, 158.

5. Marc Raeff, "The Enlightenment in Russia and Russian Thought in the Enlightenment," in J. G. Garrard, ed., *The Eighteenth Century in Russia* (Oxford: Clarendon, 1973), 25–47.

6. Raeff, "The Well-Ordered Police State," 1221–1235, 1226.

7. On the concept of social disciplining and its practice in early modern Europe, see Sheilagh Ogilvie, "'So that Every Subject Knows How to Behave': Social Disciplining in Early Modern Bohemia," *Comparative Studies in Society and History* 48, no. 1 (2006): 38–78, especially 38; on social disciplining in the Russian cultural context, see Mark Raeff, "Transfiguration and Modernization: The Paradoxes of Social Disciplining, Pedagogical Leadership, and the Enlightenment in Eighteenth-Century Russia" in idem, *Political Ideas and Institutions in Imperial Russia* (Boulder: Westview, 1994), 334–347; Lars Behrisch, "Social Discipline in Early Modern Russia, the Seventeenth to the Nineteenth Centuries," in Heinz Schilling and Lars Behrisch, eds., *Institutionen, Instrumente und Akteure sozialer Kontrolle und Disziplinierung im frühneuzeitlichen Europa* (Frankfurt am Main: Vittorio Klostermann, 1999), 325–357; and Paul Keenan. *St Petersburg and the Russian Court, 1703–1761* (Basingstoke: Palgrave Macmillan, 2013), 36–38.

8. Similar processes have been described by Daniel Gordon in the context of the Old Regime in France in *Citizens without Sovereignty: Equality and Sociability in French Thought, 1670–1789,* (Princeton: Princeton University Press, 1994), 39.

9. F. Veselago, *Ocherk istorii morskogo kadetskogo korpusa s prilozheniem spiska vospitannikov za 100 let* (St. Petersburg: Tipografiia Morskogo Kadetckogo Korpusa, 1852), 22–23.

10. Nicholas Hans, "The Moscow School of Mathematics and Navigation (1701)," *Slavonic and East European Review* 29, no. 73 (June 1951): 535; Alexander Boldyrev, "English Sundial Makers in Russia," *British Sundial Society (BSS) Bulletin* 18 (iii), October 2006, 105; Anthony Cross, *By the Banks of the Neva* (Cambridge: Cambridge University Press, 1997), 175; Smith, *Working the Rough Stone*, 78; Hughes, *Russia in the Age of Peter the Great*, 251; John. H. Appleby, "Mapping Russia: Farquharson, Delisle and the Royal Society," *Notes and Records of the Royal Society* 55, no. 2 (2001): 192; Robert Collis, "Alchemical Interest at the Petrine Court,"

Esoterica 7 (2005): 52–77; idem, *The Petrine Instauration: Religion, Esotericism and Science at the Court of Peter the Great, 1689–1725* (Leiden: Brill, 2012).

11. Hans, "The Moscow School of Mathematics and Navigation (1701)," 535; Smith, *Working the Rough Stone*, 78; Collis, "Alchemical Interest at the Petrine Court," 59, 62; Appleby, "Mapping Russia," 192; Hughes, *Russia in the Age of Peter the Great*, 251; Muireann Maguire, "The Wizard in the Tower: Iakov Brius and the Representation of Alchemists in Russian Literature," *Slavonic and East European Review* 90, no. 3 (2012): 406. For the English experimental tradition, see Steven Shapin, "The House of Experiment in Seventeenth-Century England," *Isis* 79, no. 3, A Special Issue on *Artifact and Experiment* (1988): 373–404, especially 376–379; Lesley Murdin, *Under Newton's Shadow: Astronomical Practices in the Seventeenth Century* (Bristol: Adam Hilger, 1985); Stephen Gaukroger, *Emergence of a Scientific Culture: Science and the Shaping of Modernity, 1210–1685* (Oxford: Oxford University Press, 2006); and idem, "Empiricism as a Development of Experimental Natural Philosophy," in Zvi Biener and Eric Schliesser, eds., *Newton and Empiricism* (Oxford: Oxford University Press, 2014), 15–38.

12. Hans, "The Moscow School of Mathematics and Navigation," 532–536; Boldyrev, "English Sundial Makers in Russia," 105; Smith, *Working the Rough Stone*, 78; Hughes, *Russia in the Age of Peter the Great*, 251.

13. Veselago, *Ocherk istorii morskogo kadetskogo korpusa*, 22–23.

14. Max J. Okenfuss, "Technical Training in Russia under Peter the Great," *History of Education Quarterly* 13, no. 4 (1973): 327; Appleby, "Mapping Russia," 192.

15. Bruce translated Christian Huygen's *Cosmotheros* into Russian, a text that contained references to the Copernican system (which was regarded as "heretical" in conservative Orthodox circles). See B. E. Raikov, *Ocherki istorii geliotsentricheskogo mirovozzreniia v Rossii* (Moscow and Leningrad: Izdatel'stvo Akademii Nauk SSSR, 1947); B. A. Vorontsov-Vel'iaminov, *Ocherki istorii astronomii v Rossii* (Moscow: Fizmatgiz, 1956); Hughes, *Russia in the Age of Peter the Great*, 311; Maguire, "The Wizard in the Tower: Iakov Brius and the Representation of Alchemists in Russian Literature," 406–407.

16. Okenfuss, "Technical Training in Russia," 328–329.

17. S. Maslikov, "Istoriia liubitel'skoi astronomii v Rossii i SSSR, chast' 1: Liubiteli-odinochki, XVII- nachalo XX veka," *Astronomiia i teleskopostroenie*. Accessed July 28, 2016. http://www.astronomer.ru/library.php?action=2&sub=2&gid=66.

18. Collis, "Alchemical Interest at the Petrine Court," 53, 57–59, 61–62.

19. L. A. Trakhtenberg, "Sumasbrodneishii, Vseshuteishii i Vsep'ianeishii sobor," in A. Ia. Gurevich, ed., *Odissei: Chelovek v istorii: Vremia i prostranstvo prazdnika*, (Moscow: Nauka, 2005): 89–118; Ernest Zitser, *The Transfigured Kingdom: Sacred Parody and Charismatic Authority at the Court of Peter the Great* (Ithaca: Cornell University Press, 2004).

20. On the seventeenth- to early eighteenth-centuries' learned societies and modes of learned entertainment, see Michael Hunter, *Science and Society in Restoration England* (Cambridge: Cambridge University Press, 1981), and Oliver Impey and Arthur MacGregor, eds., *The Origins of Museums: The Cabinet of Curiosities in Sixteenth- and Seventeenth-Century Europe* (Oxford: Clarendon, 1985); J. V. Golinski, "A Noble Spectacle: Research on Phosphorus and the Public Culture of Science in the Early Royal Society," *Isis* 80, no. 1 (1989): 11–39; Geoffrey V. Sutton, *Science for a Polite Society: Gender, Culture, and the Demonstration of Enlightenment* (Boulder: Westview, 1995).

21. Lotman, "Ocherki po istorii russkoi kul'tury XVIII-nachala XIX veka," 95; G. A. Gukovskii, *Russkaia Literatura XVIII veka* (Moscow: Gosuchpedgiz, 1939), 21–22; D. D. Blagoi, *Istoriia russkoi literatury XVIII v.* (Moscow: Gosuchpedgiz, 1951), 103, 141; G. V. Plekhanov, *Istoriia russkoi obshchestvennoi mysli*, vol. 2 (Moscow: Izdanie Tovarishchestva "Mir," 1925), 97–102; P. P. Epifanov, "'Uchenaia druzhina' i prosvetitel'stvo XVIII veka," *Voprosy istorii*,

no. 3 (1963): 37–53. The name *Uchenaia Druzhina* is occasionally translated as the "Learned Guard." See the English translation of Plekhanov's study, *History of Russian Social Thought* (New York: Howard Fertig, 1967), 58–68.

22. S. M. Solov'ev, *Istoriia Rossii s drevneishikh vremen*, book 10, vol. 20 (Moscow: Izdatel'stvo sotsial'no-ekonomicheskoi literatury, 1963), 550, 561.

23. Gukovskii, *Russkaia Literatura XVIII veka*, 21. Tatishchev's *History of Russia* was published originally under the title *Istoriia Rossiiskaia s samykh drevneishikh vremen, neusypnymi trudami cherez tridtsat' let sobrannaia pokoinym tainym sovetnikom i astrakhanskim gubernatorom Vasil'em Nikitichem Tatishchevym*, bk. 1, pts. 1 and 2 (Moscow Imperatorskii Moskovskii Universitet, 1768 and 1769). On Tatishchev as a historian, see N. A. Popov, *Tatishchev i ego vremia* (Moscow, 1861); idem, *Uchenye i literaturnye trudy V. N. Tatishcheva* (St. Petersburg, 1886); K. Bestuzhev-Riumin, "V. N. Tatishchev, administrator i istorik XVIII veka," in idem, *Biografii i kharakteristiki* (St. Petersburg, 1882), 94–140; Edward C. Thaden, "Tatishchev, German Historians, and the Academy of Sciences," in idem, with the collaboration of Marianna Forster Thaden, *Interpreting History: Collective Essays on Russia's Relations with Europe* (Boulder: Social Science Monographs/New York: Columbia University Press, 1990), 21–52; Aleksei Tolochko, "*Istoriia rossiiskaia*" *Vasiliia Tatishcheva: istochniki i izvestiia* (Moscow: Novoe literaturnoe obozrenie; Kiev: Kritika, 2005); M. B. Sverdlov, *Vasilii Nikitich Tatishchev—avtor i redaktor "Istorii Rossiiskoi"* (St. Petersburg: Evropeiskii dom, 2009).

24. Lotman, "Ocherki po istorii russkoi kul'tury," 95, 102.

25. Plekhanov, *Istoriia russkoi obshchestvennoi mysli*, 2: 97–102.

26. Ia. D. Betiaev, *Obshchestvenno-politicheskaia i filosofskaia mysl' v Rossii v pervoi polovine XVIII v.* (Saransk: Mordovskoe knizhnoe izdatel'stvo, 1959), 209, 214, 273, 286; M. I. Radovskii, *Kantemir i Peterburgskaia Akademiia Nauk* (Moscow-Leningrad: Izdatel'stvo AN SSSR, 1959), 32.

27. Epifanov, "'Uchenaia druzhina,'" 38.

28. Antioch Kantemir, "Satira I. Na khuliashchikh uchenie: K umu svoemu," in A. D. Kantemir, *Sobranie stikhotvorenii* (Leningrad: Sovetskii pisatel', 1956), 57–67, 361, 442, 501.

29. "Feofan Arkhiepiskop Novgorodskii k avtoru satiry," in Feofan Prokopovich, *Sochineniia* (Moscow-Leningrad: Izdatel'stvo Akademii Nauk SSSR, 1961), 215–17, 482–83.

30. F. I. Priima, "Antiokh Dmitrievich Kantemir: Vstupitel'naia stat'ia," in Kantemir, *Sobranie stikhotvorenii*, 5–56.

31. For the biography and literary activity of Antioch Kantemir, see V. Pokrovskii, ed., *Antiokh Dmitrievich Kantemir, Ego zhizn' i tvorchestvo: Sbornik istoriko-literaturnykh statei* (Moscow: V. Spiridonov and A. Mikhailov, 1910); Radovskii, *Antiokh Kantemir*; I. Z. Serman, "Prosvetitel'stvo i russkaia literatura pervoi poloviny XVIII veka," in P. N. Berkov, ed., *Problema russkogo prosveshcheniia v literature XVIII veka* (Moscow: Akademiia Nauk, 1961), 28–44; A. V. Zapadov, "A. Kantemir," in *Poety XVIII veka* (Moscow: Izdatel'stvo Moskovskogo Universiteta, 1984).

32. Priima, "Antiokh Dmitrievich Kantemir," 8; N. Popov, *Uchenye i literaturnye trudy V. N. Tatishcheva* (St. Petersburg, 1886), 10.

33. On the succession crisis, see D. M. Korsakov, *Votsarenie imperatritsy Anny Ioanovny* (Kazan': n.p., 1880); David L. Ransel, "The Government Crisis of 1730," in Robert O. Crummey, ed., *Reform in Russia and U.S.S.R.: Past and Prospects* (Urbana and Chicago: University of Illinois Press, 1989), 45–71; Marc Raeff, *Plans for Political Reform in Imperial Russia, 1730–1905* (Englewood Cliffs: Prentice-Hall, 1966); Alexander Lipski, "Some Aspects of Russia's Westernization during the Reign of Anna Ioannovna, 1730–1740," *American Slavic and East European Review* 18, no. 1 (1959): 1–11.

34. V. N. Tatishchev, "Proizvol'noe i soglasnoe rassuzhdenie i mnenie sobravshegosia shliakhetstva russkogo o pravlenii gosudarstva," first published in *Utro: Literaturnyi sbornik* (Moscow, 1859), 359–369; On Tatishchev's project, see Popov, *Uchenye i literaturnye trudy V. N. Tatishcheva*, 13–14; Rudolph L. Daniels, "V. N. Tatishchev and the Succession Crisis of 1730," *Slavonic and East European Review* 49, no. 117 (1971): 550–559; Raeff, *Plans for Political Reform in Imperial Russia*, 44.

35. Daniels, "V. N. Tatishchev and the Succession Crisis," 556.

36. F. I. Priima, "Antiokh Dmitrievich Kantemir: Vstupitel'naia stat'ia," in Kantemir, *Sobranie stikhotvorenii*, 11, 14; Betiaev, *Obshchestvenno-politicheskaia i filosofskaia mysl'*, 209, 214, 273, 286.

37. Popov, *Uchenye i literaturnye trudy V. N. Tatishcheva*, 15, 24.

38. Antioch Kantemir, Satira III, "O razlichii strastei chelovecheskikh. K arkhiepiskopu Novgorodskomu"; "Blagodaritel'nye stikhi Feofanu Prokopovichu ('Ustami ty menia obiazal i rukoiu . . .')"; "Epodos Consolatoria ad oden Rastoris Pimini sortem gregis sub tempestatem deplorantis," in Kantemir, *Sobranie stikhotvorenii*, 89–108, 448; 260, 477; 261, 477.

39. Popov, *Uchenye i literaturnye trudy V. N. Tatishcheva*, 16; Bestuzhev-Riumin, "V. N. Tatishchev," 94–140.

40. Popov, *Uchenye i literaturnye trudy V. N. Tatishcheva*, 38.

41. L. N. Maikov, *Materialy dlia biografii kniazia A. D. Kantemira, Sbornik otdeleniia russkogo iazyka i slovesnosti Imperatorskoi Akademii Nauk*, vol. 73 (St. Petersburg, 1903), 21–25, 103–104.

42. On "uchenaia druzhina" as "a community of writers with a sense of solidarity and mission," see Derek Offord, *Journeys to a Graveyard: Perceptions of Europe in Classical Russian Travel Writing* (Dordrecht: Springer, 2005), 50; W. Gareth Jones, "The Image of the Eighteenth-Century Russian Author," in Roger Bartlett and Janet M. Hartley, eds., *Russia in the Age of the Enlightenment: Essays for Isabel de Madariaga*, (Basingstoke: Macmillan, 1990), 59–60.

43. James Cracraft, "Feofan Prokopovich," in J. G. Garrard, ed., *The Eighteenth Century in Russia* (Oxford: Clarendon, 1973): 89.

44. Popov, *Uchenye i literaturnye trudy V. N. Tatishcheva*, 15–6; Lipski, "Some Aspects of Russia's Westernization during the Reign of Anna Ioanovna, 1730–1740," 3; S. N. Valk, "V. N. Tatishchev i nachalo novoi russkoi istoricheskoi literatury" in D. S. Likhachev, G. P. Makogonenko, I. Z. Serman, eds., *Rol' i znachenie literatury XVIII veka v istorii russkoi kul'tury: k 70-iu so dnia rozhdeniia P. N. Berkova* (Moscow-Leningrad: Nauka, 1966), 66–73, especially 70–71; I. V. Valkina, "K voprosu ob istochnikakh Tatishcheva," in ibid., 74–85, especially 83; Viktor Tsvirkun, "Nauchnye sviazi Antiokha Kantemira s Sankt-Peterburgskoi Akademiei nauk," *Rossiiskaia istoriia*, 2013 no. 2 (2013): 97–101.

45. This is how the academy was defined in the charter granted by Alexander I in 1803. See "Ustav Akademii Nauk, 20863, Iiulia 25 [1803]," in *Polnoe sobranie zakonov Rossiiskoi Imperii*, 27: 788.

46. A. Lipski, "The Foundation of the Russian Academy of Sciences," *Isis* 44, no. 4 (1953): 349–354.

47. "Draft of Leibniz's Memorandum on the Improvement of Arts and Sciences in Russia, 1716," in George Vernadsky, ed., *A Source Book for Russian History from Early Times to 1917*, vol. 2, *Peter the Great to Nicolas I* (New Haven: Yale University Press, 1972), 368.

48. "Draft of Leibniz's letter or oral memorandum to Peter the Great, January 16, 1712," in Vernadsky, *A Source Book for Russian History*, 2: 366; see also Lipski, "The Foundation of the Russian Academy of Sciences," 349; Michael D. Gordin, "The Importation of Being Earnest: The Early St. Petersburg Academy of Sciences," *Isis* 91, no. 1 (2000): 6.

49. On the development of Leibniz's views on scientific academies, see Ayval Ramati, "Harmony at a Distance: Leibniz's Scientific Academies," *Isis* 87, no. 3 (1996): 430–452.

50. J. R. R. Christie, "The Development of Historiography of Science," in R. C. Olby, G. N. Cantor, J. R. R. Christie, and M. J. S. Hodge, *Companion to the History of Modern Science* (London: Routledge, 1990), 11. The French Académie Royale des Sciences was founded in 1666. The Royal Society of London was chartered in 1662. See Roger L. Emerson, "The Organization of Science and Its Pursuit in Early Modern Europe," in Olby, et.al., *Companion to the History of Modern Science*, 971; the Berlin Society of Sciences was founded in 1700. See Ramati, "Harmony at a Distance," 449; Marry Terrall, "The Culture of Science in Frederick the Great's Berlin," *History of Sciences* 28, no. 4 (Dec. 1990): 333–365. For a useful comparative analysis of the patterns of these institutions' organizational structure, see James Edward McClellan III, *The International Organization of Science and Learned Societies in the Eighteenth Century* (Ann Arbor: University Microfilms International, 1982), 61–95.

51. On the distinction between old universities and new scientific societies, see Ernan McMullin, "The Development of Philosophy of Science, 1600–1900," in Olby, et al., *Companion to the History of Modern Science*, 802–805.

52. Quoted in Alexander Vucinich, *Science in Russian Culture: A History to 1860* (Stanford: Stanford University Press, 1963), 69.

53. Emerson, "The Organization of Science," 972 (this article includes an appendix [977–979] with a list of selected academies and societies); Roger Hahn, *The Anatomy of Scientific Institution: The Paris Academy of Sciences, 1666–1803* (Berkeley and Los Angeles: University of California Press, 1971).

54. "Proekt polozheniia Akademii nauk i khudozhestv, 22 ianvaria 1724," *Istoriia SSSR*, no. 2 (1974): 97. For an English translation, see "The Decree on the Founding of the Academy of Sciences, January 28, 1724" in Vernadsky, ed., *A Source Book for Russian History*, 2: 369. (Quotes taken from the English translation.) Nonetheless, the seventeenth-century French private academies where young nobles were taught riding, fencing, dancing, and military mathematics constituted a distinctive type of academies as learning institutions in Western Europe. See Mark Edward Motley, *Becoming a French Aristocrat: The Education of the Court Nobility, 1580–1715* (Princeton: Princeton University Press, 1990), 123–168. I am grateful to Oded Rabinovitch for drawing my attention to this phenomenon.

55. "Proekt polozheniia Akademii nauk i khudozhestv," 97–98; Vernadsky, *A Source Book for Russian History*, 2: 369.

56. Vucinich, *Science in Russian Culture*, 47. On the difference between the English term "science" and the German "Wissenschaft," see Ernan McMullin, "The Development of the Philosophy of Science, 1600–1900," in Olby, et al., *Companion to the History of Modern Science*, 802. According to McMullin, the term *Wissenschaft* "corresponds more closely to the epistemological concept of *scientia* or *philosophia*, denoting a methodology rather than area of study."

57. "Proekt polozheniia Akademii nauk i khudozhestv," 98. This post was initially offered to Theophilus Siegfried Bayer, who, however, preferred antiquities and eastern languages. See V. O. Kliuchevskii, "Lektsii po russkoi istoriographii," in V. O. Kliuchevskii, *Sochineniia*, vol. 8, *Issledovaniia, retsenzii, rechi (1890–1905)* (Moscow, Izdatel'stvo sotsial'no-ekonomicheskoi literatury, 1959), 396. On Bayer, see also M. N. Tikhomirov et. al., *Ocherki istorii istoricheskoi nauki v SSSR*, vol. 1 (Moscow: AN SSSR Institut Istorii, 1955); M. N. Tikhomirov, "Russkaia istoriografiia: XVIII vek," *Voprosy istorii*, no. 2 (1948): 95–97; N. L. Rubinshtein, *Russkaia istoriografiia* (Moscow: OGIZ Gospolitizdat, 1941); V. K. Iatsunskii, *Istoricheskaia geografiia* (Moscow: AN SSSR, 1955).

58. A. B. Kamenskii, "Sud'ba i trudy istoriografa Gerarda Fridrikha Millera (1705–1783)," in G. F. Miller, *Sochineniia po istorii Rossii: Izbrannoe* (Moscow: Nauka, 1996), 376.

59. Lipski, "Some Aspects of Russia's Westernization," 6.

60. Kamenskii, "Sud'ba i trudy istoriografa Gerarda Fridrikha Millera," 377–378. See also Hans Rogger, *National Consciousness in Eighteenth Century Russia* (Cambridge, MA: Harvard University Press, 1960), 203.

61. Kamenskii, "Sud'ba i trudy istoriografa Gerarda Fridrikha Millera," 387.

62. Hans Rogger observed that, with the resumption of the *Sammlung*, many of the articles that were first published there were translated into Russian and appeared in *Monthly Essays*. See Rogger, *National Consciousness in Eighteenth Century Russia*, 211.

63. R. J. W. Evans, "Learned Societies in Germany in the Seventeenth Century," *European Studies Review*, 7 (1977): 145; and David S. Lux and Harold J. Cook, "Closed Circles or Open Networks? Communicating at a Distance during the Scientific Revolution," *History of Science* 36, no. 2 (1998): 179–211.

64. McClellan, *The International Organization of Science and Learned Societies*, viii.

65. Evans, "Learned Societies in Germany," 144. This book, Demetrii Cantemirii, *Principis Moldaviae* (Petropoli, 1727), was later published in Russian as: *Dmitriia Kantemira, byvshego kniazia v Moldavii, istoricheskoe, geograficheskoe i politicheskoe opisanie Moldavii s zhizn'iu sochinitelia, s nemetskogo perelozheniia perevel Vasilii Levshin* (Moscow: Universitetskaia Tipografiia u N. Novikova, 1789). His earlier historical work, *Historia incrementorum atque descrementorum Aulae Ottomanicae*, was written in 1714–1716 in Moscow. In 1734–1735 Antioch Kantemir published this manuscript together with his father's biography in English in London (where he served as Russian ambassador) under the title *The Life of Demetrius Cantemir Prince of Moldavia*. P. V. Gusterin, *Pervyi russkii vostokoved Dmitrii Kantemir* (Moscow: Vostochnaia kniga, 2008). On Dmitrii Kantemir's scholarly works see also: Tsvirkun, "Nauchnye sviazi Antiokha Kantemira s Sankt-Peterburgskoi Akademiei nauk," 98–100; P. P. Panaitescu, *Dimitrie Cantemir, His Life and Work* (Bucharest: Romanian Academy's Printing House, 1958), and Gabriela Pohoață, "Dimitrie Cantemir and G. W. Leibniz: Encyclopedists with European Vocation," *Cogito: Multidisciplinary Research Journal* 2, no. 4 (2010): 13–20.

66. Hans Aarsleff, "The Berlin Academy under Frederick the Great," *History of the Human Sciences* 12, no. 2 (1989): 193.

67. McClellan, *The International Organization of Science and Learned Societies in the Eighteenth Century*, 95; on Euler in the Berlin Academy see also Aarsleff, "The Berlin Academy under Frederick the Great," 194, 200, 203, 204. In 1744 the Berlin Society of Sciences merged with the "ex-officio" New Literary Society (*Nouvelle Société Littéraire*) into the Royal Academy of Sciences (*Königliche Akademie der Wissenschaften*), officially inaugurated by Frederick the Great in 1746. See McClellan, *The International Organization of Science and Learned Societies in the Eighteenth Century*, 96.

68. Gordin, "The Importation of Being Earnest," 21, 2.

69. "Proekt polozheniia Akademii nauk i khudozhestv," 99, Vernadsky, *A Source Book for Russian History*, 2: 369.

70. "Proekt polozheniia Akademii nauk i khudozhestv," 101.

71. Gordin, "The Importation of Being Earnest," 15.

72. "Proekt polozheniia Akademii nauk i khudozhestv," 100. For the significance of such assemblies for Peter's etiquette reform, see Gordin, "The Importation of Being Earnest," 15–17.

73. Smith, *Working the Rough Stone*, 71; K. V. Ostrovitianov, ed., *Istoriia Akademii Nauk SSSR*, 1: 1724–1803 (Moscow-Leningrad: Izdatel'stvo Akademii Nauk SSSR, 1958), 52, 172–174, 330.

74. Keith Michael Baker, "Enlightenment and Revolution in France: Old Problems, Renewed Approaches," *Journal of Modern History* 53, no. 2 (1981): 295; and Daniel Gordon, *Citizens without Sovereignty: Equality and Sociability in French Thought, 1670–1789* (Princeton: Princeton University Press, 1994), 35.

75. Solov'ev, *Istoriia Rossii s drevneishikh vremen*, book 10, vol. 20, 526–527. Lipski, "Some Aspects of Russia's Westernization," 3–4.

76. M. I. Sukhomlinov, *Istoriia Rossiiskoi Akademii* (St. Petersburg: Tipografiia Imperatorskoi Akademii Nauk, 1874), 6.

77. V. K. Trediakovskii, "Rech' skazannaia Trediakovskim 14 marta 1735 g. po sluchaiu otkrytiia Rossiiskogo sobraniia," in A. Kunik, ed., *Sbornik materialov dlia istorii Imperatorskoi Akademii Nauk v XVIII v.*, pt. 1 (St. Petersburg, n.p., 1865), 7–16; Gary Marker, *Publishing, Printing and the Origins of Intellectual Life in Russia, 1700–1800* (Princeton: Princeton University Press, 1985), 53.

78. Vucinich, *Science in Russian Culture*, 90, 105. For the Russian Conference, see Marker, *Publishing, Printing and the Origins of Intellectual Life in Russia*, 50–58; Rogger, *National Consciousness in Eighteenth Century Russia*, 96; Lotman, "Ocherki po istorii russkoi kul'tury," 95.

79. Kamenskii, "Sud'ba i trudy istoriografa Gerarda Fridrikha Millera," 380. According to Sukhomlinov, "in 1743 it was reported to the Senate that the Russian Conference had been dismantled and its members had received other appointments." Sukhomlinov, *Istoriia Rossiiskoi Akademii*, 6.

80. G. F. Müller, "Proekt sozdaniia Istoricheskogo departamenta Akademii nauk," in idem, *Sochineniia po istorii Rossii: Izbrannoe* (Moscow: Nauka, 1990), 358.

81. Ibid., 361.

82. Müller's classification included (1) all types of Russian chronicles, whether concerning Russia as a whole or specific regions; (2) texts (*pis'mennye knigi*) about Tatar history written in Turkish or Persian; (3) archives in St. Petersburg, Moscow, and other large Russian cities; (4) works of church hagiography (lives of the Russian saints); (5) documents regarding the foundation of churches, monasteries, and convents; (6) inscriptions on tombs; (7) the family registers of nobility together with other genealogical materials; (8) Russian antiquities; (9) oral stories; and (10) foreign printed books on Russia, Lithuania, Courland, Prussia, and other German states, as well as on Poland, Sweden, Denmark, Turkey, Persia, and China. Such books, Müller believed, might include "fragmentary descriptions of Russian history," especially in those cases when "neighboring countries communicated with Russian history via wars, treaties, and alliances." See ibid., 360–361.

83. Ibid., 360.

84. Ibid., 360–62.

85. P. P. Pekarskii, *Istoriia Imperatorskoi Akademii Nauk v Peterburge*, vol. 1 (St. Petersburg: Tipografiia Imperatorskoi Akademii nauk, 1870), 346–347; "Iz protokolov istoricheskogo sobraniia Peterburgskoi Akademii Nauk (obsuzhdenie knigi G. F. Millera 'Istoriia Sibiri'), June 3 and 6, 1748" in V. V. Fomin, *Lomonosov: Genii russkoi istorii* (Moscow: Russkaia panorama, 2006), 441–443.

86. V. V. Krestinin, *Kratkaia istoriia o gorode Arkhangel'skom* (St. Petersburg: pri Imperatorskoi Akademii nauk, 1792), 243–247; A. A. Ivanov, "V. V. Krestinin, Osnovatel' pervogo chastnogo istoricheskogo obshchestva," *Nasha starina* (St. Petersburg), no. 11 (1916): 779; F. I. Cherniakhovskii, *Vasilii Vasil'evich Krestinin* (Arkhangel'sk: Arkhangel'skoe Knizhnoe Izdatel'stvo, 1956), 15.

87. Ivanov, "V. V. Krestinin," 779.

88. A. A. Kizevetter, *Istoricheskie ocherki* (Moscow: 1912), 101.

89. V. Rudakov, "Krestinin Vasilii Vasil'evich (Po povodu stoletiia so dnia smerti)," *Zhurnal Ministerstva Narodnogo Prosveshcheniia* 299, no. 5 (May 1895): 219–225; Cherniakhovskii, *Vasilii Vasil'evich Krestinin*, 15–16.

90. The titles of these works were "Istoricheskie nachatki o dvinskom narode drevnego, srednego i novogo vremeni" (1784) and "Istoricheskii opyt o sel'skom starinnom domostroitel'stve dvinskogo naroda na severe" (1785). In addition, Krestinin also authored "Nachertanie istorii g. Kholmogor" (1790) and the above-mentioned "Kratkaia istoriia o gorode Arkhangel'skom" (1792). See also U. M. Poliakova, "V. V. Krestinin i obshchestvennaia bor'ba v Arkhangel'skom posade v 60-kh-90-kh gg. XVIII v.," *Istoriia SSSR*, no. 2 (1958): 78–102; S. L. Peshtich, *Russkaia istoriografiia XVIII v.* (Leningrad: Izdatel'stvo LGU, 1965), pt. 2.

91. Adrian Jones, "A Russian Bourgeois's Arctic Enlightenment," *Historical Journal*, 48, no. 3 (September 2005): 623–640.

92. One of the first societies of this kind, the Honorable Society of Improvers of the Knowledge of Agriculture, was established in Edinburgh in 1723. It aimed "to serve members with general instruction on scientific agriculture and offer advice on specific problems." See R. J. Morris, "Clubs, Societies and Associations," 404. See also Henry Ernst Lowood, *Patriotism, Profit, and the Promotion of Science in the German Enlightenment: The Economic and Scientific Societies, 1760–1815* (Berkeley: University of California Press, 1987), 1–11; Roger Hahn, "The Application of Science to Society: The Societies of Arts," *Studies on Voltaire and the Eighteenth Century* 25 (1963): 829–863; James E. McClellan III, *Science Reorganized: Scientific Societies in the Eighteenth Century* (New York: Columbia University Press, 1985); Charles C. Gillispie, *Science and Polity in France at the End of the Old Regime* (Princeton: Princeton University Press, 1980).

93. V. V. Oreshkin, *Vol'noe ekonomicheskoe obshchestvo v Rossii (1765–1917)* (Moscow: Izdatel'stvo Akademii nauk SSSR, 1963), 14.

94. Ibid., 15; P. S. Biliarskii, ed., *Materialy dlia biografii Lomonosova* (St. Petersburg, 1865), 616; Bradley, *Voluntary Associations in Tsarist Russia*, 47.

95. James Arthur Prescott, "The Russian Free Economic Society: Foundation Years," *Agricultural History* 51, no. 3 (July, 1977): 505–506; Leckey, "Patronage and Public Culture in the Russian Free Economic Society," 364.

96. N. P. Cherepnin, *Imperatorskoe vospitatel'noe obshchestvo blagorodnykh devits: Istoricheskii ocherk, 1714–1914*, vols. 1–3 (St. Petersburg/Petrograd, 1914–1915). For the decree that founded the Society and formulated its statutes see vol. 3, 26, 27–51.

97. Leckey, "Patronage and Public Culture in the Russian Free Economic Society," 364.

98. D. G. C. Allan, "The Society of Arts and Government, 1734–1800: Public Encouragement of Arts, Manufactures, and Commerce in Eighteenth-Century England," *Eighteenth-Century Studies* 7, no. 4 (1974): 434–452.

99. A. I. Khodnev, *Istoriia Imperatorskogo vol'nogo ekonomicheskogo obshchestva s 1765 do 1865 goda (sostavlennaia po porucheniiu obshchestva sekretarem ego)* (St. Petersburg, 1865), 1.

100. "Preduvedomlenie," in *Ustav Imperatorskogo Vol'nogo Ekonomicheskogo Obshchestva, udostoennyi vysochaishego utverzhdeniia 27 fevralia 1859 goda* (St. Petersburg, 1859), 5–6.

101. Khodnev, *Istoriia Imperatorskogo vol'nogo ekonomicheskogo obshchestva*, 1.

102. "Preduvedomlenie," 6–7.

103. "Vsemilostiveishii otvet Imperatritsy Ekateriny II," in *Ustav Imperatorskogo Vol'nogo Ekonomicheskogo Obshchestva*, 7–8.

104. Leckey, "Patronage and Public Culture in the Russian Free Economic Society," 361–362; Khodnev, *Istoriia Imperatorskogo vol'nogo ekonomicheskogo obshchestva*, 34.

105. Leckey, "Patronage and Public Culture in the Russian Free Economic Society," 364.

106. Joan Klobe Pratt, "The Free Economic Society and the Battle against Smallpox: A 'Public Sphere' in Action," *Russian Review* 61, no. 4 (2002): 561–562.

107. "Nakaz," 22, clauses 148, 149; 39, clauses 245, 248; 54, clause 356; 20–21, clause 138; 1, clause 2.

108. Trentmann, "Paradoxes of Civil Society," 25–26.

109. The orientation toward the future makes it possible to consider the *Nakaz* a document relating to *Sattelzeit*, that period of time from the mid-eighteenth to the nineteenth century when, according to Reinhart Koselleck, modern political and social concepts were reformulated or created. The term *Sattelzeit* was central for *Begriffsgeschichte*. For a useful analysis of Koselleck's approach to *Sattelzeit* see Melvin Richter, "Reconstructing the History of Political Languages: Pocock, Skinner, and the *Geschichtliche Grundbegriffe*," *History and Theory* 29, no. 1 (1990): 38–70, especially 44–45. Although *Begriffsgeschichte* addresses German historical concepts, this methodological approach has proved useful in a variety of national contexts, Russian history included. See Koposov, ed., *Istoricheskie poniatiia i politicheskie idei v Rossii XIV–XX veka* for a fine example of how Koselleck's ideas can be productively applied to the Russian historical context.

110. On the distinctiveness of the modern concepts see Reinhart Koselleck, *Futures Past: On the Semantics of Historical Time* (Cambridge, MA: MIT Press, 1985); Terence Ball, *Transforming Political Discourse: Political Theory and Critical Conceptual History* (Oxford: Basil Blackwell, 1988), especially 10; N. E. Koposov, "Istoriia poniatii vchera i segodnia," in idem, ed., *Istoricheskie poniatiia i politicheskie idei v Rossii XIV–XX veka*, 18–19.

111. Leckey, "Patronage and Public Culture," 366, 379; Joseph Bradley, "Subjects into Citizens: Societies, Civil Society, and Autocracy in Tsarist Russia," *American Historical Review* 107, no. 4 (2002): 1102–1106.

112. Khodnev, *Istoriia Imperatorskogo vol'nogo ekonomicheskogo obshchestva*, 4.

113. On the *Trudy* see J. H. Brown, "The Publication and Distribution of the *Trudy* of the Free Economic Society, 1765–1796," *Russian Review* 36, no. 3 (1977): 341–350.

114. James L. Rice, "The Bolotov Papers and Andrei Timofeevich Bolotov, Himself," *Russian Review* 35, no. 2 (1976): 125–144.

115. Smith, *Working the Rough Stone*, 61.

116. On the Free Economic Society's contribution to the development of associational life in Russia, see Bradley, *Voluntary Associations in Tsarist Russia*, 51–58.

117. Sukhomlinov, *Istoriia Rossiiskoi Akademii*, 6–7.

118. Marker, *Publishing, Printing and the Origins of Intellectual Life in Russia*, 91.

119. For Kozel'skii, see Vucinich, *Science in Russian Culture*, 175–176.

120. Marker, *Publishing, Printing, and the Origins of Intellectual Life in Russia*, 91.

121. Smith, *Working the Rough Stone*, 82–83.

122. Sukhomlinov, *Istoriia Rossiiskoi Akademii*, 7.

123. V. O. Kliuchevskii, "Iubilei Obshchestva Istorii i Drevnostei Rossiiskikh," in idem, *Neopublikovannye proizvedeniia* (Moscow: Nauka, 1983), 191.

124. Sukhomlinov, *Istoriia Rossiiskoi Akademii*, 9–10; see also Smith, *Working the Rough Stone*, 84; Rogger, *National Consciousness in Eighteenth Century Russia*, 115.

125. Kamenskii, "Sud'ba i trudy istoriografa Gerarda Fridrikha Millera," 393–394, 402; Rogger, *National Consciousness in Eighteenth Century Russia*, 213; Marker, *Publishing, Printing, and the Origins of Intellectual Life in Russia*, 123–124.

126. Rogger, *National Consciousness in Eighteenth Century Russia*, 85; Marc Raeff, "At the Origins of a Russian National Consciousness: Eighteenth Century Roots and Napoleonic Wars," *History Teacher* 25, no. 1 (1991): 7–18.

127. *Ecclesiastical Dictionary* (*Tserkovnyi slovar' ili istolkovanie rechenii drevnikh, takozh inoiazychnykh, bez perevoda polozhennykh v tserkovnom pisanii i drugikh tserkovnykh*

knigakh) was published in 1773. Its author, Petr Alekseev, combined his service as archpriest of Arkhangel'skii cathedral in Moscow with teaching Divine Law (*Zakon bozhii*) in Moscow University. He was elected as a member of the Free Russian Assembly in 1771 and later became a member of the Russian Academy. See Evgenii (Bolkhovitinov), *Slovar' istoricheskii o byvshikh v Rossii pisateliakh dukhovnogo china* (St. Petersburg, 1827); Sukhomlinov, *Istoriia Rossiiskoi Akademii*, 336–343.

128. Rogger, *National Consciousness in Eighteenth Century Russia*, 115.

129. Stepanskii, *Istoriia nauchnykh uchrezhdenii i organizatsii dorevoliutsionnoi Rossii*, 9.

130. Raeff argues that this attitude became fully developed in the early 1800s. See Raeff, "At the Origins of a Russian National Consciousness," 12.

131. V. O. Kliuchevskii, "Iubilei Obshchestva Istorii i Drevnostei Rossiiskikh," 191; G. N. Moiseeva, "'Slovo o polku Igoreve' i Ekaterina II," *XVIII vek*, vol. 18 (St. Petersburg: Nauka, 1993), 9.

132. Dmitrii Kobeko, "Uchenik Vol'tera: Graf Andrei Petrovich Shuvalov (1744–1789)," *Russkii arkhiv*, no. 2 (1881): 277.

133. Kliuchevskii, "Iubilei Obshchestva Istorii i Drevnostei Rossiiskikh," 192.

134. See also Kobeko, "Uchenik Vol'tera," 277–278.

135. E. P. Dashkova, *Zapiski. Pis'ma sester M. i K. Vil'mont iz Rossii* (Moscow: Izdatel'stvo MGU, 1987), 160–161.

136. Sukhomlinov, *Istoriia Rossiiskoi Akademii*, 14.

137. Ibid., 20, 29, 40, 15–19. For M. M. Shcherbatov and I. N. Boltin as historians see Kliuchevskii, "Lektsii po russkoi istoriografii," 420–438.

138. "Kratkoe nachertanie imperatorskoi Rossiiskoi Akademii," in Sukhomlinov, *Istoriia Rossiiskoi Akademii*, 360.

139. "Protocol of the meeting of the Russian Academy on February 14, 1790," cited in ibid., 376.

140. Marker, *Publishing, Printing, and the Origins of Intellectual Life in Russia*, 93; A. I. Serkov and M. V. Reizin, eds., *Pis'ma N. I. Novikova* (St. Petersburg: Izdatel'stvo im. N. I. Novikova, 1994), 275.

141. A. A. Govorov and T. G. Kupriianova, eds., *Istoriia knigi: Uchebnik dlia vuzov* (Moscow: Izdatel'stvo MGPU "Mir knigi," 1998). Accessed August 3, 2015. www.hi-edu.ru/e-books/HB/15-1.htm.

142. Marker, *Publishing, Printing, and the Origins of Intellectual Life in Russia*, 93–94.

143. *Razmyshleniia o grecheskoi istorii, ili o prichinakh blagodenstviia i neschastiia grekov; sochinenie g. abbata de Mabli. Perevedeno s frantsuzskogo [A. N. Radishchevym], Izhdiveniem Obshchestva Staraiushchegosia o napechatanii knig. Prodaetsia v Lugovoi Milionnoi ulitse u knigoprodavtsa K. V. Millera* (St. Petersburg: Pri Imp. Akademii Nauk, 1773). See also Thomas Riha, ed., *Readings in Russian Civilization*, vol. 2, *Imperial Russia, 1700–1917*, 2nd rev. ed. (University of Chicago Press, 1969), 262.

144. Serkov and Reizin, eds., *Pis'ma N. I. Novikova*, 277.

145. V. Bogoliubov, *N. I. Novikov i ego vremia* (Moscow: Izdatel'stvo M. i S. Sabashnikovykh, 1916), 133.

146. W. Gareth Jones, "The *Morning Light* Charity Schools, 1777–1780," *Slavonic and East European Review*, 56, no. 1 (1978): 49.

147. Kamenskii, "Sud'ba i trudy istoriografa Gerarda Fridrikha Millera," 402.

148. G. N. Moiseeva, "Arkheograficheskaia deiatel'nost' N. I. Novikova," in G. P. Makagonenko, ed., *XVIII vek*, vol. 11, *N. I. Novikov i obshchestvenno-literaturnoe dvizhenie ego vremeni* (Leningrad: Nauka, Leningradskoe otdelenie, 1976), 24–36, especially 29–33.

149. Bogoliubov, *N. I. Novikov i ego vremia*, 133.

150. N. I. Novikov, "Preduvedomlenie," in A. L. Rychkov, ed., *Utrennii svet Nikolaia Novikova* (Moscow: Tsentr knigi Rudomino, 2012), 13–21; *Obshchestvo staraiushchimsia o spomoshchestvovanii zavedeniiu uchilishch* (St. Petersburg: Utrennii svet, 1777–1780).

151. G. A.Sagalakova, "Samosoznanie soobshchestva rossiiskikh martinistov i rozenkreitserov v otechestvennoi kul'ture poslednei chetverti XVIII veka" (PhD diss., Altai State University, 2004); L. I. Kulakova, "Kheraskov," in *Istoriia russkoi literatury*, vol. 4, pt. 2 (Moscow-Leningrad: Izdatel'stvo Akademii Nauk, 1947), 320; idem, "Vstupitel'naia stat'ia," in M. N. Murav'ev, *Stikhotvoreniia* (Leningrad: Sovetskii pisatel', 1967), 6–7.

152. Mikhail Murav'ev, "Pis'ma ottsu i sestre 1777–1778," in L. I. Kulakova, ed., *Pis'ma russkikh pisatelei XVIII veka* (Leningrad: Nauka, Leningradskoe otdelenie, 1980), letters of Aug. 10, 15, 25 ; Oct. 26, 30; Nov. 2, 6, 1777; Jan. 1, 4, 18, 1778: 270, 274, 308–312, 333–335, 338.

153. Isabelle de Madariaga, *Russia in the Age of Catherine the Great* (London: Weidenfeld and Nicholson, 1981), 494–495.

154. S. E. Usova, *N. I. Novikov, Ego zhizn' i obshchestvennaia deiatel'nost'* (St. Petersburg: Tipografiia tovarishchestva "Obshchestvennaia pol'za," 1892), 42; Bogoliubov, *N. I. Novikov i ego vremia*, 276.

155. P. N. Miliukov, *Ocherki po istorii russkoi kul'tury*, vol. 3 (Moscow: Progress-Kul'tura, 1995), 353.

156. Bogoliubov, *N. I. Novikov i ego vremia*, 277.

157. According to Isabel de Madariaga, in 1784 the Commission on National Schools was ordered to inspect all private schools and boarding schools. As a result all private schools were closed and their pupils advised or compelled to transfer to the new national schools, which were opened in the two capitals from 1783 onward. "Novikov's schools," she wrote, "were now absorbed into the state system." Madariaga, *Russia in the Age of Catherine the Great*, 496.

158. Rafaella Faggionato, *A Rosicrucian Utopia in Eighteenth Century Russia: The Masonic Circle of N. I. Novikov* (Dordrecht, Netherlands: Springer, 2005), 32.

159. On Murav'ev's attitude to Masonry see A. N. Pashkurov, O. V. Miasnikov, *M. N. Murav'ev: Voprosy poetiki, mirovozzreniia i tvorchestva* (Kazan': Izdatel'stvo Kazanskogo gosudarstvennogo universiteta, 2004), 42–77; V. A. Zapadov, "M. N. Murav'ev," *Slovar' russkikh pisatelei XVIII veka*, vol. 2 (St. Petersburg: Nauka, 1999), 308–309.

160. The "princess" Murav'ev referred to was identified as E. B. Urusova by L. I. Kulakova, "N. I. Novikov v pis'makh M. N. Murav'eva," in Makagonenko, ed., *N. I. Novikov i obshchestvenno-literaturnoe dvizhenie ego vremeni*, 17.

161. Jones, "The *Morning Light* Charity Schools," 58; on V. P. Petrov and his political influence, see Andrei Zorin, *Kormia dvuglavogo orla . . . : Literatura i gosudarstvennaia ideologiia v Rossii v poslednei treti XVIII- pervoi treti XIX veka* (Moscow: Novoe literaturnoe obozrenie, 2004), 67–94.

162. Jones, "The *Morning Light Charity* Schools," 59.

163. Ibid., 58.

164. Some sociologists drew a distinction between associations whose activities were self-contained, that is, took place within the association, and those whose activities were carried on outside the association. Associations whose goals and activities transcended the immediate interests of their members and which sought to make an impact on society at large became identified as "instrumental" or "social influence" organizations. See C. Wayne Gordon and Nicholas Babchuk, "A Typology of Voluntary Associations," *American Sociological Review* 24, no. 1 (1959): 22–29, here 22–23, 25–28; Arnold Rose, *Theory and Method in the Social Sciences* (Minneapolis: University of Minnesota Press, 1954), 50–71.

165. Liah Greenfeld, "The Formation of the Russian National Identity: The Role of Status Insecurity and *Ressentiment*," *Comparative Studies in Society and History* 32, no. 3 (1990): 567.

166. Marc Raeff, *Origins of the Russian Intelligentsia: The Eighteenth-Century Nobility* (New York: Harcourt, Brace & World, 1966), 122–147; Iu. M. Lotman, "The Poetics of Everyday Behavior in Russian Eighteenth Century Culture," in Ann Shukman, ed., *The Semiotics of Russian Culture* (Ann Arbor, University of Michigan, 1984), 231–256.

167. Charles Horton Cooley, *Social Organization: A Study of the Larger Mind* (New York: Shocken Books, 1962), 23–26; on togetherness, see also Georg Simmel: "above and beyond their [specific] content, all . . . associations are accompanied by a feeling for, by a satisfaction in, the very fact that one is associated with others and that the solitariness of the individual is resolved into togetherness, a union of others." Georg Simmel, "The Sociology of Sociability," *American Journal of Sociology* 55, no. 3 (1949): 254–261, quote on 255.

168. Raeff, *Origins of the Russian Intelligentsia*, 122–147.

169. Gordon defined sociability as "egalitarian interaction among individuals with different corporate standing" and as "a bond among equal individuals—a system of coordination for people who stepped outside of the hierarchy of estates in search of less ontologically grounded forms of interaction." See *Citizens without Sovereignty*, 33, 38, 242. For another perception of sociability, which focuses on the leisure habits of the political elite, see Antoine Lilti, "The Kingdom of *Politesse*: Salons and the Republic of Letters in Eighteenth-Century Paris," *Republics of Letters: A Journal for the Study of Knowledge, Politics, and the Arts* 1, no. 1 (2009), http://arcade.stanford.edu/rofl/kingdom-politesse-salons-and-republic-letters-eighteenth-century-paris.

170. Raeff, *Origins of the Russian Intelligentsia*, 140–141.

171. S. N. Glinka, *Ocherki zhizni i izbrannye sochineniia A. P. Sumarokova*, pt. 1 (St. Petersburg: n. p., 1831), 10; P. Berkov, "U istokov dvorianskoi literatury XVIII veka: Poet Mikhail Sobakin," *Literaturnoe nasledstvo*, no. 9–10 (1933): 421–422.

172. G. A. Gukovskii, "Sumarokov i ego literaturno-obshchestvennoe okruzhenie," in G. A. Gukovskii and V. A. Desnitskii, eds., Istoriia russkoi literatury, vol. 3 (Moscow-Leningrad: Izdatel'stvo AN SSSR, 1941), 350–351. The existence of a literary circle created by the pupils of the Cadet Corps was mentioned also in a memorandum of the Cadet Corps, January 11, 1735, in Materialy dlia istorii imperatorskoi Akademii Nauk II (St. Petersburg: n. p., 1885–1890), 572, and S. A. Vengerov, Russkaia poeziia, vol. 1 (St. Petersburg: n. p., 1897), 151. Cited in Alexander Lipski, "The Beginnings of General Secondary Education in Russia," *History of Education Journal* 6, no. 3 (1955): 209.

173. A. P. Kulakova, *Universitetskoe prostranstvo i ego obitateli: Moskovskii Universitet v istoriko-kul'turnoi srede XVIII veka* (Moscow: Novyi khronograf, 2006), 288.

174. Smith, *Working the Rough Stone*, 66–67; Kulakova, *Universitetskoe prostranstvo i ego obitateli*, 289.

175. Lotman, "Ocherki po istorii russkoi kul'tury," 100; Catriona Kelly, *Refining Russia: Advice Literature, Polite Culture, and Gender from Catherine to Yeltsin* (Oxford: Oxford University Press, 2001), 58–59, 61.

176. Lotman, "Ocherki po istorii russkoi kul'tury," 100–102; Kulakova, *Universitetskoe prostranstvo i ego obitateli*, 287. Kulakova also mentions predecessors (and alternatives) to the friendly societies—"narrow home circles," which appeared as an extension to the family. See her quotation from I. M. Dolgorukii's memoirs, where the latter described such circles as "consisting of five-six people, who constantly engaged in free conversation and witty jokes, but without venom," Ibid., 287.

177. The Turgenev brothers' Friendly Literary Society (*Druzheskoe Literaturnoe Obshchestvo*), which has inspired some excellent pieces of historical scholarship, might serve as an example of such a circle. See Marc Raeff, "Russian Youth on the Eve of Romanticism: Andrei I. Turgenev and His Circle," in idem, *Political Ideas and Institutions in Imperial Russia*,

42–64; Andrei Zorin, "The Perception of Emotional Coldness in Andrei Turgenev's Diaries," *Slavic Review* 68, no. 2 (2009): 238–258.

178. See Rebecca Friedman, "Romantic Friendship in the Nicholaevan University," *Russian Review* 62, no. 2 (2003): 262–280.

179. Gordon proposed five ideal types of sociability: (1) *sociability as the love of exchange*, i.e., a pure love of fellowship that had no political significance; (2) *sociability as the propagation of absolutism*, based on a view of the absolutist state as a zone of inter-group dynamics, with specific reference to royal scientific academies as state-oriented institutions of sociability; (3) *sociability as a bond among strangers*, i.e., as a means for instituting stable norms in an urban milieu where old hierarchical frames of reference were blurred and where "fixed conventions of the group allowed one to classify both oneself and others according to a consistent scale of values"; (4) *sociability as socialization and education*—in this case, institutions of sociability served as "centers of adult education" where individuals became accustomed to the norms of a particular milieu and where persons from various backgrounds could acquire speaking and writing skills or could polish their manners; and (5) *sociability as the recovery of logos* (logos meaning speech *per se*, which amounted to the "art of conversation" in the seventeenth and eighteenth centuries). Gordon saw this distinctive cultural situation as a function of the political domination of the absolutist state, which stripped corporate bodies of their administrative functions and, as a result, prevented them from serving as a small forum for reasoned debate among members. In response, "reason and speech turned toward philosophical, aesthetic, and moral concerns that were unrelated to the direct exercise of sovereign authority." From this perspective, Gordon claimed, sociability "may be defined as the effort to create a sphere of behavior in which humans can be human without becoming self-governing citizens." See Gordon, *Citizens without Sovereignty*, 33–42.

180. Lotman, "Ocherki po istorii russkoi kul'tury," 99.

181. Ibid., 105.

182. *Ukaz ob uchrezhdenii Moskovskogo universiteta i dvukh gimnazii s prilozheniem vysochaishe utverzhdennogo proekta po semu predmetu, 12 ianvaria 1755 goda.* Accessed August 4, 2015. http://www.runivers.ru/philosophy/chronograph/156896/ ; Vera Kaplan, "The History of Reform in Russian Higher Education," in Joseph Zajda, ed., *Higher Education in the Russian Federation* (pt. 1), special issue of *European Education* 39, no. 2 (2007): 40–42.

183. On the category of *raznochintsy*, see Elise Kimerling Wirtschafter, *Structures of Society: Imperial Russia's "People of Various Ranks"* (DeKalb: Northern Illinois University Press, 1994).

184. *Ukaz ob uchrezhdenii Moskovskogo universiteta i dvukh gimnazii,* clauses 21, 28, 39. There was a disagreement between nineteenth-century experts about the organization of study in the University's gymnasia. While N. V. Sushkov claimed that pupils of both gymnasia studied together, N. S. Tikhonravov argued that in the first years of the university there were separate classes, and that the curriculum of the noble gymnasium was much broader than that of the commoners, but that this separation was later abandoned de facto. N. V. Sushkov, *Moskovskii Universitetskii Blagorodnyi Pansion i vospitanniki Moskovskogo Universiteta, gimnazii ego, universitetskogo blagorodnogo pansiona i Druzheskogo obshchestva* (Moscow: Universitetskaia tipografiia, 1858), 5; N. S. Tikhonravov, "Novye svedeniia o N. I. Novikove i chlenakh kompanii Tipograficheskoi," in *Sochineniia*, vol. 3, pt. 2, *Russkaia literatura XVIII–XIX vv: Prilozheniia* (Moscow: Izdanie M. and S. Sabashnikovykh, 1898), 89–90. According to the history of the gymnasia written by P. I. Strakhov and published on the University's centenary in 1855, the gymnasia's first curricula included the same list of subjects but different teachers; Strakhov also mentioned that initially the two gymnasia were completely separated, with different classes and different teachers, but the increase in the number of pupils made it

technically impossible to maintain this separation. P. I. Strakhov, *Kratkaia istoriia akademicheskoi gimnazii byvshei pri Imperatorskom Moskovskom Universitete* (Moscow: Izdatel'stvo MGU, 2000), 6–7, 29–30.

185. *Ukaz ob uchrezhdenii Moskovskogo universiteta i dvukh gimnazii,* clause 5.

186. Ibid., clause 26.

187. For the educational activity of the Russian Freemasonry, see P. N. Miliukov, *Ocherki po istorii russkoi kul'tury,* vol. 3, *Natsionalizm i Evropeizm* (Moscow: Progress-Kul'tura, 1995) 364–366; Gilbert H. McArthur, "Freemasonry and Enlightenment in Russia: The Views of N. I. Novikov," *Canadian-American Slavic Studies* 14, no. 3 (Fall 1980): 361–375; and, especially, Faggionato, *A Rosicrucian Utopia,* 46–60.

188. A. Zapadov, "Tvorchestvo Kheraskova" in M. M. Kheraskov, *Izbrannye proizvedeniia* (Moscow-Leningrad: Biblioteka poeta, 1961), 1.

189. "Voprosnye punkty Sheshkovskogo, otvety Novikova, napisannye v Shlissel'burge v iiune 1792 g. i vozrazheniia na eti otvety," in N. I. Novikov, *Izbrannye sochineniia* (Moscow-Leningrad: Gosudarstvennoe izdatel'stvo khudozhestvennoi literatury, 1954), 610–611; Serkov and Reizin, eds., *Pis'ma N. I. Novikova,* 13; McArthur, "Freemasonry and Enlightenment in Russia," 364; Faggionato, *A Rosicrucian Utopia,* 47.

190. Faggionato, *A Rosicrucian Utopia,* 48.

191. Tikhonravov, "Novye svedeniia o N. I. Novikove i chlenakh kompanii Tipograficheskoi," 93–95; Miliukov, *Ocherki po istorii russkoi rul'tury,* 3: 357; Bogoliubov, *N. I. Novikov i ego vremia,* 195–196.

192. M. Longinov, *Novikov i Shvarts: Materialy dlia istorii russkoi literatury v kontse XVIII veka* (Moscow: V tipografii Katkova i K°, 1857), 7.

193. Jones, "The Morning Light Charity Schools," 64.

194. Miliukov, *Ocherki po istorii russkoi kul'tury,* 3: 357–358; V. N. Tukalevskii, "N. I. Novikov i I. G. Schwarz," in *Istoriia Masonstva* (Moscow, EKSMO-Press, 2002), 278; Usova, *N. I. Novikov, ego zhizn' i obshchestvennaia deiatel'nost',* 49.

195. Bogoliubov, *N. I. Novikov i ego vremia,* 195.

196. Tukalevskii, "N. I. Novikov i I. G. Schwarz," 278.

197. [I. V. Pomialovskii], "Zapiski Mikhaila Ivanovicha Antonovskogo," *Russkii arkhiv,* no. 2 (1885): 151.

198. M. Poludenskii, *Materialy dlia istorii Druzheskogo uchenogo obshchestva, 1782* (Moscow: Tipografiia Lazarevskogo instituta vostochnykh iazykov, 1863), 3; Bogoliubov, *N. I. Novikov i ego vremia,* 330–331; Usova, *N. I. Novikov, Ego zhizn' i obshchestvennaia deiatel'nost',* 56; Longinov, *Novikov i Shvarts,* 10.

199. M. N. Longinov, *Novikov i Moskovskie Martinisty* (Moscow: Tipografiia Gracheva i Komp., 1867), 185.

200. A. G. Cross, *N. M. Karamzin: A Study of His Literary Career, 1783–1803* (London and Amsterdam: Southern Illinois University Press, 1971), 21.

201. Its members included, in addition to the circle's core group (Prince N. N. Trubetskoi, M. M. Kheraskov, I. P. Turgenev, A. M. Kutuzov, I. G. Schwarz and N. I. Novikov), Prince A. A. Cherkasskii and Prince K. M. Engalychev. Prince Iu. N. Trubetskoi, P. A. Tatishchev, I. V. Lopukhin and S. I. Gamaleia also joined the lodge and became part of the circle. See Bogoliubov, *N. I. Novikov i ego vremia,* 194; "Voprosnye punkty Sheshkovskogo, otvety Novikova," 611–612.

202. "Voprosnye punkty Sheshkovskogo, otvety Novikova," 608–609; I use here Gilbert H. McArthur's translation of Novikov's writing in his "Freemasonry and Enlightenment in Russia," 365.

203. Madariaga, *Russia in the Age of Catherine the Great,* 522–523; Smith, *Working the Rough Stone,* 107–109; In-Ho L. Ryu, "Moscow Freemasons and the Rosicrucian Order," in J. G.

Garrard, ed., *The Eighteenth Century in Russia* (Oxford: Clarendon, 1973), 198–232, especially 210–211.

204. Ryu, "Moscow Freemasons and the Rosicrucian Order," 199–213; Bogoliubov, *N. I. Novikov i ego vremia*, 199–202.

205. Ryu, "Moscow Freemasons and the Rosicrucian Order," 209–213; Faggionato, *A Rosicrucian Utopia*, 60–67; 82.

206. Poludenskii, *Materialy dlia istorii Druzheskogo uchenogo obshchestva*, 1782, 5; "Voprosnye punkty Sheshkovskogo, otvety Novikova," 616.

207. Poludenskii, *Materialy dlia istorii Druzheskogo uchenogo obshchestva, 1782*, 8–10.

208. Longinov, *Novikov i Shvarts*, 11; idem, *Novikov i Moskovskie Martinisty*, 194; Tikhonravov, "Novye svedeniia o N. I. Novikove i chlenakh kompanii Tipograficheskoi," 95–96.

209. Poludenskii, *Materialy dlia istorii Druzheskogo uchenogo obshchestva, 1782*, 11; Bogoliubov, *N. I. Novikov i ego vremia*, 1916, 331.

210. *Zapiski nekotorykh obstoiatel'stv zhizni i sluzhby deistvitel'nogo tainogo sovetnika, senatora I. V. Lopukhina* (Moscow, 1860), 15.

211. N. S. Tikhonravov, "Chetyre goda iz zhizni Karamzina," in idem, *Sochineniia*, vol. 3, pt. 1 (Moscow, 1899), 273; idem, "Novye svedeniia o N. I. Novikove i chlenakh kompanii Tipograficheskoi," 96; G. P. Shtorm, "Novoe o Pushkine i Karamzine," *Izvestiia AN SSSR, Otdel literatury i iazyka* 19, no. 2 (1960): 144–150; N. D. Kochetkova, "Ideino-literaturnye pozitsii masonov 80–90kh godov XVIII i N. M. Karamzin," in P. N. Berkov and I. Z. Serman, eds., *Russkaia literatura XVIII veka: epokha klassitsizma, XVIII vek*, vol. 6 (Moscow-Leningrad: Nauka, 1964), 177. This opinion, however, has been rejected by the prominent expert on Russian masonry, M. N. Longinov, *Novikov i Moskovskie Martinisty*, 298–299.

212. Faggionato, *A Rosicrucian Utopia*, 131.

213. Longinov, *Novikov i Moskovskie Martinisty*, 184, 203; Sushkov, *Moskovskii Universitetskii Blagorodnyi Pansion*, 21; Strakhov, *Kratkaia istoriia akademicheskoi gimnazii*, 57.

214. *Vzgliad na moiu zhizn': Zapiski deistvitel'nogo tainogo sovetnika Iv. Iv. Dmitrieva* (Moscow: Tipografiia V. Got'e, 1866), 42.

215. Longinov, *Novikov i Moskovskie Martinisty*, 202–203.

216. Miliukov, *Ocherki po istorii russkoi kul'tury*, 3: 368; Marker, *Publishing, Printing, and the Origins of Intellectual Life in Russia*, 128; Faggionato, *A Rosicrucian Utopia*, 83.

217. "Zapiska I. G. Shvartsa ob otnoshenii k nemu I. I. Melissino," quoted in A. D. Tiurikov, "Podvizhnik russkoi kul'tury: I. G. Shvarts—filosof, pedagog, obshchestvennyi deiatel' XVIII veka," in I. G. Shvarts, *Lektsii* (Donetsk: Izdatel'stvo "Veber," Donetskoe otdelenie, 2008), 145.

218. See "Voprosnye punkty Sheshkovskogo, otvety Novikova," 616, 622.

219. Bogoliubov, *N. I. Novikov i ego vremia*, 331.

220. Vucinich, *Science in Russian Culture*, 178.

221. Kulakova, *Universitetskoe prostranstvo i ego obitateli*, 293.

222. Raeff, "Preface," in Faggionato, *A Rosicrucian Utopia*, xiii.

223. Miliukov, *Ocherki po istorii russkoi kul'tury*, 3: 361. Miliukov claimed also that the *Evening Glow* was the first journal edited by the graduates of the Translators' Seminary.

224. McArthur, "Freemasonry and Enlightenment in Russia," 374.

225. Shvarts, "Rassuzhdeniia v sobraniiakh Druzheskogo Uchenogo Obshchestva," in Shvarts, *Lektsii*, 102, 103.

226. Shvarts, "O trekh poznaniiakh: liubopytnom, priiatnom i poleznom" in Shvarts, *Lektsii*, 22.

227. V. P. Kozlov, *Rossiiskaia arkheografiia kontsa XVIII- pervoi chetverti XIX veka* (Moscow: Rossiiskii Gosudarstvennyi Gumanitarnyi Universitet, 1999), 50–53, 112–114; V. V. Viatkin, "Aleksei Ivanovich Musin-Pushkin," *Voprosy istorii*, no. 9 (2013): 22.

228. N. S. Tikhonravov, "K istorii Moskovskogo Universiteta: Professor F. G. Bauze" in idem, *Sochineniia*, vol. 3, pt. 1 (Moscow: Izdanie M. and S. Sabashnikovykh, 1898), 22.

229. On the collecting of historical artifacts in the contemporary Germany, see Susan A. Crane, *Collecting and Historical Consciousness in Early Nineteenth-Century Germany* (Ithaca and London: Cornell University Press, 2000): 64–71.

230. Ibid., 15.

231. G. N. Moiseeva, "Arkheograficheskaia deiatel'nost' N. I. Novikova," 36. For N. N. Bantysh-Kamenskii and A. F. Malinovskii, see Kozlov, *Rossiiskaia arkheografiia*, 52–53.

232. Tikhonravov, "Chetyre goda iz zhizni Karamzina," 258–275.

233. Nil Popov, *Istoriia Imperatoskogo Moskovskogo obshchestva istorii i drevnostei Rossiiskikh, chast' I (1804–1812)* (Moscow: Imperatorskoe Obshchestvo Istorii i Drevnosti Rossiiskikh, 1884), 14.

234. Kliuchevskii, "Iubilei obshchestva istorii i drevnostei rossiiskikh," 192–193.

235. N. S. Tikhonravov, "Moskovskii Universitetskii Blagorodnyi Pansion," in idem, *Sochineniia*, 97.

236. Iu. M. Lotman, "Vstupitel'nye zametki," in Iu. M. Lotman and M. G. Al'tshuller, *Poeziia 1790–1810- kh godov* (Leningrad: Sovetskii pisatel', 1971), 46.

237. Faggionato, *A Rosicrucian Utopia*, 146.

238. Zorin, *Kormia dvuglavogo orla*, 217–222.

239. "Proekt ustava obshchestva liubitelei rossiiskoi uchenosti," 1789, *Istoricheskii arkhiv*, vol. 5 (Moscow-Leningrad, 1950): 304–305.

240. Anufriev, "Pravitel'stvennaia reglamentatsiia," 18; Bradley, *Voluntary Associations in Tsarist Russia*, 43.

241. This notion is taken from Susan Crane's discussion of the role of collecting in making history perceptible: "And yet, the historical perception had to be awakened in people, and others had to be urged to be won to the cause of collecting." See Crane, *Collecting and Historical Consciousness in Early Nineteenth-Century Germany*, 18.

242. Stephen Bann, *The Clothing of Clio: A Study of the Representation of History in Nineteenth-Century Britain and France* (Cambridge: Cambridge University Press, 1984), 2.

243. On the development of history as a profession, see Stephen Bann, "History and Her Sibling: Law, Medicine and Theology," in idem, *The Inventions of History: Essay on the Representation of the Past* (Manchester: Manchester University Press, 1990), 13.

2 Historical Societies at the Juncture of Scholarship, Politics, and Education

THE FOUNDATION OF the Society for Russian History and Antiquities in 1804 signified the beginning of a new stage in the development not only of historical societies, but of learned societies in Russia in general. In comparison with their eighteenth-century predecessors, learned societies in the nineteenth century saw their educational tasks mainly as an extension of their scholarly pursuits. More public-oriented educational activity was left to philanthropic educational associations, while the tradition of humanistic syncretism was continued by the free societies of lovers of literature and art that once again made an appearance in the first quarter of the nineteenth century.[1] The situation changed after the Great Reforms, especially in the last decades of the nineteenth century, when the learned societies launched their own educational programs. This trend eventually led to the appearance of a new category of historical societies which undertook to combine scholarly and educational goals. Throughout the century, each new historical association consciously adopted some elements of the organizational structure and patterns of activity characteristic of its predecessors but no less consciously modified the existing models in order to adapt them to its specific aims. In this way the procedures and practices of various societies eventually consolidated into shared norms and patterns of activity, which formed the basis for the emerging community of historians.

The Society for Russian History and Antiquities

The Society for Russian History and Antiquities (*Obshchestvo istorii i drevnostei rossiiskikh* [OIDR]) was founded in the course of the major educational reform launched in the early years of Alexander I's reign. Its emergence was enabled by the charter of Moscow University, which was issued in 1804 and served as a model for the new universities established in 1802–1819.[2] The charter defined Moscow University as "the highest learning estate founded for the teaching of science" and authorized it to establish learned societies that would engage in "Russian and ancient philology (*slovesnost'*)" and disseminate "the experimental and exact sciences." The university was to support such societies by publishing their works and periodicals.[3] In this document, the study of history was placed under the rubric of "philological science." Remarkably, history became the first field in which the right to establish a learned society was realized.[4]

The authors of later histories of Moscow University and the OIDR provided different explanations for this phenomenon. Stepan Shevyrev, whose monumental history of Moscow University was written to mark its centennial, ascribed the key role in establishing the historical society to the curator of Moscow University, Mikhail Murav'ev. This was the same Murav'ev who thirty years earlier had enthusiastically cooperated with Kheraskov and Novikov in their publishing and philanthropic endeavors. In the course of the following three decades he had made an impressive state career and in 1785 had been appointed by Catherine the Great to teach Russian language, history, and moral philosophy to her grandchildren, the future Emperor Alexander I and his younger brother Konstantin. It was in this capacity as the grand dukes' teacher that Murav'ev formulated his views on history in a number of essays, especially in his "Letter to a young man on topics related to history and the description of Russia" addressed to Grand Duke Alexander.[5] In these essays Murav'ev presented his thoughts about the nature of the historian's work, Russia's distinctive historical destiny, and the role of cultural borrowings in Russian history.[6] With Alexander's accession to the Russian throne Murav'ev was appointed a senator and played an important role in carrying out the educational reform—in the beginning as a member of the commission for the preparation of new statutes for the academy and the universities, and later as a deputy of the minister of education and, from 1803, as a curator of Moscow University. It is therefore not surprising that the former royal history teacher supported establishing a historical society before any other institution of that kind. Shevyrev, however, pointed to a further aspect of Murav'ev's approach—his desire to surround the university with learned associations in order to create a link between scholarship and broader society, to "connect representatives of the former with educated members of the latter" and, in so doing, to stimulate the professors' scholarly activity.[7]

Another version of the founding tale was provided by Nil Popov, the author of a book on the OIDR published to mark its eightieth anniversary in 1884. Popov ascribed the initiative to launch the society to a fellow historian, the German expert on Russian chronicles August Ludwig von Schlözer, who, he claimed, raised the idea of establishing a historical society in a letter to Alexander I.[8] Schlözer, who at that time was a distinguished professor at Göttingen University, began his academic career in Russia. In 1762 he became an adjunct of the St. Petersburg Academy, three years later he was awarded the title of professor, but in 1767 he left the Russian capital for Göttingen. Although he never came back to Russia, Schlözer continued to study Russian chronicles and started to teach Russian history at Göttingen even before such a course was included in the curriculum of any Russian university.[9] In 1802 Schlözer published his magnum opus—the first part of his magisterial translation and critical analysis of the *Russian Primary Chronicle*.[10] This work brought him not only scholarly recognition, but also a valuable award from the young Russian monarch, who bestowed upon the German scholar the Order of St. Vladimir, which gave him the rights of a Russian nobleman. In his letter of thanks Schlözer offered to cooperate with Russian scholars in publishing ancient Russian chronicles—now in Russian. For this purpose, Popov argued, Alexander I instructed the Minister of Education P. V. Zavadovskii to establish a historical society "attached to one of the learned estates (*pri odnom iz uchenykh soslovii*)." Zavadovskii appointed Murav'ev to fulfill this task.[11] Despite their different versions of the founding story, both Shevyrev and Popov saw the historical society as a framework in which historical knowledge would be accumulated and turned into a public asset.

Since no such society existed in the German states in this period, the idea to establish it, even if inspired by Schlözer, was not based on the German experience. It was only ten years later, in 1814, after the fateful years of the Napoleonic wars, that Prussian officials and literati, including Goethe and the Grimms, started to discuss this idea.[12] However, four more years would elapse before the Society for the Study of Early German History (*Gesellschaft für ältere deutsche Geschichtskunde*) was founded in Frankfurt in 1819.[13] The crucial role in the society's establishment was played by Baron Karl vom Stein, who spent the year of 1812 as a political émigré in Russia, on the personal invitation of Alexander I.[14] Arriving in Moscow on July 24, 1812, just two months before the city was destroyed by fire, he "was among the last travelers who beheld it" and described it in his letters.[15] In early 1813 vom Stein came back to Germany as a superintendant of the administration for the liberated territories, remaining in this post until the end of the Congress of Vienna. Throughout these years, and even later, after his retirement, when vom Stein devoted himself to the historical society, Alexander I remained his patron. When Stein's society struggled to find the means for issuing its anthology, Alexander I offered to finance the undertaking, but Stein declined his offer because he found it humiliating to receive help from abroad for publishing sources of German history.[16] Although there are no sources at our disposal that can clarify whether vom Stein was aware of the OIDR and its activity, it is clear that the OIDR did not have any German example to emulate at the time of its establishment.

The documents relating to the first years of the OIDR's existence reveal how its search for a collective *modus operandi* led to a growing awareness of the historian's distinctive skills, on the one hand, and to increasing sophistication in the structure of the society, on the other. The University's Council, which took the preliminary decision to found the society, defined its main task as "critical publication of the ancient Russian chronicles," and stipulated that its members should have scholarly experience and historical erudition.[17] In practice, however, it was evident that the future members were not expected to possess both these qualities. The council elected the university's rector, Chebotarev, a professor of history, ethics and rhetoric, as the society's chairman, and nominated four professors as full members (*deistvitel'nye chleny*); three of them were former alumni of the Friendly Learned Society, but only one, N. E. Cherepanov, taught history.[18] The university's Council also recommended inviting Schlözer and some other individuals who were "enlightened and versed (*svedushchie*) in ancient Russian history" to be honorary members of the society.[19] The latter included the third (and last) official historiographer Karamzin, as well as the dignitary and collector (*sobiratel'*) of ancient manuscripts Musin-Pushkin, the head of the Foreign Affairs Archive Bantysh-Kamenskii, and his deputy and fellow-collector, Malinovskii, none of whom had formal education as historians, but all of whom were commonly recognized as experts (*znatoki*) in Russian history.[20] Hence, at the very outset of its activity, the society recognized two modes of "being a historian": that of the academic scholar whose status arose from formal training, and that of the nonacademic connoisseur, whose informally acquired knowledge endowed him with expertise in the field. Over the following years the society contributed to both developing and challenging these modes.

The very first meeting of the society chose the manuscript to be prepared for publication—not surprisingly, this was the *Russian Primary (Nestor) Chronicle*— and suggested the way in which its members could collaborate in this work. It was decided to print the most ancient version of the manuscript in a special format—with each page printed separately on half a folio, with wide spaces between the lines—and to send the pages to members of the society for comparison with other versions of the same document and for comments. Each portion of the ancient text, was to be examined by each member and then passed on to another for his amendments and criticism. This process was to take two weeks, culminating in a session of the society where corrections would be summarized and the best version chosen. In the final stage, comments on differences in interpretation were to be inserted into the approved portions of the text, which would subsequently be proofread by members of the society—again page by page.[21] This kind of work emphasized one particular criterion for "being a historian": members were expected to demonstrate special skills in examining ancient chronicles. Not all intended members of the society, however, agreed with this cumbersome procedure. In particular, it was criticized by Karamzin, who, although ready to cooperate with the society, rejected taking part in such time-consuming collective labor. Karamzin saw his main purpose as writing Russian history: according to him, "ten societies cannot do what one man completely devoted to historical subjects can do."[22] Questioning the view of the historian as a commentator of the ancient chronicles, Karamzin represented his own vision of the historian as a writer able to compose an attractive modern narrative of the national past.

The image of the historian was further elaborated in the course of the first contest organized by the society.

The practice of contests organized by learned societies had been initiated by the Free Economic Society in 1765, so that by the early nineteenth century such events had become familiar to the Russian educated public. The Moscow University Council and the OIDR announced its first contest in June 1805. The following question was suggested: "The chronicler Nestor said that the Slavs who populated Russia came from the shores of the Danube, out of Bulgaria and the Ugrian land, having been forced out by the Wallachians. [The question] to resolve: (1)When could such resettlement most likely have taken place? (2) Whom does Nestor refer to by the name Wallachians? Are these Romans, Langobards, Bulgarians or indeed Wallachians?"[23] The very formulation of the problem shows that the contest's organizers expected the participants (who were to submit their answers under pseudonyms) to demonstrate far more than an accurate interpretation of the ancient texts. The question assumed a profound acquaintance with various historical sources and the ability to examine them critically. When announcing the results of the contest, the society publicized its assessment of the submitted essays, in which special attention was paid to the author's method of work and argumentation, thereby contributing to the contemporary discourse on the role and limits of criticism in general and scholarly criticism in particular.[24] Not surprisingly, it was a member of the OIDR, Moscow University Professor of History Mikhail Kachenovskii, who later formulated what Allison Y. Katsev called "an exclusive definition of the historian" based on the notion of scientific criticism. Kachenovskii insisted that the historian, contrary to the novelist or epic poet, should be able to apply the technique of scholarly criticism in order to "cleanse" historical sources and elicit from the documents "an authentic history."[25] The society therefore played a remarkable role in consolidating the view of history as a "science." In Thaden's words, "during the 1820s and 1830s, the word 'science' became almost a commonplace in referring to history in both Europe and Russia."[26] In addition, as a result of the society's activity, the notion of "auxiliary sciences for history" (*vspomogatel'nye nauki dlia istorii*) emerged. By the early 1830s this subject was already being taught at Moscow University by Kachenovskii's student, Mikhail Gastev.[27]

While playing an important role in fashioning history as a science and establishing the image of the historian as a specialist, the society had no intention of turning into a self-contained clique of experts: in its everyday practice it acted as an inclusive rather than exclusive institution. Thus, the society's report on the results of its contest addressed not only the participants' scientific skills, but also their "historical talent" and "love of history." Moreover, the very idea of the contest assumed that it would attract those who were not yet formally associated with the society. Therefore its organizers found themselves in a real quandary when they discovered that the winning author was one of its own members, Moscow University Professor Christian Schlözer, the son of the Göttingen pundit. Despite the embarrassment involved, the contest's organizers decided not to confer the prize upon him, explaining that its members were to be excluded from participation in such competitions.[28] In the announcement of its next contest, published in March 1812, the society mitigated this condition and permitted a new category of its members—competitors (*sorevnovateli*)—to participate.[29]

The very appearance of this category indicated that the society's membership had become open not only to experts, but also to amateur "lovers" of history. Indeed, while the initial documents of the society mentioned only full or honorary members, its statutes (approved in 1811) listed four categories of membership: "members," "competitors," "corresponding members" (*korrespondenty*) and "benefactors" (*blagotvoriteli*).[30] The description of their rights and duties revealed the elaborate structure of the society and a broader vision of its members' desirable qualities. Prospective members were expected to be "well known in the world of scholarship" either for their knowledge of Russian history and antiquity or for their writings. They were expected to be diligent and to conduct a "restrained (*nerasseiannyi*) way of life" so as to have enough time to contribute to the society's work. However, each member could choose in what way he wished to make this contribution. Unlike the initial attempts to organize close collaboration among all members, the statutes assumed that each member could develop his own particular subject and maintain his own work schedule. There was also another novelty: the statutes prescribed that members should deliver papers on aspects of Russian history at the society's sessions and make a material donation to the society's archive and library. While full members were given a broad range of opportunities for participation, the statutes ascribed narrower duties and a supplementary status to newly created categories of membership. Thus, the title of *sorevnovatel'* was given to persons who regularly provided the society with information on new findings and studies. In order to become a *blagotvoritel'*, the member had to make a personal endowment of some kind, whether in the form of books, manuscripts, or money. The status of *korrespondenty* applied to those who resided in different areas of the country or abroad and were able to collect information about sources on Russian history available in their localities.[31] In addition, the statutes defined the duties of the society's new officials—a secretary and a treasurer: both posts were created in order to help the chair in his administrative tasks. These structural innovations were intended to improve the society's effectiveness.

Indeed, the problem of the society's efficiency loomed large in 1810 when the new curator of the university, Pavel Golenishchev-Kutuzov, claiming that the society's activity was far from effective, made the dramatic decision to close it down. He declared a cessation of the society's work on December 14, 1810—only in order to reorganize it and to establish a new society under the same name a week later, on December 22.[32] The head of the reformed society, who was elected by its members, not appointed by Moscow University, turned out to be neither a university professor nor an official of the archive, but an educated amateur, the collector and publisher Platon Beketov.[33] This choice (made on the curator's recommendation) was explained by Beketov's personal qualities, such as "tireless activity" and "devotion to the public good."[34] Both Golenishchev-Kutuzov and the members of the society apparently considered "antiquarian" to be no less estimable than "scholar" at that time. The reorganized society changed its methods of work and expanded its activities. The editing of the Primary Chronicle was now assigned to Professor Roman Timkovskii, who was charged with verifying the text and then supervising its printing together with Beketov and Kachenovskii.[35] In addition to continuing this major project, the society started to build its own library and archival collection. The materials from this collection were published in its first periodical, *Russkie dostopamiatnosti* (*Russian Memorabilia*), which began to appear in 1815, shortly followed by its second periodical, *Zapiski i trudy Obshchestva Istorii i Drevnostei Rossiiskikh* (*Notes and Works of the OIDR*).[36] Furthermore, the society's members (who numbered up to twenty-seven by 1811) undertook various personal projects.[37] Thus, according to the protocols of the session of December 22, 1810, Golenishchev-Kutuzov, who joined the society as a rank-and-file member, suggested his study of ancient Russian poetry; other members planned to explore subjects as diverse as ancient Russian coins and medals, factories and crafts in pre-Petrine Russia, and the development of medicine from ancient *Rus'* to Peter the Great. One of the society's new members, the translator Iakov Bordovskii, intended to search for ancient manuscripts in Moscow's monasteries and to conduct a comparison between Polish and Russian documents, while Kachenovskii was assigned with examining information about chronicles and chronographs kept in ecclesiastical consistories throughout Russia.[38] Although these plans were interrupted by Napoleon's invasion, their very formulation prepared a fertile ground for future—and more impressive—projects. In 1823 a student of Timkovskii and Kachenovskii, Pavel Stroev, proposed launching a special program for the systematic study and publication of all ancient manuscripts, which was followed by the organization of the first archeographic expeditions.[39]

Nonetheless, these more diversified and particularistic methods of operation were not combined with aspirations for greater autonomy. On the contrary, the reorganized society tried to strengthen its status as an extension of the university and as such to obtain special privileges, as revealed by the correspondence between Golenishchev-Kutuzov and Minister of Education Aleksei Razumovskii. In the preliminary draft of the society's statutes that he submitted to the minister, Golenishchev-Kutuzov included a number of exclusive rights, such as the right to receive documentary and published materials from all state archives and libraries and the right to censor all history books issued in the Russian Empire. Furthermore, he added the designation "Imperial" to the society's name and requested that all members of the society be permitted to wear the university's uniform. The minister rejected all these requests and canceled the corresponding clauses from the draft; he also reminded Golenishchev-Kutuzov of the necessity to apply the same rules and rights to all learned societies. He thus implicitly moved the emphasis from the society's statist origins to its public role. Moreover, in accordance with the liberal principles of the early period of Alexander I's reign, Razumovskii warned Golenishchev-Kutuzov against the oppressive (*pritesnitel'nyi*) character of excessive censorship.[40] The situation changed in the reign of Nicholas I, when the society itself became the object of harsh censorship.

From 1837 until 1874 the OIDR was headed by Count Sergei Stroganov, who successfully played the role of its enlightened patron. Due to his patronage the society attained the desired title of "Imperial" and was also awarded a permanent monetary grant, which made it possible to expand the society's publishing activity. In 1837 the society launched the *Russkii istoricheskii sbornik* (*Russian Historical Anthology*), edited by its secretary, Mikhail Pogodin, professor of Russian history at Moscow University. This periodical followed the practice of publishing historical sources that had been initiated by Novikov and continued by *Russian Memorabilia* (whose second volume, which was still under preparation at that time, finally appeared in 1843). However, the standard of such publications became more demanding in the wake of the appearance of the first volumes of the *Monumenta Germaniae Historica* (MGH) published by the Society for the Study of Early German History. These volumes, issued in 1826, 1829 and 1835 as an "archive" of documentary materials on the national past, marked "an epoch in historical study" since "it was the first time that German texts had been edited on the same critical principles as the works of classical writers."[41] This attitude to historical sources influenced Russian historians, who remained deeply connected with the German scholarly world, and strengthened the OIDR's basic principle of "critical publication"of ancient Russian documents. Yet, while adhering to the method of textual criticism, the OIDR expanded the scope of its interests. In 1846 it launched a new periodical, *Chteniia MOIDR* (*Readings of the Moscow Society for Russian History and Antiquities*), which became its most influential publication.[42] It was edited by the society's new secretary, Osip Bodianskii, one of the first Russian Slavicists and the chair of the Department of Slavic History and Literature at Moscow University, who eventually became the society's unofficial scholarly leader.[43] Due to his efforts, twenty-three volumes of *Chteniia* were issued over the next three years. Each volume was divided into four parts—historical studies, Russian documents, foreign documents, and miscellaneous—thereby constituting a new, comprehensive type of historical journal. However, the publication in 1848 of one of the foreign manuscripts—Giles Fletcher's notes on the Russian state at the time of Ivan the Terrible (entitled in English *Of the Russe Commonwealth* [1591])—proved fatal for both *Chteniia* and its editor. The time of publication was far from propitious: in the atmosphere of growing political reaction the attempt to publish Fletcher's critical account was perceived as a political gesture. *Chteniia* was closed, while Bodianskii lost his post in the society and, temporarily, even at the university.[44] His reinstatement as secretary of the society and the resumption of *Chteniia* in 1858 were a sign of the new atmosphere of Alexander II's reign.[45]

The political stance that had been ascribed to *Chteniia*'s publishing strategy in the 1840s–1850s became a reality in the following decade of the Great Reforms, when Bodianskii took part in the discussions on the new statutes for the universities, which drew the attention of the entire Russian academic world. In the early 1860s Bodianskii published a number of articles on this subject, some of them in *Chteniia*.[46] About ten years later, when attempts were made to repeal the liberal statutes of 1863, *Chteniia* again became a tribune of discussion after it published in 1873 a polemical article, "A trilogy on a trilogy: A historical essay from the contemporary life of the Russian university."[47] The article, which appeared under the pen name K. Mutsii Stsevola, was actually written by a former student of Bodianskii, Apollon Aleksandrovich Maikov, as was recently discovered by O. N. Khokhlova.[48] Nevertheless, both Bodianskii's contemporaries and generations of researchers held him responsible for the appearance of the paper and were even convinced that he had written it himself.[49] In the course of the subsequent conflict between the society and Minister of Education Dmitrii Tolstoi, the most fundamental aspects of the society's operation were questioned. State officials attacked the society, claiming that the number of its members exceeded the limit of thirty persons laid down by the statutes, demanded reconsideration of the rights and duties of the society's officials, and criticized the division of functions between its chair and secretary. At one point, its very existence seemed to be in danger. However, despite the pressure of the Ministry of Education, the society did not dismiss Bodianskii from his post and, unlike in 1848, the minister of education refrained from ordering his removal. As V. I. Chesnokov concluded in his analysis of this case, the ministry, while encroaching on the society's existence, had to take into consideration the norms of the governmental bureaucracy's behavior toward the learned societies that had consolidated during the previous decades.[50] These norms, it should be added, were both reconfirmed and reformed in the course of such crises. If in 1811 the dramatic decision to close the society had been implemented in one day, in 1848 the closure of the society's journal and dismissal of its leading functionary required the involvement of the whole chain of the bureaucratic command structure, while in 1873 the bureaucratic machine's freedom of action was limited both by public opinion and by the new informal code of interaction between governmental bodies and voluntary scientific societies.

Despite these crises, the OIDR proved its endurance; by the end of the nineteenth century it was a solid scholarly institution that included the leading Russian historians. The author of the history of the society, written eighty years after its establishment, was able to base his research on the OIDR's numerous publications, including eight volumes of *Zapiski i trudy*, three volumes of *Russkie dostopamiatnosti*, seven volumes of *Istoricheskii sbornik*, twenty-five volumes of *Vremennik*, and 127 volumes of *Chteniia*.[51] *Chteniia* retained its status as the leading historical journal until the end of the nineteenth century, even though new journals, the popular *Russkii arkhiv* and *Russkaia starina*, entered the field.[52] From the 1880s *Chteniia* attracted young scholars as a respected tribune for publishing their dissertations: thus, in 1893 it published the master's dissertation of Alexander Lappo-Danilevskii, and at one point Pavel Miliukov considered publishing his dissertation there.[53] The OIDR continued to grow in numbers: in 1890 it comprised 15 honorary members, 116 full members, 24 competitors, and one corresponding member; the category of benefactors was included in the list of membership, but remained empty.[54] Although they were spread throughout various cities inside and, in some cases, even outside the Russian Empire, the society's members were still divided into the same categories defined by the statutes of 1811. Similarly, the official posts created in 1811 remained unchanged.[55] Nonetheless, in the 1880s-1890s, the OIDR began to undergo a fundamental transformation: from being the privileged beneficiary of enlightened patronage, it evolved into a more independent institution of the emerging professional community.

This tendency appeared first in growing attention to procedural aspects of the society's activity. A striking example was the scandal that erupted in the society in late 1892–early 1893 around a seemingly minor issue. In October 1892 the Moscow Archeological Society sent a letter to the OIDR announcing the forthcoming celebration of fifty years of scholarly work of Ivan Zabelin, a historian and archeologist, who was a member of both societies. Yet the temporary head of the OIDR, Iurii Filimonov, an archeologist and historian of art, did not convey this letter to the members of the society. As a result, no representative of the OIDR attended the celebration, and its participation in the event was limited to sending an official telegram of greetings. Following this incident, a prominent member of the society, the former rector of Moscow University Nikolai Tikhonravov, sent Filimonov a personal letter demanding that he convene an immediate session of the OIDR, but Filimonov concealed this letter as well. By this stage, however, Tikhonravov had already appealed to all members of the OIDR over Filimonov's head, requesting that they find a way to restore the society's damaged reputation. The following discussion went beyond the immediate question of Filimonov's behavior to address the broader issue of the society's proper self-government. Finally, in February 1893, Filimonov resigned from his post and the highly respected Vasilii Kliuchevskii was elected as the new chair.[56]

Another sign of the society's aspiration for greater autonomy can be seen in its demonstrative disregard for members' involvement in the kind of political activity that was considered unlawful by the state bodies. Thus, Pavel Miliukov, a member of the OIDR since 1887, continued his work on editing the seventeenth-century books of appointments (*razriadnye knigi*) to be published in *Chteniia* even though he was fired from the Moscow University in February 1895, prohibited to teach anywhere in the Russian Empire, and exiled from Moscow to Riazan'.[57] From the society's point of view, the only problem in this situation was the necessity to ask another member to compare the printed text with the original manuscript before sending it to Miliukov for the final proofreading.[58] Such blatant detachment from politics, however, could in itself be interpreted as politically motivated and could not be maintained for long. Politics inevitably interfered in the society's everyday work, embodied not only in the decisions of governmental bodies, but also in the judgment of public opinion. Thus, when after the death of Alexander III, Kliuchevskii delivered a flattering farewell speech to the emperor at the society's session, it immediately aroused public reaction. "Somebody," Miliukov related, "obtained a copy of this speech, added a hectographed text of Krylov's fable (something about 'a fox flattering a lion') and disseminated it among the public."[59]

By continuing and developing the eighteenth-century traditions and, at the same time, fashioning and negotiating new rules and norms of learned associational activity, the OIDR served as a model of emulation for the historical societies that appeared in its wake. The latter adopted its categories of membership, organizational structure, and patterns of publication, but concentrated their activity on more specific goals.

Local and Archeological Societies: Why Archeology?

Local historical societies were the next kind of voluntary associations to emerge in the field: the Society for History and Antiquities of the Baltic Provinces (*Gesellschaft für Geschichte und Altertumskunde der Ostseeprovinzen Russland*) appeared in Riga in 1834, followed by the Estonian Learned Society (*Gelehrte Estnische Gesellschaft*) founded in Derpt (1838) and another Society for History and Antiquities established in Odessa (1839).[60] The latter devoted a large part of its activity to archeology; in a sense, the establishment of the Odessa Society for History and Antiquities marked the beginning of a period when most voluntary historical associations took the form of archeological societies. A number of such societies were founded in the following decades: the Russian Archeological Society in St. Petersburg in 1846, the Archeological Society in Vilna in 1856, the

Moscow Archeological Society in 1865, the Church Archeological Society at the Kiev Ecclesiastical Academy in 1872, the Society of Lovers of Caucasian Archeology in Tiflis in 1873, and the Society for Archeology, History, and Ethnography at Kazan' University in 1878.[61] From the 1880s local archeological societies emerged in Pskov (1880), Novgorod (1894), and Cherdyn', the district (uezd) town of Perm' gubernia (1903). In the last years of the nineteenth century and the early years of the twentieth century, smaller archeological circles were established in the recently annexed regions of Central Asia; the first and most prominent of these was Turkestan's Circle of the Lovers of Archeology founded in 1895 in Tashkent.[62] This was followed some years later, in 1901, by Ashkhabad's Trans-Caspian Circle of the Lovers of History and Archeology of the East, and then, in 1907, by Samarkand's Circle of the Lovers of Archeology, History, and Ethnography.[63] Why did archeology become the basis for the emergence of a new cohort of learned historical associations, and what was archeology's relation to history at that stage?

This phenomenon was connected, first and foremost, to the emergence of "historical-mindedness" among broad circles of the European educated public. Russia, in this case, experienced the same developments that Philippa Levine identified in nineteenth-century Britain, where "antiquarian, historical and archeological studies of the past attracted a body of enthusiastic and committed devotees . . . who, whether able to involve themselves full-time or only in their leisure hours in their pursuit, formed a highly motivated self-taught élite on familiar and friendly terms with one another and sharing a common body of knowledge."[64] In that period "historical" and "archeological" were almost synonymous. Indeed, as experts on nineteenth-century Russian historical studies have demonstrated, at that time "archeology" meant "the science of antiquities" (*nauka drevnostei*) and was regarded as a subdiscipline of history. The first textbook on this topic, translated from French into Russian in 1807, divided archeology into "the study of ancient manners and ceremonies" on the one hand, and archeography, which "explained the meaning of memorabilia (*pokazyvaiushchaia ob'iasnenie pamiatnikov*)" and was mainly concerned with the ancient literary texts, on the other hand.[65]

In the 1820s–1830s the term archeography began to be applied to the practice of collecting, describing, and publishing written historical sources. Its transformation into a separate historical discipline can be largely attributed to the archeographic expedition for collecting ancient manuscripts initiated by Stroev. Stroev had originally presented his proposal for such an expedition to the OIDR, but the latter had merely organized one short journey to the Novgorod *Sofiiskaia* library. An extended archeographic expedition in accordance with Stroev's original plan was launched later, in 1828, by the Academy of Sciences. During the five-and-a-half-year journey undertaken by Stroev and his assistants through North and Central Russia, they collected and described a huge quantity of ancient sources. In the wake of their success it was decided to found the Archeographic Commission in order to study and publish the collected materials. Established in 1834 as a temporary body for this particular purpose, the commission turned into a permanent institution three years later. From 1837 it functioned as the Imperial Archeographic Commission at the Ministry of Education, dealing with the discovery and publication of historical documents. In the following decades regional archeographic commissions were established in Kiev (1843), Vilna (1864), and the Caucasus (1864).[66] In 1859 the Imperial Archeological Commission was established in order to supervise the excavations on state, peasants', and urban lands. The activity of these commissions contributed to the institutionalization of archeography and archeology as separate disciplines with diverse spheres of interest. Thus Ikonnikov in his fundamental book on Russian historiography, which was published in the 1890s, distinguished between archeology and history, but asserted that knowledge of the former was essential for historical research. He broke down the discipline of archeology into several fields—paleography, diplomatics, sigillography (or sphragistics, the study of seals and signets), heraldry, numismatics, and, last but not least, the study of ancient art and everyday life.[67] According to Ikonnikov, this broad definition of archeological knowledge had practical importance in training qualified historians. In order to strengthen his claim, he represented it as a tendency characteristic of all European states, noting in particular, the high level of training undergone by the experts of the British Museum and the methods of teaching in the French École des Chartes.[68] Considering the study of archeology as essential for acquiring basic professional skills, Ikonnikov underlined the contribution made by both the archeological societies and the more specialized voluntary bodies such as the Society for Ancient Russian Art (*Obshchestvo drevnerusskogo iskusstva*), founded in 1864, and the Society for Ancient Russian Literature (*Obshchestvo liubitelei drevnei pis'mennosti*), founded in 1878.[69] The cofounder of the latter, we should note, was the future chair of the Society of Zealots of Russian Historical Education, Count Sergei Dmitrievich Sheremetev.

The perception of archeology as a basis for the historian's professional training found its practical expression in the establishment of the Archeological Institutes—in St. Petersburg in 1877 and in Moscow in 1907. Both institutes, although subordinated to the Ministry of Education, were supported by private funds. Their aims, as formulated in the Regulations (*Polozhenie*) of the Moscow Archeological Institute, included not only "the scholarly development of archeology, archeography and Russian history with its auxiliary disciplines," but also the preparation of specialists for "offices in state, public, and private archives, museums and libraries."[70] The institutes were modeled on the École des Chartes and their curricula included special courses on ancient (especially Russian) and Christian archeology, Russia's historical geography and ethnography and a cluster of courses on various branches of paleography.[71] The foundation of these institutes contributed to strengthening the scholarly status of the archeological societies.

Meanwhile, the archeological societies' expanding scope of activities led to changes in their organizational structure. Thus, in 1851 the Russian Archeological Society had been divided into the Department of Russian and Slavic Archeology, the Department of Oriental Archeology, and the Department of Ancient Classical, Byzantine, and West European Archeology. The Moscow Archeological Society adopted a different organizational strategy and gradually created a number of commissions attached to its core body. The first one was the Oriental Commission established in 1887, followed by the Slavic Commission (1892), the Archeographic Commission (1896), and the Commission for the Study of Old Moscow (1909).[72] These organizational changes facilitated further specialization in the societies' scholarly work while also broadening the domain of archeological studies. In the last decade of the nineteenth century a new agent—the Orthodox Church—intervened in the field. From the mid-1890s the Holy Synod started to launch ecclesiastical historical and archeological committees, commissions, and societies in dioceses.[73]

In order to overcome the problem of communication among the growing number of specialized archeological societies, archeological congresses began to be organized on the initiative of the Moscow Archeological Society.[74] The first congress was convened in Moscow in 1869, after which they were held every three years in various localities throughout the Russian Empire until the beginning of World War I—the last archeological congress (the sixteenth in number), which was scheduled to be held in Pskov in 1914, never took place.[75] These events aroused public interest in local history and led to the formation of local archeological expeditions and historical societies. Ivan Petrovich Khrushchov, the cofounder of the Society of Nestor the Chronicler, who would later be a prominent member of the Society of Zealots of Russian Historical Education, provided a striking example of the impact of archeological congresses when he noted how three separate projects for establishing historical societies in Kiev were proposed on the very same day that the participants of the second archeological congress in St. Petersburg started to talk about planning the third one in Kiev.[76]

These congresses also contributed to the development of local historical institutions of a new kind: the gubernia scholarly archival commissions, which had begun to be established in 1884 on the initiative of Nikolai Kalachov, a member of the Academy of Sciences and the founder of the St. Petersburg Archeological Institute.[77] Their initial aims were to locate materials of scholarly value among the documents destined for destruction by gubernia and uezd governmental, estate (*soslovnye*), and public (*obshchestvennye*) bodies and to deposit these documents in historical archives (to be set up at the commissions) in order

Fig. 2.1 Participants of the archeological congress in Iaroslavl', August 12, 1901. Courtesy of the Department of Manuscripts, Russian National Library.

to make them available for scholarly purposes. These commissions were also permitted to "explore other relics (*pamiatniki stariny*) of the past."[78] At first, four gubernia scholarly archival commissions were established in Orel (June 11, 1884), Tambov (June 12, 1884), Riazan' (June 15, 1884), and Tver' (June 22, 1884), and subsequently in other, mainly central gubernias. The Iaroslavl' gubernia scholarly archival commission was created in the course of the preparations for the seventh archeological congress which was held there in 1887.[79] The decree (*polozhenie*) of 1884 on the gubernia scholarly archival commissions conceived them as private (*chastnye*), not governmental bodies: each of them was to be established by agreement between the director of the St. Petersburg Archeological Institute and the local governor, who was given the status of custodian (*popechitel'*) of the commission. The commission's chair, his deputy and secretary were to be elected by the commission itself, while the commissions as a whole were subordinated to the Archeological Institute and, via the latter, to the Academy of Sciences. The Archeological Institute was to subsidize the commissions from its own budget, with additional funding to be raised from "local donations to the benefit of scholarship."[80] The members of the commission were expected to be "well educated"—a condition that the Ministry of the Interior's official documents interpreted as "holding a university degree," but no particular historical education was required. However, these documents also made it clear that the members were not supposed to serve in the gubernia's administration, in other words, they were not expected to be *chinovniki*.[81] The gubernia scholarly archival commissions were originally envisioned, therefore, as voluntary learned societies under the auspices of the local governors. The commissions' essentially voluntary character enabled local "enthusiasts for the past" (*liubiteli stariny*) to join the community of historians.

The provincial Russian amateurs of history constituted a heterogeneous and steadily growing group. Viktor Berdinskikh, an expert on nineteenth-century local history, has linked their emergence to the activity of the governmental gubernia statistical committees, whose establishment began in 1834.[82] These committees created an initial agenda of local studies by conducting the first surveys on the history, archeology, and ethnography of the various gubernias. In the 1830s–1860s the statistical committees served as a kind of hub for local amateurs of history, who occasionally published their materials in the official *Gubernskie vedomosti* (*Gubernia News*) issued by local governments since 1837. In the 1860s–1870s the spread of populist ideas and the emergence of the notion of *oblastnichestvo* (regional cultural and historical distinctiveness) considerably increased the interest in local history. According to Berdinskikh, the Kazan' historian Afanasii Shchapov played a special role in formulating the concept of *oblastnichestvo*. Interpreting Russian history as a process of the "self-development" of regions (*oblasti*), Shchapov insisted on the need to focus historical studies on the history of particular regions where the people's creative activity was fully expressed.[83] Vera Tolz, who has discussed these ideas in her analysis of the projects of the 1870s to integrate the minority nationalities, pointed to a certain similarity between the notion of *oblastnichestvo* and the contemporary German movement of *Heimat*, which focused on the study of local traditions and history. She also noted that the Russian enthusiasts of the "little motherland" approach (that is, study of their home region) were interested in the French experience in this field.[84] All these new trends and ideas attracted the local educated public— teachers, physicians, clerics, and petty officials—to studying the history of local life (*narodnaia zhizn'*) in their own region. This provincial *intelligentsia* later constituted the "first echelon" of the gubernia scholarly archival commissions. Indeed, according to the very critical assessment of the commissions' activity by Dmitrii Samokvasov, written at the beginning of the twentieth century, most of their members were former students of ecclesiastical seminars or former gymnasia pupils, elementary school teachers, officers, landowners (*pomeshchiki*), merchants, booksellers, and local governmental officials who rarely had the university degrees that had been initially envisioned.[85] Sometimes, these commissions were launched by the same people who served in the local statistical committees, as in Nizhnii Novgorod in 1887.[86] It was the steady rise in the number of gubernia scholarly archival commissions in the following decades that made ties among the capital's academic scholars and provincial nonacademic practitioners (*kraevedy*) increasingly important.

The State Duma's report of 1908 mentioned "the hundreds of members in each of the local archival commissions," and claimed that, taken together, the members of all the twenty-five commissions (that existed at that time) constituted "an archival and archeological force (*druzhina*) of some thousands of activists."[87] By 1914 there were already twenty-seven commissions, including that of Irkutsk, opened in 1911, which provided information on the state of archives in western and eastern Siberia, Sakhalin, Kamchatka and Manchuria.[88] The growing "density" of the archival commissions made it possible to organize regional activity. In 1903 the gubernia archival commission of Iaroslavl' initiated the first local archeological conference, followed by those of Tver' (1904), Vladimir (1906), and Kostorma (1909).[89] Addressing the Iaroslavl' conference, Sergei Fedorovich Platonov, a distinguished professor of St. Petersburg University, outlined the desirable pattern of cooperation between scholars from leading universities and local amateur historians. According to him, "the more broadly and actively the local past is studied, the more national history as a whole benefits from this." But he insisted that "local studies will be useful only if they are conducted in full accordance with scholarly standards and deliberately apply the methods of historical scholarship."[90]

All these voluntary archeological societies, state archeographic and archeological commissions, gubernia scholarly archival commissions, and church *tserkovno-istoricheskie* and *tserkovno-arkheologicheskie* commissions and committees constituted a basic network of institutions involved in the exploration of the ancient past of the Empire's heterogeneous population. In light of the special significance attributed by twentieth- and early twenty-first century historiography to the role of the nineteenth century's "fascination with the past" in the formation of national identity, these institutions can be seen as pivotal agents in this process.[91]

Nineteenth-century historians, however, noted another (and more immediate) reason for the prevailing interest in ancient times—the political circumstances. Russian historians, claimed Ikonnikov, felt themselves less constrained when writing about the history of the pre-Petrine period, where freedom of research was rarely hampered by external influences.[92] Starting from the same assumption, but taking it in a different direction, the head of the Moscow Archeological Society, Count Aleksei S. Uvarov, wrote in 1869 to the Minister of

Fig. 2.2 Sergei F. Platonov (on right) with head of the Tver' gubernia scholarly archival commission, Ivan A. Ivanov, early 1900s. Courtesy of the Department of Manuscripts, Russian National Library.

Education, Count Tolstoi, about the usefulness of the first archeological congress which could "guide minds" (*napravit' umy*) to scholarly aims and, in so doing, distract them from materialistic tendencies.[93] Miliukov in his *Memoirs* pointed to another aspect of the same phenomenon when he wrote that he "finally learned how to conduct archeological excavations properly" only when he was exiled to Riazan', under the supervision of "the patriarch of local historical studies, Aleksei Ivanovich Cherepnin."[94] This view of studies of the ancient past as a refuge from political problems was already being criticized at the end of the 1850s. One of the results of this tendency, claimed the author of the *Otechestvennye zapiski*'s bibliographical survey of 1858, was a lack of knowledge about modern history, including the eighteenth century. The need for research into this period was explained in terms of the current situation: "In the present time historical investigations are essential for resolving a multitude of vital questions that have been raised in our society; the necessity for comprehensive knowledge of the more recent era of the past is increasing by the minute. That is why we consider that the eighteenth century should soon give rise to serious studies."[95] Ikonnikov quoted this observation in his own survey of the development of "Russian historical science" in 1855–1880. In retrospect, he confirmed that the study of modern Russian history had indeed begun in the 1860s and also made explicit the political overtones that had only been implicit in the article in *Otechestvennye zapiski*. Writing in 1880, Ikonnikov defined history as a social science and underlined the connections between historical research and the course of governmental policy.[96] Examining the developments of contemporaneous historiography from the perspective of modernization and politicization, Ikonnikov ascribed particular importance to the establishment in 1866 of the Russian Historical Society. Indeed, this society was the first, and most influential, of the voluntary associations that undertook research into modern—eighteenth- and nineteenth-century—Russian history.

The Russian Historical Society

The Russian Historical Society (*Russkoe istoricheskoe obshchestvo* [RIO]) was founded in St. Petersburg in 1866. According to its statutes, the goal of the society was "to collect, process, and disseminate materials and documents on Russian history" located in both state and private archives and libraries.[97] Thanks to the support of the Ministry of Foreign Affairs to which the Russian Historical Society was officially subordinated, it managed to gain access to valuable diplomatic materials from foreign archives located in London, Vienna, Paris and Berlin. From 1867 the RIO started to publish its *sborniki*, anthologies of historical sources, mainly from the eighteenth and early nineteenth centuries, of which 148 volumes appeared over the next fifty years. These anthologies were distinguished by the fact that they included only previously unpublished materials and were edited according to the most rigorous contemporaneous archeographic standards. Starting from the seventh volume, each of the RIO's *sborniki* contained full collections of documents on a particular topic.[98] From the 1880s the RIO worked on the *Russian Biographical Dictionary*, whose actual publication began only in 1896.[99] The society thereby provided the reading public with valuable sources on the recent past and contributed to shaping the very concept of modern Russian history. However, the mode of the RIO's foundation and its everyday practice seemed to be at odds with its essentially modernizing mission and with the trend toward increasing autonomy that could be seen in the activity of the OIDR and some other historical societies.

Indeed, the establishment of the Russian Historical Society was initiated by two high-ranking officials: Count Peter Viazemskii, a friend of Pushkin and Karamzin, and the senator and millionaire Alexander Polovtsov. Their idea to create a new historical society was supported by a group of well-educated bureaucrats from the highest echelon of the imperial power structure who constituted the core group of the society's founding members.[100] Only three of the twelve founders of the society were historians, the most prominent figure among them being Afanasii Bychkov, a member of the Imperial Archeographic Commission and head of the Russian Department of the Imperial Public Library.[101] The other two historians were the military history expert, Modest Bogdanovich, and the Chair of the Department of Russian History at St. Petersburg University, Konstantin Bestuzhev-Riumin, who would subsequently become the director of the first Russian institution for women's higher education, known as Bestuzhev's higher courses.[102] Seventy-four-year-old Viazemskii was elected the first chair of the RIO's council. By that time he was a kind of "living history" himself. His *Zapisnye knizhki* (*Notebooks*) of 1865–1877 as well as his essays of this period reveal that he devoted much of his time to talks and writing about his brilliant youth. Viazemskii worked intensively on his own memoirs and commented extensively on memoirs and papers of other memoirists and writers.[103] Nonetheless, his participation in the RIO's everyday activity was limited by his prolonged trips abroad, and his chairmanship in the society was to a certain extent symbolic. After Viazemskii's death in 1879, Polovtsov, who had at first served as the RIO's secretary, became its chair. Polovtsov remained RIO's leading figure (and the main private sponsor of its publications) until his death in 1909.

In addition to the chair, the RIO's statutes provided the possibility of appointing an honorary chair if "any member of the Imperial family would honor the society by accepting this designation."[104] None other than the heir, Grand Duke Alexander Alexandrovich (the future Emperor Alexander III), took this task upon himself. His participation in the society, which was originally expected only to symbolize imperial patronage, developed into active involvement. Alexander's interest in history had already emerged in his adolescence, had been nurtured by Sergei Solov'ev's lessons in Russian history, and encouraged by the heir's tutor, Konstantin Pobedonostsev. The latter took care of his royal pupil's reading and included historical studies and historical novels in his list of recommended literature.[105] The post of honorary chair suited Alexander's interest in history and gave him the opportunity to express it. Alexander hosted the RIO's annual meetings in the library of his residence in Anichkov Palace from the time he was *Tsesarevich* (heir to the throne) and continued this practice after his ascendance to the throne. He received (and read) the reports and publications of the society and approved the election of new members and the selection of materials for its anthologies. In private conversations with his son, he called the RIO "our society" and did not hesitate to interfere in rather technical questions about lists of invitees and the schedule of its events.[106] Polovtsov even mentioned an instance when Alexander III "ordered" him to organize the 1889 meeting of the Historical Society on the very next day.[107] The future head of the Society of Zealots of Russian Historical Education, Count Sheremetev, who served as the tsar's messenger on this occasion, confirmed Alexander III's genuine interest and personal involvement in the RIO's activity in general, and in that specific case in particular.[108] Sheremetev, who joined the RIO in 1873, explained the tsar's frequent intervention in a way that was rather unflattering to Polovtsov. He blamed Polovtsov for lack of interest in the orderly running of the society and presented Alexander III as the one who urged the irresponsible chair to carry out his functions properly. Moreover, according to Sheremetev, Alexander III had a particular vision of the RIO as a channel of direct communication between the monarch and representatives of the educated public. The tsar expected that the publication of historical documents would be accompanied by "a lively exchange of ideas among the members of the society gathered around their honorary chair." It was Polovtsov's fault, Sheremetev argued, that this goal was not achieved.[109]

In 1884 the sixteen-year-old *Tsesarevich* Nicholas, who was to be the last Russian emperor, was invited by the RIO to join it as an honorary member.[110] Nicholas was fascinated by the explorations of the national past to which he became exposed at the society's meetings, and he once told the RIO's secretary, Georgii Shtendman, that if he had been a private person he would have devoted himself to historical studies. In 1889 Nicholas considered preparing an essay of his own for one of the society's annual meetings. His uncle, Grand Duke Vladimir Aleksandrovich, also a member of the RIO, recommended that he base his study on the works of Alexander N. Popov on the Patriotic War of 1812.[111] Like his father, Nicholas retained his interest in the RIO after becoming emperor and managed to astonish Polovtsov by requesting to convene the society's annual meeting at the height of the revolutionary events in the winter of 1905–1906.[112] After Polovtsov's death in 1909, the tsar's uncle, Grand Duke Nikolai Mikhailovich, was elected chair of the RIO, which further increased the involvement of the royal family in the society's activity.[113] The designation "Imperial," which was bestowed on the RIO in 1873, had a literal meaning in this case. Not surprisingly, when it was decided to publish Nicholas I's personal papers, this sensitive mission was entrusted to the Russian Historical Society.[114] However, the direct involvement of royal figures not only gave access to valuable sources, but also introduced an element of court ceremonialism into the RIO's practice. Polovtsov's description of the annual meeting of the society in 1885 provides a striking example of this phenomenon, and for this reason is quoted here in full:

At 8.30 we [Polovtsov and Shtendman] set off to Anichkov Palace where about ten members of the society have already gathered for the meeting. Together with the Emperor, Tsesarevich, and Grand Duke Vladimir Alexandrovich, there are 26 persons present. His Majesty appears at 9 p.m., greets everybody and notes that there has never been a meeting attended by so many people. I notice that the "Muscovites," Bartenev, Biuler, Karpov, Count Sheremetev, are in attendance. I introduce to the Tsesarevich each of the members he comes across. A lackey Kulomzin tells him that he had the pleasure of seeing him in Moscow.

His Majesty sits Vladimir Alexandrovich next to him and orders the Tsesarevich to take a seat between me and Shtendman. I open the meeting by reading my report. Then A. F. Bychkov reads excerpts from unpublished and partly unknown letters of Peter the Great, while describing one of the letters, rather tactlessly, as presenting a perfectly correct (that is, unflattering) evaluation of the Poles' character. Grot delivers a rather boring article on negotiations during the Swedish war of 1788. Dubrovin reads a very nice report (*premiloe soobshchenie*) on the Empress Catherine's historical studies and her attempts to found a historical society under her chairmanship with Count Shuvalov's help. Martens suffocates us with a tale that would befit a village schoolteacher about Russia's relations with Prussia during the Patriotic War. With difficulty I interrupt his pedantic, undistinguished tale and move to the re-election of members whose turn it is to leave the council.[115] At this moment Kulomzin pulls a manuscript out of his pocket and wants to begin reading it, but I stop him because he did not inform me about his intention in advance. After each presentation His Majesty most kindly says a few words to the speaker, while the Tsesarevich is enthusiastic about this pastime which is completely new to him and tells me that he will write down everything he has heard today in the diary that he has been keeping for the past 4 years. The meeting finishes at 10.45. His Majesty most graciously expresses once again his pleasure to each of the members present.[116]

Polovtsov's account clearly demonstrates that the tsar's presence, not the papers presented, was the focal point of this meeting. Consequently, meetings of the RIO that were not attended by Alexander III were far less attractive. "I have held the annual meeting of the Historical Society; we waited half an hour for Grand Duke Vladimir Aleksandrovich, but it then transpired that he had gone hunting," wrote Polovtsov about such a "work only" meeting of 1884.[117] In 1886 Bychkov and Grot, who had intended to talk at the annual meeting, "went back on their promises" when they found out that the event would be held in Polovtsov's home (one of the most fashionable in St.Petersburg), but not in Anichkov Palace, and without the RIO's honorary chair. "Only 11 persons came," Polovtsov noted in his diary.[118] Moreover, Polovtsov himself exploited his chairmanship of the RIO as a pretext for approaching Alexander III unofficially with different problems connected to his official duty as the State Secretary, and even Alexander III used the RIO's meetings as an opportunity to settle various issues informally.[119]

At the annual meeting of 1887, for example, as reported by Polovtsov, Sheremetev saw the tsar reprimanding his closest advisor, the Ober-Procurator of the Synod, Pobedonostsev, for lack of order in the Alexander Nevsky Monastery.[120] Thus, while remaining a voluntary association, the RIO became interwoven into the dynamics of court life. Coming into contact with the rulers in this particular context provided numerous opportunities for gaining benefits of various kinds, including service promotion for the society's members. The examples are impressive: the secretary of the society, Shtendman, was given the rank of Actual State Councilor (*deistvitel'nyi statskii sovetnik*) as an award for his work on the RIO's anthologies, while the Moscow scholar, Gennadii Karpov, asked to be appointed a member of the Council for Printed Matter as a reward for preparing for publication two volumes of the *Sbornik* on Russia's relations with England and the Tatars in the sixteenth century.[121] This perception of the RIO as a place for establishing useful connections and obtaining valuable favors made it seem a rather outdated body, reminiscent of the "societies" of Catherine's time rather than a nineteenth-century scholarly association.

Nonetheless, this apparent revival of an old-fashioned model was in fact a new and essentially political phenomenon. Polovtsov described the RIO's founders as motivated by a strong sense of the need to confront the nihilist interpretation of history which, he argued, had consolidated in the 1860s. In a speech in memory of Alexander II he presented his view of the situation as follows: "The Russian people, craving to know their past, were provided only with an unsightly picture of weaknesses and shortcomings that influenced its fate. The lofty, significant aspects of our state's important activity that created the great Russia, so dear to us all, were, with rare exceptions, passed over in silence in the literature of the 1860s, thus destroying the people's belief in themselves and in the forces that have governed them."[122] Sheremetev described the situation of the 1860s in greater detail, but in the same spirit, claiming that "the aspiration to destroy and remove from the pedestal names that were dear to us prevailed in the historical studies of that time." Unlike Polovtsov, Sheremetev provided some specific examples of this tendency:

> Kostomarov, for all his talent, expressed quite blatantly in his works his biased view of pre-Petrine Rus', focusing his fulminations on Moscow. Moscow was a word of abuse for Kostomarov, who at that time was an oracle for the university's youth. . . . Pavlov did not conceal his sympathies and hatreds in his article on Russia's thousandth anniversary. Semevskii began denouncing Peter the Great as soon as he launched the publication of *Russkaia starina*. In Moscow Bartenev, who in 1863 started the *Russkii arkhiv* journal, promised a great deal and had the wherewithal for it, but very quickly revealed himself as a panderer to public taste and a stooge for other people. . . . Bodianskii was the only one who tirelessly continued to publish in his *Chteniia* materials that were

as rich in content as they were poor in presentation. The spirit of destruction penetrated everything and influenced the writings of our researchers. Only Solov'ev's monumental, conscientious work was not affected: every year he produced a new volume of his history, one after the other. Unfortunately, his work lacked any "spirit" at all, because the deadening dryness of the exposition is not redeemed by its positive merits.[123]

Although neither Polovtsov nor Sheremetev ever used the definition of history as *obshchestvennaia nauka* that had already appeared in the lexicon of their contemporary Ikonnikov, they emphasized history's social function. Furthermore, their vision of the society's activity as a counter-force to the liberal criticism of Russia's recent past presented the RIO as a reactionary body in the most fundamental meaning of the word—one that sought to counteract a new and undesirable development. Sheremetev explicitly stated this view when he wrote that the RIO stood "against the current."[124] Yet while Sheremetev saw the RIO's goal as resisting liberal ideas, Polovtsov emphasized the necessity to counter not only liberal but also ultra-nationalist political tendencies. Polovtsov's diary of the 1880s reflects his concern with the rapid increase in anti-German and anti-Polish sentiments among Russian officialdom which, he noted, led to "pseudo-national persecution" of the non-Russian population of the Empire.[125] He condemned "the indulgence (*potakanie*) of the weaknesses of the common people" as criminal and was especially concerned by the growing influence of Mikhail Katkov, editor of the popular *Moskovskie Vedomosti* newspaper, whom he described as "an irresponsible journalist, whose impertinent self-esteem damages the dignity of the government and compromises it in the eyes of both the Russian people and other states."[126] The RIO's careful publication of historical documents according to the highest scholarly standards was intended to juxtapose a more balanced conservative narrative of Russia's historical development to both liberal and ultra-nationalist interpretations of Russia's past and present. Moreover, some of these documents related to historical events or processes that were still relevant to fin-de-siècle Russian society. Thus, in 1890 Polovtsov sent Alexander III the first copy of the RIO's new volume containing materials of the Committee of December 6, 1826, which had examined measures for reforming the state apparatus in the wake of the Decembrists' revolt. In his cover letter, Polovtsov drew the tsar's attention to the fact that some of the reforms suggested by that committee were yet to be implemented. As he noted in his diary on that day, "I wrote about the significance of the proposed reforms, about the benefit of joint collegial discussions of the reforms and their gradual realization, as well as about the fact that some of them, first and foremost the abolition of the Table of Ranks, are still waiting their turn."[127] Polovtsov's intention to maintain a moderate but activist political line was, however, challenged by the vicissitudes of Russia's actual political life: the same political stance that had appeared to be conservative but modern in the mid-1880s was perceived as completely outdated twenty years later. "Both our *sbornik* and my dictionary [Russian Biographical Dictionary] are regarded as reactionary; not only do they meet with no sympathy in the press, but almost nobody buys them," Polovtsov complained to Nicholas II in 1906. Still, even in this situation he found consolation in his personal conviction that the society's volumes presented "the true, correct view" of Russian history.[128]

The RIO's implicit political purpose suggests that the royal participation in its activity had a new element. The last Russian monarchs' personal involvement in the RIO differed from the model of enlightened patronage typical of Catherine II and her successors. This might be better understood in the context of the changes undergone by the tsarist "scenario of power" (in Richard Wortman's term) after the accession of Alexander III. According to Wortman, Alexander's way of exercising power implied repudiation of the post-Petrine image of the Westernized monarch striving to make Russia a part of the European cultural world. The Russian emperor was instead to be presented as a non-Western national ruler, whose legitimacy derived from the Russian historical tradition, not from modern judicial institutions. Wortman defines this scenario as a "national myth" and emphasizes both its novelty and its intrinsic paradox: the very concept of the "national ruler" derived from the modern Western doctrine of nationalism. While analyzing the formation of this nationalist scenario, Wortman ascribes a crucial role to the influence of what he calls "the Russian party"—"a diverse group of writers, journalist and officials" that consolidated around Katkov, so hated by Polovtsov.[129] However, Alexander III's involvement in the Russian Historical Society indicates that his scenario of power was more sophisticated, and its internal paradox more profound. Despite Katkov's notorious impact on Alexander III's politics, Polovtsov still had some justification for calling himself the emperor's "historical secretary," and, in this capacity, for giving Alexander III political advice during the crisis in Russia's relations with England in 1885.[130] In addition, the tsar's participation in the RIO's activity adds another nuance to the "national myth" scenario—the notion of the monarch's direct connection with his people, without the mediation of bureaucratic institutions. In the RIO's case this connection took the form of the tsar's participation in the process of forming a proper narrative of the national past. Both the mode of his involvement and his very cooperation with a voluntary historical society contributed to modernizing the image of the monarchy without challenging its status as a traditional institution deeply rooted in national history.

This modernizing effect was strengthened by the RIO's aspiration to act as an association of experts. Both Polovtsov and Sheremetev repeatedly employed the notion of expertise while evaluating their comembers' input or ability. The way in which they employed this term indicates that, unlike in the early nineteenth

century, it had now come to refer to the knowledge stemming from formal education. Both men described the RIO's secretary, Shtendman, as an expert. Polovtsov
praised his erudition (*uchenost'*) and sense of responsibility, which excused, in
his eyes, Shtendman's rather weak organizational abilities. Sheremetev, for his
part, characterized Shtendman as "a pupil of [Theodor] Mommsen, a person with
multifaceted historical education, able to work laboriously and diligently" and
assigned him the main role in producing the RIO's anthologies.[131] While com-
plimenting Shtendman for his expertise, Polovtsov sharply criticized another
member of the RIO, Petr Bartenev, the well-known publisher of the *Russkii
arkhiv* journal, for lack of this quality. Despite Bartenev's respected reputation,
Polovtsov accused him of ignorance. Polovtsov's sarcastic exchange with the
Minister of Education, Delianov, regarding Bartenev's prospective promotion, as
recorded in Polovtsov's diary, is revealing in this respect:

> POLOVTSOV: "Is it true that you have promoted Bartenev, the editor of the
> *Russkii arkhiv,* to the rank of Actual State Councilor (*Deistvitel'nyi statskii
> sovetnik*)?"
>
> DELIANOV: "Yes."
>
> POLOVTSOV: "What for? Was it for publishing documents disgracing the
> government or for the extreme ignorance with which he published
> them?"[132]

Polovtsov used even harsher language when writing about Bartenev's request
that the RIO entrust him with the task of publishing Nicholas I's papers: "Of
course, I have no intention of getting involved with this profit-seeking, coarse,
uneducated man."[133]

The situation depicted in this episode points to another aspect of the aspiration for expertise: Polovtsov took special care in choosing editors for each volume of the RIO's anthologies from among specialists in the particular period or
field of study. Both Polovtsov's notes and a glance at the full list of the volumes
reveal that their editing was gradually entrusted to academic historians, namely,
those who held the degree of magister or doctor and were associated with one of
the academic institutions (most typically as a university professor).[134] A number
of the RIO's *Sborniki* of 1910–1915 were edited by Nikolai Chechulin, who at that
time also served as head of the Historical Department of the Society of Zealots of
Russian Historical Education.[135]

The dynamics of the RIO's membership demonstrated the same tendency
of "academization." While at the time of the society's establishment there were
only three historians among its twelve founding members, in 1912 thirteen of the
twenty-nine full members were historians. Among them were professors from
the main universities, including such leading figures in the field as Platonov and
Ikonnikov. [136] The desire to maintain the level of expertise apparently led to the

society's increasing professionalization—a tendency that could also be discerned in the development of the OIDR in this period. Combined with the RIO's unique closeness to the tsar's court, this pursuit of historical excellence turned the Russian Historical Society into a kind of elitist club, where respected historians mingled with high-ranking civil servants. The list of members for 1912 included, among others, the former Minister of Foreign Affairs, and since 1910 the Russian ambassador to France, Alexander Izvol'skii; his deputy in the Ministry of Foreign Affairs, Konstantin Gubastov; and Deputy Minister of Education Mikhail Taube, along with other distinguished holders of the highest bureaucratic offices. What is striking, however, is not only the eminence of the members, but also the brevity of the list. In addition to the twenty-nine full members, it comprised only one corresponding member, the Russian military attaché in London, N. S. Ermolov, and three honorary members: an additional representative of the tsarist family, Grand Duke Konstantin Konstantinovich, and two French historians, Frédéric Masson and Gabriel Hanotaux.[137] The Russian Historical Society was apparently reluctant to expand its membership, preferring to remain a small select group.

Yet this distinctive feature of the RIO's membership did not lead to the formation of close relationships or "a sense of comradeship (*soobrazheniia tovarishchestva*)" within the society; Polovtsov, who occasionally used the latter term, never applied it to the RIO.[138] The atmosphere within the society was one of mutual mistrust. Thus, Sheremetev suspected Polovtsov of having intentionally postponed the RIO's meetings in order to prevent him, Sheremetev, from presenting his own research on the Times of Trouble.[139] Polovtsov was sarcastic about the alleged "disinterestedness (*beskorystie*) of the Russian scholars," believing their participation in the historical society to be actually motivated mainly by vanity. "They all want to lick honey—to sit in the library of the Anichkov Palace; frankly, I am tired of this, but it is the only enticement that I have at my disposal for the scholars who participate in issuing the *Sbornik*," Polovtsov concluded in his diary in 1890.[140] When Nicholas II, much less charismatic than his father, accepted the post of honorary chair of the society, and when its meetings were moved from the splendid Anichkov to the modest Aleksandrovskii Palace, even this lure lost its former appeal. In 1906 Polovtsov complained to Nicholas II about the difficulty of organizing the RIO's meetings in the face of general apathy. His description of the society's meeting in that year conveyed the aura of indifference and alienation among its members. Polovtsov wrote about the silence that followed the first lecture and his attempt to ease the embarrassment with a flattering remark: "I hastened to say that the paper was very interesting." Another person who tried to save the situation was Nicholas II: he asked the lecturer about his sources.[141] This instance appears not only embarrassing but also puzzling in view of the fact that the lecturer was none other than Platonov, greatly admired by his students and highly respected by his colleagues, and that his lecture had been devoted to a topic that had become popular as a result of his research—the first years of Mikhail Fedorovich Romanov's reign. The problem probably had more to do with the relations among the society's members than with Platonov's lecturing abilities.

Through all these successes and failures, the Russian Historical Society continued its activity until 1917, contributing not only to the formation of the concept of modern Russian history and the modernization of the image of the Russian monarchy, but also to the very notion of what it meant to "be a historian." Furthermore, in 1911 Nicholas II, acting in his capacity of honorary chair of the Russian Historical Society, suggested that the society take upon itself the task of supervising the gubernia scholarly archival commissions in developing a network of local archives.[142] From 1912 the RIO served as a channel through which information about the preservation of documents by local bodies was conveyed by gubernia commissions to the center, and governmental financial support was transferred from the Council of Ministers to gubernias.[143] It thus also played an important role in strengthening connections with local segments of the historical community.

Acting as a venue of ongoing interaction between scholars and statesmen and as a channel of political influence, the RIO exposed the challenges confronting a voluntary society that sought to build its membership on a combination of scholarly expertise and royal patronage. Somewhat paradoxically, its very failure to provide a framework for nurturing friendly relations contributed to the emergence of new kinds of voluntary historical associations. The mid-1880s– early 1890s saw the appearance, in St. Petersburg and later in Moscow, of circles (*kruzhki*) of historians based on the principle of friendly cooperation between students of history or on informal communication between students and their professors. Not surprisingly, some of the members of these circles also participated in the activity of the Russian Historical Society, but their behavior and their relations in the less formal associations differed strikingly from what they experienced in the RIO.

Circles (*kruzhki*) of Historians

It is hard to determine precisely when the historical circles first appeared as they were not officially established like the earlier societies, but gradually took shape in the course of informal meetings among university lecturers and graduate students. Consequently, these circles never formulated any kind of regulations. Their main forms of activity consisted of meetings and discussions held in private houses. However, since these discussions revolved around the participants' research interests and career advancement, they contributed to fostering a sense of professional identity while displaying a variety of particular modes of relations among their members.

The first "circle of Russian historians" appeared in St. Petersburg in 1884 among the students of Bestuzhev-Riumin.[144] Evgenii Shmurlo listed the members of the circle on the occasion of its fifth anniversary in 1889:

> On January 2 our circle celebrated its fifth anniversary. . . . Almost everybody attended, including Simonov, even though he is permanently resident in Vyborg and is detached from the circle both because he lives in another town and because of his occupation: he has become a teacher and is now removed from scholarly history. I don't even know him very well, but he is the spiritual father of the circle—the very idea of establishing it belongs to him. Our members are now (I will list them in the approximate order in which they joined since I was not in the circle from the very beginning): V. G. Druzhinin, S. F. Platonov, A. I. Barbashev, N. M. Bubnov, N. D. Chechulin, S. M. Seredonin, I. A. Shliapkin, A. S. Lappo-Danilevskii, M. A. Diakonov, A. I. Solov'ev, me, N. M. Lisovskii, I. F. Annenskii, S. D. Stepanov, I. A. Kozeko—all in all, fifteen members, not counting Simonov.[145]

The circle's meetings took place twice a month in the spacious house of Vasilii Druzhinin, a son of a rich merchant who was the wealthiest member of the circle. Miliukov, who attended the circle's meetings as a Moscow guest in the course of his visits to St. Petersburg, described the atmosphere of conviviality at these meetings: "On the ground floor of the large mansion young historians talked about the news in their field of scholarship and exchanged opinions while partaking of tea and good refreshments."[146] The same impression of conviviality and young comradeship was conveyed by Shmurlo, who underscored the "good exchange of ideas" and the friendly nature of the circle's gatherings, with a mixture of serious talk and light banter.[147] Indeed, the members of the circle were young in terms of both their age and academic standing. Almost all of them were in their early thirties, and all of them were at the beginning of their scholarly careers: they were, as Miliukov formulated it, "*sverstniki i aspiranty*," namely graduate students of more or less the same age. By 1889 four members—Barbashev, Platonov, Bubnov, Shmurlo—had already defended their dissertations and gained their *magister* (master's) degree; in March 1889 Druzhinin's dissertation defense took place, while it was expected that Diakonov, Lappo-Danilevskii, Chechulin and Shliapkin would soon complete their writing.[148] The dissertation defense constituted the most important procedure of initiation into the academic world: it signified the end of studentship and opened the doors to the post of privat-docent (*privat-dotsent*), which constituted the first rung on the academic ladder.[149] "For the first time I was sitting among the throng of the faculty by virtue of being a privat-docent," wrote Shmurlo after Druzhinin's defense on March 5, 1889. The celebration of dissertation defenses was, therefore, the circle's central event and had its own joyful ritual, which Shmurlo described in detail when writing about Druzhinin's celebration:

On that same evening of March 5 we celebrated a new *magister* (*magistr*) in the luxurious residence of his parents... There were a lot of people. The huge dining room was full. In the course of the dinner I congratulated Druzhinin on behalf of the historical circle and presented him with a *magister*'s badge (*magisterskii znachok*). Since the number of *magisters* in our circle is now growing, we decided to club together and give these badges to each other as a sign of our good relations. This was done for the first time when Platonov obtained his *magister*'s degree (*magisterstvo*); badges were presented to him and to the "old" *magister*, Barbashev, and later to me, and now to Druzhinin. During the same dinner Platonov recited a comic poem about the morning's defense. Druzhinin spoke very warmly about Bestuzhev, and also mentioned Vasilevskii and Karpov who were attending the dinner. . . . After dinner we went down to the rooms of the young magister and did a lot more reveling (*brazhnichali*) there.[150]

The next celebration took place in December of that year after Diakonov's dissertation defense: "in the evening we greeted the young *magister* and, as usual, endowed him with the *magister*'s badge," Shmurlo wrote.[151] The circle, therefore, played the role of a support group providing its members with emotional support in the state of liminality that each of them experienced while standing on the threshold of their professional career.

Striving to cross the invisible line that separated advanced students from the group of the initiated who had already entered the ranks of the university's teaching staff, the members of the circle were aware of their destiny to be the "next" generation of Russian historians.[152] This generational identity was particularly evident at the celebration of the circle's fifth anniversary, which took the form of paying symbolic respect to the "elders." In order to commemorate this day, wrote Shmurlo, all members of the circle went to the photo studio to have a collective picture taken and presented copies of it to their former teachers: "Three copies of the pictures were presented to Bestuzhev, Zamyslovskii, and V. G. Vasilevskii; the latter was given one not only as an *hommage* from Russian historians, but also because there are two of his students among us, Bubnov and Stepanov, specialists on general history. The group came out well in this picture. Shliapkin brought parchment rolls (*stolbtsy*) of the seventeenth century with which we decorated ourselves, and an abundant stock of laughter and jokes made up the rest."[153] This demonstration of respect for their teachers interwoven with an element of intentional distancing from "the elders" represented an attitude that Stephen Lovell has defined as "cohort thinking" and increased the sense of solidarity among the members of the circle.[154] This attitude is reflected in Miliukov's use of the term "generation" when describing his first encounter with the circle: "a generation of Petersburg historians, of my own age and slightly younger, met my arrival with understandable interest and anticipation: I was preceded by my reputation as Kliuchevskii's favorite pupil and a representative of his approach."[155] Later Miliukov considered that the members of the circle played an important role in introducing new ideas into the Petersburg historiographic tradition:

> In Petersburg the view (established by Schlözer) still prevailed that it was impossible to write Russian history without a prior critical study of its sources. This was quite correct, of course, with regard to ancient history, from which Schlözer started and where he stopped: this approach signified the transition from the compilers of the eighteenth century to scientific research. Yet the Moscow school, which dealt with historical materials of a later period, had progressed much further. First, it did not confine itself to studying the ancient period, but included in its work a huge amount of archival materials on whose basis it was possible to draw direct conclusions about the history of everyday life and the evolution of political and social institutions. The Petersburg school, even after it submitted to the influence of the Moscow school, retained its connections with the views of the older generation. In particular, this was characteristic of E. F. Shmurlo's works. . . . Even S. F. Platonov made a compromise and resolved the problem brilliantly by dedicating the first half of his work on the seventeenth-century Time of Troubles to a critical examination of the sources and presenting the history of the Time of Troubles, according to the Moscow approach (*po-moskovski*), only in the second part.[156]

The members of the circle, according to Milukov, sympathized with "the Moscow approach" but were still reluctant to express their views openly.[157] Despite its informal character, therefore, the circle functioned as a new kind of scholarly framework, in which young historians were able to present new ideas without endangering their status in the formal academic institution, in this case—in their alma mater, St. Petersburg University. This role of the circle was even recognized by the university's "elders." In the course of D'iakonov's dissertation defense, wrote Shmurlo, Sergeevich unintentionally made a flattering remark about the circle of historians when he noted that because of its influence, D'iakonov, a legal expert, had been able to write a work on the "Power of Moscow's Rulers" that exceeded the scope of a strictly juridical study.[158]

This scholarly and generational identity shared by the society's members, together with the emotional support the society provided, contributed to the atmosphere of equality among them. "Generation is horizontal: it constructs a community of coevals," noted Lovell, and this feeling of community was discernible in the circle's discourse.[159] Shmurlo constantly depicted the circle as a comradeship of equals in his *Notes*: while assigning the role of the circle's "spiritual father" to its founder, who lived far away, he did not mention any actual head or leader. All the members of the circle, he underlined, published their works in the same publishing house of Skorokhodov, which he defined as "our, the circle's, 'dissertational' printing-house."[160] Together they supported "their" *Bibliograf* (*The Bibliographer*), a professional journal founded and edited by one of

С.-ПЕТЕРБУРГЪ — St. Pétersbourg   Императорскій Университетъ
L'université

Fig. 2.3 St. Petersburg University; postcard from the early twentieth century. Courtesy of the Department of Manuscripts, Russian National Library.

the members, Lisovskii, although, as Shmurlo lamented, the circle's help was not regular enough: "The circle pays the obligations that it took upon itself on a very irregular basis. At the end of 1887 we had the idea of supporting the publication of the *Bibliograf* financially in order to enable the editor to increase its size. . . . Each of us voluntarily determined his monthly payment according to his means."[161] The same theme of a collective based on the mutual interests and equality of its members also prevailed in Platonov's letters to Miliukov. Platonov described the circle's activities as entirely dependent on the presence or absence of its members. "'Russian historians' became less convivial after the departure of Shmurlo and Bubnov," he wrote in October 1891. "Seredonin is very busy with the exams, and his absence, along with that of the other two mentioned above, has reduced the number of the circle's habitués by half."[162]

Yet the image of equality, so carefully nurtured by the members of the society, was challenged by the observant outsider Miliukov. Miliukov regarded Platonov as the head of the circle, who "absolutely deserved" to play the leading role.[163] His description of Platonov, however, was rather ambivalent. Platonov was "intelligent and talented, but, at the same time, cautious enough not to rupture relations with 'the elders' and to preserve his chances of an academic career. This prevented him from being entirely frank even in private conversations.

Yet he listened to his guest from Moscow [i.e. Miliukov] attentively and established amicable relations between me and his surrounding group of coevals and graduate students."[164] Milukov thus noted the main components of Platonov's emerging leadership, the first being his successful career: Platonov climbed the academic ladder much faster than other members of the circle. Shmurlo's melancholy reflections regarding his own future at St. Petersburg University included a description of Platonov's rapid advancement, in which recognition of his friend's success was mingled with a touch of envy:

> My position vis-à-vis the members of the faculty remains unclear to me. I am not one of those who know how "to test the ground," how to take the initiative etc., I take what others give me, and you don't get far like that. I do not know, for example, whether I'll be given something in this semester like the last one. Obviously, Platonov is in a much better and firmer position than I. After all, it is said that both the dean and the rector have a good opinion of him. . . . This December Platonov was especially lucky: on December 2 Zamyslovskii had a stroke that he won't recover from very soon. As a result, the Philological Institute charged Platonov with delivering lectures instead of Zamyslovskii in the coming semester. On Zamyslovskii's suggestion, Platonov has already been sharing lectures with him for the last three years: Zamyslovskii gave up two hours for him from the usual six and paid him forty rubles per month (I think that's the figure) *out of his own pocket*; our faculty did the same. So by now he will have seventeen lectures altogether![165]

In practice, Platonov's "luck" was even greater than Shmurlo thought: in September 1890, after Zamyslovskii's resignation, Platonov was appointed acting head and professor of the Department of Russian History even before he had obtained his doctoral degree.[166] Yet while advancing successfully up the "vertical" academic ladder, Platonov carefully maintained and strengthened his "horizontal" friendly connections established in the circle, and this was the second component of his leadership. Platonov's correspondence with Miliukov in 1891–1892 creates an impressive picture of his constant care for his colleagues and students. He asked Miliukov to "arrange" a subscription of *Chteniia MOIDR* for Druzhinin, reminded him about the documents that had been promised to be sent to D'iakonov, sent Miliukov his protégé, Alexander Presniakov ("one of the best of our students"), and requested him "to take under his patronage in the archival and academic sphere" another student, Sergei Rozhdestvenskii. The latter request was accompanied by a friendly compliment: "since January 1890 I know that you are able to supervise very well those *peterburzhtsy* who happen to be in Moscow, and that you do not refuse to take this burden upon yourself."[167]

The word "patronage" (*pokrovitel'stvo*) in this note is revealing. Platonov not only ascribed this role to Miuliukov, but also played it himself, investing considerable time and effort in managing the exchange of favors and appeasement of

Fig. 2.4 Sergei F. Platonov (standing), with (sitting, from left to right): Sergei M. Seredonin, Nikolai. D. Chechulin, and his brother, the *zemstvo*'s physician, Sergei D. Chechulin, during a summer vacation on the Chechulins' estate near Cherepovets, near the village of Borisoglebsk (Irma), Novgorod gubernia, ca. 1888. Courtesy of the Department of Manuscripts, Russian National Library.

conflicts between his friends and colleagues, as shown by his attempt to prevent a clash between Chechulin and Miliukov provoked by the latter's review of the former's work.[168] The story of this conflict is especially important for us given the significant role that Chechulin was to play some years later in the Society of Zealots of Russian Historical Education.

In 1889 the *Zhurnal Ministerstva Narodnogo Prosveshcheniia* (*Journal of the Ministry of Education [ZhMNP]*) published Chechulin's study on "Russian Provincial Society in the Eighteenth Century" which was simultaneously issued as a monograph.[169] This study stemmed from Chechulin's earlier work, "Andrei Bolotov's *Notes* as a Historical Source," carried out in the framework of Bestuzhev-Riumin's seminar on Russian history and awarded a silver medal as the best student essay in 1883. When deciding to publish this piece Chechulin could hardly have anticipated any trouble, which made the impact of a devastating review that appeared in the liberal journal *Russkaia mysl'* (*Russian Thought*) even stronger.[170] Chechulin's work was dismissed as immature student writing of little value, while Chechulin himself was accused of having joined ("probably unintentionally") the "nationalist and conservative party." The last accusation was formulated in especially insulting terms. In particular, the reviewer wrote: "The author is too far from reality, from the real ground for us to be able to consider him a member of the party; we are rather willing to suppose that he is 'living without consciousness' of contemporary life and does not know what he is doing (*ne vedaet chto tvorit*). . . . He is also 'without consciousness' with regard to the theory that he undertook to defend."[171] Although the review was anonymous, at least two members of the circle of Russian historians, Platonov and Lappo-Danilevskii, knew the name of the author: it was Miliukov, and he informed them personally about the appearance of this review. They reacted to this information differently. As emerges from Lappo-Danilevskii's letters to Miliukov, he completely agreed with the review's harsh critique and lauded its publication. Moreover, he also drew Miliukov's attention to another book by Chechulin—*Cities of the Moscow State in the Sixteenth Century*, characterizing that study as "unworked raw material with some, not always reliable, comments."[172] When he learned of Chechulin's intentions to reply to the criticism, he warned Miliukov not to get into trouble with him, writing with venomous sarcasm: "Your review has made the author of *Provincial Society* quite furious. He has decided to answer you and will probably send or has already sent his response to *Russkaia Mysl'*. He is a man of a rather tempestuous nature and poorly educated; do not waste your time on polemics with him."[173] Platonov's response to the conflict was quite different: he tried to mitigate it. When writing to Miliukov two weeks after Lappo-Danilevskii's first letter, he mainly addressed the possible impact of the review on Miliukov's Petersburg connections and, while trying to play down its destructive effect, did not regard it as anything to joke about: "I don't think your decision regarding Chechulin's brochure will affect your Petersburg relations, as you seem to have expressed this concern. Its tone is found to be angry and agitated, just as was to be expected from you. I must confess, I myself was convinced that it had been written by Gol'tsov [V.A. Gol'tsov, editor of *Russkaia mysl'* and an expert on eighteenth-century Russia] and assumed that he could stand up for himself. I await with great interest your review of Chechulin's *Cities*."[174] At the same time, Platonov supported Chechulin as a friend and tried to help him cope with the unpleasant situation. His main aim seemed to be to calm Chechulin so as not to exacerbate the conflict further. Chechulin did not know who the author of the review was but strongly felt that he had to defend his scholarly reputation and was therefore determined to publish his—rather belligerent—response. Platonov tried to prevent him from doing this and even revealed to Chechulin the identity of the reviewer: Chechulin was sure that the review had been written by the liberal St. Petersburg historian Semevskii. Chechulin, however, could not be deterred, so Platonov helped him to publish his response in the *Journal of the Ministry of Education,* where Platonov had recently became a member of the board, but managed to postpone its appearance until May 1890 and forewarned Miliukov about it. Moreover, Platonov published his own review of Chechulin's book on the *Cities of the Moscow State* in the same issue of that journal, also informing Miliukov beforehand of his intention. In his letters, Platonov let Miliukov know that his own assessment of Chechulin' research, based on his talk as an official disputant at Chechulin's dissertation defense in March 1890, would be more moderate ("not panegyric, but adequate") and would focus "seriously" on his research methods. Platonov therefore elegantly but clearly hinted at the political nuances in Miliukov's review. When Chechulin's response finally appeared in May 1890, Miliukov preferred not to continue his polemic.[175]

Not surprisingly, Platonov's unofficial leading position became accepted by other members of the circle: a later humoristic definition of the circle as "Platonov and retinue" which derived from a pun on Druzhinin's name (*druzhina* being both a retinue and a prince's armed force in Russian) reflected this situation.[176] Sometimes the soirées that were held by Platonov and his wife on Wednesdays (known as Platonov's "sredy") served as a substitute for the regular meetings at Druzhinin's house. Thus, Platonov's wife, Nadezhda Nikolaevna, mentioned in her diary that in 1892 the circle's annual meeting on January 2 had been transferred to their house on Druzhinin's request. This meeting was attended by Miliukov, who had arrived in St. Petersburg on the very same day, and it was there that he encountered Chechulin, whom he had so severely attacked in his review and with whom he had not been personally acquainted before. Some days later, on January 7, Platonova noted in her diary: "The literary enemies (*literaturnye vragi*), Miliukov and Chechulin, met for the first time at our home, and the encounter was amicable. Yesterday they played chess the whole day." She also noted that Lappo-Danilevskii's absence, which "was noticed by everybody," annoyed Sergei Fedorovich and upset herself as the hostess of the house.[177]

As the dynamics of the conflict between Chechulin and Miliukov demonstrated, the circle of Russian historians under Platonov's leadership played a stabilizing role in the growing professional community due to its ability to contain

Fig. 2.5 Members of the Circle of Russian Historians: (from left to right) Sergei.M. Seredonin, Nikolai D. Chechulin, Vasilii G. Druzhinin, and Sergei F. Platonov, late 1890s. Courtesy of the Department of Manuscripts, Russian National Library.

(and, ideally, to "smooth out") some personal conflicts between its members. In so doing, the unofficial circle of Russian historians also contributed to the effective functioning of its alma mater—the university. This aspect of the circle's position was accentuated by Miliukov who mentioned the occasional tasks entrusted to the circle's members "from above." Politically conscious Miliukov acknowledged that the circle of Russian historians could not be called "rightist" but was certainly regarded as "loyal" (*blagonadezhnyi*), in contrast to what he called the "leftist" circle of Petersburg historians headed by Vasilii Semevskii.[178]

Contrary to Platonov's group, which was broadly perceived as affiliated with the university, Semevskii's circle appeared to stand apart from the university and its loyal adherents. Miliukov characterized the relation between Platonov's and

Semevskii's circles as mutually exclusive: "whoever was in contact with the former, by this very fact was excluded from the latter."[179] Moreover, as revealed by Nadezhda Nikolaevna's diary, at least once "the task entrusted" to Platonov "from above" was connected directly with Semevskii's activity and concerned a very sensitive matter. On January 11, 1891, she wrote: "At the moment S. F. is polishing his report on the works of Semevskii, which he prepared on Anichkov's (confidential) instructions. Concerning this, Maikov told Serezha: 'if people from liberal circles get to know about it you will be forever ruined in their opinion; even now the boys (*mal'chishki*) are shouting that you are marked by conservatism.' It would be interesting to know, who these boys are. Personally, I recall Nikitenko; I think it is much more worthy to act honestly and with integrity in the Ministry than to 'wash one's hands.'"[180] A little over two weeks later, on January 29, 1891, Nadezhda Nikolaevna returned to the topic, which now looked more troubling from the ethical point of view:

> Yesterday it became clear why the department of the Ministry of Education has demanded from Serezha a report on V. I. Semevskii's works. The latter asked the Ministry of Interior for permission to work in one of the archives (probably, the state one). The Ministry asked Delianov [the Minister of Education] whether such permission was desirable. The latter decided: "No, it is not desirable; to request from Prof. Platonov a report on Semevskii's works." Probably, Delianov himself needed this report in order to have a point of support, but his decision not to admit Semevskii to the archives was made before he received the report.[181]

The situation that Platonova describes and her attempt to explain—or rather, excuse—her husband's reluctant participation in this unpleasant event demonstrates Semevskii's peculiar position. Vasilii Semevskii, a historian of the Russian peasantry and social movements, was known for his liberal political views. Due to the political implications of his *magister* dissertation, which was devoted to the socially charged issue "Peasants in the Reign of the Empress Catherine the Great," he was prevented from defending it at St. Petersburg University; his *magister* dispute took place at Moscow University. Thomas Sanders has described the complicated amalgam of political, scholarly, and personal aspects of Semevskii's dissertation defense of February 1882: "The dissertation had encountered innumerable obstacles at St. Petersburg University, where Konstantin N. Bestuzhev-Riumin was shocked by the political connotations of Semevskii's subject, his treatment of it, and its 'dangerous thoughts,' and ultimately refused to accept it. Forced to submit the work to another university, Semevskii won the right to present it at Moscow, despite the 'cool' (Kliuchevskii) and 'hostile' (N. A. Popov) reception accorded it."[182] The combination of "political notoriety and scholarly appeal" characteristic of Semevskii's *magister* dispute complicated the latter's academic career but contributed to his becoming a public figure. Sanders has provided a picturesque description of the atmosphere at Semevskii's dispute, which "attracted many members of the public [*massa publiki*]" and where "everyone wanted to get more closely acquainted with the contents of the book and to judge on the basis of the evidence of the author himself the truth of the stupid rumors that have been so zealously set in circulation."[183] As a result of this successful and publicly acclaimed dispute Semevskii received his *magister*'s decree and was even given an opportunity to teach in St. Petersburg University as a privat-docent for four years. In January 1886, however, his course was canceled, as Sanders put it, "owing to Bestuzhev's inveterate backdoor politicking."[184] Given the demonstrative way in which Semevskii was dismissed, this step was perceived as politically motivated, an impression that was reinforced by the explanations provided by the Minister of Education Delianov. The latter accused Semevskii of inciting "in young minds a feeling of indignation against the past without enriching their basic concepts" and expressed his concern that Semevskii's announced course on the period of Alexander I would open for him "a vast field" for "transmitting to his audience events that are quite out of place in the halls of an institution which is being supported by Treasury funds and which has the honor of being called Imperial."[185]

Ironically, it was Semevskii's dismissal, not his lectures, that stirred up the students: several hundreds of them signed a letter of appreciation to Semevskii.[186] It was in this atmosphere that Semevskii's home circle was formed, where he continued to teach his students on a voluntary basis. As follows from the number of signatures under another letter of appreciation presented to Semevskii in 1899, altogether over seven hundred students attended his home circle during the first decade of its existence. The most prominent among them was Venedikt A. Miakotin, whom Miliukov characterized as an "incorruptible idealist who was very close to the populist movement at this time."[187] For Semevskii his home circle provided the opportunity for an alternative scholarly career: as David Sanders noted, "he remained an academic, but from 1886 until his death in 1916 he worked outside the university system."[188] In 1889 Semevskii successfully defended his doctoral dissertation on the topic "The Peasant Question in the Late Eighteenth and the First Half of the Nineteenth Century," once more in Moscow. This work earned its author both the Academy of Sciences' Uvarov award (*Uvarovskaia premiia*) and the Free Economic Society's golden medal.[189] His home circle proved itself a supportive framework for fruitful historical research not only for Semevskii himself. As Mikhail Pokrovskii later said, Semevskii "became a dean of all those historians who did not belong to any faculty."[190] To some extent, his home circle might be regarded as the cradle for the school of history of the Russian peasantry developed under Semevskii's influence.

Alongside Platonov's and Semevskii's groups, another historical circle, that of Georgii Forsten, appeared in St. Petersburg in the early 1890s. Forsten, who received his *magister* degree in 1885, specialized in the history of the Baltic region and Scandinavian countries and on this basis was granted a two-year study trip to continue his research in the archives of northern Europe. During his stay abroad in 1885–1886, Forsten visited some German universities in order to become acquainted with "the methods of historical education and of organizing historical seminars."[191] This interest in university seminars was characteristic of the young historians who embarked on research trips in the second half of the 1880s. Indeed, the very perception of the seminar's role in academic life underwent profound changes in the late nineteenth century.[192] Seminars appeared in the Russian universities in the second half of the nineteenth century as "practical classes" (*prakticheskie zaniatiia*), and initially served as a "provisional complement to professorial lectures." Eventually, however, they turned into what Andy Byford defined as "serious tutor-directed students' study groups, modeled on learned societies and mimicking the organizational and communicational patterns of professional scholarship." As a result, "seminars became the most advanced part of the university course, preparing students for independent research and potentially a scholarly career."[193] In introducing seminars as advanced study groups, Russian scholars were influenced by the models of research seminars existing in French and German universities. During his research trip Forsten attended lectures and seminars of such well-known German historians as Alfred Wilhelm Dove at Bonn University, August von Druffel at Munich University and Karl Peter Wilhelm Maurenbrecher of Leipzig University.[194] As former students of Leopold von Ranke and Heinrich von Sybel, these historians continued and embodied the tradition of Ranke's historical school; it seems probable that Forsten's acquaintance with the academic practice of the leading German historians had an impact on his perception of the mode of communication between the scholar and his students.

In 1887 Forsten started to teach at St. Petersburg University as a privat-docent and, not unlike other privat-docents, also taught history in some gymnasia, in particular at Princess Obolenskaia's girls' gymnasium, which was founded in 1870 and was reputed to be one of the best grammar schools.[195] Leading representatives of the capital's intellectual elite taught there, and in the 1870s–1880s the future great actress, Vera Komissarzhevskaia, and Lenin's future wife, Nadezhda Krupskaia, were among its pupils. Its 8th, pedagogical grade trained girls to teach in elementary schools and thus gave them some basic professional qualification. Forsten joined its teaching staff in 1891 and shortly became one of the most admired teachers both there and at A. Ia. Gurevich's boys' gymnasium, where he started to teach in the same year. In Obolenskaia's pedagogical grade Forsten delivered a course on "Humanism and Reformation" based on his university courses.[196] Therefore it is not surprising that his pupils from these two gymnasia constituted the nucleus of the circle that met on Saturdays at Forsten's home.

Later this group was joined by Forsten's students from the university, students from Bestuzhev's women's higher courses, and some university privat-docents; in this way a circle came into being, as Platonov said jokingly, "even before anybody had noticed that it was being formed."[197] The *Bestuzhevki* humorously dubbed the circle "forsteniata," and this affectionate nickname conveys its intimate, almost family-like atmosphere. As one of its first members, Alexander Presniakov (about whom Platonov had approached Miliukov some years before), wrote in February 1895: "We are Forsten's circle . . . it is a circle of eight comrades and four *kursistki* headed by Forsten."[198]

As Forsten's academic reputation became established (he successfully defended his doctoral thesis in 1894), his home circle assumed a more serious character. The memoirs of its participants reveal the process by which the gatherings at Forsten's home were transformed into an informal scholarly study group. Thus, Il'ia Borozdin described the meetings at Forsten's apartment as "conversations," in the course of which "G. V.'s listeners expanded the knowledge they obtained at the lectures and seminars and were gradually made into his students." Another participant, Ivan Grevs, characterized these meetings as "intimate home seminars."[199] The notion of a scholarly seminar presumed the exclusion of any political agenda and adoption of the norms of communication characteristic of the academic milieu. These traits, which were also typical of Platonov's previously established circle, opened up the opportunity for a growing closeness between the two groups. Although they never merged, the two circles occasionally cooperated and "shared" some of their members. In a letter to his mother, Presniakov described this cooperation as a most pleasant and inspiring instance of scholarly comradeship: "Forsten's and Platonov's young people have suddenly become bunched together into a circle that is unable to take a single step separately. It's a most unexpected and curious phenomenon. For me this company is the best means of recreation and diversion. All of us belong to the same school, we all have more or less the same cast of mind, our relations are simple, our mood is light-hearted when we are together; the sphere of our interests is serious, and I find the general tone very likeable."[200]

While Forsten's circle was modeled on the ideal of the scholarly seminar, the circles of Moscow historians which appeared in the early 1890s emerged as an extension of the existing university seminars. Miliukov used the example of his own university course to describe this process: "My audience was not numerous, but it consisted of students who were really interested in learning and wanted to work; as a result I was even able to divide special topics among certain students and then to listen to the results of their works in a kind of seminar (*seminarii*). I wanted our work to be done together, my only condition was that it would be dynamic. Having thus come closer to my students and younger comrades who came to listen to me, I organized *jours fixes* at our home so that we could maintain contact."[201] One of these younger colleagues, a future professor of Moscow University, Alexander Kizevetter, who at that time was a student in the historical-philological faculty, later described these meetings at Miliukov's "modest apartment" as both pleasant and instructive "due to the unconstrained nature of the friendly relations being formed": "There unfolded before our eyes a picture of the feverish work of a scholar completely immersed in his study. His modest apartment resembled a second-hand bookshop. You couldn't move without brushing against a book. His desk was piled high with every possible kind of documents and special publications. In this environment we spent entire evenings engaged in pleasant and interesting conversation."[202] Nonetheless, despite the regular character of these meetings, neither Miliukov nor Kizevetter referred to them as a *kruzhok*, a term that they applied to the more numerous meetings at the home of their teacher, Professor Pavel Vinogradov.[203] Kizevetter provided a detailed description of this circle in which he emphasized the tight connection between the particular nature of Vinogradov's university seminar and his home circle:

> Vinogradov organized the work in his historical seminar brilliantly. Neither Kliuchevskii nor [Vladimir] Ger'e could compare with him in this respect. Kliuchevskii overloaded his seminars with his own improvisations. There his every word was priceless—just try to catch these brilliant sparks of scholarly thought in their flight—while the members of the seminar were relegated to a merely passive role. Ger'e was not resourceful enough and was unable to transform the seminar into collective work. Vinogradov turned his seminar into a real school of research work where one could learn how to become a scholar. He was able to bring all the participants to work together on studying historical sources, and used his own leading role only in order to stimulate the independent work of the seminar's members. . . . Vinogradov was endowed with the gift of being able to gather devoted students around himself, to form a school based on shared academic interests. These relations continued even after the end of the course. The members of Vinogradov's seminar (*pavlikane*, as they were called, after Pavel Gavrilovich's name) were invited to the professor's home, where they met more senior historians and where scholarly meetings of a higher level took place. New historical publications were discussed there and students who were working on their dissertations presented their preliminary findings there; and novices (*neofity*) of historical sciences who had just left the university's benches met there historians of previous generations. Thus, P. G. Vinogradov's hospitable apartment in the small house of priest Slovtsov in *Mertvyi pereulok* [Dead Lane] was at that time the center of lively contacts among Moscow historians. At these meetings we listened to talks by Miliukov, Fortunatov, Vipper and many others. The host himself always had a number of most interesting comments on each talk, and the evening was spent in fascinating scholarly discussion.[204]

Another participant of Vinigradov's home circle, Dmitrii Petrushevskii, who would later become one of the leading Soviet medievalists, defined these meetings as seminars in the literal sense of the word, with a rather rigid structure: "These seminars are held at his [Vinogradov's] home each Tuesday. . . . Matters proceed as follows. An essay (*referat*) is submitted some time in advance. Vinogradov reads it, prepares, and then in the course of the meeting presents the theses of the *referat* and his comments on them. The *referent* has to defend his thesis. Students are free to participate in the discussion."[205] Thus, in their memoirs, members of Vinogradov's circle highlighted the distinctive nature of the Moscow circles—their multigenerational character, their focus on interactive communication, and their tendency to model themselves on the scholarly seminars.

In some ways the St. Petersburg and Moscow circles of historians were reminiscent of the friendly circles (*kruzhki*) that had emerged in the eighteenth century and become the "main institutions of intelligentsia culture" by the 1840s.[206] The historians' informal associations shared the basic characteristics of the nineteenth-century *kruzhki*, as described by Herzen in his *My Past and Thoughts*. Irina Paperno, on the basis of Herzen's account, has defined these *kruzhki* as "an intimate circle of intellectuals, alienated from the state and society, who are bound by a sense of historical significance of shared familiarity," thereby underlining the internal solidarity and emotional ties between members of the circle.[207] A different perspective has been suggested by Barbara Walker who described the distinctive "circle culture" as originating in "the somewhat informal and haphazard institutional life of the pre-Revolutionary educated elite," and consisting of "a complex pattern of networking and clientelist behaviour which centred on the intelligentsia circle or kruzhok." These circles, she claimed, played the key role in modernizing the existing patronage system: "The direct vertical lines of patronage relations had been blurred—but by no means eradicated—by an increasing number of horizontal, more egalitarian networking relations among intellectuals which often manifested themselves in the formation of informal circles, or kruzhki, of mutual support and assistance. The system of patronage was being recontextualized in terms of the kruzhok, and working it involved grasping the principles of a highly complex system of cultural norms."[208] The main feature of what she has called "the games of kruzhok culture" was the presence of a leading personality who had the qualities needed to bring people together with a sense of a common goal and to encourage harmonious interactions and to soothe quarrels. *Kruzhok* leaders, according to Walker, "were not patrons in the classic economic sense of providing mere financial support to intellectual endeavour. Rather, they were skilful organisers of intelligentsia social, professional and emotional life—charismatic fathers, disciplinarians and mentors."[209] For our purposes, Paperno's and Walker's notions of intelligentsia circles complement one another and provide a useful prism for exploring the distinctiveness of the circles of historians. While sharing the combination of egalitarian comradeship and voluntary submission to an informal leader that was typical of the *kruzhki* of the intelligentsia as such, the circles of historians had one striking difference: their members were bound together by devotion to a common scholarly discipline. This interplay of scholarly devotion with egalitarian and hierarchical elements enabled the circles of historians to become the nuclei of the St. Petersburg and Moscow historical schools that took shape in these very years.

As Thomas M. Bohn has noted, it was Miliukov who first used the term "historical school" with reference to Russia in a paper on "The Chief Currents of Russian Historical Thought" that he delivered at the annual session of the American Historical Association in Chicago in December 1904.[210] Describing the differences between the approaches of the Moscow and St. Petersburg historians, he contrasted the "St. Petersburg school of 'the critical study of sources,'" to the Moscow school which was engaged in the "study of institutions, social history and economic history." Stressing the preeminence of Moscow, he asserted that "The Moscow school has influenced also specialists in other universities, and now its position is generally accepted in Russia."[211] When examined through the prism of later theoretical models of the "scientific school," the circles can be seen as playing a significant part in fashioning both the St. Petersburg and Moscow historical schools. It was during the discussions that took place in their meetings that the research problems that engaged their members were formulated and the informal connections between "teachers and students" strengthened. [212] Yet, as demonstrated by the lively communication between Miliukov and Platonov, and the complex interpersonal dynamics among St. Petersburg historians, the circles of historians contributed to the formation not only of exclusive research schools, but also of a broader professional community which comprised various circles and schools. Philippa Levine, in her study on historians in Victorian England, described "the network of social contacts among historians" as generating "a sense of a close-knit fraternity dedicated to particular ends" and claimed that "acceptance into the circle brought with it the advantages of collective commitment." Noting the importance of "freely criticizing and praising," she determined that the "fusion of conviviality and utility" was a basic characteristic of the historians' professional communication. [213] These same features can be discerned in the contemporaneous circles of Russian historians whose members shared the common ethos of an academic profession. In their practice, therefore, the circles of historians embodied apparently contradictory trends of exclusivity and inclusivity which remained in a precarious but effective equilibrium due to the flexibility created by the circles' informal nature and their essential openness. The situation, however, became much more problematic when more formal historical societies were established at the universities.

The Historical Societies at St. Petersburg and Moscow Universities

The idea to establish the Historical Society at St. Petersburg University was proposed in March 1889 by Nikolai Kareev. Kareev, who was a newcomer to St. Petersburg University, did not belong to any of the existing circles of historians. He had been a student of Ger'e (with whom he maintained an intensive correspondence) at Moscow University, where he had successfully defended his *magister*'s dissertation in 1879.[214] He had then taught at Warsaw University in 1879–1885, defended his doctoral dissertation (once again in Moscow) in 1884 and joined the academic staff of St. Petersburg University only in 1885.[215] By that time he had already authored two major books based on his dissertations. The first study, *Krest'iane i krest'ianskii vopros vo Frantsii v poslednei chetverti XVIII veka (Peasants and the Peasant Question in France in the Last Quarter of the Eighteenth Century)*, brought Kareev scholarly recognition not only among Russian specialists in European history, but also among his French colleagues.[216] The second one, *Osnovnye voprosy filosofii istorii: Kritika istoriosofskikh idei i opyt nauchnykh teorii istoricheskogo protsessa (The Main Questions of the Philosophy of History: A Critique of Historiosophical Ideas and a Test of the Scholarly Theories of the Historical Process)*, put him at the forefront of the ongoing debates about the nature of historical scholarship. Wladimir Bérélowitch—who was the first to investigate the establishment of the Historical Society at St. Petersburg University in the broader context of the development of historical studies in late imperial Russia—noted Kareev's "great interest in the theory of knowledge in history" as well as his fascination with sociology and his attempts "to define the specific place of history and sociology within the 'social sciences.'"[217] Indeed, in 1899 Kareev became vice-president of the International Institute of Sociology.

The idea to establish a historical society focusing on the theory of history and on ways of improving history teaching was, therefore, a natural outcome of his scholarly inclinations. It was less obvious, however, that his colleagues would be willing to support his initiative. Interest in the philosophy of history was not widespread among late nineteenth-century Russian historians: Miliukov, for example, wrote later that he never applied the word "philosophy" to historical scholarship because he was afraid that it disguised an outdated "metaphysical" approach to history. From his perspective, the concept of history was opposed to the concept of philosophy; modern historical research, he argued, was to become closer to "experimental science."[218] Kareev himself wrote later that only one of his colleagues—Lappo-Danilevskii—was genuinely interested in the theoretical aspects of history, and noted the rather skeptical attitude to sociology among contemporary historians.[219] And yet, even such a firm adherent to traditional empirical research as Shmurlo praised Kareev for conceiving of "a good plan" and commended his "energy and commitment to work." Moreover, according to Shmurlo's *Notes*, the members of St. Petersburg University's Department of History supported Kareev's idea almost unanimously:

> On March 14 [1889] Kareev invited [some people] to discuss a draft of the [society's] statutes. Forsten, Vasilevskii, Platonov, Gurevich, E.A. Belov, Druzhinin, and myself attended this meeting. Both a memorandum [on the establishment of the society] and a draft of the statutes were accepted with minor changes. In addition, Kareev had already talked with the rector about both documents in order to obtain his consent in advance. The statutes are the usual statutes, with all that they are supposed to include (*so vsemi onërami*). The memorandum, which was submitted to the faculty on March 15 and signed by all the University's professors and privat-docents of history except for Regel', presented the reasons for establishing the society as follows: "It is not possible to study Western and recent Russian history in the framework of the existing Petersburg societies; the proposed society will enable scholarly exchange and make it possible to follow recent scholarly developments, etc. The society, in addition to the empirical (factual) study of history, will also develop theoretical aspects of this science; and, finally, discussion of issues in the field of teaching and pedagogy.[220]

One possible explanation for this supportive attitude might be found in Kareev's later works. In his memoirs, he described the concept of social evolution as the basic component of the development of sociological thought in Russia, and linked the "intervention" of Western sociology in Russian scholarship to Russian historians' growing interest in the social aspect of history. Kareev listed among the first representatives of the social approach to history such powerful figures as his teachers Ger'e and Kliuchevskii at Moscow University as well as Ivan Luchitskii at Kiev University.[221] Kareev's thesis was indirectly confirmed by Miluikov who defined the new historical trend to which he assigned followers of Vinogradov and to which he himself adhered as the "shift from a history of events to a history of ways of life (*istoriia byta*)" and a "history of institutions." For him, the notion "ways of life" (*byt*) also included the "economic way of life" (*ekonomicheskii byt*) while he occasionally substituted the term "history of *byt*" for "social history" in his writings.[222] Kareev's conception of the historical society therefore corresponded to a new—social—trend of Russian historical scholarship and accorded with an existing vision of history as social science (*obshchestvennaia nauka*). Bohn characterized these developments as part of a more general (and profound) intellectual current, arguing that the development of "sociological thought" in Russia at the end of the 1860s was influenced by the works of Auguste Comte and Herbert Spencer and, as a result, positivism "began to fulfill the main function in the humanities, replacing Hegelianism which had been advocated since the 1840s."[223] Furthermore, the positive response to Kareev's initiative demonstrated that theoretical competence had become recognized as an additional—and significant—component of historical knowledge. The establishment of a learned society that strove to lay the theoretical foundations of historical scholarship thus drew a line between theoretically minded academic historians and well-versed amateurs, a distinction that enhanced the status of history as a profession. It was hence not so surprising that Kareev's idea to establish a historical society was embraced by his colleagues.

Shmurlo's account indicates that Kareev succeeded in mobilizing both formal and informal networks in order to prepare the ground for the proposed society. His efforts to seek the cooperation of Forsten and Platonov, the leaders of the informal circles, should have paved the way for future productive collaboration among its members. These hopes were strengthened even more when Semevskii and Miakotin joined the society (the latter appeared in the list of its founding members).[224] In accordance with the existing historical societies' practice, the statutes of the new association suggested several ways in which its members could contribute, including the delivery of regular scholarly lectures open to the public, organizing "paid and unpaid public courses," convening conferences, publishing their works in the Society's periodicals, proposing topics for scholarly competitions, and bestowing awards on the winners.[225] Yet the impression of harmony was already challenged at the first meeting of the society on November 26, 1889, when, contrary to Kareev's expectations, Vasilevskii was elected chair. Kareev was offered the post of his deputy, but, deeply hurt, he rejected the offer. Lappo-Danilevskii described the subsequent dramatic developments in a letter to Miliukov:

> Kareev conceived of the idea to establish a historical society at the University. Recently there was the first meeting of the founding members—Vasilevskii, Bershadskii, Sergeevich, Platonov, Grevs, and various "small fry" like me. Vasilevskii was elected chair (almost at the instigation of the most honorable Platonov and company). Kareev, who was organizing the society, was seriously offended (*ne na shutku obidelsia*) and even displayed it! Then Vasilevskii and the whole committee resigned. Today [on December 6] we had to hold the elections again. Kareev has been elected. Vasilevskii and Platonov, among others, have been elected members of the committee, but both refused outright to accept the posts. It is not very excusable for the elderly Vasilevskii to behave capriciously, and it is entirely unbefitting for such a young but already renowned scholar as Platonov to be always quarreling and to introduce a lust for power and sectarian [*partiinye*] considerations into something good. All these squabbles create a bad, terribly bad impression.[226]

In a letter to Lappo-Danilevskii in response to the "incident that your historical society began its activity with," Miliukov accused Kareev of lack of tact and even defined his behavior as a *coup d'état.*[227] While such phrases as "lust for power" and *coup d'état* related mainly to the participants' personal ambitions, the expression "sectarian considerations" (*partiinye raschëty*) pointed to the tensions within the society, which were caused not only by the participants' membership in various personal networks but also by their diverse ideological orientations and indicated a growing awareness of the political implications of historical scholarship. The combination of personal ambitions with ideological disagreements hampered the activity of the Historical Society in the first years of its existence. Although the society achieved an impressive membership, established its own journal, *Istoricheskoe obozrenie* (*Historical Review*), and created a number of effective specialized commissions, the frequent internal conflicts were hardly conducive to successful collaborative work.

According to the society's annual report for 1890, by the end of that year it comprised 162 members.[228] These included, in addition to Petersburg historians, such distinguished Muscovites as Ger'e, Vinogradov, and Miliukov: "yesterday we had a meeting of the Historical Society where, inter alia, you were elected a member, *ne vous en déplaise*," wrote Lappo-Danilevskii to Miliukov on December 27, 1889.[229] On February 22, 1890, Kareev officially informed Ger'e that he had been elected a member of the society.[230] In the course of 1890 the society held ten sessions with scholarly lectures, seven of which were open to a wider audience. The lecture program reflected an aspiration to maintain a balance between Russian and universal, or general (*vseobshchaia*) history,[231] a tendency that continued in the following years as well: according to Bérélowitch's calculation, among the 359 papers that were delivered at the society's meetings between 1890 and 1915, "109 dealt with universal history, 172 were on Russian history, and 25 on the 'theory of history,' with the remainder divided among teaching-related issues, reports on current events in academia, and topics from disciplines other than history (philology, ethnography, sociology)."[232] The society's efforts to advance a more sophisticated perception of historical scholarship were demonstrated by its attempt to compile a systematic guide (*spravochnik*) to historical literature. A special bibliographical commission was established for this purpose. Its suggestions regarding content reflected a new vision of history as a discipline where the old-fashion "philological" perspective was juxtaposed with a new "social" paradigm.

The guide was supposed to begin with bibliographical annotations on studies in the theory and philosophy of history followed by writings on historical geography and primitive (*pervobytnyi*) culture. Topics connected with different aspects of "history proper" were divided into such rubrics as "universal history," "history of the East," "European history," "America and Australia" and, finally, "history of Russia."[233] The commission emphasized that the Russian history section would make up about a third of the volume. The outline of this section vividly demonstrated the mixture of traditional and novel perceptions of history. It was to start with the usual survey of historical sources, but then a rubric of ethnography was to appear followed by a section on the history of colonization and the regions. The basic chronological arrangement of the reviewed items suggested by Platonov was combined with the topical divisions proposed by Miliukov and was further subdivided into more detailed categories such as "general works," "politics," "law," "economy" (*khoziaistvo*), "culture," and "church" for each distinctive historical epoch (namely, the prehistorical [*doistoricheskaia*] epoch, the Kievan era, the period of principalities [*udel'naia epokha*], and the Muscovite and Imperial periods).[234] Thus, whereas the proposed draft confirmed the existing division between Russian and universal history and retained the conventional periodization of history, it also moved the emphasis to the social, economic, and anthropological facets of historical scholarship. Moreover, the society intended to survey historical literature published not only in Russian but also in other languages such as Latin, French, German, English, Italian, and Polish. Two "model surveys" (literally, "trial pages" or *probnye stranitsy*), one of recent French and German publications on medieval history written by Vinogradov and another of recent Polish historiography devoted to the Fall of Poland (*Istoriia padeniia Pol'shi*) submitted by Kareev, were attached to the commission's proposal.[235]

This sophisticated bibliographical project suggested that the founders were able to overcome their initial conflicts and to collaborate for the sake of a common professional goal. Indeed, as follows from correspondence between Lappo-Danilevskii and Miliukov as well as from Pavel A. Tribunskii's comments on their letters, the preliminary version of the plan was prepared in early 1890, amended by Miliukov in April 1890, discussed and confirmed at the society's meeting of October 3, 1890, and shortly afterward printed and sent to those "specialists in different fields of history" who had already agreed or been invited to participate in the project.[236] All in all the bibliographic commission met four times in the course of the first year of the society's existence, which creates the impression of diligent work and effective cooperation.[237] The letters of Lappo-Denilevskii, who became the society's secretary, confirmed this impression: "The Historical Society is blossoming," he wrote to Miliukov in December 1890.[238] Yet Platonov's letters to the same addressee spoil this optimistic picture. Thus, Platonov wrote on May 10, 1890:

> Your question regarding the bibliographical commission of Kareev's society put me in a real quandary. I have been invited to participate in this commission, but I am not aware whether it has a permanent composition. Its meetings are attended by anyone who wants to, and, personally, I do not know whether I am a member of the commission or have just been invited on the side. I can't participate actively in [preparing] the bibliography, which seems to annoy Kareev. He is dragging me into this business, but is unwilling to talk to me

personally, face-to-face. That is why I have no reliable information either about the progress of the work or about Kareev's intentions. Moreover, I confess that I dislike talking about it. Kareev should be rather scorned or ridiculed for the methods he employs for managing the Society, but I am unable to do either the former or latter due to my personal misunderstandings with the "enlightened" chair. In addition, there are some delicate aspects even beyond these personal troubles. How is it possible to condemn something that is positive in its essence, but negative in its realization? Special honor is due to Kareev for his energetic initiative in launching the praiseworthy endeavor of gathering together the "dispersed temple" (*sobiranie rasseiannoi khraminy*) of St. Petersburg's historians, and this fact disarms me. I am also disarmed by the fact that Kareev is persecuted and hunted enough outside the [Historical] Society: he is an outcast among his colleagues.[239]

Platonov's problematic relations with Kareev, confirmed also by Shmurlo's *Notes*, both reflected and impacted on the society's internal atmosphere: it was fraught with personal rivalry and cliquish enmity. The internal tensions intensified even more in the following years as a result of generational changes among the university's professors: as the influence of the "older generation" of historians—Vasilevskii, Bestuzhev-Riumin and Zamyslovskii—declined, the rival cliques or "parties" among their successors multiplied.[240] Presniakov's letters to his mother (which have already attracted the attention of many students of late imperial Russia's academic life) give a vivid description of these rivalries. Thus, in February 1894 Presniakov wrote:

On Wednesday [at Platonov's soirée] we talked a lot about the university's relations which have become more strained. In January, at one of the Historical Society's meetings, there was a clash between Chechulin and Semevskii, who behaved very improperly. As a result Russian historians have completely broken with Kareev and his society. The society's matters are being run in a frivolous manner; its "committee" is composed in a biased way, from among "their own people"; voting results are almost juggled with. Some people were persuaded to put forward their candidacy but were intentionally rejected in the elections. The society's meetings are ceasing to be scholarly and turning into public lectures for a broader audience. There's a deluge of such accusations, and there are reasons for them. Now only the chair, secretary, treasurer, two or three members, and a lot of strangers—students and *kursistki*—attend the society's meetings. Things are bad. Before there was a flimsy peace, but now the quarrel is in the open.[241]

Presniakov defined the appearance of rival factions as *kruzhkovshchina*, thereby connecting this phenomenon with the existing *kruzhki*. The society's factions, however, were not identical to the informal circles that were described in the previous section. Thus, with the establishment of the society, Lappo-Danilevskii, who initially belonged to the circle of Russian historians, became the unofficial head of the "governing" faction, which included also Kareev and Grevs, and played the leading role in the society's decision making; this faction was opposed by Platonov's circle. Although all members of the society recognized that *kruzh-kovshchina* was detrimental to the society's reputation and its effective functioning, their ways of dealing with the problem were different. While the younger Presniakov made efforts to reconcile the factions, the more experienced Platonov and Lappo-Danilevskii regarded *kruzhkovshchina* as an inevitable and ineradicable evil, as Presniakov depicted in his letters of March 1894. Platonov, according to him, was rather positive, but not optimistic:

> He explained to me that the circles—his and Lappo-Danilevskii's—differ in two parameters. The latter belong to the nobility according to their upbringing, received a good education at home, possess extensive scholarly tools; they are democrats by conviction and according to their theoretical approaches, people with political aspirations, with particular political views in which they believe dogmatically and are therefore intolerant of the opinions of others. The others, (that is, the *platonovtsy*) are *raznochintsy*, belonging to a different society and with a different upbringing, with fewer scholarly resources, with a wide variety of opinions, who are bound only by personal friendship. They [*platonovtsy*] are skeptics according to their intellectual inclination; they are no less dissatisfied with the dominant order of things than the other group, but they see no means of fighting it and thus bear it with ostensible indifference, carrying out their teaching and scholarly duties without proclaiming their lack of satisfaction, without constantly demanding from others to agree with them and calmly accepting contradictions and opposite opinions, even the least attractive. They [*platonovtsy*] do not shun the other circle, but the latter ignores them; there were attempts to approach them but they ended in an insult to themselves.[242]

When Presniakov tried to discuss the same issue with Lappo-Danilevskii, the latter responded briefly, but very plainly:

> After finishing my talk with Platonov I was unable to resist talking with Lappo-Danilevskii. Unfortunately, we were disturbed when I visited him on Thursday. He managed to speak out (and, thank God, did so with absolute candor) about his relations with Platonov and Co. My God, what an absurd confusion of concepts there is! They regard [Platonov] as ultra-conservative à la *Novoe vremia* and, recalling Platonov's "earlier liberal thoughts," see him as a renegade (?!!), and, what is more, apparently under the influence of his wife. This "beautiful" label is attached to the whole circle, and—readers, don't laugh—also . . . to myself! All this is very annoying, but so absurd as to be more amusing than insulting.[243]

Both Platonov's and Lappo-Danilevskii's mutual accusations and Presniakov's reaction to his being labeled a "conservative" reveal, besides the antagonism between the society's factions, significant new developments in the historian's professional identity. The refashioning of history as a social science meant that the historian not only had to be aware of modern social theories, but also had to choose his social position and public role, including his political leanings. Moreover, as demonstrated by Presniakov's case, those who tried to avoid "taking sides" could eventually find themselves being ascribed an unexpected "label" by others. At the same time, the very necessity to explain, define, and redefine every historian's political position testified to the arbitrariness of such divisions. Indeed, as Rostovtsev argued in his study on Lappo-Danilevskii, in the 1890s the development of the St. Petersburg historical school had a rather paradoxical trait: the younger generation of the capital's historians became split into conservative and liberal "camps," but there was no clear "dividing line" between the camps.[244]

The use of political markers inevitably charged historians' professional discourse with ethical considerations, as demonstrated by Platonov's reluctance to criticize Kareev for what Platonov saw as his poor management of the Historical Society. Kareev's populist (*narodnicheskie*) political views made him susceptible to political persecution (this threat was realized in 1899 when he was dismissed from his position at the university in the wake of the student unrest), and Platonov was apparently unwilling to add his voice to the chorus of Kareev's official persecutors (*goniteli*). Platonov's inclination to use hints and euphemisms with regard to his opponent's political views, in striking contrast to Lappo-Danilevskii's straightforward claim about Platonov's "ultra-conservatism," can also be understood in this light. Vladimir Gurko has described the late imperial educated elite's "timid bashfulness about openly confessing to their rightist opinions," which, he claims, stemmed from the unequal positions of both sides, namely those who criticized the existing order of things and those who supported it: "While the former risked going rather too far in the direction of the rising sun, the latter talked as if they were under police protection."[245]

The increasing politicization of history was also reflected in the emerging correlation between historians' research interests and their ideological inclinations. Thus, according to Sanders's analysis of the "Chechulin affair," "there was no great stretch from Nikolai Kareev's research in Parisian archives on the peasantry in eighteenth-century France (in the course of which he befriended the revolutionary Petr Lavrov) to the troubled rural environment of contemporary Russia."[246] Similarly, Rostovtsev has pointed to the political overtones in the expressions of interest in the theory of history, which was seen as connected with Western intellectual traditions, and noted the link between scholarly preferences and ideological opinions among the St. Petersburg academic community in the 1890s: while the "system-builders" prevailed among the liberal historians, the "empiricists" dominated the conservative camp.[247] Even though Platonov and Presniakov rejected the label of "conservative" and regarded the very division of historians into "liberals" and "conservatives" as shallow and superficial, the impact of the historian's ideological views on his professional status was barely disputed in the 1890s. Miliukov's and Lappo-Danilevskii's negative assessment of Chechulin's earlier works in 1889 as well as Kareev's and Miakotin's sharp criticism of Chechulin's doctoral dissertation in 1896 demonstrated that their comments on the poor quality of his research were inseparable from their view of him as a conservative ultra-nationalist.[248] Thus, the professionalization and politicization of history became interwoven in the last decades of the nineteenth century.

Years later Alexander Kizevetter described in detail the combination of personal, scholarly, and ideological considerations that influenced his decision on the field and topic of his future research:

> In summer 1894 I got married, traveled for the second time (this time with my wife) through the Caucasus and Crimea and in the autumn finally entered the place to which my secret thoughts had long aspired. I started to work in the huge archive of the Ministry of Justice where the records of the ancient state institutions of the Muscovite Rus' and of the eighteenth-century [Russian] Empire are concentrated. . . . I had already planned the topic and Kliuchevskii had approved it. I had decided to plough an enormous field [urban history] that had not been touched by anyone before me. This archive holds the records of the Main Magistrate for the entire eighteenth century—an institution responsible for the administration of the towns—and documents of some of the towns' magistrates. There were innumerable quantities of bundles of various papers and books. Until now nobody had touched this archive. . . . I was faced with a tempting task: to open for scholarship an absolutely new corner of Russian historical life. This fact alone was enough to make work on this topic extremely attractive for me. Nevertheless, there were also other considerations that strengthened my intention. Although I had not yet embarked on political activity, as I was still completely immersed in my theoretical scholarly studies and had not yet entered politics, my political views had already taken shape. Being a convinced constitutionalist, I had no doubts that sooner or later the Russian political regime would also be transformed on the basis of political freedom. Here arose a question that was natural for a historian: what prerequisites for enabling such a transformation might be found in our political past? Neither Muscovite Russia nor the eighteenth- or nineteenth- century [Russian] Empire had any constitutional institutions, but in both Muscovite Russia and the Empire there was local self-government—rural and urban. We know that in the West European countries the medieval towns' self-government served to a considerable extent as a prototype for the state constitutional institutions. This fact stimulated my interest in studying the communal institutions of the Russian towns, especially from the moment when Peter made an attempt to reconstruct urban self-government in accordance with West European models. The topic I envisaged suited both my scholarly-theoretical and public-political interests. There was, however, one more reason behind my choice of that topic, which related not to the possible results, but to the very process of my future research. I was attracted by a particular mode of work

that demanded recreating a picture of a certain historical process by collecting, like for a mosaic, the tiniest facts portraying the everyday current of a past reality. I was well aware that this kind of work would be more time-consuming and thus postpone the longed-for moment of attaining the scholarly degree, but this did not bother me at all. I anticipated the pleasure of creation in such work, and it is surely only natural to aspire to prolong, rather than shorten pleasure! The material that I selected for analytical examination . . . perfectly satisfied this need as well. I would be working with a countless number of documents, each of which reflected different facets of eighteenth-century urban life. My creative task was to find unity in that motley variety, a task that turned the archive for me into the most attractive place that I could possibly imagine.[249]

Kizevetter's view that it was natural for historians to seek the political usefulness of the past, along with his attempt to harmonize his political views with his vision of historical research as creative and essentially aesthetic work, enables us to understand the enormous challenges faced by fin-de-siècle historians. The fascination with the ancient texts ("special charms are hidden in the archival documents," wrote Kizevetter on the same occasion),[250] the attraction of documentary research, the anticipation of archival discoveries, personal aspirations, hopes, and ambitions, together with more sophisticated scholarly requirements and more demanding public expectations, created enormous pressure and contributed to the emergence of what might be defined as "professional anxiety." This anxiety and tension provided fertile ground for the conflicts that afflicted the Historical Society at St. Petersburg University in its early years and underlay the "founding conflict" that took place when the Historical Society at Moscow University was established some years later.

The idea to establish a Historical Society at Moscow University, inspired by the St. Petersburg example, emerged in 1889.[251] It was first discussed in Vinogradov's circle, but a concrete proposal was made only three years later, in January 1892, by Vladimir Ger'e when a large group of his former students (including Miliukov) presented Ger'e with a letter of appreciation to mark his thirty years of scholarly endeavor. In his response, Ger'e suggested founding a new historical society and insinuated that he was ready to head such a society.[252] From the very beginning, therefore, the society had two "initiating centers," Ger'e on the one hand and Vinogradov's circle on the other—and herein lay the nucleus of the future conflict. The process of establishing the society took more than a year; its founding meeting took place on March 9, 1893, and, although Ger'e was elected as the society's chair almost unanimously, his relations with Vinogradov's circle and particularly with Miliukov became increasingly tense. The main cause of disagreement concerned membership in the society. Vinogradov's circle, which by that time included thirty-five participants, decided "to join the society *in corpore* [in their entirety] or not to join at all"; Vinogradov and Miliukov, who were elected to the society's committee alongside Kliuchevskii, M. C. Korelin, R. Iu. Vipper, and V. M. Mikhailovskii, insisted on the immediate admittance of the *pavlikane*. Ger'e, on the contrary, suggested that the first members should be the eighty signatories to the jubilee letter that he had received, despite the fact that not all of them had any scholarly status. In addition, he asked that four places in the committee should be reserved for gymnasium history teachers and generally preferred that the society's bodies should be formed more gradually and slowly. In order to resolve this seemingly technical matter, a meeting of the committee was scheduled for March 18, 1894, at Ger'e's apartment, but instead of reaching an agreement it ended in a rupture between the rival sides. At one point in the meeting Ger'e became annoyed by the stubbornness of his former student and main opponent Miliukov and told him patronizingly: "You have completely forgotten who you are talking to." Insulted, Milukov replied that he apparently had indeed forgotten with whom he was dealing and walked out, having announced that he was leaving both the committee and the society. As a result of the conflict only a small number of Vinogradov's circle joined the Historical Society, where Ger'e's leadership was now indisputable.[253]

Although the witnesses to the conflict and the participants in it described this incident as a clash of personal ambitions, the issue that triggered the quarrel (the composition of the society's membership) was not insignificant and represented two different visions of the society. Vinogradov and Miliukov envisioned the Historical Society as a scholarly association intended to bring together academic historians—more or less according to the St. Petersburg model. Ger'e's desire to expand its membership to include gymnasium history teachers provided an opportunity for more direct interaction between academic historians and secondary school educationists. The latter model was certainly relevant to the society's interests since, like its St. Petersburg predecessor, it regarded the teaching of history as one of its central issues, while its statutes suggested that the society would bring together "young persons preparing for academic degrees" and "history teachers from Moscow and the provinces."[254] In practice, however, none of the proposed models were realized. In retrospect Kizevetter described the Historical Society at Moscow University as "a modest and orderly (*chinnoe*) society completely dominated by its patriarchal chair," whose meetings were attended only by his devoted students; on another occasion he portrayed Ger'e's society as "a still backwater which the echoes of life's noise never reached."[255] Kizevetter attributed such stagnation in a newborn society to its chair's attitude to voluntary activity. By the 1890s Ger'e was well known in Moscow due to his significant involvement in the city's public life. His pioneering role in the establishment of women's higher courses, of which he also served as a director during 1872–1888, was especially appreciated by his contemporaries. Being a restless public activist, Ger'e, according to Kizevetter, "liked and knew how to create new sophisticated organizations." Unfortunately, he started to undermine his creations as soon as he undertook their supervision. Ger'e, Kizevetter claimed, was unable to administer a public enterprise by any other method than "patriarchal personal despotism."[256] This problem of leadership became especially disturbing in the Historical Society which mainly comprised Ger'e's current and former students. Thus, Kizevetter described a characteristic episode of the Society's everyday practice:

> I remember an extremely comical story told me by my late friend O.P. Gera-simov. Once he entered a meeting of the Historical Society and saw the fol-lowing scene: members of the society, all young scholars, were sitting at the table; Ger'e was sitting in the middle, drinking his tea and chewing a biscuit. Deep silence reigned in the room. "Hasn't the meeting started yet?" Gera-simov asked after sitting in this silence for some time. Ger'e cast him an angry look and stated didactically: "The meeting has been open for a long time," and lapsed into silence again. Some more minutes passed in deathly silence, and then Gerasimov stood up and left the room. Later we found out that Ger'e had been angered by something and had stopped talking, but did not close the meeting. All the participants were struck dumb and nobody dared to speak. This mute meeting continued for quite a long time.[257]

However, the suffocating effect of the Chair's "patriarchal despotism" disap-peared when the topic of a lecture or a particular lecturer attracted the interest of the broader public. In these cases the society's tedious meetings turned into well-attended—and sometimes stormy—public events. This sudden transformation took place, for example, in February 1896 when the society announced a lecture by Ger'e's former student and a founder of the St. Petersburg Historical Society, Kareev. His reputation as an incisive polemicist and his populist ideological views attracted a politically minded audience. In the atmosphere of the fierce disputes between populists and Marxists that characterized the mid-1890s, Kareev's pub-lic lecture turned into a battle between them, while the society's meeting served as the battlefield.[258] Kizevetter described this event as extremely dramatic:

> Long before the beginning of the meeting the entrance door started to bang incessantly, letting in more and more visitors, mainly young students. There was an immense crowd, and it was clear that the topic of the lecture by itself could not have attracted such a huge and diverse audience. According to the bellicose mood of many of those who gathered there, one could draw the con-clusion that either an ovation or a hostile demonstration was to be anticipated, depending on which camp the majority of the audience belonged to. Ger'e walked around quite in dismay and deeply agitated. He had not expected such an influx of people and, as usual, had not informed the police about the forth-coming event, and now—what a thing to happen! "Why don't you inform the police as required by the rules?" asked those with whom he shared his con-cern. "Why would I inform them," he answered in despair, "if usually nobody turns up!"[259]

Irrespective of the circumstances of that particular event, the fact that the society's meetings were open to a broader audience demonstrated the nature of its relations with the Moscow educated public. Indeed, in comparison to the earlier historical associations, the new historical societies of the universities were much more receptive to the public despite their emphasis on their strictly academic character. This reveals the dual nature of these societies, whose tasks enabled them to function both as "self-contained" learned associations focusing on their specific scholarly aims and as "social influence" organizations pursuing broader educational goals that transcended the immediate interests of their members. The combination of these two facets made the historical societies more public oriented; however, the involvement of the public in the societies' activity presented some difficulties.

As noted in the previous chapter, the concept of the public played a significant role in forming Russian academic culture even before a "real" public had developed. It was especially important for learned societies which, notwithstanding their differences, shared the goal of enlightening the public. Yet the public was not only the object but also the active subject of and participant in the learned activity. By the end of the nineteenth century, the educated public constituted an important, albeit unofficial actor in academic life. It served, according to Thomas Sanders' catchy definition, as "a third opponent" at dissertation disputes, transforming this academic procedure into an attractive, well-attended and, frequently politically charged social event.[260] The public's attitude was crucial for creating a scholar's reputation and, more broadly, for establishing a scholar's social status. A positive public response to a junior scholar's "trial lectures" was conducive to his attaining the position of privat-docent, and was most valuable for opening doors into elite educated society. Miliukov demonstrated this on the basis of his own experience: "The public's impression [of his trial lectures] was favorable: *dignus est intrare* [he is worthy to enter]. . . . And I happily crossed the border from student to scholar. It also strengthened my social position in Moscow society where, contrary to military and official Petersburg, the academic sphere was traditionally in the forefront."[261] The practice of the university societies was apparently based on that tradition of the public's involvement in academic life and enabled its further institutionalization. The bylaws of the historical societies stipulated their right to hold public events and to organize public courses; the societies' publishing activity was intended to take into consideration "the needs of the educated public, including history teachers and students."[262] Nevertheless, as demonstrated by Ger'e's dissatisfaction with the unexpectedly large turnout at the meeting of the Moscow Society and by Platonov's and Presniakov's disgruntled remarks about the prevalence of "strangers" at the meetings of the St. Petersburg Society, the public could be perceived as an intrusive element if its involvement threatened to undermine the hierarchy of its relations with the academic elite.

Scholars carefully protected their status as enlighteners of the public and, while investing considerable efforts in creating new frameworks for communication with the public, remained reluctant to yield control of them. This implicit problem of hierarchy underlay both the historical societies' persistent search for a balance between what they saw as their inclusive public role and exclusive scholarly tasks. Neither of the societies managed to achieve this balance.

The Historical Society at St. Petersburg University succeeded in maintaining its membership (by the end of 1904 it numbered 170 members, apart from those in other towns and countries), continued the regular publication of *Istoricheskoe obozrenie*, and gained international recognition. [263] In 1913 its leading members, Lappo-Danilevskii, Kareev, and Presniakov, played a central role in organizing the Fourth International Historical Congress scheduled to be held in St. Petersburg in 1918.[264] According to the preliminary report on preparations for the congress, published in the *Nauchnyi istoricheskii zhurnal* (*Scholarly Historical Journal*, 1913–1914)—which was edited by Kareev, but issued by the famous Brokgauz-Efron publishers and not affiliated with the Historical Society—it was to be organized more or less according to the divisions within the broader field of history that had been elaborated years ago by the society's bibliographical commission.[265] However, by this time the society itself consisted only of sections on Russian and universal history; the section on the theory of history and sociology had ceased its activity, and there was no mention in the society's papers of the section on history teaching, which had been formed in 1891.[266] After fifteen years of existence, therefore, the society's organizational structure had become more traditional and more "self-contained" than in its early years. The Historical Society at Moscow University, which from the outset was less structured and less active, practically stopped functioning in 1904 (without being officially closed), but was revived in 1916 thanks to the energetic efforts of Mikhail Bogoslovskii.[267] In the atmosphere of war and revolution the society managed to issue six volumes of its new historical-bibliographical journal, *Istoricheskie izvestiia*, but both the society and the journal finally ceased their existence after 1917.[268]

Despite their lack of success in achieving their goals, the historical societies at St. Petersburg and Moscow Universities had a deep impact on the formation of history as a profession and on the strengthening of historians' public status. As Stephen Bann wrote about the development of history in Europe in general, "An article of faith for the contemporary specialist in historical research is the assumption that before 1800 there were indeed historians, but only after that date does it become possible and necessary to speak of the *professional* historian." In Russia, as in Victorian England and preunified Germany, this process was characterized by "the eventual separation of the 'professional' and the 'amateur'" combined with growing interaction between both groups in the context of local history. [269] The formation of the university historical societies was one more step in shaping history as a profession. Comprising historians with a similar educational background and belonging to the same university but who adhered to different methodological cal approaches, these formal societies constituted complementary frameworks to the informal "historical schools." While "historical schools," according to Russian experts on the subject, brought together scholars who worked in the same institution, had studied under the same teacher, or adhered to similar methods of historical research, [270] the university historical societies provided an opportunity for fruitful cooperation among representatives of different schools, despite the frequent conflicts. Moreover, such conflicts had the important function of giving expression to the ideological differences of the historical schools. This kind of ideology has been defined by Sveshnikov as "a certain ideal image" comprising "both the representation of the school itself in terms of its aims, tasks, history, participants, and distinctiveness as well as the foundations out of which it emerged" or "the sum total of worldviews—political, religious, cultural, aesthetic, and ethical—which the members held in varying degrees."[271] The historical societies therefore provided a platform for the interaction and clash of different worldviews which became part of contemporary intellectual discourse.

The Russian nineteenth-century historical circles and societies thus played a crucial role in the transformation of history as a discipline from a branch of philology to social science and highlighted the question of the historian's public role. In so doing, they fashioned new modes of cooperation between members of the academic community and the broader educated public and prepared fertile ground for historians' participation in public educational activity beyond the framework of the universities—as both professionals and public activists (*obshchestvennye deiateli*).

Notes

1. The most active of these societies were *Vol'noe obshchestvo liubitelei slovesnosti, nauk i khudozhestv* established in 1801 and officially approved in 1803; *Beseda liubitelei russkogo slova*, whose first session took place in 1807, and *Vol'noe obshchestvo liubitelei rossiiskoi slovesnosti* created in 1816. See Kozlov, *Rossiiskaia arkheografiia*, 32; Mark Al'tshuller, *Beseda liubitelei russkogo slova: U istokov russkogo slavianofil'stva* (Moscow: Novoe literaturnoe obozrenie, 2007).

2. New universities in Vilna and Dorpat (now Tartu), Kazan', Kharkov, and St. Petersburg, in addition to Moscow, were established between 1802 and 1819. See Vucinich, *Science in Russian Culture*, 190, 193; Kaplan, "The History of Reform in Russian Higher Education," 43.

3. *Ustav imperatorskogo moskovskogo universiteta 5 noiabria 1804 goda*, 11, clause 1. Accessed August 4, 2015. http://museum.guru.ru/ustavy/ustav1804/glava_i.phtml.

4. Moscow University's Society for the Comparative Study of the Medical and Physical Sciences was established in 1805, followed by the Society of Mathematicians founded in 1811. See Vucinich, *Science in Russian Culture*, 195.

5. "Pis'ma k molodomu cheloveku o predmetakh kasaiushchikhsia istorii i opisaniia Rossii," in M. N. Murav'ev, *Sochineniia*, vol. 1 (St. Petersburg: Izdanie Aleksandra Smirdina, 1847), 375–445.

6. I. Iu. Fomenko, "Istoricheskie vzgliady M. N. Murav'eva," in G. P. Makagonenko, A. M. Panchenko, eds., *XVIII vek, Sbornik 13, Problemy istorizma v russkoi literature. Konets XVIII-nachalo XX v.* (Leningrad: Nauka, Leningradskoe otdelenie, 1981), 167–184: 172, 175.

7. S. P. Shevyrev, *Istoriia imperatorskogo moskovskogo universiteta, napisannaia k stoletnemu ego iubileiu* (Moscow: Izdatel'stvo MGU, 1998), 349.

8. Popov, *Istoriia Imperatorskogo Moskovskogo obshchestva istorii i drevnostei Rossiiskikh*, 4. See also Kliuchevskii, "Iubilei Obshchestva istorii i drevnostei rossiiskikh," 187–195.

9. Vucinich, *Science in Russian Culture*, 194.

10. The book was entitled *Nestor: russische Annalen in ihrer slawonischen Ursprache verglichen, gereinigt und erklärt*; it was translated into Russian as A. L. Shlözer, *Nestor: Russkie letopisi na drevne-slavianskom iazyke*, pts. 1–3 (St. Petersburg, 1809–1819). See also "On podgotovil razvitie istoricheskoi nauki XIX veka: Avgust Ludvig Shletser," in Sakharov, ed., *Istoriki Rossii: XVIII- nachalo XX veka*, 61–75.

11. Popov, *Istoriia Imperatorskogo Moskovskogo obshchestva istorii i drevnostei Rossiiskikh*, 4.

12. G. P. Gooch, *History and Historians in the Nineteenth Century* (London: Longmans, Green and Co., 1913), 64–65. Crane, *Collecting and Historical Consciousness in Early Nineteenth-Century Germany*, 83.

13. Gooch, *History and Historians in the Nineteenth Century*, 65.

14. V. K. Nadler, *Imperator Alexander I i ideia Sviashchennogo Soiuza* (Riga: N. Kimmel, 1886), 68–73.

15. John Robert Seeley, *Life and Times of Stein, or Germany and Prussia in the Napoleonic Age*, vol. 2 (London: Cambridge University Press, 1879), 483–486.

16. Seeley, *Life and Times of Stein*, vol. 3, 490.

17. "Ot obshchego sobraniia professorov Imperatorskogo Moskovskogo Universiteta," Prilozhenie k I glave, in Popov, *Istoriia Imperatorskogo Moskovskogo obshchestva istorii i drevnostei Rossiiskikh*, part 1, 68; *Sostav Imperatorskogo Obshchestva Istorii i Drevnostei Rossiiskikh pri Moskovskom Universitete* (Moscow, 1890), 1.

18. Popov, *Istoriia Imperatorskogo Moskovskogo obshchestva istorii i drevnostei Rossiiskikh*, 28–48.

19. "Ot obshchego sobraniia professorov Imperatorskogo Moskovskogo Universiteta," in Popov, *Istoriia Imperatorskogo Moskovskogo obshchestva istorii i drevnostei Rossiiskikh*, 68.

20. For Karamzin's "path to history," see Edward C. Thaden, *The Rise of Historicism in Russia* (New York: Peter Lang, 1999), 49–62; on Musin-Pushkin's career and his collecting activity, see Kozlov, *Rossiiskaia arkheografiia*, 62–80.

21. Popov, *Istoriia Imperatorskogo Moskovskogo obshchestva istorii i drevnostei Rossiiskikh*, 15.

22. Quoted in ibid., 14.

23. "Ob'iavlenie o konkurse na zadachu, predlozhennuiu Obshchestvom Istorii i Drevnostei Rossiiskikh v 1805 godu, i o posledstviiakh ego," in Popov, *Istoriia Imperatorskogo Moskovskogo obshchestva istorii i drevnostei Rossiiskikh*, Appendix to chap. 1, 77.

24. Ibid., 77–82. For a survey of the contemporaneous discussions on criticism, including criticism in historical writing, see William Mills Todd III, *Fiction and Society in the Age of Pushkin* (Cambridge, MA: Harvard University Press, 1986), 89–90; Allison Y. Katsev, "In the Forge of Criticism: M. T. Kachenovskii and Professional Autonomy in Pre-Reform Russia," in Thomas Sanders, ed., *Historiography of Imperial Russia: The Profession and Writing of History*

in a Multinational State (Armonk, New York: M.E. Sharpe, 1999), 52–57; and, especially, the chapter "Osnovnye iavleniia v teorii i metodike kritiki i vvedenie v obshchestvennyi oborot istoricheskikh istochnikov v Rossii v kontse XVIII-pervoi polovine XIX veka" in Kozlov, *Rossiiskaia Arkheografiia*, 231–352.

25. Katsev, "In the Forge of Criticism," 55. On Kachenovskii's critical commentary of Karamzin's *magnum opus*, *The History of the Russian State*, see also V. P. Kozlov, "Polemika vokrug 'Istorii gosudarstva Rossiskogo' N. M. Karamzina v otechestvennoi periodike (1818– 1830 gg.), *Istoriia SSSR*, no. 5 (1984): 88–102; and Thaden, *The Rise of Historicism in Russia*, 61.

26. Thaden, *The Rise of Historicism in Russia*, 87.

27. M. S. Gastev, "O vspomogatel'nykh naukakh dlia istorii," *Vestnik Evropy*, no. 19/20 (1830): 161–202. Gastev also authored the first Russian textbooks on auxiliary historical disciplines, *Materialy dlia vspomogatel'nykh nauk istorii: Knizhka pervaia dlia khronologii* (Moscow, 1833) and *Knizhka vtoraia dlia genealogii* (Moscow, 1835). For Gastev's teaching courses, see N. G. Abramova and T. A. Kruglova, *Vspomogatel'nye istoricheskie distsipliny* (Moscow: Izdatel'skii tsentr "Akademiia," 2008), 37–39.

28. "Ob'iavlenie o konkurse na zadachu, predlozhennuiu Obshchestvom Istorii i Drevnostei Rossiiskikh," in Popov, *Istoriia Imperatorskogo Moskovskogo obshchestva istorii i drevnostei Rossiiskikh*, 82.

29. "Dnevnaia zapiska zasedaniia obshchestva, proiskhodivshego 13 marta 1812 g.," in Popov, *Istoriia Imperatorskogo Moskovskogo obshchestva istorii i drevnostei Rossiiskikh*, 238–239.

30. *Ustav obshchestva istorii i drevnostei Rosiiskikh utverzhdennyi fevralia 11 dnia, 1811 goda* (Moscow, 1811), 5.

31. Ibid., 6–7, 16–19.

32. Popov, *Istoriia Imperatorskogo Moskovskogo obshchestva istorii i drevnostei Rossiiskikh*, 58–59; "Dnevnaia zapiska zasedaniia obshchestva, 1810 goda dekabria 22 dnia," in ibid., 214–15. There were probably some other reasons for closing the society as well: thus, Kozlov noted Kutuzov's hostility to Karamzin and Musin-Pushkin as influencing his decision to reform the society. See Kozlov, *Rossiiskaia arkheografiia*, 35–36. For Golenishchev-Kutuzov's antagonism to Karamzin, see P. I. Golenishchev-Kutuzov, "Pis'mo ministru narodnogo prosveshcheniia gr. Razumovskomu (1810)," in L. A. Sapchenko, ed., *Karamzin: Pro et contra* (St. Petersburg: RKhGA, 2006), 491–492. On the causes of this conflict, see M. G. Al'tshuller and Iu. M. Lotman "P. I. Golenishchev-Kutuzov: Biograficheskaia spravka" in idem, eds., *Poety 1790–1810kh godov* (Leningrad: Sovetskii pisatel', Leningradskoe otdelenie, 1971), 475–476.

33. In the protocols of the society's session Beketov appeared as a retired major and an honorary member of Moscow University. See "Dnevnaia zapiska zasedaniia Obshchestva Istorii i Drevnostei Rossiiskikh 1810 goda dekabria 22 dnia," in Popov, *Istoriia Imperatorskogo Moskovskogo obshchestva istorii i drevnostei Rossiiskikh*, 215.

34. "Dnevnaia zapiska zasedaniia Obshchestva Istorii i Drevnostei Rossiiskikh 1810 goda dekabria 22 dnia" and "Vtoraia rech' popechitelia Moskovskogo Universiteta P. I. Kutuzova v zasedanii 22 dekabria 1810," in ibid., 216, 220.

35. F. Ia. Priima, "Timkovskii kak issledovatel' 'Slova o polku Igoreve'" in V. I. Malyshev, ed., *Trudy Otdela drevne-russkoi literatury, Akademiia nauk SSSR, Institut Russkoi literatury (Pushkinskii Dom)*, vol. 14 (Moscow-Leningrad: Izdatel'stvo Akademii Nauk SSSR, 1958), 89; "Dnevnaia zapiska zasedaniia Obshchestva Istorii i Drevnostei Rossiiskikh byvshego 1811 goda marta 13 dnia," in Popov, *Istoriia Imperatorskogo Moskovskogo obshchestva istorii i drevnostei Rossiiskikh*, 226.

36. *Russkie dostopamiatnosti, izdavaemye OIDR* (Moscow, 1815); Kozlov, *Rossiiskaia arkheografiia*, 37–38; V. S. Ikonnikov, *Opyt russkoi istoriografii*, vol. 1, part 1 (Kiev: Tipografiia Imperatorskogo Universiteta sv. Vladimira, 1891), 298.

37. "Spisok chlenov Obshchestva Istorii i Drevnostei Rossiiskikh, nyne sie Obshchestvo sostavliaiushchikh," in Popov, *Istoriia Imperatorskogo Moskovskogo Obshchestva Istorii i Drevnostei Rossiiskikh*, 221.

38. "Dnevnaia zapiska zasedaniia Obshchestva Istorii i Drevnostei Rossiiskikh 1810 goda dekabria 22 dnia," 217.

39. "Rech' govorennaia v zasedanii Obshchestva Istorii i Drevnostei Rossiiskikh pri Imperatorskom Moskovskom universitete 14 iiunia 1823 goda deistvitel'nym chlenom onogo Pavlom Stroevym," *Severnyi arkhiv*, no. 19 (1823): 9–21. The most detailed biography of Stroev was written by a future member of the Society of Zealots of Russian Historical Education, N. P. Barsukov, *Zhizn' i trudy P. M. Stroeva* (St. Petersburg, 1878); on the significance of Stroev's initiative in the context of the quest for Russian national identity, see Bradley, *Voluntary Associations*, 91–92; on the implementation of Stroev's program by the Academy of Sciences, see S. F. Platonov, "Obzor istochnikov russkoi istorii," in idem, *Polnyi kurs lektsii po russkoi istorii*, 10th ed. (Petrograd, 1917), 23–26.

40. "Pis'mo Ministra Narodnogo Prosveshcheniia k popechiteliu Moskovskogo Universiteta," in Popov, *Istoriia Imperatorskogo Moskovskogo Obshchestva Istorii i Drevnostei Rossiiskikh*, 222–224.

41. Gooch, *History and Historians in the Nineteenth Century*, 67.

42. S. A. Belokurov, *Ukazatel' ko vsem periodicheskim izdaniiam OIDR pri Imperatorskom Moskovskom Universitete, 1815–1883* (Moscow: Tipografiia E. I. Pogodinoi, 1883), 3–6; A. D. Stepanskii, "K istorii nauchno-istoricheskikh obshchestv v dorevoliutsionnoi Rossii," *Arkheograficheskii ezhegodnik za 1974 g.* (Moscow: Nauka, 1975), 41.

43. The topics of Bodianskii's dissertations were "The folk poetry of the Slavic tribes" and "On the time of origin of the Slavic characters." See L. I. Nasonkina, "Bodianskii, Osip Maksimovich," in E. M. Zhukov, ed., *Sovetskaia istoricheskaia entsiklopediia*, vol. 2 (Moscow: Sovetskaia entsiklopediia, 1962), 515.

44. Nasonkina, "Bodianskii, Osip Maksimovich," 515, and Ikonnikov, *Opyt russkoi istoriografii*, vol. 1, part 1, 300. For a more detailed description of the case, see Fedor Buslaev, *Moi vospominaniia* (Moscow: Izdanie V. G. Fon Boolia, 1897), chap. 24, and V. V. Boiarchenkov: "Obshchestvo istorii i drevnostei rossiiskikh v seredine 1840-kh gg," *Voprosy istorii*, no. 4 (2008): 114–121; idem, "S. G. Stroganov, S. S. Uvarov i 'Istoriia Fletchera' 1848," *Rossiskaia istoriia*, no. 5 (2009): 144–149; idem, "'Sekretar' antikvarnogo sosloviia': O. M. Bodianskii v Obshchestve istorii i drevnostei rossiiskikh," *Slavianovedenie*, no. 2 (2009): 91–102, as well as chapter two of his dissertation *Istoricheskaia nauka v Rossii 1830–1870kh gg.: poisk novoi kontseptsii russkoi istorii* (Riazan': Riazanskii gosudarstvennyi universitet, 2009).

45. V. S. Ikonnikov, *Russkaia istoricheskaia nauka v dvadtsatipiatiletie 1855–1880 gg.* (St. Petersburg, 1880), 425.

46. O. M. Bodianskii, "Zamechaniia na proekt obshchego ustava imperatorskikh universitetov," *Chteniia v Obshchestve istorii i drevnostei rossiiskikh*, no. 2 (1862), 217–242; idem, "Istoricheskaia zapiska o dele Sankt-Peterburgskogo universiteta," ibid., no. 3 (1862), 179–205; "Otdel'noe mnenie professora Bodianskogo po voprosam, kasaiushchimsia shtatnykh prepodavatelei universiteta po ustavu 1863," *Moskovskie universitetskie izvestiia*, no. 37 (1867), 417–420.

47. "Trilogiia na trilogiiu: Istoricheskii ocherk iz sovremennoi zhizni russkogo universiteta K. Mutsiia Stsevoly (s predisloviem O. Bodianskogo)," *Chteniia v Obshchestve istorii i drevnostei rossiiskikh*, no. 1 (1873): 3–31; an offprint (*ottisk*) of this paper was published in the same year.

48. O. N. Khokhlova, "O. M. Bodianskii i A. A. Maikov: K voprosu o vzaimootnosheniiakh v universitetskoi srede," *Vestnik Tverskogo gosudarstvennogo universiteta*, no. 34 (2008): 77–83.

49. N. A. Kondrashov, *Osip Maksimovich Bodianskii* (Moscow: Izdatel'stvo Moskovskogo Universiteta, 1956); Chesnokov, *Pravitel'stvennaia politika i istoricheskaia nauka Rossii*, 72–78.

50. Chesnokov, *Pravitel'stvennaia politika i istoricheskaia nauka Rossii*, 78.

51. Popov referred to *Zapiski i Trudy* as *Trudy i Letopisi*, which was its title from 1828 until 1837.

52. Ikonnikov, *Opyt russkoi istoriografii*, 302.

53. A. V. Makushin and P. A. Tribunskii, *Pavel Nikolaevich Miliukov: Trudy i dni (1859–1904)* (Riazan', 2001), 59, 61–62.

54. *Sostav Imperatorskogo Obshchestva Istorii i Drevnostei Rossiiskikh*, 35–42.

55. Ibid., 35.

56. Makushin and Tribunskii, *Pavel Nikolaevich Miliukov: Trudy i dni*, 77–78.

57. P. N. Miliukov, *Vospominaniia* (Moscow: Izdatel'stvo politicheskoi literatury, 1991), 122.

58. Makushin and Tribunskii, *Pavel Nikolaevich Miliukov: Trudy i dni*, 78–79.

59. Miliukov, *Vospominaniia*, 122.

60. Toivo Miljan, *Historical Dictionary of Estonia* (Lanham, Maryland and Oxford: Scarecrow Press 2004), 221; A. Markov, *Imperatorskoe Odesskoe Obshchestvo Istorii i Drevnostei: Obzor ego deiatel'nosti za 1839–1888 g.* (St. Petersburg: St. Peterburgskii Arkheologicheskii Institut, 1888); V. Iurgevich, *Istoricheskii ocherk piatidesiatiletiia imperatorskogo Odesskogo obshchestva istorii i drevnostei 1839–1889* (Odessa, 1889); Ikonnikov, *Opyt russkoi istoriografii*, 302, 318; Stepanskii, "K istorii nauchno-istoricheskikh obshchestv v dorevoliutsionnoi Rossii," 39, 54.

61. Ikonnikov, *Opyt russkoi istoriografii*, 306–313.

62. "Protokoly zasedanii i soobshcheniia chlenov Turkestanskogo kruzhka liubitelei arkheologii: god vosemnadtsatyi (11 dekabria 1912–11 dekabria 1913) - god dvadtsatyi (11 dekabria 1914–11 dekabria 1915)" in *Zapiski vostochnogo otd. Imperatorskogo Russkogo arkheologicheskogo obshchestva*, no. 23 (1915): 217–226; B. V. Lunin, *Iz istorii russkogo vostokovedeniia i arkheologii v Turkestane: Turkestanskii kruzhok liubitelei arkheologii (1895-1917 gg.)*, (Tashkent: Izdatel'stvo Akademii Nauk UzSSR, 1958); Stepanskii, "K istorii nauchno-istoricheskikh obshchestv," 53.

63. B. A. Litvinskii, "K istorii zakaspiiskogo kruzhka liubitelei arkheologii i istorii Vostoka," *Izvestiia Akademii Nauk Tadzhikskoi SSR, Otdelenie obshchestvennykh nauk*, vol. 14 (1957), 157–167.

64. Philippa Levine, *The Amateur and the Professional: Antiquarians, Historians and Archeologists in Victorian England, 1838–1886* (Cambridge: Cambridge University Press, 1986), 7.

65. *Rukovodstvo k poznaniiu drevnostei g. Al. Millenia, izdannoe s pribavleniiami i zamechaniiami v pol'zu uchashchikhsia v Imp. Mosk. Un-te Nik. Koshanskim, Iziashchnykh nauk Magistrom i Filosofii Doktorom* (Moscow, 1807), quoted in Kozlov, *Rossiiskaia Arkheografiia*, 258–259. On the appearance of the concept of archeography, see also S. N. Valk, "Sud'by 'arkheografii,'" in M. N. Tikhomirov, ed., *Arkheograficheskii ezhegodnik za 1961 god* (Moscow: Nauka, 1962), 453–465.

66. Platonov, "Obzor istochnikov russkoi istorii," 23–28.

67. Ikonnikov, *Opyt russkoi istoriografii*, vol. 1, part 1, 92–93.

68. Ibid., 156.

69. Ibid., 306, 312

70. "Polozhenie o Moskovskom Arkheologicheskom Institute," *Sobranie uzakonenii i rasporiazhenii pravitel'stva, izdavaemoe pri Pravitel'stvuiushchem Senate*, February 20, 1907 (St. Petersburg, 1907), part 1, 414. See also M. F. Khartanovich, *Gumanitarnye nauchnye uchrezhdeniia Sankt-Peterburga XIX veka* (St. Petersburg: Izdatel'stvo St. Peterburgskogo otdeleniia Instituta Istorii RAN "Nestor-Istoriia," 2006), 188–200.

71. Tsentral'nyi gosudarstvennyi istoricheskii arkhiv St. Petersburga (TsGIA Spb), f. 119, Arkheologicheskii Institut, op. 2, d. 48, O reorganizatsii instituta, l. 20, 47, 11.

72. Stepanskii, "K istorii nauchno-istoricheskikh obshchestv," 51; *Istoricheskaia zapiska o deiatel'nosti imperatorskogo Moskovskogo arkheologicheskogo obshchestva za pervye 25 let sushchestvovaniia* (Moscow: Sinodal'naia tipografiia, 1890), 23–24.

73. K. Ia. Zdravomyslov, *Svedeniia o sushchestvuiushchikh v eparkhiiakh tserkovno-arkheologicheskikh uchrezhdeniiakh i konsistorskikh arkhivakh* (Petrograd, 1917); Stepanskii, "K istorii nauchno-istoricheskikh obshchestv," 53.

74. Ikonnikov, *Russkaia istoricheskaia nauka v dvadtsatipiatiletie 1855–1880*, 446.

75. On archeological congresses, see *Istoricheskaia zapiska o deiatel'nosti imperatorskogo Moskovskogo arkheologicheskogo obshchestva, 79–114*; "Arkheologicheskie s'ezdy," in I. E. Andreevskii (ed.), *Entsiklopedicheskii Slovar'*, vol. 2 (St. Petersburg: F.A. Brokgauz and I.A. Efron, 1890), 229; Chesnokov, *Pravitel'stvennaia politika i istoricheskaia nauka Rossii*, 56–72.

76. I. P. Khrushchov, "Ob'iasnenie," *Kievlianin*, no. 138 (1872); quoted in N. P. Dashkevich, *25-letie Istoricheskogo Obshchestva Nestora-Letopistsa* (Kiev, 1899), 21.

77. For a general survey of the commissions' establishment and activity, see V. S. Ikonnikov, *Gubernskie uchenye arkhivnye komissii, 1884–1890* (Kiev: Tipografiia universiteta sv. Vladimira, 1892) and V. P. Makarikhin, *Gubernskie uchenye arkhivnye komissii Rossii* (Nizhnii Novgorod: Volgo-Viatskoe knizhnoe izdatel'stvo, 1991).

78. "Proekt polozheniia o gubernskikh istoricheskikh arkhivakh i uchenykh arkhivnykh komissiiakh [April 13, 1884]" in *Sbornik materialov otnosiashchikhsia do arkhivnoi chasti v Rossii*, vol. I (Petrograd: Russkoe Istoricheskoe Obshchestvo, 1916), 662–663.

79. "Proekt polozheniia o gubernskikh istoricheskikh arkhivakh i uchenykh arkhivnykh komissiiakh" and "Vypiska iz zhurnala Komiteta Ministrov 3 Aprelia 1884 g." in *Sbornik materialov otnosiashchikhsia do arkhivnoi chasti v Rossii*, I: 662–664; Ikonnikov, *Gubernskie uchenye arkhivnye komissii*, 2, 5, 10, 17; "Arkheologicheskie s'ezdy," *Entsiklopedicheskii Slovar'*, 2: 229.

80. *Sbornik materialov otnosiashchikhsia do arkhivnoi chasti v Rossii*, 1: 663.

81. "Predstavlenie Ministra Vnutrennikh Del 17 marta 1884 g. no. 7867," in *Sbornik materialov otnosiashchikhsia do arkhivnoi chasti v Rossii*, I: 661.

82. V. A. Berdinskikh, *Uezdnye istoriki: Russkaia provintsial'naia istoriografiia* (Moscow: Novoe literaturnoe obozrenie, 2003), 44–66. See also the interesting and rather sarcastic comments on the beginning of the gubernia statistical committees' activity in the memoirs of Alexander Herzen, who in 1835 was appointed the clerk (*deloproizvoditel'*) of such a committee in Viatka, where he was in political exile. A. I. Hertzen, *Byloe i dumy*, vol. 1 (Moscow: Khudozhestvennaia literatura, 1982), 222, quoted by Berdinskikh, *Uezdnye istoriki*, 46–47.

83. Berdinskikh, *Uezdnye istoriki*, 40–44, 49. For representative, albeit incomplete collections of Shchapov's writings, see N. Ia. Aristov, *A. P. Shchapov: Zhizn' i sochineniia* (St. Petersburg, 1883); and A. P. Shchapov, *Sochineniia*, vols. 1–3 (St. Petersburg: Izdatel'stvo M. V. Pirozhkova, 1906–1908). V. V. Boiarchenkov has suggested a perceptive analysis of Shchapov's ideas in the context of the contemporary historiographic approaches to local history in his *Istoriki-federalisty: Kontseptsiia mestnoi istorii v russkoi mysli 20–70kh godov XIX veka* (St. Petersburg: Dmitrii Bulanin, 2005), 6–17, 107–163. On the ideology of *oblastnichestvo* (and of the powerful Siberian *oblastnichestvo* in particular), see also A. V. Malinov, *Filosofiia i ideologiia oblastnichestva* (St. Petersburg: Intersotsis, 2012), especially 5–17.

84. Vera Tolz, *"Sobstvennyi Vostok Rossii": Politika identichnosti i vostokovedenie v pozdneimperskii i rannesovetskii period* (Moscow: Novoe literaturnoe obozrenie, 2013), 69–79. On the Heimat movement, see Celia Applegate, *A Nation of Provincials: The German Idea of Heimat* (Berkeley: University of California Press, 1990); Alon Confino, *The Nation as a Local*

Metaphor: Würtemberg, Imperial Germany and National Memory, 1871–1918 (Chapel Hill: University of North Carolina Press, 1997).

85. D. Ia. Samokvasov, *Arkhivnoe delo v Rossii* (Moscow: Tovarishchestvo tip. A. I. Mamontova, 1902), 26.

86. A. S. Gatsiskii, *Istoricheskaia zapiska ob uchrezhdenii v Nizhnem Novgorode gubernskoi uchenoi arkhivnoi komissii* (1884–1887) (Nizhnii Novgorod, 1887); cited in Berdinskikh, *Uezdnye istoriki*, 90–91.

87. "Doklad Komissii po napravleniiu zakonodatel'nykh predpolozhenii Gosudarstvennoi Dumy po vnesennomu Ministrom Vnutrennikh Del zakonoproektu ob assignovanii iz kazny denezhnykh sredstv na vydachu gubernskim uchenym arkhivnym komissiiam ezhegodnykh posobii (predstavlenie ot 23 Oktiabria 1908 goda za no. 19868), 12 Dekabria 1908 g.," in *Sbornik materialov otnosiashchikhsia do arkhivnoi chasti v Rossii*, 1: 669.

88. "Izvlechenie iz otchëta godovogo sobraniia Imperatorskogo Russkogo Istoricheskogo Obshchestva, 13 Marta 1914," in ibid., 1: 688.

89. "Doklad Komissii po napravleniiu zakonodatel'nykh predpolozhenii Gosudarstvennoi Dumy," 670.

90. S. F. Platonov's address to Iaroslavl's regional archeological conference (a conference of researchers of history and antiquities of Rostov-Suzdal region), August 12, 1901, supplement to Ia. E. Smirnov, "S. F. Platonov i iaroslavskoe kraevedenie," in S. O. Shmidt, ed., *Arkheograficheskii ezhegodnik za 2009–2010 gg.* (Moscow: Nauka, 2012), 282.

91. This view was developed mainly in regards to the role of the Russian Geographical Society. See, in particular, Nathaniel Knight, "Science, Empire and Nationality: Ethnography in the Russian Geographical Society, 1845–1855" in Jane Burbank and David Ransel, eds., *Imperial Russia: New Histories for the Empire* (Bloomington: Indiana University Press, 1998), 108–142; idem, "Ethnicity, Nationality and the Masses: Narodnost' and Modernity in Imperial Russia," in Hoffmann and Kotsonis, eds., *Russian Modernity*, 41–66; Bradley, *Voluntary Associations in Tsarist Russia*, chap. 3, "The Quest for National Identity: The Russian Geographical Society," 86–127. For the role of nineteenth-century historical and archeological associations in forming national and local identities in various national contexts, see Applegate, *A Nation of Provincials*; Confino, *The Nation as a Local Metapor*; Levine, *The Amateur and the Professional*; M. Diaz-Adreu and T. Champion, eds., *Nationalism and Archeology in Europe* (Boulder: Westview, 1996).

92. Ikonnikov, *Russkaia istoricheskaia nauka v dvadtsatipiatiletie 1855–1880*, 427.

93. Cited in Chesnokov, *Pravitel'stvennaia politika i istoricheskaia nauka Rossii*, 60.

94. Miliukov, *Vospominaniia*, 123.

95. "Novosti nauk, iskusstv i literatury," *Otechestvennye zapiski*, no. 4 (1858): 80–81.

96. Ikonnikov, *Russkaia istoricheskaia nauka v dvadtsatipiatiletie 1855–1880*, 423.

97. *Ustav Russkogo istoricheskogo obshchestva* (St. Petersburg, 1866), 3.

98. M. Iu. Agapova, "Sborniki Russkogo istoricheskogo obshchestva kak istoricheskii istochnik," *Russkii istoricheskii sbornik*, vol. 2 (Moscow, 2010): 349–356.

99. "Azbuchnyi ukazatel' imen russkikh deiatelei dlia Russkogo Biograficheskogo Slovaria, chast' 1 (A-L)," *Sbornik Imperatorskogo Russkogo istoricheskogo obshchestva*, vol. 60 (St.Petersburg, 1887), and "Azbuchnyi ukazatel' imen russkikh deiatelei dlia Russkogo Biograficheskogo Slovaria, chast' 2 (M-O)," ibid., vol. 62 (St. Petersburg, 1888); P. A. Zaionchkovskii, "A. A. Polovtsov: Biograficheskii ocherk," in A. A. Polovtsov, *Dnevnik Gosudarstvennogo Sekretaria*, vol. 1, 1883–1886 (Moscow: Tsentrpoligraf, 2005), 15–16.

100. A. A. Polovtsev was the secretary (1866–1879) and then the chair of the society (1879–1909). Other high-ranking officials among the RIO's founding members were *chinovniki* of the Ministry of Foreign Affairs Baron A. G. Zhomini and A. F. Gamburger, Director of the archive

of the Ministry of Foreign Affairs K. K. Zlobin, Chair of the Department of Laws of the State Council, Baron M. A. Korf, the tutor of the Heir, Count B. A. Perovskii, the Ober-Procurator of the Synod, Count D. A. Tolstoi, and an official of the Ministry of Education (who was also a journalist), E. M. Feoktistov. See "Spisok uchreditelei Russkogo istoricheskogo obshchestva," in *Ustav russkogo istoricheskogo obshchestva*, 13; and Zaionchkovskii, "A. A. Polovtsov: Biograficheskii ocherk," 14.

101. G. A. Voskresenskii, "Akademik A.F. Bychkov, pochetnyi chlen Moskovskoi Dukhovnoi Akademii," *Bogoslovskii vestnik* 2, no. 5 (1899): 114–126.

102. *Slushatel'nitsy S.-Peterburgskikh Vysshikh zhenskikh (Bestuzhevskikh) kursov: Po dannym perepisi (ankety), vypolnennoi Statisticheskim seminariem v noiabre 1909* (St. Petersburg, 1912); *Nasha dan' Bestuzhevskim kursam: Vospominaniia byvshikh bestuzhevok za rubezhom* (Paris: Ob'edinenie byvshikh Bestuzhevok za rubezhom, 1971); E. P. Fedosova, *Bestuzhevskie kursy—pervyi zhenskii universitet v Rossii (1878–1918 gg.)* (Moscow: Pedagogika, 1980).

103. See, for example, Viazemskii's essays: "Knizhki 29–32 (1865–1877 gg.)," in idem, *Staraia zapisnaia knizhka* (Moscow: Zakharov, 2003); "O pis'makh Karamzina" (1866) in Sapchenko, ed., *Karamzin*, 82–86; "Po povodu zapisok grafa Zenfta (Mémoires du comte de Senfft, ancien ministre de Saxe. 1868)," in P. A. Viazemskii, *Polnoe sobranie sochinenii* (St. Petersburg, 1882), 7: 425–464; "Vospominaniia o 1812 gode" (1869) in idem, *Estetika i literaturnaia kritika* (Moscow: Iskusstvo, 1984), 262–270; "Mitskevich o Pushkine" (1873), in idem, *Polnoe sobranie sochinenii*, 7: 306–332; "Griboedovskaia Moskva (1874–1875) in ibid., 7: 374–382; "Moskovskoe semeistvo starogo byta," *Russkii arkhiv* 1, no. 3 (1877): 305–314; "Kharakteristicheskie zametki i vospominaniia o grafe Rastopchine," *Russkii arkhiv* 2, no. 5 (1877): 69–78.

104. *Ustav Russkogo istoricheskogo obshchestva*, 4.

105. Richard Wortman, *Scenarios of Power: Myth and Ceremony in Russian Monarchy from Peter the Great to the Abdication of Nicholas II* (Princeton: Princeton University Press, 2006), 254.

106. Polovtsov, *Dnevnik Gosudarstvennogo Sekretaria*, 1: 77, 98, 201, 241, 297–298, 317, 319, 438–439; 2: 30, 265–266, 281, 449, 457.

107. Ibid., 1: 317; 2: 183.

108. "Once—he wrote—His Majesty ordered me to go to him [Polovtsov] and to declare his desire to hold the meeting on the next day." See S. D. Sheremetev, "Imperator Aleksandr III," in K. A. Vakh and L. I. Shokhin, eds., *Memuary grafa S. D. Sheremeteva*, vol.1 (Moscow: Indrik, 2005), 488–489.

109. S. D. Sheremetev, "Imperator Aleksandr III," 488.

110. Polovtsov, *Dnevnik Gosudarstvennogo Sekretaria*, 1: 240–241, 266

111. Ibid., 2: 31, 184.

112. *Memuary grafa S. D. Sheremeteva*, vol. 1, 489; "Dnevnik A. A. Polovtsova," *Krasnyi arkhiv* no. 4 (1923): 92. Nicholas II even mentioned the meetings of the RIO in his personal diary; thus the note of March 8, 1903, referred to an especially lengthy session which took place in the fabulous Malakhitovyi hall of the Winter Palace—*Dnevniki Imperatora Nikolaia II (1894–1918)*, vol. 1 (Moscow: ROSSPEN, 2011), 717.

113. *Sostav Imperatorskogo Russkogo istoricheskogo obshchestva 12 marta 1912 g.* 3.

114. Nicholas I's papers were transferred to Polovtsov in 1886 and were published by the RIO in 1910–1911. See Polovtsov, *Dnevnik Gosudarstvennogo Sekretaria*, 1: 405, 414, 449; D. F. Kobeko, ed., "Perepiska Imperatora Nikolaia Pavlovicha s Velikim Kniazem Konstantinom Pavlovichem, chast' 1 (1825–1829)," *Sbornik Imperatorskogo Russkogo istoricheskogo obshchestva*, vol. 131 (St. Petersburg, 1910); K. A. Gubastov, "Perepiska Imperatora Nikolaia Pavlovicha s Velikim Kniazem Konstantinom Pavlovichem, chast' 2 (1830–1831)," ibid., vol. 132 (St. Petersburg, 1911).

115. According to the RIO's statutes, the member of its council who was supposed to leave was chosen by casting lots (*po zhrebiiu*). See *Ustav Russkogo istoricheskogo obshchestva*, 7.

116. Polovtsov, *Dnevnik Gosudarstvennogo Sekretaria*, 1: 319.

117. Ibid., 1: 234.

118. Ibid., 1: 444.

119. Ibid., 2: 17, 22.

120. Ibid., 2: 37.

121. Cited in ibid., 1: 80, 438. By the Council for Printed Matter (*Sovet po delam pechati*) Polovtsov apparently meant the Main Administration for Printed Matter (*Glavnoe upravlenie po delam pechati*)—see V. G. Chernukha, "Glavnoe upravlenie po delam pechati v 1865–1881 gg." in *Knizhnoe delo v Rossii vo vtoroi polovine XIX-nachale XX veka*, vol. 6 (St. Petersburg, 1992), 20–40.

122. *Imperatorskoe Russkoe istoricheskoe obshchestvo, 1866–1916: Obzor piatidesiatiletnei deiatel'nosti* (Petrograd, 1916), 5.

123. Sheremetev, "Peterburgskoe obshchestvo 60-kh gg (1863–1868)," in *Memuary grafa S. D. Sheremeteva*, 1: 156.

124. Ibid., 1: 157.

125. Polovtsov, *Dnevnik Gosudarstvennogo Sekretaria*, 1: 391, 392.

126. Ibid., 1: 419, 432–433, 435, 498, 499; 2: 28, 44, 46.

127. Ibid., 2: 308.

128. "Dnevnik A. A. Polovtsova," 94.

129. Wortman, *Scenarios of Power*, 245.

130. Polovtsov, *Dnevnik Gosudarstvennogo Sekretaria*, 1: 332.

131. Ibid., 1: 319, 438; S. D. Sheremetev, "Peterburgskoe obshchestvo 60kh gg. (1863–1868)," and "Aleksandr III," in *Memuary grafa S. D. Sheremeteva*, 1: 157, 489.

132. Polovtsov, *Dnevnik Gosudarstvennogo Sekretaria*, 1: 405.

133. Ibid., 1: 441.

134. Ibid., 2: 54; *Imperatorskoe russkoe istoricheskoe obshchestvo 1866–1916* (Petrograd, 1916), Prilozhenie no. 5, 165–186.

135. V. V. Maikov and N. D. Chechulin, eds., "Pamiatniki diplomaticheskikh snoshenii Moskovskogo gosudarstva so Shvedskim gosudarstvom, chast'1-ia (gody s 1556 po 1586)," *Sbornik Imperatorskogo Russkogo istoricheskogo obshchestva*, vol. 129 (St. Petersburg, 1910); N. D. Chechulin, ed., "Istoricheskie svedeniia o Ekaterininskoi Zakonodatel'noi Komissii dlia sochineniia proekta Novogo Ulozheniia, chast' 12-aia," ibid., vol. 134 (St. Petersburg, 1911); idem, ed., "Protokoly Konferentsii pri Vysochaishem dvore, chast' 1-aia (gody s 1756 po 1757)," ibid., vol. 136 (St. Petersburg, 1912); idem, ed., "Istoricheskie svedeniia o Ekaterininskoi Zakonodatel'noi Komissii dlia sochineniia proekta Novogo Ulozheniia, chast' 13-ia," ibid., vol. 144 (St. Petersburg, 1914); idem, ed., "Materialy Ekaterininskoi Zakonodatel'noi Komissii, chast' 14-aia," ibid., vol. 147 (Petrograd, 1915).

136. *Sostav Imperatorskogo Russkogo Istoricheskogo Obshchestva, 12 marta 1912 g.* 3–7.

137. Ibid., 3–7.

138. Polovtsov, *Dnevnik Gosudarstvennogo Sekretaria*, 2: 255.

139. S. D. Sheremetev, "Aleksandr III," 488–489.

140. Polovtsov, *Dnevnik Gosudarstvennogo Sekretaria*, 1: 80; 2: 280.

141. "Dnevnik A. A. Polovtsova," 95.

142. "Protokol zasedaniia Imperatorskogo Russkogo Istoricheskogo Obshchestva 3 Maia 1911," in *Sbornik materialov otnosiashchikhsia do arkhivnoi chasti v Rossii*, 1: 680–681.

143. "Izvlechenie iz godovogo otchëta Imperatorskogo Russkogo Istoricheskogo Obshchestva, 13 Marta 1914," in ibid., 1: 688.

144. Korzun, *Obrazy istoricheskoi nauki na rubezhe XIX–XX vv.*, 85.

145. L. I. Demina, "'Mne kak istoriku pozvolitel'no otsenivat' sobytiia istoricheskoi merkoi': Iz 'Zapisok' E. F. Shmurlo o Peterburgskom Universitete. 1889 g." *Otechestvennye arkhivy*, no. 1 (2006): 78, note of February 11, 1889; hereafter "Iz 'Zapisok' E. F. Shmurlo." Shmurlo's *Notes* were neither a diary nor memoirs, but something "in between." Shmurlo himself characterized them as "not a diary which has a personal interest only, but the kind of observations that would be not without significance for others. I have an opportunity to see, hear, participate—and everything together makes up, if not a picture, then good material for a picture." Ibid., 77.

146. Miliukov, *Vospominaniia*, 109.

147. "Iz 'Zapisok' E. F. Shmurlo," 83, note of August 29, 1889.

148. Ibid., 78, 80, notes of February 11 and March 18.

149. For the procedure and significance of the dissertation defense and the institution of *privat-docentura*, see Samuel D. Kassow, *Students, Professors, and the State in Tsarist Russia* (Berkeley: University of California Press, 1989), 32–36; Thomas Sanders, "The Third Opponent: Dissertation Defense and the Public Profile of Academic History in Late Imperial Russia," in Sanders, ed., *Historiography of Imperial Russia*, 69–97; Tomas M. Bon [Thomas Bohn], *Russkaia istoricheskaia nauka: Pavel Nikolaevich Miliukov i Moskovskaia shkola* (St. Petersburg: Olearius Press, 2005), 34–44; N. N. Alevras and N. V. Grishina, "Rossiiskaia dissertatsionnaia kul'tura XIX-nachala XX veka v vospriiatii sovremennikov: K voprosu o natsional'nykh osobennostiakh," *Dialog so vremenem*, no. 36 (2011): 221–247; and idem "Dissertatsii istorikov i zakonodatel'nye normy (1860–1920-e gg.) *Rossiiskaia istoriia*, no. 2 (2014): 77–90.

150. "Iz 'Zapisok' E. F. Shmurlo," 81, note of March 18, 1889.

151. Ibid., 95, note of December 30, 1889.

152. For general background on the historians' intergenerational relations, see A. A. Sinenko, "Mezhpokolencheskie kommunikatsii i formirovanie obraza uchitelia russkimi istorikami kontsa XIX v.," in V. P. Korzun and A.V. Iakub, eds, *Mir istorika: istoriographicheskii sbornik*, vol. 5 (Omsk: Izdatel'stvo OmGU, 2009), 140–151; and A. A. Serykh, "Pokolencheskaia identichnost' istorikov Rossii v kontse XIX-nachale XX vv." (PhD diss., Omsk State Pedagogical University, 2010)

153. "Iz 'Zapisok' E. F. Shmurlo," 78, note of February 11, 1889.

154. Stephen Lovell, "From Genealogy to Generation: The Birth of Cohort Thinking in Russia," *Kritika: Explorations in Russian and Eurasian History* 9, no. 3 (Summer 2008): 567–594.

155. Miliukov, *Vospominaniia*, 109.

156. Ibid., 108.

157. Ibid., 108–109.

158. "Iz 'Zapisok' E. F. Shmurlo," 94, note of December 30, 1889.

159. Lovell, "From Genealogy to Generation," 567.

160. "Iz 'Zapisok' E. F. Shmurlo," 84, note of August 29, 1889.

161. "Iz 'Zapisok' E. F. Shmurlo," 83, note of August 29, 1889. The *Bibliograf* was issued in St. Petersburg from 1884 until 1914. Its full title was *Bibliograf: Vestnik literatury, nauki i iskusstva* (*The Bibliographer: Herald of Literature, Science and Art*). From 1890 it was issued periodically and in 1892 became a historical and literary bibliographical monthly.

162. "Pis'ma S. F. Platonova P. N. Miliukovu" [edited by V. P. Korzun and M. A. Mamontova], in A. N. Sakharov, ed., *Istoriia i istoriki. 2003. Istoriograficheskii vestnik* (Moscow: Nauka, 2003), 326.

163. Miliukov, *Vospominaniia*, 108–109. Miliukov's opinion was accepted and reinforced by the later historiography. See, for example, Boris Anan'ich and Viktor Paneiakh, "The St. Petersburg School of History and Its Fate," in Sanders, ed., *Historiography of Imperial Russia*, 148; S. O. Shmidt, "Sergei Fedorovich Platonov," in G. N. Sevast'ianova and L. T. Mil'skaia,

eds., *Portrety istorikov: vremia i sud'by*, vol. 1, *Otechestvennaia istoriia* (Moscow-Jerusalem: Universitetskaia kniga/Gesharim, 2000), 107.

164. Miliukov, *Vospominaniia*, 109.

165. "Iz 'Zapisok' E. F. Shmurlo," 93, note of December 30, 1889.

166. A. N. Tsamutali, "Sergei Fedorovich Platonov (1860–1933)" in Sanders, ed., *Historiography of Imperial Russia*, 316; Alevras and Grishina, "Dissertatsii istorikov i zakonodatel'nye normy (1860–1920-e gg.)," 83–84.

167. "Pis'ma C. F. Platonova P. N. Miliukovu," *Istoriia i istoriki. 2003*, 328, 330, 332.

168. For conflicts in the Russian academic world in general, and among historians in particular, in the late nineteenth-early twentieth century, see A. V. Sveshnikov, "'Vot Vam istoriia nashei istorii': k probleme tipologii nauchnykh skandalov vtoroi poloviny XIX-nachala XX veka," in V. P. Korzun and G. K. Sadretdinova, eds., *Mir istorika: Istoriograficheskii sbornik*, vol. 1 (Omsk: Izdatel'stvo OmGU, 2005), 231–262; idem, "Kak possorilsia Lev Platonovich s Ivanom Mikhailovichem: Istoriia odnogo professorskogo konflikta," *Novoe literaturnoe obozrenie*, no. 96 (2009): 42–72.

169. N. D. Chechulin, "Russkoe provintsial'noe obshchestvo vo vtoroi polovine XVIII veka," *Zhurnal Ministerstva Narodnogo Prosveshcheniia*, no. 3 (1889): 45–71; no. 4 (1889): 241–268; no. 5 (1889): 55–96; no. 6 (1889): 261–281.

170. [B/a], "Retsenziia na ocherk: N. D. Chechulin, 'Russkoe provintsial'noe obshchestvo vo vtoroi polovine XVIII veka,'" *Russkaia mysl',* no. 9 (1889): 381–387. Miliukov described *Russkaia mysl'* as a "leftist camp of social thought." Miliukov, *Vospominaniia*, 113.

171. Retsenziia na ocherk: N. D. Chechulin, 'Russkoe provintsial'noe obshchestvo vo vtoroi polovine XVIII veka,'" 386–387; quoted in P. A. Tribunskii, "Perepiska A. S. Lappo-Danilevskogo i P. N. Miliukova," *Journal of Modern Russian History and Historiography*, no. 3 (2010): 87.

172. A. S. Lappo-Danilevskii to P. N. Miliukov, St. Petersburg, September 24, 1889, in Tribunskii, "Perepiska A. S. Lappo-Danilevskogo i P. N. Miliukova," 87–88; A. S. Lappo-Danilevskii to P. N. Miliukov, St. Petersburg, December 4 and 6, 1889, in ibid., 97.

173. A. S. Lappo-Danilevskii to P. N. Miliukov, St. Petersburg, December 4 and 6, 1889, in ibid., 97.

174. S. F. Platonov to P. N. Miliukov, October 7, 1889, in "Pis'ma S. F. Platonova P. N. Miliukovu," *Istoriia i istoriki. 2002. Istoriograficheskii vestnik* (Moscow: Nauka, 2002), 170. Miliukov's review of Chechulin's *Cities of the Moscow State in the Sixteenth Century* appeared in *Russkaia mysl'* in December 1889: [P. N. Miliukov], "Rets. na: Chechulin N. D., Goroda Moskovskogo gosudarstva v XVI veke, St. Petersburg, 1889," *Russkaia mysl'* no. 12 (1889): 522–524.

175. S. F. Platonov to P. N. Miliukov, March 1, 1890, in "Pis'ma S. F. Platonova P. N. Miliukovu," *Istoriia i istoriki. 2002*, 172; N. D. Chechulin, "Otvet retsenzentu 'Russkoi mysli,'" *Zhurnal Ministerstva Narodnogo Prosveshcheniia*, no. 5 (1890): 203–213; S. F. Platonov, "Rets. na: Chechulin N. D., Goroda Moskovskogo gosudarstva v XVI veke, St. Petersburg, 1889," ibid., 140–154; Tribunskii, "Perepiska A. S. Lappo-Danilevskogo i P. N. Miliukova," 97 nn. 49, 50.

176. Anan'ich and Paneiakh, "The St. Petersburg School of History and Its Fate," 160.

177. Otdel rukopisei Rossiiskoi natsional'noi biblioteki (OR RNB), f. 585, Platonov S.F., op.1, d. 5691, Dnevnik N. N. Platonovoi, l. 81 ob.-82.

178. Miliukov, *Vospominaniia*, 109.

179. Ibid., 109.

180. OR RNB, f. 585, op.1, d. 5691, l. 33 ob. Nikolai Milievich Anichkov (1844–1916) was the director of a department in the Ministry of Education; A. V. Nikitenko (1804–1877) was a historian of literature, professor at St. Petersburg University, and a member of the Academy of Sciences who also served as a censor and was widely respected for his combination of liberalism and responsibility in carrying out his duties as censor. See V. P. Zotov, "Liberal'nyi tsenzor

i professor-pessimist (Biograficheskii ocherk)," *Istoricheskii vestnik* 54, no. 10 (1893), 194–210; and A. V. Tsyganov, "Rossiiskii tsenzor Nikitenko: po materialam dnevnika," *Molodoi uchenyi* 2, no. 4 (2011): 51–54.

181. OR RNB, f. 585, op.1, d. 5691, l. 36 ob.-37.

182. Sanders, "The Third Opponent," 83, 96. Sanders noted especially the inappropriate timing of Semevskii's first presentation of his work to Bestuzhev-Riumin "in the immediate wake of the assassination of Alexander II," on March 9, 1881.

183. Ibid., 83. Sanders is here quoting from the description of Semevskii's dispute in Z., "Disput g. V. I. Semevskogo v Moskve," *Vestnik Evropy* (May 1882): 442–444.

184. Sanders, "The Third Opponent," 84.

185. Michael B. Petrovich, "V. I. Semevskii (1848– 1916): Russian Social Historian," in John Shelton Curtiss, ed., *Essay in Russian and Soviet History: In Honor of Geroid Tanquary Robinson* (New York: Columbia University Press, 1968), 70.

186. Petrovich notes that "the signatures included A. Ulianov, Lenin's brother, and P. Shevyrev—both members of the terrorist Will of the People, as well as P. N. Miliukov and M. I. Tugan-Baranovskii." Ibid., 70.

187. Miliukov, *Vospominaniia*, 109. For Miakotin's membership in Semevskii's circle, see also Melissa Kirshke Stockdale, *Pavel Miliukov and the Quest for Liberal Russia, 1880–1918* (Ithaca: Cornell University Press, 1996), 23.

188. David Sanders, "The Political Ideas of Russian Historians," *The Historical Journal* 27, no. 3 (1984): 764.

189. A. A. Kizevetter, "V. I. Semevskii v ego uchenykh trudakh," *Golos minuvshego*, no. 1 (1917): 199–200.

190. A. G. Slonimskii, "Semevskii, Vasilii Ivanovich" in *Sovetskaia Istoricheskaia Entsiklopediia* vol. 12 (Moscow: Sovetskaia Entsiklopediia, 1969), 727.

191. A. S. Kan, *Istorik G. V. Forsten i nauka ego vremeni* (Moscow: Nauka, 1979), 14.

192. Andy Byford, "Initiation to Scholarship: The University Seminar in Late Imperial Russia," *Russian Review* 64, no. 2 (2005): 299–323; A. V. Antoshchenko, A. V. Sveshnikov, "Istoricheskii seminarii kak mesto znaniia," in A. N. Dmitriev, ed., *Istoricheskaia kul'tura imperskoi Rossii: formirovanie predstavlenii o proshlom* (Moscow: Izdatel'skii dom Vysshei shkoly ekonomiki, 2012), 138–160. For the historical seminars at Russian universities in the nineteenth century, see also V. I. Chesnokov, "Puti formirovaniia i kharakternye cherty sistemy universitetskogo obrazovaniia v dorevoliutsionnoi Rossii," in ibid., 113–137, especially 126–128; A. V. Antoshchenko, "Das Seminar: nemetskie korni i russkaia krona (o primenenii nemetskogo opyta 'seminariev' moskovskimi professorami vo vtoroi polovine XIX v.)," in A. Iu. Andreev, ed., *"Byt' russkim po dukhu i evropeitsem po obrazovaniiu": Universitety rossiiskoi imperii v obrazovatel'nom prostranstve Tsentral'noi i Vostochnoi Evropy XVIII-nachala XX v.* (Moscow: ROSSPEN, 2009), 263–278.

193. Byford, "Initiation to Scholarship," 300.

194. Kan, *Istorik G. V. Forsten i nauka ego vremeni*, 14.

195. E. M. Tikhomirova, "Obrazovannoe serdtse: kniaginia Aleksandra Alekseevna Obolenskaia," in G. A. Tishkin, ed., *Rossiiskie zhenshchiny i evropeiskaia kul'tura: materialy konferentsii, posviashchennoi teorii i istorii zhenskogo dvizheniia* (St. Petersburg: St. Peterburgskoe Filosofskoe Obshchestvo, 2001), 130–131.

196. Kan, *Istorik G. V. Forsten i nauka ego vremeni*, 91.

197. Platonov's remark was quoted by A. E. Presniakov in a letter to his mother of February 5, 1895. A. N. Tsamutali, ed., *Aleksandr Evgen'evich Presniakov: Pis'ma i dnevniki, 1889–1927* (St. Petersburg: IISPb RAN and Dmitrii Bulanin, 2005), 172.

198. Ibid., 172.

199. Kan, *Istorik G. V. Forsten i nauka ego vremeni*, 80.

200. *Aleksandr Evgen'evich Presniakov: Pis'ma i dnevniki 1889–1927*, 177.

201. Miliukov, *Vospominaniia*, 105.

202. Alexander Kizevetter, *Na rubezhe dvukh stoletii: Vospominaniia 1881–1914* (Prague: Orbis, 1929; republished: Cambridge: Oriental Research Partners, 1974), 87.

203. L. S. Moiseenkova, "Pavel Gavrilovich Vinogradov," in G. N. Sevast'ianov, L. P. Marinovich and L. T. Mil'skaia, eds., *Portrety istorikov: Vremia i sud'by*, vol. 2, *Vseobshchaia istoriia* (Moscow-Jerusalem: Universitetskaia kniga/Gesharim, 2000), 120. For an intellectual biography of Vinogradov, see A. V. Antoshchenko, "Pavel Gavrilovich Vinogradov: Stanovlenie prepodavatelem," in N. N. Alevras, ed., *Istorik v meniaiushchemsia prostranstve rossiiskoi kul'tury: sbornik statei* (Cheliabinsk: Kamennyi poias, 2006): 24–30; idem, *Russkii liberal-anglofil Pavel Gavrilovich Vinogradov* (Petrozavodsk: Izdatel'stvo Petrozavodskogo Universiteta, 2010).

204. Kizevetter, *Na rubezhe dvukh stoletii*, 70–71. A biographer of Ger'e noted the same dynamic of a university seminar continuing in the form of meetings at the home of the professor with regard to Ger'e's courses. See D. A.Tsygankov, *Professor V. I. Ger'e i ego ucheniki* (Moscow: ROSSPEN, 2010), 58–61.

205. Quoted in M. M. Mandrik, "D. M. Petrushevskii i ego uchitelia: k voprosu o lichnykh i nauchnykh vzaimootnosheniiakh," in A. A. Meshchanina and P. A. Sokolov, eds., *Prizvanie—istoriia: Sbornik nauchnykh statei k 55-letiiu professora Iu.V. Krivosheeva: Trudy istoricheskogo fakul'teta Sankt-Peterburgskogo gosudarstvennogo universiteta*, vol. 2 (St. Petersburg: Izdatel'skii dom Sankt- Peterburgskogo Universiteta, 2010), 65.

206. Irina Paperno, "Personal Accounts of the Soviet Experience," *Kritika: Explorations in Russian and Eurasian History* 3, no. 4 (2002): 584.

207. Ibid., 585–586.

208. Barbara Walker, "Kruzhok Culture: The Meaning of Patronage in the Early Soviet Literary World," *Contemporary European History* 11, no. 1 (2002): 107, 111.

209. Ibid., 112–113.

210. Bon, *Russkaia istoricheskaia nauka*, 97; Charles H. Haskins, "Report on the Proceedings of the Twentieth Annual Meeting of the American Historical Association," *Annual Report of the American Historical Association for the Year 1904* (Washington: Government Printing Office, 1905), 35.

211. P. N. Milyoukov, "The Chief Currents of Russian Historical Thought," *Annual Report of the American Historical Association for the Year 1904*, 114.

212. For the concept of "scientific school" in general and "historical school" in particular, see Bon [Bohn], *Russkaia istoricheskaia nauka*, 11–14, as well as I. G. Dezhina and V. V. Kiseleva, *Tendentsii razvitiia nauchnykh shkol v sovremennoi Rossii* (Moscow: IEPP, 2009), especially chapter 2, "'Nevidimyi kolledzh' i ego sviaz' s nauchnoi shkoloi," 25–75; G. P. Miagkov, *Nauchnoe soobshchestvo v istoricheskoi nauke: Opyt "russkoi istoricheskoi shkoly,"* (Kazan': Izdatel'stvo Kazanskogo universiteta, 2000); D. A. Gutnov, "O shkolakh v istoricheskoi nauke," in I. P. Smirnov, ed., *Istoriia mysli: Istoriografiia* (Moscow: Vuzovskaia kniga, 2002), 65–72; A. N. Shakhanov, *Russkaia istoricheskaia nauka vtoroi poloviny XIX- nachala XX veka: Moskovskii i Peterburgskii universitety* (Moscow: Nauka, 2003); D. A. Tsygankov, "Issledovatel'skie traditsii moskovskoi i peterburgskoi shkol istorikov," in I. P. Smirnov, ed., *Istoriia mysli: Russkaia myslitel'naia traditsiia*, (Moscow: Vuzovskaia kniga, 2005); idem, *Professor V. I. Ger'e i ego ucheniki*; T. N. Ivanova, *Nauchnoe nasledie V. I. Ger'e i formirovanie nauki vseobshchei istorii v Rossii (30-e gg. XIX- nachalo XX veka)* (Cheboksary: Izdatel'stvo Chuvashskogo Universiteta, 2010), especially 307–322.

213. Levine, *The Amateur and the Professional*, 26, 27, 46.

214. Kareev's sixty-seven letters to Ger'e have been published as an appendix in Tsygankov, *Professor V. I. Ger'e i ego ucheniki*, 110–147.

215. V. P. Zolotarev, "Nikolai Ivanovich Kareev (1850–1931)," in Sevast'ianov, Marinovich, and Mil'skaia, eds., *Portrety istorikov: Vremia i sud'by*, 2: 279–281.

216. Ibid., 279; Wladimir Bérélowitch, "History in Russia Comes of Age: Institution-Building, Cosmopolitanism, and Theoretical Debates among Historians in Late Imperial Russia," *Kritika: Explorations in Russian and Eurasian History* 9, no. 1 (2008): 127–128.

217. Ibid., 128. See also V. P. Zolotarev, *Istoricheskaia kontseptsiia N. I. Kareeva: soderzhanie i evoliutsiia* (Leningrad: Izdatel'stvo Leningradskogo Universiteta, 1988); and B. G. Safronov, *N. I. Kareev o structure istoricheskogo znaniia* (Moscow: Izdatel'stvo moskovskogo universiteta, 1995).

218. Miliukov, *Vospominaniia*, 75.

219. N. I. Kareev, "Otnoshenie istorikov k sotsiologii," *Rubezh: al'manakh sotsial'nykh issledovanii*, no. 3 (1992): 6.

220. According to Shmurlo, the memorandum was signed by Vasil'ev, Zamyslovskii, Kareev, Sokolov, Forsten, Platonov, Lamanskii, Veselovskii, Minaev and himself. V. E. Regel was a privat-docent and an editor of the journal *Vizantiiskii vremennik*. See "Iz 'Zapisok' E. F. Shmurlo," 82, note of March 18, 1889.

221. Kareev, "Otnoshenie istorikov k sotsiologii," 5–13.

222. Miliukov, *Vospominaniia*, 76, 92, 98.

223. Bon [Bohn], *Russkaia istoricheskaia nauka*, 105–106. On positivism's appeal to the Russian intelligentsia of the 1870s, see also S. A. Ermishina, "Nauka ili nauchnost'?" in Smirnov, *Istoriia mysli*, 18–35, especially 25–28.

224. *Spisok chlenov Istoricheskogo Obshchestva pri Imperatorskom S.-Peterburgskom universitete k 1 oktiabria 1904* (St. Petersburg, 1905), 1, 5.

225. *Ustav Istoricheskogo Obshchestva pri Imperatorskom S.- Peterburgskom Universitete* (St. Petersburg, 1889), clause 3, 3

226. A. S. Lappo-Danilevskii to P. N. Miliukov, St. Petersburg, December 4 and 6, 1889, in Tribunskii, "Perepiska A. S. Lappo-Danilevskogo i P. N. Miliukova," 99–101.

227. P. N. Miliukov to A. S. Lappo-Danilevskii, Moscow, December 10, 1889, in ibid., 103.

228. *Otchët o sostoianii i deiatel'nosti Istoricheskogo Obshchestva pri Imperatorskom S.-Peterburgskom Universitete v 1890 godu* (St. Petersburg, 1890), 1.

229. A. S. Lappo-Danilevskii to P. N. Miliukov, St. Petersburg, December 27, 1889, in Tribunskii, "Perepiska A. S. Lappo-Danilevskogo i P. N. Miliukova," 105; Bérélowitch, "History in Russia Comes of Age," 130.

230. N. I. Kareev to V. I. Ger'e, St. Petersburg, February 22, 1890, in Tsygankov, *Professor V. I. Ger'e i ego ucheniki*, 132.

231. *Otchët o sostoianii i deiatel'nosti Istoricheskogo Obshchestva . . . v 1890 godu*, 54. The lectures on theory and didactics of history were delivered by Kareev and Ia. G. Gurevich; the former spoke on "The development of the theoretical aspects of historical scholarship" (*O razrabotke teoreticheskikh voprosov istoricheskoi nauki*) and "The new endeavor in the sphere of history teaching in the institutions for secondary education" (*O novom predpriiatii v oblasti prepodavaniia istorii v sredneuchebnykh zavedeniiakh*); and the latter on "History as a science and as a teaching subject" (*Ob istorii kak nauke i kak predmete prepodavaniia*). The lectures of a more empirical nature were devoted to such topics as S. A. Bershadskii, "On the peasant household in Lithuania in the late fifteenth and early sixteenth century" (*O krest'ianskom khoziaistve v Litve v kontse XV i nachale XIV veka*); S. L. Stepanov, "On the Athens higher school in the fourth century AD" (*Ob Afinskoi vysshei shkole v IV v. po R. Khr.*)"; Kh. M. Loparev, "On

F. Kabrit's diary of 1788" (*O dnevnike F. Kabrita 1788 g.*); E. A. Belov, "On the question of the significance of Ivan the Terrible's reign in Russian historical literature" (*Po voprosu o znachenii tsarstvovaniia Groznogo v russkoi istoricheskoi literature*); P. D. Pogodin, "On Paspati's book on the capture of Constantinople by the Turks" (*Po povodu knigi Paspati o vziatii Konstantinopolia turkami*); E. N. Shchepkina, "On the Tula uezd in the sixteenth and seventeenth centuries" (*O Tul'skom uezde v XVI–XVII vekakh*); A. M. Onu, "On the historical significance of Josef II's reign" (*Ob istoricheskom znachenii tsarstvovaniia Iosifa II*); G. E. Afanas'ev, "On pacte de famine" (*O pacte de famine*), ibid., 54.

232. Bérélowitch, "History in Russia Comes of Age," 132.

233. Arkhiv Sankt-Peterburgskogo instituta istorii Rossiiskoi Akademii Nauk (ASpbII RAN), f. 219, Istoricheskoe obshchestvo pri St. Peterburgskom Universitete, op. 1, d. 25, Plan izdaniia sistematicheskogo obzora istoricheskoi literatury Istoricheskim obshchestvom, sostoiashchim pri St. Peterburgskom Universitete, l. 1 ob.

234. ASpbII RAN, f. 219, op. 1, d. 25, l. 2.

235. ASpbII RAN, f. 219, op. 1, d. 25, l. 1, 3–6.

236. A. S. Lappo-Danilevskii to P. N. Miliukov, St. Petersburg, between May 10 and 20, 1890, in Tribunskii, "Perepiska A. S. Lappo-Danilevskogo i P. N. Miliukova," 121–123; ASpbII RAN, f. 219, op. 1, d. 25, l. 1. One of the intended participants was Ger'e: in October 1890 Kareev reminded him that he was waiting for his list of books on the Roman Republic and medieval culture to be reviewed in the *spravochnik*. N. I. Kareev to V. I. Ger'e, St. Petersburg, October 13, 1890, in Tsygankov, *Professor V. I. Ger'e i ego ucheniki*,133.

237. *Otchët o sostoianii i deiatel'nosti Istoricheskogo Obshchestva*, 54.

238. A. S. Lappo-Danilevskii to P. N. Miliukov, St. Petersburg, December, 5, 1890, Tribunskii, "Perepiska A. S. Lappo-Danilevskogo i P. N. Miliukova," 138.

239. "Pis'ma S. F. Platonova P. N. Miliukovu," *Istoriia i istoriki. 2002*, 177.

240. E. A. Rostovtsev, "N. I. Kareev i A. S. Lappo-Danilevskii: iz istorii vzaimootnoshenii v srede peterburgskikh uchenykh na rubezhe XIX–XX vv.," *Zhurnal sotsiologii i sotsial'noi antropologii* 3, no. 4 (2000): 110.

241. Quoted in Rostovtsev, "N. I. Kareev i A. S. Lappo-Danilevskii," 110.

242. *Aleksandr Evgen'evich Presniakov: Pis'ma i dnevniki, 1889–1927*, 133.

243. Ibid., 135.

244. E. A. Rostovtsev, *A. S. Lappo-Danilevskii i peterburgskaia istoricheskaia shkola* (Riazan': NRIID, 2004), 66.

245. V. I. Gurko, *Cherty i siluety proshlogo: pravitel'stvo i obshchestvennost' v tsarstvovanie Nikolaia II v izobrazhenii sovremennika* (Moscow: Novoe literaturnoe obozrenie, 2000), 510.

246. Thomas Sanders, "The Chechulin Affair or Politics and *nauka* in the History Profession of Late Imperial Russia," *Jahrbücher für Geschichte Osteuropas* 49, no. 1 (2001): 2.

247. Rostovtsev, *A. S. Lappo-Danilevskii i peterburgskaia istoricheskaia shkola*, 66.

248. "Retsenziia na ocherk: N. D. Chechulin, 'Russkoe provintsial'noe obshchestvo vo vtoroi polovine XVIII veka,'" 381–387; A. S. Lappo-Danilevskii to P. N. Miliukov, St. Petersburg, September, 24; December 4 and 6, 1889, in Tribunskii, "Perepiska A. S. Lappo-Danilevskogo i P. N. Miliukova," 87–88, 97.

249. Kizevetter, *Na rubezhe dvukh stoletii*, 266–269.

250. Ibid., 275.

251. P. N. Miliukov to A. S. Lappo-Danilevskii, Moscow, December 10, 1889; P. N. Miliukov to A. S. Lappo-Danilevskii, Moscow, December 28, 1889-January 9, 1890, in Tribunskii, "Perepiska A. S. Lappo-Danilevskogo i P. N. Miliukova," 103; 109–110; Makushin and Tribunskii, *Pavel Nikolaevich Miliukov: Trudy i dni*, 81.

252. Makushin and Tribunskii, *Pavel Nikolaevich Miliukov: Trudy i dni*, 82; V. G. Bukhert, "Osnovanie Istoricheskogo obshchestva pri Moskovskom universitete," S. O. Shmidt, ed., *Arkheograficheskii ezhegodnik za 2000 god* (Moscow: Nauka, 2001), 197, 200.

253. Makushin and Tribunskii, *Pavel Nikolaevich Miliukov: Trudy i dni*, 82–84.

254. Quoted in Bukhert, "Osnovanie Istoricheskogo obshchestva pri Moskovskom universitete," 201.

255. Kizevetter, *Na rubezhe dvukh stoletii*, 217–218.

256. Ibid., 67, 68.

257. Ibid., 69.

258. A. V. Makushin and P. A. Tribunskii, "Dnevnikovye zapisi M. S. Korelina o P. N. Miliukove," in S. O. Shmidt, ed., *Arkheograficheskii ezhegodnik za 2005 god* (Moscow: Nauka, 2007): 428.

259. Kizevetter, *Na rubezhe dvukh stoletii*, 218.

260. Sanders, "The Third Opponent," 69–97.

261. Miliukov, *Vospominaniia*, 99.

262. "Plan izdaniia sistematicheskogo obzora istoricheskoi literatury," ASpbII RAN, f. 219, op. 1, d. 25, l. 1.

263. *Spisok chlenov Istoricheskogo Obshchestva pri Imperatorskom S.-Peterburgskom universitete*, 1–6.

264. ASpbII RAN, f. 193, Presniakov A. E., op. 3, d. 2, Protokoly zasedanii predvaritel'nogo soveshchaniia po voprosu ob ustroistve Mezhdunarodnogo Istoricheskogo S'ezda v St. Petersburge v 1918, l. 21–22 ob.

265. "Spisok delegatov, komandirovannykh uchenymi uchrezhdeniiami i obshchestvami i pribyvshikh na predvaritel'noe Soveshchanie po ustroistvu IV mezhdunarodnogo istoricheskogo s'ezda," *Nauchnyi istoricheskii zhurnal*, no. 3 (1913): 11.

266. ASpbII RAN, f. 219, op. 1, d. 28, Otchët o sostoianii Istoricheskogo Obshchestva pri Imperatorskom St. Peterburgskom Universitete za 1913, l. 1.

267. "Protokoly Istoricheskogo Obshchestva pri Imperatorskom Moskovskom Universitete, Zasedanie 10 ianvaria 1916 g.," *Istoricheskie izvestiia, izdavaemye Istoricheskim obshchestvom pri Imperatorskom moskovskom Universitete*, no. 1 (1916): 191–194.

268. *Istoricheskie izvestiia*, no. 1, 2, 3–4 (1916); no. 1, 2 (1917).

269. Stephen Bann, *The Inventions of History: Essays on the Representation of the Past* (Manchester and New York: Manchester University Press, 1990), 14.

270. Gutnov, "O shkolakh v istoricheskoi nauke," 69. See also N. N. Alevras, "Problema liderstva v nauchnom soobshchestve istorikov XIX-nachala XX veka," in idem, ed., *Istorik v meniaiushchemsia prostranstve rossiiskoi kul'tury*, 117–126.

271. Sveshnikov, *Peterburgskaia shkola medievistov nachala XX veka*, 33–35, quoted in (and translated by) Nethercott, "Reevaluating Russian Historical Culture," 432.

3 From the University Societies to the "University Extension": Historians as Public Activists

THE PARTICIPATION OF Russian historians in voluntary educational enterprises in the late nineteenth century in many ways continued the tradition of combining scholarly and educational activity that had been established by eighteenth-century scholars. Yet voluntary educational activity now implied fulfillment of the scholar's public duty and was broadly perceived as oppositional, rather than complementary, to state educational policy. The distinctiveness of this situation was explained later by Miliukov, who played the leading role in public educational projects in the early 1890s:

> There can be no doubt that the political activity of such influential advisers of the two last tsars as K. P. Pobedonostsev and D. A. Tolstoi was intentionally aimed at holding back the enlightenment of Russian people. . . . The progressive part of the Russian cultured class vigorously opposed this anti-historical and, as could be predicted, dangerous position. Its work to raise the level of knowledge and consciousness among the Russian people proceeded in two directions in the 1880s. Those who were closer to the mass of the people organized a public campaign among them. Their activity concentrated around the progressive elements of the *zemstvo,* especially among the so-called "third element"—teachers, agronomists, statisticians, physicians—in brief, all the professional circles involved in culture. Yet in order to bring education to the masses they first had to complete their own education. This part of the task fell to the lot of the university intelligentsia. Of course, both detachments of "enlighteners" were in permanent contact and worked for the same aims.[1]

As Miliukov makes clear, the involvement of professionals became one of the main characteristics of voluntary educational activity from the 1880s. Miliukov and Kizevetter noted in their memoirs some turning points in the development of the *obshchestvennyi* educational movement, in particular, the launching of nongovernmental programs for people's literature in the 1880s, the public's involvement in the campaign against famine in 1891–1892, and the development of the self-education movement in the mid-1890s, which reached its zenith in the "university extension" project.

The Circle for People's Literature, "Priiutintsy," and the Concept of the Scholar's Cultural Mission

The *obshchestvenniki*-educators of the 1880s were certainly not the pioneers in the field of people's education, for numerous governmental and public bodies had been involved in such activity since the early 1860s. Joseph Bradley has provided an impressive picture of the earlier developments in this sphere in his study of the St. Petersburg Literacy Committee:

> During the Era of the Great Reforms, the ministries of education, finance, and war endorsed philanthropic efforts to found schools and libraries, organize public lectures and museums, and open Sunday schools. Ivan Turgenev and Lev Tolstoy, to cite only the most famous, were engaged in schemes to disseminate education. In addition to the St. Petersburg Literacy Committee, the Imperial Russian Technical Society, the Society to Disseminate Technical Knowledge, and the Moscow Pedagogical Society were all founded in the 1860s in order to spread education and facilitate the more productive use of human and material resources. All of these projects gained the support of a newly vigorous Russian press.[2]

The *Kulturträgers* of the 1880s, however, perceived people's education not as intermittent philanthropic activity but as a life-long vocation and strove to combine their professional aspirations with their progressive *obshchestvennyi* ideals. Writing in the capacity of both observer and historian, Miliukov ascribed special significance to the emergence of what he called the "St. Petersburg circle for people's literature of F. F. Oldenburg, D. I. Shakhovskoi, and N. A. Rubakin" in the mid-1880s.[3] This circle was organized by the students and graduates of St. Petersburg University belonging to the Students' Scientific-Literary Society (*Studencheskoe nauchno-literaturnoe obshchestvo pri St. Peterburgskom Universitete*),[4] which was established in 1882 as a loyal (*blagonamerennyi*) alternative to the radical students' revolutionary groups. The latter had been active at St. Petersburg University between 1878 and March 1881, when university life was characterized by sporadic outbursts of student unrest. At that time, recalled Platonov (then a young student), the political leaflets printed by the underground press could be read or bought in the *shinel'naia* (cloak-room), where they "lay in piles on the window-sills" and where "political conversations took place, gatherings (*skhodki*) were prepared, and agitators operated."[5] Writing in 1921, Platonov mentioned that he himself had experienced a certain temptation to join these revolutionary circles: "I did not like the gatherings (may their participants and supporters forgive me); to me, they seemed to be just chaotic assemblages intended to win over the vulgar masses. The propaganda in the cloak-room, in small circles, through lengthy and calm conversation, was another matter. If my personal life had not turned out the way it already had at that time, and if by nature I had been at all suited to party organizations, 'the cloakroom' could have won me over and drawn me in."[6] A similarly uneasy attraction to the revolutionary movement was also described by Ivan Grevs, eventually a well-known medievalist and one of the prominent members of the university's Historical Society. Grevs participated in revolutionary circles during the first year of his university studies; later, in 1918, he analyzed his complex feelings in the early 1880s when "a sense of civic duty" drew him "toward revolutionary politics," but his personal "temperament" fought against it.[7] The assassination of Alexander II on March 1, 1881, stripped the revolutionary circles of their allure in the eyes of such students as Platonov and Grevs; the latter described the "frightening emptiness" that prevailed after the assassination in the *Narodnaia volia* circles with which he was involved.[8] In the gloomy atmosphere of that time, the founders of the Students' Scientific-Literary Society, and Platonov among them, strove to turn students away from politics and send them back to their scholarly tasks.

The idea of establishing a students' society had first been suggested by Platonov's colleague at the university (*sokursnik*), Count Alexander Geiden, in May 1881. Initially only "philologists and some jurists" supported this initiative; then students from other faculties joined them, and when the society came into being on January 25, 1882, its membership included 117 students from all departments of the university.[9] The society's activity was coordinated by its scientific department consisting of twenty elected members from all academic units. Ironically, at that time the future bitter rivals, Chechulin and Lappo-Danilevskii, who represented the field of Russian history in this society in the first years of its existence, worked effectively and devotedly together.[10] The society's popularity among the students increased along with its membership; at one point it reached three hundred members. Among those who joined the society at that stage was Alexander Ul'ianov (Lenin's elder brother) and three other students who would later participate in the attempt to assassinate Alexander III on March 1, 1887.[11] In the fall of 1886, Ul'ianov—at that time a promising student of natural science—was even elected secretary of its scientific department, which proved to be fatal for the society. Although Ul'ianov quit his post about three months before the assassination attempt ("despite the fact that we [unaware of the reason] asked him not to leave," noted Grevs, who remembered him very well), the students' society was banned in the wake of its members' involvement in the attempt on the emperor's life.[12] During its five years of existence, however, the society provided a fertile ground for numerous emerging circles that focused on more specific scholarly subjects. Among the circles that appeared between 1884 and 1886 were the Spencer Circle (*Spenserovskii kruzhok*) devoted to psychology and sociology, which was inspired by the works of Herbert Spencer; a circle of Russian and Western literature whose central figure was a young poet Dmitrii Merezhkovskii; a circle for the scientific study of the Motherland (*otchiznovedenie*); a circle for examining the "university question" and higher education in Russia and abroad; and some other more or less significant students' projects. A circle for studying and publishing people's literature, organized by a group of members of the students' society known as the Oldenburg circle, emerged in the same way but eventually expanded its activity far beyond the university's walls.[13]

The Oldenburg circle consisted of the brothers Sergei and Fedor Oldenburg and their close friends Aleksandr Kornilov, Prince Dmitrii Shakhovskoi, Ivan Grevs, and Vladimir Vernadskii; they joined the Students' Scientific-Literary Society in its first year and quickly started to play a leading role.[14] As Grevs wrote later, the members of the Oldenburg circle considered the students' society as a most appropriate framework for developing students' independence, cooperation, and mutual aid through nonpolitical scholarly and educational activity.[15] Their opposition to involvement in politics did not mean that they rejected the notion of the scholar's public duty. According to Grevs, the slogan of the Oldenburg circle in the mid-1880s was "not to participate in the present political struggle" but "to prepare themselves for future public activity through serious scholarly work and the attentive study of life." Almost forty years later, he defined the circle's aims as instilling in its members a kind of "progressive idealism," which would liberate youth from "premature partisanship" and lead them, via devotion to scholarship and comradeship, to commitment to an ideology based on moral principles (*ideinost'*) and selflessness.[16] This perception of scholarship as a cultural mission assumed that scholarly knowledge should be used for ethical purposes. It was thus quite logical that the Oldenburg circle's next step was to launch an educational endeavor that gave them an opportunity to apply their academic knowledge to enlightening the people. In early 1884, Dmitrii Shakhovskoi suggested setting up a circle for studying and publishing people's literature, which began its activity in the same year.

The circle for people's literature started, like other student circles, with the study of a particular topic and presenting papers on its various aspects at weekly meetings. The circle's next step, however, was to produce catalogues of existing literature and publish bibliographic reviews in various journals; at some point the members of the circle even considered launching their own "people's journal" entitled *Gorod i derevnia* (*Town and Countryside*). They also adapted classical literature for less educated readers, selecting a remarkably varied list of works for this purpose. Thus, Alexandra Timofeeva-Oldenburg, Sergei Oldenburg's wife, "composed" an adapted version of Chateaubriand's *Les Martyrs*; her husband, who would later become a leading expert on Indian culture, translated Indian legends, while another member of the circle, the artist Ekaterina Zarudnaia, illustrated them. Anna Sirotkina, who eventually married Shakhovskoi, adapted Andersen's fairy tales; Sveshnikova modified Ostrovskii's plays and prepared a book on St. Francis of Assisi, while Staritskaia, Vernadskii's wife, produced a book based on Heinrich Zschokke's *Das Goldmacherdorf* (*The Goldmakers' Village*).[17] Members of the circle were particularly proud of women's participation in its activity. "The presence of women," wrote Grevs, "contributed to the feeling of plenitude and intimacy. An impeccably pure, idealistic, and serious attitude to women reigned among us. We enthusiastically supported the idea of complete equality between the sexes. There was no excessive 'feminism,' but women's influence became more and more perceptible."[18]

Eventually, the circle's members established connections with other groups and prominent figures involved in the field of people's education. The first were Lev Tolstoy and his closest collaborator at that time, Vladimir Chertkov. In the same year that the circle for people's literature was launched, Tolstoy and Chertkov founded the *Posrednik* (*Intermediary*) publishing house for people's literature in cooperation with a young publisher, Ivan Sytin.[19] Their aim was to create a special collection of literature for peasants that would combine excellent content with a low price. One of the first items accepted for publication, alongside stories by Tolstoy and Nikolai Leskov, was a book on Socrates written by the pedagogue and publicist Alexandra Kalmykova, since 1885 a member of the circle for people's literature.[20] Kalmykova had already written chapters on history and geography for the three-volume bibliographic handbook *Chto chitat' narodu?* (*What to Read to the People?*), compiled by the teachers of the famous Alchevskaia Sunday School for Women in Kharkov, where she had taught before moving to St. Petersburg, and was therefore able to make a significant contribution to the circle's work.[21]

The appearance of the new voluntary educational initiatives raised the question of how the "old" and "new" educational bodies could cooperate with each other. The Literacy Committees proved to be the most appropriate venues for such cooperation. The oldest among them were the Moscow Literacy Committee, which had been established in 1845 at the Moscow Agricultural Society, and the St. Petersburg Literacy Committee, founded by the Free Economic Society in 1861; subsequently, such committees appeared in Kharkov (1869), Tbilisi (1879), Kiev (1882), Tomsk (1882), and Samara (1886).[22] The participation of the new cohort of educational activists injected new life into these committees. "Beginning in the mid-1880s," wrote Bradley about the St. Petersburg Literacy Committee, "government officials and highly placed notables gave way to public figures (*obshchestvennye deiateli*); patrons of science gave way to public policy activists."[23] In 1890 Kalmykova assumed the post of secretary of the St. Petersburg Literacy Committee and in the late 1880s Nikolai Rubakin, a librarian, bibliographer, and writer associated with the populist movement, became an active member.[24] Starting with his first *Program on the Study of Literature for the People* (*Opyt programmy issledovaniia literatury dlia naroda*) published in 1889, Rubakin wrote widely on people's literature and on the people's reading habits and, in so doing, "was influential in shaping the attitudes of thousands of educators and schoolteachers toward books and proper reading for the lower classes."[25] In the early 1890s the Moscow Literacy Committee invited Kizevetter to head its historical commission; years later he wrote about the breadth of the committee's work:

> At the time when I was invited to participate in the Committee's works, its activity extended over the whole of Russia. Village schools, libraries and reading-rooms in all regions of the Empire were connected in one way or another to the Committee which served them as an inexhaustible source of books and other aids. The Committee's annual critical surveys of recently published educational and popular scientific literature were also very useful for educators. Many Moscow pedagogues from different spheres of expertise took part in writing these surveys; the experts were divided into various commissions for that purpose. I was invited to head the historical commission and thus observed the Committee's work very closely. There were no political undercurrents or propaganda in this activity. It was purely cultural work, with an impressively enormous range of connections spread throughout the whole of Russia.[26]

The *obshchestvennost*'s "purely cultural work" was animated by a sense of moral obligation shared by all its participants. In some cases, as happened with the Oldenburg circle, this sense of obligation even became a dominant factor in its members' lives. Two of them, Dmitrii Shakhovskoi and Fedor Oldenburg, decided to relinquish the opportunity of an academic career and to become *zemstvo* educators. In 1885 Shakhovskoi assumed responsibility for *zemstvo* schools in Ves'egonsk uezd of Tverskaia gubernia; in 1887 Fedor Oldenburg started to teach in the Tver' *zemstvo*'s school for women teachers. Both of them, however, retained their connection with the circle of friends, which supported their decision.[27] At the same time, some female members of the circle started to work as teachers in St. Petersburg schools. One of them was Grevs's wife, who taught at a school attached to a cartridge factory (*patronnyi zavod*), where she also established a library intended for both children and adults.[28] Meanwhile, in early 1886 those members of the Oldenburg circle who had opted for an academic career (and eventually became eminent experts in their particular fields), namely, Sergei Oldenburg, Vernadskii, and Grevs, together with their wives, decided to strengthen their bonds by creating a new association that they called a fraternity (*bratstvo*). This association became known as the *Priiutinskoe bratstvo* after the name of the landed estate *Priutino* that the members of the *bratstvo* dreamt of buying together in order to turn this "piece of land and house" into the "shared spiritual motherland of all current and future members of the fraternity."[29] The replacement of the customary term "circle" by the more demanding designation *bratstvo* reflected its members' changing aspirations. In addition to pursuing certain concrete goals, they now aspired to live in accordance with the highest ethical principles through maintaining their friendly bonds.[30] "The *priiutintsy*," wrote G. M. Humburg, "embodied the best traditions of the liberal intelligentsia: commitment to truth, social equality, nonviolence, and the hope for political freedom to be achieved by patient labor on behalf of the people."[31]

In her study on the *Priiutinskoe bratstvo*, S. A. Eremeeva underlined the religious-like devotion in their concept of cultural mission, along with the importance that the initiators of the *bratstvo* ascribed to the ideal of a family-like union.[32] These two aspects of the *priiutintsy*'s perception of their association contributed to the sense of moral perfection to which they aspired. However, these idealist inclinations and the moralizing stance seemed rather problematic from the point of view of the broader academic community. The *priiutintsy*'s missionary-like posture was interpreted as a claim to moral superiority and as a presumption to set themselves up as judges toward those who contributed less to the self-imposed *obshchestvennyi* tasks. Nadezhda Nikolaevna Platonova described this attitude most touchingly (and indignantly) in her diary in 1891:

> [November 2, 1891] Stepanov visited us some days ago, and we talked about the Grevs and Oldenburg circle, which Lappo-Danilevskii has apparently also joined. According to Stepanov, the members of this circle are so convinced that they are the vessels of truth, good, and beauty that they are condescending toward all other people and very easily and readily criticize their way of thinking and work. They are evidently unfavorably disposed toward us, that is to S[ergei] F[edorovich] and me; maybe they consider us backward and ignorant. Among others, they reproach S. F. for devoting little time to the university, but how did they come to this conclusion? S.F. always comes to his lectures well prepared; every student who is interested in his subject is always heartily welcomed and given advice, instructions, and books. His seminar on Kotoshikhin is very lively. It is the same with the [Higher Women's] Courses; only recently a student, Kolianovskaia, told me that no other course is as lively as his course in Russian history, and rarely has anything afforded me such pleasure as this response. If so, what is it about S.F.'s teaching that has aroused such reproach on the part of the circle? Is it because apart from the university and the courses, S.F. also works at the Educational Committee and the editorial board [of the journal of the Ministry of Education]? But surely no one can say that S.F. takes more work upon himself out of cupidity, that we live in luxury. All our *pia desideria* [pious longings] amount to attempts to make ends meet without counting every kopeck, so that S.F. would be able to replenish his library, and we could afford to go to the theater four or five times during the winter. Are these wishes illegitimate? Do we deserve condemnation for them? Perhaps, they think that I personally am a woman immersed in humdrum concerns without any *obshchestvennyi* ideals because I do not teach in school like Grevs's wife, who can't live without her classes? But she has only one child, while I have three, and will soon have a fourth. According to Stepanov, this circle has an unfavorable opinion of Kareev, but maintains relations with him because they consider him to be a useful instrument for attaining their goals.[33]

Platonova's attempt to defend her and her husband's way of life—which was perfectly decent and proper according to the standards of the academic community but did not meet the missionary demands of the Oldenburg circle—and her
highly emotional tone, indicate the importance of the moral code of *obshchestvennost'* for the academic historian's reputation. Moreover, as follows from this
and other comments by Platonova, the positive opinion of members of the Oldenburg circle, who were perceived as the bearers of that moral code, was very
important to her and her husband's self-esteem and psychological well-being.
This attitude is manifest in her description of a surprise visit Grevs made to their
home two years later, in January 1893:

> [January 13, 1893] Grevs visited us absolutely unexpectedly on January 5; he
> did not stay long. I showed him the children, and he talked with S. F. about
> the [Higher Women's] Courses and the university; it is interesting that he is
> far from being in complete agreement with the Committee of which he was a
> member. I can't put in words how much Grevs's visit pleased me. It gave me
> moral satisfaction in a very particular sense. Grevs, undoubtedly, is an honest,
> truth-seeking man. He had never visited us before his trip abroad, which I saw
> as a sign of his lack of appreciation and respect towards S. F. personally and
> towards his work. Of course, such an attitude hurt and even insulted us. The
> fact that he himself has now come to visit us means that he has recognized that
> S.F.'s work is worthy of respect. I may be exaggerating the significance of his
> visit, but I am still very pleased.[34]

Platonova's explanation makes it clear that the moral principles symbolized by
Grev's figure meant so much to her because they embodied the intelligentsia's
basic values, which were personal integrity and "truth seeking." This was the reason why one could not feel comfortable in the academic milieu without following
the moral code of *obshchestvennost'*. Furthermore, although the shared moral
norms did not prevent professional and political conflicts among university
historians (a hint regarding the tension between Platonov's and Grevs's groups
inside the university's historical society can be discerned in the way Kareev is
mentioned in Platonova's diary), it endowed their professional community with
a quality that Jane Burbank has defined as "moralized collectivism."[35] The mutually accepted moral code guided historians' public behavior in situations when
a choice between political loyalty, academic reputation, and the norms of the
intelligentsia's ethics became inevitable. Thus, Platonova noted in her diary that
her husband, loyal and cautious as he was, nevertheless ignored a warning not to
participate in a series of public lectures that the Ministry of Education was unfa-
vorably disposed to, because he found the minister's "wish" inappropriate from
the ethical point of view:

> [February 5, 1891] Three days ago S. F. received an official offer from Kak-
> hovskii to deliver public lectures on Russian history in Solianoi gorodok next

year.[36] When S. F. talked about this with Pomialovskii [Dean of the Faculty of History and Philology], the latter told him that since the committee at Solianoi gorodok included Trachevskii, whom the Minister regarded as a complete good-for-nothing, it would be "unorthodox" (*ne pravoslavno*) (i.e. undesirable from the Ministry's point of view) to deliver public lectures there. S. F. will not, of course, be guided by such considerations. He has not yet given his consent because in his opinion the composition of the committee is very bad. If he agrees to lecture, the subject will be "Russian society before the reform of Peter the Great."[37]

Paradoxically, Platonov's hesitation stemmed from the same circumstances that bothered the Minister, namely, the personal composition of "the committee"— more precisely, of the scholarly department of the Pedagogical Museum of Military-Educational Institutions created on the initiative of the museum's director, Major General V. P. Kakhovskii, in the 1890/1891 academic year.[38] However, as follows from Platonov's letters to Miliukov, he was concerned about the organizers' professionalism, not the political implications of being involved in this project: he had doubts about the success of an endeavor in which "Trachevskii and Mikhail Semevskii are taken for historians," and where, Platonov claimed, there were "neither connections to the university nor order or system."[39] Nevertheless, despite these doubts and the Minister's displeasure, Platonov agreed to deliver not one, but a series of six public lectures on pre-Petrine society; the first of them was scheduled for November 25, 1891.[40]

Another example of the historian's uneasy but resolute choice—this time between political loyalty, professional ethics, and a desire for a certain public status—might be found in the case of Platonov's critical review of Dmitrii Ilovaiskii's *History of Russia*. Ilovaiskii, the author of school textbooks from which generations of Russian pupils learned history, an "educated rodent" as Kliuchevskii dubbed him, labored for more than thirty years on his five-volume *History of Russia*. [41] Its first volume had appeared in 1876; in 1890 the third volume was issued and, although approved by the Ministry of Education, was severely criticized by academic historians who considered it as a mere compilation of Karamzin's and Solov'ev's works.[42] The first harsh reviews, written by Moscow historians P. V. Bezobrazov and V. N. Storozhev, appeared in *Russkoe obozrenie* and *Vestnik Evropy*; Ilovaiskii responded furiously, and in early 1891 the polemics around his book became the sensation of the day. It was in these circumstances that Platonov wrote his review, which was first presented at a meeting of the university's Historical Society on January 13, 1891. The event attracted unusual attention, about which Nadezhda Nikolaevna wrote anxiously: "The turnout was so large that there were not enough places for everyone, and masses of people were standing. . . . Thus, the die is cast: S. F. read his incisive and disapproving review of [Ilovaiskii's] book; an expanded version will be published in *ZhMNP*. . . . *Novosti* has already published a two-column report on Serezha's

Fig. 3.1 Sergei F. Platonov with his wife, Nadezhda N. Platonova (1915). Courtesy of the Department of Manuscripts, Russian National Library.

lecture in yesterday's issue (January 15), and today we read a telegram about it in *Russkie vedomosti*. What a scandal there is going to be!"⁴³ Platonov's senior colleagues were disturbed by the possible consequences of its publication. One of them, Zamyslovskii, tried to convince Platonov to refrain from publishing the review—his point was that since "Ilovaiskii was on good terms with the Minister of Education," the latter "might reprimand the journal" because of the review, and even "His Majesty (*gosudar'*) would be displeased."[44]

Platonov himself was very annoyed at being involved in an "all-Russian scandal" around Ilovaiskii's book and was especially disturbed by the press's distorted reports on his lecture. "The rumpus I've created with this book has resounded in *Russkie vedomosti*, which found nothing better to do than to clumsily shorten *Novosti's* idiotic report," he wrote to Miliukov on February 18. The latter, however, drew Platonov's attention to the positive impact of the press coverage of this "scandal" on Platonov's reputation among the Moscow public, where his critique of Ilovaiskii, Miliukov claimed, had very favorable repercussions (*progremelo na slavu*).[45] In the end, Platonov's critical review of Ilovaiskii's book was published in the third issue of the *Journal of the Ministry of Education* of 1891—but not before its editor-in-chief, Vasilevskii, had informed Platonov that the Minister of Education would not be especially irritated by its appearance.[46]

The Public Campaign Against Famine

The guiding role of the *obshchestvennost'*-approved moral code for historians' public behavior became especially evident in the course of the campaign against famine, which contemporaries considered as a turning point in the history of Russia's public life. The famine of 1891–1892 started in the Volga region and eventually spread to sixteen (according to some sources, eighteen or even twenty) gubernias with a population of about thirty-five million. It had an especially devastating impact on villages in the densely populated central Black Earth region, including the gubernias of Nizhnii Novgorod, Riazan', Tula, Kazan, Simbirsk, Saratov, Penza, Samara, and Tambov.[47] In view of the disaster, the government launched an extensive relief campaign during which nearly thirteen million people received some form of aid; this campaign included permission, and even support, for public initiatives in the struggle against famine.[48] As a response, wrote Kizevetter, "the call 'to the famine' resounded along the entire front of Russian *obshchestvennost'*. Local committees appeared everywhere; dining rooms were opened with private funds, while the intelligentsia rushed in droves to the famine-stricken regions in order to organize aid." The two years' work on the famine, Kizevetter believed, "had a profound impact on public sentiments." Miliukov drew a similar conclusion when he wrote in the British journal *The Athenaeum* about the rise in Russia's "social temperature" in 1896.[49]

Academic historians participated actively in this campaign, first and foremost by charging a fee for their public lectures and donating the entire income to the famine relief committees. St. Petersburg University launched a series of such lectures in the 1891–1892 academic year; the practical and, at the same time, highly humanitarian goal of these lectures meant that they were assessed less by strictly academic criteria than by their turnout and the money collected, while the lecturer's ability to attract a wide audience enhanced his public reputation. In this particular situation, lecturers chose topics that could appeal to the Petersburg public. Thus, Kareev's lecture "for the benefit of the starving" (*v pol'zu golodaiushchikh*), which was entitled "The Sources of Historical Change," attracted an audience of over two hundred, while privat-docent Iosif Senigov managed to raise 330 rubles from tickets to his lecture on "The Popular View of Ivan the Terrible."[50] However, this exposure to a broader audience and the attempt to increase its size raised the question of the ethical limits to the quest for public attention. Failure to collect a considerable sum of money was seen as regrettable ("Yesterday the economist Georgievskii delivered a lecture for the benefit of the starving and collected only 20 rubles," Platonova noted on February 28, 1892), but the use of such philanthropic lectures for self-advertisement was scorned as inappropriate despite their profitability. Thus, Senigov's colleagues criticized him for personally giving tickets to his lecture to the minister, his deputy, and other powerful figures, which they saw as an attempt to draw too much attention to a talk that they judged to be shallow and inept from the academic point of view.[51]

The famine relief campaign not only changed the character of the existing academic practice of public lectures but also opened new channels of communication among public activists and led to scholars' deeper involvement in expanding networks of *obshchestvennost'*. In one of her essays N. M. Pirumova described a meeting of *zemstvo* representatives and Moscow *obshchestvennye deiateli* with Lev Tolstoy in January 1892. The meeting was organized by Dmitrii Shakhovskoi and was attended, inter alia, by *priiutintsy* Vernadskii and Kornilov, who were active in the campaign.[52] Miliukov's biographers described another meeting of that kind which took place in January 1893, with thirty-five participants, including Vernadskii, Shakhovskoi, Miliukov, and Kornilov, as well as the editor of *Russkaia mysl'* Viktor Gol'tsov and the well-known economist Ivan Ianzhul, who contributed both academic and practical expertise: in 1882–1887 he had combined his position of professor at Moscow University with that of factory inspector of the Moscow district.

Ianzhul initiated a project intended to resolve fundraising problems and to lay the ground for expanding public educational activity in the future. He suggested the publication of a comprehensive bibliographical handbook in order to transfer profits from its sale to the starving gubernias.[53] The decision to publish such a book was made in January 1892; 130 scholars from various academic fields undertook to provide materials on 112 disciplines within three weeks. Ianzhul served as chief editor of this project, while Miliukov made his input as a coeditor and was responsible for the chapter on history. The book, entitled *Kniga o knigakh* (*The Book on Books*), appeared in May 1892 and was met with both approval and criticism: the rightist *Moskovskie vedomosti*, for example, responded with a review entitled "A Guide to Muddle-Headed Reading."[54] The very idea of this book, however, indicated the growing attention to "educating the educated." Its editors aimed to produce a complete guide intended to replace the regularly issued "systematic catalogues" for various academic disciplines, which would provide readers with comprehensive, almost encyclopedic, information. They therefore envisaged a kind of readership different from the target audience of previous educational initiatives. As Ianzhul noted in the editor's introduction, the guide was supposed to serve the interests of two groups of readers: those who had completed at least secondary school, and university students. The readers of the *Book on Books* were expected to belong to "educated society" rather than to the *narod*.

"Self-Education" as the Slogan of the Day

Indeed, in 1893–1894, when the famine was over and cultural work returned to being the main focus of public voluntary activity, its new addressee was conceived as a "person with serious intellectual interests taken by fate to the provincial backwoods, . . . pining from solitude," who would eagerly welcome the opportunity to improve his, or even more significant, her level of education.[55] This new vision made "self-education" (*samoobrazovanie*) the slogan of the day. In retrospect, Kizevetter described the emphasis on self-education as primarily a political phenomenon: "At that time the aspiration for active work, which awakened in society, pending the opportunity for politic activity, found an outlet in participation in various organizations assisting self-education."[56] Kareev, who started to write on self-education in 1894 and authored the entry on this topic in Brokgauz-Efron's widely used *Encyclopedic Dictionary* in 1900, linked this awareness of the need for self-education to social changes in Russian society—the appearance of a new "class of intelligent readers consisting of workers, master-craftsmen, salesmen, clerks, doctor's assistants and petty bureaucrats." [57] He also referred to the "young women" who had no opportunity to continue their formal education beyond the level of secondary school due to the scarcity of institutions of higher education for women in Russia.[58] Miliukov, whose contribution to the campaign for the development of self-education was especially significant, regarded it as a manifestation of the trend toward the democratization of education characteristic of modern culture throughout the world.[59] Despite their slightly different approaches, all these participants-cum-observers viewed the campaign for self-education as a progressive public movement.

In practice, the campaign was launched as an attempt to adopt the model of distance learning (known as "university extension") that had been in wide use in Britain and the United States since the 1870s and had already attracted the attention of Russian *kulturträgers* in the 1880s. [60] According to Grevs, the members of the Students' Scientific-Literary Society studied the experience of the Chautauqua College of Liberal Arts in organizing a "traveling university" in the United States and surveyed the beginning of the "university extension movement" in Britain.[61] Looking at the English and American experience through the prism of the contemporary Russian discussions on education, its Russian supporters focused primarily on the social aspect of this new trend. As Miliukov wrote in an article of 1896, the essence of the idea of distance learning lay in "bringing the university closer to the people and turning education, which had hitherto been acquired only by particular social groups, at a certain age, and primarily for professional goals, into the property of all the people and the task of an entire life, into its essential component, along with music and theater."[62]

The idea to apply the model of university extension in Russia was proposed by Elizaveta Orlova, who was a granddaughter of Mikhail Orlov (a hero of 1812 and one of the first Decembrists), great-granddaughter of the famous General Raevskii, and great-great-granddaughter of the renowned scientist and writer Mikhail Lomonosov. In the early 1890s Orlova was, according to Kizevetter, "a respected public activist (*obshchestvennaia deiatel'nitsa*)." Familiar with the British and American practice of university extension, she assumed that it would be even more appropriate for Russia with its vast territory and scarcity of institutions for higher education.[63] Orlova suggested this idea to Miliukov, and he undertook the organization of the project. Years later he described their first steps: "Elizaveta Nikolaevna Orlova might be regarded as a pioneer of this endeavor. She drew our attention to English examples of assistance to self-education through supervision of home reading, and university extension, which was a much more serious movement with a promising future. We adopted both ideas combined together. I devoted one of my summer vacations to a trip to England in order to become acquainted with the practical application of these ideas. I attended the summer conference of the university extension's professors and students in Cambridge and collected literature pertaining to the movement."[64] Miliukov published a series of articles on the topic between 1894 and 1902. They presented the results of his "field work" in Cambridge and of his examination of the available literature in order to find elements of the existing projects that could be adopted in Russia. In his first article, written in the wake of his trip to Cambridge and published in spring 1894 in the monthly *Mir Bozhii,* a literary and popular scientific journal for self-education established only two years before, Miliukov described the methods of popularizing scholarly knowledge used by the lecturers at the summer conference.[65] A more detailed article appeared in the influential populist journal *Russkoe bogatstvo* two years later, after the first attempts to realize the idea of distance learning in Russia had been undertaken.[66] In this article he drew attention to the main social actors behind the English and American university extension projects. He noted the joint efforts of society and university, supported by the county councils (which he translated as "zemstvo"), to launch such a project in Britain, and the role of the church in the United States, claiming that "the movement started [there] from the church as it started from the university in Britain." He also pointed to the growing interest in the project on the part of governmental bodies in both countries, citing in particular the Law on university extension that was adopted "unanimously, irrespective of the religious and political differences among the parties," by the state of New York in 1891 and was the first law "in the entire world" to recognize the "dissemination of university education" as part of the state system of education.[67] In his entry on university extension in the *Encyclopedic Dictionary* in 1902, Miliukov considered the pedagogical and didactic aspects of the English and American systems. He described the essence of distance learning as a mode of interpersonal communication based on students' supervision by university professors both through correspondence between them and lecture courses held close to the students' place of residence. The basic elements of this system, Miliukov wrote, were a syllabus, or a detailed description of each course (including a list of literature and questions for independent study), "classes" or tutorial meetings between the professor and his students after the lectures, and essays which students wrote on their own and sent to the professor for assessment. "'Syllabus,' 'class,' 'written essays' and permission to take an exam for those students who attended two-thirds of the lectures and completed two-thirds of the written exercises were the main traits that distinguished the lectures delivered in the framework of the university extension's project from ordinary public lectures," Miliukov concluded.[68] It was therefore decided by the initiators of the project in Russia to begin it by producing guides for home reading on a few subjects. "Moscow professors willingly joined our plan, and soon the first volume of the 'Programs for Home Reading' appeared, with a list of books and sets of test questions for students," Miliukov later wrote in his memoirs. At the same time, "V. I. Semevskii and N. A. Rubakin launched a similar publication project in St. Petersburg at the center for public lectures in Solianoi gorodok."[69]

However, there was a significant difference between the Anglo-American model of university extension and the way it was implemented in Russia. In both Britain and the United States, universities played the key role in developing this method of distance learning, while in Russia it was university professors acting as private persons and public activists, rather than the universities as educational institutions, who undertook the initiative. Any attempt to involve the *zemstva* could be seen as a violation of the latter's sphere of authority, and governmental support was out of the question. As a result, the problem of affiliation arose. "It was absolutely impossible to get permission to establish any kind of independent organization," Kizevetter recalled. Therefore, "there was only one possible solution: to become attached to an already existing institution, one that was solid enough, inspired no suspicion in the eyes of the authorities, and had a right to establish its own commissions with tasks of an educational nature."[70] According to these criteria, the Society for Dissemination of Technical Knowledge (*Obshchestvo rasprostraneniia tekhnicheskikh znanii* [ORTZ]) was chosen to serve as an umbrella organization in Moscow; the Russian Technical Society (*Russkoe tekhnicheskoe obshchestvo* [RTO]) played a similar role in St. Petersburg.[71]

ORTZ had been established in 1869 under the aegis of Grand Duke Aleksei Aleksandrovich with the aim of opening Sunday and evening schools for workers and their children and developing educational programs for technical and trade education in Russia and abroad, but it did not limit its activity to vocational education. From 1888 its educational department started to establish permanent commissions of teachers in various subjects, including a commission of history teachers, which from 1892 was headed by Pavel Vinogradov. The four-volume *Reader on the History of the Middle Ages*, which was produced on Vinogradov's initiative, was awarded a special prize by the Ministry of Education in 1895 and was widely used by history teachers.[72] Some years later, in 1898, the Moscow University Pedagogical Society was founded on the basis of ORTZ's educational department; Vinogradov, who was one of its founding members, was elected head of its council.[73] This particular direction of ORTZ's activity can explain why the initiators of the university extension project decided to approach ORTZ's educational department with their idea of founding a commission for organizing home reading. The first session of the new commission, which Kizevetter described as highly impressive, took place in April 1893:

> The organizational meeting of the newly established commission was convened in the spacious hall of the Polytechnic Museum. A brilliant array of participants attended the meeting. The most esteemed and energetic of Moscow's professors, those most responsive to public needs, were present: Miliukov went from one to the other, arousing their interest and attracting them to this initiative. There were Chuprov, Vinogradov, Veselovskii, Storozhenko, Umov, Mlodzeevskii, Tseraskii, almost all the young privat-docents, and many secondary school teachers. Miliukov and Orlova cochaired the meeting. It was decided unanimously to establish a real "university outside the university walls," that is, to develop programs of learning embracing the university curricula in all departments except medical sciences.[74]

Miliukov was chosen to head the new commission. When planning its future activity, the commission for home reading considered only one aspect of its target population—their level of knowledge—and ignored all social or gender limitations. "All the commission's instructions," wrote Kareev, "were written on the assumption that they would be used by three categories of people: (1) those who had no formal (*pravil'nyi*) secondary education, but were becoming accustomed to reading serious books; (2) those whose education was limited to secondary school only; (3) those who had completed a course at an institution for higher education, but wanted to refresh their memory of what they had learnt, to fill in the gaps, or to acquire new information in fields of scholarship previously unknown to them."[75] Miliukov described the potential participant in the project in less sociological and more anthropological terms. This would be a "person chained to an occupation or employment that does not satisfy his intellectual needs; a person who does not content himself with what he is told about a subject and desires to delve into it himself, but does not know, and does not have the opportunity to find out, how to do this."[76]

The first syllabi for home reading were published in 1894. They were devoted to six scholarly disciplines: physics and chemistry, biology, philosophy, law and economics, history, and literature. Later mathematics was added to the list. Each syllabus was designed for four years of study; Vinogradov was responsible for the history courses.[77] According to Miliukov's data, between 1895 and 1899, 1,473 people applied to the commission for home reading; by 1899 there were 585 active students, of whom 419 were in the first year, 128 were studying the materials of the second year (73 of whom had continued after finishing the first year), and 43 were in their third year (of whom 31 had successfully completed the first and second years of study). Only a few of the participants submitted written essays (8% in 1895, a percentage that doubled by 1899). Despite these modest numbers, the organizers of the program were pleased with its development.[78] Their optimism stemmed from two main reasons. The first was the readers' evident interest in the special book series named *Library for Self-Education* launched by the commission in cooperation with Sytin's publishing house. "Sytin published these books magnificently," Kizevetter recalled, "each volume had a pleasing stylish look, excellent paper, lilac-colored cardboard binding, an elegant format—all this attracted the reader by its external appearance alone."[79] These books, edited by the leading Moscow scholars, embodied the main principle that Sytin had pronounced at the beginning of his career as a publisher, namely, "the best content at the lowest price." Indeed, about 6,000 books were ordered by readers during the first four years of the commission's activity despite the high cost of postage.[80] As Miliukov noted in an article of 1896, the most popular fields were "the socio-juridical and philosophical sciences," followed by history.[81] The second, even more encouraging reason for the organizers' optimism was the success of the first lecture courses, which took place in the provincial city of Nizhnii Novgorod in late December 1894-January 1895.

The commission for home reading ascribed particular significance to lectures in the provincial cities since the lack of university affiliation prevented it from convening summer conferences like those that took place in British universities to mark the end of the year's university extension activity. The decision to hold the first lecture course in Nizhnii Novgorod was not made randomly, as Miliukov subsequently explained: "At that time public lectures in the provinces encountered all kinds of obstacles. We tried to overcome them. The first place chosen for the trial lectures (*dlia proby*) was Nizhnii Novgorod since there was a circle of local and exiled intelligentsia who could help us."[82] Miliukov's biographers add another important detail: the commission's idea of "guest lectures" was supported and even partly financed by the Teachers' Mutual Aid Society of the Nizhnii Novgorod gubernia.[83]

The "University Extension" Guest Lectures: Scholarly Status, Educational Goals, and Political Effects

The first two systematic courses (each consisting of six lectures) were delivered by Miliukov and a privat-docent of Moscow University, Ivan Ivanov, who wrote widely on the history of literature and theater (his master's dissertation was devoted to the political role of French theater in the eighteenth century) and was renowned for his lecturing abilities.[84] The topics that the Moscow lecturers chose for their courses were similar to the politically charged subjects that their St. Petersburg colleagues had presented during the famine-relief campaign. Ivanov, who was the first to lecture on December 30 and 31, 1894, and January 1, 1895, defined his topic as "The Enlightenment Movement of the Last Century" (*Prosvetitel'noe dvizhenie proshlogo veka*), focusing on intellectual life in France on the eve of the French Revolution. Miliukov, whose course took place on January 4–6, 1895, devoted five of his lectures to "Russian Public Movements of the Eighteenth and Nineteenth Centuries" (*Russkie obshchestvennye techeniia XVIII i XIX vv.*); the topic of his last, sixth lecture was "The Dissemination of University Education in England and the United States." The length of the courses was defined after careful examination of and comparison between the English and American models as presented by Miliukov:

> Cambridge adopts the position of serious, systematic classes according to the model of higher education. That is why it offers long lecture courses: a typical Cambridge course consists of twelve lectures. Oxford, on the contrary, tries to attract participants by the entertaining nature (*zanimatel'nost'*) of the courses and counts more on the curiosity than on the serious intentions of the audience. Until recently, it usually offered either short courses or single public lectures on topics of general interest. America has chosen the prudent golden mean in this regard. A typical course in Philadelphia or Chicago is made up of six lectures.[85]

Miliukov chose the American model for his own course, assuming that it would better suit the inclinations of the Russian public.[86]

Ivanov and Miliukov's courses took place just two months after the death of Alexander III, which, according to Miliukov, was perceived by *obshchestvennost'* as a new turning point: it seemed that "the heavy slab of stone that he had placed on Russian public life and culture had to shift."[87] Other contemporaries, however, described the atmosphere of transition from Alexander III's to Nikolai II's reign in more nuanced terms. "The mood in St. Petersburg is gloomy and anxious, there is a lot of whispering. His Majesty (*Gosudar'*) is seriously ill, he has a dangerous kidney disease and a profound nervous disorder," wrote Presniakov to his mother on September 15, 1894.[88] Indications of sympathy for the emperor became even stronger in his letter of October 29, 1894, some days after Alexander III's death: "Petersburg has fallen silent in mourning, waiting for the arrival of the sovereigns—the old one in the coffin and the new living one. In Moscow people are collecting money for a monument to Alexander III. Many are sincerely sorry for him."[89] Around the same time, on October 22, Platonova mentioned her husband's impression of what he saw as the excessively loyal (*vernopoddan-nicheskii*) character of the celebration of Nikolai II's accession at St. Petersburg University.[90] At some point, however, a distinction began to be made between sympathy for the deceased emperor as a man and the negative assessment of him as a ruler. "Now Petersburg is waiting for His Majesty's funeral. A lot of people pity him, but expect a turn for the better from the new tsar. Alexander III was good as a private person, but he was not cut out to be a ruler (*kak pravitel' nikuda ne godilsia*). Now everybody anticipates that the former people will be replaced by better ones," wrote Presniakov on October 31.[91] This optimistic note characterized both Presniakov's letters and Platonova's diary during November 1894. Nadezhda Nikolaevna described the rumors regarding the new tsar which were circulating among the capital's educated public and depicting the destined ruler as being strikingly different from Alexander III:

> [November 3, 1894] Surprisingly unexpected impressions are being received now about the personality of the new sovereign. Until now he seemed to lack character, but it now turns out that this apparent lack of personality might be explained by his perfect inscrutability. It is interesting that his responses to telegrams [of condolence], which have probably not been written by him but have undergone his censorship, are surprisingly good: brief, rich in content, and really intelligent. Grand Duke Konstantin Kostantinovich told the members of the Academy that His Majesty likes to speak and speaks very freely and easily. In addition, according to common opinion, His Majesty is a man of perfectly correct behavior and, finally, it is nice to know that among all the Grand Dukes he is closest to Konstantin Konstantinovich and Alexander Mikhailovich, who are both most decent and intelligent persons, and that his seemingly closest non-royal friend—Kochubei—is, without doubt, a decent man. Furthermore, there is a story (which seems to be nothing but a story) that when he was still the heir, His Majesty somehow listened to the lectures that Kliuchevskii read to Grand Duke Georgii in Abbas-Tuman [the Grand Duke's residence in Georgia], was very impressed by them, and conducted the-oretical discussions for nights on end. There are also some gratifying rumors about Alice, that she is undoubtedly from a good family, that her mother was a wonderful woman; Alice is said to be very well educated. She even attended

courses of the Red Cross in her motherland, people say that she is a keen philosopher (*bol'shaia filosofka*) and even writes philosophical essays of her own
(but the latter is probably just a fable); in light of all this, it is hoped that medical courses will be opened soon. Please God! In general, we are on the threshold of something new and, hopefully, something good.[92]

Not surprisingly, Nadezhda Nikolaevna Platonova's account of gossip about the
royal couple mostly reflected the ideal of a meaningful life which guided the *priiutintsy*, the Platonovs, Miliukovs, and many other academic families in their own
lives. Yet imagining the new tsar and his wife as embodying a successful combination of educated interests, devoted public service, and harmonious conjugal
relations also indicated the variety of hopes that emerged in the first months of the
new reign. A vague aspiration for the liberalization of public life was the common
denominator in the expectations for a "new and better" future that were expressed
in different ways. Thus, the "spirit of the new times" caused students of the Moscow
University to hiss Kliuchevskii off the university's pulpit when he delivered a panegyric lecture on Alexander III and led students of St. Petersburg and some other
universities to organize a petition for a change in the universities' statutes and for
expanding their autonomy.[93] The same "new trends" even caused the conservative
Minister of Justice, Nikolai Murav'ev, to speak of the national equality of all subjects of the empire and the necessity for the courts' independence in his speeches
of early 1895.[94] This period of liberal expectations reached an apogee on January
17, 1895, when representatives of *zemstva*, noble societies and urban Dumas presented the young tsar with their greetings in which they expressed their hopes
for political reforms. But such hopes were immediately dispelled by the tsar who,
in his response, defined them as "senseless dreams" (*bessmyslennye mechtaniia*).[95]
"His Majesty's rude and tactless speech made a strong impression. . . . Some representatives of the old noble gentry (*stolbovoe dvorianstvo*) say that they have never
experienced such an insult," wrote Presniakov some days later.[96]

Miliukov's and Ivanov's lectures in Nizhnii Novgorod took place in the short
span of time when liberal expectations were at their peak. This can probably
explain the distinct nature of the event, during which the politically laden topics
of the lectures were easily approved by the local governor, the heads of the local
commercial and *vsesoslovnyi* (open to all estates) clubs willingly provided their
premises for the lectures, and vice governor A. I. Chaikovskii (the brother of the
well-known composer) and the local bishop Aleksii attended the lectures as if
they were perfectly official events. By contrast, the teachers who were transported
en masse from the districts (uezdy) to Nizhnii Novgorod due to the support of
the local *zemstva*, came to the same lectures in expectation of what Miliukov
defined as "a public demonstration" (*obshchestvennaia demonstratsiia*).[97] The
lecturers, in their turn, tried to fill the "solid courses," fashioned on the chosen
American model, with politically evocative content. As a result, Ivanov's lectures

on eighteenth-century France established the link between the French Enlightenment and the revolution of 1789 and emphasized the necessity of educating the people (*narod*) in order to achieve civic freedom.[98] In his lectures Miliukov described how public movements in Russia had developed since the time of Catherine II; "the conclusion," he wrote in his memoirs, "followed logically by itself, without my having to emphasize the implications or depart from the ground of factual narrative."[99] His last talk, devoted to the history of the university extension movement in Britain and the United States, underlined its difference from the Russian situation where the movement was not supported by any governmental agency and depended only on the public's enthusiasm.[100]

The lectures apparently aroused a warm response from the local audience. Kizevetter, who lectured in Nizhnii Novgorod a year later, assessed the results of Ivanov's and Miliukov's lecture trip as "a huge success." He especially noted its broader inspiring effect: "The public flocked to the lectures. The lectures were followed by parties and banquets with visiting lecturers and a torrent of speeches; all of Nizhnii Novgorod's intelligentsia were roused and animated as if they had been sprinkled with the magical water of life."[101] Comments by those who attended the lectures suggest that it was a combination of the lecturers' scholarly status and their openly liberal stance that caused their success. "Never before had Moscow professors made such pronouncements at a public event, in the province, in the presence of young people, teachers, and students," wrote one of the participants.[102]

Yet, as Miliukov implies in his memoirs, his lecturing strategy was influenced by the audience's anticipations: in early 1895, he claimed, "a speaker who talked on the topic of 'public movements' could not fail to somehow reflect the general elated mood in his lectures."[103] The expression of progressive ideas in public lectures reinforced the lecturers' and their audience's sense of belonging to the intelligentsia as "the advanced part of the cultured class." Both Miliukov and Kizevetter also noted the impact this experience had on their own professional maturation. Kizevetter emphasized the numerous advantages of participating in the *obshchestvennye* educational enterprises for those who were at the beginning of their academic careers. The university youth of the 1890s, he claimed, had received an invaluable opportunity to practice teaching at university level and to systematize their knowledge through compiling the public courses' curricula and teaching aids. While participating in the activity of the Commission for Home Reading, "young armchair scholars" became acquainted with Russia's "inner life" and with people belonging to different social strata and thus expanded their horizons and enriched their own intellectual world. He also argued that voluntary educational practice contributed to the integration of young scholars into the academic community:

> The Commission for Home Reading became the focal point around which the majority of young scholars from different disciplines united into a friendly community through participation in lively and meaningful public activity.

How many people became acquainted and drew closer in the course of this joint work precisely during the meetings of this commission! Moreover, this joint work in the commission brought together these young scholars and prestigious professors. Here we met our teachers, so to say, on an equal footing, as collaborators in the common enterprise, and the closer we became in these circumstances, the easier our communication was.[104]

Nevertheless, the case of the university extension also demonstrated that this public educational activity, which was perceived by participants as valuable from the scholarly point of view, could be devastating to their careers. Thus, in February 1895, when the short period of liberal hopes had ended, Miliukov's leading role in organizing the Nizhnii Novgorod courses led to his dismissal from the university, a ban on his teaching anywhere in the Russian empire, and subsequent exile from Moscow to Riazan'.[105] At the same time, the response of the academic community to Miliukov's punishment revealed once again the prevalence of the intelligentsia's moral norms in the historians' code of professional behavior. The officially disgraced Miliukov was openly supported by his university colleagues, including those with whom he had recently quarreled: "V. I. Ger'e behaved like a hero in this affair, he even visited Miliukov," noted Platonova in her diary.[106] The Platonovs did not hesitate to show Miliukov's wife every possible hospitality when she came to St. Petersburg in order to plead for her husband. Platonov, despite his reputation as a "conservative," was convinced that to prevent such a prominent scholar (*krupnaia nauchnaia sila*) as Miliukov from teaching would cause a profound loss to Russian historical scholarship, and he did not hesitate to share his thoughts with his colleagues.[107] In Moscow the liberal intelligentsia's annual commemoration of the abolition of serfdom on February 19 turned into a celebration of Miliukov. In his speech in Miliukov's honor at this event, Kizevetter declared that an opportunity for an alternative career, one that was public, rather than strictly academic, had now opened for the historian. One such alternative was suggested to Miliukov by the liberal newspapers: "*Russkie vedomosti* asked me to become a regular contributor with a fixed monthly salary; Petersburg's *Mir Bozhii* offered to publish my lectures on the history of culture," he recalled.[108] Miliukov indeed accepted this option of becoming a journalist. In addition, however, he used his membership in the historical societies (OIDR and the Moscow Archeological Society) and the opportunity to join the gubernia scholarly archival commission of Riazan' in order to continue his scholarly work during his exile. Hence, despite the official deprivation of his university status, Miliukov continued to be a member of the professional community and was treated as such by his former colleagues. Already in August 1895 a privat-docent of Novorossiisk University, G. E. Afanas'ev, informed Miliukov that he had recommended his candidacy to the Department of History of the Sofia Higher School in Bulgaria. The support of such influential colleagues as Vasilevskii, Platonov, and the vice president of the Academy of Sciences, L. N. Maikov, enabled him to obtain the necessary permission. In February 1897 Miliukov left Riazan' and Russia for a professorship in Sofia.[109]

Furthermore, Miliukov's exile did not put an end either to the activity of the commission for home reading or to its lecture program. A well-known expert in chemistry, V. F. Lungin, became the commission's chair after Miliukov's resignation, and two years later another historian, Pavel Vinogradov, assumed this post.[110] When the first part of Miliukov's *Essays on the History of Russian Culture* appeared in 1896 under the aegis of *Mir Bozhii*, the commission added it to its reading list as a basic text on Russian history.[111] In 1896 Kizevetter delivered a new course of the university extension lectures in Nizhnii Novgorod, and he was then chosen to be the first head of the commission's lecture office, which was established to coordinate the commission's courses in the provincial towns. Later, Kizevetter characterized the lecture office's activity as "a lecture academy" which "traveled throughout the country and brought a strong breath of fresh air to provincial life."[112] This practice, in which liberal historians played a leading part, contributed to institutionalizing scholars' public activity.

Yet, the growing public involvement of academic historians and the apparent politicization of history led to a reaction not only from the government, but also from that part of the "cultured class" that did not identify itself with the liberal *obshchestvennost'*. From the mid-1890s, historical societies of a new kind began to appear. Founded by conservative aristocrats and scholars, they had a salient nationalist and monarchist ideological profile. Yet, while distancing themselves from the liberal intelligentsia, these associations propounded a vision of society as a sphere existing outside the realm of government, whose policy they criticized no less sharply than their liberal rivals. One of the first, and the most influential, of these new voluntary bodies was the Society of Zealots of Russian Historical Education in Memory of Alexander III (*Obshchestvo Revnitelei Russkogo Istorichesk-ogo Prosveshcheniia v Pamiat' Imperatora Aleksandra III*), which was established in 1895, during the ambiguous first months of the new reign. The activity of this historical society, whose foundation signified a distinctively new tendency in late imperial Russia's associational life, will be the focus of the following chapter.

Notes

1. Miliukov, *Vospominaniia*, 116.
2. Joseph Bradley, "The St. Petersburg Literacy Committee and Russian Education: Government Tutelage or Public Trust?" *The Russian Review* 71 no. 2, (2012): 268.
3. Ibid.
4. On the Students' Scientific-Literary Society, see E. G. Oldenburg, "Studencheskoe nauchno-literaturnoe obshchestvo pri S.-Peterburgskom Universitete," *Vestnik Leningradskogo*

Universiteta, no. 2 (1947), 145–155, especially 146–148; I. M. Grevs, "V gody iunosti. Za kul'turu. Iz universitetskikh let. Studencheskoe Nauchno-Literaturnoe Obshchestvo v Peterburge, 1880-e gody," *Byloe*, no. 12 (1918), 42–88; S. F. Platonov, "Neskol'ko vospominanii o studencheskikh godakh," *Dela i dni*, no. 2 (1921) ; 104–133; D. A. Zav'ialov, *Studencheskie nauchnye obshchestva Sankt-Peterburgskogo Universiteta v kontse XIX-nachale XX v.* (PhD diss., St. Petersburg University, 2006).

5. Platonov, "Neskol'ko vospominanii o studencheskikh godakh," 118.

6. Ibid., 118, 125.

7. Grevs, "V gody iunosti," 48.

8. Ibid., 47–48. Grevs mentioned, in particular, that he had been in touch with persons among whom Sergei Degaev (notorious for being a police double agent in the *Narodnaia Volia*) worked and that he had even met Degaev himself.

9. Platonov, "Neskol'ko vospominanii o studencheskikh godakh," 126; Oldenburg, "Studencheskoe nauchno-literaturnoe obshchestvo," 145.

10. Oldenburg, "Studencheskoe nauchno-literaturnoe obshchestvo," 149.

11. These were Vasilii Generalov, Pakhomii Andreiushkin, and Petr Shevyrev; they were executed together with Ul'ianov on May 8, 1887. See Grevs, "V gody iunosti," 85.

12. Zav'ialov, "Studencheskie nauchnye obshchestva Sankt-Peterburgskogo Universiteta"; Grevs, "V gody iunosti," 85.

13. I. M. Grevs, "Za kul'turu (Otryvok Vtoroi). Posle studenchestva. Nashe bratstvo," *Byloe*, no. 16 (1921): 159–160.

14. Oldenburg, "Studencheskoe nauchno-literaturnoe obshchestvo," 148.

15. Grevs, "V gody iunosti," 58.

16. Ibid., 78.

17. Grevs, " Za kul'turu (Otryvok Vtoroi)" 158.

18. Ibid., 151.

19. V. K. Lebedev, "Knigoizdatel'stvo 'Posrednik' i tsenzura (1885–1889)," *Russkaia literatura*, no.2 (1968), 163; Grevs, "Za kul'turu (Otryvok Vtoroi)," 158.

20. A. M. Kalmykova, *Grecheskii uchitel' Sokrat* (Moscow: Posrednik, 1886); Lebedev, "Knigoizdatel'stvo 'Posrednik' i tsenzura," 164; Brooks, *When Russia Learned to Read*, 337; Grevs, "Za kul'turu (Otryvok Vtoroi)," 155.

21. Kh. D. Alchevskaia et.al., eds., *Chto chitat' narodu? Kriticheskii ukazatel' knig dlia narodnogo i detskogo chteniia*, vol. 1–3 (St. Petersburg: Tipografiia tovarishchestva "Obshchestvennaia pol'za," 1884, 1887, 1906); for Alchevskaia and her school, see Brooks, *When Russia Learned to Read*, 324.

22. E. D. Dneprov, "Komitety i obshchestva gramotnosti," in *Bol'shaia Sovetskaia Entsiklopediia*, vol. 12 (Moscow: Izdatel'stvo "Sovetskaia Entsiklopediia," 1973), 515; for the Moscow Literacy Committee, see Bradley, *Voluntary Associations in Tsarist Russia*, 77–79.

23. Bradley, "The St. Petersburg Literacy Committee," 277.

24. Ibid., 279. On Rubakin, see Alfred Erich Senn, *Nicholas Rubakin: A Life for Books* (Newtonville, MA: Oriental Research Partners, 1977); A. N. Rubakin, *N.A. Rubakin: Lotsman knizhnogo moria* (Moscow: Molodaia gvardiia, 1967).

25. Brooks, *When Russia Learned to Read*, 326.

26. Kizevetter, *Na rubezhe dvukh stoletii*, 229.

27. V. V. Shelokhaev, "Dmitrii Ivanovich Shakhovskoi," *Otechestvennaia istoriia*, no. 5 (2001): 107–120; A. A. Zlatopol'skaia, "D. I. Shakhovskoi—istorik russkoi filosofii i obshchestvennoi mysli," in T. V. Artem'eva and T. V. Mikeshin, eds., *Filosofskii vek: Almanakh*, no. 26, *Istoriia idei v Rossii: Issledovaniia i materialy* (St. Petersburg: Sankt-Peterburgskii Tsentr Istorii Idei, 2004), 116; V. U. Slanevskii, "K istorii tverskoi uchitel'skoi shkoly P. P. Maksimovicha,"

Sovetskaia pedagogika, no. 4–5 (1946): 75–83, especially 79–82; idem, "Fedor Fedorovich Olden-burg," in V. V. Davydov, ed., *Rossiiskaia pedagogicheskaia entsiklopediia v 2-kh tomakh* (Moscow: Bol'shaia Rossiiskaia Entsiklopediia, 1999), 2: 83.

28. Grevs, " Za kul'turu (Otryvok Vtoroi)," 159.

29. I. M. Grevs to his friends, St. Petersburg, December 30, 1887, in O. B. Vakhromeeva, ed., *Avtobiograficheskoe i epistoliarnoe nasledie I. M. Grevsa* (St. Petersburg: St. Petersburgskii filial Arkhiva RAN, 2004), 212.

30. S. A. Eremeeva, "V prostranstve vospominanii: memuary chlenov Priiutinskogo brat-stva," in *Dialog so vremenem*, no. 20 (2007): 209–218, especially 210–212; see also, by the same author, "Priiutinskoe bratstvo," *Vysshee obrazovanie v Rossii*, no. 1 (2007): 157–166; *Priiutins-koe bratstvo kak fenomen intellektual'noi kul'tury Rossii poslednei treti XIX - pervoi poloviny XX veka* (PhD diss., Russian State University for the Humanities, Moscow, 2007). For a history of *Priiutinskoe bratsvo*, see G. V. Vernadskii, "Priiutinskoe bratstvo," *Novyi zhurnal*, no. 93 (1968): 147–171; no. 95 (1969): 202–215; no. 96 (1969): 153–171; no. 97 (1969): 218–237; F. F. Perchenko, A. B. Roginskii, and M. Iu. Sorokina, eds., "D. I. Shakhovskoi: Pis'ma o bratstve," *Zven'ia: Istoricheskii al'manakh*, no. 2 (1992): 174–318.

31. G. M. Hamburg, "A. S. Lappo-Danilevsky and the Writing of History in Late Imperial Russia," introduction to E. A. Rostovtsev, *A. S. Lappo-Danilevskii i peterburgskaia istoriches-kaia shkola* (Riazan': NRIID, 2004), 13.

32. Eremeeva, "V prostranstve vospominanii," 212, 216–217.

33. OR RNB, f. 585, op. 1, d. 5691, l. 67 ob.- 69 ob. Grigorii Kotoshikhin was the author of an important account of seventeenth-century Muscovite society.

34. OR RNB, f. 585, op. 1, d. 5692, l.12 ob.-13.

35. Jane Burbank, "Discipline and Punish in the Moscow Bar Association," *Russian Review*, 54 (January 1995): 53.

36. Solianoi gorodok was a St. Petersburg neighborhood where a number of museums were located, including the Pedagogical Museum of Military-Educational Institutions. From 1872 the Pedagogical Museum organized public lectures in various fields. See Ia. P. Barsu-kov, ed., *Pedagogicheskii muzei voenno-uchebnykh zavedenii, 1864–1914* (St. Petersburg, 1914); Z. A. Maksheev, *50-letie Pedagogicheskogo muzeia voenno-uchebnykh zavedenii: Kratkaia istoricheskaia zapiska* (St. Petersburg, 1914).

37. OR RNB, f. 585, op. 1, d. 5691, l. 41–41 ob.

38. "Publichnye lektsii po istorii v Peterburge," *Istoricheskoe obozrenie*, no. 1 (1890): 275–276; "Publichnye lektsii po istorii," ibid., no. 2 (1891): 187, no. 3 (1891): 261.

39. S. F. Platonov to P. N. Miliukov, St. Petersburg, January 24, 1891, in P. A. Tribunskii and V. A. Makushin, eds., *Akademik S. F. Platonov: Perepiska s istorikami* vol. 2, pt. 1, *Perepiska S. F. Platonova i P. N. Miliukova, 1886–1901* (Moscow: Feoriia, 2011), 75. Alexander Trachevskii (1838–1906) specialized in eighteenth- and nineteenth-century Russian history; Mikhail Semevskii (1837–1892), an older brother of Vasilii Semevskii, was a publisher and an editor of the journal *Russkaia starina*. See ibid., 216.

40. OR RNB, f. 585, op. 1, d. 5691, l. 72.

41. V. O. Kliuchevskii, "Istoriograficheskie etiudy: D. I. Ilovaiskii i I. E. Zabelin," in Kli-uchevskii, *Neopublikovannye proizvedeniia* (Moscow: Nauka, 1983), 117. Marina Tsvetaeva gave an unusual and extremely interesting portrait of Ilovaiskii in her autobiographical essay *Dom u starogo Pimena*. See M. I. Tsvetaeva, "Avtobiograficheskaia proza," in *Sobranie Sochinenii v 7 tomakh*, vol. 5, book 1 (Moscow: Terra—Knizhnaia lavka—RTR, 1997), 104–140.

42. D. I. Ilovaiskii, *Istoriia Rossii*, vol. 3, *Moskovskii tsarskii period* (Moscow: Tipografiia M.T. Volchaninova, 1890).

43. OR RNB, f. 585, op. 1, d. 5691, l. 43–43 ob.

44. Ibid., l. 43 ob.
45. S. F. Platonov to P. N. Miliukov, St. Petersburg, February 17, 1891; P. N. Miliukov to S. F. Platonov, Moscow, February 18 or 19 [*sic*], 1891, in *Perepiska S. F. Platonova i P. N. Miliukova*, 79–81.
46. OR RNB, f. 585, op. 1, d. 5691, l. 43 ob.
47. V. A. Obolenskii, "Vospominaniia o golodnom 1891 gode," *Sovremennye zapiski*, no. 7 (1921): 261–285; Richard G. Robbins, *Famine in Russia, 1891–1892: The Imperial Government Responds to a Crisis* (NY: Columbia University Press, 1975), especially 185–189; James Y. Simms, "'The Crop Failure of 1891: Soil Exhaustion, Technological Backwardness, and Russia's 'Agrarian Crisis,'" *Slavic Review* 41, no. 2 (1982): 236–250.
48. Simms, "The Crop Failure of 1891," 237.
49. Kizevetter, *Na rubezhe dvukh stoletii*, 186, 188, P. Milyoukov, "Russia," *The Athenaeum*, no. 1894, July 7 (1894): 22–24, cited in Makushin and Tribunskii, *Pavel Nikolaevich Miliukov*, 133, 212.
50. OR RNB, f. 585, op. 1, d. 5691, l. 84, 88 ob.
51. Ibid., l. 87 ob., 89 ob.
52. N. M. Pirumova, "L. N. Tolstoy na moskovskikh 'Besedakh' 90-kh godov," *Izvestiia AN SSSR, Seriia literatury i iazyka* 37, no. 4 (1978): 314–317.
53. Makushin and Tribunskii, *Pavel Nikolaevich Miliukov*, 125. For Ianzhul's biography and works, see Ia. Ia. Ianzhul, *Iz vospominanii i perepiski fabrichnogo inspektora pervogo prizyva* (St. Petersburg, 1907); idem, *Vospominaniia o perezhitom i videnom v 1864–1909 gg.*, v[ypuski] 1–2 (St. Petersburg: Elektro-Tipografiia N. Ia. Stoinovoi, 1910–1911).
54. I. I. Ianzhul with P. N. Miliukov, P. V. Preobrazhenskii, and L. Z. Morokhovets, eds., *Kniga o knigakh: Tolkovyi ukazatel' dlia vybora knig po vazhneishim otrasliam znanii (v pomoshch' golodaiushchim)*, pts. 1 and 2 (Moscow, 1892); Nespetsialist, "Rukovodstvo k bestolkovomu chteniiu," *Moskovskie vedomosti*, May 31, 1892.
55. Kizevetter, *Na rubezhe dvukh stoletii*, 287.
56. Ibid.
57. N. I. Kareev, *Pis'ma k uchashcheisia molodezhi o samoobrazovanii* (St. Petersburg, 1894).
58. N. I. Kareev, "Samoobrazovanie," in K. K. Arsen'ev and F. F. Petrushevskii, eds., *Entsiklopedicheskii slovar',* vol. 28a (St. Petersburg: Brokgauz-Efron, 1900), 220–223.
59. P. Miliukov, "University Extension," in K. K. Arsen'ev and F. F. Petrushevskii, eds., *Entsiklopedicheskii slovar',* vol. 34a (St. Petersburg: Brokgauz-Efron, 1902), 803–809.
60. P. Miliukov, "Rasprostranenie universitetskogo obrazovaniia v Anglii, Amerike i Rossii," *Russkoe bogatstvo*, no. 3 (1896): 81–83.
61. Grevs, "Za kul'turu (Otryvok Vtoroi)," 161–162.
62. Miliukov, "Rasprostranenie universitetskogo obrazovaniia," 79.
63. Kizevetter, *Na rubezhe dvukh stoletii*, 288.
64. Miliukov, *Vospominaniia*, 117.
65. P. Miliukov, "Letnii universitet v Anglii (iz poezdki v Kembridzh)," *Mir Bozhii*, no. 5 (May 1894): 194–206; for *Mir Bozhii*, see L. A. Skvortsova, "Mir Bozhii" in B. A. Bialik, *Literaturnyi protsess i russkaia zhurnalistika kontsa XIX - nachala XX veka. Sotsial-demokraticheskie i obshchedemokraticheskie izdaniia* (Moscow: Nauka, 1981), 136–197.
66. P. Miliukov, "Rasprostranenie universitetskogo obrazovaniia," 79–121. For *Russkoe bogatstvo*, see S. Ia. Makhonina, *Istoriia russkoi zhurnalistiki nachala XX veka* (Moscow: Nauka-Flinta, 2002), 7–99.
67. Miliukov, "Rasprostranenie universitetskogo obrazovaniia," 81–84, 88.
68. Miliukov, "University Extension," 803–809.
69. Miliukov, *Vospominaniia*, 117.

70. Kizevetter, *Na rubezhe dvukh stoletii*, 288.

71. For the Russian Technical Society, see Bradley, *Voluntary Associations in Tsarist Russia*, 169–210.

72. Antoshchenko, *Russkii liberal-anglofil Pavel Gavrilovich Vinogradov*, 74–75.

73. Ibid., 83; *Otchët o deiatel'nosti Pedagogicheskogo obshchestva, sostoiashchego pri imperatorskom Moskovskom universitete, za 1898/9 god (sushchestvovaniia obshchestva god pervyi)* (Moscow, 1899).

74. Kizevetter, *Na rubezhe dvukh stoletii*, 289–290.

75. Kareev, "Samoobrazovanie," 222.

76. Miliukov, "Rasprostranenie universitetskogo obrazovaniia," 108.

77. *Programmy domashnego chteniia na 1894–95 god* (Moscow: Tipograpfiia I. D. Sytina, 1894); *Otchët Komissii po organizatsii domashnego chteniia, sostoiashchei pri Uchebnom otdele Obshchestva rasprostraneniia tekhnicheskikh znanii za 1894 i 1895 g.* (Moscow, 1897), 3, 17; Kareev, "Samoobrazovanie," 222–223.

78. Miliukov, "University Extension," 807.

79. Kizevetter, *Na rubezhe dvukh stoletii*, 292.

80. Miliukov, "University Extension," 807–808.

81. The figures provided by Miliukov (probably relating to 1895) were as follows: sociojuridical sciences—118 subscribers; philosophy—110; history—74; literature—55; physics and chemistry—49; biology—29; and mathematics—8. See Miliukov, "Rasprostranenie universitetskogo obrazovaniia," 108.

82. Miliukov, *Vospominaniia*, 117.

83. Makushin and Tribunskii, *Pavel Nikolaevich Miliukov*, 139.

84. I. I. Ivanov, *Politicheskaia rol' frantsuzskogo teatra v sviazi s filosofiei XVIII veka* (Moscow: Universitetskaia tipografiia, 1895).

85. Miliukov, "Rasprostranenie universitetskogo obrazovaniia," 90–91.

86. Ibid., 102.

87. Miliukov, *Vospominaniia*, 117.

88. *Aleksandr Evgen'evich Presniakov: Pis'ma i dnevniki 1889–1927*, 145.

89. Ibid., 154.

90. OR RNB, f. 585, op. 1, d. 5692, l. 53.

91. *Aleksandr Evgen'evich Presniakov: Pis'ma i dnevniki 1889–1927*, 155.

92. OR RNB, f. 585, op. 1, d. 5692, l. 57 ob. - 58 ob. It is worth noting, however, that the empress's image as "a nurse" played a most negative role in the attitude to the Imperial family during World War I. See Boris Kolonitskii, *"Tragicheskaia erotika": Obrazy imperatorskoi sem'i v gody Pervoi mirovoi voiny* (Moscow: Novoe literaturnoe obozrenie, 2010), 246–289.

93. Kizevetter, *Na rubezhe dvukh stoletii*, 60; OR RNB, f. 585, op. 1, d. 5692, l. 66; *Aleksandr Evgen'evich Presniakov: Pis'ma i dnevniki 1889–1927*, 162–63.

94. Gurko, *Cherty i siluety proshlogo*, 92.

95. Nine *zemstva*—those of Tver', Tula, Ufa, Poltava, Tambov, Saratov, Kursk, Orel, and Chernigov gubernias—submitted their greetings along with moderate political demands; the action was initiated by the members of Tver' *zemstvo*. See N. M. Pirumova, *Zemskoe liberal'noe dvizhenie: sotsial'nye korni i evoliutsiia do nachala XX veka* (Moscow: Nauka, 1977), 158–61.

96. *Aleksandr Evgen'evich Presniakov: Pis'ma i dnevniki 1889–1927*, 170.

97. Miliukov, *Vospominaniia*, 117; A. V. Makushin and P. A. Tribunskii, "Iz istorii dvizheniia za rasprostranenie universitetskogo obrazovaniia v Rossii (Nizhegorodskie lektsii V. A. Goltseva, I. I. Ivanova, P. I. Miliukova i ikh posledstviia)," in M. D. Karpachev, ed., *Obshchestvennaia zhizn' Tsentral'nogo Chernozem'ia Rossii v XVII - nachale XX veka: Sbornik nauchnykh trudov* (Voronezh: Voronezhskii gosudarstvennyi universitet, 2002), 174–175.

98. Makushin and Tribunskii, "Iz istorii dvizheniia za rasprostranenie universitetskogo obrazovaniia v Rossii," 175.

99. Miliukov, *Vospominaniia*, 118.

100. Makushin and Tribunskii, "Iz istorii dvizheniia za rasprostranenie universitetskogo obrazovaniia v Rossii," 177.

101. Kizevetter, *Na rubezhe dvukh stoletii*, 300.

102. Quoted in Makushin and Tribunskii, *Pavel Nikolaevich Miliukov: Trudy i dni*, 142.

103. Miliukov, *Vospominaniia*, 118.

104. Kizevetter, *Na rubezhe dvukh stoletii*, 292–293.

105. Miliukov, *Vospominaniia*, 122.

106. OR RNB, f. 585, op. 1, d. 5692, l. 80 ob.

107. Ibid.

108. Miliukov, *Vospominaniia*, 121.

109. Makushin and Tribunskii, *Pavel Nikolaevich Miliukov: Trudy i dni*, 89, 164–174; Miliukov, *Vospominaniia*, 124–125.

110. Kizevetter, *Na rubezhe dvukh stoletii*, 294–296.

111. P. Miliukov, *Ocherki po istorii russkoi kul'tury, chast' 1, Izdanie redaktsii zhurnala "Mir Bozhii"* (St. Petersburg: Tipografiia I. N. Skorokhodova, 1896); *Programmy domashnego chteniia na 3-i god sistematicheskogo kursa* (Moskow: Tipografiia I. D. Sytina, 1897), XVI, 220–231.

112. Kizevetter, *Na rubezhe dvukh stoletii*, 303.

4 The Society of Zealots of Russian Historical Education: Conservative Activism and the Quest for Useful History

THE FOUNDERS OF the Society of Zealots of Russian Historical Education saw themselves as defenders of Russia's type of autocracy, embodied in the image and policies of Alexander III. They therefore launched a society intended to commemorate the late tsar, to promote knowledge about the historical significance of his reign, and to advance studies in national history "in the spirit of Russian principles (*v dukhe russkikh nachal*)."[1] Contrary to the existing historical associations, the Zealots subordinated their society's scholarly aims to its educational goals, conceiving the latter in overwhelmingly political terms. In accentuating their ideological motivation, the Zealots made explicit those political aspects of history that had already been implicit in the practice of other historical societies; moreover, the Zealots' choice of ideology as a common denominator had a decisive impact on the society's composition. The Society of Zealots did not grow "organically" from a friendly circle or the expanding academic community but was carefully constructed by a group of ideology-driven courtiers, high-ranking bureaucrats, and conservative historians with the express intention of combating the growing influence of liberal sentiments among the Russian public. In their political views the members of this group represented a new kind of ultranationalist conservatism, whose basic thrusts were activism, opposition to the hegemony of the liberal *obshchestvennost'* in public life, and a distinctive kind of populism.

Remaining active until 1918, the Zealots could boast of some remarkable achievements. Created in 1895 by a group of twelve people, the society numbered 976 members five years later, a figure that increased to 1,084 in the following year (1901). The Zealots founded local branches in major gubernias of the Russian empire, established a network of libraries extending from the Baltic region to Siberia, published their own historical journal and newsletters, and issued books and booklets devoted to various aspects of history and contemporary politics.[2] Yet while trying to create a new type of association, the founders of the Zealots utilized the experience of the existing societies, adopting some well-established elements of their organizational structures and patterns of functioning. By reproducing and modifying the existing modes of voluntary activity, the Zealots contributed to broadening and diversifying associational life. An examination of the Zealots' historical and political views and the inner workings of their society sheds light on a hitherto overlooked component in the mosaic of Russia's historical societies, and in the Russian associational world in general.

The Crusade Against the Literacy Committees and the Idea for a Society of Historical Education

The idea of establishing the Society of Zealots arose at the beginning of the new reign when the liberals' rising hopes for reforms were causing growing anxiety among those who proudly defined themselves as conservatives. Among the latter was the "architect" of the Society of Zealots, Count Arsenii Arkad'evich Golenishchev-Kutuzov (or just Kutuzov, as he signed his letters). Kutuzov was not a historian; he was a well-known poet, whose literary success had led to his being elected a corresponding member of the Department of Russian Language and Literature of the Academy of Sciences in 1891.[3] Yet this refined poet, whose lyrical texts were used by Musorgskii in his famous vocal cycles, was also a high-ranking state official. In 1889–1895 Kutuzov headed the Nobles' Land Bank and Peasants' Land Bank (*Gosudarstvennyi Dvorianskii zemel'nyi i Krest'ianskii pozemel'nyi Banki*), both of which were state bodies created in the 1880s for promoting state agrarian policy.[4] In 1895 he was appointed head of the private chancellery of Alexander III's widow, Maria Fedorovna, a post he held until his death in 1913. As a part and parcel of the conservative elite, Kutuzov represented that segment of the Russian "cultured class" that perceived the intellectual ferment of the winter of 1894–1895 as a revival of the "spirit of the seventies," with the expansion of the liberal voluntary educational projects as its most dangerous manifestation, and believed that they should be combated by means of alternative educational enterprises promoting the values of monarchism. Significantly, his original idea had been to propose the establishment of a new governmental publishing committee at the Main Administration for Printed Matter rather than a voluntary society. According to this initial plan, the committee would be responsible for issuing books, textbooks, and brochures "especially for the people" (*dlia naroda*) and would be able to create its own public network by holding essay competitions, awarding prizes for essays on specific topics, and collaborating with private persons, including students, on the publication of provincial newspapers.[5] Kutuzov shared this plan with Lev Tikhomirov, who belonged neither to his social circle nor to the capital's literary milieu but professed the same ideological stance.

A former leading figure in *Narodnaia Volia*, Tikhomirov had publicly renounced his revolutionary past in the late 1880s and become a devoted defender of the Russian monarchy, writing widely in the conservative Moscow newspapers

Moskovskie vedomosti and *Russkoe obozrenie* (*Russian Review*).[6] It was the liminal nature of those months that enabled the aristocrat Kutuzov and the former revolutionist Tikhomirov to become acquainted and form surprisingly close relations. Kutuzov first contacted Tikhomirov in November 1894 following the appearance of the latter's article "The Sign of the Time: The Bearer of the Ideal" (*Znamenie vremeni—Nositel' ideala*).[7] Written immediately after Alexander III's death, this article attracted the attention of the conservative part of the educated public with its eloquent historical and religious evaluation of Alexander III's reign, so different from the disapproving criticism of the liberal *obshchestevennost'*. Kutuzov's favorable response to the article, to which he attached a poem he had written on Alexander III, was not the only letter that Tikhomirov received at that time. "I have gotten a lot of flattering comments regarding 'Bearer of the Ideal,' including from such persons as Apol[lon] Maikov, Prince [N. V.] Shakhovskoi, and S[ergei] Rachinskii with whom I have not previously been acquainted," he noted in his dairy on November 13, 1894.[8] Even though Kutuzov's letter contained an embarrassing error—"not having the pleasure of being personally acquainted" with Tikhomirov, he addressed him as "Lev Nikolaevich" instead of "Lev Aleksandrovich"—Tikhomirov responded immediately and in the most effective way: he suggested including Kutuzov's poem in an anthology in memory of Alexander III that he was compiling on behalf of *Moskovskie vedomosti*. The anthology was produced in a very short time, during 18 working days from November 12 to December 5, 1894. On December 14 Tikhomirov already shared with his new correspondent his hopes that the anthology "would, for some time, be the best reference book on the biography and history of the deceased sovereign."[9]

Two weeks after this first promising collaboration, Kutuzov informed Tikhomirov of his proposal for a publishing committee, explaining the need for a broad positive governmental program of action that would complement the inevitable "prohibitive" steps:

> I feel strongly that the government must defend society and *especially the people* from the plague of *iskariotsvo* ["Iscariotism," i.e., betrayal], from all kinds of falsehood and hypocrisy. However, the preservation of the people's moral health is only one side of the coin. When destroying harmful food, the government must provide the people and society with healthy nutrition. Negative activity (censorship) without positive activity (providing the people with good books and journals) will always look odious and make the entire government look like a persecutor of enlightenment. If only the appropriate people could be convinced of this and such a committee would be established! Just think what a broad field of activity would be opened up! It takes one's breath away.[10]

Tikhomirov thought this was "an excellent idea" and suggested how it could be implemented, albeit in a slightly different way from Kutuzov's initial intention: he drew his attention to the St. Petersburg and Moscow Literacy Committees. Although Tikhomirov described these committees as agents of dangerous influences and as a "safe haven for people who should not have been allowed to come anywhere near people's education," he argued that they could be made into useful tools for the people's enlightenment if the proposed new body intervened in their activity and improved it. Yet, while supporting the idea of state intervention in the voluntary public educational movement, Tikhomirov also advised that the planned governmental committee itself should be of a semipublic character. He recommended including journalists and men of letters in the proposed body in order to prevent its bureaucratization: "Your Committee could serve as a center for rallying literature and journalism, but only on condition that, at least in the beginning, its work would be conducted by convinced and enthusiastic people, not just by bureaucrats (*chinovniki*). For this purpose the committee would need to periodically appoint members from among professional writers, and above all to stipulate that all writers and publishers would have the right to submit proposals to the committee and that these proposals would have to be considered."[11] In accordance with this advice, Kutuzov examined the publications of both the Literacy Committees and the *Posrednik* publishing house for people's literature and agreed that they "corrupted the people."[12] But he also criticized the government for "resting on its laurels" and thought that the problem could be solved by placing the literacy committees under the Ministry of Education's direct control; the proposal for establishing a new publishing committee was apparently set aside in view of the new task.[13]

The idea to modify the status of the literacy committees was far from new at this time. As Joseph Bradley has described in his study on the St. Petersburg Literacy Committee, as a result of the conservative politicians' growing anxiety regarding "the unsupervised (*bezkontrol'noe*) interference of ill-intentioned private persons and societies in public education," a special interagency conference (*osoboe mezhduvedomstvennoe soveshchanie*) was convened in summer 1894. The conference had already recommended "to transfer the literacy committees to the Ministry of Education and to rewrite their charters," and on February 12, 1895, the Minister of Internal Affairs, Ivan Durnovo, submitted a memorandum on the conference's findings to Nicholas II.[14] Kutuzov was aware of these official steps but did not rely on them. On February 20, 1895, he informed Tikhomirov of the forthcoming hearing on the literacy committees at the session of the Committee of Ministries and simultaneously expressed his concern about the results. "The local liberals," he claimed, "are intensifying their campaign in order to thwart this matter and to keep everything as it was, i.e., to continue the practice whereby committees publish books for the people *without supervision* and open schools with libraries without any governmental involvement."[15] Kutuzov took the main argument of the "liberals" quite seriously: "Messrs. liberals are frightening everybody by claiming that public opinion is allegedly very satisfied with the committees' activity and won't hear of their transfer to the Ministry of Education. Unfortunately, there is no newspaper in Petersburg except *Grazhdanin* that would dare to speak out for the right cause." He therefore tried to use his influence in the "corridors of power," that is, he wrote a memorandum on the issue and submitted it "to the appropriate persons" (*kuda sleduet*), as he was wont to say. At the same time, he asked Tikhomirov for help and, in so doing, implicitly confirmed and strengthened the notion of public opinion's crucial importance for the committees' fate:

> It is essential that the Moscow newspapers, *Vedomosti* and *Russkoe slovo*, should publish as soon as possible articles in support of the propitious idea of the need to establish governmental control over the activity of the committees. Surely the autocratic power, responsible before God and history for the moral and intellectual health of the people entrusted to its hands, cannot be indifferent to the way these self-styled volunteers are throwing their weight around in such an important matter as the dissemination of literacy and elementary education among the people. . . . Please, pay attention to today's articles in *Novoe vremia* and the articles that will appear tomorrow in *Grazhdanin*. You would do a truly good deed if you could assist in ensuring a favorable reaction to these articles in the Moscow press.[16]

Tikhomirov eagerly fulfilled the assignment: as Kizevetter wrote in his memoirs, "*Moskovskie vedomosti* pronounced their *caveant consules* and began a crusade against the literacy committee."[17] On March 6, 1895, a grateful Kutuzov informed Tikhomirov that the campaign he had aroused had been a success: "Many thanks to you for the articles in *Moskovskie vedomosti* and *Russkoe slovo*; they made the most fitting impression. I bought some copies and sent them to the appropriate persons." In the same letter Kutuzov wrote that the hearing on the literacy committees by the Committee of Ministers had been postponed yet again. However, his annoyance at this delay was mitigated by some "good news," to be kept in "strict confidence," that the Minister of Finance had promised him to allot an annual sum of 25,000–30,000 rubles for the publication of "appropriate" books for the people. The announcement was to be made at the next session of the Committee of Ministries devoted to this issue and was expected to play a decisive role in achieving supervision over the literacy committees' activities. In addition, Kutuzov also informed his Moscow ally of his new plan to found "a special society" in memory of Alexander III, intended to be "the center of active opposition to all present and future constitutionalists": "Finally, the most important point: I am currently writing the memorandum (*Zapiska*) and a draft of the statutes (*Ustav*) of the special society that I will write to you about in more detail later, asking for your advice and, subsequently, also your cooperation in Moscow. Now I will just say that I want to establish a Society in memory of the late sovereign with the aim of studying his reign in connection with the whole of Russian history."[18] The idea to establish the Society of Zealots emerged, therefore, in the context of the struggle against the educational activity of the liberal *obshchestvennost'* and the dissatisfaction with the sluggish pace of the state bureaucratic machinery in resolving what the conservative activist saw as the most burning problem. However, it seems that its appearance at this time was influenced by developments that Kutuzov had not informed Tikhomirov about. According to the diary of Grand Duke Konstantin Konstantinovich, on March 20, 1895, Nicholas II suggested that he become head of the St. Petersburg Literacy Committee. The Grand Duke, who was very enthusiastic about this project, proposed to transform the literacy committees into a Russian Society of Zealots of Peoples' Education (*Rossiiskoe obshchestvo revnitelei prosveshcheniia naroda*), but this plan was thwarted—as a result, he suspected, of Pobedonostsev's intrigues.[19] The striking similarity between the names of the society proposed by Konstantin Konstantinovich and the one that was promoted by Kutuzov suggest that the Grand Duke's project may have had an impact on Kutuzov's plans. In any event, the *Zapiska* that Kutuzov mentioned in his letter declared "the peaceful winning of minds and hearts by means of education" as the main goal of the society-in-the-making, and emphasized that this task might be better fulfilled by "social forces" (*obshchestvennye sily*) than by the state.[20] At the same time, the future Zealots' attitude to the literacy committees became more sophisticated. Although Kutuzov continued to urge that the literacy committees should be placed under governmental control, he and his new collaborators—the head of the Society of Lovers of Ancient Russian Literature and a member of the RIO, Count Sergei Sheremetev, the poet Apollon Maikov and the future Interior Minister, Dmitrii Sipiagin—closely scrutinized the committees' experience in promoting educational projects imbued with an ideological message. Instructive in this regard was Kutuzov's response to accusations made against the Orel Literacy Committee (*Komitet narodnykh chtenii*). This committee, which played a leading role in the city's cultural life, was used as a tribune for propagandist activity by an underground revolutionary group, the Party of the People's Rights (*Partiia "Narodnogo prava"*), whose "political headquarters," headed by veteran Populist Mark Natanson, were located in Orel.[21] The arrest of the group in 1894 led to the collective resignation of the committee's leaders and a temporary cessation of its activity.[22] Kutuzov saw this case as extremely useful for exerting pressure on the government and, to some extent, as a model for the planned Society of Zealots: "The information on the Orel Literacy Committee published by *Moskovskie vedomosti* is truly striking! I will disseminate it intensively in various spheres—perhaps this will wake them up! There are no doubts—the forces of darkness have begun to intensify their work, and they are conducting their activity in a very clever and effective way. This means only one thing—that we too should not be dreaming and should go in their footsteps, step by step."[23] Therefore, although regarding as a "great and important victory" the final decision to turn the St. Petersburg and Moscow Literacy Committees into societies of literacy at the Ministry of Education (which meant, as Kizevetter formulated it, their reorganization "into a kind of bureaucratic office"), the Zealots conceived their own society as "an absolutely private union (*chastnyi soiuz*)," an association of private people who had voluntarily come together in order to pursue certain educational goals.[24]

By defining historical education as their main field of activity, the founders of the society envisioned that it would undertake some of the tasks that the proposed governmental publishing committee had been intended to fulfill. At the same time, they deliberately appropriated the methods of work employed by the literacy committees and commissions for home reading. As a result, the declared goals of the Society of Zealots included "the collection of information and materials, which in future might be conducive to composing the history of the reign of Alexander III"; the publication of periodicals, essays, and anthologies on Russian history and related aspects of general history; the establishment of libraries, reading rooms, and storehouses for books; and the supply of educational institutions with the society's publications and other relevant literature.[25] The society's first task was planned to be the publication of programs for home reading on history, philosophy, and law, intended to serve as a "counterbalance" to what the Zealots called "the extremely absurd and tendentious programs" of the ORTZ's commission for home reading and of the scholarly committee of the Military-Educational Institutions in St. Petersburg. In May 1895, four months before the establishment of the Society of Zealots was officially announced, Kutuzov and Maikov were already considering the compilation of "a list of essays on Russian history" and attempting to locate existing materials appropriate for the aims of the society, including catalogues and reference books for students.[26] They thus emulated the methods of the liberal *obshchestvennost'* in order to combat the latter's growing influence.

Yet the Society of Zealots was not merely a negative copy of the liberal societies. The very idea to establish a historical society for the purposes of commemoration and historical education was essentially innovative. Furthermore, while advancing an ideologized conception of Russian historical development, the Zealots also stressed the "scientific" aspect of their planned activity in an attempt to endow their concept of "Russian historical education" with scholarly legitimacy. Thus, in a letter to Sheremetev in March 1895, when the society was still at the planning stage, Kutuzov explained that

> It should be proved, not through dialectical polemics but scientifically, on the basis of firm historical facts, like two times two is four, that cosmopolitism is hoisting the deceptive and sham flag of freedom that tempts the mob and whose illusory character is being exposed by the whole of contemporary

Europe, and that on the contrary, only the triumph and incarnation of the Russian state idea of autocracy, as the reign of Alexander III demonstrated brilliantly, guarantees to both the people in its entirety and to each individual person the greatest portion of freedom, tranquility, and well-being that is possible on earth.[27]

Drawing heavily on the ideas of contemporary conservative thinkers (first and foremost Tikhomirov and Pobedonostsev) and combining the concepts of science and politics with the notions of Russian tsarsdom and Orthodoxy, the Zealots introduced a new—reactionary, conservative but also essentially modern—perspective into contemporary historical discourse.

Politicizing History, Historicizing Politics

The Zealots' intention to base their society on a shared *Weltanschauung* can explain their effort to formulate a clear and coherent historical and ideological platform, which was presented in a number of the society's documents starting from its founding *Zapiska*. Unlike the usually formal *zapiski* that were duly submitted by organizers of voluntary associations as part of their authorization procedure, this text was conceived as a manifesto. All the society's cofounders gradually became involved in its preparation. Their number continued to grow in spring and summer 1895 and included, inter alia, the doyen of St. Petersburg historians, Bestuzhev-Riumin, and a rising star in the capital's conservative circles, Prince Esper Ukhtomskii.[28] The main ideas presented in this memorandum were further elaborated and negotiated in the society's documents and its everyday practice.

The Zealots' basic principle was conservatism, which they saw as first and foremost a "historical" worldview. Thus, in one of the society's unsigned and undated documents conservatism was defined as "love of the Motherland, not as it is conceived intellectually, but as it really is, as a result of its historical past, the character and religion of the people and other conditions of its progress." In this context progress entailed "the development of those truths that the country's state and popular life has at its disposal." For Russia, the document claimed, these were Orthodoxy and autocracy, while "the moral bond between the autocrat and his people" signified "the cultural expression of progress."[29]

Another basic principle was monarchism. Alexander III, whom the Zealots regarded as embodying the quintessence of Russian autocracy and to whom they ascribed unique historical significance, was compared in the society's *Zapiska* to Russia's most influential rulers, Ivan III and Peter the Great. If Ivan III had laid the foundations of the Russian autocracy and Peter the Great had brought Russia closer to the European Enlightenment, Alexander III had "inaugurated a period in which the national consciousness blossomed." Yet, while establishing a direct line of succession between Peter the Great and Alexander III, the memorandum also drew a line separating the thirteen-year reign of Alexander III from the "Petrine period" of Russian history, during which Russia had absorbed Western culture. Alexander had ended this period. "The Russian people had already internalized those principles of Western Enlightenment that they needed for the formation of the state," the memorandum maintained, "and now the Russian nation is entering world history and the family of other nations as an equal member, in full possession of its rights for independence and uniqueness." In order to strengthen Alexander III's image as a national monarch, the *Zapiska* assigned him the role of savior in the struggle against "hostile trends" that, it claimed, had defeated "the bearers of national consciousness" during the reign of his predecessor, Alexander II. [30] Consequently, in a language that combined the terminology of contemporaneous political discourse with images of faith and miracle, the *Zapiska* described Alexander III's ascension to the throne as a moment of salvation: "A dark night descended over Russia; in the deep darkness of ethical and intellectual turmoil the event of the First of March erupted. And it was precisely then, amidst the darkness and total despair, that like the peal of a mighty bell, there broke from the lips of Tsar Alexander III the word of a revived and resurrected Russian national consciousness calling to prayer and salvation." [31] It is significant that when presenting Alexander III as the incarnation of both Russian national identity and the Orthodox Righteous ruler, the *Zapiska* used the title of the Russian monarch in its Old Russian form, "tsar," instead of the modern official designation "emperor." Although these terms were synonymous in everyday discourse, their cultural and even juridical meanings were not identical. Since the assumption of the title of emperor by Peter the Great in 1721, the title "tsar" had remained in use as the official designation of the Russian monarch only with relation to his sovereignty over a certain part of the empire. Thus, the full title of the Russian monarch from 1815 to 1917 was abbreviated as: "Emperor and Autocrat of All-Russia, Tsar of Poland, Great Prince of Finland etc., etc., etc." [32] Therefore, from the juridical point of view, the title of tsar was subordinate to that of emperor and had a limited sphere of application and lesser significance. From the cultural point of view, however, the two titles had a very different connotation. In his study on the semantics of the monarch's titles, B. A. Uspenskii noted that Peter I's assumption of the title of emperor was an act of "cultural reorientation, not expansion of power," linked to the general course of Russia's Europeanization. [33] The memorandum's persistent use of the title "tsar" might therefore suggest an attempt at a reverse "cultural reorientation," intended to detach the image of the Russian monarch from the "Europeanized" context of recent historical developments and reconnect it with the "Russian" cultural and historical context.

Placing the image of Alexander III in an Old Russian context made it possible to exploit the huge emotional and political potential embedded in the concept of the Orthodox tsar-autocrat. Furthermore, by constantly invoking pre-Petrine cultural symbols alongside modern political terminology, the *Zapiska* could present the reign of Alexander III both as "a great miracle" and as a political success. His deep religious feelings ("he believed in the Justice of his power, in the Justice of the Russian national ideal") were depicted, therefore, as crucial both for overcoming "the twenty-five years of trouble which took possession of minds and hearts" and for "reviving authority in all branches of state government" for financial stabilization and for strengthening Russia's international position.[34] Similarly, the *Zapiska* portrayed Alexander III's popularity among the people both in emotional terms, as "the people's love" (*narodnaia liubov'*), and in quasi-scientific terms, as an expression of the deep connection between tsar and people, the two repositories of national consciousness (*natsional'noe samosoznanie*).

This attempt to redeem the "historical" image of tsardom placed the Zealots' conception of monarchy in the context of the "national myth" which, according to Richard Wortman, had developed during Alexander III's reign. Nonetheless, in their attempt to elaborate the image of the late tsar so soon after his death, the Zealots introduced new elements into the narrative structure of the national myth and accentuated its difference from the previously dominant doctrine of Official Nationality. As Wortman has explained, whereas the Official Nationality doctrine "had sought to establish a national grounding by adorning the European myth with national motifs derived from Russia's past," the national myth "was more sweeping in its repudiation of the heritage of the eighteenth and nineteenth centuries, delegitimizing the judicial institutions, the intelligentsia, and the dynamic of reform that had reached its culmination in the previous reign."[35] Yet despite its theme of return to the pre-Petrine past, the national myth was an essentially modern phenomenon, and the *Zapiska* strikingly reflected this element of neotraditionalism. In keeping with the revisionist idea of a popular autocracy "emancipated from legal formalities and the manipulations of the intelligentsia," as it was formulated by the main ideologists of conservatism in the 1880s–1890s,[36] the *Zapiska* suggested an innovative program for commemorating Alexander III, intended to adapt the national myth to the conditions of the new reign and new public sentiments. The modern character of the proposed program can be seen in its author's suggestion to employ scholarly expertise and contemporary modes of learning in order to reestablish the ideal of the monarchy as a godly community based on a direct bond between tsar and people.

The notion of such bonds was not confined to conservative thinkers but was characteristic of late nineteenth-century Russian populist social thought as a whole. Elise Kimerling Wirtschafter has observed that "in its radical, liberal and conservative forms, the populist orientation attempted to establish (or imagine) bonds across the breadth of society, either through the transmission of Enlightenment civilization to the people or through submersion in local folkways."[37] Indeed, both conservative populism and reactionary activism characterized the

Zealots' perception of history and their program of action. While ascribing to Alexander III a crucial role in molding Russian national identity, the memorandum argued that the further development of that identity depended on the intellectual and moral advance of the Russian nation, but it assigned to society, not to the state, the main agency in Russia's cultural progress. The task was depicted as being too elusive to be implemented by the state: "only social forces, which would voluntarily and consciously join together under the banner (*khorugv'*) of Russian national identity, would be able to fulfill this difficult, but urgent task, this sacred service," the memorandum asserted. The *Zapiska* depicted society as consisting of several components such as the "common people" (*narodnye massy*), the governing classes, educated society, and "the so-called intelligentsia," which were distinguished by their respective attitudes to Western influence. According to the *Zapiska*, the "common people" were the only sector of society that adhered (albeit emotionally, not rationally) to the idea of a strong and powerful Orthodox Russia, while the intelligentsia were a transmitter of foreign influence, who "have ceased to understand their own history and its sacred behests (*zavety*)." As a result, "the intelligentsia embarked upon their destructive labor of forcing alien ideals upon the Russian people, and alien ideas into state, social, and family life."[38]

This view of the intelligentsia as an antinational entity was by no means a new phenomenon. Boris I. Kolonitskii, who has written on the hostility to the intelligentsia (or "intelligentofobiia") among certain segments of Russian educated society, discerned such a perspective already in Katkov's writings of the late 1870s.[39] More important, for our particular case, was the blending of social, national, and religious elements characteristic of the Zealots' approach. Furthermore, the *Zapiska* rejected the assumption that the intelligentsia could be identified as consisting of educated society as a whole. Claiming that the former constituted only a small part of the latter, it suggested creating "an association of like-minded Russian people" from among that segment of educated society which distanced itself from the Westernized intelligentsia. While subscribing to an anti-intelligentsia stance, the *Zapiska* positioned the Zealots in a particular—right-wing, or *okhranitel'nyi*—political camp. It is therefore not surprising that Kutuzov and his collaborators did not use the word *obshchestvennost'*, associated with the liberal intelligentsia, but employed such terms as *obshchestvo* and *narod*, with *obshchestvo* signifying the field of struggle between contesting social forces over the soul of the *narod*. Yet, while presenting themselves as a vanguard in the battle against the Western-oriented intelligentsia, the Zealots appropriated from the latter both the notion of social activism and the insistence on the need for a particular moral code that would guide the behavior of the society's future members. The *Zapiska* called upon the Zealots to follow the principles of cooperative activity not only in public but also in private life, and compared the proposed association to a "harmonious family."[40] In this respect, therefore, the Zealots' conservative manifesto resembled the ideas of the liberal *priiutintsy*, who based their association on the model of the family. In so doing, it also imbued the *Zapiska*'s notion of "like-mindedness" with *ideinost'*, a term signifying a combination of ideological and moral principles. In the Zealots' case, however, the proposed moral code stemmed directly from the norms of Russian Orthodoxy, and not from their secularized version expressed in the intelligentsia's moral values. The founders of the society thus envisaged a version of "moralized collectivism" based on religious ethics alongside selected elements of the discourse of *obshchestvennost'*.[41]

Seeking "to make the Russian people aware rationally, not only emotionally (*razumom, a ne serdtsem*), of the greatness of the deceased Tsar," the Zealots outlined their program for shaping an inclusive mode of collective memory centered on the image of Tsar Alexander III. They thus placed themselves in a rather ambiguous position toward the new ruler, who was depicted mainly as the "crowned successor" of Alexander III, whose mission was merely "to continue His cause for the benefit of Russia and the whole of mankind."[42] The cover letter that Count Sheremetev sent to the tsar together with the *Zapiska* in October 1895 stated this attitude quite bluntly. "The Society of Zealots," Sheremetev informed Nicholas, "is an association of people who strongly believe that the path of the Emperor Alexander III is the only way of securing the happiness and welfare of Russia." Any deviation from this path in either foreign or domestic policy, he continued, "could have disastrous results and would deprive our Fatherland of the tranquility and the power that were its happy lot (*schastlivyi udel*) during the unforgettable reign of the Great and Wise Sovereign, Alexander III."[43] Their strict adherence to the monarchist outlook, therefore, led the founders of the society to assume the pose of mentors toward Alexander's successor, to whom they seemed to be dictating a certain line of behavior. This was by no means a sign of their lack of loyalty to the young ruler. Nicholas had read an early draft of the *Zapiska* in May 1895 and made some—essentially positive—remarks of his own. "There have been few such happy days in my life as yesterday, when Dmitrii Sergeevich [Sipiagin] showed me His Majesty's comments on my *Zapiska*," Kutuzov wrote to Sheremetev on May 12, 1895, noting in particular Nicholas's reference to the idea of establishing the society as a "sacred cause." Yet in addition to describing his joy, Kutuzov mentioned that Nicholas had agreed to the absolutely independent status of the society. This may have meant that the Zealots, contrary to the Russian Historical Society, were not promised the emperor's personal patronage.[44] Indeed, twelve years later Sheremetev wrote: "it is an indubitable fact that during all this time no question has been asked from above about the Society's activity!"[45] Although, as we shall see later, Sheremetev rather exaggerated the ruler's indifference to the Zealots, his personal feeling reflected a remarkable situation. The young monarch apparently kept his distance from the Zealots and their patronizing stance, which led to the latter's greater independence. Paradoxically, the society established by high-ranking bureaucrats and courtiers, who belonged to the very core of the Russian monarchy, thus contributed to enhancing the autonomous status of voluntary associations.

Formalized Equality and Hierarchy of Membership

The Zealots' documents, therefore, presented the society as a voluntary association of private people who shared a particular ideology, entailing certain moral obligations. This vision also assumed compliance with certain rules, as outlined in the society's statutes (*Ustav*). Kutuzov, who wrote the *Ustav* at the same time as the *Zapiska*, mentioned in his letters to Sheremetev that the statutes were modeled on those of existing learned societies such as the Free Economic Society, the Society of the Lovers of Russian Literature, and, especially, the Society of the Lovers of Ancient Literature, which Sheremetev himself had headed since 1888.[46] Yet as a result of the emphasis placed on the political significance of the Zealots' goals, their statutes were more elaborate than those of other associations, and thus more revealing.

The statutes envisaged the Society of Zealots as a voluntary but disciplined organization, based not only on its members' free desire to contribute, but also on solid financial foundations, sophisticated methods of control, and a carefully designed structure. The statutes imposed no explicit restrictions on membership. A potential member, it was implied, was supposed to share the society's aims, but there were no educational or professional requirements, nor any limitations based on social status, religion, nationality, or gender. On joining the society, members were eligible to take part in the meetings of the society, to participate in the elections to its offices, and to be informed of the state of its budget. Imposition of assignments on the society's members was subject to their agreement. The desire of local members of the society, and the agreement of the local authorities, were presented as preconditions for opening a local branch of the society. The statutes, therefore, invented its membership as a network of participation, cooperation, and feedback.[47]

Nonetheless, the same structure could easily be transformed from a channel of cooperation into a means of subordination and restraint: it was as divisive as it was cohesive, and as exclusive as it was inclusive. Thus, the lack of preliminary conditions for joining the society meant also a lack of clear-cut criteria for admitting new members, which in practice depended on the preferences of the society's managing body—its council. The members of the society were divided into "full members" (*deistvitel'nye chleny*), "corresponding members" (*chleny-sotrudniki*), and "honorary members" (*pochëtnye chleny*). At the top of the membership hierarchy were the founders (*uchrediteli*)—the twelve people who had founded the society, set up its council, and become the society's first full members. Other full members were to be elected by the council from among candidates proposed by the chairman or by three members of the council. The same principle of selection from above characterized the process of designating honorary members.

The different ranks of membership were expressed in different rights and duties. Only full members had the right to vote at the society's meetings, while corresponding members had the right to speak at the meetings but not to vote, and honorary members were to be "invited to participate in the society's general meetings, but remain free from any duty." Full members also had more opportunities for active participation: they could enroll into one of the society's three departments (the historical, publishing, or executive department). The full members could be given assignments by the council, such as managing libraries and reading rooms, organizing discussions and meetings, and issuing and distributing the society's publications. They were also granted the right "to make written proposals regarding what they thought was useful for the society."[48] In the case of corresponding members, the statutes did not designate any specific responsibilities or spheres of activity, while honorary members were not obliged to fulfill any duties at all. Despite these differences in rights and obligations, there was a noteworthy common denominator among all members: they did not have the right to elect the council of the society.

The council would determine its own composition (*sam obrazuet svoi sostav*)— in other words, it would be formed by the founders of the society. In the future, the statutes assumed rotation among the council members and the cooptation of new associates into this upper body. Every three years one member of the council, who would be chosen by drawing lots (*po zhrebiiu*), would be replaced by a new one, selected from the list of the full members. This procedure was characterized by meticulous attention to its formal aspects, on the one hand, and the deliberate exclusion of any element of competition between candidates, on the other. Not only did chance determine which member would be removed from the council, but there was only one candidate to replace him. This procedure may have been intended to reduce personal conflicts, painful choices, and possible arguments among the members, and, consequently, to strengthen the role of the council and its chairman. The council's preeminent role in determining the society's personal composition constituted only one aspect of its power. In practice, the statutes endowed this body with overarching authority in all spheres of the society's activity. Its fields of responsibility included establishing the society's new institutions and opening its new branches; controlling its financial operations; and even, if necessary, preparing suggestions for changing the statutes of the society. With such a wide scope of responsibilities, the council thus had the ability both to maintain the proposed procedural frameworks and, potentially, to change "the rules of the game." However, the statutes also stated that the council should inform the general meetings in advance of the most important matters "in order to utilize the personal opinions and diligence of the Society's members."[49] In some (mainly financial) cases, the general meeting had to approve the council's decisions.

The same interplay between authoritative and corporative components was reflected in the clauses relating to the functions of the chairman of the society and of the chairmen of the local branches and the departments. While giving them broad authority, the statutes also presented a detailed election procedure at the different levels based on the principles of election from among the members of the society and secret ballots but with different periods of tenure.[50] Since they were elected by their peers, chairmen had to be accountable to them, being obliged to report on their activities not only to the council of the society but also to a meeting of the members at the appropriate level.[51] Combined with the regular reports to the council by the secretary and treasurer, this type of accountability included elements of both bureaucratic subordination and peer control.

The conception of the Society of Zealots, as it emerges from the statutes, contained, therefore, an intrinsic contradiction. While the society was undoubtedly formed as a voluntary association, based on the notions of free will, electiveness, and accountability, the memorandum's demand for like-mindedness was translated in the statutes into principles of hierarchy and domination. The founders of the society concentrated in their hands considerable power and levers of influence over its members. This extensive authority was supposed to enable the council to fulfill its main obligation, formulated as "advancing the Society's aims in all relevant areas."[52] This vague definition was in striking contrast to the meticulous elaboration of its structure and procedures. The statutes were surprisingly reticent about the educational and historical aspects of the society's activity. Indeed, the design of the society seemed suited to a political organization no less than to an educational association. Its structure enabled it to serve any aim, while remaining under the strict control of its founders. Kutuzov had all the reasons to write proudly to Tikhomirov: "I am sending you these statutes, from which you will see that the founders have taken all necessary measures to make sure that this society will not repeat the eternal story of all the other societies, which in the beginning had first-class forces and the best goals, but, as a result of the penetration of undesirable elements, are now serving completely opposite goals (the Society of Lovers of Russian Literature, the Literacy Committees, etc.)."[53] The founders of the society demonstrated remarkable skill in using the considerable potential for manipulation provided by the society's statutes.

Constructing the Zealots: From Controlled Fellowship to Inclusive Participation

The society's membership policy was characterized by a combination of openness and selectivity, starting from the founders' efforts to select appropriate candidates for the society's council. These were invited on the basis of both ideological and pragmatic considerations—"like-mindedness" on the one hand, and their ability to contribute to the society (inter alia, because of the official positions they held) and to appeal to certain target groups, on the other. Thus, it was decided to include the editor of the *Tserkovnye vedomosti* (*Church News*), Archpriest (*protoierei*) Peter Smirnov, in the society's council: his presence, it was believed, would turn the society into a kind of spiritual focus for "nationally minded youth."[54] For the same reason, the founders also considered inviting the architect Nikolai Sultanov, whose participation, Kutuzov suggested, could serve "as a link to the world of artists," and Alexander Kireev, who, although described as "not especially gifted and not especially serious," was still regarded as "a representative of Slavophilism."[55] In the end, neither Sultanov nor Kireev was included in the group of the society's founders, while choosing candidates on the basis of their representativeness led to some surprising results. First, Sheremetev, and not Kutuzov, was elected chair of the society: as a personal friend of Alexander III, a scion of one of the most ancient Russian families, an amateur historian, and a respected member of some existing historical societies, Sheremetev was seen as more closely representing the values that the Zealots sought to promote.[56] Second, Tikhomirov was welcomed as a member of the society, but not as a member of its council: "It was hard to propose a former participant in the affair of March 1, 1881, as a guardian of our most cherished principles!" Sheremetev wrote years later, in 1913.[57]

On the basis of these combined criteria of representativeness, influence, and conservative views, the founders of the society constructed the council from people who could promote its agenda in the court and in certain academic circles. As a result, the list presented to the first meeting of the society comprised, alongside its original core group (namely, Sheremetev, Kutuzov, Sipiagin, Bestuzhev-Riumin, Ukhtomskii, Smirnov, and Apollon Maikov), also the vice-president of the Academy of Sciences, Leonid Maikov, who was an expert on Russian literature, and the head of the emperor's hunting office, Prince Dmitrii Golitsyn. Two other members of the council were Prince Sergei Gorchakov and Peter Gesse, both of whom, like Sipiagin, stood on the threshold of a promising court career. In 1895 Sipiagin was appointed head of His Majesty's Private Chancellery for the Receipt of Petitions and thus gained direct access to the emperor; in May 1896 Gorchakov became the court's Master of Ceremonies, while Gesse, who had served with Nicholas in the Preobrazhenskii regiment and, as Witte wrote in his memoirs, had taught the future emperor "the manual of arms," assumed in May 1896 post of the commandant of the emperor's palace and was thus responsible for the emperor's guard.[58] The last member of the council was its secretary Alexander Kartsov, who served at the Nobles' Land Bank and Peasants' Land Bank and eventually rose to become head of this governmental body.[59]

The Zealots had considered inviting Kliuchevskii, the most prominent Russian historian of the time, to join the society's council, but had relinquished the idea as "not very convenient *for the initial period*." Kliuchevskii, as Kutuzov wrote in April 1895, had "recently aroused too much talk," referring to the episode when Kliuchevskii had been hissed off the podium by Moscow University students because of his panegyric lectures on Alexander III. [60] Nadezhda Niko-laevna Platonova noted in her diary in December 1894 that "sixty-nine students and *magistranty* of Moscow University have been expelled because of the scandal over Kliuchevskii's lectures."[61] This incident was compounded by his behavior following Miliukov's dismissal from the university and exile in February 1895. On March 10, 1895, Presniakov wrote about the "sad news" from Moscow and connected Kliuchevskii to Miliukov's troubles, accusing him of failing to help his former student.[62] The sensitivity demonstrated by the Zealots in this case testi-fied not only to their concern with the image of the new society, but also to their attentiveness to public opinion.

Indeed, as demonstrated by earlier correspondence between Kutuzov and Tikhomirov, the organizers of the society were well aware of the importance of public opinion and how it was formed. They therefore made an attempt to place one of the council's members in a position that would enable him to influ-ence the views of the capital's public. In May 1895 Kutuzov endeavored to have a young and promising member of the society's council, Prince Esper Esperovich Ukhtomskii, appointed as editor of the popular *Sankt-Peterburgskie vedomosti*. Ukhtomskii, an official at the Department of Spiritual Affairs of Foreign Confes-sions in the Ministry of Interior, had accompanied the *Tsesarevich* Nicholas on his Grand Tour to the East in 1890–1891. He subsequently described this trip in a three-volume book, which was personally vetted by Nicholas II; the book started to appear in 1893 and was immediately translated into the main European lan-guages.[63] In the Zealots' correspondence of spring 1895, Ukhtomskii was referred to as "a very serious and resolute man, able to dedicate himself completely to the good cause." Kutuzov explained the rationale of his appointment in a letter to Sheremetev of May 12, 1895:

> I am making efforts to transfer the *Peterburgskie vedomosti* newspaper, which belongs to the Ministry of Education and whose current term of lease expires next December, to Prince Ukhtomskii, who has already expressed his willing-ness to take on this work. In this way we would have the ready-made organ that some of our co-members are thinking and talking about. Prince Ukhtom-skii is most appropriate for this purpose: he is full of energy, intelligent, well-educated, and wields a skillful pen. I am sure that he will be successful, and it will be very useful for our society to have at our disposal a newspaper where we can express our opinions on all topical issues. Of course, this newspaper will be the completely private, that is, personal undertaking of Prince Ukh-tomskii, for I still think that no society can have, and ours certainly should not have, its own newspaper, because collective management is unthinkable in newspapers and journals.[64]

The plan was successful: in October 1895 the Minister of Education Delianov informed Ukhtomskii of his forthcoming appointment as editor of

Sankt-Peterburgskie vedomosti with an annual subsidy of 35,000–45,000 rubles.[65] However, it soon turned out that Uktomskii was much more moderate in his political views than the rightist and nationalist majority of the society's council. By 1896 Kutuzov had already abandoned his hope of using Ukhtomskii's newspaper for the Zealots' purposes.[66] This did not mean, however, that the Zealots gave up the idea of mobilizing one of the popular newspapers for the society's aims.

Another opportunity occurred in 1909 when Tikhomirov assumed editorship of *Moskovskie vedomosti*.[67] The society's council celebrated this event with an open letter of congratulations to Tikhomirov and by publishing his programmatic letter to the newspaper's readers as a special booklet in the Zealots' book series.[68] Tikhomirov, for his part, published both the Zealots' letter and his official response in his newspaper and also transmitted his own confidential suggestions for possible cooperation between *Moskovskie vedomosti* and the society. Despite his proclaimed promise that the newspaper would not be connected with any "corporations, circles, or associations," Tikhomirov asked the council of the Zealots for help in "reviving the newspaper" and underlined the possible benefit his newspaper could bring. Claiming that "Russia has quite fallen out of the habit of reading *Moskovskie vedomosti*," he suggested that "the council and the society would help enormously if they could take every step to restore the newspaper to the public's memory, to spread the news that the unlucky era of its stagnation is over for ever, and that the newspaper has once again become a living organ of the Russian Cause."[69] Explaining how this could be done, Tikhomirov stressed the need for "names" that would indicate its spirit and direction: "To put it bluntly (*ne obinuias'*), even now, the very fact of my name means more than all the articles that have been published hitherto. The same applies to other NAMES. And the members of the council are a veritable bouquet of names that reveal a lot to the public."[70] He, therefore, asked the Zealots to send letters, essays, and articles to the newspaper. Although it is difficult to assess whether this appeal had any practical results, its very existence demonstrates both the Zealots' awareness of the role of publicity and their expectations regarding the different ways in which its members could contribute to the society's cause.

In order to construct the Society of Zealots as an effective but, at the same time, manageable body, its founders did not initially aspire to expand its membership, preferring to create a kind of cohesive fellowship. As Kutuzov explained to Tikhomirov in November 1895: "In the beginning, until a strong enough contingent of members is consolidated, any publicity regarding the initial activity or composition of the society, and, consequently, excessive dissemination of its statutes are absolutely undesirable."[71] At this stage the founders personally invited desirable candidates to join the Zealots. Thus, in November 1895 Sheremetev approached Viktor Vasnetsov, a well-known artist and a protagonist of a new Russian style in painting. Vasnetsov was expected to produce graphic images for the society's future publications, thereby giving visual form to the Zealots' ideas.[72] However, he was reluctant to accept the invitation. While emphasizing his deep sympathy with the aims of the Zealots and stressing that membership in such a society would be a great honor, Vasnetsov nevertheless declined Shereme- tev's offer on the pretext that "in view of the complex and difficult character" of his artistic work he would not have the time to take upon himself the duties of a full member and did not find it appropriate "to be a member of the Soci- ety in name only."[73] Since Vasnetsov repeated his refusal in his following letters, Sheremetev resorted to other means of persuasion, offering his help in arranging an audience for the artist with the Dowager Empress Maria Fedorovna, which would provide Vasnetsov with an opportunity to acquaint her with his plan for a monument to Alexander III.[74] In June 1898 Vasnetsov duly joined the Zealots as a corresponding member.[75] His next exchange of letters with Sheremetev was already concerned with illustrations for the Zealots' publications. Very much in line with the society's guiding principles, its council asked the artist to create an ex-libris that would serve as "a symbolic image of the main idea [of the soci- ety]: loyal service to the Holy Orthodox Faith, Russian nationality and the Tsar's autocratic power personified by the Tsar as the Church's loyal son." This official request was followed by a personal note from Sheremetev: "Please do this, dear Viktor Mikhailovich, and in so doing you will support a good cause which has the prospect of extensive development."[76] The artist fulfilled the task: the Zealots' publications bore their own graphic symbol.

The case of Vasnetsov reveals the possible benefits of membership in such an association as the Society of Zealots. Participation in the Zealots' project endowed Vasnetsov with Sheremetev's personal support. The powerful count not only introduced him to such a key figure as the empress, but also promoted Vastnetsov's artistic projects in the other governmental and public institutions he headed, the Committee of Guardianship of Russian Icon-painting (*Komitet popechitel'stva o russkoi ikonopisi*) and the Society of Lovers of Ancient Litera- ture. Later Sheremetev also helped him to obtain some attractive (and profitable) private commissions.[77]

The leaders of the society, in particular Sheremetev, made a special effort to attract historians to its ranks. On January 2, 1896, the Council elected a number of historians of varying status and educational background to full membership. These included Anatolii Aleksandrov, a privat-docent at Moscow University and the publisher of the journal *Russkoe obozrenie* and the newspaper *Russkoe slovo*, Petr Bartenev (previously mentioned in chapter 2), publisher of *Russkii arkhiv*, the brothers Alexander, Ivan, and Nikolai Barsukov, who were eminent archivists and genealogists, Dmitrii Ilovaiskii (whose works Platonov was so critical of), the historian of literature Ivan Khrushchov, and Nikolai Chechulin, a member of the circle of Russian historians, the University Historical Society, and the Russian

Historical Society, with whom we have already became acquainted in the previous chapters.[78] By that time Chechulin's situation at St. Petersburg University was far from promising. His lecturing début as a privat-docent in 1891 had been a failure: as Platonova wrote in her diary, "the general responses" assessed it as "weak, consisting of commonplaces, and unsuccessful."[79] Chechulin's almost scandalous doctoral defense in December 1896 (which has been examined in Thomas Sanders's article devoted specifically to that event) demonstrated not only the critical, but even the disparaging attitude to him on the part of his more successful colleagues.[80] In view of his problematic career prospects, Chechulin preferred to leave the university for the quieter but less prestigious work of librarian in the Imperial Public Library, where he started on January 1, 1896, from the very bottom of the service hierarchy, as a junior assistant of the librarian in the Department of History, a position he remained in for five years.[81] By joining the Zealots just one day after beginning to work at the Imperial Library, and by continuing to be a member of the RIO, Chechulin was able to maintain and eventually to develop his career as a historian despite having left the university.[82]

From this perspective, the case of the conservative Chechulin was similar to that of his liberal opponent Miliukov and the populist Semevskii, demonstrating that the historical societies of the late nineteenth century, irrespective of their specific goals, served as a venue where historians could realize their scholarly interests and ambitions. Moreover, in Chechulin's case membership in the Society of Zealots provided him with the opportunity to develop exclusive connections among the higher echelons of society that could to a certain extent compensate for his troubled relations within the university community. Chechulin himself referred to this possibility in a letter to his mother written in February 1897, when he was still trying to cope with the devastating effect of his doctoral dissertation defense. He began with an attempt to explain to his mother (and himself) the reasons for the harsh criticism that he regarded as personally insulting, but continued with a piece of information that, he thought, "would be flattering" to his mother's pride:

> There is the Society of Zealots of Russian Historical Education in memory of Alexander III in St. Petersburg; it consists of three departments. I have been elected deputy chair in one of them, where our dean is the chair, and the members consist of such persons as the secretary of the Empress M[aria] F[edorovna], the head of the commission for receipt of petitions sent to the highest authority, and the vice-president of the Academy of Sciences. Yet, for God's sake, please, dear mother, do not draw any special conclusions from this. Frankly speaking, I am very much afraid of such conclusions, but I thought I had no right to conceal from you the news which could make you happy.[83]

In practice, the expectations that Chechulin had been afraid of admitting even to himself were realized: his close relations with Sheremetev enabled him to advance his official career in the library and later in the Ministry of Education. Moreover, membership in the Society of Zealots could be attractive not only as an alternative career, but also as a valuable supplement to an official career. Thus, in December of the same year, 1896, none other than Ivan Pomialovskii, the Dean of the historical and philological faculty of St. Petersburg University whom Chechulin mentioned in his letter and who was also a member of the council of the Ministry of Education, a member of the educational committee of the Holy Synod, and a corresponding member of the Academy of Sciences, informed Sheremetev of his agreement to join the Zealots as a full member and to accept the post of chairman of the publishing department.[84] Both the number and the diversity of historians among the Zealots grew steadily in the following years. By 1900 they included such people as Sergei Tatishchev, a high-ranking official and court historian (and great-grandson of the author of the first *Russian History,* Vasilii Tatishchev, who has been discussed in chapter 1); Konstantin Gubastov, a diplomat (and later deputy foreign minister), genealogist, and member of various historical societies; Nikolai Selifontov, head of both Kostroma's scholarly archival commission and the Department of Civil and Spiritual Affairs of the State Council; Nikolai Dubrovin, a military historian, member of the Academy of Sciences and, from 1896, editor of the journal *Russkaia starina*; and Boris Turaev, a historian of the Ancient East and the founder of Egyptology in Russia.[85]

Yet, this wide range of historians did not satisfy the head of the society, Count Sheremetev. Although he was an amateur historian, Sheremetev adhered to an essentially modern perception of history as a field of expertise and a scholarly profession, and this attitude was shared by his collaborators. For example Gubastov, who was invited to be deputy head of the historical department, enthusiastically accepted this offer but felt obliged to warn the elected head, Selifontov, that he "had never dealt with history seriously" and therefore thought that he would "prove to be a very poor assistant."[86] Ascribing special importance to the historian's status in the academic community, Sheremetev strove to attract solid university scholars who were both respected in the academic world and shared the Zealots' political stance. It was rather hard, however, to find in the mostly liberal university milieu people who would be willing to subscribe to the Zealots' militant conservatism. After Bestuzhev-Riumin's death in early 1897, Sheremetev saw only one potential candidate who could replace him in the Society of Zealots: Sergei Fedorovich Platonov. Sheremetev explained his considerations in Platonov's favor in a note of December 1900, apparently addressed to a person very close to him:

> I would consider Platonov as a man with a name, and also not an extreme (*krainii*) person, cautious, even diplomatic with a tinge of the courtier (he reads to M[ikhail] A[leksandrovich]), and not without legitimate ambition. If he resolved [to join the society], regardless of *quoi qu'en dirait* [whatever

anyone might say] in the scholarly and university spheres, this would be an acquisition. . . . I would destine him for deputy head of the historical department and would go even further and immediately select such a man as Platonov to be a member of the council where Bestuzhev's place is vacant, and it is strange for a society of historical education to remain without a historian. Yet it is very hard for me to influence him [Platonov], despite the very best personal relations.[87]

Platonov did agree to join the society, and was, as planned, rapidly elected to its council on December 23, 1900, remaining in this post for the next three years.[88] In November 1903, however, he informed Sheremetev of his resignation from the council. Some hints in the distressed count's response—he mentioned, inter alia, "everyone's right to his own convictions and views regarding certain activity"— suggest that Platonov's decision stemmed from his unease in being identified with the rightist Zealots. [89] Indeed, in view of Platonov's sensitivity about his public reputation, it would probably have been hard for him to stay in a society whose members included such notorious ultra-right figures as Boris Iuzefovich and Vladimir Gringmut, absolutely odious from the *obshchestvennost'* perspective, and Ilovaiskii, who was an outcast from the university scholars' point of view. Yet Platonov's resignation did not mean his complete detachment from the society's activity. In 1910 Platonov's name appeared in the list of the members of the society's publishing department and, as Sheremetev's letters to him reveal, Platonov continued to advise the Zealots on their publishing endeavors.[90] Later, when he was director of the Women's Pedagogical Institute, Platonov took care to order the Zealots' anthology of historical materials, *Starina i novizna* (*Past and Present*), issued twice a year, for the institute's library, thereby contributing to the dissemination of the Zealots' publications.[91]

Nevertheless, the principle of selecting the society's members on an individual basis eventually confronted its founders with a serious dilemma, since its membership was growing too slowly to carry out their ambitious program. This seems to be the reason why, by the end of the first year of the society's existence, the Zealots started to talk about "recruiting members" (*verbovka chlenov*).[92] For this purpose, a number of local branches were established: in 1897 they appeared in Bezhetsk and Moscow, in 1898 in Podol'sk and Serpukhov, in 1899 in Tula and Vil'na, in 1900 in Tomsk and Tiflis, and in 1902 in Kiev.[93] The council of the society instructed the local branches "to expand the circle of persons participating in the Society by approaching those from whom assistance and sympathy regarding the society's aims could be expected."[94] It also provided the branches with considerable autonomy in the field of membership, duly confirming decisions made by the local bodies. The head of the Bezhetsk branch, for example, expressed gratitude to the council for unanimously electing all candidates recommended by him for admittance to full membership.[95] At some point Sheremetev even suggested to Gubastov, who since 1900 had been Russian minister-resident at the Papal Court in Rome, that he establish a branch of the society in Italy. "There are many Russian residents in Rome. Surely there must be some who sympathize with the Society of Zealots," Sheremetev wrote in December 1900. "It would be a good initiative to establish a 'world branch' abroad, but it could be possible only with your energy and support for the Russian cause (*sochuvstvie delu russkomu*)."[96] Although the society's documents do not reveal whether this idea was realized, some of its members served in official positions outside Russia, such as Archimandrite Climent and Dmitrii Berezhkov, who were located in Rome and in the Russian Church in Florence, respectively; Vladimir Maikov and Peter Maksimov of the Russian embassy in Constantinople; Count Sergei Golitsyn of the Russian embassy in Berlin; Archpriest Peter Maksimov of the Berlin Russian church; and Sergei Verigin, a priest of the Russian church in Menton, France.[97] Their membership was not merely formal: Kutuzov mentioned in his correspondence with Tikhomirov some "letters from abroad offering to contribute to the society's undertakings."[98]

At this stage the question of new members and their possible contribution began to be considered in terms of social groups rather than individuals. Thus, Pomialovskii, responding to the council's request, promised to make efforts to convince young scholars to participate in the Zealots' activity as corresponding members.[99] A new member of the society's council, the scholar and pedagogue Sergei Rachinskii, recommended focusing on educators and suggested exempting both "University and Ecclesiastical Academy lecturers" and school teachers from membership fees, explaining that the teachers' influence on the younger generation would enable them "to be of use to the society in very many ways."[100] At the same time, one of the society's provincial activists advised concentrating efforts on recruiting teachers of church parish schools (*tserkovno-prikhodskie shkoly*), but warned against teachers of *zemstvo* schools, whom he regarded as undesirable elements.[101] Special attention was paid to the clergy: in 1901 the church's official weekly, *Tserkovnye vedomosti*, published a call to take part in the society's activities.[102] The Zealots were evidently aware of the "social Christianity" movement which had been developing since the 1880s and was characterized by "a renewed emphasis on the church's teaching role (*uchitel'stvo*)."[103] By seeking to involve clergy in their activity, the Zealots gave them the opportunity to assume the position of social actors while remaining loyal servants of the church.

As a result, the society's membership gradually increased. If at the time of the first general meeting of the society on April 7, 1896, it numbered, in addition to the founders, 114 full members and 37 corresponding members, by the end of 1899 these figures had risen to 603 and 273 respectively. According to the last published statistics, in 1903 the society numbered 724 full members and 442 corresponding members.[104] The conservative Zealots, therefore, contributed to expanding and diversifying the public educational movement and in effect took part in challenging the state's dominance in the sphere of education.[105]

Even more significant than the steady rise in membership was the society's growing inclusiveness. The Society of Zealots comprised on an apparently equal footing the scions of the most noble families (the Sheremetevs, Golitsyns, Iusupovs, Viazemskiis), wealthy merchants and industrialists (Aleksei Bakhrushin and Ivan Rukavishnikov), along with provincial nobles, petty *chinovniki*, and clerics from all levels of the church hierarchy, including numerous village priests. It also admitted women to its ranks: in 1900 there were 153 women among the 946 registered Zealots.[106] Women participated in establishing and maintaining the society's libraries, were welcomed by its publishing department as translators, and were members of the society's commissions and committees. Nadezhda Sergeevna Timasheva, a corresponding member of the society, eventually became a member of the society's important committee responsible for publishing *Starina i novizna*.[107] Women—E. P. Sheremeteva, I. I. Sheremeteva, A. P. Sipiagina and A. S. Saburova—constituted half of the members of the special commission on preparing a catalogue of literature for the society's libraries, and E. P. Sheremeteva's major contribution to producing this catalogue was noted in particular.[108]

However, all the women who participated in the society's elected bodies were related to the Zealots' leading male members. Nor did all members of the society see such signs of gender equality as beneficial to the society. Thus, an organizer of its Moscow branch, Ivan Fedorovich Tiutchev (the son of the famous poet), mentioned in one of his letters that he did not rely too much on the society's "ladies' (*damskii*) element": women, he believed, were capable of deeds of pure charity but hardly suited to a task such as the Zealots were undertaking.[109] Perhaps because of such doubts, one of the Zealots' subsequent official documents stated that the society was interested in admitting new members of both sexes, without any limitations in regard to their status, but with concern for their ability to contribute.[110] Moreover, as follows from the rather cumbersome title of the manuscript submitted to the council of the society by a priest, Simeon Pospelov—"On the mission of the Russian woman in the field of public activity in the spirit of Orthodoxy" (*O missii russkoi zhenshchiny na pochve obshchestvennoi deiatel'nosti v dukhe pravoslavnykh nachal*)—the Zealots sought to reconcile women's new public role with the traditional status of women prescribed by the Orthodox church.[111] The society also demonstrated an opportunity for such reconciliation when in May 1897 it admitted a new corresponding member, mother-superior Dorofeia, prioress of the Bogoroditsk-Tikhvin convent, which had been established in the eighteenth century by Sheremetev's famous great-grandfather, Boris Petrovich Sheremetev, and thus enjoyed the Sheremetev family's special patronage.[112] It is also interesting that, despite this emphasis on the Russian and Orthodox character of the society, the Zealots were proud to admit the Emir of Bukhara and some of his high officials—all of them Muslims—to their ranks.[113]

What is most striking, however, is the fact that among the members of the society were people who might be seen as border-crossers. In addition to Tik-homirov, they included Rachinksii, a former university professor who had left Moscow to become the founder of a village school; Iosif Fudel', who had abandoned his promising career as a *chinovnik* in order to become a priest (at the time he joined the society he was serving in that capacity at the Moscow transit [*Butyr-skaia*] prison); and last but not least, Vladimir Gringmut, an ethnic German, converted Protestant, and future leader of the Black Hundreds.[114] Joining the Society of Zealots—and, in the cases of Rachinskii and Tikhomirov, attaining eminent status among its members—might be seen as part of a quest for a new identity instead of the one that they had so radically rejected. Does this mean that the Society of Zealots was one of the social institutions where another pattern of being an *obshchestvennyi deiatel'*—in the case of the Zealots, of an overwhelmingly conservative and nationalist thrust—was molded? Its rules, procedures, and membership composition suggest that this was indeed the case. However, the picture becomes more complicated if we shift the focus from the society's regulations and official procedures to its everyday practices and forms of sociability.

The Zealots in the Mirror of Sociability

Following Daniel Gordon's definition, the term sociability is employed here in the sense of "a mode of exchange free of the ritualistic constraints of corporate hierarchy" or "egalitarian interaction among individuals with different corporate standing," where egalitarianism is limited, however, to the sociable environment that produces it. Delineating sociability as "a system of coordination for people who had stepped out from the hierarchy of estates in search of less ontologically grounded forms of interaction," Gordon examined models of associational activity in eighteenth-century France.[115] This notion is no less useful, however, for understanding the specific nature of associational life in late nineteenth-century Russia.

The Zealots' particular way of "stepping out" from their official ranks and statuses in order to fulfill the ideal of being members of a "like-minded harmonious family" created a new form of sociability that was neither the "friendly comradeship" or "intimate seminar" model of the circles of historians nor the "research workshop" model of the university historical societies. The Zealots also made every effort to avoid what they saw as the suffocating elitism of the Imperial Russian Historical Society. Nonetheless, they did not become a kind of fraternity bound together, like the *Priiutinskoe bratstvo*, by emotional ties. In comparison with other historical societies, the relationships among the Zealots seemed quite formal. The society's documents demonstrated that it duly adhered to the principles of electiveness and accountability in its daily routine. Protocols and agendas (*povestki dnia*) of the council's meetings recorded regular elections of its full and corresponding members as well as heads of its departments and local branches. They also indicated that the meetings of the society, its departments, and local branches were held with sufficient frequency.[116] In due time (in November 1904), the council of the society reminded its members that the nine-year term of the society's chairman and his deputy had come to an end and hence new elections had to be arranged.[117]

Yet, the new formal connections between the members created by these practices were interwoven with preexisting or newly created bonds of kinship, friendship, or patronage. Despite (or, probably, because of) the formal election and rotation procedure, the same person—Count Sergei Dmitrievich Sheremetev—served as head of the society throughout its existence, while the core of the society's leadership consisted of people connected to him personally. The informal communications within this cliquish group underlay the Zealots' official deliberations. Thus, the formal election of new heads of the societies' departments in December 1901 was preceded by an exchange of letters between Sheremetev and his relative and friend Sipiagin on the one hand, and between Sheremetev and Platonov, on the other hand. "I propose Chechulin as head of the Historical Department," wrote Sheremetev to Sipiagin. "With regard to the head of the Publishing Department, it might be Khrushchov. In the land of the blind the one-eyed man is king (*na bezryb'e i rak ryba*), if we do not proceed the situation will be even worse. Khrushchov is free now, he is looking for a post (*ishchet dolzhnosti*). . . . He is very familiar with publishing matters. What do you say?"[118] The dialogue, according to Sipiagin's note, was supposed to be continued during a subsequent meeting between them, and we do not know what Sipiagin's answer was. However, Sheremetev discussed the same issue in a less informal tone, but with the same combination of intimacy and determination, in a letter to Platonov on November 23, 1901:

> I am writing you regarding the vacant position of the head of the Historical Department. It is very inconvenient for us to wait any longer, and it is desirable to finally nominate someone at the next meeting of the Council. That military person, whom we talked about earlier, is inappropriate for many reasons. I see no other solution than to ask N. D. Chechulin to rescue us and to agree to be head of the Historical Department, which would in all respects be desirable.
>
> Regarding the Publishing Department, I would suggest a person who, first, is free, second, has some experience, and third, is interested in demonstrating his activity.
>
> I think this combination at present would be the best way out of a complicated situation. I will name you this man when we meet and if you are surprised, my explanation may satisfy you at least partly. Of course, it is not what we need, but the times are difficult.[119]

Two days later, on November 25, 1901, the council of the society proposed a list of three candidates for election to each of the departments. Surprisingly, the list intended for the historical department originally included the names of Chechulin, Platonov, and the supervisor (*zaveduiushchii*) of the Tsarskoe Selo royal palaces Milii Milievich Anichkov. Platonov's name, however, was deleted from the final draft of the council's document, and the name of Prince M. S. Putiatin, an as yet undistinguished Guard officer, was inserted instead.[120] We can only surmise what considerations caused the appearance and disappearance of Platonov's name although the preceding exchange of letters points to some possible explanations. In any event, both Chechulin and Khrushchov were elected in December 1901 as heads of the corresponding departments via strictly formal procedures, each of them competing against two other candidates.[121]

Indeed, belonging to the voluntary Society of Zealots also meant entering into a sophisticated network of personal connections. Resembling, in this particular regard, the practice of the RIO, the everyday activity of the Society of Zealots provided myriad opportunities for seeking support and protection which extended far behind the boundaries of this particular association. Thus, in a letter to Sheremetev in July 1897 on the society's libraries, Ivan Barsukov included a request to help him obtain the post of supervisor of the Palace Archives: "Oh, if only you, Your Excellency, would help me gain a position that I have been waiting for so long! You would be doing a truly good deed, because you would thereby rescue me by extricating me from the *Ksenievskii* Institute, where I feel like a fish out of water, and where I have perforce found myself for a while."[122] Chechulin, during his ongoing correspondence with Sheremetev as editor of *Starina i novizna* and as head of the publishing and subsequently the historical department, asked for the powerful count's help in advancing his position in the Imperial Public Library. From 1901 Chechulin steadily climbed the library's ladder of ranks, eventually asking Sheremetev to help him obtain an appointment as its deputy director.[123] The head of the Moscow branch Tiutchev inserted into his correspondence a request for Sheremetev's help in obtaining his son's appointment to the post of land captain in the county where their family estate was located.[124] Yet appeals to the powerful count from his fellow Zealots stemmed not only from their private needs, but also from public interests. Thus, Tiutchev apologized for bothering Sheremetev with his son's matter and even suggested that he not deal with it "if its fulfillment may cause the slightest difficulty or inconvenience," but was extremely insistent in demanding Sheremetev's assistance in another mutual public project, namely, the establishment of a new institute for noble girls in Moscow.[125]

Furthermore, Sheremetev's readiness to provide his backing depended on his colleagues' ability to contribute to the public enterprise. Thus, he never rejected appeals from the diligent Chechulin, who served devotedly as head of the

society's historical department until 1915. Chechulin continued asking Sheremetev for his support even after he left this voluntary work in 1915 and became a
popechitel' of the Vil'na educational district.[126] In his last request of January 1917,
which proved to be too late in view of the imminent revolution, Chechulin even
asked Sheremetev's help in moving from Vil'na to Petrograd, also as a *popechitel'*,
but now of the capital's district.[127] Yet Sheremetev did not hesitate to use the same
instrument of personal influence in order to remove a no longer desirable member from his post, despite the lack of a formal procedure of enforced removal in
the society's statutes.[128] Thus, disappointed by Pomialovskii's poor performance
as head of the publishing department, Sheremetev sent him a personal letter on
October 27, 1900, formulated in terms of both private and public concern and
dictating clear-cut action:

> How is your health? I called on you, but did not find your house, everything
> has been rebuilt, and is unrecognizable.
> I would like to talk to you about the Publishing Department's activity,
> although I am ashamed to bother you. But since it is a public, and not a private
> matter, and in light of the necessity of the report to the council, I am forced
> to ask you a question and request that you answer it frankly: Will you find it
> possible, in view of your health circumstances, to continue as chairman of
> the Publishing Department? Or, maybe you would prefer to remain a mem-
> ber of the council, but to resign from your position as chairman and thereby
> enable the council to bring new forces and vigor to the society's publishing
> activity, which comprises the most important goal of our *obshchestvennaia
> deiatel'nost'*?
> Please help us, dear Ivan Vasil'evich, to find a way out of a difficult and, in
> a sense, crucial situation.[129]

Not surprisingly, on November 19, 1900, the council of the society already discussed Pomialovskii's letter informing them of his willingness to resign from
his position.[130] On December 23, 1900, his deputy Chechulin was elected to
replace him as head of the publishing department, a position he retained until
his election to the historical department a year later. In due course, the Zealots'
newsletter announced the council's consent to Pomialovskii's wish to resign and
expressed its gratitude to him for his work.[131]

Sheremetev insisted on the priority of public interests not only over private
matters but also over official duties of a purely ceremonial nature, as he put it
bluntly in a letter to none other than Kutuzov: "What you say in your letter, that
you do not take off your [civil servant's] uniform (*vits-mundir*) and are snowed
under with work (*zavalen delami*), made a sad impression on me and even worried me when I thought about the Society of Zealots and those interests which
in their essence are much more serious than most of the matters that require
a uniform."[132] When claiming, in the same letter, that "for me, the interests of

the Society of Zealots take precedence over all others," the conservative and authoritarian Sheremetev expressed the same perception of *obshchestvennaia deiatel'nost'* as a mission that guided the Zealots' liberal rivals and served as a moral yardstick for the moderate Platonov. Public and private were deeply interwoven in the Zealots' practice, while the hidden command structure, based on patronage connections, underlay the formal organizational edifice of a voluntary association.

Alongside its salient paternalistic tendency, the Zealots' mode of sociability was based on a distinct code of behavior, which can be described as noble etiquette animated by the language of mission and devotion.[133] This distinct pattern of behavior is reflected both in the minutest details of the society's daily routine and in the ways it dealt with internal conflicts. Hence, while having an opportunity, as formally equal members of a voluntary society, to communicate in what Gordon terms "a mode of exchange free of the ritualistic constraints of corporate hierarchy," the Zealots nonetheless adhered to the manners associated with the noble estate (*soslovie*). To some extent, this was entirely natural for a body that was conceived during Kutuzov's "soirées" on glamorous Admiralty Embankment, and whose offices and meetings were hosted in Count Sheremetev's palace on 34 Fontanka River Embankment—the famous *Fontannyi Dom*. Such an arrangement was anything but unique: one can recall Nabokov's colorful description of the Kadet party leadership's meetings in his father's fashionable home on Great Morskaya Street, and some recent studies have described the role of private salons as frameworks for the consolidation of political *kruzhki* and pre-party organizations of that time.[134] Although the location was chosen partly for reasons of expediency, it inevitably added a touch of conviviality to the supposedly formal events and helped to wrap even the fiercest arguments in the cloak of kindness and hospitality.

Nonetheless, the prevailing norms of noble etiquette in the Zealots' interpersonal relations did not have an exclusionary effect. The society's everyday activities provided numerous opportunities for its members of diverse social origins to become familiar with these norms, which, in turn, helped them to overcome invisible *soslovnye* barriers. The society's socialization function was reflected in a letter from Rachinskii concerning his former pupil, the peasant artist Nicholas Bogdanov-Bel'skii, who joined the Society of Zealots in 1898. Rachinskii expressed his cordial appreciation for Sheremetev's attention to the young man and, while mentioning gratefully Sheremetev's commission of Bogdanov-Bel'skii's paintings, also referred to the importance of admitting someone from his background into Sheremetev's close circle. "You understand the danger that lies in transferring a boy from the peasant environment to the artistic and fashionable milieu. But in this case, he is evidently helped by God's grace—among others, through you."[135]

Fig. 4.1 Guests of Count Sergei D. Sheremetev on the Ostaf, evo estate, July 7, 1908. Courtesy of the Department of Manuscripts, Russian National Library.

The society's adherence to the norms of noble etiquette made its style of interpersonal communication very different from both the friendly conviviality of the Petersburg circle of Russian historians and the almost monastic modesty of the Moscow historical associations. This style was not, however, unique to the Zealots. As indicated in recent research, an alternative standard of polite behavior had not yet been established among the Russian cultural elite even though it already included representatives of different *sosloviia*.[136] Therefore, mixed social groupings of literati, irrespective of their ideological affiliation, tended to follow the etiquette of noble behavior, which had a certain stabilizing and integrating effect. Probably the most paradoxical example of the predominance of this code of behavior was provided by Sheremetev in one of his last letters to Platonov written in February 1918. While describing the expropriation of his family property, the old count added ironically: "Lunacharskii's behavior toward me was quite proper in the matter of the requisition (*byl so mnoiu korrekten v dele rekvizitsii*). An aesthete (*estet*)!"[137]

Yet in the Zealots' case, the adherence to the nobility's patterns of behavior also affected the society's routine activities. Not only might a council session be canceled when, for example, one of its members, N. A. Zverev, informed his colleagues that he was "not going out" (*ne vyezzhaet*) on that day, or when it coincided with the Sheremetevs' day for receiving visitors, but the entire time-table of the society's sessions was adapted to the calendar of noble life.[138] The statutes assumed a long break in the Zealots' meetings in the period between March and October, when noble families habitually moved from the capital cities to their estates (*imeniia*). This did not mean that the society ceased its activity for six months every year since the stay in the *imenie* provided opportunities for engaging in other kinds of activities beneficial to the society, such as exploring the estates' archives and establishing public libraries in the estates or nearby villages. These undertakings expanded the scope of the Zealots' associational practice and also gave a leading role to those among them who were local landlords. In these cases, belonging to a voluntary society placed them in a position of cultural leadership and consequently strengthened their *soslovnyi* status.

Associationalism, Soslovnost', and Multifaceted Identities

The predominance of the noble code of behavior and the estate-oriented chrono-tope of the society's activities suggest that in the case of the Zealots a voluntary association provided an institutional framework not only for creating new social arrangements, but also for preserving the existing ones. If so, did the quest for new ways of restoring the nobility's cultural leadership in a period when its political influence and economic dominance were being seriously challenged mean also subscribing to the idea of *soslovnost'* as such, even though this notion was absent from the society's founding *Zapiska*? Some of the Zealots' practices confirm this assumption.

When the society launched its program of special awards for historical studies on Alexander III's reign in 1898, the list of recommended topics included "The Restoration and Strengthening of the Estate Principle in Russia's Governmental Practice (*Vosstanovlenie i ukreplenie soslovnogo nachala v gosudarstvennoi zhizni Rossii*)," with the recommendation that candidates write about changes in the local administrations and the introduction of *zemskie nachal'niki* (land captains) as well as the *krest'ianskoe delo* in 1881–1894 and the struggle against the 1891–1892 famine.[139] Concern with the particular *soslovnyi* dimension of contemporary public life can also be discerned in the society's publishing practice. While aiming its publications at two different audiences—"advanced readers" and the *narod*—it actually applied the latter term to literate peasants, or, as Khrushchov defined them, *sel'skie gramotniki*.[140] The Zealots thus transformed the ideologically constructed *narod* of the society's founding memorandum into a *soslovie*-bound peasantry. Moreover, the society's main organ, *Starina i novizna*, which was targeted at the "advanced readers," became a kind of tribune for presenting the nobility as a leading estate, since it endeavored to publish materials from the archives of individual noble families. A precedent was created when the collection of Rachinskii's family materials was published as a special supplement to *Starina i novizna* under the title *Tatevskii sbornik*.[141] Rachinskii drew the attention of the society's council to the potential that private archives offered the society, which, he claimed, "by its very composition included representatives of the families that have played a prominent role in Russia's political and intellectual life."[142]

Despite the neutrality of the term "family materials," the element of *soslovnost'* embedded in such publications was obvious both to the editors and readers of the anthology. While involving their potential readers in the process of collecting and publicizing their family archives, the Zealots created what Frederick C. Corney has defined as "the best case scenario" for forming a successful foundation tale when "the listener becomes the storyteller," retelling its major elements.[143] The society thus made a significant contribution to developing the nobility's collective memory. A survey of the first issues of *Starina i novizna* published in the society's *Newsletter* (*IOR*) stressed the special "national and educational" significance of publishing these documents, claiming that "in a society that has attained intellectual maturity, there is particular enthusiasm for documentary historical reading . . . since this is the means for acquiring the most independent and direct knowledge of the fate of its country." Such "living knowledge," the author claimed, "is the best condition for a strong, healthy conservatism in which the past and the future are combined with the present in one meaningful whole."[144] In the atmosphere of the late 1890s, such publications were interpreted as a political statement. Thus, a member of *Starina i novizna*'s editorial commission, Nikolai Platonovich Barsukov, wrote to Sheremetev in 1897, when the first issue of the anthology was published: "You are participating in a difficult endeavor. . . . It is difficult because it is uncertain and very unpopular. Just remember the enthusiasm and unanimity with which the noble way of life was destroyed forty years ago! . . . And, most important: how few remain of those who are noble in their feelings, principles, and actions (*Kak malo ostalos' dvorian po chuvstvam, pravilam, deistviiam*)." In addition to this transparent hint at the allegedly antinoble policy of Alexander II's early years, Barsukov also referred to internal disagreements about the anthology, noting that "despite Tikhomirov's assertion that *Starina i novizna* might be interesting only for specialists, it has already attracted, and will increasingly attract, the attention of people from all estates (*liudei vsekh soslovii*)." A year later Barsukov sent Sheremetev a list of provincial marshals of the nobility who had expressed their desire to join the Zealots; all of them, he believed, could be "useful and decent" members of the society.[145] Later, in 1902, when local branches of the society were established, a conference of marshals and delegates of the nobility from Tul'skaia gubernia decided to award the Tula branch of the Zealots with a 300-ruble grant to be used for "any of the society's needs."[146]

The Zealots' adherence to the principle of *soslovnost'* acquired even greater political significance when Sipiagin, one of the most active members of the society, became Minister of Interior in 1900. Sipiagin was identified with the *soslovie*-oriented tendency of governmental policy: Gurko characterized him in his well-known memoirs as "a representative of the old Russian gentry (*barstvo*)" who in the early twentieth century still viewed Russia as a patrimony (*votchina*) that "should be governed paternalistically (*otecheski*) by the Russian Tsar."[147] Kizevetter's sarcastic description of Sipiagin's policy may serve also as a succinct summary of the Zealots' views: "Assigning to the landowning nobility a privileged position in all fields of the state's life, and subjecting all other segments and groups of the population to the nobility as the ruling class, were now declared to be the historical distinctiveness of the Russian way of life. Efforts were made to present the policy of 'counter-reforms' as a return to the national traditions of pre-Petrine Moscow olden times (*starina*). . . . Liberal fantasies were proclaimed a leprosy brought from foreign lands, while retrograde politics was declared to be traditional Russian wisdom."[148] This, however, was *soslovnost'* in a cultural and social, rather than a legal sense, which might be seen as one of the signs of what Gregory Freeze defined as the reconceptualization of *sosloviia* as *kul'turno bytovye gruppy* or "social groups defined by their subculture and peculiar life styles."[149] This approach was clearly articulated by Sheremetev in a memorandum on establishing special institutes for noble girls (an additional project of his, not directly related to the Society of Zealots). While claiming that "it cannot be doubted that education as such should not be the privilege of any single estate (*soslovie*)," he also insisted on the necessity of preserving the estate principle (*soslovnoe nachalo*) in the school system.[150] Some years later, in 1905, Kutuzov put it even more plainly at the Peterhof Conference (*Petergofskoe Soveshchanie*) when he referred to the nobility and peasantry as *bytovye* rather than juridical groups, which "despite the laws that blur the borders dividing them, remain fully organized, united not only by their material interests, but also for the sake of more fundamental spiritual ideals."[151] "Soslovnost' as mentalité," as Freeze defined it, was intrinsic, therefore, to the Zealots' concepts and practice.[152]

Yet, the salient features of paternalism, patronage, and noble etiquette in the Zealots' practices and their attempts to strengthen *soslovnost'* did not make the society's egalitarian stance entirely devoid of meaning. Rather, there was constant tension between formalized equality and the *soslovie*-bound code of behavior, between the formal structure and personal ties, and, essentially, between old hereditary and new voluntary, ideology-driven frames of social grouping. There was also the possibility of choosing which norms or rules should be employed in each particular situation.

This freedom of choice and interpretation created some serious conflicts in the society. Thus, Tiutchev, whom Sheremetev had personally asked to organize the society's Moscow branch, was shocked to discover that some participants in

Fig. 4.2 Count Arsenii A.
Golenishchev-Kutuzov dressed
as a seventeenth-century
boiarin at a costume ball of
1903. *Albom kostiumirovannogo
bala v Zimnem dvortse v fevrale
1903 g., 21 geliograviura i 174
svetopechati/ Album du bal
costume au Palais d'hiver,
Féevrier 1903, 21 photogravures et
174 phototypies* (St. Petersburg:
Ekspeditsiia Zagotovleniia
gosudarstvennykh bumag, 1904).

the founding session had taken the election rules literally and proposed another candidate for the post he had been invited to assume. Tiutchev (who was finally elected) described this unpleasant incident in a letter to Sheremetev: "Gringmut, Tikhomirov, and priest Fudel' attended the session and proposed V. K. Isto-min for the post of chair; Gringmut excluded me completely from the list of the branch's officials, while one of the others granted me the position of deputy chair (*zhaloval menia tovarishchem predsedatelia*)."[153]

Fig. 4.3 Count Sergei D. Sheremetev dressed as a seventeenth-century *boiarin* at a costume ball of 1903. *Albom kostiumirovannogo bala v Zimnem dvortse v fevrale 1903 g., 21 geliograviura i 174 svetopechati/ Album du bal costume au Palais d'hiver, Février 1903, 21 photogravures et 174 phototypies* (St. Petersburg: Ekspeditsiia Zagotovleniia gosudarstvennykh bumag, 1904).

On another occasion Tiutchev and Sheremetev tried desperately to prevent Gringmut—who, Tiutchev claimed, "had the gift of soiling everything that he touched"—from delivering a paper at the annual meeting of the society on February 26, 1898. [154] As head of the Zealots' Moscow branch, Tiutchev discussed with Sheremetev how this could be done without breaching the rules of the society:

I entirely share your opinion that it is undesirable to let Gringmut read his memoirs on Alexander III at the society's [annual] meeting, but how can it be prevented? After all, Gringmut is a full member of the society. He can hardly be forbidden to use his rights; the only thing that can be done is to postpone this lecture at the council on one pretext or another and thus to put it off for an indefinite time. My idea is as follows: memoirs, speeches, papers, etc., that are intended to be read out at the meeting of February 26 should be considered beforehand by the council of the society; and the council, judging Gringmut's memoirs "untimely" can postpone them to a more appropriate time.[155]

Although clashes of ambition formed an element in these conflicts, the most heated arguments revolved around ideological issues. The very format of a voluntary association, which made it possible to discuss the society's goals and activities, eventually led to disputes about the meaning of its fundamental ideological precepts, presented in the Zealots' programmatic memorandum as "Russian principles." These disputes demonstrated that membership in a voluntary association provided an opportunity not only for identifying with a new social grouping or for confirming preexisting identification with older social frameworks, but also for developing an array of available identities. The Ukhtomskii affair was most revealing in this regard.

As we have seen, the society's founding fathers had assigned special significance to Ukhtomskii's membership. The fact that he belonged to the old Russian aristocracy (Ukhtomskii's family traced its lineage to the Rurik Dynasty), his friendly relations with the Tsar, Nicholas II, and, especially, his position as the publisher and editor of the popular newspaper *Sankt Peterburgskie vedomosti* (obtained, as Kutuzov claimed, with his support and for the society's possible benefit) made Ukhtomskii almost an ideal Zealot. Yet his editorial policy failed to meet their expectations. The newspaper criticized the Russification of the empire's Polish subjects, objected to the enforced dissemination of Russian Orthodoxy among non-Orthodox groups of the empire's population, and called for religious tolerance. The last straw from his fellow Zealots' point of view was his publication of an article by Sergei Trubetskoi, "The Mortar Case" ("Delo Mortara") attacking the enforced removal of children from members of some religious sects. The author compared this practice to the notorious Mortar case of 1858 when an Italian Jewish boy was secretly christened by the family's maid and then taken from his parents by Papal decree in order to be adopted by a Catholic family. "If we have an especially harmful sect that endangers the church and the state, it is first and foremost the one that commits crime and sacrilege under cover of Orthodoxy's sacred truth," Trubetskoi declared.[156] The article appeared on November 7, 1897, and on the very same day one of the ultra-rightist Zealots, Boris Iuzefovich, sent a furious letter to the council of the society, accusing Ukhtomskii of propagating "national discord" and "kindling the animosity of the

Russian empire's non-Orthodox population (*inovertsy*) to Orthodoxy." Claiming that Ukhtomskii had nothing in common with the Zealots' worldview, Iuzefovich suggested "releasing" him from membership in the society on the basis of a rather convoluted argument. Since the Zealots' activity could only be effective if it was based on the "sincere and full agreement of opinions of all its co-members," the society could not afford "even the smallest violation of the opinions of those members who had joined the society mistakenly and found themselves face to face with activity that does not accord with their personal views on Russia's political goals." Consequently, Iuzefovich recommended "releasing" Ukhtomskii from the moral obligations stemming from the status of founding member and suggested that he should resign from the society. Iuzefovich attached a copy of an even more vehement letter that he had sent to Ukhtomskii himself a few days earlier in which he explicitly attacked Ukhtomskii's anti-Russian sentiments, claiming that the newspaper's articles, written by journalists "of Polish and Jewish origin," insulted the "religious and patriotic feelings" of "us Russians."[157] In response, Ukhtomskii wrote a number of letters in which he expressed a different notion of Russian nationalism, based on citizenship rather than ethnicity and religion, each time emphasizing different aspects of his own identity. In a personal letter to Sheremetev, Ukhtomskii presented himself first and foremost as a Russian nobleman: "It is not for me to judge how many generations of various Gringmuts and company have served Orthodoxy and Russia, but I am deeply and piously aware of my thousand-year-long ancestral connection, in spirit and blood, with those who founded, built, and created our Motherland from the dawn of our historical life." In another, more official letter, Ukhtomskii presented himself as a supporter of conservative ideology and as an *obshchestvennyi deiatel'* (the latter with somewhat ironical overtones). In a subsequent letter, deeply disappointed with the position of the society's leadership, Ukhtomskii shifted the emphasis from his noble status and ideological credo to his professional work. Declining an invitation to a meeting of the council, he sarcastically requested that the matter of his expulsion be postponed until he had finished his editorial duties.[158]

Ukhtomskii's ability to maneuver among these various identities was, in a sense, confirmed by Kutuzov, who wrote in response to Ukhtomskii's earlier letter:

> Your letter has finally convinced me that there are two men inside you. One, my dear Esper Esperovich, whom I have known and loved for more than twenty years. . . . This one is our fellow member who who—not for a moment do I doubt this—will remain as he has always been until his and our last days. And there is another one I hardly know—the editor of *Sankt-Peterburgskie vedomosti*, who changed the word "I" to "a group of people" in my first article and who wrote a sharp and unjust response not only about Gringmut (with whom he is hardly acquainted) but even about Tikhomirov (whom he has never seen!).[159]

When accusing Ukhtomskii-the-editor, Kutuzov used the term "our party" to describe the Zealots and their ideological allies; but he used the language of comradeship when he promised that Ukhtomskii's friends would wait patiently until he changed his mind. Ukhtomskii did not waver and left the Society of Zealots; about ten years later he joined Ivan Tolstoi's Circle for Equal Rights and Brotherhood (*kruzhok ravnopraviia i bratstva*).[160] Nonetheless, this victory of the Zealots' radical members confronted the society's leaders with a new dilemma: to become a political association or to continue functioning as a learned and educational historical society. Sheremetev and his close circle chose the second path. As a result, in 1900 a group of ultra-nationalists that had emerged within the society took part in launching a new voluntary association with an overwhelmingly political agenda: the Russian Assembly (*Russkoe sobranie*), which was intended to become the first Russian ultra-monarchist party.[161]

Following this internal split, the Society of Zealots underwent what Sheremetev termed a certain "academization" which enabled those members who were (and perceived themselves as) amateur historians both to obtain semiprofessional status and to acquire the identity of public activists in the field of education (*obshchestvennye deiateli po narodnomu obrazovaniiu*).

The Zealots as Educators

The notions of public activism, associationalism, and *soslovnost'* became interwoven in a very distinctive manner in what the Zealots saw as the society's most successful educational enterprise—its network of free public libraries. From 1898, the society invested considerable financial and human resources in establishing such libraries in different regions of the Russian empire, mainly in the rural areas of central and western gubernias, but also in more remote locations; in spring 1903, for example, its council approved opening a library at the Algachinsk convict prison in Siberia.[162] Although these libraries were intended to challenge the leading role played by the "liberal" literacy committees, the Zealots in effect became part of the public movement initiated in 1893 by the St. Petersburg Literacy Committee, which had "launched a campaign to open one hundred free public libraries all across the empire, as well as to assist local agricultural societies and private persons desiring to open same, as the first step in an effort to organize a network of public libraries."[163] The participation of numerous educational societies, committees, village communities, and, especially, *zemstva* in establishing rural libraries made this movement an impressive example of joint associational activity. The rapid increase in the number of such libraries was noted by V. P. Vakhterov—about 300 in 1896 as compared with a few dozen in the early 1890s.[164] By 1898 there were already more than 3,000 public libraries in thirty-four *zemskie* gubernias, and their number had risen to 4,500 by 1904.[165]

The Zealots themselves established 81 libraries in sixteen gubernias between 1898 and 1902. Since this was the period in which there was the greatest increase in the number of rural libraries, the Zealots' project was very timely. The reports of the society's executive department show that its libraries were well attended. According to the reports submitted by twenty-nine of the society's libraries, in 1901 10,795 readers had borrowed 19,429 items (books and journals); two-thirds of the readers were adults, and one third were adolescents.[166] Rachinskii described the particular popularity of the library opened on the society's behalf at his school in Glukhov by a former pupil, the artist Bogdanov-Bel'skii.[167] A provincial educator and local historian (*kraeved*) from Tula, Valerii Liaskovskii, enthusiastically welcomed the society's libraries as a "direct educational aid for the peasantry."[168]

The Zealots' libraries proved to be a durable enterprise: the last time they were mentioned was in a letter from Sheremetev to Platonov in May 1918. The libraries were still operating, but Sheremetev was worried that they were being targeted by the new government.[169] Yet, while the libraries exemplified the society's affiliation with the associational movement, they also revealed the distinctiveness of the Zealots' policies. Whereas the literacy committees endeavored to encourage cooperation with *zemstva* and other public institutions, the Society of Zealots strove to establish libraries independently and to retain complete control of their collections and staff. The liberal leaders of the library movement viewed libraries as transmitters of social progress intended to renew rural life and considered the libraries' councils, comprising representatives of the *zemstvo*, *volost'*, village community, educational institutions and readers, as representing the united forces of progress.[170] The Zealots, who conceived of rural libraries as a buttress against social change and a channel for safeguarding the traditional way of life, sought to create a network of libraries that was completely subordinated to one body, the society's council.[171]

In the beginning, two possible models for the Zealots' libraries were discussed. Rachinskii's suggestion that they should be established at local church schools meant that they would be placed under the control of a local priest. According to Rachinskii, the main advantage of that model lay in the existing policy of stocking the church libraries, which was "exclusively in the spirit of the Zealots," as he wrote to Sheremetev: "a mediocre book or a book that is beyond the average reader's comprehension could probably find its way into this library, but a harmful book never." According to Rachinskii's plan, the Zealots should adapt the collection of each library to local needs. For example, in areas where there was a tendency for peasants to migrate to the eastern regions, the libraries should be provided with literature on Siberia, Central Asia, and "matters of resettlement," while in areas with cottage industries, they should be provided with books related to those industries.[172] The council of the society, however, opted for the other model developed by Sipiagin, which proposed an entirely new (and completely uniform) type of library, not based on existing ones. The society assigned an identical sum of 133 rubles and 45 kopeeks for establishing each library and demanded that each of them be stocked with exactly the same books; unlike Rachinskii's proposal, there was no room for any diversity. Only full members of the society were allowed to open libraries on its behalf. The society's executive department encouraged the society's members to provide new libraries with appropriate premises and to give them private financial support. As a result, the majority of the libraries were located in or near the estates of its landowning members, who were personally responsible for supervising and subsidizing their activities. Nonetheless, the society's rules (written by Sipiagin) did permit the libraries' day-to-day administration to be transferred to someone else with proved qualifications, usually a local priest. [173]

The involvement of local landowners and priests in the supervision of the society's libraries gave them control over an important channel of the peasants' extracurricular education, which the Zealots employed skillfully. The reading material was carefully chosen in accordance with the society's compulsory, meticulously compiled catalogues. The catalogue for 1899, for example, included 151 books and three periodicals: *Dosug i delo* (*Leisure and Work*), *Sel'skii vestnik* (*Village Messenger*), and *Troitskie listki* (*Troitsk Leaflets*). Its first section comprised books with "spiritual and moral content"; the second section, entitled "Ecclesiastical and Civil History," included Karamzin's *History of the Russian State* alongside Pobedonostsev's *History of the Orthodox Church before the Division of the Churches*, and K. K. Abaza's *Popular Military-Historical Reader*. Most of this section, however, consisted of popular histories and "conversations" in history, such as *Saint Peter and Alexius, Metropolitans of Moscow and the Glorious Battle of Mamaevo*, *The Times of Trouble*, and *Peter the Great*. Only three items from this section related to modern history: a brochure entitled *The Tsar-Peacemaker Alexander III* by D. I. Loman, a collection of stories *Examples from the Last War, 1877–1878* by L. M. Chichagov, and a small booklet, *October 17, 1888*, devoted to the survival of the tsar's family in a railway accident on that date. A book on Tsesarevich Nicholas's journey to the East appeared in the third section "Geography and Knowledge of the World" (*Geografiia i mirovedenie*), while some historical novels were included in the catalogue's fourth section, "Books of Literary Content" (*Knigi literaturnogo soderzhaniia*).[174]

The choice of these books projected a particular vision of a literate but traditionally minded Russian peasant. A vivid example of this ideal image can be found in a report of the executive department, which described a peasant who borrowed books from the library of Countess N. N. Meshcherskaia located in the village of Khot'kovo in Sychevsk uezd, Smolensk gubernia, in order to read them aloud at *posidelki* (peasants' leisure gatherings): "In so doing, he read 12 volumes of Karamzin's *Istoriia gosudarstva rossiiskogo*, 28 volumes of the journal *Dosug i delo*, 20 volumes of *Troitskie listki*, and 10 volumes of the *Bog pomoshch'* (*God's Help*) supplement to *Sel'skii vestnik*."[175] This image of a peasant who borrowed books from the library of the enlightened countess and read volumes of historical writings and moralistic journals at traditional *posidelki* reflected the Zealots' notion of rural libraries as a bastion of the traditional way of life. The problem was that this kind of peasant reader was already disappearing. Thus, the manager of the society's library in the uezd town of Bolkhov of Orel gubernia wrote about the emergence of "a *muzhik* with a new mentality" and urged the council to pay more attention to the urban population: "The uezd town is very authoritative for the new kind of *muzhik*; the patriarchal way of life has almost disappeared; the model of the miner and factory-worker has emerged, and street notions of local centers are gaining ever more influence on village life every year. Nowadays it is increasingly rare to meet muzhiks of the old cast who rather look down on the bustle of the city."[176] A similar picture emerged from the libraries' reports, which indicated that the periodical press was more popular than books, while among the latter, historical novels by Alexei Tolstoi, Mikhail Zagoskin, and Ivan Lazhechnikov were the most in demand. Books of religious and moral content, the reports noted, were mainly read during Lent. They also conveyed the regret expressed by readers that there was no daily newspaper to provide information about current events.[177]

The society's local activists suggested different ways for resolving this problem. The abovementioned manager of the Bolkhov library insisted that the Zealots' libraries should not resemble "a miniature version of the eparchial library" and recommended expanding their collections of fiction and historical literature, to supplement them with novels by the best writers, and to provide newspapers and journals selected by the council.[178] A similar request was made by the supervisor of the Zealots' library at the Nizhnii Novgorod Fairs Committee, the wealthy merchant Andrei Titov—a respected *kraeved* and a member of both the Society of Zealots and the Nizhnii Novgorod gubernia scholarly archival commission—who noted the increasing demand for such materials among the visitors to his library.[179] Vladimir Vostokov, a village priest from Moscow gubernia, suggested that the dearth of popular historical literature could be overcome if priests and teachers took upon themselves the task of holding popular religious and historical readings. Explaining his proposal, Vostokov drew the council's attention to the popularity of the genre of hagiography among "the people" and assumed that it could be used in order to depict "in passing" those historical events "that were most valuable from the educational point of view." In the future he hoped to compose a course on "Russian popular ecclesiastical history" (*Kurs russkoi tserkovno-narodnoi istorii*) based on the materials of those readings.[180] The society's council attempted to combine all proposals: it immediately implemented Titov's request and provided his library with "the books of our best writers" and subscriptions to *Novoe vremia, Moskovskie vedomosti, Russkii vestnik,* and *Svet,* established a commission for producing a supplementary catalogue for the society's libraries, and gave permission to hold "popular readings" (*narodnye chteniia*) on the society's behalf.[181]

The very decision to organize popular readings was far from simple. According to the government rules of 1894, public readings of already published materials were under the strict control of central and local governmental offices. For such events in gubernia cities, it was necessary to obtain the permission of the *popechitel'* of the educational district and of the governor, while only the Minister of Education in agreement with the Minister of Interior and the Ober-Procurator of the Holy Synod could authorize popular readings in uezd towns. In addition, the organizers had to receive the approval of the local administrative, church, and educational authorities.[182] The Zealots actually added another layer to the existing structure of prohibitions and permits by stipulating that the readings could be organized only by full members and only if their initiative were approved by the council.[183] Despite this complicated procedure, the first popular reading took place in early 1899 in the uezd town of Bezhetsk. It was organized by a local priest, Ioann Khil'tov, and was based on an essay entitled "The Behest of the Tsar-Peacemaker," by one of the Zealots' founding members, archpriest Smirnov. According to the society's newsletter, "The local population reacted very favorably to this reading: the spacious hall of the *zemstvo* building, which could accommodate an audience of over a thousand, was so packed that many people were unable to enter. This initiative of the society's local branch was supported by the town authorities (*uprava*), who purchased a lantern for slides and books containing the designated reading material."[184] In the wake of this success the Tula branch undertook to organize "traveling readings in Russian history," while the society's newsletter launched a new section on "The experience of popular historical readings" (*Opyt narodnogo istoricheskogo chteniia*).[185]

Sipiagin, who in March 1900 became the Minister of Interior, supported this idea and offered to elaborate rules for the popular readings, which were duly approved by the society's council in May 1901.[186] These rules accorded with the new governmental regulations on public readings approved by the Committee of Ministries on January 28, 1901, which simplified the bureaucratic procedure by authorizing the director of the local elementary schools (*direktor narodnykh uchilishch*), with the approval of the governor, to grant permission for popular readings. Moreover, in some cases it was now possible to use books that had not yet been included in the Ministry of Education's catalogues of public readings.[187] The Zealots' rules went even further: they allowed the members of the society to organize popular readings without the council's authorization in each particular case, requiring only that it be informed of the event and receive a report on it. The council, however, maintained strict control over the reading materials: only books and booklets included in the Zealots' catalogue could be used.[188] Although there is no documentary evidence, it is possible that the fact that the Minister of Interior was personally involved in the Zealots' libraries and popular readings projects played a role in the relaxation of governmental regulations, and subsequently of the Zealots' rules. The Society of Zealots may have served as a kind of experimental laboratory in this matter. In any event, the easier procedure led to an increase in the number of popular readings in general and of the Zealots' readings in particular. In 1902 the Bezhetsk branch of the society already reported that four readings had been held on "Emperor Alexander III," "The Christian Church from the times of the Apostles to Constantine the Great," "Suvorov," and "The coronation of Their Majesties." The local clergy was closely involved in these readings, as exemplified by the case of the Bezhetsk branch, where Father Khil'tov organized popular readings with the assistance of N. P. Plotnikov, a teacher from a local church school, and with the financial support of Archpriest Ioann Sergiev (later canonized as Saint John of Kronstadt), a full member of the Society of Zealots.[189]

These readings also testified to changes in the target groups of the Zealots' educational activity: alongside literate peasants, they were increasingly aimed at the illiterate population of the villages and city suburbs. The use of simple texts accompanied by lantern slides made it possible "to show" historical events and demanded no literacy from the audience. In the early 1900s this practice already seemed outdated: the governmental regulations of 1901 defined popular readings as a means of elementary education, while theoreticians of extracurricular education proposed their gradual transformation into preparatory courses for the people's university.[190] The latter proposal actually envisioned popular readings as the future basis for a system of extracurricular education crowned by the "university extension" courses. From this perspective, the Zealots' attempt to maintain the mode of popular readings that had been elaborated by eparchial councils two decades earlier looked extremely conservative. Nonetheless, this old-fashioned practice provided the Zealots with an opportunity to appeal to a mass audience and even engendered some innovative ideas, such as a suggestion to conduct performances and shows intended "to acquaint people with their Motherland's historical past." Another proposal, submitted by members of the Tiflis branch, suggested installing show-cases of reading matter (*chital'ni-vitriny*) near churches and at other public places, in particular in the villages of sectarians and the settlements of Russian peasant migrants to the Caucasus, since these displays could provide new settlers with "a spiritual link to the Motherland," and give them support in a land that was "not always hospitable toward these true bearers of Russian missions."[191]

The quest for new ways of making history meaningful to the people led to a new perception of how the society could contribute to disseminating knowledge about the past. On February 17, 1910, one of the rank-and-file Zealots proposed a method for combining educational tasks with the idea of commemoration, implicitly based on the notion of "sites of memory":

> Constant references to the sites of glorious historical events is undoubtedly one of the best means of disseminating historical knowledge. But in Russia it is the custom to keep silent about historical sites, and they can be learned about only from information that is not available to everyone. Thus, nothing reminds the millions of passengers traveling on the Riazan'-Ural railway of the famous Kulikovo field [the site of the Kulikovo battle of 1380] located 20 versts to the north of Kurkino station, although they can see from the compartment window the top of the column erected on "Red Hill" [near the field]. However, it is very easy to arouse these passengers' interest in the historical site. It is enough to change the station's name from Kurkino to "Kulikovo field" (*Kulikovo pole*). Then, as part of their duties, the railway employees would mention this historical site every time that a train approached the station. Changing the name does not involve great expense, and, without doubt, the Minister of Transportation, as a Russian who loves his native history, will support this endeavor if the Society of Zealots finds it possible to bring up the issue.[192]

The council of the society adopted this proposal, and in 1911 the *Kurkino* station was renamed *Kulikovo pole*. The Zealots' role did not remain invisible: the protocols of the council's session of January1912 recorded a letter from land-captain Zhdanovich of Bogucharskii uezd in Voronezh gubernia, requesting "the society's possible help in the historical and patriotic education of the local population."[193]

While pursuing conservative political goals and employing seemingly outdated methods of "people's enlightenment," the Zealots demonstrated an essentially modern attitude to creating images of the past as a means for molding the desired collective memory. For the Zealots, however, the visualization of history remained an auxiliary method: the society saw its main task as providing its expanding audience with popular historical literature.[194] For this purpose, they had to define what popular history should be composed of.

Popularizing History

The attempt to mold a particular kind of popular history led the Zealots to become involved in the crowded field of publishing activity. According to the official list of publications authorized for use by public libraries and popular readings in 1902, 46 governmental and voluntary public bodies—committees for popular readings, publishing cooperatives (*tovarishchestva*), historical societies (in particular, the Historical Society at Moscow University), journals, and private publishers—were already engaged in producing this kind of historical literature.[195] The Zealots adopted the principle of "excellent content at a low price" that had previously been established by the *Posrednik* and the activists of the literacy committees. Like their liberal opponents, the Zealots sought to protect readers from worthless commercial literature: their definition of excellence combined ideological relevance with high-quality historical information. The Zealots' first criterion was accessibility (*dostupnost'*). Thus, when discussing the topic for the society's proposed award in military history, the members of its publishing department removed subjects that seemed too narrow (such as "The role of the Tsesarevich as a combat officer in training the army for combat in peacetime") or too bookish (such as "Russian military-historical scholarship"), and retained only a more general and descriptive subject, "The actions of the Rushchuk detachment under the command of the Tsesarevich Alexander, future Emperor Alexander III, during the military campaign of 1877–1878." One of the department's members, Mikhail Solov'ev, doubted whether even this topic could be addressed in sufficient detail, but two other members, Chechulin and Peter Maikov, argued that an account intended for a broader audience should not be too detailed, but had to be *populiarnyi*, which in this case meant both accessible and appealing.[196] The department's commission subsequently established criteria for essays competing for the society's awards. They were to be of a scholarly character, written in an unbiased way and "accessible not only to specialists in a particular field of knowledge, but also to a wider readership."[197]

Another significant aspect of the society's publishing policy was the question of circulation, which arose in November 1898, when the Zealots decided to publish Liaskovskii's manuscript on the Slavophile Kirievskii brothers (*Brat'ia Kirievskie*). Solov'ev suggested issuing a number of copies equal to the number of the society's members and distributing the book among them, citing the example of the Imperial Orthodox Palestinian Society which distributed its *Reports* (*Soobshcheniia*) in that way. The secretary of the department reminded him, however, that the society's publications were intended for an "average audience" (*sredniaia publika*), not only for the Zealots, and thus recommended a larger number of copies. Finally, the publishing department decided to issue 3,000 copies of the book.[198] Some months later, the commission on the society's awards suggested that works published under the society's auspices would be issued in 1,200 copies.[199] This decision set precedents for the society's future publishing policy. Its most significant aspect, however, concerned the preferred genre and format of the proposed publications.

At first the publishing department proposed reprinting popular works by eminent Russian historians, such as Solov'ev's *Public Readings on Peter the Great*, Kostomarov's *Venerable (Prepodobnyi) Feodosii Pecherskii*, and Kliuchevskii's *Beneficial Educator of the Russian National Spirit: Venerable Sergei Radonezhskii*.[200] This selection demonstrated a marked preference for the genre of historical biography. As the department's future head, Ivan Khruchshov, argued, it accorded with the reading habits of the Zealots' target audience since "an essay on historical events is beyond the comprehension of readers whose education is below the level of secondary school, whereas a historical figure as a focus of the events, as a vivid type of the hero or public activist, attracts their attention."[201] However, the society's council rejected this plan, noting that the publishing department had failed to check whether the previous editions of the works he suggested were already out of print or, even more important, whether the authors or their heirs would agree to grant the society the right to reprint their writings.[202] The publishing department therefore tried to elaborate a different strategy, proposing, on the one hand, to issue a number of memoirs (including that of the society's cofounder Bestuzhev-Riumin) and biographies and, on the other hand, to commission the writing of a concise history of Russia.[203] The council of the society adopted the first proposal intended to personalize history and eventually published the biographies of "peasant writer" Ivan Pososhkov, the Kirievskii brothers, and Rachinskii.[204] Regarding the second task, the council considered inviting Nikolai Kvashnin-Samarin, a local historian from Tver' and a cofounder of the Tver' gubernia scholarly archival commission, to write such a history but dropped the whole plan in favor of a more promising project.[205] It was decided to produce a series of "Tales on Russian History" based on adaptations of well-known historical works devoted to the "heroic deeds of the Russian people in their struggle for territorial conquest: of Finland in the north; of the Kazan' and Astrakhan kingdoms, Siberia, Bukhara, Khiva, Amur, and the Ussuri region, and Central Asia, in the east; of the Caucasus and Crimea in the south; of the kingdom of Poland and the Baltic borderlands (*okrainy*) in the west." Other proposed topics reflected the nationalist and religious aspects of the society's program. These included "The Patriotic War of 1812," "The Fall of Tsargrad [the old Russian name for Constantinople] and the Holy City of Jerusalem," "Stories from the Times of the Christians' Persecution in the First Centuries of our Era," and "Christianity in Central Asia in the Middle Ages." In addition, the collections were to include "essays with geographical and ethnographic content." The department stressed that the "tales" should be "vivid and absorbing" and advised using published materials that had already proved their "readability." Thus, the writings of A. I. Mikhailovskii-Danilevskii were suggested as an appropriate source for the article on the 1812 War, *The Travels of Marco Polo* for an essay on Nestorianism in Asia, and Sigizmund Herbershtein's *Rerum Moscovitarium* (which four decades earlier had created such serious troubles for OIDR) for one on sixteenth-century Moscow. [206]

Practical work on the society's collections started in 1902, when Khrushchov became head of the publishing department and made this project his main task. Khrushchov, an expert on the history of ancient Russian literature and a high-ranking *chinovnik* of the Ministry of Education, was also an experienced activist in the public educational movement. In the late 1870s he had been secretary of the Historical Society of Nestor the Chronicler in Kiev, had served as head of the St. Petersburg commission for popular readings in the 1880s, and played a leading role in founding the Society for Popular Readings (*Obshchestvo po ustroistvu narodnykh chtenii*) in Tambov gubernia in 1893. Khrushchov had his own vision regarding the nature of the proposed popular collections (in 1900 the society published his *Conversations on Ancient Russian Literature*) and even his own funds for realizing the project.[207] In March 1902 he transferred to the Society of Zealots a special endowment of the Publishing Society that he had established together with Count Pavel Stroganov in 1882 for issuing books for the people and which they had now decided to bestow on the Zealots.[208] In particular, Khrushchov planned to issue a three-volume collection of tales on Russian history from ancient times to the end of the nineteenth century, which would appeal to readers of various levels of education, from "those who like reading lives of the saints and the *School of Piety* (*Uchilishche blagochestiia*) to those who are partial to newspapers."[209] Khrushchov was particularly insistent that great care should be taken in editing the chosen texts in order to remove "anything that is not essential or clear to the readers," and to add necessary comments and explanations.[210] For this purpose, each version of the proposed chapters was reviewed by historians who were members of the society, thereby going through a peer review procedure characteristic of scholarly practice. For example, the chapter "Ioann III and Sophia Paleoplog," composed by historian and archivist Count Nicholas Golitsyn on the basis of Solov'ev's *History of Russia*, Zabelin's *History of the City of Moscow*, and Paul Pierling's *La Russie et le Saint-Siège: études diplomatiques*, was read by Chechulin, Ilovaiskii, and military historian Platon Geisman, whose comments were to be taken into consideration in the final version of the piece. The scrupulous Chechulin also volunteered to check the proofs.[211]

This method of work made the process of preparation rather slow but enabled Khrushchov to maintain historical quality. The results were impressive and somewhat surprising. The first and, contrary to the original plans, the only volume of the collection, the *Reader on Russian History from Ancient Times to the End of the Sixteenth Century* (*Sbornik chtenii po russkoi istorii s drevneishikh vremen do XIV veka*), published in 1907, was exemplary from the pedagogical point of view. Each chapter of the book was preceded by a list of sources intended to serve as a guide for further reading. The bibliography for the section on the Eastern Slavs also included, alongside works by Bestuzhev-Riumin, Zabelin, Kliuchevskii and Solov'ev, Miliukov's chapter on the ancient Slavs from the *Reader on the History of the Middle Ages* produced by the Society for Dissemination of Technical Knowledge (ORTZ), against which the Zealots vehemently struggled.[212] This reader, which had been composed by the ORTZ's commission of history teachers headed by Vinogradov and comprising, according to Kizevetter, "all the young lecturers most interested in their subjects," was widely perceived as one of the most successful educational projects carried out by the *obshchestvennost'* (an "important deed," as Kizevetter put it).[213] Nonetheless, neither its association with the liberal *obshchestvennost'* nor Miliukov's problematic political reputation prevented the Zealots from using his piece as a source in their own volume. In this particular case the Zealots clearly demonstrated their preference for scholarly rather than political criteria, which enabled them to appeal to an audience from different age groups and social strata. In the forewords to its *Reader on Russian History*, the society's council recommended it as both a teaching aid for school pupils and as reading matter for those "with no access to scholarly works and original historical documents," thereby demonstrating a more sophisticated perception of the term "popular readers."[214]

This promising beginning generated ideas for other publications. In 1903 an active member of the publishing department, the poet and ultra-nationalist journalist Vasilii Velichko, whose historical drama *Menshikov* was published by the society in the same year, suggested issuing a collection entitled *Russian History in Poems and Songs*.[215] Maybe inspired by his proposal, Khrushchov suggested a similar but much broader project of a *Reader on Russian Literature*, which would present the "best of modern Russian writers" and consist of three sections—fiction, ethnography, and historical novels. Chechulin, who enthusiastically supported this idea, recommended including some poems as well. It was eventually decided to produce two separate collections, a literary collection based on excerpts from historical novels, and an "ethnographic" collection, including travel notes (*putevye zametki*). In addition, Khrushchov suggested preparing a collection of biographies of Russian historical figures, from Prince Mstislav *Udaloi* to Count Murav'ev-Amurskii.[216] From early 1904, therefore, the society worked on the "historical," "literary," "ethnographic," and "biographical" volumes simultaneously. This new publishing strategy signified the emergence of a new, broader concept of popular historical literature, which transcended the borders of history as a discipline to include a survey of cultural life in its wider anthropological sense, as reflected in the suggestions for the ethnographic volume. The latter included such titles as "Uncle Semenych's Story on Solovki" by E. K. Somova, "Street Life in Constantinople" by Francis Marion Crawford, "At-Davan—A Story from Life in Yakutsk Region" by V. G. Korolenko and "At the Chinese Dinner" by A. V. Vereshchagin.[217] The intensive work on the four collections was, however, interrupted by Khrushchov's illness; the first parts of the "literary" and "historical" collections were published only after his death. The literary volume was finally entitled *Collection of Stories on Russian and Foreign Life (Sbornik rasskazov iz russkoi i chuzhezemnoi zhizni)* and included fragments from *War and Peace* by Tolstoy, *The Karamazov Brothers* by Dostoevsky, *Uncle Tom's Cabin* by Harriet Beecher Stowe, and *Les Misérables* by Victor Hugo, alongside excerpts from historical novels by Alexei Tolstoi and Zagoskin.[218] Khrushchov and his coeditors, therefore, not only took into consideration their prospective audience's reading habits, but tried to educate future readers by exposing them to the best of contemporary Russian and Western literature.

Despite the success of the first volumes of this project, the publication of subsequent collections was postponed and eventually canceled altogether.[219] The new head of the publishing department, Konstantin Grot, a well-known expert on Slavic studies and former professor of Warsaw University, changed the Zealots' publishing policy once again in accordance with the new political situation and his own scholarly interests; the Zealots demonstrated sufficient flexibility in both respects.

Introducing his program at the session of the publishing department in March 1905, when revolutionary unrest was shaking Russia, Grot based it on "contemporary Russian society's essential need for the development of national and political self-consciousness," which, he claimed, "underlay the cultural work of any nation." The aim of the society's publishing activity should therefore consist in clarifying "Russia's place and role in the Slavic world, and the role of the Slavic people in world history," rather than in disseminating factual information about the historical past. Thematic books and booklets, not collections of adapted texts, he argued, would better meet this aim. Furthermore, Grot apparently rejected Khrushchov's concept of popular books that appealed to all readers and proposed publishing books in two different categories: for "so-called people's reading" and for "broader circles of the reading public." Nonetheless, he completely shared his predecessor's interest in the ethnographic approach to history, which became one of the main thrusts of his program. In practical terms, Grot suggested issuing two or three brochures in the first category on such topics as "Russia in the Slavic World: A Historical-Ethnographic Study;" "Cyril and Methodius—Apostles of the Slavonic Peoples;" and "Russia, Turkey and the South Slavs." Regarding the books of the second category, he proposed, first and foremost, to issue a number of "truthful and vivid" essays providing historical-ethnographic data on Galician Ruthenia and the Carpatho-Ruthenians (or, as he put it, on "the Carpathian part of the Slavic tribe torn away from our people and our national state") and, in so doing, "to fill the gap in public knowledge" about it. Second, he suggested popularizing the ideas and writings of "appropriate" Russian political thinkers such as Iurii Samarin. Last, but not least, Grot advised reprinting the political and philosophical essay, "Slavdom and the World of the Future," by the leading figure of the Slovak national revival, Ľudovít Velislav Štúr, which had been published in Lamanskii's translation in the *Readings of the Moscow Society for Russian History and Antiquities* in 1867.[220]

The publishing department readily embraced all of Grot's suggestions, adopting his proposal regarding Štúr with special enthusiasm. Professor P. A. Kulakovskii, Grot's deputy and future successor as head of the publishing department (from 1909), noted that Štúr's ideas on "the vocation of the Russian people, the essence of the Eastern Church, the meaning of the unity between the autocratic Russian tsar and the people" could be a powerful tool in "awakening our political consciousness."[221] Publication of the three items from the proposed program (Štúr's study and the essays on Cyril and Methodius and on Galician Ruthenia) over the next four years testified both to the pan-Slavist turn in the Zealots' nationalist ideology and the greater weight assigned to the political dimension of their effort to popularize history.[222] The publishing department's recommendations to the author of the book on Galician Ruthenia—who preferred to remain anonymous and wrote this text under the pen-name "Eyewitness" (*ochevidets*)—are instructive in this regard:

> In accordance with the conclusion of A. S. Budilovich, the council of the society finds it necessary to remove from the manuscript "Galician Ruthenia" (*Galitskaia Rus*) the following paragraphs: p. 29—the reproach to Galician-Ruthenian priests for their "loyalty" to the government and neglect of the people's "cultural and national needs"; p. 110—the author's reference to the extenuating circumstances of the orthographic reform; p. 204—comments regarding the scholarly merits of the leader of Galician Ukrainophiles, Professor Grushevanyi; p. 242—ascribing an anti-Muscovite song to Volyn peasants; p. 243—the author's opinion on the necessity for education in the mother tongue for South- and White-Russians (*dlia iuzhnorossov i belorossov*).[223]

The society undertook this severe censorship quite voluntarily on the basis of comments by a fellow Zealot, the philologist Anton Budilovich, who was active in the Russian Assembly and whose views were more rightist than governmental policy of that time.[224] Some months earlier Budilovich had submitted to the society an essay on *Non-Russians in Russia: Contemporary Questions (Inorodtsy v Rossii: Sovremennye voprosy)* by A. E. Alektorov, a provincial educator, director of the elementary schools in the Akmolinsk and Semipalatinsk regions. The essay was published with an introduction and supplementary chapter by Budilovich, and both Alektorov's and especially Budilovich's texts expressed an ultra-nationalist stance. [225] The reactionary tendency was seen not only in the Zealots' choice of manuscripts but also in the channels through which the publications were distributed. In May 1908 the council decided "to establish closer relations with the Russian Assembly by means of mutual services, while retaining organizational independence"; "to contact a bookshop of the right-wing press in order to cooperate on the sale of the society's publications;" and "to organize public readings and lectures at special meetings of the Society of Zealots open to non-members."[226]

The Zealots' efforts to publicize their projects therefore became primarily political; the temptation to transform the society into a rightist political association loomed large once again. Yet, this tendency did not please the society's conservative but more scholarly minded members, and the mechanism of negotiations and votes that characterized the procedure of a voluntary association enabled them to prevent future development in this direction. While avoiding a direct confrontation, they proposed less politically laden publishing opportunities, and thereby partly foiled the society's radicalization. At the publishing department's session of April 1909, Grot (who at that time had already resigned as head of the department) informed the participants that Professor Timofei Florinskii had agreed to write a popular essay on the connections between Russia and Southern Slavdom from ancient times, and reminded members of the idea to publish a series of popular biographies of the first Slavophiles, such as Khomiakov, Samarin, and the Aksakovs. A member of the Academy of Sciences, Aleksei Sobolevskii, suggested that the society should issue a short popular booklet on the *History of the Northern War* to mark the approaching 200th anniversary of the battle of Poltava and should produce an album of Russian antiquities intended to inform "a wider readership" about monuments of ancient Russian architecture. He also recalled the earlier plans to publish biographies of figures from ancient Russian history. The newly elected head of the publishing department, Kulakovskii, recommended preparing a popular biography of Jan Hus.[227] This plethora of proposals, with a marked emphasis on the more distant past, indicated, if not synchronized action, then at least a joint desire to preserve the image of the Zealots as a learned rather than an outright political society. This effort to protect the Zealots' status as a historical society was strengthened by a debate that took place at the council's meeting in May 1909. Its participants questioned the prevalence of pan-Slavist topics in the latest proposals and also the relevance of Hus's biography but reminded their fellow members that the Zealots' task would be best served by publishing literature on the "Russian present and historical past."[228]

Indeed, in the following years the society returned to its earlier policy of personified accounts of Russian history: in 1912–1913 it published the memoirs of Count Komarovskii, while the last book it issued was a biography of Metropolitan Platon (1737–1812) by N. P. Rozanov.[229] Gradually, the society began to concentrate its efforts on producing periodical issues of *Starina i novizna* containing unique historical documents, carefully prepared for print by Chechulin or the Barsukovs. This trend gave the *Starina i novizna* great archeographic value, but actually meant an end to the Zealots' plans to publish popular books on Russian history. This did not mean, however, that the society gave up its aspiration to combine the "popular" and the "scholarly" facets of its activity: this aspect remained crucial for the Zealots' persistent attempts to produce a history of Alexander III's reign, which was perceived as the society's main research task.

Who Should Write a History of the Monarch and the Monarchy?

From the very outset, the society's founders regarded the task of writing a history of Alexander III's reign as their highest priority and tried to make it their exclusive privilege. For this purpose, the society's historical department started to create its own archive and library intended to bring together materials on the late tsar. The first documents were transferred to the Zealots' archive directly by Dowager Empress Maria Fedorovna and Nicholas II.[230] Representatives of the capital's high society followed their example, providing the Zealots with invaluable sources: thus, the heirs of a maid of honor (*freilina*), A. A. Akulova, gave the society 103 letters written by members of the Imperial family in 1836–1855, including a letter by Nicholas I which had never been published.[231] The society also made every effort to obtain materials from the archives of the governmental offices.[232] One of the most significant donations was made in 1899 by the Commission for Printing State Documents and Treaties of the Main Archive of the Ministry of Foreign Affairs, which submitted to the Society of Zealots "three bales" of its publications.[233] Encouraged by the increasing inflow of "publications and manuscripts containing official acts, eyewitness testimonies of events or memoirs of contemporaries," the society's council hoped that "with further diligence of the society's members, its gradually expanding archive and library will eventually become a precious depository of sources on the history of the life and reign of Emperor Alexander III."[234] The first head of the historical department, Nicholas Selifontov, even prepared a kind of guide to searching for relevant documents in the state archives.[235]

Nonetheless, the main questions were who would use the archival materials for writing a history of the late tsar and how this would be done. The persistent attempts to produce a biography of Alexander III—which never came to fruition—revealed both the complex interrelations among the Zealots and their distinctive relations with the Imperial court. The society's efforts to "monopolize" the writing of Alexander III's biography reflected the Zealots' desire to enhance the image of the Russian monarchy as an enduringly relevant institute embodying Russia's historical fate. Although they were unable to realize their main project, the Zealots' quest for the best ways in which to fulfill their ambitious task led them to experiment with a variety of models. During this process, they contributed to defining the notion of modern history and gave new meanings to the popularization of history.

It took almost three years for the council of the society to choose its candidate for writing a history of Alexander III: Sergei Spiridonovich Tatishchev, a diplomat, publicist, and, as Sheremetev defined him, "a historical writer." By that time Tatishchev had already published a number of historical essays, was working on a biography of Alexander II, and had authored the first short biographical brochure on Alexander III, which was issued in 1894.[236] In addition, Tatishchev was involved in research on the revolutionary movement in Russia, which was carried out under the supervision of the Department of Police and was intended to be its internal source of information.[237] On March 22, 1898, Tatishchev was admitted to the society as a full member, and three weeks later A. S. Stishinskii, head of the society's executive department, invited him to visit Sheremetev at the latter's home.[238] This first meeting was followed by an exchange of letters between Sheremetev and Tatishchev in which the idea of the future book was discussed. In December 1898 Sheremetev finally informed Tatishchev of the council's "expression of interest" in his writing a biography of Alexander III on the society's behalf and asked Tatishchev to present a short essay on Alexander III's reign at the society's annual meeting on February 26, 1899.[239] In the next month Tatishchev was also provided with a detailed description of the society's archive which was now available to him.[240]

Yet Tatishchev's diplomatic service as an *attaché* of the Russian Ministry of Finance in London caused serious delay in carrying out his voluntary obligations. Sheremetev's numerous telegrams to London remained unanswered. "Can we rely on your presence and lecture on the anniversary day? I have written to London three times, your answer is needed," he wrote desperately on January 12, 1899.[241] Tatishchev presented a chapter of his planned book only in 1900, a year later than the society's council had expected.[242] He barely made any progress in the following year: no additional chapter from his work was presented at the society's ceremonial meeting in 1901, and Liaskovskii read the introduction to his own biographical essay on Alexander III instead.[243] This lack of progress led to understandable tension in the relations between the two men, and it was probably for this reason that Tatishchev made an attempt to secure his status as biographer of Alexander III. In January 1903, upon his appointment to a new official post in St. Petersburg, he submitted a formal request to the emperor via the Minister of the Imperial Court, Baron Vladimir Frederiks, to permit him "to compose the late sovereign's history" which would be "a natural continuation" of his historical research on Alexander II. Tatishchev emphasized in particular that the writing would be carried out under the supervision and guidance of the council of the Society of Zealots and of its head, Sheremetev, personally.[244] His request was granted. Both Sheremetev and Tatishchev were informed by a letter from Frederiks that the emperor had assigned to the council of the society and to Sheremetev as its chair the right to examine and approve Tatishchev's work plan, and placed the council in charge of the final censorship of his manuscript. The tsar thus confirmed the society's supervisory role (and, in so doing, undermined Sheremetev's later accusation of his indifference to the Zealots' activity) but at the same time recommended that Sheremetev should approach Nicholas II or his mother, Empress Maria Fedorovna, for guidance and advice in every instance of uncertainty— and, therefore, subordinated him to the higher, royal censors. In addition, Tatishchev received permission to work in the court archive and libraries and was granted an allowance of 12,000 rubles for the next two years of work.[245]

Tatishchev was justifiably pleased with the favorable decision, but his delight was marred by Sheremetev's message of displeasure with his apparently unexpected initiative, conveyed to him by Sheremetev's close associate and fellow Zealot, one of the three Barsukov brothers, Nikolai Platonovich. Acting in this situation not as a functionary of the society but as Sheremetev's proxy (*doverennoe litso*), Barsukov warned Tatishchev "not to publish even a single line about Alexander III before submitting it to the council of the society." Tatishchev, who had no intention of coming into conflict with the powerful Sheremetev, accepted these conditions "with unquestionable obedience" but, as the following events demonstrated, did not fully understand the harshness of this warning.[246] In the following year he worked enthusiastically, searching for historical materials in the numerous civil and military archives.[247] In addition to extensive archival search, Tatishchev tried to contact people who could provide him with their own personal memories of the late emperor. At some point he acquired the notes of the wife of Alexander III's teacher, Iakov Grot (Konstantin Grot's father), about the lessons he had given Alexander and his older brother Nicholas and even asked Sofia Andreevna Tolstaia to provide him with information about her meeting with Alexander III.[248] As a result of this intensive work, Tatishchev managed to finalize the first two chapters of the book and write the drafts of the eight additional chapters by January 1904, when he duly submitted them to Sheremetev's judgment, expressing his hope that a date for presenting the manuscript at a session of the society's council would be fixed as soon as possible. Yet something strange happened with the council's timetable in the following months. As revealed by Sheremetev's letters and telegrams to Tatishchev of April 1903–January 1904, this event was postponed several times under a variety of pretexts, from Sheremetev's obligation to attend an event at which "the highest presence" was expected to the funeral of an old maidservant in his house.[249] Nor did Sheremetev hasten to inform the "highest office" about Tatishchev's work. While ostensibly abiding by the society's official rules, Sheremetev stressed the private nature of their relations and thereby downplayed Tatishchev's ambitions to achieve public recognition and to strengthen his status as Imperial biographer. Tatishchev, however, was not prepared to wait long. On October 30, 1904, Sheremetev received a letter from Tatishchev informing him of another unexpected step the historian had taken:

> I consider it my duty to inform Your Highness (*Vashe Siiatel'stvo*) that on October 20, the tenth anniversary of Emperor Alexander III's decease, I had the pleasure of presenting the manuscript of the first volume of my work on the life and reign of the late sovereign to His Majesty the Emperor via the Minister of the Imperial Court. This volume covers the first twenty years of the life of the Tsar-Peacemaker, from his birth to his declaration as heir to the

throne, i.e., from 1845 to 1865. It consists of ten chapters. I have read you the first five of them, but they too have been significantly revised and expanded on the basis of new materials. I wrote the remaining five chapters during the last summer. In its current form this volume constitutes a complete literary whole and could be published and circulated immediately, which would meet not only my personal expectations as author, but, I dare to think, also the state interest at a time of unsteadiness in public thought such as we are currently experiencing. Therefore I would be inexpressibly grateful to you, Count, if you would consider it possible to begin immediately the censorship of my work that His Imperial Majesty has entrusted you with.[250]

Sheremetev's reaction to this move was very harsh. From his point of view, Tatishchev had breached not only the Zealots' formal rules but also their informal hierarchy, which could undermine the relations within the society. The recalcitrant historian therefore had to be punished, or, as Sheremetev formulated it years later, "it was necessary to put him in his place (*prishlos' osadit' ego i postavit' na mesto*)."[251] Immediately after receiving Tatishchev's message, Sheremetev sent him an irate telegram: "I am utterly astounded by the fact that you presented your work without my knowledge, which entirely contradicts the conditions that I informed you of in the guidelines." Tatishchev's first response was equally caustic: "I am no less astounded by your strange pretension to guide me in fulfillment of my duty," he wrote in a telegram on the next day.[252] However, on the following day, November 1, 1904, Tatishchev sent a more moderate letter, in which he not only tried to explain his step but, what is more significant for our case, pronounced his credo as a historian. "Being a historian" still meant for him a sublime vocation rather than a modern profession, while "the right to submit literary works to His Imperial Majesty's opinion" was perceived as "the Russian writer's innate right, limited only by the sovereign's will." Yet, at the same time, Tatishchev proclaimed the importance of the writer's freedom and the historian's independence: "Being an enlightened man, you cannot fail to understand that it cannot be otherwise; that the writer's free creative work cannot be equated with ordinary bureaucratic labor which is done at someone else's bidding (*po ukazke*)," he wrote to Sheremetev, reminding him that "non-independent historical work would be of no value and significance."[253] Sheremetev was not convinced by Tatishchev's plea of not guilty and proceeded in his crusade against him. Paradoxically, his actions reflected the same perception of the historian's distinctive status as one who was dependent on a higher patron while at the same time being an independent researcher and writer—and, as such, vulnerable to criticism.

First, Sheremetev sent telegrams to the Minister of the Court Frederiks and to the supervisor of the Winter Palace's library, Vasilii Shcheglov, informing them of Tatishchev's "extremely unseemly behavior" (*krainiaia nekorrektnost'*). In particular, he asked Frederiks "to report" the matter, hinting at his willingness to let the highest censors know about it.[254] In response, Shcheglov cleverly suggested his own initiative: "Upon receiving Your Highness's telegram concerning Tatishchev, I thought it would be useful to bring to the notice of the Minister of the Imperial Court some details regarding Tatishchev's usage of documents from the library under my supervision, and also to inform him of the distinctive ethics of the biographer and of the dowager empress's displeasure regarding the assignment of the task of writing this historical work to him."[255] After preparing the ground, Sheremetev took the next step, now apparently fulfilling his censorial duty: on November 8, 1904 he submitted his review of Tatishchev's work. His assessment was quite malicious. Although recognizing Tatishchev's "good, and sometimes even talented manner of writing" and acknowledging his ability to attract the potential readers' interest, he expressed serious doubts regarding the manuscript's historical value. Sheremetev found its documentary basis "one-sided and even sparse" and noted the "inaccurate and uninteresting" representation of Alexander III's mother and her role in the future tsar's education. He questioned the author's criteria for "giving the floor" to certain voices of the past while ignoring "more precise and modest" pieces of evidence, and sharply criticized the shift of emphasis from the personality of Alexander Alexandrovich to the figure of his older brother, Nicholas Alexandrovich. In addition, Sheremetev pointed to a number of facts that were not substantiated by documentary sources and questioned the author's arbitrariness in assigning either central or subordinate roles to people around the young Alexander. His conclusion was disapproving. While recognizing that "it is hard to make a final assessment on the basis of one fragment, which undoubtedly reads in an interesting manner," he nevertheless pronounced that Tatishchev's manuscript laid "the wrong basis for Alexander III's biography." Therefore he recommended its revision, suggesting, as the first step, that it be sent to additional reviewers. Remarkably, he advised that the manuscript should also be read by those people who, as he claimed earlier in his review, did not receive sufficient attention in Tatishchev's text.[256]

It is hard to know what transpired regarding Tatishchev's manuscript in the following month, but on December 18, 1904 Frederiks dispatched him the third and last letter about his work. Tatishchev was informed that Nicholas II had decided to give him an opportunity to finalize his historical research on Alexander III according to the original conditions, that is, with an annual allowance of 6,000 rubles over the next two years and under the censorship of the council of the Zealots. The first two volumes of the book were expected to be finished by 1907, and permission to write two additional volumes was granted. However, the tsar opposed the manuscript's publication as "untimely."[257] Tatishchev died two years later, in 1906, and in 1908 Sheremetev concluded this story with satisfaction: "The decision of the sovereign, who definitely opposed the publication of Tatishchev's work, was absolutely justified. Tatishchev's manuscript is now held in the archive of the society [of Zealots] as material for the future, although the material is rather one-sided."[258]

The story of the conflict around writing the historical biography of Alexander III revealed, first and foremost, the mechanisms by which a dissident member of a voluntary association could be disciplined by its leadership. By employing a variety of tactics—the possibility of cooperating with governmental offices, the exploitation of networks of personal relationships and of the society's formal rules—the council of the Zealots and its authoritarian chair appropriated the right of policing a disobedient member's historical writing and thereby had a profound impact on his fate as a historian. Despite the distinctiveness of Tatishchev's case, it revealed the potential for discipline and punishment lurking in the very idea of a voluntary association that subordinated its members to self-imposed rules for the sake of a mutually accepted goal. Furthermore, by delegating the task of censorship to a voluntary historical society, Nicholas II created a precedent that heralded those governmental practices which seemingly enhanced society's agency, but in fact bound it to the governmental institutions and thus contributed to the paradoxical hybridity of state and society in late imperial Russia. Yet, despite its rejection of Tatishchev's work, the council of the society had no intention of abandoning the project of writing a history of Alexander III's reign. Rather, it employed another instrument at the disposal of a voluntary historical society— the mechanism of awards and contests, which in the Zealot's case was intended to produce a cadre of fresh (and more obedient) "literary forces" who would be willing to write on the recent past in accordance with the society's guidelines.

Even in the period when the council of the society still pinned its hopes on Tatishchev's study, it supported voluntary initiatives by members of the society who undertook to write their own memoirs or biographical notes on Alexander III. In 1897 the society's historical department already decided to place in its archive notes written by a teacher, Nevzorov, on Alexander III's visit to the Lutheran school at the Church of St. Anna in St. Petersburg and by Colonel Del'sal' on the tsar's visit to the Guards' camp.[259] At the same time Liaskovskii submitted to the historical department his project entitled "Emperor Alexander III as a human being: a draft plan for his personal biography," while A. V. Prakhov delivered a lecture on "Alexander III's impact on the revival of Russian national art" at the society's annual meeting on February 26, 1897.[260] The following year, probably as a result of these first promising items, Sheremetev sent an open letter to the members of the society asking them to submit "unpublished diaries and memoirs" on Alexander III for the period 1845–1894, as well as notes and essays describing "the sphere of public activity in Russia and the impact of the Highest Authority on this sphere in the period from 1865 up to 1894" and "Russia's relations with foreign states" during the same period.[261] In this letter, the notion of "the history of Alexander III" was already much broader than a biography proper, and it was further developed in the rules governing the society's awards for the best essays on the reign of Alexander III. The list of preferred topics included—alongside the previously mentioned *soslovie*-oriented subject of "the estate principle in Russia's governmental practice"—a wide range of themes such as the "Russian navy," "education," "religious life," "Russian art," and "the Siberian railway" in the time of Alexander III.[262] An even broader approach was suggested by Chechulin upon his election to head of the historical department in December 1901. The Society of Zealots, he claimed, should expand its historical activity beyond the chronological borders of Alexander III's period in order to demonstrate the significance of his role in Russian history. "The late sovereign embraced the whole life of the Russian people," Chechulin explained, "he expressed their eternal ideals and, at the same time, left behests to be implemented in the future." For this reason the best way of commemorating his name would be "to study all facets of Russian history, on condition that this study be animated by a love of Russia and the truth."[263] While introducing the scholarly practice of presenting research papers at the meetings of the historical department, Chechulin proposed that the papers should focus on the history of the eighteenth and nineteenth centuries and, in so doing, strengthened the status of the Society of Zealots as a center for the study of modern Russian history, which he interpreted as history of the last centuries, not decades.

This steady expansion of the society's sphere of interests attracted a growing number of authors who were willing to participate in the Zealots' writing projects. They proposed a wide variety of topics, from local history to the history of the Cossacks, religious communities, and monasteries. The genres of writing were also diverse: thus, Andrei Belaiev, who taught history at the Vifanskaia ecclesiastical seminary of Spaso-Vifanskii monastery in the town of Sergiev Posad, sent the society the prospectus of his history textbook for secondary schools, while a priest, Iakov Temnogrudov, from the village of Staro-Novaia Tolkovka in Krasnoslobodskoi uezd of Penza gubernia submitted his own autobiography.[264] Only a small number of submissions were awarded grants or accepted for publication, but all of them underwent an evaluation procedure intended to locate suitable works. The council of the society endeavored to make this procedure more flexible while nonetheless retaining complete control. The case of Beliaev's textbook is helpful for understanding how this mechanism of selection worked.

Beliaev's textbook proposal took the society's historical department completely by surprise. Therefore its evaluation began with an inquiry into the author's qualifications and, first of all, his identity. In January 1898 the puzzled head of the department, Selifontov, asked the chief of the Moscow branch, Tiutchev, via whom this proposal had been sent, to provide him with information about the author, including his permanent place of residence, who had guided him in preparing the textbook's prospectus, and "most important, what help, excepting consideration of the prospectus of the textbook, Mr. Beliaev expected."[265] The preliminary investigation took a long time, and it was only in spring 1899 that the proposal was discussed by members of the historical department. Their opinions were divided. Even before the unexpected appearance of Beliaev's prospectus, the idea of a history textbook had been circulating among the Zealots. In December 1896 Iuzefovich had already spoken of the need for school textbooks that would "present the historical past in the national spirit," which led to the council's decision to prepare a plan for such textbooks and to launch a search for possible writers and means for subsidizing the project.[266] Since no progress was made in the following years, some members of the historical department saw Beliaev's initiative to write a textbook emphasizing the Russian people's "adherence to the Orthodox church" and "devotion to autocracy" as a chance to realize previous plans. Yet Selifontov's deputy, the university historian Nikolai Petrovich Likhachev, pointed out certain difficulties: textbook writing, he claimed, demanded "profound pedagogical experience and erudition, especially in view of the current state of scholarly knowledge." Therefore, the department asked Beliaev to send them a chapter of the proposed text and a list of his other writings so that they could reach a decision.[267]

Beliaev fulfilled both requests, and, in addition, attached a letter explaining his vision of the history textbook's educational role. He started with a statement that could have been easily adopted both by adherents of progressive pedagogy and by liberal university scholars:

> The study of history usually leaves only the memory of some events, dates, and names, but the pupil acquires neither a clear notion of the development of the Russian people's historical life and its distinctive characteristics nor any meaningful opinions or convictions stemming from the painstakingly studied facts. This is why we need a textbook that will give pupils a clear idea of the fundamental principles and distinctive characteristics of Russian history without burdening them with an abundance of historical facts. I agree with you that producing such a textbook is quite a difficult task. Not only deep knowledge of the historical material and a correct historical understanding are needed, but also the ability to transmit this knowledge and understanding to pupils.[268]

Yet Beliaev subsequently contradicted the progressive spirit of his basic postulate. While assuming that pupils should analyze the material independently, he feared that they would be unable to formulate their conclusions and thus planned to include in his textbook the "right conclusions" leading to "correct opinions." Although he promised to base his account on "scholarly authorities" and to choose the material according to its importance and educational value, he planned to avoid "disputed" issues since exposure to "doubts" could create in pupils an unfavorable impression of scholarship as such.[269] He nonetheless included in his textbook additional materials intended for the best pupils, and left the decision of when and how to use these materials to the teacher, thereby strengthening the latter's role in the educational process. Beliaev's explanations hardly made the task of assessing his textbook any easier.

The historical department agreed to consider all the materials, including this controversial letter, two chapters of the proposed textbook and Beliaev's not very impressive list of publications consisting of a few compilations such as the *Illustrated History of the Russian Church* and a *List of Heads, Teachers and Students of the Vifanskaia Seminary in 1800–1897.*[270] Now it was time for the next, crucial stage of the evaluation process, namely, for an expert's review. The committee entrusted this task to the critically minded Likhachev, whose review (absent from the Zealots' surviving documents) was in all probability unfavorable since the department subsequently decided to compensate Beliaev for his time and effort, but not to commission him to write the textbook. Yet the same decision of December 31, 1899, also included the suggestion to hold a contest for the best history textbook in which Beliaev was invited to participate together with other candidates.[271] The department's decision, therefore, introduced an element of openness and competitiveness into the Zealots' selection process. Although this particular contest never took place, the same principles were applied to the contest for the best essays on the reign of Alexander III, the rules of which were publicized in *Moskovskie vedomosti*, *Russkii vestnik*, and *Novoe vremia* in May–June 1899. The Zealots announced their intention to grant a prize of 500 rubles in 1901, 1903, and 1905; both manuscripts and published works on relevant subjects and of appropriate length (not less than ten printer's sheets) could be nominated.[272] The society apparently sought a way to find—or create—a kind of "author from among the people."

The first of such awards was granted to a book that had already been published, *The Life and Reign of Emperor Alexander III (1881–1894)* by a priest of Kiev's Zlatoustovskaia church, Konstantin Korol'kov.[273] The society's evaluation commission consisting of Stishinskii, Khrushchov, Chechulin, Platonov, and Peter Maikov explained that Korol'kov had succeeded in satisfying the Zealots' combined criteria of quality and popularity. The commission noted his "intelligent and sufficiently complete account," elegance of style, and, especially, the vividness of the narrative "warmed by patriotism." The commission's conclusion hinted at a certain deficiency in the book, which its members, nevertheless, readily excused in this case:

> Although none of the topics recommended in the rules and given preference for the award has been developed in detail, all of them are included in the essay and addressed from the perspective of their historical significance. As a result, the author has succeeded in portraying a well-constructed general picture of the reign and depicted an image of the sovereign with all the attractiveness of his personal qualities and with a faithful assessment of the great service he rendered to his people as a pacifier of internal order and bearer of peace and truth. The narrative style of this work makes it accessible to a wide circle of readers.[274]

Yet this first award, which was granted only in 1903, and not in 1901 as initially planned, was also the last: amateur "historical writers" failed to meet the society's expectations. Although in practical terms the results were rather disappointing, the Zealots' call for writings on the recent past did stimulate creative activity among its target audience, especially clerics of various ranks. Priest Temnogrudov's submission of his autobiography—inspired, as he explained in his letter, by the society's announcement in the *Tserkovnye vedomosti* and accompanied by a rather peculiar offer that the society buy the rights to its first publication—demonstrated that at least in his case the transformation of a "reader from among the people" into an "author from among the people" had taken place. Temnogrudov, however, strove to express himself, not to fulfill the society's political goals. He saw the Zealots' historical project as a way of exposing his writing to the same audience to which he belonged. Temnogrudov expressed his views with remarkable candor when promising to join the society as a corresponding member if his proposal was accepted.[275] This, however, did not happen: Chechulin, who reviewed this manuscript on the society's behalf, found nothing interesting in Temnogrudov's autobiography, which he dismissed as the life story of an ordinary man, who "was certainly not distinguished by anything notable" and whose writing was even "not always grammatically correct."[276]

Despite the rejection, the very fact that a village priest decided to publish his autobiography in the wake of the Zealots' call demonstrated that the society had succeeded in opening a channel of interactive communication with its audience and had indeed created a pool of people willing to be involved in the society's project of writing modern history. The Zealots' attempts to collect accounts of the recent past contributed to the ongoing process of forming the grand narrative of the Russian monarchy, which the Society of Zealots strove to steer and control via the mechanisms of selection, assessment, and awards to suitable "histories."

A Modern Narrative for Russian Tsardom

The narrative of the Russian autocracy that the Zealots sought to create was based on the explanatory model which had been outlined in their founding *Zapiska* and was subsequently elaborated in the society's various publications. This model determined the choice of particular "instruments of persuasion" and factual data that shaped their distinctive story of the fin-de-siècle monarchy. Through the different channels at their disposal, including book series, newsletters, and a historical journal, the Zealots created an image of a popular (*narodnyi*) Orthodox tsardom, whose historical roots stretched back to the ancient Slavs and which now occupied a key position between East and West. While emphasizing the traditional character of the Russian monarchy, the Zealots insisted on its relevance for modern conditions. Thus, they devoted a special section of the journal *Starina i novizna* to contemporary materials, carefully selected topics for their contests and award programs and—most intriguingly—connected the issue of the Russian monarchy with the discussions on socialism and democracy that were agitating the educated public in 1890s. Relevant essays appeared regularly in the society's newsletters (*Izvestiia*), mainly in the form of bibliographic surveys of what was being published on the topic by the foreign press. This mode of presentation enabled the editor of the *Izvestiia* (who was none other than Kutuzov) to introduce the Russian public to the voices of Western critics of socialist ideas, to warn about the Western states' "inadequate" response to the danger of socialism, and to describe Russia as a better alternative to the flawed West. A review of a dystopian novel, *The Triumph of Socialism*, in the first issue of *Izvestiia* in February 1900 provided an instructive example of this strategy.

The Triumph of Socialism was written by the Russian author Alexander Velitsyn, who had previously translated a study by the contemporary English publicist William Hurrell Mallock on the negative economic aspects of social equality.[277] Velitsyn (whose real name was Alexander Paltov) was well known in nationalist circles for his articles on "Foreign Colonization in Russia" and "The German Invasion of the South of Russia" published in *Russkii vestnik* in 1889–1890, where he presented the German colonists as the vanguard of the forces of "Germanism" advancing on Russia. The *Triumph of Socialism* was based on the writings of the German politician Eugen Richter and French journalist Hippolyte Verly.[278] Velitsyn borrowed from Verly the title of the novel and the location of the fictitious events—twentieth-century France. The plot and even the genre of his book—dystopian fiction—were taken from Richter's *Pictures of the Socialistic Future*, and it was written, like the latter, as the diary of a devoted socialist workman, who after a victorious socialist revolution (in Richter's version—in Germany) gradually became disenchanted with its results and finally fell victim to post-revolutionary chaos and anarchy. Similar to Richter's hero, the protagonist of Velitsyn's book was depicted as an "honest and diligent social-democrat, who sincerely believed in the rightness of his cause," but started to grasp the painful truth when revolution hurt his own family. His son was forced to leave the country, his small daughter died, his wife went mad, and the hero finally realized the dimension of his tragic mistake shortly before he was killed in the street unrest. Yet, while following Richter's plot in general, Velitsyn made one particular—and significant—change. In his version of the story, the hero's son flees from France to Russia, and his letters from the Russian "safe haven" conveyed the main idea of the novel. This was the reason why Velitsyn's by no means original work attracted the Zealots' attention. The *Izvestiia*'s review of the *Triumph of Socialism* accordingly focused on these two aspects of the novel: its claim that any attempt to realize the socialist ideal would inevitably lead to disaster and its depiction of Russia as a domain of freedom.

The reviewer presented Richter/Velitsyn's argumentation in detail, explaining the inevitable progression from the allegedly promising beginning when the "capitalists and bourgeoisie were destroyed, power was in the hands of the workers' party, and the latter sought to establish life on the principles of collectivism" to the disappointing end when the initial hopes were ousted by "horror and suffering." Special attention was paid to the various stages in this process: deepening dissatisfaction when resources accumulated in the "capitalist period" disappeared; the emergence of a "barrack-like (*kazarmennyi*) style of life," and economic deterioration following the enforced imposition of the principle of equality; unprecedented debauchery as a result of the abolition of the institution of the family; and increasing disobedience to the new rules that ensued in "the resurrection of the kind of punishment that the world has long forgotten." In these circumstances, a group of "energetic scoundrels" seized power and imposed a tyrannical regime. Nonetheless, it was emphasized that such a regime could not endure for long. A few months later, when "all the supplies had run out, hunger loomed large, workers refused to work, despotism reached the highest level, the bloody hydra of anarchy raised its head," the "social republic" for which "the stupefied European working class had striven so hard" came to an end.[279]

This apocalyptic (and in some points strikingly prescient) description was the perfect backdrop for portraying Russia as a realm of security and protected human rights via the "letters" of a French émigré. One of these fictitious letters was quoted in the review:

> When we arrived here we felt as if we had awoken from a terrible nightmare. . . . We are free—we cannot stop repeating it, and it fills our hearts with exaltation. . . . We are no longer obliged to eat when and what we are told; we are no longer obliged to go at a certain hour to work that we detest, in the company of antipathetic strangers; we are not obliged to rejoice and dance on command or go to sleep at a certain hour. Finally, we do not feel that terrible control over us which in France made us scared to utter a superfluous word for fear of administrative exile. . . . Now we do what we want, we read whatever we please, we eat whatever we find tasty, and we choose work at our own discretion—in short, we are free![280]

This interpretation of freedom as a basic existential, "everyday" value, and not as a political right, was followed by praise for the Russian government's defense of personal security, contrasted to the "great falsehood" of the socialist ideas. *Izvestiia* thus presented a new perspective on the debates about the nature of the Russian state. The Zealots' insistence on the latter's advantages in protecting individual freedom provided a basis for suggesting a more sophisticated (and problematic) notion—that of the potential of the Russian monarchy to become a pristine "social state" where the unity between the monarch and the people, not democratic elections, would guarantee its citizens' rights and freedoms. For this purpose the third issue of *Izvesiia* published a review of a book by Gaston Deschamps devoted to the "malady" of contemporary democracy, followed by a survey of recent English articles on the contemporary socialist and anarchist movements. Pointing to their sharp criticism of the deficiencies of the democratic form of government, it paid particular attention to an article by Geoffrey Langtoft, who argued, inter alia, that most freedom-loving, honest people had always preferred monarchy which, although theoretically limiting political rights, still guaranteed the inviolability of private property and personal freedom. The reviewer concluded his essay with a recommendation to disseminate the "sober views" of the Western authors among Russian society. Otherwise, he warned, someone in Russia might fight for the triumph of ideas regarded as "the last word of science," even though their "false and unrealistic character is well known to every intelligent person in the West."[281]

The Zealots mobilized the voices of Western critics of democracy (including those who, like Richter, were confirmed liberals) in order to demonstrate the scientific credentials of their critique. They were thus able to condemn socialist, democratic, and "constitutionalist" views not only as politically dangerous, but also as unscientific. Their manipulative use of modern political and scholarly language alongside the lexicon of patriarchy and *soslovnost'* made the Zealots' narrative both eclectic and flexible. In this framework it was possible to depict Alexander III's personal patronage of a mental hospital in Udel'naia, a poor suburb of Petersburg, both as a manifestation of the traditional quality of the tsar's benevolence to his most miserable subjects and, simultaneously, as a humanistic act intended to protect the rights of the mentally ill. Employing the same logic, the conservative pedagogue, Ivan Kornilov—who in his capacity of *popechtel'* of the Vil'na educational district in the turbulent 1860s had made every effort to russify the school system there—in 1900 suggested establishing pupils' patriotic circles on the model of German "Vereins" in Russian schools.[282]

The Zealots drew on a variety of political, scholarly, and religious discourses but did not subscribe completely to any of them, freely employing the rhetorical tools that seemed appropriate to the narrative they wished to inculcate. In so doing, they also played a role in shaping the concept of contemporary history and produced a "conservative" account of the national past that challenged the views of the liberal historians.

Notes

1. *Ustav Obshchestva revnitelei russkogo istoricheskogo prosveshcheniia v pamiat' Imperatora Aleksandra III s izmeneniiami i dopolneniiami* (St. Petersburg, 1904) (hereafter *Ustav*), 1–2.

2. "Otchët obshchestva revnitelei russkogo istoricheskogo prosveshcheniia v pamiat' imperatora Aleksandra III za 1900–1901," in *Izvestiia Obshchestva Revnitelei russkogo istoricheskogo prosveshcheniia v pamiat' imperatora Aleksandra III* (hereafter *IOR*), no. 4,

Feb. 26, 1902, 2; "Otchët obshchestva revnitelei . . . za 1901–1902 god" in *IOR*, no. 5, Feb. 26, 1904, 2; *Izdaniia Obshchestva Revnitelei russkogo istoricheskogo prosveshcheniia v pamiat' imperatora Aleksandra III* (St. Petersburg, 1908).

3. On A. A. Golenishchev-Kutuzov as a poet, see P. P. Pertsov, "Graf A. A. Golenishchev-Kutuzov," in idem, *Filosofskie techeniia russkoi poezii* (St. Petersburg: Tip. M. Merkusheva, 1896), 365–378; I. I. Vysotskii, *Poeziia grafa A. A. Golenishcheva-Kutuzova* (Riga, Tip. A. Nitavskogo, 1913); A. Krukovskii, "Pevets bezmiatezhnykh perezhivanii," *Filologicheskie zapiski*, no. 4 (1915): 523–60.

4. The Peasants' Land Bank was founded in 1882 as a state mortgage bank intended to provide peasants with long-term loans for purchasing land. The State Nobles' Land Bank was established in 1885 according to a proposal of the Minister of Finance H. Kh. Bunge; it gave long-term loans to noble landowners on the security of their land. In 1895 the Peasants' Bank acquired the right to buy noble land properties for their following piecemeal resale. See N. P. Sokolov's index of names in V. I. Gurko, *Cherty i siluety proshlogo* (Moscow: Novoe literaturnoe obozrenie, 2000), 702; *Entsiklopedicheskii slovar'*, vol. 9 (St. Petersburg, 1893), 43.

5. A. A. Golenishchev-Kutuzov to L. A. Tikhomirov, Dec. 29, 1894, Rossiiskii gosudarstvennyi arkhiv literatury i iskusstva (RGALI), f. 143, Golenishchev-Kutuzov Arsenii Arkad'evich, graf (1848–1913), op. 1, d. 150, Pis'ma Tikhomirovu L. A., l. 5.

6. L. A. Tikhomirov, *Pochemu ia perestal byt' revoliutsionerom* (Moscow: Tipografiia Vilde, 1895); idem, *Monarkhicheskaia gosudarstvennost'* (Moscow: Alir, 1998); idem, *Kritika demokratii* (Moscow: Moskva, 1997); idem, *Religiozno-filosofskie osnovy istorii* (Moscow: Moskva, 1997); Abbott Gleason, "The Emigration and Apostasy of Lev Tikhomirov," *Slavic Review* 26, no. 3 (1967): 414–429; V. N. Kostylev, "Vybor L'va Tikhomirova," *Voprosy istorii*, no. 6–7 (1992): 30–46; O. A. Milevskii, "L. A. Tikhomirov i K. Leont'ev: k istorii vzaimootnoshenii," *Vestnik Tomskogo gosudarstvennogo pedagogicheskogo universiteta*, no.1 (1997): 70–74; O. A. Milevskii, "K istorii ideinoi evoliutsii L. Tikhomirova: poslednie gody emigratsii (1885–1888)," in A. M. Salagaev and F. N. Podustov, eds., *Problemy otechestvennoi i vseobshchei istorii: sbornik statei posviashchennyi 70-letiiu prof. L. I. Bozhenko* (Tomsk: Izdatel'stvo Tomskogo pedagogicheskogo universiteta, 1999), 96–111; A. V. Repnikov, "Lev Tikhomirov—ot revoliutsii k apokalipsisu," *Rossiia i sovremennyi mir*, no. 3 (1998), 189–198; A. V. Repnikov, ed., *Dnevnik L. A. Tikhomirova, 1915–1917 gg* (Moscow: ROSSPEN, 2008); A. V. Repnikov and O. A. Milevskii, *Dve zhizni L'va Tikhomirova* (Moscow: Academia, 2011).

7. *Moskovskie vedomosti*, October 30, 1894.

8. L. A. Tikhomirov, *Vospominaniia* (Moscow-Leningrad: Gosudarstvennoe Izdatel'stvo, 1927), 428.

9. A. A. Golenishchev-Kutuzov to L. A. Tikhomirov, November 30, 1894, RGALI, f. 143, op. 1, d. 150, l. 1–1 ob.; Tikhomirov, *Vospominaniia*, 430; L. A. Tikhomirov to A. A. Golenishchev-Kutuzov, December 4, 14, 1894, RGALI, f. 143, op. 1, d. 211, Pis'ma L. A. Tikhomirova, l. 1–2 ob., 3.

10. A. A. Golenishchev-Kutuzov to L. A. Tikhomirov, Dec. 29, 1894, RGALI, f. 143, op. 1, d. 150, l. 5.

11. L. A. Tikhomirov to A. A. Golenishchev-Kutuzov, Jan. 1, 1895, RGALI, f. 143, op. 1, d. 211, l. 4–5.

12. A. A. Golenishchev-Kutuzov to L. A. Tikhomirov, Jan. 18, 1895, RGALI, f. 143, op. 1, d. 150, l. 9-9 ob. On the activity of the *St. Petersburg Literacy Committee* in the early 1890s, see Bradley, "The St. Petersburg Literacy Committee," 281–289.

13. "I am writing a memorandum on the publishing commission, but it is no easy task: not all the details have to be revealed but it is essential not to leave out anything important. " A. A. Golenishchev-Kutuzov to L. A. Tikhomirov, Jan. 13, 1895, RGALI, f. 143, op. 1, d. 150, l. 7 ob.

14. The full name of this conference was "Osoboe mezhduvedomstvennoe soveshchanie dlia obsuzhdeniia voprosov o peredache Peterburgskogo komiteta gramotnosti v vedenie Ministerstva narodnogo prosveshcheniia i o podchinenii pravitel'skomu kontroliu vsekh chastnykh obshchestv, presleduiushchikh tseli narodnogo obrazovaniia." See Bradley, "The St. Petersburg Literacy Committee," 288–290.

15. A. A. Golenishchev-Kutuzov to L. A. Tikhomirov, February 20, 1895, RGALI, f. 143, op. 1, d. 150, l. 17–17 ob.

16. Ibid., l. 18–18 ob.

17. Kizevetter, *Na rubezhe dvukh stoletii*, 230.

18. A. A. Golenishchev-Kutuzov to L. A. Tikhomirov, March 6, 1895, RGALI, f. 143, op. 1, d. 150, l. 20–20 ob.

19. V. G. Bukhert, "Pavlovskie kursy (1899–1997 gg.)," in S. O. Shmidt, ed., *Arkheograficheskii ezhegodnik za 2004* (Moscow: Nauka, 2005), 281–282.

20. "Ot redaktsii:[Zapiska s podrobnym izlozheniem osnovanii i sposobov deiatel'nosti predpolagaemogo obshchestva]," (hereafter "Zapiska"), *IOR*, no. 1, Feb. 26, 1900, 3.

21. O. V. Aptekman, "Partiia 'Narodnogo prava': Po lichnym vospominaniiam," *Byloe*, no. 7 (19) (1907): 177–206; V. M. Chernov, *Pered burei: Vospominaniia* (New York: Izdatel'stvo im. Chekhova, 1953), 75–78.

22. *Pamiatnaia knizhka Orlovskoi gubernii na 1897 g.: Izdanie Orlovskogo gubernskogo statisticheskogo komiteta* (Orel: Tipografiia gubernskogo pravleniia, 1897), 90; O. M. Trokhina, "Iz istorii narodnogo obrazovaniia v Orlovskoi gubernii," *Obrazovanie i obshchestvo*, no. 1 (1999), http://www.jeducation.ru/1_1999/44.html; A. M. Gularian, *Obshchestvenno-politicheskaia zhizn' v Orlovskoi gubernii v kontse XIX-nachale XX veka* (PhD diss., Orel State Agrarian University, 2006), 47–60, 80–97; R. I. Reutskaia and V. G. Sidorov, eds., *Deiateli knizhnoi kul'tury Orlovskogo kraia* (Orel: Izdatel'skii dom "Orlik," 2003), 13–15.

23. A. A. Golenishchev-Kutuzov to L. A. Tikhomirov, Apr. 12, 1895, RGALI, f. 143, op. 1, d. 150, l. 21 ob.

24. A. A. Golenishchev-Kutuzov to L. A. Tikhomirov, Nov. 8, 1895, RGALI, f. 143, op. 1, d. 150, l. 25 ob; Kizevetter, *Na rubezhe dvukh stoletii*, 281; A. A. Golenishvev-Kutuzov to S. D. Sheremetev, May 12, 1895, Rossiiskii gosudarstvennyi arkhiv drevnikh aktov (RGADA), f. 1287, Sheremetevy, Lichnyi arkhiv S. D. Sheremeteva, op. 1, d. 411, Pis'ma S. D. Sheremetevu ot A. A. Golenishcheva-Kutuzova, l. 31 ob.

25. "Zapiska," *IOR*, no. 1 (1900), 5.

26. A. A. Golenishchev-Kutuzov to L. A. Tikhomirov, May 12, 1896, RGALI, f. 143, op. 1, d. 150, l. 26 ob.-27.

27. A. A. Golenishchev-Kutuzov to S. D. Sheremetev, March 5, 1895, RGADA, f. 1287, op. 1, d. 411, l. 7 ob.–8.

28. A. A. Golenishchev-Kutuzov to S. D. Sheremetev, April 6, 20, 21, 24; May 3, 12, 24; July 7, 17, 1895, RGADA, f. 1287, op. 1, d. 411, l. 18–18 ob., 22, 23, 23 ob., 27–28 ob., 30 ob., 32, 35 ob.-36, 39 ob.–40, 41.

29. Rossiiskii gosudarstvennyi istoricheskii arkhiv (RGIA), f. 747, Obshchestvo revnitelei russkogo istoricheskogo prosveshcheniia, op. 1, d. 16, Tetrad' so stat'ei ob obshchestve revnitelei russkogo istoricheskogo prosveshcheniia, l. 3–4.

30. "Zapiska," *IOR*, no. 1 (1900), 3–4.

31. Ibid., 4.

32. "Imperator i samoderzhets Vserossiiskii, Tsar' Pol'skii, Velikii kniaz' Finliandskii, i prochaia, i prochaia, i prochaia." See B. A. Uspenskii, *Tsar' i Imperator: Pomazanie na tsarstvo i semantika monarshikh titulov* (Moscow: Iazyki russkoi kul'tury, 2000), 52.

33. Uspenskii, *Tsar' i Imperator*, 48. On the reduced significance of the title "tsar" after 1721 and the changes in its application to the different parts of the empire, see ibid., 49–52.

34. "Zapiska," *IOR*, no. 1 (1900), 4.

35. Wortman, *Scenarios of Power*, 264.

36. Wirtschafter, *Social Identity in Imperial Russia*, 172. Konstantin Pobedonostsev was the main supporter of the idea of popular monarchy. See K. P. Pobedonostsev, *Moskovskii sbornik* (Moscow: Russkaia simfoniia, 2009); idem, *Pis'ma Pobedonostseva k Aleksandru III* (Moscow: Novaia Moskva, 1925–1926), vols. 1–2; idem, *Reflections of a Russian Statesman* (Ann Arbor: University of Michigan Press, 1965).

37. Wirtschafter, *Social Identity in Imperial Russia*, 172.

38. "Zapiska," *IOR*, no. 1 (1900), 4.

39. B. I. Kolonitskii, "Identifikatsiia rossiiskoi intelligentsii i intelligentofobiia (konets XIX-nachalo XX veka)," in D. A. Sdvizhkov, ed., *Intelligentsiia v istorii: Obrazovannyi chelovek v predstavleniiakh i sotsial'noi deistvitel'nosti*, (Moscow: RAN, Institut Vseobshchei istorii, 2001), 150–170; for the phenomenon of hostility to the intelligentsia, see also Knight, "Was the Intelligentsia Part of the Nation?", 733–758; Gary Saul Morson, "The Intelligentsia and Its Critics," in Abbott Gleason, ed., *A Companion to Russian History* (Chichester, UK; Malden, MA: Wiley Blackwell, 2009), 261–278.

40. "Zapiska," *IOR*, no. 1 (1900), 5–6.

41. As mentioned in the previous chapter, the notion of "moralized collectivism" was suggested and discussed by Burbank in "Discipline and Punish in the Moscow Bar Association," 53.

42. "Zapiska," *IOR*, no. 1 (1900), 3.

43. Draft of a letter from Count S. D. Sheremetev to Nicholas II, October 7, 1895, RGADA, f. 1287, op. 1, d. 4119, Chernoviki pisem S. D. Sheremeteva Nikolaiu II po voprosam, sviazannym s deiatel'nost'iu Obshchestva revnitelei, l. 1. As follows from the diaries of both Nicholas II and Sheremetev, the latter was quite close to the young emperor in the initial stage of his reign. Sheremetev frequented the tsar's intimate family breakfasts and the tsar visited his house on some occasions; in a note of March 15, 1896, Nicholas mentioned "prolonged talks with Sheremetev and Count Ignat'ev." However, some of the tsar's notes hint at his irritation about the timing (or frequency) of Sheremetev's visits. See, for example, his note of January 19, 1898: "Before the reports there was a visit from Count Sheremetev, which deprived me of an opportunity to go for a walk," *Dnevniki Imperatora Nikolaia II*, vol. 1, 261, 389; see also ibid., 135, 166, 183, 188, 213, 657, 714, 717, 794, 811; RGADA, f. 1287, op. 1, d. 5041, Dnevnik S. D. Sheremeteva, l. 47, 51–52 ob., 60–60 ob.

44. A. A. Golenishchev-Kutuzov to S. D. Sheremetev, May 12, 1895, RGADA, f. 1287, op. 1, d. 411, l. 31.

45. RGADA, f. 1287, op. 1, d. 4145, l. 4 ob.

46. RGADA, f. 1287, op.1, d. 411, l. 14, 15 ob.

47. *Ustav*, 13, clauses 46, 47, 49; 14, clauses 51, 53, 55; 15, clause 56; 22, clause 93.

48. Ibid., 1–2, clause 2; 3–4, clause 10; 5–6, clauses 16–19, 21, 22; 7, clauses 25, 26.

49. Ibid., 8, clause 31.

50. The chairman of the society (as well as his deputy) was to be elected for a term of nine years; the tenure of department chairmen was not defined at all; and chairmen of the branches would be elected for a term of three years. Ibid., 15, clause 59; 17, clause 67; 22, clause 95.

51. Ibid., 14, clause 51; 17, clause 65; 17–18, clause 69; 23–24, clauses 102–103.

52. Ibid., 8, clause 31.

53. A. A. Golenishchev-Kutuzov to L. A. Tikhomirov, November 6, 1895, RGALI, f. 143, op. 1, d. 150, l. 23–24.

54. A. A. Golenishchev-Kutuzov to S. D. Sheremetev, March 29, 1895, RGADA, f, 1287, op. 1, d. 411, l. 11 ob.-12.

55. A. A. Golenishchev-Kutuzov to S. D. Sheremetev, Mar. 29, 1895, Apr. 5, 12, 1895, RGADA, f. 1287, op. 1, d. 411, l. 12, 17, 20 ob.-21. For Kireev's public role, see A. A. Kireev, *Sochineniia*. 2 vols. (St. Petersburg, 1912); John D. Basil, "Alexander Kireev and Theological Controversy in the Russian Orthodox Church, 1890–1910," in Geoffrey A. Hosking, ed., *Church, Nation and State in Russia and Ukraine* (Houndmills, Basingstoke and London: Macmillan in association with the School of Slavonic and East European Studies, University of London, 1991), 131–147.

56. S. D. Sheremetev, "Imperator Aleksandr III," in *Memuary grafa S. D. Sheremeteva*, 414–620. For Sheremetev's biography, see Douglas Smith, *Former People: The Final Days of the Russian Aristocracy* (Farrar, Straus and Giroux, 2012), 34–43; for the complete list of his governmental and court posts, see A. D. Alekseeva and M. D. Kovaleva, eds. *Sheremetevy v sud'be Rossii: Vospominaniia, dnevniki, dokumenty* (Moscow: "Zvonnitsa", 2001), 414–415; for his public activity including his participation in historical societies, see A. A. Meshchenina, *S. D. Sheremetev: deiatel'nost' v oblasti organizatsii russkoi istoricheskoi nauki kontsa XIX-nachala XX veka* (PhD diss., St. Petersburg State University, 2004); and O. V. Belousova, *Graf S. D. Sheremetev v obshchestvennoi i politicheskoi zhizni Rossii vtoroi poloviny XIX-nachala XX veka* (PhD diss., Lomonosov Moskow State University, 2012). For Sheremetev's works, see N. V. Timofeev, *Izdaniia grafa S. D. Sheremeteva* (St. Petersburg: Tipografiia M. N. Aleksandrova, 1913), and L. I. Shokhin, "Neopublikovannaia rabota S. D. Sheremeteva o Smutnom vremeni: Lev Sapega i Fedor Sheremetev," in S. O. Shmidt, ed., *Arkheograficheskii ezhegodnik za 1994* (Moscow: Nauka, 1996), 185–191. For his activity as a nonacademic historian, see idem, "S. D. Sheremetev-istorik v svoikh dnevnikovykh zapisiakh," in ibid., 191–222; A. V. Krasko, "Zhiznennyi put' i tvorcheskoe nasledie grafa S. D. Sheremeteva (k 150-iu so dnia rozhdeniia)," *Izvestiia russkogo genealogicheskogo obshchestva*, no. 2 (1995): 13–19.

57. RGADA, f. 1287, op. 1, d. 4116, Chernovaia zametka S. D. Sheremeteva 'Iz vospominanii o vozniknovenii Obshchestva revnitelei, 1913, l. 4 ob.

58. On L. N. Maikov and D. B. Golitsyn, see S. D. Sheremetev, "Imperator Aleksandr III," in *Memuary grafa S. D. Sheremeteva*, 508–509, 560, 587–588. For an insightful portrayal of Sipiagin in that period of his life, see Gurko, *Cherty i siluety proshlogo*, 84–91. On Gorchakov, see V. A. Ivanov, "Materialy k biografiiam dvorian Kaluzhskoi gubernii sluzhivshikh po vyboram: Kniaz' Sergei Dmitrievich Gorchakov," in *Letopis' istoriko-rodoslovnogo obshchestva v Moskve*, no. 4–5 (48–49) (1997): 50–52; on Gesse, see S. Iu. Vitte, *Vospominaniia*, vol. 2, *Tsarstvovanie Nikolaia II: 1894-oktiabr' 1905* (Moscow: Izdatel'stvo sotsial'no-ekonomicheskoi literatury, 1960), 40–41; see also V. I. Fedorchenko, *Imperatorskii Dom: Vydaiushchiesia sanovniki. Entsiklopediia biografii*, vol. 1 (Krasnoiarsk: Bonus & Moscow: Olma-Press, 2003), 286.

59. Kartsov was appointed head (*upravliaiushchii*) of the Nobles' and Peasants' Banks in 1915. See *Ves' Petrograd na 1915: Adresnaia i spravochnaia kniga g. Petrograda* (Izdatel'stvo Tovarishchestva A. S. Suvorina "Novoe Vremia"), st. [stolbets] 125; and O. V. Erokhina, "Krest'ianskii Pozemel'nyi Bank i likvidatsiia nemetskogo zemlevladeniia v oblasti Voiska Donskogo," in *Novyi istoricheskii vestnik*, 27, no.1 (2011): 40. He was fired from this post by the decree of the Provisional Government of March 27, 1917. See Gosudarstvennyi arkhiv Rossiiskoi Federatsii (GARF), f. 1779, Kantseliariia Vremennogo pravitel'stva, op.2, d. 1, Zhurnaly zasedanii Vremennogo pravital'stva s no. 3 po 67, l. 133–135.

60. A. A. Golenishchev-Kutuzov to S. D. Sheremetev, Apr. 5, 1895, RGADA, f. 1287, op. 1, d. 411, l. 17. (Original emphasis.)

61. OR RNB, f. 585, op. 1, d. 5691, l. 71 ob.

62. "A multitude of students saw Miliukov off. He himself wept, and his wife was brought into the [train] compartment in a faint. Miliukov is the remains of the movement launched by Kliuchevskii and Vinogradov, but these generals shunned him quite openly . . . and thus made the blow even heavier." *Aleksandr Evgen'evich Presniakov: Pis'ma i dnevniki 1889–1927*, 179.

63. E. E. Ukhtomskii, *Puteshestvie na Vostok ego imperatorskogo vysochestva gosudaria naslednika tsesarevicha: 1890–1891* (St. Petersburg and Leipzig, 1893–1897), vols. 1–3. The first English translation was Hesper Ookhtomsky, *Travels in the East of Nicholas II, emperor of Russia when cesarewitch, 1890–1891*: Written by order of His Imperial Majesty; and tr. from the Russian by R. Goodlet; edited by Sir George Birdwood (Westminster: Constable, 1900). For Nicholas II's involvement in the work on this book, see David Schimmelpenninck van der Oye, *Toward the Rising Sun: Russian Ideologies of Empire and the Path to War with Japan* (Dekalb: Northern Illinois University Press, 2001), 49, 230.

64. A. A. Golenishchev-Kutuzov to S. D. Sheremetev, May 12, 1895, RGADA, f, 1287, op. 1, d. 411, l. 32 ob.–33.

65. Schimmelpenninck van der Oye, *Toward the Rising Sun*, 48.

66. A. A. Golenishchev-Kutuzov to E. E. Ukhtomskii, Mar. 20, 1896, RGIA, f. 1072, Ukhtomskii Esper Esperovich, op. 1, d. 10, Pis'ma E. E. Ukhtomskomu, l. 1.

67. At that time Tikhomirov was a member of the society's publishing department. RGIA, f. 747, op. 1, d. 29-2, Kopii protokolov i vypiski iz zhurnalov zasedanii, perepiska o deiatel'nosti Izdatel'skogo otdela, l. 353.

68. *Ot Soveta Obshchestva Revnitelei Russkogo Istoricheskogo Prosveshcheniia v pamiat' Imperatora Aleksandra III po sluchaiiu priniatiia L. A. Tikhomirovym rukovodstva gazetoi "Moskovskie vedomosti"* (St. Petersburg, 1909).

69. RGADA, f. 1287, op. 1, d. 4147, Kopiia pis'ma L. Tikhomirova v Sovet Obshchestva ob okazanii podderzhki gazete "Moskovskie vedomosti," l. 2-2ob.

70. RGADA, f. 1287, op. 1, d. 4147, l. 2-2ob.

71. A. A. Golenishchev-Kutuzov to L. A. Tikhomirov, Nov. 6, 1895, RGALI, f. 143, op. 1, d. 150, l. 23–24.

72. S. D. Sheremetev to V. M. Vasnetsov, Nov. 15, 1895, Otdel rukopisei Gosudarstvennoi Tret'iakovskoi galerei (OR GTG), f. 66 V. M. Vasnetsov, d. 279 Pis'ma V. M. Vasnetsovu ot S. D. Sheremeteva, l. 1.

73. V. M. Vasnetsov to S. D. Sheremetev, Nov. 17, 1895, RGADA, f. 1287, op. 1, d. 256, Pis'ma V. M. Vasnetsova to S. D. Sheremetevu, l. 1.

74. V. M. Vasnetsov to S. D. Sheremetev, Nov. 27, 1895, Nov. 1, 1896, RGADA, f. 1287, op. 1, d. 256, l.4-4 ob, 5–6; V. M. Vasnetsov to S. D. Sheremetev, December 27, 1898, RGADA, f. 1287, op. 1, d. 256, l. 7–8; S. D. Sheremetev to V. M. Vasnetsov, Feb. 3, 1899, OR GTG, f. 66, d. 281, l. 1.

75. "Spisok chlenov obshchestva," *IOR*, no. 2 (1900), 32.

76. V. M. Vasnetsov to S. D. Sheremetev, Nov. 20, 1899, RGADA, f. 1287, op. 1, d. 256, l. 9–10 ob.; S. D. Sheremetev to V. M. Vasnetsov, Nov. 29, Dec. 18, 1899, May 9, 1900, OR GTG, f. 66, d. 285, l.1–1 ob., d. 292, l. 1 ob.-2, d. 405, l. 1, d. 406. l. 1.

77. S. D. Sheremetev to V. M. Vasnetsov, February 24, March 2, July 29, 1899, OR GTG, f. 66, d. 282, l. 1; d. 283, l.1–1 ob., d. 284, l. 1.

78. "Spisok chlenov obshchestva," *IOR*, no. 2 (1900): 22, 23, 25, 31.

79. OR RNB, f. 585, op. 1, d. 5691, l. 39.

80. Thomas Sanders, "The Chechulin Affairs or Politics and *nauka* in the History Profession of Late Imperial Russia," *Jahrbücher für Geschichte Osteuropas* 49, no. 1 (2001): 1–23.

81. N. D. Chechulin to M. P. Chechulina, January 5, 1896, OR RNB, f. 838, Chechulin N. D., op. 1, d. 94, Chechulin Nikolai Dmitrievich, Pis'ma k materi, Marii Pavlovne Chechulinoi,

8 iiulia 1896–18 dekabria 1899, l. 3. For Chechulin's work in the Imperial Public Library, see also Ts. I. Grin, "Chechulin Nikolai Dmitrievich," in *Sotrudniki Rossiiskoi natsional'noi biblioteki—deiateli nauki i kul'tury: Biograficheskii slovar'*, vol. 1, *Imperatorskaia Publichnaia Biblioteka* (St. Petersburg: Rossiiskaia natsional'naia biblioteka, 1995), 565–569; P. L.Vakhtina and O. S. Ostroi, "Nikolai Dmitrievich Chechulin i ego kniga," in N. D. Chechulin, *Russkaia provintsiia vo vtoroi polovine XVIII veka* (St. Petersburg: Rossiiskaia natsional'naia biblioteka, 2010), 5–20; and my article, "Weathering the Revolution: Patronage as a Strategy of Survival," *Revolutionary Russia*, 26, no. 2 (2013): 97–127.

82. According to one of Chechulin's biographers, he finally resigned from St. Petersburg University on February 14, 1898. See E. V. Pinaeva, "Peterburgskii period v zhizni N. D. Chechulina (1881–1915): Biograficheskii ocherk," in *Nikolai Dmitrievich Chechulin—uchenyi, kraeved, bibliotekar': Materialy nauchno-prakticheskoi konferentsii* (Cherepovets: Tsentral'naia gorodskaia biblioteka im. V. V. Vereshchagina, 2002), 26.

83. N. D. Chechulin to M. P. Chechulina, Feb. 4, 1897, OR RNB, f. 838, op. 1, d. 94, l. 11–11 ob.

84. I. V. Pomialovskii to S. D. Sheremetev, Dec. 6, 1896, RGADA, f. 1287, op. 1, d. 4112, Pis'ma po obshchestvu revnitelei, l. 23.

85. For Turaev's professional biography, see O. D. Berlev and R. A. Gribov, "Egiptologiia i assirologiia v Leningradskom Universitete," *Uchenye zapiski Leningradskogo Universiteta*, no. 236 (1960): 160–176. Dubrovin's major works were N. F. Dubrovin, *Istoriia voiny i vladychestva russkikh na Kavkaze*, vols. 1–6 (St. Petersburg, Tip. Departamenta udelov, 1871–1888); *Pugachev i ego soobshchniki: Epizod iz istorii tsarstvovaniia imperatritsy Ekateriny II, 1773–1774, po neizdannym istochnikam*, vols. 1–3 (St. Petersburg, Tip. I. N. Skorokhodova, 1884); *Nikolai Mikhailovich Przheval'skii: Biograficheskii ocherk* (St. Petersburg: Voennaia tipografiia, 1890); *Istoriia Krymskoi voiny i oborony Sevastopolia*, vols. 1–3 (St. Petersburg: Tipografiia tovarishchestva "Obshchestvennaia pol'za," 1900).

86. K. A. Gubastov to N. N. Selifontov, January 16, 1897, OR RNB, f. 682, Selifontov N. N., Bakhtin I. N., op. 1, d. 74, Gubastov K. A., Chlen Soveta Ministrov, Pis'mo Nik. Nik. Selifontovu, l., 1–1 ob. Gubastov, as was noted in chapter 2, edited RIO's anthologies, including "Perepiska Imperatora Nikolaia Pavlovicha s Velikim Kniazem Konstantinom Pavlovichem, part 2 (1830–1831)," *Sbornik Imperatorskogo Russkogo istoricheskogo obshchestva*, vol. 132 (St. Petersburg, 1911) and wrote a number of biographical essays. See, for example, K. A. Gubastov, *K portretu kniazia Nikity Ivanovicha Odoevskogo* (St. Petersburg: Tip. "Sirius," 1909); idem, *Iz lichnykh vospominanii o K. N. Leont'eve* (St. Petersburg: tip. "Sirius," 1911).

87. RGADA, f. 1287, op. 1, d. 4115, Zapiska S. D. Sheremeteva o deiatel'nosti otdelenii Obshchestva revnitelei russkogo istoricheskogo prosveshcheniia, l. 3–4. Gubastov had already left this post by that time due to his diplomatic obligations; Platonov taught Russian history to Grand Dukes Mikhail Aleksandrovich, Dmitrii Pavlovich, Andrei Vladimirovich and Grand Duchess Olga Aleksandrovna in 1895–1902. See Shmidt, "Sergei Fedorovich Platonov," 116.

88. S. D. Sheremetev to S. F. Platonov, Dec. 24, 28, 1900, OR RNB, f. 585, op. 1, d. 4615, Pis'ma S. D. Sheremeteva S. F. Platonovu, l. 51, 56; OR RNB, f. 585, op. 1, d. 5027, Sovet obshchestva revnitelei russkogo istoricheskogo prosveshcheniia, l. 1, 3; S. F. Platonov to S. D. Sheremetev, Jan. 22, 1901 in S. O. Shmidt and V. G. Bukhert, eds., *Akademik S. F. Platonov: perepiska s istorikami*. vol. 1 (Moscow: Nauka, 2003), 71.

89. S. D. Sheremetev to S. F. Platonov Nov. 7, 1903, OR RNB, f. 585, op. 1, d. 4616, l. 30.

90. RGIA, f. 747, op. 1, d. 29-2, l. 352 ob.; S. D. Sheremetev to S. F. Platonov, Jan. 15, 1910, August 13, 1911, October 12, 1911, Dec. 15, 1912, OR RNB, f. 585, op. 1, d. 4620, l.1; d. 4621, l. 13 ob., 18 ob.; d. 4622, l. 18.

91. S. D. Sheremetev to S. F. Platonov, Feb. 14, 1914, Mar. 5, 1916, OR RNB, f. 585, op. 1, d. 4624, l. 4; d. 4626, l. 2.

92. RGADA, f. 1287, op. 1, d. 4112, l. 5, 8 ob.

93. *IOR*, no. 1, Feb. 26, 1900, 7; ibid., no. 2, Oct. 20, 1900, 3–4; ibid., no. 5, Feb. 26, 1904, 16.

94. *Ocherk glavnykh osnovanii deiatel'nosti mestnykh otdelov Obshchestva revnitelei russkogo istoricheskogo prosveshcheniia v pamiat' imperatora Alexandra III* (St. Petersburg, 1900), 8–9.

95. P. M. Kaznacheev to S. D. Sheremetev, Dec. 4, 1896, RGADA, f. 1287, op. 1, d. 4112, l. 22-22 ob.

96. S. D. Sheremetev to K. A. Gubastov, Dec. 29, 1900, Rukopisnyi otdel Instituta russkoi literatury (Pushkinskii dom) Akademii nauk (PO IRLI), f. 463 Gubastov K. A., d. 44 Pis'ma Sheremeteva S. D., l. 5.

97. "Spisok chlenov obshchestva," *IOR*, no. 2 (1900): 26–35.

98. A. A. Golenishchev-Kutuzov to L. A. Tikhomirov, May 12, 1896, RGALI, f. 143, op. 1, d. 150, l. 26 ob.

99. I. V. Pomialovskii to S. D. Sheremetev, December 16, 1896, RGADA, f. 1287, op. 1, d. 4112, l. 24.

100. RGADA, f. 1287, op. 1, d. 4124, l. 1.

101. RGADA, f. 1287, op. 1, l. 4112, l.4 ob.

102. RGIA, f. 747, op.1, d. 28, l. 55.

103. Simon Dixon, "The Church's Social Role in St. Petersburg, 1880–1914," in Geoffrey A. Hosking, ed., *Church, Nation and State in Russia and Ukraine* (Houndmills, Basingstoke and London: Macmillan in association with the School of Slavonic and East European Studies, University of London, 1991), 167–192, here 167. A fundamental study of the Russian Orthodox clergy is Gregory L. Freeze, *The Parish Clergy in Nineteenth-Century Russia: Crisis, Reform and Counter-Reform* (Princeton: Princeton University Press, 1983); more recent research on the Russian clergy's social activism focusing on the capital's priesthood is Jennifer Hedda, *His Kingdom Come: Orthodox Pastorship and Social Activism in Revolutionary Russia* (DeKalb: Northern Illinois University Press, 2008).

104. "Spisok chlenov Obshchestva revnitelei russkogo istoricheskogo prosveshcheniia v pamiat' imperatora Aleksandra III," 33–40; RGIA, f. 747, op. 1, d. 3, O sbore svedenii dlia sostavleniia godovogo otcheta o deiatel'nosti obshchestva za 1896-04 gg., l. 11; "Otchët obshchestva revnitelei . . . za 1902–1903 god," *IOR*, no. 5 (1904): 16.

105. For the possible results of such a challenge and the European governments' desire to retain control over education, see chapter one, "European Societies and the State: Russia in Comparative Perspective," in Bradley, *Voluntary Associations in Tsarist Russia*, 17–37.

106. "Spisok chlenov obshchestva," *IOR*, no. 2, Oct. 20, 1900, 22–36.

107. *Otchët Obshchestva revnitelei . . . za 1897–1898 god* (St. Petersburg, 1898), 18–21; *Otchët Obshchestva revnitelei . . . za 1898–1989 god* (St. Petersburg, 1899), 21; RGIA, f. 747, op.1, d. 33, Delo komissii po izdaniiu sbornika "Starina i novizna."

108. *IOR*, no. 2 (1902): 8.

109. I. F. Tiutchev to S. D. Sheremetev, March 25, 1898, RGADA f. 1287, op. 1, d. 1754, Pis'ma S. D. Sheremetevu ot I. F. Tiutcheva, l. 30 ob.

110. *Ocherk glavnykh osnovanii deiatel'nosti mestnykh otdelov Obshchestva revnitelei russkogo istoricheskogo prosveshcheniia v pamiat' Imperatora Aleksandra III* (St. Petersburg, 1900), 8–9.

111. RGIA, f. 747, op.1, d. 28, l. 81 ob.

112. "Spisok chlenov obshchestva," *IOR*, no. 2, October 20, 1900, 33; Arkhimandrit Leonid (Kavelin), *Istoricheskoe opisanie Borisovskoi pustyni, sostavlennoe po monastyrskim*

dokumentam i zapisiam (n.p., 1884); V. Puzanov, Nekrolog [nastoiatel'nitse Borisovskoi obiteli igumen'e Dorofei]," *Kurskie eparkhial'nye vedomosti*, no. 4 (1902).

113. *Otchët Obshchestva revnitelei . . . za 1898–1899 god* (St. Petersburg, 1899), 3–4, 55–56.

114. "Spisok chlenov obshchestva," *IOR*, no. 2 (1900): 22–36.

115. Daniel Gordon, *Citizens without Sovereignty: Equality and Sociability in French Thought, 1670–1789* (Princeton: Princeton University Press, 1994), 29, 33, 242.

116. RGIA, f. 747, op. 1, d. 12, Povestka dnia zasedanii soveta Obshchestva revnitelei russkogo istoricheskogo prosveshcheniia, l. 1, 2, 3, 4, 5, 7, 13, 17, 18, 22, 38, 39.

117. Ibid., l. 8.

118. S. D. Sheremetev to D. S. Sipiagin, [no date, approximately late Nov. 1901], RGADA, f. 1287, op. 1, d. 1554, Pis'ma S. D. Sheremetevu ot D. S. Sipiagina, l. 55.

119. S. D. Sheremetev to S. F. Platonov, November 23, 1901, OR RNB, f. 585, op. 1, d. 4616, l. 13–13 ob.

120. RGIA, f. 747, op. 1, d. 12, l. 3, 4.

121. "Otchët Obshchestva revnitelei russkogo istoricheskogo prosveshcheniia v pamiat' imperatora Aleksandra III za 1901–1902 god," in *IOR*, no. 5 (1904): 2. Khrushchov's rivals were Nikolai Milievich Anichkov and Pavel Dmitrievich Akhlestyshev. See RGIA, f. 747, op. 1, d. 12, l. 3.

122. RGADA, f. 1287, op.1, d. 67, Pis'ma S. D. Sheremetevu ot I. P. Barsukova, July 3, 1897, l. 17 ob.

123. RGADA, f. 1287, op.1, d. 1898, Pis'ma S. D. Sheremetevu ot N. D. Chechulina, May 13, 1914, l. 57–57 ob.

124. I. F. Tiutchev to S. D. Sheremetev, Jan. 26, 1898, RGADA, f. 1287, op.1, d. 1754, l.24 ob.–25.

125. I. F. Tiutchev to S. D. Sheremetev, Feb. 12, June 26, 1896, RGADA, f. 1287, op.1, d. 1754, l. 5 ob., 7; Nov. 10, 1896, RGADA, f. 1287, op. 1, d. 4112, l. 12- 13 ob., 80–80 ob.

126. RGIA, f.747, op. 1, d. 12, l. 40.

127. N. D. Chechulin to S. D. Sheremetev, [Jan.] 20, 1917, RGADA, f. 1287, op.1, d. 1898, l. 64–65.

128. The statutes of the society proposed no procedure of enforced removal; functionaries who completed their tenure were eligible for reelection. The personal desire of a chairperson to resign or to transfer part of his authority to his deputy was mentioned as the only reason for his "departure"(*vybytie*). Members of the society were considered as having resigned only after they had not paid their fees for three years. *Ustav*, 21, clause 90; 16, clause 60; 17, clause 66; 8, 30.

129. S. D. Sheremetev to I. V. Pomialovskii, October 27, 1900, RGADA, f. 1287, op.1, d. 4126, Chernoviki pisem Sheremeteva k raznym litsam po obshchestvu revnitelei, l. 24–24 ob.

130. RGIA, f. 747, op. 1, d. 12, l. 1.

131. *IOR*, no. 2 (1902): 2.

132. S. D. Sheremetev to A. A. Golenishchev-Kutuzov, late Jan. 1901, RGADA, f. 1287, op.1, d. 4126, l. 28.

133. The importance of etiquette and its various codes depending on the formal or informal nature of social interaction was described by Erving Goffman in his classical study, *The Presentation of Self in Everyday Life* (New York: Doubleday Anchor Books, 1959), especially 89–91. For the special significance of etiquette and decorum in the Russian cultural context, see Lotman, "Ocherki po istorii russkoi kul'tury XVIII-nachala XIX veka" and Catriona Kelly, *Refining Russia: Advice Literature, Polite Culture, and Gender from Catherine to Yeltsin* (Oxford: Oxford University Press, 2001).

134. Vladimir Nabokov, "Drugie berega," in *Sobranie sochinenii v chetyrekh tomakh*, vol. 4 (Moscow: Izdatel'stvo "Pravda", 1990), 242; D. I. Stogov, *Pravomonarkhicheskie salony Peterburga-Petrograda (konets XIX - nachalo XX veka)* (St. Petersburg: Dmitrii Bulanin, 2007); K. A. Solov'ev, *Kruzhok "Beseda": v poiskakh novoi politicheskoi real'nosti 1899–1905* (Moscow: ROSSPEN, 2009), especially 4–5.

135. S. A. Rachinskii to S. D. Shremetev, May 15, 1898, RGADA, f. 1287, op.1, d. 1420, Pis'ma S. D. Sheremetevu ot S. A. Rachinskogo, l. 3 ob.

136. S. A. Chuikina, *Dvorianskaia pamiat': "byvshie" v sovetskom gorode (Leningrad, 1920–30-e gody)* (St. Petersburg: Izdatel'stvo Evropeiskogo Universiteta v Sankt-Peterburge, 2006), 200–201.

137. S. D. Sheremetev to S. F. Platonov, February 3 (16), 1918, OR RNB, f. 585, op. 1, d. 4627, l. 4.

138. RGIA, f. 747, op. 1, d. 12, l. 30; RGADA, f. 1287, op.1, d. 2082, Pis'ma S. D. Sheremetevu ot B. M. Iuzefovicha, l. 3-3 ob.

139. *Otchët Obshchestva revnitelei . . . za 1898–1899 god*, 13.

140. RGADA, f. 1287, op. 1, d. 1420, l. 2 ob.; *IOR*, no. 5 (1904): 7.

141. S. A. Rachinskii to S. D. Sheremetev, Nov. 6, 1898, RGADA, f. 1287, op. 1, d. 1420, l. 22 ob., 28, 28 ob.; *Otchët Obshchestva revnitelei . . . za 1898–1899 god*, 11.

142. S. A. Rachinskii to S. D. Sheremetev, June 1, 1898, RGADA, f. 1287, op. 1, d. 1420, l. 40b.

143. Frederick C. Corney, *Telling October: Memory and the Making of Bolshevik Revolution* (Ithaca, NY: Cornell University Press, 2004), 4.

144. *IOR*, no. 2, Oct. 20, 1900, 21.

145. RGADA, f. 1287, op. 1, d. 71, Pis'ma S. D. Sheremetevu ot N. P. Barsukova, l. 14, 14 ob., 52 ob.

146. "Otchët Obshchestva revnitelei . . . za 1901–1902 god," *IOR*, no. 5 (1904): 5.

147. Gurko, *Cherty i siluety proshlogo*, 84.

148. Kizevetter, *Na rubezhe dvukh stoletii*, 320–321.

149. Gregory L. Freeze, "The *Soslovie* (Estate) Paradigm and Russian Social History," *American Historical Review* 91, no. 1 (1986): 34; see also Confino's discussion of *kul'turno-bytovye gruppy* in his "The *Soslovie* (Estate) Paradigm," 690.

150. *Zapiska grafa S. Sheremeteva o sozdanii osobykh dvorianskikh zhenskikh uchebno-vospitatel'nykh zavedenii*, Nov. 24, 1898 g. 5.

151. The Peterhof Conference was convened by the tsar in July 1905 for deliberations on the composition and competence of the future State Duma. See *Petergofskie soveshchaniia o proekte Gosudarstvennoi Dumy* (Petrograd, 1917), 78–161.

152. Freeze, "The *Soslovie* (Estate) Paradigm," 35.

153. I. F. Tiutchev to S. D. Sheremetev, March 25, 1898, RGADA, f. 1287, op. 1, d. 1754, l. 30 ob.

154. I. F. Tiutchev to S. D. Sheremetev, January 7, 1898, April 23, 1901, RGADA, f. 1287, op. 1, d. 1754, l. 21, 76 ob.

155. I. F. Tiutchev to S. D. Sheremetev, January 7, 1898, RGADA, f. 1287, op. 1, d. 1754, l. 21–21 ob.

156. Kn. S. Trubetskoi, "Delo Mortara," *St. Peterburgskie vedomosti*, Nov. 7, 1897. This article was later included in S. N. Trubetskoi, *Sobranie sochinenii*, vol. 1, *Publitsisticheskie stat'i, napechatannye s 1896 g. po 1905 g. vkliuchitel'no* (Moscow: Tipografiia G. Lissnera i D. Sobko, 1907), 20–22, here 21. On the Zealots' reaction to this article, see B. M. Iuzefovich to S. D. Sheremetev, Nov. 18, 1897, and N. N. Selifontov to S. D. Sheremetev, Nov. 18, 1897, RGIA, f. 1088, Sheremetevy, op. 2, S. D. Sheremetev, d. 26, Perepiska gr. S. D. Sheremeteva s redaktorom-izdatelem St. Peterburgskikh Vedomostei kn. E. E. Ukhtomskim i chlenom soveta obshchestva revnitelei B. M. Iuzefovichem, l. 6–7 ob., 10–11 ob.

157. B. M. Iuzefovich to S. D. Sheremetev, Nov. 7, 1897, RGIA, f. 1088, op. 2, d. 26, l. 2, 2 ob.; B. M. Iuzefovich to E. E. Ukhtomskii, Oct. 22, 1897, RGIA, f. 1088, op. 2, d. 26, l. 4.

158. E. E. Ukhtomskii to S. D. Sheremetev, Nov. 30, 1897, RGIA, f. 1088, op. 2, d. 26, l. 18; E. E. Ukhtomskii to S. D. Sheremetev, Feb. 21, 1898, ibid., l. 79–81; E. E. Ukhtomskii to S. D. Sheremetev, February 23, 1898, ibid., l. 29–30 ob.

159. A. A. Golenishchev-Kutuzov to E. E. Ukhtomskii, Mar. 20, 1896, RGIA, f. 1072, op. 1, d. 10, l. 1 ob.–2.

160. B. V. Anan'ich, *I. I. Tolstoi i peterburgskoe obshchestvo nakanune revoliutsii* (St. Peters-burg: Liki Rossii and St. Peterburgskii institut istorii RAN, 2007), 67–82; I. I. Tolstoi, *Dnevnik 1906–1909*, vol. 1 (St. Petersburg: Liki Rossii, 2010), 302–303, 307.

161. RGADA, f. 1287, op. 1, d. 4116, l. 2; RGADA, f. 1287, op. 1, d. 4146, Chernovaia zametka S. D. Sheremeteva o Russkom Sobranii, l. 1–1 ob.; *Spisok uchreditelei Russkogo Sobraniia* (St. Petersburg, 1901); *Programma Russkogo Sobraniia* (St. Petersburg, 1907). For secondary sources on the Russian Assembly, see I. V. Lukoianov, "Russkoe sobranie" in A. A. Fursenko, ed., *Rossiia v XIX–XX vv.: Sbornik statei k 70-iu R. Sh. Ganelina* (St. Petersburg: Dmitrii Bulanin, 1998), 165–171; Iu. I. Kir'ianov, *Russkoe Sobranie, 1900–1917* (Moscow: ROSSPEN, 2003).

162. *IOR*, no. 5 (1904): 20.

163. Bradley, "The St. Petersburg Literacy Committee," 284.

164. V. P. Vakhterov, *Vneshkol'noe obrazovanie naroda* (Moscow: Tipografiia tovarishchestva Sytina, 1896), 33.

165. Mary Stuart, "'The Ennobling Illusion': The Public Library Movement in Late Imperial Russia," *Slavonic and East European Review*, 76, no. 3 (1998): 411. On the library movement, see also Ben Eklof, "The Archaeology of 'Backwardness' in Russia: Assessing the Adequacy of Libraries for Rural Audiences in Late Imperial Russia," in Miranda Remnek, ed., *The Space of the Book: Print Culture in the Russian Social Imagination*, (Toronto: University of Toronto Press, 2011), 108–141.

166. *IOR*, no. 5 (1904): 8.

167. S. A. Rachinskii to S. D. Sheremetev, Nov. 30, 1901, RGADA, f. 1287, op. 1, d. 1421, Pis'ma S. D. Sheremetevu ot S. A. Rachinskogo, l. 71 ob.; *IOR*, no.5 (1904): 14.

168. *IOR*, no. 1 (1900): 30.

169. S. D. Sheremetev to S. F. Platonov, May 7 (20), 1918, OR RNB, f. 585, op. 1, d. 4627, l. 18–18 ob.

170. V. Charnoluskii, *Osnovnye voprosy organizatsii vneshkol'nogo obrazovaniia v Rossii* (St. Petersburg, 1909), 67.

171. In her study of the public library movement, Mary Stuart contrasts the position of the Russian library activists with that of the leaders of the public library movement in America who, she claims, "conceptualized libraries as a bulwark against social change." The Zealots, who constituted a conservative minority in an overwhelmingly liberal movement, assumed a standpoint more resembling the American approach. See Stuart, "The Public Library Movement," 440.

172. S. A. Rachinskii to S. D. Sheremetev, June 14, 1898, RGADA, f. 1287, op. 1, d. 1420, l. 8–10 ob.

173. "Pravila o besplatnykh narodnykh bibliotekakh Obshchestva Revnitelei Russkogo Istoricheskogo Prosveshcheniia v pamiat' Imperatora Aleksandra III," in *Narodnye Biblioteki Obshchestva Revnitelei Russkogo Istoricheskogo Prosveshcheniia v pamiat' Imperatora Aleksandra III* (St. Petersburg, 1899), 29–35.

174. "Katalog besplatnykh narodnykh bibliotek Obshchestva revnitelei," in ibid., 19–27.

175. *IOR*, no. 5 (1904): 8.

176. Sviatoslav Volodimerov, "Sel'skie i gorodskie narodnye biblioteki," *IOR*, no. 2 (1900): 10.

177. "Otchët Obshchestva revnitelei . . . za 1901–1902 god," *IOR*, no. 5 (1904): 8–9.

178. Volodimerov, "Sel'skie i gorodskie narodnye biblioteki," *IOR*, no. 2 (1900): 10.

179. "Otchët Obshchestva revnitelei . . . za 1899–1900 god," *IOR*, no. 3 (1901): 7.

180. V. Vostokov, "Pis'mo sel'skogo sviashchennika k chlenam obshchestva revnitelei russk-ogo istoricheskogo prosveshcheniia," *IOR*, no.2 (1900): 10–12.

181. "Otchët Obshchestva revnitelei . . . za 1899–1900 god," 7; "Otchët Obshchestva revnitelei . . . za 1900–1901 god," *IOR*, no. 4 (1902): 7–8.

182. T. V. Leont'ev, *Narodnye chteniia* (Petrograd: Kul'turno-prosvetitel'noe kooperativnoe tovarishchestvo "Nachatki znanii," 1919), 9–10.

183. "Otchët Obshchestva revnitelei . . . za 1900–1901 god," 8.
184. *IOR*, no. 3 (1901): 8, 28.
185. V.Vostokov, "Zaria zemli russkoi," *IOR*, no. 3, June 10, 1901, 23–28; ibid., no. 4 (1902): 40–44.
186. "Otchët Obshchestva revnitelei . . . za 1900–1901 god," *IOR*, no. 4 (1902): 4.
187. Leont'ev, *Narodnye chteniia*, 10–11.
188. "Otchët Obshchestva revnitelei . . . za 1900–1901 god," 8–9.
189. "Otchët Obshchestva revnitelei . . . za 1901–1902 god," *IOR*, no. 5 (1904): 9.
190. Leont'ev, *Narodnye chteniia*, 13.
191. "Deiatel'nost' otdelenii obshchestva za 1895–1899 goda," *IOR*, no. 1 (1900): 28; "Otchët Obshchestva revniteleii . . . za 1900–1901," ibid., no. 4 (1902): 4; "Otchët Obshchestva revnitelei . . . za 1901–1902 god," *IOR*, no. 5 (1904): 11.
192. G. Kamenskii v Sovet Obshchestva Revnitielei, Feb. 7, 1910, RGIA, f. 747, op. 1, d. 72, O raznykh predpolozheniiakh zaiavlennykh chlenami obshchestva, l. 18.
193. RGIA, f. 747, op. 1, d. 72, l. 19–20; ibid., d. 12, l. 17.
194. In the following years the idea of the visualization of history as a means of disseminating historical knowledge was appropriated and developed by some new historical societies, in particular by the Society for Familiarization with Russian Historical Events (*Obshchestvo oznakomleniia s istoricheskimi sobytiiami Rossii*). See *Kratkii obzor deiatel'nosti obshchestva oznakomleniia s istoricheskimi sobytiiami Rossii za 1911–1912 gody* (Moscow: 1913), 3, 18–19.
195. *Ukazaniia ob izdaniiakh razreshennykh dla narodnykh chtenii i besplatnykh narodnykh chitalen, a takzhe dramaticheskikh sochineniiakh, odobrennykh k predstavleniiu narodnykh teatrov* (St. Petersburg, 1902); the series of the Historical Society at Moscow University edited by Ger'e was entitled "Historical Tales for Public Readings and Schools" (*Istoricheskie rasskazy dlia narodnykh chtenii i shkol*) and included such booklets as *Liudovik IX, Korol'-podvizhnik*; *Atilla, bich bozhii*; *V pervyi raz krugom sveta*; *Rabstvo i osvobozhdenie negrov*. Ibid., 15.
196. Protokol zasedaniia izdatel'skogo otdeleniia Obshchestva revnitelei russkogo istoricheskogo prosveschenia v pamiat' imperatora Aleksandra III, Mar. 2, 1899, RGIA, f. 747, op. 1, d. 28, Kopii protokolov i vypiski iz zhurnalov zasedanii, perepiski o deiatel'nosti Izdatel'skogo otdeleniia, l. 21 ob.
197. Zasedanie komissii [po razrabotke polozheniia o premiiakh obshchestva], Mar. 9, 1899, RGIA, f. 747, op. 1, d. 28, 1, 24. The commission was established on March 2, 1899 and included M. P. Solov'ev, N. D. Chechulin, P. M. Maikov and Kh. M. Loparev.
198. Protokol zasedaniia izdatel'skogo otdeleniia, Nov. 18, 1899, RGIA, f. 747, op. 1, d. 28, l. 1, 14–14 ob.
199. The list included also Zabelin's *Venerable Old Man Irinarkh* (*Starets Irinarkh*); Buslaev's *Ideal Women Characters of the Ancient Rus'*(*Ideal'nye zhenskie kharaktery Drevnei Rusi*), and *Lives of the Fathers of the Kievo-Pecherskii Monastery* (*Kievo-Pecherskii Paterik*). RGIA, f. 747, op. 1, d. 28, 1, 25 ob.
200. I. Pomialovskii v Sovet Obshchestva Revnitielei, March 13, 1899, RGIA, f. 747, op. 1, d. 28, l. 22.
201. Protokol zasedaniia izdatel'skogo otdeleniia, February 18, 1902, RGIA, f. 747, op. 1, d. 28, l. 81 ob.
202. Vypiska iz zhurnala Soveta, [no date, approximately Mar. 1899], RGIA, f. 747, op. 1, d. 28, l. 27.
203. Zasedanie izdatel'skogo otdeleniia obshchestva, Apr. 16, 1901, RGIA, f. 747, op. 1, d. 28, l. 50.
204. V. N. Liaskovskii, *Brat'ia Kirievskie: zhizn' i trudy ikh* (St. Petersburg, 1899); I. S. Beliaev, *Krest'ianin-pisatel' nachala XVIII veka I. T. Pososhkov* (Moscow, 1902); N. M. Gorbov, S. A.

Rachinskii (St. Petersburg, 1903); Vypiska iz zhurnala soveta obshchestva revnitelei, Mar. 16, 1903, RGIA, f. 747, op. 1, d. 29, l. 31.

205. Kvashnin-Samarin may have been recommended by I. P. Khrushchov, who had given the council of the society the former's essay "Chronicles of Russian History" (*Letopisi Russkoi Istorii*), which had been included as a chapter in the popular *People's Handbook* edited by Khrushchov. I. P. Khrushchov, ed., *Nastol'naia kniga dlia naroda* (St. Petersburg: Izdatel'stvo postoiannoi komissii po ustroistvu narodnykh chtenii v St. Peterburge i ego okrestnostiakh, 1887–1891).

206. Protokol zasedaniia izdatel'skogo otdeleniia, May 1, 1898, RGIA, f. 747, op. 1, d. 28, l. 13 ob.

207. I. P. Khrushchov, *Zamechaniia na Slovo o Polku Igoreve kniazia Pavla Petrovicha Viazemskogo* (St. Petersburg, 1875); idem, *Ksenia Ivanovna Romanova (Velikaia staritsa Inokinia Marfa)* (St. Petersburg, 1877); idem, *Ocherk iamskikh i pochtovykh uchrezhdenii ot drevnikh vremen do tsarstvovaniia Ekateriny II* (St. Petersburg, 1884); and idem, *Besedy o drevnei russkoi literature* (St. Petersburg, 1900). On I. P. Khrushchov, see A. I. Sapogov, "Khrushchov Ivan Petrovich," in L. G. Protasov, ed., *Tambovskaia Entsiklopediia* (Tambov; Iulis, 2004), 650.

208. For the earlier activity of the Publishing Society, see I. P. Khrushchov, *Ob izdatel'skoi deiatel'nosti Postoiannoi komissii narodnykh chtenii i uchrezhdennogo pri nei obshchestva za piatnadtsat' let, 1881–1896* (St. Petersburg, 1901). The endowment contained capital and property including 9,000 rubles in interest-bearing securities, 2,000 rubles in cash, and a stock of books and brochures worth 40,000 rubles. Vypiska iz zhurnala zasedaniia soveta obshchestva, March 24, 1902, RGIA, f. 747, op. 1, d. 28, l. 82–83.

209. Protokol zasedaniia izdatel'skogo otdeleniia, February 18, 1902 goda, RGIA, f. 747, op. 1, d. 28, l. 81 ob. Khrushchov was referring to the popular digest *Uchilishe Blagochestiia ili primery khristianskikh dobrodetelei vybrannykh iz zhitii sviatykh* (St. Petersburg: Sinodal'naia tipografiia, 1903).

210. Vypiska iz zhurnala zasedaniia soveta obshchestva revnitelei russkogo istoricheskogo prosveshcheniia v pamiat' imperatora Aleksandra III, February 10, 1902, RGIA, f. 747, op. 1, d. 28, l. 83.

211. Protokol zasedaniia izdatel'skogo otdeleniia, January 21, 1903, RGIA, f. 747, op. 1, d. 29-1, Kopii protokolov i vypiski iz zhurnalov zasedanii, perepiska o deiatel'nosti izdatel'skogo otdela, l.22 ob.

212. For example, the chapter "Vostochnye slaviane" was based on K. Bestuzhev-Riumin, *Russkaia istoriia*, vol. 1 (St. Petersburg, 1872); I. Zabelin, *Istoriia russkoi zhizni*, vol. 1 (Moscow, 1876); V. Kliuchevskii, *Posobie po russkoi istorii* (Moscow, 1899); S. Solov'ev, *Istoriia Rossii s drevneishikh vremen*, vol. 1 (Moscow, 1874); P. Miliukov, "Rasselenie slavian," "Drevneishii byt slavian," "Religiia slavian," in P. Vinogradov, *Kniga dlia chteniia po istorii srednikh vekov*, vol. 1 (Moscow, 1896). See I. P. Khrushchov, ed., *Sbornik chtenii po russkoi istorii s drevneishikh vremen do XIV veka* (St. Petersburg, 1907), 78.

213. Kizevetter, *Na rubezhe dvukh stoletii*, 289.

214. Khrushchov, ed., *Sbornik chtenii po russkoi istorii*, iii.

215. V. L. Velichko, *Menshikov: istoricheskaia drama v piati deistviiakh* (St. Petersburg, 1903); Vypiska iz zhurnala Soveta Obshchestva, May 4, 1903, RGIA, f. 747, op. 1, d. 29-1, l. 43.

216. Protokol zasedaniia izdatel'skogo otdeleniia, October 16, 1903, RGIA, f. 747, op. 1, d. 29-1, l. 49–49 ob., 55, 56; January 27, 1904, RGIA, f. 747, op. 1, d. 29-1, l. 64 ob.

217. Protokol zasedaniia izdatel'skogo otdeleniia, March 17, 1904, RGIA, f. 747, op. 1, d. 29-1, l. 66 ob.

218. I. P. Khrushchov, ed., *Sbornik rasskazov iz ruskoi i chuzhezemnoi zhizni: Chasy dosuga* (St. Petersburg, 1905); idem, ed., *Sbornik chtenii po russkoi istorii s drevneishikh vremen do XIV*

veka (St. Petersburg, 1907); Doklad sovetu obshchestva sekretaria izdatel'skogo otdeleniia S. N. Khrushchova [I. P. Khrushchov's nephew], Oct. 10, 1904, RGIA, f. 747, op. 1, d. 29-1, l. 104.

219. The proposed title of the ethnographic volume was "Through Russia and Foreign Lands" (*Po Rusi i chuzhim kraiam*). See Vypiska iz zhurnala soveta obshchestva, Oct. 10, 1904, RGIA, f. 747, op. 1, d. 29-1, l. 83; Protokol zasedaniia izdatel'skogo otdeleniia, March 31, 1905, ibid., l. 221–222.

220. RGIA, f. 747, op. 1, d. 29-1, l. 222 ob.–223.

221. RGIA, f. 747, op. 1, d. 29-1, l. 223 ob.

222. Ochevidets, *Galitskaia Rus' prezhde i nyne. Istoricheskii ocherk i vzgliad na sovremennoe sostoianie* (St. Petersburg, 1907); E. I. De-Vitte, *Sviatye pervouchiteli slavianskie Kirill i Mefodii i kul'turnaia rol' ikh v slavianstve i Rossii* (St. Petersburg, 1908); Liudvig Shtur, *Slavianstvo i mir budushchego*, translated by V. I. Lamanskii, second edition (St. Petersburg, 1909).

223. Vypiska iz zhurnala soveta obshchestva, Dec. 10, 1906, RGIA, f. 747, op. 1, d. 29-2, l. 272.

224. On A. S. Budilovich see: "Budilovich A. S. [Nekrolog]," *Moskovskie vedomosti*, Dec. 14, 16, 18, 21, 1908; "Budilovich kak politicheskii myslitel'," *Moskovskie vedomosti*, Dec. 20, 1908. Surprisingly, some of Budilovich's writings have been reprinted in recent years, including A. S. Budilovich, *Statisticheskie Tablitsy Raspredieleniia Slavian: a. Po Gosudarstvam i Narodnostiam, b. Po Veroispoviedaniiam, Azbukam i Literaturnym Iazykam (Narechiiam)*, (St. Petersburg, 1875); "Mozhet li Rossiia otdat' inorodtsam svoi okrainy?", *Bibilioteka okrain Rossii* no. 4 (1907): 67–75; *Nauka i politika: Tri stat'i po zlobodnevnym voprosam* (St. Petersburg: Pushkinskaia skoropechatnia, 1905).

225. A. E. Alektorov, *Inorodtsy v Rossii: Sovremennye voprosy. Finliandtsy. Poliaki. Latyshi. Evrei. Nemtsy. Armiane. Tatary. S predisloviem i dobavleniem A. S. Budilovicha* (St. Petersburg, Tipografiia I. V. Leont'eva, 1906).

226. Vypiska iz zhurnala soveta obshchestva, May 11, 1908, RGIA, f. 747, op. 1, d. 29-2, l. 309.

227. Protokol zasedaniia izdatel'skogo otdeleniia, Apr. 16, 1909, RGIA, f. 747, op. 1, d. 29-2, l. 358 ob.–359.

228. Vypiska iz zhurnala soveta obshchestva, May 3, 1909, RGIA, f. 747, op. 1, d. 29-2, l. 343.

229. *Zapiski grafa Nikolaia Egorovicha Komarovskogo* (Moscow: Synodal'naia tipografiia, 1912); N. P. Rozanov, *Moskovskii mitropolit Platon (1737–1812)* (St. Petersburg: Sinodal'naia tipografiia, 1913). On the preparation for publication of Komarovskii's memoirs, see notes and telegram of June 27–29, 1912, RGIA, f. 747, op. 1, d. 29-2, l. 371–373; for Rozanov's book, see Protokol izdatel'skogo otdeleniia obshchestva, Apr. 7, 1913, RGIA, f. 747, op. 1, d. 29-2, l. 375–375 ob.

230. *Otchët Obshchestva revnitelei... za 1896–1897* (St. Petersburg, 1897), 3–4; "Deiatel'nost' otdelenii obshchestva za 1895–1899 goda," *IOR*, no. 1, 1900, 22; "Otchët Obshchestva revnitelei... za 1901–1902," *IOR*, no. 5 (1904): 2; RGIA, f. 747, op. 1, d. 23, Otchëty, protokoly i perepiska o deiatel'nosti Istoricheskogo otdeleniia, l. 57–57 ob.; 69 ob., 70; 72 ob., 74–74 ob.

231. N. N. Selifontov to I. V. Pomialovskii, May 26, 1900, RGIA, f. 747, op. 1, d. 28, l. 41, 42.

232. Otchët o deiatel'nosti Istoricheskogo Otdeleniia Obshchestva za pervuiu polovinu 1897, RGIA, f. 747, op. 1, d. 23, l. 46, 48, 54, 95.

233. P. A. Golitsyn to the council of the Society of Zealots, April 13, 1899, RGIA, f. 747, op. 1, d. 23, l. 98.

234. *Otchët Obshchestva revnitelei... za 1897–1898* (St. Petersburg, 1898), 5.

235. RGIA, f. 747, op. 1, d. 23, l. 96–97, 159–162.

236. S. S. Tatishchev, *Pamiati imperatora Aleksandra III* (St. Petersburg, Tip. Tovarishchestva "Obshchestvennaia pol'za", 1894). His work on Alexander II was published in 1903: *Imperator Aleksandr II, ego zhizn' i tsarstvovanie*, vols. 1–2 (St. Petersburg, A. S. Suvorin, 1903). Tatishchev mentioned in his preface (dated July 28, 1902) that the book was based on his short biography of Alexander II written for the *Russian Biographical Dictionary* "six years ago," i.e., in 1896. See

reprint of the book produced in 1996 from the second edition of 1911 (Moscow: Algoritm, 1996), 6. For Tatishchev's biography, see Iu. S. Kartsov, *Sergei Spiridonovich Tatishchev: Stranitsa Vospominanii* (Petrograd, Tip. Tovarishchestva gazety "Svet," 1916) and V. V. Shevtsov, "Sergei Spiridonovich Tatishchev: istorik i diplomat na strazhe ofitsial'noi pechati, ili kak tsarskoe pravitel'stvo proigralo informatsionnuiu voinu," in V. P. Zinov'ev and E. E. Dutchak, eds., *Chelovek-tekst-epokha: Sbornik nauchnykh statei i materialov*, vyp. 2: *Sovremennye problemy istochnikovedeniia* (Tomsk: Izdatel'stvo Tomskogo Universiteta, 2006), 302–313.

237. RGIA, f. 878, S. S. Tatishchev, op. 1, dd. 27–31, Obzor sotsial'no-revoliutsionnogo dvizheniia v Rossii, 1894–1905 and Otdel'nye glavy raboty S. S. Tatishcheva; dd. 32–44, Materialy dlia raboty, sobrannye S. S. Tatishchevym. Tatishchev managed to write five chapters of his study on the revolutionary movement, focusing mainly on *zemstvo* activity, the students' movement, and the emergence of the workers' movement in 1895–1896. For a historiographical assessment of Tatishchev's unfinished research, see N. A. Troitskii, *Russkoe revoliutsionnoe narodnichestvo 1870-kh godov: istoriia temy* (Saratov: Izdatel'stvo Saratovskogo universiteta, 2003), 7; O. M. Khlobustov, "Iz istorii bor'by s terrorizmom v Rossii v XIX- nachale XX veka: Istoriko-kriminologicheskii aspekt," *Istoriia gosudarstva i prava*, no. 5 (2006): 19–24, here 20–21.

238. "Spisok chlenov Obshchestva Revnitelei," *IOR*, no. 2 (1902): 30; A. S. Stishinskii to S. S. Tatishchev, Apr. 13, 1898, RGIA, f. 878, op. 1, d. 69, Pis'mo A. S. Stishinskogo S. S. Tatishchevu s priglasheniem k gr. S. D. Sheremetevu, l. 1. In the same years (1896–1899) A. S. Stishinskii was also deputy of the state secretary; for an outline of his career and personality, see Gurko, *Cherty i siluety proshlogo*, 181–183, 191–198.

239. S. D. Sheremetev to S. S. Tatishchev, July 20, Dec. 29 1898; Jan. 12, 1899, RGIA, f. 878, op.1, d. 74, Pis'ma, telegrammy i vizitnye kartochki gr. S. D. Sheremeteva S. S. Tatishchevu po povodu ego raboty po istorii tsarstvovaniia Aleksandra III, l. 1–5; S. D. Sheremetev to S. S. Tatishchev, December 29, 1898, RGIA, f. 878, op.1, d. 74, l. 3–3ob.

240. RGIA, f. 878, op. 1, d. 74, Spisok knig i dokumentov po russkoi istorii khraniashchikhsia v biblioteke i arkhive Obshchestva revnitelei russkogo istoricheskogo prosveshcheniia, l. 1-8ob.

241. S. D. Sheremetev to S. S. Tatishchev, Jan. 12, 1899, RGIA, f. 878, op.1, d. 74, l. 4.

242. The chapter presented at his reading was devoted to Alexander III's accession to the throne and was named "Votsarenie Imperatora Aleksandra III. Mart–Avgust 1881 g." See "Obshchie sobraniia obshchestva," *IOR*, no. 3 (1901): 6.

243. The title of Liaskovskii's essay was "K opytu lichnoi biografii imperatora Aleksandra III"; it was published in the third issue of the society's newsletters. See *IOR*, no. 3, June 10, 1901, 17; no. 4 (1902): 6.

244. RGIA, f. 878, op. 1, d. 59 Dokladnaia zapiska S. S. Tatishcheva ministram dvora, vnutrennikh del, finansov i gr. Serg. Dm. Sheremetevu s prilozheniem uslovii raboty nad knigoi po istorii tsarstvovaniia Aleksandra III, Jan. 28, 1903, l. 1–2; S. S. Tatishchev to S. D. Sheremetev, July 4, 1903, RGIA, f. 1088, op. 2, d. 28, Perepiska S. D. Sheremeteva s Tatishchevym S. S. o knige ob Aleksandre III, l. 1.

245. RGIA, f. 878, op.1, d. 73, Pis'ma ministra dvora gr. V. B. Frederiksa S. Tatishchevu o ego rabote nad istoriei tsarstvovaniia Aleksandra III, l. 1, 1 ob., 2, 2 ob.

246. S. S. Tatishchev to S. D. Sheremetev, November 1, 1904, RGIA, f. 1088, op. 2, d. 28, l. 17 ob.–18; and July 4, 1903, ibid., l. 1–2.

247. V. P. Tselebrovskii to S. S. Tatishchev, June 12, 1903, RGIA, f. 878, op.1, d. 72, Pis'mo general-leitenanta V. P. Tselebrovskogo S. S. Tatishchevu o razreshenii emu zaniatii v voennykh arkhivakh, l. 1–1 ob.; S. S. Tatishchev to the Council of the Society of Zealots, July 24, 1903, f. 1088, op. 2, d. 18, Retsenziia [S. D. Sheremeteva] na knigu S. S. Tatishcheva "Imperator Aleksandr III. Ego zhizn' i tsarstvovanie," l. 2–5.

248. RGIA, f. 878, op. 1, d. 23, Zapiska Natalii Petrovny Grot ob urokakh ee muzha, Iakova Karlovicha Grota, nasledniku Nikolaiu Aleksandrovichu i v. kn. Aleksandru Aleksandrovichu v 1853–1858 gg; S. A. Tolstaia to S. S. Tatishchev, Feb. 14, 1904, RGIA, f. 878, op. 1, d. 71, Pis'mo gr. S. A. Tolstoi S. S. Tatishchevu o svoem svidanii s imperatorom Aleksandrom III, l. 1–1 ob. The list of books and archival files used by Tatishchev in 1903–1904 completes the picture of Tatishchev's research. See RGIA, f. 878, op. 1, d. 24, Spisok knig i arkhivnykh del poluchennykh S. S. Tatishchevym dlia raboty po "Istorii zhizni i tsarstvovaniia imp. Aleksandra III."

249. S. D. Sheremetev to S. S. Tatishchev, Apr. 1, Dec. 15, 18, 1903, Jan. 6, 1904, RGIA, f. 878, op. 1, d. 74, l. 11, 13 ob., 16, 17.

250. S. S. Tatishchev to S. D. Sheremetev, October 29, 1904, RGIA, f. 1088, op. 2, d, 28, l. 14–14 ob.

251. RGADA, f. 1287, op. 1, d. 4144 Chernovik zametok S. D. Sheremeteva o trudakh Liaskovskogo i Tatishcheva ob Aleksandre III, 1908 g., l. 1 ob.

252. S. D. Sheremetev to S. S. Tatishchev, Oct. 30, 1904, RGIA, f. 878, op. 1, d. 74, l. 20; S. S. Tatishchev to S. D. Sheremetev, Oct. 31, 1904, RGIA, f. 878, op. 1, d. 56, l. 7.

253. S. S. Tatishchev to S. D. Sheremetev, Nov. 1, 1904, RGIA, f. 1088, op. 2, d. 28, l. 18.

254. S. D. Sheremetev to V. B. Frederiks and to V. V. Shcheglov, Oct. 30, 1904, RGIA, f. 1088, op. 2, d. 28, l. 13.

255. V. V. Shcheglov to S. D. Sheremetev, Nov. 2, 1904, RGIA, f. 1088, op. 2, d. 28, l. 12.

256. RGIA, f. 1088, op. 2, d. 18, l. 36–38 ob.

257. V. B. Frederiks to S. S. Tatishchev, 18 Dec. 1904, RGIA, f. 878, op. 1, d. 73, l. 3–3 ob.

258. RGADA, f. 1287, op. 1, d. 4144, l. 2.

259. Otchët o deiatel'nosti Istoricheskogo Otdeleniia Obshchestva za pervuiu polovinu 1897, RGIA, f. 747, op. 1, d. 23, l. 48, 69.

260. RGIA, f. 747, op. 1, d. 23, l. 48, 69; *Otchet Obshchestva revnitelei . . . za 1896–1897* (St. Petersburg, 1897), 18.

261. S. D. Sheremetev, Circular letter (*Tsirkuliarnoe pis'mo*), Mar. 31, 1898, RGIA, f. 747, op. 1, d. 23, l. 57–57 ob.

262. "Deiatel'nost' Obshchestva v 1898–9 godu," *IOR*, no. 1, Feb. 26, 1900, 17–18.

263. Protokol zasedaniia istoricheskogo otdeleniia obshchestva, Mar. 5, 1902, RGIA, f. 747, op. 1, d. 23, l. 145 ob.

264. Programma uchebnika russkoi istorii, RGIA, f. 747, op. 1, d. 68 O programme uchebnika po russkoi istorii, l. 1-16 ob.; S. D. Sheremetev to N. D. Chechulin, Apr. 25, 1901, RGIA, f. 747, op. 1, d. 28, l. 47.

265. N. N. Selifontov to I. F. Tiutchev, Jan. 21, 1898, RGIA, f. 747, op. 1, d. 68, l. 17 ob.

266. *Otchët Obshchestva revnitelei . . . za 1896–1897*, 15.

267. N. N. Selifontov to A. A. Beliaev, Mar. 28, 1899, RGIA, f. 747, op. 1, d. 68, l. 23–24.

268. A. A. Beliaev to I. F. Tiutchev, July 1899, RGIA, f. 747, op. 1, d. 68, l.29-29 ob.

269. Ibid., l. 30-30 ob.

270. A. A. Beliaev, *Illiustrirovannaia istoriia russkoi tserkvi* (Moscow, 1894); idem, *Spiski nachal'nikov, nastavnikov i vospitannikov Vifanskoi seminarii s 1800 do 1897 goda* (Sergieva Lavra, 1898); for the whole list of Beliaev's publications, see RGIA, f. 747, op. 1, d. 68, l. 26–26 ob.

271. N. N. Selifontov to the Council of the Society, January 8, 1900, RGIA, f. 747, op. 1, d. 23, l. 105–106.

272. Pravila o premiiakh obshchestva; Ot Soveta Obshchestva revnitelei russkogo istoricheskogo prosveshcheniia, May 27, 1899; S. D. Sheremetev to A. M. Katkov, June 25, 1899; S. D. Sheremetev to V. A. Gringmut, June 1899; RGIA, f. 747, op. 1, d. 65, Ob uchrezhdenii premii za istoricheskie sochineniia, l. 1–2; 5,6.

273. K. N. Korol'kov, *Zhizn' i tsarstvovanie Imperatora Aleksandra III: 1881–1894* (Kiev, 1901).

274. Ob'iasnenie o prisuzhdenii uchrezhdennoi Obshchestvom premii za sochinenie, posviashchennoe zhizni i tsarstvovaniiu imperatora Aleksandra III, Feb. 26, 1904, RGIA, f. 747, op. 1, d. 65, l. 28.

275. Iakov Temnogrudov to the Society of Zealots, Apr. 8, 1901, RGIA, f. 747, op. 1, d. 28, l. 55-55 ob.

276. N. D. Chechulin to the Council of the Society, Nov. 23, 1901, RGIA, f. 747, op. 1, d. 28, l. 62.

277. W. H. Mallock, *Social Equality: A Short Study in a Missing Science* (London: Richard Bentley & Son: 1882). Velitsyn's translation appeared seventeen years later: V. H. Mellok, *Sotsial'noe ravenstvo. Perevod s angliiskogo A. Velitsyna* (Moscow: Sotsial'no-politicheskaia biblioteka, 1899).

278. Hippolyte Verly, *Le Triomphe du Socialisme: Journal d'un Ouvrier Révolutionnaire: imité de Richter* (Paris: Librairie H. Le Soudier, 1897). Richter's novel was published in German in 1891. Its first English translation appeared in 1893 and was reissued in 1897 and 1907. I have used the later edition: Eugene Richter, *Pictures of the Socialistic Future (Freely adapted from Bebel)* (London, Swan Sonnenschhein & Co., 1907).

279. [No author], Review of "A. A. Velitsyn, *Torzhestvo sotsializma (po E. Rikhteru i I. Verli)*, Moskva, 1899 g. Sotsial'no-politicheskaia biblioteka," *IOR*, no. 1 (1900): 38–39.

280. Ibid., 39.

281. "O sovremennoi demokratii," *IOR*, no.3, 10 June 1901, 30–31 (review of Charles Pierre Gaston Napoléon Deschamps, *Le Malaise de la démocratie* [Paris: A. Colin, 1899]); "Obzor inostrannykh zhurnalov za 1900 god," ibid., 31–35. The articles surveyed included Geoffrey Langtoft, "Socialism and Anarchism," *Fortnightly Review*, no. 406 (1900); Ambros Paré Winston, "Socialism in the United States," *Contemporary Review*, no. 409 (1900); Wiliam Clarke, "The Social Future of England," *Contemporary Review*, no. 420 (1900); G. M. Fiamingo, "Italian Anarchism," *Contemporary Review*, no. 417 (1900).

282. M. E. Nirod, "V Sovet Obshchestva Revnitelei Russkogo Istoricheskogo Prosveshcheniia v pamiat' imperatora Alexandra III," *IOR*, no. 3 (1901): 13–14l; Kornilov, "Pis'mo v redaktsiiu," ibid., 28–29. For Kornilov's pedagogical views, see I. P. Kornilov, *Ocherk istorii Russkoi shkoly, ee sovremennoe sostoianie i na kakikh nezyblemykh nachalakh ona dolzhna byt' utverzhdena* (St. Petersburg, 1901).

Conclusion: Voluntary Historical Societies in the Fin-de-Siècle Associational World

THE ALMOST TWO centuries of associational life in Russia in which historians played a prominent part—including over a century in which the historical societies were active—constituted a remarkable chapter in the social history of Imperial Russia. Yet the Russian voluntary societies were not isolated from the dynamics of the European associational world whose borders extended in the early nineteenth century "from Boston to Saint Petersburg."[1] By the beginning of the twentieth century, they had expanded even further in both directions: voluntary societies had become an essential factor of social life both in remote Russian provinces and in the new American states as a basic characteristic of modern European—or European-oriented—culture. This was how they were described by Alexis de Tocqueville, who first discovered associationalism as a social phenomenon during his trip to the United States in the early 1830s. For him, it was the most appropriate answer to one of the challenges of modernity, namely, the democratization of public life: "Among the laws that rule human societies there is one which seems to be more precise and clear than all others. If men are to remain civilized or to become so, the art of associating together must grow and improve in the same ratio in which the equality of conditions is increased."[2] According to P. J. Morris, voluntary associations are characterized, among others, by the ability to act as an integrative agency in societies "experiencing rapid and disturbing change," "to assert status for those outside of the established institutions and networks of state power," and to provide their members with an opportunity for gaining "ideological, cultural and moral dominance" via "achieving prominence." Morris also noted the role of voluntary societies in forming an alliance between the social elite and the leaders of the professions and argued that the networks of voluntary societies "served and exploited local community and urban identities," while at the same time molding them into national identities.[3]

In eighteenth-century Russia, voluntary associations of the educated, which at that time embodied the Enlightenment's longing for universal knowledge, functioned as agents of cohesiveness in a society undergoing social and political reforms. At the beginning of the century, the first informal sodalities of the reform-minded minority provided their participants with emotional support and useful patronage connections. By the last third of the century, there were already numerous formal and informal voluntary associations that offered a supportive environment both to those who advocated the reforms and to those who felt confused and disturbed by their results. Despite the differences in the structures, aims, and agendas of the various circles and societies, they all shared two common traits: their voluntary nature and their ethos of knowledge and education. This ethos can explain why state-sponsored institutions such as the St. Petersburg Academy of Sciences and Moscow University played a pivotal role in Russian eighteenth-century associational life. Although they were established by the state and acted under its aegis, these bodies advanced norms of educated sociability characteristic of the learned societies throughout Europe. Both the Academy of Sciences and Moscow University served as a hothouse and a center of gravitation for associations of literati; the involvement of these high-standing bodies endowed the seemingly egalitarian associations of the educated with elements of prestige and exclusivity. This elitist aura was enhanced even more by the appearance of semiprivate societies enjoying imperial patronage. Yet, while providing their members with multiple opportunities for achieving social prominence, these voluntary associations also accentuated the social value of education and contributed to the further development of the concept of knowledge. Furthermore, the emphasis gradually shifted from the universalistic nature of knowledge to the particularity of its specific branches. The emerging perception of history as a field of knowledge and a scholarly discipline was part of this process.

The growing awareness of history's distinctive status as knowledge about the past found expression in the attempt to create an autonomous historical department at the St. Petersburg Academy of Sciences and the experience of the short-lived local historical society in the provincial town of Arkhangel'sk in the mid-eighteenth century. In the following years it was reflected in Catherine II's "historical assembly," boosted by Novikov's *Ancient Russian Library* and personified by the erudite antiquarians who enthusiastically collected Russian medieval chronicles. This increasing interest in the national past was stimulated by diverse but interconnected factors such as the emergence of a national consciousness, the admiration for "ancient knowledge" inculcated by the Masonic circles, and the fashion of antiquarianism which gripped the educated public throughout Europe. Indeed, this "historical awakening," which led, *inter alia*, to the appearance of the first historical societies, was a Pan-European phenomenon which began in the late eighteenth century and blossomed in the nineteenth century.

The Russian historical societies—from the academically solid Society for Russian History and Antiquities and the elitist Russian Historical Society to the politically engaged liberal Historical Society at St. Petersburg University and the conservative Society of Zealots of Russian Historical Education—all constituted distinctive examples of the phenomenon of modern voluntary associations. While collecting and publishing documents, establishing awards, and issuing books and journals, they produced multifaceted narratives of the Russian past and thus reflected and fashioned the sentiments and opinions of their time. Through their extensive discussions of the meaning of national history and their persistent quest for the best methods of writing and popularizing that history, members of historical societies contributed to shaping the notion of national identity and at the same time developed and strengthened their identities as public activists. This process inevitably had a profound impact on the structure of older estate (*soslovnye*) identities, creating ways in which they could be reconfigured and reinterpreted. This was especially meaningful in the case of the nobility: active participation in various historical and educational societies contributed to sustaining its public status through "achieving prominence" in the cultural sphere at a time when the nobility's economic and political significance was in decline. Furthermore, as a venue where historians of different status and educational background met, argued, and cooperated, the historical societies played a vital role in transforming personal ambitions, interests, and expectations into collective activities and projects, thereby contributing to the emergence of a professional community of historians.

The gradual professionalization of history took almost the entire nineteenth century, and the proliferation of historical societies was part of that process. However, this general trend had diverse manifestations in different national contexts.[4] The distinct nature of the Russian historical societies is particularly striking when their development is compared with that of their counterparts on another frontier of the European cultural universe—the United States.

* * *

The first American historical society appeared in Boston in 1791, almost four decades after the emergence of the first Russian historical society in Archangel'sk and about a decade before the establishment of the Moscow Society for Russian History and Antiquities. Contrary to the latter, the Massachusetts Historical Society (MHS) had no connection with any institution of higher education; among its founders were representatives of the Boston educated elite—Protestant ministers, a lawyer, a librarian, but not a single historian. The founding fathers of the MHS saw its main mission as preserving documents that could be useful for writing histories. Their concept of preservation, however, differed from the idea of an archive as it was conceived in Russia by Gerhard Müller. They sought to publish historical documents in order to disseminate knowledge about the past "among the general populace."[5] Accordingly, their first journal, the *American Apollo*, was intended for broad public consumption. Yet three years later this format was changed, and from 1795 the MHS published the *Collections of the*

Massachusetts Historical Society oriented to a more exclusive audience of educated gentlemen.

The model of the MHS was adopted by other historical societies that appeared in the following years. The New York Historical Society (1804) was the second American historical society to be founded, and by the mid-nineteenth century around twenty-five historical societies already existed in the northeast and the mid-Atlantic states. Approximately twenty more societies were established between 1850 and 1860, and about the same number were established in the next decade. [6] On the eve of the Civil War, almost every society issued its own *Collections* intended, first and foremost, for consumption by other historical societies, thus fostering communication "among a national-wide network of historically minded gentlemen's clubs." In addition to this network of private associations, the first state-sponsored public societies started to appear. The precedent was created when the State Historical Society of Wisconsin (SHSW) was established in 1846 and when Minnesota Territory's legislature founded the Minnesota Historical Society in 1849, nine years before Minnesota's status was upgraded from territory to state.[7] However, the *modus operandi* of the new public societies, whose number grew rapidly in the last third of the nineteenth century, resembled that of their private predecessors: they also collected and preserved books and historical documents, publicizing their activities in their own collections. This pattern began to change only in the 1870s, when American universities established the first departments of history and a new generation of historians appeared who subscribed to a "scientific" approach to the study of the past. A large proportion of these "new historians" had studied in Germany, which they saw as possessing "the sole secret of scholarship," and had thus obtained their doctoral degrees from the same German universities as the Russian scholars.[8] However, the backgrounds from which the Russian and American students came to Germany were strikingly different. While the Russian system of higher education was built on the German model and German professors used to teach at Russian universities, the American students felt as if they had arrived in a completely different world. As Peter Novick described in his seminal study on the American historical profession,

> In Germany, young American students of history found institutions of higher education whose structure and values were totally unlike anything they had known at home. The colleges they had attended in America were still primarily moral academies for the inculcation of "discipline"—mental, behavioral, religious. Student life was strangled in meticulously arrayed and rigidly enforced regulations; classroom work consisted, for the most part, of mechanical recitation; intellectual innovation was viewed as a threat to Protestant piety. In Germany they found the models that were to inspire a revolution in American higher education: the creation of new universities,

like Johns Hopkins, Clark, and Chicago; the transformation of older ones, like Columbia, Harvard, Michigan, and Wisconsin. A "proper" university was a community of investigators, concerned with pursuing their researches while training the next generation of *Gelehrten* [scholars]; rigorous scholarship, rather than religious or philosophical orthodoxy, was the criterion of academic excellence.[9]

On their return home, these American graduates of German universities tried, with the zeal of the newly converted, to advance their vision of history as a science and their perception of the historian as a competent professional with knowledge certified by a university diploma. This was the same positivist ideal of scholarship that guided contemporary Russian historians, but the situation in the United States was much more dramatic. While Kareev and Vinogradov identified themselves as belonging to a new generation of Russian historians that was different from but still connected to their teachers, their American counterparts saw themselves as pioneers of historical scholarship in their country. They fiercely criticized "gentlemen amateurs" for the "'intrusive' authorial presence" and "explicit moralizing" of their writings, and distanced themselves from their "history as literature" approach.[10] The new academic historians were no less critical of the activity of the existing historical societies, which they despised for their "too localized subjects with little or no bearing on general American history; too much emphasis upon the colonial and Revolutionary periods; too much concern with genealogy; and too little attention paid to economic history."[11] The "new historians" therefore advocated a different kind of historical society, which would be "composed of specialists alone and working in unhampered devotion to intellectual ends."[12] This aspiration lay behind the establishment of the American Historical Association (AHA) in 1884; one of the papers presented at its very first meeting was rather symbolically entitled "Narrative and Critical History of America."[13]

Unlike the local private and state societies, the AHA was conceived as a national historical society, and its status was enhanced even more by the Act of Incorporation of 1889, which defined it as "a body corporate and politic" created "for the promotion of historical studies, the collection and preservation of historical manuscripts, and for kindred purposes in the interest of American history and of history in America." According to the act, the AHA was to report annually to the US Congress on "the condition of historical study in America."[14] Its national status, however, also obliged the AHA to enable cooperation with and among the state and private historical societies—the very societies whose perceived deficiencies had led to its establishment. Hence, it was not surprising that twenty years elapsed until the annual meeting of the American Historical Association held in Chicago in 1904 devoted one of its sessions to a conference of representatives of local societies. While the delegates from the veteran historical societies talked about preserving documents and the various ways of interaction with local governments, Professor Henry E. Bourne delivered a paper in which he critically analyzed the societies' activity. As it was elegantly formulated in the AHA report for that year, in the conclusion he "dwelt on the desirability of cooperation, and especially on the need of good understanding between the local societies and the general association."[15] Bourne substantiated his argument by citing the example of the French societies: "In France the historical societies, with the other scientific associations, hold an annual congress which is much like the annual meetings of this Association. The congress is directed by the *comité des travaux historiques* which is appointed by the ministry of public instruction. If some common direction is needed in a highly centralized country like France, where the intellectual life centers in Paris, it is much more necessary here."[16]

This comparison with European, in particular German and French, scholarly life also underlay the discussions at other sessions, including the one devoted to the procedure of obtaining a doctoral degree in history at American universities. It is interesting that Miliukov participated in this debate as a visiting lecturer at the University of Chicago; he claimed that "in his country the attainment of a degree is too difficult, and here [is] too easy."[17] The very fact that Miliukov attended the AHA's meeting of 1904 vividly demonstrates the growing cooperation between voluntary associations and universities in the United States. It also indicated the American historical community's progress from merely emulating European examples to adapting those elements that they saw as useful for fashioning the modern American historical enterprise.[18] This new trend included inviting European historians to deliver courses in American institutions of higher education. Miliukov became one such guest lecturer, and his invitation was also connected with the American "university extension" program, which served as the model for the similar Russian project from the mid-1890s.

In early 1900, the businessmen Charles R. Crane donated the substantial sum of $10,000 to the University of Chicago for the purpose of holding an annual lecture series "Russian Literature and Institutions" (*Lektsii po russkoi literature i uchrezhdeniiam*). The lectures were to be held during the following five years in the framework of the "university extension" summer courses. In order to select the appropriate candidates, a special delegation headed by the president of the University, William P. Harper, went on a two-month trip through Europe in April 1900.[19] Having become acquainted with Miliukov at one of St. Petersburg's social gatherings, Harper and Crane invited him to participate in the project. Miliukov taught during the third "Russian season," following Maxim Kovalevskii, who had delivered a course "Russian Political Institutions" in 1901, and Thomas Masaryk, who had addressed some issues related to Russia in his lectures on the more general topic of the historical philosophy of small nations in summer 1902. Miliukov's course, under the general title "Russia and Its Crisis," was held in Chicago from

June 23 to July 25, 1903, after which he continued to the Lowell Institute in Boston where he delivered a further course in the fall semester of that year. Invited by Crane to deliver a new series of lectures on the Balkan Slavs in the next academic year, Miliukov left the United States in order to collect the necessary materials and returned to Chicago in the late fall of 1904.[20] He therefore participated in the AHA meeting on December 28–30, 1904, while teaching his new course at the University of Chicago and was able to speak as an observant outsider who had already became acquainted with American university life from the inside. In his lecture "The Chief Currents of Russian Historical Thought" at the AHA session, Miliukov not only described the distinct features of the St. Petersburg and Moscow historical schools, but also identified a new trend in Russian historical scholarship, which he defined as sociological, and revealed his awareness of similar developments in the United States, even pointing to American influence on contemporary Russian historical thought: "I need not dwell upon the theoretical foundations of that new current, as it is chiefly from America that we borrowed our most widely spread and most relevant sociological doctrines, Mr. Lester Ward and Mr. Giddings exercising the greatest influence in that line."[21] One of the important decisions of the Chicago meeting was to appoint a committee to prepare a report on "the best methods of organization and work of the state and local historical societies" for the next AHA meeting in 1905. The committee began by sending an elaborate questionnaire to the local societies, whose number already fluctuated between four hundred and five hundred. Although only less than a half of the societies responded to the questions, the committee had enough data to draw the conclusion that there was "an increasing tendency toward a closer alliance between state historical societies and departments of history in the state universities."[22] Indeed, this trend, alongside the AHA's increasing coordinating role, characterized both American associational life and the process of the professionalization of history in this period. It was the ability of the American historical community to develop the European tradition and to adapt it to their distinctive needs and conditions that paved the way for the historical enterprise to flourish in the twentieth-century United States.

* * *

In comparison with the American societies' steady development from disparate local groups of amateurs to a national network of state and private societies under the aegis of a scholarly association headed by academic historians, the Russian historical societies followed a less coherent path. On the one hand, the Russian societies were from the outset closely connected with the universities and thus became involved earlier (and more easily) in the process of the professionalization of history. This kind of affiliation provided them with the protection of governmental institutions but also made them less autonomous than the American historical associations. On the other hand, there was neither an organized national network of historical societies nor one umbrella association analogous to the AHA. Nonetheless, although there were fewer historical societies in Russia, their organizational structure and concrete modes of operation were more varied. Moreover, the very pattern of their development was different. The first and the most important Russian nineteenth-century historical societies appeared in the capital cities, Moscow and St. Petersburg, with local historical and archeological societies emerging only later, followed by the gubernia scholarly archival commissions. Although the trend toward greater cooperation appeared in Russia even earlier than in America—heralded by the first archeological congress of the 1860s—it remained sporadic, and only a few of the plans to strengthen it were implemented in practice.

One episode from the history of the Society of Zealots of Russian Historical Education, in which various figures who have appeared in this book were involved, exemplifies this process. In 1899, the society considered the possibility of launching a historical-bibliographical anthology to be entitled the *Chronicle of Russian Historical Literature* (*Letopis' russkoi istoricheskoi literatury*). This idea was reminiscent of the guide to historical literature that had been planned some years before by the historical society at St. Petersburg University but had been only partially realized in the publication of its journal, *Istoricheskoe obozrenie*. In the Zealots' case, however, the proposal came from none other than the arch-conservative of the era, the Ober-Procurator of the Holy Synod, Konstantin Pobedonostsev, who did not conceal the fact that one of his aspirations was to create a tribune for presenting works by church historians from ecclesiastical institutions whose studies frequently "remained without attention and appreciation."[23] Remarkably, he suggested including in this anthology surveys of such foreign journals as "*Athenaeum, Liter. [Literarisches] Centralblatt [für Deutschland], Revue Critique*, etc."[24] The society's council discussed Pobedonostsev's proposal and decided to conduct a kind of opinion poll regarding the feasibility of such a project among fifty-eight scholars, archivists, bibliographical experts, and editors of historical journals. The list they drew up began with the names of Korsakov, Ikonnikov, Kliuchevskii, and Zabelin, included Platonov, Chechulin, and Forsten but excluded Miliukov, Kizevetter, and Semevskii. The head of the society, Sheremetev, sent a letter to all the people selected, translating Pobedonostsev's proposal into the broader idea of the need for a professional organ that would present "unbiased criticism that would embrace the entirety of historical writings."[25]

The council of the society received forty-two detailed responses to this letter, which conveyed the impression of a professional community that was becoming consolidated. Whether they supported or had reservations about the Zealots' proposal, the respondents regarded historical journals as a channel of professional communication and popularization of history. Kliuchevskii recommended that the proposed journal should provide information about the activity of the gubernia scholarly archival commissions, drawing attention to these comparatively new institutions. The Kazan' historian Dmitrii Korsakov, the bibliographer Aleksander Braudo, the archeologist Nikodim Kondakov, and the secretary of the Russian Historical Society, Georgii Shtendman, compared the Zealots' proposal with the practices of German and French historical societies and journals and thus placed the project in the broader European context. In particular, Shtendman recommended studying the practice of the Historical Society of Berlin (*Historische Gesellschaft zu Berlin*), which since 1878 had published annual reports, *Jahresberichte der Geschichtswisssenschaft*. He also drew the Zealots' attention to the *Historische Zeitschrift* issued by the Munich Historical Society, which was considered the leading historical journal of the time. Shtendman noted that it would be advisable to obtain the help of the Academy of Sciences and recommended cooperation with the *Journal of the Ministry of Education*. Vladimir Lamanskii provided a detailed plan of how the proposed anthology could be organized and managed and suggested a possible mode of cooperation among experts in particular branches of historical scholarship. Nikolai Likhachev suggested that they could collaborate with the state institutions engaged in collecting and preserving historical documents by devoting a special section of the anthology to an annotated catalog of the manuscripts held by the Academy of Sciences, the Imperial Public Library, and the Library of the Archive of the Ministry of the Foreign Affairs.[26]

All these different proposals outlined a variety of ways in which cooperation between voluntary and governmental bodies involved in historical scholarship could be strengthened. However, since it was evident that a huge amount of work was needed in order to launch and maintain such a project, the council of the Society of Zealots decided that the time and effort required for publishing a bibliographical anthology would be at the expense of the society's other tasks and gave up the idea. Instead, it opted to launch a newsletter with a special section devoted to critical reviews of new historical literature. The council also decided to publish excerpts from the correspondence on its unrealized bibliographic project in the Zealots' newsletter. This decision was implemented in 1902, and publicizing the proposals placed the entire discussion in the broader context of the debates on the fate of Russian historical studies in the new, twentieth century.[27] Furthermore, the idea of coordination and cooperation among voluntary societies and governmental offices connected with the preservation and publication of historical documents was eventually realized in another way.

As a result of Nicholas II's suggestion to transfer part of the responsibility for the gubernia scholarly archival commissions to the Russian Historical Society (RIO), the latter not only started to serve as a channel for funding the commissions, but eventually became perceived as the institution that would be responsible for supervising them. Indeed, the first conference of local archival commissions was organized by the RIO in May 1914.[28] The conference suggested that the gubernia commissions' members should be affiliated with the special archival committee of the RIO, which could have "upgraded" the ties between the commissions and the society, but the proposal was not implemented because of the outbreak of the First World War.[29] Another project that could have had a significant impact on the interaction among the Russian historical associations was the Fourth International Historical Congress scheduled to be held in St. Petersburg in 1918. Planning started in 1913, and the various committees and commissions involved in the preparations became the new center of the historical community's life, but their activity was curtailed when it became clear that there was no chance of holding the congress at the scheduled time because of the war.[30] Despite the war, in March 1915, a conference of Russian history professors took place at Moscow University. It decided to organize congresses of Russian historians every five years—to be called Russian Historical Congresses in the Name of Emperor Nicholas II—which were defined as a "new institution, extremely important for the development of Russian historical scholarship." They were planned to be held in one of the university cities; the corresponding university would be responsible for the preparations. The first congress was scheduled for December 1919 in Moscow, to coincide with the twenty-fifth anniversary of Nicholas II's reign. It was during the preparations for this congress that the Historical Society at Moscow University launched its journal *Istoricheskie izvestiia* (*Historical News*): as Moscow University Rector Matvei Liubavskii explained, the members of the society could not tolerate the idea that the future congress would take place without Russian historians having their own "scholarly and informative organ."[31] A year later, in 1916, a group of Petrograd historians associated with the Historical Society at Petrograd University, including Lappo-Danilevskii and Presniakov, launched their own *Russkii istoricheskii zhurnal* (*Russian Historical Journal*) with the similar aim of informing all "workers in Russian history" about recent developments in the field.[32] Yet, when in October 1915 the Society of Zealots of History, which had been founded only in 1911 (evidently inspired by the Society of Zealots of Russian Historical Education), suggested that the activity of all the historical, archival and archeological societies should be "unified" in order to enhance their "greater productivity" without limiting their independent status, the more established societies regarded this proposal as the insolent initiative of a novice body and furiously rejected it.[33]

The trend toward greater cooperation among the historical societies and their increased collaboration with the governmental bodies intensified during the First World War and the turbulent years of the revolution. As early as March 1917, a few days after the fall of the monarchy in Russia, Petrograd historians and archivists

Fig. 5.1 Representatives of the gubernia scholarly archival commissions at their April 1914 conference. Courtesy of the Department of Manuscripts, Russian National Library.

launched a new kind of voluntary body—the Union of Russian Archive *Deiateli* (*Soiuz Rossiiskikh Arkhivnykh Deiatelei*).³⁴ The word *deiateli* (activists) in its title implied both a strong element of activism and broad eligibility for membership. The union included both archive employees and university professors; Lappo-Danilevskii was elected chairman, while its council comprised representatives of the capital's governmental, court, and academic archives. All in all, "more than 30 bodies from the capital and provinces participated in the Union," Presniakov noted a year later.³⁵ Although the establishment of the union was primarily the result of the widely recognized urgent necessity to preserve archival documents in the critical circumstances of the revolutionary unrest, its bylaws included the protection of archive employees' professional interests. This new theme in the historians' discourse was closely connected with the tendency to professional self-organization characteristic of this period of revolutionary development. For the community of historians, however, this call for unification reverberated with the already existing trend toward closer cooperation among its various segments. At the same time, the revolutionary events stimulated the appearance of another new kind of historical association—commissions and societies for the study of the revolution. These voluntary bodies embodied and expressed an additional significant trend that had emerged in the prerevolutionary historical societies—increased interest in contemporary events along with historians' involvement in public educational and commemorative projects. However, after the fall of the monarchy these ideas were expressed in a new form and by the new actors in the field, as Presniakov described in 1918:

> From the very first days of the February revolution various groups of society, swept up by the huge significance of the events being experienced, became filled with the aspiration to collect and preserve materials that could serve as a means for studying these events in future, when the time will come to look back on the path of struggle, revolutions, and experiences of new political and social creativity. This tendency was particularly salient in some army units and military circles. In several regiments of the Petrograd garrison "historical commissions" were formed by soldiers and young officers in order to preserve the memory of the actions of military units and their role in the [revolutionary] movement. The short-lived Union of Republican Soldiers attempted to organize this matter systematically and asked for the help of the intelligentsia—the young forces from the universities. In that way, on the initiative of the Union of Republican Soldiers, the Society for the Study of the Revolution of 1917 was formed, which undertook not only to collect various printed materials, of a fluctuating and ephemeral (*tekuchii i letuchii*) nature, which reflected the rapidly changing events, but also to create sources for the future study of the Russian revolution by interviewing its prominent activists and rank-and-file participants in order to preserve the factual traces of the events while they are still fresh in memory.[36]

The appearance of this and other historical-revolutionary societies—according to Presniakov, similar "circles and bodies" existed in the capital cities and the provinces—reflected the increased role of voluntary public initiatives in the study of history. The trend toward closer professional cooperation, combined with the willingness to involve new public forces, intensified the historical societies' activity in the period of the Provisional Government and even in the first years of Soviet power. However, they were hampered by the harsh economic conditions and the difficulties of the civil war while the atmosphere in early Soviet Russia, in which the ideas of "centralization" and "nationalization" were becoming dominant, appeared hostile to voluntarism. The "old" historical associations gradually curtailed their activity and the Union of Archive *Deiateli* was swallowed up by the new governmental structures, while the spontaneously created societies for the study of the revolution were ousted by the party-controlled Commission on the History of the October Revolution and the Russian Communist Party (the notorious Istpart).[37] Not surprisingly, the informal circles of historians proved to be the most resilient during the postrevolutionary years, and "numerous scholarly *kruzhki*" continued to meet "primarily at participants' homes, just as they had in the pre-revolutionary period," despite the difficult conditions of the early 1920s.[38]

However, even when historians became Soviet *sluzhashchie*, they retained their professional and personal networks and brought their norms, values, and codes of behavior into the Soviet institutions. They thus made a deep impact on those institutions' mode of operation—at least until the first wave of repression of the late 1920s heralded the fateful changes in the nature of the Soviet system, dealing a harsh blow to academic life in general and the historical community in particular.

Notes

1. Hoffmann, "Democracy and Associations in the Long Nineteenth Century: Toward a Transitional Perspective," 275.

2. Alexis de Tocqueville, *Democracy in America*, vol. 2 (New York: Vintage Books, 1945), 118.

3. Morris, "Clubs, Societies and Associations," 400, 408, 410, 414.

4. For a survey of this process in various national contexts, see Ilaria Porciani and Jo Tolle-beek, eds., *Setting the Standards: Institutions, Networks, and Communities of National Historiography* (Basingstoke, UK: Palgrave Macmillan, 2012).

5. Ryan Schumacher, "The Wisconsin Magazine of History: A Case Study in Scholarly and Popular Approaches to American State Historical Society Publishing, 1917–2000," *Journal of Scholarly Publishing* (2013): 117.

6. Julian P. Boyd, "State and Local Historical Societies in the United States," *American Historical Review* 10, no. 1 (1934): 18, 21, 24.

7. Schumacher, "The Wisconsin Magazine of History," 118–119.

8. "That Germany possessed the sole secret of scholarship was not doubted by us young fellows in the eighteen eighties than it had been doubted by George Ticknor and Edward Everett when they sailed from Boston, bound for Göttingen, in 1814." Bliss Perry, *And Gladly Teach: Reminiscences* (Boston: Hoghton Mifflin Company, 1935), 88–89, quoted in Peter Novick, *That Noble Dream: The "Objectivity Question" and the American Historical Profession* (Cambridge: Cambridge University Press, 1988), 21.

9. Novick, *That Noble Dream*, 22.

10. Ibid., 40, 46.

11. Boyd, "State and Local Historical Societies in the United States," 27. Scholarly historians saw one of their aims as expanding the scope of historical studies. In 1896, for example, the *American Historical Review* published an article urging the study of Scandinavian and Russian history, given, among others, "the importance of Russia in the world today." See Archibald Cary Coolidge, "A Plea for the Study of the History of Northern Europe," *American Historical Review* 2, no. 1 (1896): 34–35.

12. J. Franklin Jameson, "The American Historical Association," *American Historical Review* 15, no. 1 (1909): 2.

13. Ibid., 8.

14. The report was to be submitted via the Secretary of the Smithsonian Institution. "Act of Incorporation [approved January 4, 1889]," in *Annual Report of the American Historical Association for the Year 1904* (Washington: Government Printing Office, 1905), 4.

15. Charles H. Haskins, "Report of the Proceedings of the Twentieth Annual Meeting of the American Historical Association" in *Annual Report of the American Historical Association for the Year 1904* (Washington: Government Printing Office, 1905), 33.

16. Henry E. Bourne, "The Work of American Historical Societies," in *Annual Report of the American Historical Association for the Year 1904*, 127.

17. Haskins, "Report of the Proceedings of the Twentieth Annual Meeting of the American Historical Association," 34.

18. The term "historical enterprise" was coined by Robert B. Townsend to denote "the broad range of activities where such knowledge about the past is produced and used in an organized or systematic way" and to explain "when, how, and why particular areas of work under the large sign of history became professional." See his *History's Babel: Scholarship, Professionalization, and the Historical Enterprise in the United States, 1880–1940* (Chicago: University of Chicago Press, 2013), 3–4.

19. Albert Parry, "Charles R. Crane, Friend of Russia," *Russian Review* 6, no. 2 (1947): 28.

20. Bon [Bohn], *Russkaia istoricheskaia nauka*, 94–96, 225; Miliukov, *Vospominaniia*, 146–149, 152, 172.

21. Milyoukov, "The Chief Currents of Russian Historical Thought," 114.

22. Boyd, "State and Local Historical Societies in the United States," 27–29.

23. RGIA, f.747, op.1, d. 43, Perepiska po povodu izdaniia Letopisi istoricheskoi literatury, l. 2–3. For an interesting source on the kind of research works produced by the students of ecclesiastical academies, see A. V. Mel'nikov, "Neopublikovannye otzyvy M. M. Bogoslovskogo o kandidatskikh sochineniiakh vypusknikov moskovskoi dukhovnoi akademii (1916–1917)," in S. O. Shmidt, ed., *Arkheograficheskii ezhegodnik za 2004 god* (Moscow: Nauka, 2005): 517–526.

24. K. P. Pobedonostsev to S. D. Sheremetev, Jan. 1899, RGIA, f.747, op.1, d. 43, l. 1-3.

25. RGIA, f.747, op.1, d. 43, l. 1–1 ob., 5.

26. V. O. Kliuchevskii to S. D. Sheremetev, January 14, 1899; D. A. Korsakov to S. D. Sheremetev, February 8, 1899; G. F. Shtendman to S. D. Sheremetev, February 9, 1899; N. P. Likhachev to S. D. Sheremetev, February 14, 1899. RGIA, f.747, op.1, d. 43, l. 13–13 ob., 28–29, 39–39 ob., 25–30 ob., 49–59.

27. "Ob izdanii 'Letopisi' russkoi istoricheskoi literatury," *IOR*, no. 4 (1902), 14–34.

28. "Protokol zasedaniia Imperatorskogo Russkogo Istoricheskogo Obshchestva 3 Maia 1911," in *Sbornik materialov otnosiashchikhsia do arkhivnoi chasti v Rossii*, 1: 680–681.

29. "Izvlechenie iz otcheta godovogo sobraniia Imperatorskogo Russkogo Istoricheskogo Obshestva 12 Marta 1915," in *Sbornik materialov otnosiashchikhsia do arkhivnoi chasti v Rossii*, 1: 691.

30. ASpbII RAN, f. 193, op. 3, d. 2 Protokoly zasedanii predvaritel'nogo Soveshchaniia po voprosu ob ustroistve Mezhdunarodnogo istoricheskogo s'ezda v Sankt-Peterburge v 1918 g., l. 21–26. The fourth international historical congress was finally held in 1923 in Brussels. See Karl Dietrich Erdmann, *Toward a Global Community of Historians: The International Historical Congresses and the International Committee of Historical Sciences, 1898–2000* (New York and Oxford: Berghahn Books, 2005); for the participation of Russian historians in these congresses, see N. S. Zonova, *Rossiiskie istoriki na mezhdunarodnykh kongressakh istoricheskikh nauk nachala XX veka* (PhD diss., Nizhnii Novgorod State University for Architecture and Civil Engineering, 2004).

31. V. G. Bukhert, "Soveshchanie professorov russkoi istorii i istorii russkogo prava Rossiiskikh universitetov (Moscow, 26–28 marta 1915 g.)," in S. O. Shmidt, ed., *Arkheograficheskii ezhegodnik za 2009–2010 gg.* (Moscow: Nauka, 2012), 184–189; "Obrashchenie Redaktsionnogo komiteta," *Istoricheskie izvestiia izdavaemye istoricheskim obshchestvom pri Imperatorskom moskovskom universitete*, no. 1 (1916), 3–4.

32. "Ot redaktsii," *Russkii istoricheskii zhurnal* 1, no. 1–2 (1917): 3–7.

33. RGIA, f. 746 Russkoe istoricheskoe obshchestvo, op. 1, d. 195 Ob organizatsii Vseros-siiskogo soiuza istoricheskikh obshchestv, l.1–5 ob.

34. Tsentral'nyi moskovskii arkhiv-muzei lichnykh sobranii (TsMAM LS), f. 110, I. L. Maiakovskii, op. 1, d. 226, Ustav soiuza Rossiiskikh arkhivnykh deiatelei, l. 6.

35. A. E. Presniakov, "Reforma arkhivnogo dela," *Russkii istoricheskii zhurnal*, no. 5 (1918): 209.

36. Ibid., 205.

37. The Union of Archive *Deiateli* ceased its activity in 1922 and was finally closed in 1924. See S. Iu. Malysheva, *Osnovy arkhivovedeniia* (Kazan': Tatarskoe respublikanskoe izdatel'stvo "Kheter," 2002); G. D. Alekseeva, "Istpart: Osnovnye napravleniia i etapy deiatel'nosti," *Voprosy istorii*, no. 9 (1982): 17–29; Corney, *Telling October: Memory and the Making of the Bolshevik Revolution*, 97–125.

38. Anan'ich and Paneiakh, "The St. Petersburg School of History and Its Fate," 149.

Bibliography

Archival and Manuscripts Collections

Arkhiv Sankt-Peterburgskogo instituta istoriii Rossiiskoi Akademii Nauk (ASpbII RAN), f. 193, Presniakov A. E., op. 3, d. 2, Protokoly zasedanii predvaritel'nogo soveshchaniia po voprosu ob ustroistve Mezhdunarodnogo Istoricheskogo S'ezda v St. Petersburge v 1918.

———. f. 219, Istoricheskoe obshchestvo pri St. Peterburgskom Universitete, op. 1, d. 25, Plan izdaniia sistematicheskogo obzora istoricheskoi literatury Istoricheskim obshchestvom, sostoiashchim pri St. Peterburgskom Universitete.

Gosudarstvennyi arkhiv Rossiiskoi Federatsii (GARF), f. 1779, Kantseliariia Vremennogo pravitel'stva, op. 2, d. 1, Zhurnaly zasedanii Vremennogo pravital'stva.

Otdel rukopisei Gosudarstvennoi Tret'iakovskoi galerei (OR GTG), f. 66, V. M. Vasnetsov, d. 279, Pis'ma V. M. Vasnetsovu ot S. D. Sheremeteva.

Otdel rukopisei Rossiiskoi natsional'noi biblioteki (OR RNB), f. 585, S. F. Platonov, op.1, d. 4615, 4616, 4627, Pis'ma S. D. Sheremeteva S. F. Platonovu; d. 5691, Dnevnik N. N. Platonovoi.

———. f. 682, Selifontov N. N., Bakhtin I. N., op. 1, d. 74, Gubastov K. A., Chlen Soveta Ministrov, Pis'mo Nik. Nik. Selifontovu.

———. f. 838, Chechulin N. D., op. 1, d. 94, Chechulin Nikolai Dmitrievich, Pis'ma k materi, Marii Pavlovne Chechulinoi, 8 iiulia 1896–18 dekabria 1899.

Rossiiskii gosudarstvennyi istoricheskii arkhiv (RGIA), f. 746 Russkoe istoricheskoe obshchestvo, op. 1, d. 195 Ob organizatsii Vserossiiskogo soiuza istoricheskikh obshchestv.

———. f. 747, Obshchestvo revnitelei russkogo istoricheskogo prosveshcheniia, op. 1, d. 12, Povestka dnia zasedanii soveta Obshchestva revnitelei russkogo istoricheskogo prosveshcheniia; d. 16, Tetrad' so stat'ei ob obshchestve revnitelei russkogo istoricheskogo prosveshcheniia; d. 23, Otchëty, protokoly i perepiska o deiatel'nosti Istoricheskogo otdeleniia; d. 28, Kopii protokolov i vypiski iz zhurnalov zasedanii, perepiska o deiatel'nosti Izdatel'skogo otdeleniia; d. 29–1 and 29–2, Kopii protokolov i vypiski iz zhurnalov zasedanii, perepiska o deiatel'nosti Izdatel'skogo otdela; d. 33, Delo komissii po izdaniiu sbornika "Starina i novizna"; d. 43, Perepiska po povodu izdaniia Letopisi istoricheskoi literatury; d. 68, O programme uchebnika po russkoi istorii; d. 72, O raznykh predpolozheniiakh zaiavlennykh chlenami obshchestva; d. 74, Spisok knig i dokumentov po russkoi istorii khraniashchiksia v biblioteke i arkhive Obshchestva revnitelei russkogo istoricheskogo prosveshcheniia.

———. f. 878, S. S. Tatishchev, d. 23, Zapiska Natalii Petrovny Grot ob urokakh ee muzha, Iakova Karlovicha Grota, nasledniku Nikolaiu Aleksandrovichu i v. kn. Aleksandru Aleksandrovichu v 1853–1858 gg; d. 24, Spisok knig i arkhivnykh del

poluchennykh S. S. Tatishchevym dlia raboty po "Istorii zhizni i tsarstvovaniia
imp. Aleksandra III"; dd. 27–31, Obzor sotsial'no-revoliutsionnogo dvizheniia
v Rossii, 1894–1905 and Otdel'nye glavy raboty S. S. Tatishcheva; dd. 32–44,
Materialy dlia raboty, sobrannye S. S. Tatishchevym; d. 59; Dokladnaia zapiska
S. S. Tatishcheva ministram dvora, vnutrennikh del, finansov i gr. Serg. Dm.
Sheremetevu s prilozheniem uslovii raboty nad knigoi po istorii tsarstvovaniia
Aleksandra III, January 28, 1903; d. 69, Pis'mo A. S. Stishinskogo S. S. Tatishchevu
s priglasheniem k gr. S. D. Sheremetevu; d. 71, Pis'mo gr. S. A. Tolstoi S. S.
Tatishchevu o svoem svidanii s imperatorom Aleksandrom III; d. 72, Pis'mo
general-leitenanta V. P. Tselebrovskogo S. S. Tatishchevu o razreshenii emu
zaniatii v voennykh arkhivakh; d. 73, Pis'ma ministra dvora gr. V. B. Frederiksa
S. S. Tatishchevu o ego rabote nad istoriei tsarstvovaniia Aleksandra III; d. 74
Pis'ma, telegrammy i vizitnye kartochki gr. S. D. Sheremeteva S. S. Tatishchevu po
povodu ego raboty po istorii tsarstvovaniia Aleksandra III.
———. f. 1072, Ukhtomskii Esper Esperovich, op. 1, d. 10, Pis'ma E. E. Ukhtomskomu.
———. f. 1088, Sheremetevy, op. 2, S. D. Sheremetev, d. 18, Retsenziia [S. D. Sheremeteva]
na knigu S. S. Tatishcheva "Imperator Aleksandr III. Ego zhizn' i tsarstvovanie";
d. 26, Perepiska gr. S. D. Sheremeteva s redaktorom-izdatelem St. Peterburgskikh
Vedomostei kn. E. E. Ukhtomskim i chlenom soveta obshchestva revnitelei B. M.
Iuzefovichem; d. 28, Perepiska S. D. Sheremeteva s Tatishchevym S. S. o knige ob
Aleksandre III.
Rossiiskii gosudarstvennyi arkhiv drevnikh aktov (RGADA), f. 1287, Sheremetevy,
Lichnyi arkhiv S. D. Sheremeteva, op. 1, d. 67, Pis'ma S. D. Sheremetevu ot I. P.
Barsukova; d. 411, Pis'ma S. D. Sheremetevu ot A. A. Golenishcheva-Kutuzova; d.
1554, Pis'ma S. D. Sheremetevu ot D. S. Sipiagina; d. 1754, Pis'ma S. D. Sheremetevu
ot I. F. Tiutcheva; d. 1898, Pis'ma S. D. Sheremetevu ot N. D. Chechulina; d. 2082,
Pis'ma S. D. Sheremetevu ot B. M. Iuzefovicha; d. 4112, Pis'ma po obshchestvu
revnitelei; d. 4116, Chernovaia zametka S. D. Sheremeteva 'Iz vospominanii o
vozniknovenii Obshchestva revnitelei, 1913; d. 4115, Zapiska S. D. Sheremeteva
o deiatel'nosti otdelenii Obshchestva revnitelei russkogo istoricheskogo
prosveshcheniia; d. 4119, Chernoviki pisem S. D. Sheremeteva Nikolaiu II
po voprosam, sviazannym s deiatel'nost'iu obshchestva revnitelei; d. 4126,
Chernoviki pisem Sheremeteva k raznym litsam po obshchestvu revnitelei; d.
4144, Chernovik zametok S. D. Sheremeteva o trudakh Liaskovskogo i Tatishcheva
ob Aleksandre III, 1908 g.; d. 4146, Chernovaia zametka S. D. Sheremeteva o
Russkom Sobranii; d. 4147, Kopiia pis'ma L. Tikhomirova v Sovet Obshchestva
ob okazanii podderzhki gazete "Moskovske vedomosti" ; d. 5041, Dnevnik S. D.
Sheremeteva.
Rossiiskii gosudarstvennyi arkhiv literatury i iskusstva (RGALI), f. 143, Golenishchev-
Kutuzov Arsenii Arkad'evich, graf (1848–1913), op. 1, d. 150, Pis'ma Tikhomirovu L. A.
Rukopisnyi otdel instituta russkoi literatury (Pushkinskii Dom) Akademii Nauk (RO
IRLI), f. 463, K. A. Gubastov, d. 44 Pis'ma Sheremeteva S. D.
Tsentral'nyi gosudarstvennyi istoricheskii arkhiv St. Petersburga (TsGIA Spb), f. 119,
Arkheologicheskii Institut, op. 2, d. 48, O reorganizatsii instituta.
Tsentral'nyi moskovskii arkhiv-muzei lichnykh sobranii (TsMAM LS), f. 110, I. L.
Maiakovskii.

Periodicals and Journals

Bibliograf: Vestnik Literatury, Nauki i Iskusstva. 1884–1914.
Drevniaia Rossiiskaia Vivliofika. St. Petersburg, 1773–1775. Moscow, 1788–1791.
Istoricheskie Izvestiia, Izdavaemye Istoricheskim Obshchestvom Pri Imperatorskom Moskovskom Universitete. 1916–1917.
Istoricheskii Vestnik. 1880–1917.
Istoricheskoe Obozrenie. 1890–1916.
Izvestiia Obshchestva Revnitelei Russkogo Istoricheskogo Prosveshcheniia v Pamiat' Imperatora Aleksandra III. 1900–1905.
Mir Bozhii. 1892–1906.
Moskovskie Vedomosti. 1756–1917.
Nasha Starina. 1914–1916.
Nauchnyi Istoricheskii Zhurnal. 1913–1914.
Novoe Vremia. 1868–1917.
Opyt Trudov Vol'nogo Rossiiskogo Sobraniia Pri Imperatorskom Moskovskom Universitete. 1771–1783
Otechestvennye Zapiski. 1818–1884.
Russkaia Mysl'. 1880–1918.
Russkie Dostopamiatnosti. 1815, 1843, 1844.
Russkie Vedomosti. 1863–1918.
Russkii Arkhiv. 1863–1917.
Russkii Istoricheskii Zhurnal. 1917–1921.
Russkoe Bogatstvo. 1876–1918.
Russkoe Obozrenie. 1890–1898, 1901, 1903.
Russkoe Slovo. 1859–1866.
Sankt-Peterburgskie Vedomosti. 1728–1917.
Starina i Novizna. St. Petersburg, 1897–1904, Moscow/St.Petersburg, 1904–1917.
Trudy Vol'nogo Ekonomicheskogo Obshchestva. 1765–1915.
Tserkovnye Vedomosti. 1888–1918.
Utrennii Svet. 1777–1780.
Vestnik Evropy. 1802–1830; 1866–1918.
Vecherniaia Zaria. 1782.
Zhurnal Ministerstva Narodnogo Prosveshcheniia. 1834–1917.

Published Documents

Annual Report of the American Historical Association for the Year 1904. Washington: Government Printing Office, 1905.
Imperatorskoe Russkoe Istoricheskoe Obshchestvo, 1866–1916: Obzor Piatidesiatiletnei Deiatel'nosti. Petrograd, 1916.
Istoricheskaia Zapiska o Deiatel'nosti Imperatorskogo Moskovskogo Arkheologicheskogo Obshchestva za Pervye 25 Let Sushchestvovaniia. Moscow: Sinodal'naia tipografiia.
Izdaniia Obshchestva Revnitelei Russkogo Istoricheskogo Prosveshcheniia v Pamiat' Imperatora Aleksandra III. St. Petersburg, 1908.

"Katalog Besplatnykh Narodnykh Bibliotek Obshchestva Revnitelei." In *Narodnye Biblioteki Obshchestva Revnitelei Russkogo Istoricheskogo Prosveshcheniia v Pamiat' Imperatora Aleksandra III*, 19–27. St. Petersburg: V gosudarstvennoi tipografii, 1899.

Kratkii Obzor Deiatel'nosti Obshchestva Oznakomleniia s Istoricheskimi Sobytiiami Rossii za 1911–1912 gody. Moscow, 1913.

Müller, G. F. "Proekt Sozdaniia Istoricheskogo Departamenta Akademii Nauk." In *Sochineniia po Istorii Rossii: Izbrannoe*, edited by A. B. Kamenskii, idem., 355–364. Moscow: Nauka, 1990.

"Nakaz Komissii o Sostavlenii Proekta Novogo Ulozheniia." In *Polnoe Sobranie Sochinenii Imperatritsy Ekateriny II*. Vol. 1, 5–84. St. Petersburg: Izdanie knizhnogo sklada "Rodina," 1893.

Ocherk Glavnykh Osnovanii Deiatel'nosti Mestnykh Otdelov Obshchestva Revnitelei Russkogo Istoricheskogo Prosveshcheniia v Pamiat' Imperatora Alexandra III. St. Petersburg, 1900.

Otchët Komissii po Organizatsii Domashnego Chteniia, Sostoiashchei pri Uchebnom Otdele Obshchestva Rasprostraneniia Tekhnicheskikh Znanii za 1894 i 1895 g. Moscow, 1897.

Otchët o Deiatel'nosti Pedagogicheskogo Obshchestva, Sostoiashchego pri Imperatorskom Moskovskom Universitete, za 1898/9 god (Sushchestvovaniia Obshchestva God Pervyi). Moscow, 1899.

Otchët o Sostoianii i Deiatel'nosti Istoricheskogo Obshchestva Pri Imperatorskom Sankt-Peterburgskom Universitete v 1890 godu. St. Petersburg, 1890.

Otchët Obshchestva Revnitelei Russkogo Istoricheskogo Prosveshcheniia v Pamiat' Imperatora Aleksandra III za 1897/8 god. St. Petersburg, 1898.

Otchët Obshchestva Revnitelei Russkogo Istoricheskogo Prosveshcheniia v Pamiat' Imperatora Aleksandra III za 1898/9 god. St. Petersburg, 1899.

"Otchët Obshchestva Revnitelei Russkogo Istoricheskogo Prosveshcheniia v Pamiat' Imperatora Aleksandra III za 1900–1901." *Izvestiia Obshchestva Revnitelei Russkogo Istoricheskogo Prosveshcheniia v Pamiat' Imperatora Aleksandra III*, no. 4 (1902): 1–10.

"Otchët Obshchestva Revnitelei . . . za 1901–1902 god." *Izvestiia Obshchestva Revnitelei Russkogo Istoricheskogo Prosveshcheniia v Pamiat' Imperatora Aleksandra III* 5 (1904): 1–12.

Ot Soveta Obshchestva Revnitelei Russkogo Istoricheskogo Prosveshcheniia v Pamiat' Imperatora Aleksandra III po Sluchaiu Priniatiia L. A. Tikhomirovym Rukovodstva Gazetoi "Moskovskie Vedomosti." St. Petersburg, 1909.

Poludenskii, M. *Materialy dlia Istorii Druzheskogo Uchenogo Obshchestva, 1782*. Moscow: Tipografiia Lazarevskogo instituta vostochnykh iazykov, 1863.

"Pravila o Besplatnykh Narodnykh Bibliotekakh Obshchestva Revnitelei Russkogo Istoricheskogo Prosveshcheniia v Pamiat' Imperatora Aleksandra III." In *Narodnye Biblioteki Obshchestva Revnitelei Russkogo Istoricheskogo Prosveshcheniia v Pamiat' Imperatora Aleksandra III*, 29–35. St. Petersburg: V gosudarstvennoi tipografii, 1899.

"Proekt Polozheniia Akademii Nauk i Khudozhestv, 22 Ianvaria 1724." *Istoriia SSSR*, no. 2 (March–April 1974): 97–98.

"Proekt Ustava Obshchestva Liubitelei Rossiiskoi Uchenosti, 1789." *Istoricheskii Arkhiv,* no. 5 (1950): 303–315.

Programma Russkogo Sobraniia. St. Petersburg, 1907.

Programmy Domashnego Chteniia na 1894–95 god. Moscow: Tipograpfiia I. D. Sytina, 1894.

Programmy Domashnego Chteniia na 3-i god Sistematicheskogo Kursa. Moscow: Tipografiia I. D. Sytina, 1897.

"Protokoly Istoricheskogo Obshchestva pri Imperatorskom Moskovskom Universitete, Zasedanie 10 Ianvaria 1916 g." *Istoricheskie Izvestiia, Izdavaemye Istoricheskim Obshchestvom pri Imperatorskom Moskovskom Universitete,* no. 1 (1916): 191–194.

Sbornik Materialov Otnosiashchikhsia do Arkhivnoi Chasti v Rossii vols. I–II. Petrograd: Russkoe Istoricheskoe Obshchestvo, 1916.

Sostav Imperatorskogo Obshchestva Istorii i Drevnostei Rossiiskikh pri Moskovskom Universitete. Moscow, 1890.

Sostav Imperatorskogo Russkogo Istoricheskogo Obshchestva 12 Marta 1912 g.

Speranskii, M. M. *Polnoe Sobranie Zakonov Rossiiskoi Imperii. Sobranie Pervoe, 1625–1825.* St. Petersburg: Tipografiia II Otdeleniia Sobstvennoi Ego Imperatorskogo Velichestva Kantseliarii, 1830.

Spisok Chlenov Istoricheskogo Obshchestva pri Imperatorskom S.-Peterburgskom Universitete k 1 Oktiabria 1904. St. Petersburg, 1905.

"Spisok Delegatov, Komandirovannykh Uchenymi Uchrezhdeniiami i Obshchestvami i Pribyvshikh na Predvaritel'noe Soveshchanie po Ustroistvu IV Mezhdunarodnogo Istoricheskogo S'ezda." *Nauchnyi Istoricheskii Zhurnal,* no. 3 (1913): 11–12.

Spisok Uchreditelei Russkogo Sobraniia. St. Petersburg, 1901.

Ukaz ob Uchrezhdenii Moskovskogo Universiteta i Dvukh Gimnazii s Prilozheniem Vysochaishe Utverzhdennogo Proekta po Semu Predmetu, 12 Ianvaria 1755 goda. Accessed August 22, 2015. http://www.runivers.ru/philosophy /chronograph/156896/.

Ukazaniia ob Izdaniiakh Razreshennykh dlia Narodnykh Chtenii i Besplatnykh Narodnykh Chitalen, a Takzhe Dramaticheskikh Sochineniiakh, Odobrennykh k Predstavleniiu Narodnykh Teatrov. St. Petersburg, 1902.

"Ustav Akademii Nauk, 20863, Iiulia 25 [1803]." In *Polnoe Sobranie Zakonov Rossiiskoi Imperii.* Vol. 27: 786–800. St. Petersburg: Tipografiia II Otdeleniia Sobstvennoi Ego Imperatorskogo Velichestva Kantseliarii, 1830.

"Ustav Blagochiniia ili Politseiskii, 15.379, Aprelia 8 [1782]." In *Polnoe Sobranie Zakonov Rossiiskoi Imperii.* Vol. 21: 461–488. St. Petersburg: Tipografiia II Otdeleniia Sobstvennoi Ego Imperatorskogo Velichestva Kantseliarii, 1830.

Ustav Istoricheskogo Obshchestva pri Imperatorskom S.—Peterburgskom Universitete. St. Petersburg, 1889.

Ustav Imperatorskogo Moskovskogo Universiteta 5 Noiabria 1804 goda. Accessed August 22, 2015. http://museum.guru.ru/ustavy/ustav1804/glava_i.phtml.

Ustav Imperatorskogo Vol'nogo Ekonomicheskogo Obshchestva, Udostoennyi Vysochaishego Utverzhdeniia 27 Fevralia 1859 goda. St. Petersburg, 1859.

Ustav Obshchestva Istorii i Drevnostei Rosiiskikh Utverzhdennyi Fevralia 11 Dnia, 1811 goda. Moscow, 1811.

Ustav Obshchestva Revnitelei Russkogo Istoricheskogo Prosveshcheniia v Pamiat' Imperatora Aleksandra III s Izmeneniiami i Dopolneniiami. St. Petersburg, 1904.

Ustav Russkogo Istoricheskogo Obshchestva. St. Petersburg, 1866.
Vernadskii, George, ed. *A Source Book for Russian History from Early Times to 1917.* Vol. 2. *Peter the Great to Nicholas I.* New Haven and London: Yale University Press, 1972.
"Vremennye Pravila ob Obshchestvakh i Soiuzakh: Vysochaishii Ukaz 4 Marta 1906 g." In *Samoderzhavie i Obshchestvennye Organizatsii v Rossii 1905–1917 gody* by A. S. Tumanova, Appendix I: 440–447. Tambov: Izdatel'stvo TGU im. G. R. Derzhavina, 2002.
Vypis' Khronologicheskaia iz Istorii Russkoi. St. Petersburg.
Zapiska Grafa S. Sheremeteva o Sozdanii Osobykh Dvorianskikh Zhenskikh Uchebno-Vospitatel'nykh Zavedenii. n.p., 1898.
"Zapiska s Podrobnym Izlozheniem Osnovanii i Sposobov Deiatel'nosti Predpolagaemogo Obshchestva." *Izvestiia Obshchestva Revnitelei Russkogo Istoricheskogo Prosveshcheniia v Pamiat' Imperatora Aleksandra III,* no. 1 (1900): 2–6.

Published Letters, Diaries and Memoirs

Aptekman, O. V. "Partiia 'Narodnogo prava': Po Lichnym Vospominaniiam." *Byloe,* no. 7/19 (1907): 177–206.
Buslaev, Fedor. *Moi Vospominaniia.* Moscow: Izdanie V. G. Fon Boolia, 1897.
Chernov, V. M. *Pered Burei: Vospominaniia.* Izdatel'stvo im. Chekhova, 1953.
Dashkova, E. P. *Zapiski. Pis'ma Sester M. i K. Vil'mont iz Rossii.* Moscow: Izdatel'stvo Moskovskogo Universiteta, 1987.
Demina, L. I. "'Mne Kak Istoriku Pozvolitel'no Otsenivat' Sobytiia Istoricheskoi Merkoi': Iz 'Zapisok' E. F. Shmurlo o Peterburgskom Universitete. 1889 g." *Otechestvennye Arkhivy,* no. 1 (2006): 72–99.
Dnevniki Imperatora Nikolaia II (1894–1918), Vols. 1–2. Moscow: ROSSPEN, 2011.
Got'e, Iu. V. "Moi Zametki." *Voprosy Istorii,* no. 6: 150–175; 7–8: 164–190; 9–10: 160–185; 11: 150–177; 12: 137–164 (1991).
———. "Moi Zametki." *Voprosy Istorii,* no. 1: 119–138; 2–3: 146–161; 4–5: 107–118; 11–12: 124–160 (1992).
———. "Moi Zametki." *Voprosy Istorii,* no. 1: 72–87; 2: 139–155; 3: 157–176; 4: 78–99; 5: 151–167 (1993).
Grevs, I. M. "V Gody Iunosti. Za Kul'turu. Iz Universitetskikh Let. Studencheskoe Nauchno-Literaturnoe Obshchestvo v Peterburge, 1880-e gody." *Byloe,* no. 12 (1918): 42–88.
———. "Za kul'turu (Otryvok Vtoroi). Posle studenchestva. Nashe bratstvo." *Byloe,* no. 16(1921): 137–166.
Ianzhul, Ia. *Iz Vospominanii i Perepiski Fabrichnogo Inspektora Pervogo Prizyva.* St. Petersburg, 1907.
———. *Vospominaniia o Perezhitom i Videnom v 1864–1909 gg.,* v[ypuski] 1–2. St. Petersburg: Elektro-Tipografiia N. Ia. Stoikovoi, 1910–1911.
Kizevetter, Alexander. *Na rubezhe Dvukh Stoletii: Vospominaniia 1881–1914.* Cambridge: Oriental Research Partners, 1974. Originally published 1929 by Orbis.
Kornilov, A. A. "Vospominaniia," *Voprosy Istorii,* no. 2: 143–159; 3: 120–139; 4: 136–149; 5: 106–124; 7: 126–152; 8; 108–128; 9: 112–122; 10: 122–134 (1994).

Korzun, V. P., and V. P. Mamontov, eds. "Pis'ma S. F. Platonova P. N. Miliukovu." In *Istoriia i Istoriki.2002. Istoriograficheskii Vestnik*, edited by A. N. Sakharov, 167–193, 311–339. Moscow: Nauka, 2003.

Kulakova, L. I. *Pis'ma Russkikh Pisatelei XVIII Veka*. Leningrad: Nauka, Leningradskoe otdelenie, 1980.

Maksakov, V., ed., "Dnevnik A. A. Polovtsova." *Krasnyi arkhiv*, no. 4 (1923): 63–128.

Miliukov, P. N. *Vospominaniia*. Moscow: Izdatel'stvo politicheskoi literatury, 1991.

Nabokov, Vladimir. "Drugie Berega." In *Sobranie Sochinenii v Chetyrekh Tomakh*, vol. 4. 133–302. Moscow: Izdatel'stvo "Pravda," 1990.

Nasha Dan' Bestuzhevskim Kursam: Vospominaniia Byvshikh Bestuzhevok za Rubezhom. Paris: Ob'edinenie byvshikh Bestuzhevok za rubezhom, 1971.

Pomialovskii, I. V. "Zapiski Mikhaila Ivanovicha Antonovskogo," *Russkii Arkhiv*, no. 2 (1885): 145–178.

Perchenko, F. F., A. B. Roginskii, and M. Iu. Sorokina, eds. "D. I. Shakhovskoi: Pis'ma o Bratstve." *Zven'ia: Istoricheskii al'manakh*, no. 2 (1992): 174–318.

Platonov, S. F. "Neskol'ko Vospominanii o Studencheskikh Godakh." *Dela i Dni*, no. 2 (1921): 104–133.

Pobedonostsev, K. P. *Pis'ma Pobedonostseva k Aleksandru III*, Vols. 1–2. Moscow: Novaia Moskva, 1925–1926.

Polovtsov, A. A. *Dnevnik Gosudarstvennogo Sekretaria*, Vol. 1, 1883–1886. Vol. 2, 1887–1892. Moscow: Tsentrpoligraf, 2005.

Perry, Bliss. *And Gladly Teach: Reminiscences*. Boston: Hoghton Mifflin Company, 1935.

Repnikov, A. V., ed. *Dnevnik L. A. Tikhomirova, 1915–1917 gg*. Moscow: ROSSPEN, 2008.

Serkov, A. I. and M. V. Reizin, eds. *Pis'ma N. I. Novikova*. St. Petersburg: Izdatel'stvo im. N. I. Novikova, 1994.

Shmidt, S. O. and V. G. Bukhert, eds. *Akademik S. F. Platonov: Perepiska s Istorikami*. Vol. 1. Moscow: Nauka, 2003.

Tikhomirov, L. A. *Vospominaniia*. Moscow-Leningrad: Gosudarstvennoe Izdatel'stvo, 1927.

Tolstoi, I. I. *Dnevnik 1906–1909*. Vol. 1. St. Petersburg: Liki Rossii, 2010.

Tribunskii, P. A., ed. "Perepiska A. S. Lappo-Danilevskogo i P. N. Miliukova." *Journal of Modern Russian History and Historiography*, no. 3 (2010): 77–160.

Tribunskii, P. A. and V. A. Makushin, eds. *Akademik S. F. Platonov: Perepiska s Istorikami*. Vol. 2, part 1. *Perepiska S. F. Platonova i P. N. Miliukova, 1886–1901*. Moscow: Feoriia, 2011.

Tsamutali, A. N., ed. *Aleksandr Evgen'evich Presniakov: Pis'ma i Dnevniki, 1889–1927*. St. Petersburg: IISPb RAN and Dmitrii Bulanin, 2005.

Tsvetaeva, M. I. "Avtobiograficheskaia Proza: Dom u Starogo Pimena." In idem. *Sochineniia v 7 tomakh*. Vol. 5, book 1, 104–140. Moscow: Terra—Knizhnaia lavka—RTR, 1997.

Vakh K. A., and L. I. Shokhin, eds. *Memuary Grafa S. D. Sheremeteva*. Vols. 1–3. Moscow: Indrik, 2004, 2005.

Vakhromeeva, O. B. *Chelovek s Otkrytym Serdtsem: Avtobiograficheskoe i Epistoliarnoe Nasledie I. M. Grevsa*. St. Petersburg: ID SPbGU, 2004.

Veselovskii, S. B. "Dnevniki 1915–1923, 1944." *Voprosy Istorii*, no. 2: 69–83; 3: 84–110; 6: 93–11; 8: 86–109; 9: 114–133; 10: 113–140; 11–12: 59–77 (2000); no. 2 (2001): 69–83.

Vernadskii, G. V. "Priiutinskoe Bratstvo." *Novyi Zhurnal*, 93 (1968): 147–171; 95 (1969): 202–215; 96 (1969): 153–171; 97 (1969): 218–237.
———. "Iz Vospominanii." *Voprosy Istorii*, no. 3 (1995): 79–103.
Viazemskii, P. A. *Staraia Zapisnaia Knizhka*. Moscow: Zakharov, 2003.
Vitte, S. Iu. *Vospominaniia*. Vol. 2. *Tsarstvovanie Nikolaia II: 1894-oktiabr' 1905*. Moscow: Izdatel'stvo sotsial'no-ekonomicheskoi literatury, 1960.
Vzgliad na Moiu Zhizn': Zapiski Deistvitel'nogo Tainogo Sovetnika Iv. Iv. Dmitrieva. Moscow: Tipografiia V. Got'e, 1866.
Zapiski Nekotorykh Obstoiatel'stv Zhizni i Sluzhby Deistvitel'nogo Tainogo Sovetnika, Senatora I. V. Lopukhina. Moscow: V Universitetskoi tipografii, 1860.

Secondary Sources

Aarsleff, Hans. "The Berlin Academy under Frederick the Great." *History of the Human Sciences* 2, no. 2 (1989): 193–206.
Abramova, N. G., and Kruglova, T. A. *Vspomogatel'nye Istoricheskie Distsipliny*. Moscow: Izdatel'skii tsentr Akademiia, 2008.
Agapova, M .Iu. "Sborniki Russkogo Istoricheskogo Obshchestva kak Istoricheskii Istochnik." *Russkii Istoricheskii Sbornik*, edited by B. M. Lavrov. Vol. 2, 349–356. Moscow: Kuchkovo pole, 2010.
Alchevskaia, Kh. D., E. D. Gordeeva, and A. P. Grishchenko, eds., *Chto Chitat' Narodu? Kriticheskii Ukazatel' Knig Dlia Narodnogo i Detskogo Chteniia*. Vol. 1–3. St. Petersburg: Tipografiia tovarishchestva Obshchestvennaia pol'za, 1884, 1887, 1906.
Alekseeva, A. D., and M. D. Kovaleva, eds. *Sheremetevy v Sud'be Rossii: Vospominaniia, Dnevniki, Dokumenty*. Moscow: Zvonnitsa, 2001.
Alekseeva, G. D. "Istpart: Osnovnye Napravleniia i Etapy Deiatel'nosti." *Voprosy Istorii*, no. 9 (1982): 17–29.
Alektorov, A. E. *Inorodtsy v Rossii: Sovremennye Voprosy. Finliandtsy. Poliaki. Latyshi. Evrei. Nemtsy. Armiane. Tatary. S predisloviem i Dobavleniem A. S. Budilovicha*. St. Petersburg, Tipografiia I. V. Leont'eva, 1906.
Alevras, N. N. "Problema Liderstva v Nauchnom Soobshchestve Istorikov XIX-Nachala XX Veka." In *Istorik v Meniaiushchemsia Prostranstve Rossiiskoi Kul'tury*, edited by idem, 117–126. Cheliabinsk: Kamennyi poias, 2006.
Alevras, N. N., and N. V. Grishina. "Rossiiskaia Dissertatsionnaia Kul'tura XIX-Nachala XX Veka v Vospriiatii Sovremennikov: k Voprosu o Natsional'nykh Osobennostiakh." *Dialog So Vremenem* 36 (2011): 221–247.
———. "Dissertatsii Istorikov i Zakonodatel'nye Normy (1860-e-1920-e gg.)." *Rossiiskaia istoriia*, 2 (2014): 77–90.
Alevras, N. N., N. V. Grishina, and Iu. V. Krasnova, eds. *Istoriia i Istoriki v Prostranstve Natsional'noi i Mirovoi Kul'tury XVIII–XIX Vekov*. Cheliabinsk: Entsiklopediia, 2011.
Allan, D. G. C. "The Society of Arts and Government, 1734–1800: Public Encouragement of Arts, Manufactures, and Commerce in Eighteenth-Century England." *Eighteenth-Century Studies* 7, no. 4 (Summer 1974): 434–452.
Al'tshuller, Mark. *Beseda Liubitelei Russkogo Slova: u Istokov Russkogo Slavianofil'stva*. Moscow: Novoe literaturnoe obozrenie, 2007.

Anan'ich, B. V. *I. I. Tolstoi i Peterburgskoe Obshchestvo Nakanune Revoliutsii.* St. Petersburg: Liki Rossii and St. Peterburgskii institut istorii RAN, 2007.

Anan'ich, Boris and Paneiakh, Viktor. "The St. Petersburg School of History and Its Fate." In *Historiography of Imperial Russia: The Profession and Writing of History in a Multinational State,* edited by Thomas Sanders, 146–162. Armonk, New York: M.E. Sharpe, 1999.

Anderson, Robert T. "Voluntary Associations in History." *American Anthropologist* 73, 1 (1971): 209–222.

Anisimov, Evgenii A. *The Reforms of Peter the Great: Progress through Coercion in Russia.* Armonk, NY: M.E. Sharpe, 1993.

Antoshchenko, A. V. "Pavel Gavrilovich Vinogradov: Stanovlenie Prepodavatelem." In *Istorik v Meniaiushchemsia Prostranstve Rossiiskoi Kul'tury,* edited by N. N. Alevras, 24–30. Cheliabinsk: Kamennyi poias, 2006.

———. "Das Seminar: Nemetskie Korni i Russkaia Krona (o Primenenii Nemetskogo Opyta 'Seminariev' Moskovskimi Professorami vo Vtoroi Polovine XIX v." In *"Byt' Russkim Po Dukhu i Evropeitsem po Obrazovaniiu": Universitety Rossiiskoi Imperii v Obrazovatel'nom Prostranstve Tsentral'noi i Vostochnoi Evropy XVIII-Nachala XX v.,* edited by A. Iu. Andreev, 263–278. Moscow: ROSSPEN, 2009.

———. *Russkii Liberal-Anglofil Pavel Gavrilovich Vinogradov.* Petrozavodsk: Izdatel'stvo Petrozavodskogo Universiteta, 2010.

Antoshchenko, A. V. and A. V. Sveshnikov, "Istoricheskii Seminarii kak Mesto Znaniia." In *Istoricheskaia Kul'tura Imperskoi Rossii: Formirovanie Predstavlenii o Proshlom,* edited by A. N. Dmitriev, 138–160. Moscow: Izdatel'skii dom Vysshei shkoly ekonomiki, 2012.

Anufriev, Nikolai. "Pravitel'stvennaia Reglamentatsiia Obrazovaniia Chastnykh Obshchestv Rossii." In *Voprosy Administrativnogo Prava,* book 1, edited by A. I. Elistratov, 15–44. Moscow, 1916.

Applegate, Celia. *A Nation of Provincials: The German Idea of Heimat.* Berkley: University of California Press, 1990.

Appleby, John. H. "Mapping Russia: Farquharson, Delisle and the Royal Society." *Notes and Records of the Royal Society* 55, no. 2 (May 2001): 191–204.

Aristov, N. Ia. *A. P. Shchapov: Zhizn' i Sochineniia.* St. Petersburg, 1883.

"Arkheologicheskie S'ezdy." In *Entsiklopedicheskii Slovar'.* Vol. 2, edited by I. E. Andreevskii, 229. St. Petersburg: F.A. Brokgauz and I.A. Efron, 1890.

Baker, Keith Michael. "Enlightenment and Revolution in France: Old Problems, Renewed Approaches." *The Journal of Modern History* 53, no. 2 (1981): 281–303.

Balzer, Harley D., ed. . *Russia's Missing Middle Class: The Professions in Russian History.* Armonk, New York: M.E. Sharpe, 1996.

Ball, Terence. *Transforming Political Discourse: Political Theory and Critical Conceptual History.* Oxford: Basil Blackwell, 1988.

Bann, Stephen. *The Clothing of Clio. A Study of Representation of History in Nineteenth Century Britain and France.* Cambridge: Cambridge University Press, 1984.

———. *The Inventions of History: Essay on the Representation of the Past.* Manchester: Manchester University Press, 1990.

Barsukov, Ia. P., ed., *Pedagogicheskii Muzei Voenno-Uchebnykh Zavedenii, 1864–1914.* St. Petersburg, 1914.

Barsukov, N. P. *Zhizn' i Trudy P. M. Stroeva*. St. Petersburg, 1878.

Basil, John D. "Alexander Kireev and Theological Controversy in the Russian Orthodox Church, 1890–1910." In *Church, Nation and State in Russia and Ukraine*, edited by Geoffrey A. Hosking, 131–147. Houndmills, Basingstoke and London: Macmillan in association with the School of Slavonic and East European Studies, University of London, 1991.

Behrisch, Lars. "Social Discipline in Early Modern Russia, Seventeenth to Nineteenth Centuries." In *Institutionen, Instrumente und Akteure sozialer Kontrolle und Disziplinierung im frühneuzeitlichen Europa* edited by Heinz Schilling and Lars Behrisch, 325–357. Frankfurt am Main: Vittorio Klostermann, 1999.

Belousova, O. V. *Graf S. D. Sheremetev v Obshchestvennoi i Politicheskoi Zhizni Rossii Vtoroi Poloviny XIX-Nachala XX Veka*. PhD diss., Lomonosov Moscow State University, 2012.

Bell, Morag, and Cheryl McEwan. "The Admission of Women Fellows to the Royal Geographical Society, 1892–1914: The Controversy and the Outcome." *Geographical Journal* 162, no. 3 (1996): 295–312.

Beliaeva, O. M. *Ervin Davidovich Grimm v Peterburgskom Universitete: Akademicheskoe Soobshchestvo Pozdneimperskogo Perioda*. PhD diss., Institute of History of the Russian Academy of Sciences, St. Petersburg, 2011.

Belokurov, S. A. *Ukazatel' ko Vsem Periodicheskim Izdaniiam OIDR pri Imperatorskom Moskovskom Universitete, 1815–1883*. Moscow: Tipografiia E. I. Pogodinoi, 1883.

Berdinskikh, V. A. *Uezdnye istoriki: Russkaia Provintsial'naia Istoriografiia*. Moscow: Novoe literaturnoe obozrenie, 2003.

Bérélowitch, Wladimir. "History in Russia Comes of Age: Institution-Building, Cosmopolitanism, and Theoretical Debates among Historians in Late Imperial Russia." *Kritika: Explorations in Russian and Eurasian History* 9, no. 1 (2008): 113–134.

Bestuzhev-Riumin, K. N. "V. N. Tatishchev, Administrator i Istorik XVIII veka." In *Biografii i Kharakteristiki* by idem, 94–140. St. Petersburg, 1882.

Berkov, P. N. "U Istokov Dvorianskoi Literatury XVIII veka: Poet Mikhail Sobakin." *Literaturnoe nasledstvo*, no. 9–10 (1933): 421–422.

Betiaev, Ia. D. *Obshchestvenno-Politicheskaia i Filosofskaia Mysl' v Rossii v Pervoi Polovine XVIII v.* Saransk: Mordovskoe Knizhnoe Izdatel'stvo, 1959.

Biagioli, Mario. "Etiquette, Interdependence, and Sociability in Seventeenth-Century Science." *Critical Inquiry* 22 (1996): 193–238.

Bibikova, L.V. "Politicheskaia Politsiia, Konservatory i Sotsialisty: Igra Liberalizmami v Publichnom i Nepublichnom Politicheskom Prostranstve Rossiiskoi Imperii v Kontse XIX-Nachale XX Veka." In *Poniatiia o Rossii: k Istoricheskoi Semantike Imperskogo Perioda*, edited by Aleksei Miller, Denis Sdvizhkov and Ingrid Shirle. Vol. 1, 514–573. Moscow: Novoe literaturnoe obozrenie, 2012.

Bilarskii, P. S. ed., *Materialy dlia Biografii Lomonosova*.St. Petersburg, 1865.

Blackbourn, David. "The Discreet Charm of the Bourgeoisie." In *The Peculiarities of German History*, edited by idem and Geoff Eley, 159–292. Oxford: Oxford University Press, 1984.

Blagoi, D. D. *Istoriia Russkoi Literatury XVIII v.* Moscow: Gosuchpedgiz, 1951.

Bodianskii, O. M. "Istoricheskaia Zapiska o Dele Sankt-Peterburgskogo Universiteta." *Chteniia v Obshchestve Istorii i Drevnostei Rossiiskikh*, no. 3 (1862): 179–205.

———. "Zamechaniia Na Proekt Obshchego Ustava Imperatorskikh Universitetov." *Chteniia V Obshchestve Istorii i Drevnostei Rossiiskikh* 2 (1862): 217–242.

———. "Otdel'noe Mnenie Professora Bodianskogo po Voprosam, Kasaiushchimsia Shtatnykh Prepodavatelei Universiteta po Ustavu 1863." *Moskovskie Universitetskie Izvestiia*, no. 37 (1867): 417–420.

Bogoliubov, V. N. I. *Novikov i Ego Vremia*. Moscow: Izdatel'stvo M. i S. Sabashnikovykh, 1916.

Boiarchenkov, V. V. *Istoriki-Federalisty: Kontseptsiia Mestnoi Istorii v Russkoi Mysli 20kh-70kh godov XIX veka*. St. Petersburg: Dmitrii Bulanin, 2005.

———. "Obshchestvo Istorii i Drevnostei Rossiiskikh v Seredine 1840-kh gg," *Voprosy Istorii*, no. 4 (2008): 114–121.

———. *Istoricheskaia Nauka v Rossii 1830-1870kh gg.: Poisk Novoi Kontseptsii Russkoi Istorii*. PhD diss., Riazan' State University, 2009.

———. "S. G. Stroganov, S. S. Uvarov i 'Istoriia Fletchera' 1848," *Rossiskaia istoriia* 5 (2009): 144–149

———. "'Sekretar' Antikvarnogo Sosloviia': O. M. Bodianskii v Obshchestve Istorii i Drevnostei Rossiiskikh," *Slavianovedenie*, no. 2 (2009): 91–102.

Bolkhovitinov, Evgenii. *Slovar' Istoricheskii o Byvshikh v Rossii Pisateliakh Dukhovnogo China*. St. Petersburg: V tipografii I. Glazunova, 1827.

Boldyrev, Alexander. "English Sundial Makers in Russia," *British Sundial Society (BSS) Bulletin* 18/3 (2006): 120–127.

Bon, Tomas M. [Bohn, Thomas]. *Russkaia Istoricheskaia Nauka: Pavel Nikolaevich Miliukov i Moskovskaia Shkola*. St. Petersburg: Olearius, 2005.

Boyd, Julian P. "State and Local Historical Societies in the United States," *The American Historical Review* 10, no. 1 (1934): 10–37.

Bradley, Joseph. "Voluntary Associations, Civic Culture and *Obshchestvennost'* in Moscow." In *Between Tsar and People: Educated Society and the Quest for Public Identity*, edited by Edit W. Clowes, Samuel D. Kassow and James L. West, 131–148. Princeton: Princeton University Press, 1991.

———. "Russia's Parliament of Public Opinion: Association, Assembly, and the Autocracy, 1906–1914." In *Reform in Modern Russian History: Progress or Cycle?* Edited by Theodore Taranovski, 212–236. Cambridge: Woodrow Wilson Center Press and Cambridge University Press, 1995.

———. "Merchant Moscow after Hours: Voluntary Associations and Leisure." In *Merchant Moscow: Images of Russia's Vanished Bourgeoisie*, edited by James L. West and Jurii A. Petrov, 133–143. Princeton: Princeton University Press, 1998.

———. "Subjects into Citizens: Societies, Civil Society and Autocracy in Tsarist Russia." *American Historical Review* 107, 4 (2002): 1094–1123.

———. *Voluntary Associations in Tsarist Russia: Science, Patriotism and Civil Society*. Cambridge, MA: Harvard University Press, 2009.

———. "The St. Petersburg Literacy Committee and Russian Education: Government Tutelage or Public Trust?" *The Russian Review* 71 no. 2 (2012): 267–294.

Brooks, Jeffrey. *When Russia Learned to Read: Literacy and Popular Literature, 1861-1917*. Evanston, IL: Northwestern University Press, 2003.

Brown, J. H. "The Publication and Distribution of the *Trudy* of the Free Economic Society, 1765–1796," *Russian Review* 36, no. 3 (1977): 341–350.

Bukhert, V. G. "Osnovanie Istoricheskogo Obshchestva pri Moskovskom Universitete." In *Arkheograficheskii Ezhegodnik za 2000 god*, edited by S. O. Shmidt, 195–206. Moscow: Nauka, 2001.

———. "Pavlovskie kursy (1899–1997 gg.)." In *Arkheograficheskii Ezhegodnik za 2004*, edited by S. O. Shmidt, 281–290. Moscow: Nauka, 2005.

———. "Soveshchanie Professorov Russkoi Istorii i Istorii Russkogo Prava Rossiiskikh Universitetov (Moscow, 26–28 marta 1915 g.)." In *Arkheograficheskii Ezhegodnik za 2009–2010 gg.*, edited by S.O. Shmidt, 179–194. Moscow: Nauka, 2012.

Burbank, Jane. "Discipline and Punish in the Moscow Bar Association," *Russian Review*, 54 (1995): 44–64.

Byford, Andy. "Initiation to Scholarship: The University Seminar in Late Imperial Russia," *Russian Review* 64, no. 2 (2005): 299–323.

Cantor, G. N., J. R. R. Christie, M. J. S. Hodge, and R. C. Olby, eds. *Companion to the History of Modern Science*. London and New York: Routledge, 1990.

Chambers, David and François Quiviger, eds. *Italian Academies of the Sixteenth Century*. London: Warburg Institute, 1995.

Charnoluskii, V. *Osnovnye Voprosy Organizatsii Vneshkol'nogo Obrazovaniia v Rossii*. St. Petersburg, 1909.

Chechulin, N. D. "Russkoe Provintsial'noe Obshchestvo vo Vtoroi Polovine XVIII Veka." *Zhurnal Ministerstva Narodnogo Prosveshcheniia* no. 3: 45–71; 4: 241–268; 5: 55–96; 6: 261–281 (1889).

———. "Otvet Retsenzentu 'Russkoi mysli'" *Zhurnal Ministerstva Narodnogo Prosveshcheniia*, no. 5 (1890): 203–213.

Cherniakhovskii, F. I. *Vasilii Vasil'evich Krestinin*. Arkhangel'sk: Arkhangel'skoe Knizhnoe Izdatel'stvo, 1956.

Chesnokov, V. I. *Pravitel'stvennaia Politika i Istoricheskaia Nauka Rossii 60-kh -70-kh godov XIX v.: Issledovatel'skie Ocherki*. Voronezh: Voronezhskii Universitet, 1989.

———. "Puti Formirovaniia i Kharakternye Cherty Sistemy Universitetskogo Obrazovaniia v Dorevoliutsionnoi Rossii." In *Istoricheskaia kul'tura Imperskoi Rossii: Formirovanie Predstavlenii o Proshlom*, edited by A. N. Dmitriev, 113–137. Moscow: Izdatel'skii dom Vysshei shkoly ekonomiki, 2012.

Christie, J. R. R., "The Development of Historiography of Science." In *Companion to the History of Modern Science*, edited by Cantor, G. N., J. R. R. Christie, M. J. S. Hodge, and R. C. Olby, 5–24. London: Routledge, 1990.

Chuikina, S. A. *Dvorianskaia Pamiat': "Byvshie" v Sovetskom Gorode (Leningrad, 1920–30-e gody)*. St. Petersburg: Izdatel'stvo Evropeiskogo Universiteta v Sankt-Peterburge, 2006.

Clark, Peter. *British Clubs and Societies, 1580–1800: The Origins of an Associational World*. Oxford: Clarendon, 2000.

Clemens, Elisabeth. "Securing Political Returns to Social Capital: Women's Associations in the United States, 1880–1920s." *Journal of Interdisciplinary History* 29, no. 4 (Spring 1999): 613–638.

Clemens, Gabriele B. "Ancestors, Castles, Tradition: The German and Italian Nobility and the Discovery of the Middle Ages in the Nineteenth Century." *Journal of Modern Italian Studies* 8, no. 1 (2003): 1–15.

Collis, Robert. "Alchemical Interest at the Petrine Court," *Esoterica* 7 (2005): 52–77.

———. *The Petrine Instauration: Religion, Esotericism and Science at the Court of Peter the Great, 1689–1725*. Leiden: Brill, 2012.

Confino, Alon. *The Nation as a Local Metaphor: Würtemberg, Imperial Germany and National Memory, 1871–1918*. Chapel Hill: University of North Carolina Press, 1997.

Confino, Michael. "The Soslovie (Estate) Paradigm: Reflections on Some Open Questions." *Cahiers du Monde russe* 49, no. 4 (October–December 2008): 681–700.

Cooley, Charles Horton. *Social Organization: A Study of the Larger Mind*. New York: Shocken Books, 1962.

Coolidge, Archibald Cary. "A Plea for the Study of the History of Northern Europe." *American Historical Review* 2, no. 1 (October 1896): 34–39.

Corney, Frederick C. *Telling October: Memory and the Making of Bolshevik Revolution*. Ithaca, NY: Cornell University Press, 2004.

Cracraft, James. "Feofan Prokopovich." In *The Eighteenth Century in Russia*, edited by J. G. Garrard, 75–105. Oxford: Clarendon, 1973.

Crane, Susan A. *Collecting and Historical Consciousness in Early Nineteenth-Century Germany*. Ithaca: Cornell University Press, 2000.

Cross, Anthony. *N. M. Karamzin: A Study of His Literary Career, 1783–1803*. Carbondale: Southern Illinois University Press, 1971.

———. *By the Banks of the Neva*. Cambridge: Cambridge University Press, 1997.

Dashkevich, N. P. *25-letie Istoricheskogo Obshchestva Nestora-Letopistsa*. Kiev, 1899.

Daniels, Rudolph L. "V. N. Tatishchev and the Succession Crisis of 1730." *Slavonic and East European Review* 49, no. 117 (October 1971): 550–559.

Daston, Lorraine. "The Academies and the Unity of Knowledge: The Disciplining of the Disciplines." *Differences* 10, no. 2 (1999): 67–86.

Davis, Belinda. "Reconsidering Habermas, Gender and the Public Sphere: The Case of Wilhelmine Germany." In *Society, Culture, and the State in Germany, 1870–1930*, edited by Geoff Eley, 397–426. Ann Arbor: University of Michigan Press, 1996.

Dezhina, I. G., and V. V. Kiseleva. *Tendentsii Razvitiia Nauchnykh Shkol v Sovremennoi Rossii*. Moscow: IEPP, 2009.

Diaz-Adreu M. and T. Champion, eds. *Nationalism and Archeology in Europe*. Boulder: Westview, 1996.

Dixon, Simon. "The Church's Social Role in St. Petersburg, 1880–1914." In *Church, Nation and State in Russia and Ukraine*, edited by Geoffrey A. Hosking, 167–192. Houndmills, Basingstoke and London: Macmillan in association with the School of Slavonic and East European Studies, University of London, 1991.

Dneprov, E. D. "Komitety i Obshchestva Gramotnosti." In *Bol'shaia Sovetskaia Entsiklopediia*. Vol. 12, 515. Moscow: Izdatel'stvo "Sovetskaia Entsiklopediia," 1973.

Dowler, Wayne. *Russia in 1913*. DeKalb: Northern Illinois University Press: 2010.

Dvornichenko, A. Iu., and S. O. Shmidt, eds., *Pamiati Akademika Sergeia Fedorovicha Platonova: Issledovaniia i Materialy*. St. Petersburg: St. Petersburg State University and OIFN RAN, 2011.

Dubrovskii, A. M. *S. V. Bakhrushin i Ego Vremia*. Moscow: Izdatel'stvo Rossiiskogo Universiteta Druzhby Narodov, 1992.

Eklof, Ben. "The Archaeology of 'Backwardness' in Russia: Assessing the Adequacy of Libraries for Rural Audiences in Late Imperial Russia." In *The Space of the*

Book: Print Culture in the Russian Social Imagination, edited by Miranda Remnek, 108–141. Toronto: University of Toronto Press, 2011.

Eley, Geoff. "Nations, Politics, and Political Cultures: Placing Habermas in the Nineteenth Century." In *Habermas and the Public Sphere*, edited by Craig Calhoun, 289–339. Cambridge, MA: MIT Press, 1992.

Ely, Christopher. "The Question of Civil Society in Late Imperial Russia." In *A Companion to Russian History*, edited by Abbott Gleason, 225–242. Chichester, UK; Malden, MA: Wiley Blackwell, 2009.

Emerson, Roger L. "The Organization of Science and Its Pursuit in Early Modern Europe." In *Companion to the History of Modern Science*, edited by Cantor, G. N., J. R. R. Christie, M. J. S. Hodge, and R. C. Olby, 960–979. London and New York: Routledge, 1990.

Engelstein, Laura. *Slavophile Empire: Imperial Russia's Illiberal Path*. Ithaca: Cornell University Press, 2009.

Epifanov, P. P. "'Uchenaia druzhina' i prosvetitel'stvo XVIII veka." *Voprosy istorii*, no. 3 (March 1963): 37–53.

Erdmann, Karl Dietrich. *Toward a Global Community of Historians: The International Historical Congresses and the International Committee of Historical Sciences, 1898–2000*. New York: Berghahn, 2005.

Eremeeva, S. A. "Priiutinskoe bratstvo." *Vysshee Obrazovanie v Rossii*, no. 1 (2007): 157–166.

———. *Priiutinskoe Bratstvo kak Fenomen Intellektual'noi Kul'tury Rossii Poslednei Treti XIX—Pervoi Poloviny XX Veka*. PhD diss., Moscow: Russian State University for the Humanities, Moscow, 2007.

———. "V Prostranstve Vospominanii: Memuary Chlenov Priiutinskogo Bratstva." *Dialog so Vremenem* 20 (2007): 209–218.

Ermishina, S. A. "Nauka ili Nauchnost'?" In *Istoriia Mysli: Istoriografiia*, edited by I. P. Smirnov, 18–35. Moscow: Vuzovskaia kniga, 2002.

Erokhina, O. V. "Krest'ianskii Pozemel'nyi Bank i likvidatsiia Nemetskogo Zemlevladeniia v Oblasti Voiska Donskogo." *Novyi Istoricheskii Vestnik*, 27, no.1 (2011): 38–48.

Evans, R. J. W. "Learned Societies in Germany in the Seventeenth Century." *European Studies Review*, 7 (1977): 129–151.

Faggionato, Raffaella. *A Rosicrucian Utopia in Eighteenth-Century Russia: The Masonic Circle of N. I. Novikov*. Heidelberg: Springer, 2005.

Fedorchenko, V. I. *Imperatorskii Dom: Vydaiushchiesia Sanovniki. Entsiklopediia Biografii*.Vols. 1–2. Krasnoiarsk: Bonus & Moscow: Olma-Press, 2003.

Fedosova, E. P. *Bestuzhevskie Kursy—Pervyi Zhenskii Universitet v Rossii* (1878–1918 gg.). Moscow: Pedagogika, 1980.

Fomenko, I. Iu. "Istoricheskie Vzgliady M. N. Murav'eva." In *XVIII vek, Sbornik 13, Problemy Istorizma v Russkoi Literature. Konets XVIII-Nachalo XX v.*, edited by G. P. Makagonenko and A. M. Panchenko, 167–184. Leningrad: Nauka, Leningradskoe otdelenie, 1981.

Fomin, V. V. *Lomonosov: Genii Russkoi Istorii*. Moscow: Russkaia panorama, 2006.

Freeze, Gregory L. *The Parish Clergy in Nineteenth-Century Russia: Crisis, Reform and Counter-Reform*. Princeton: Princeton University Press, 1983.

———. "The Soslovie (Estate) Paradigm and Russian Social History." *American Historical Review* 91, no. 1 (February 1986): 11–36.

Friedman, Rebecca. "Romantic Friendship in the Nicholaevan University." *Russian Review* 62, no. 2 (April 2003): 262–280.

Gatsiskii, A. S. *Istoricheskaia Zapiska ob Uchrezhdenii v Nizhnem Novgorode Gubernskoi Uchenoi Arkhivnoi Komissii* (1884–1887). Nizhnii Novgorod, 1887.

Gamm, Gerald, and Robert D. Putnam. "The Growth of Voluntary Associations in America, 1840–1940." *Journal of Interdisciplinary History* 29, no.4 (Spring 1999): 511–537.

Gastev, M. S."O Vspomogatel'nykh Naukakh Dlia Istorii." *Vestnik Evropy* 19/20 (1830): 161–202.

———. *Knizhka Vtoraia dlia Genealogii*. Moscow, 1835.

———. *Materialy dlia Vspomogatel'nykh Nauk Istorii: Knizhka Pervaia dlia Khronologii*. Moscow, 1833.

Gaukroger, S. *The Emergence of a Scientific Culture: Science and the Shaping of Modernity, 1210–1685*. Oxford: Oxford University Press, 2006.

———. "The Académie des Sciences and the Republic of Letters: Fontenelle's Role in the Shaping of a New Natural-Philosophical Persona, 1699–1734." *Intellectual History Review.* Special Issue: The Persona of the Philosopher in the Eighteenth Century, 18, no. 3 (2008): 385–402.

———. "Empiricism as a Development of Experimental Natural Philosophy." In *Newton and Empiricism*, edited by Zvi Biener, Eric Schliesser, 15–38. Oxford: Oxford University Press, 2014.

Gleason, Abbott. "The Emigration and Apostasy of Lev Tikhomirov." *Slavic Review* 26, no. 3 (September 1967): 414–429.

———. "The Terms of Russian Social History." In *Between Tsar and People: Educated Society and the Quest for Public Identity*, edited by Edit W. Clowes, Samuel D. Kassow and James L. West, 15–27. Princeton: Princeton University Press, 1991.

Gillispie, Charles C. *Science and Polity in France at the End of the Old Regime*. Princeton: Princeton University Press, 1980.

Glinka, S. N. *Ocherki Zhizni i Izbrannye Sochineniia A. P. Sumarokova*. Chast' 1. St. Petersburg, 1831.

Goffman, Erving. *The Presentation of Self in Everyday Life*. New York: Doubleday Anchor Books, 1959.

Golinski, J. V. "A Noble Spectacle: Research on Phosphorus and the Public Culture of Science in the Early Royal Society." *Isis* 80, no. 1 (March 1989): 11–39.

Grin, Ts. I. "Chechulin Nikolai Dmitrievich." In *Sotrudniki Rossiiskoi Natsional'noi Biblioteki—Deiateli Nauki i Kul'tury: Biograficheskii Slovar'*. Vol. 1. *Imperatorskaia Publichnaia Biblioteka*, 565–569. St. Petersburg: Rossiiskaia natsional'naia biblioteka, 1995.

Gooch, G. P. *History and Historians in the Nineteenth Century*. London: Longmans, Green and Co., 1913.

Goodman, Dena. "Public Sphere and Private Life: Toward a Synthesis of Current Historiographical Approaches to the Old Regime." *History and Theory* 31, no. 1 (February 1992): 1–20.

Gordin, Michael D. "The Importation of Being Earnest: The Early St. Petersburg Academy of Sciences." *Isis* 91, no. 1 (March 2000): 1–31.

Gordon, Daniel. *Citizens without Sovereignty: Equality and Sociability in French Thought, 1670–1789*. Princeton: Princeton University Press, 1994.

Gordon, C. Wayne and Nicholas Babchuk. "A Typology of Voluntary Associations." *American Sociological Review* 24, no. 1 (February 1959): 22–29.

Govorov, A. A. and T. G. Kupriianova, eds. *Istoriia Knigi: Uchebnik dlia Vuzov.* Moscow: Izdatel'stvo MGPU "Mir knigi," 1998.

Greenfeld, Liah. "The Formation of the Russian National Identity: The Role of Status Insecurity and *Ressentiment.*" *Comparative Studies in Society and History* 32, no. 3 (July, 1990): 549–591.

Grosul, V. Ia. "Rossiiskaia obshchestvennost' XVIII–XX vv. Osnovnye etapy stanovleniia i uchrezhdeniia." In *Samoorganizatsiia Rossiiskoi Obshchestvennosti v Poslednei Treti XVIII- Nachale XX vv.*, edited by A. S. Tumanova, 28–165. Moscow: ROSSPEN, 2011.

Gukovskii, G. A. *Russkaia Literatura XVIII veka.* Moscow: Gosuchpedgiz, 1939.

———. "Sumarokov i Ego Literaturno-Obshchestvennoe Okruzhenie." In *Istoriia Russkoi Literatury.* Vol. 3, edited by G. A. Gukovskii and V. A. Desnitskii, 349–420. Moscow-Leningrad: Izdatel'stvo AN SSSR, 1941.

Gularian, A. M. *Obshchestvenno-Politicheskaiia Zhizn' v Orlovskoi Gubernii v Kontse XIX-Nachale XX Veka.* PhD diss., Orel State Agrarian University, 2006.

Gusterin, P. V. *Pervyi Russkii Vostokoved Dmitrii Kantemir.* Moscow: Vostochnaia kniga, 2008.

Gurko, V. I. *Cherty i Siluety Proshlogo: Pravitel'stvo i Obshchestvennost' v Tsarstvovanie Nikolaia II v Izobrazhenii Sovremennika.* Moscow: Novoe literaturnoe obozrenie, 2000.

Gutnov, D. A. "O Shkolakh v Istoricheskoi Nauke." In *Istoriia mysli: Istoriografiia*, edited by I. P. Smirnov, 67–72. Moscow: Vuzovskaia kniga, 2002.

Habermas, Jürgen. *The Structural Transformation of the Public Sphere: An Inquiry into a Category of Bourgeois Society.* Cambridge, MA: MIT Press, 1989.

Hahn, Roger. "The Application of Science to Society: The Societies of Arts." *Studies on Voltaire and the Eighteenth Century* 25 (1963): 829–863.

———. *The Anatomy of Scientific Institution: The Paris Academy of Sciences, 1666–1803.* Berkeley: University of California Press, 1971.

Hamburg, G. M. "A. S. Lappo-Danilevsky and the Writing of History in Late Imperial Russia." Introduction to *A. S. Lappo-Danilevskii i Peterburgskaia Istoricheskaia Shkola* by E. A. Rostovtsev, 7–17. Riazan': NRIID, 2004.

Hans, Nicholas. "The Moscow School of Mathematics and Navigation (1701)." *Slavonic and East European Review* 29, no. 73 (June 1951): 532–536.

Hasegawa, Tsuyoshi. "Gosudarstvennost', Obshchestvennost', and Klassovost': Crime, the Police, and the State in Russian Revolution in Petrograd." *Canadian-American Slavic Studies* 35, nos. 2–3 (Summer-Fall 2001): 157–188.

Häfner, Lutz. "Civil Society, Bürgertum, and 'Local Society': In Search for Analytical Categories for Studies of Public and Social Modernization in Late Imperial Russia." *Ab Imperio*, no. 3 (2002): 161–208.

———. "'The Temple of Idleness': Associations and the Public Sphere in Provincial Russia." In *Russia in the European Context 1789–1914: A Member of the Family* edited by Susan P. McCaffray and Michael Melancon, 141–160. Basingstoke, UK: Palgrave Macmillan, 2005.

Hedda, Jennifer. *His Kingdom Come: Orthodox Pastorship and Social Activism in Revolutionary Russia.* DeKalb: Northern Illinois University Press, 2008.

Hertzen, A. I. *Byloe i Dumy*. Moscow: Khudozhestvennaia literatura, 1982.

Hoffmann, David L. "European Modernity and Soviet Socialism." In *Russian Modernity: Politics, Knowledge, Practices*, edited by idem and Yanni Kotsonis, 245–261. London: Macmillan, 2000.

Hoffmann, Stefan-Ludwig. "Democracy and Associations in the Long Nineteenth Century: Toward a Transnational Perspective." *Journal of Modern History* 75, no.2 (June 2003): 269–299.

Hosking, Geoffrey A. "Patronage and the Russian State." *Slavonic and East European Review* 78 (April 2000): 301–320.

Hughes, Lindsey. *Russia in the Age of Peter the Great*. New Haven: Yale University Press, 1998.

Hunter, Michael. *Science and Society in Restoration England*. Cambridge: Cambridge University Press, 1981.

Ianzhul, Ia. Ia., P. N. Miliukov, P. V. Preobrazhenskii, and L. Z. Morokhovets, eds. *Kniga o Knigakh: Tolkovyi Ukazatel' dlia Vybora Knig po Vazhneishim Otrasliam Znanii (V Pomoshch' Golodaiushchim)*, chasti 1 and 2. Moscow, 1892.

Iatsunskii, V.K. *Istoricheskaia Geografiia*. Moscow: AN SSSR, 1955.

Ikonnikov, V. S. *Russkaia Istoricheskaia Nauka v Dvadtsatipiatiletie 1855–1880 gg*. St. Petersburg, 1880.

———. *Opyt Russkoi Istoriografii*. Vol. 1, part 1. Kiev: Tipografiia Imperatorskogo Universiteta Sv. Vladimira, 1891.

———. *Gubernskie Uchenye Arkhivnye Komissii, 1884–1890*. Kiev: Tipografiia universiteta Sv. Vladimira, 1892.

Il'ina, I. N. *Obshchestvennye Organizatsii Rossii v 1920-e gody*. Moscow: Rossiiskaia Akademiia Nauk, Institut rossiiskoi istorii, 2001.

Impey, Oliver, and Arthur MacGregor, eds. *The Origins of Museums: The Cabinet of Curiosities in Sixteenth- and Seventeenth-Century Europe*. Oxford: Clarendon, 1985.

Iurgevich, V. *Istoricheskii Ocherk Piatidesiatiletiia Imperatorskogo Odesskogo Obshchestva Istorii i Drevnostei 1839–1889*. Odessa, 1889.

Ivanov, A. A."V. V. Krestinin, Osnovatel' Pervogo Chastnogo Istoricheskogo Obshchestva." *Nasha Starina*, no. 11 (1916): 775–781.

Ivanov, I. I. *Politicheskaia Rol' Frantsuzskogo Teatra v Sviazi s Filosofiei XVIII Veka*. Moscow: Universitetskaia tipografiia, 1895.

Ivanov, V. A. "Materialy k Biografiiam Dvorian Kaluzhskoi Gubernii Sluzhivshikh po Vyboram: Kniaz' Sergei Dmitrievich Gorchakov." *Letopis' Istoriko-Rodoslovnogo Obshchestva v Moskve*, no. 4–5 (48–49) (1997): 50–52.

Ivanova, T. N. *Nauchnoe Nasledie V. I. Ger'e i Formirovanie Nauki Vseobshchei Istorii v Rossii (30-e gg. XIX-Nachalo XX Veka)*. Cheboksary: Izdatel'stvo Chuvashskogo Universiteta, 2010.

Jameson, J. Franklin. "The American Historical Association." *American Historical Review* 15, no. 1 (October 1909): 1–20.

Jones, Adrian. "A Russian Bourgeois's Arctic Enlightenment." *Historical Journal* 48, no. 3 (September 2005): 623–640.

Jones, W. Gareth. "The *Morning Light* Charity Schools, 1777–1780," *Slavonic and East European Review* 56, 1 (1978): 49–60.

———. "The Image of the Eighteenth-Century Russian Author." In *Russia in the Age of the Enlightenment: Essays for Isabel de Madariaga*, edited by Roger Bartlett and Janet M. Hartley, 57–74. Basingstoke: Macmillan, 1990.

Kaganovich, B. S. *Evgenii Viktorovich Tarle i Peterburgskaia Shkola Istorikov*. St. Petersburg: Dmitrii Bulanin, 1995.

———. *Russkie Medievisty Pervoi Poloviny XX Veka*. St. Petersburg: Giperion, 2007.

Kalashnikov, M. V. "Poniatie *liberalism* v Russkom Obshchestvennom Soznanii XIX Veka." In *Poniatiia o Rossii: k istoricheskoi semantike imperskogo perioda*, edited by Aleksei Miller, Denis Sdvizhkov and Ingrid Shirle. Vol. 1, 464–513. Moscow: Novoe literaturnoe obozrenie, 2012.

Kamenskii, A. B. "Sud'ba i Trudy Istoriografa Gerarda Fridrikha Millera (1705–1783)." In G. F. Miller, *Sochineniia po Istorii Rossii: Izbrannoe*, 374–416. Moscow: Nauka, 1996.

Kan, A. S. *Istorik G. V. Forsten i nauka ego vremeni*. Moscow: Nauka, 1979.

Kaplan, Vera. "The History of Reform in Russian Higher Education." In *Higher Education in the Russian Federation* (pt. 1) edited by Joseph Zajda. Special issue of *European Education* 39, 2 (2007): 37–59.

———. "From *Soslovie* to Voluntary Associations: New Patterns of Collective Identities in Late Imperial Russia." *Cahiers du Monde russe*, 51, 2–3 (2010): 369–396.

———. "Weathering the Revolution: Patronage as a Strategy of Survival." *Revolutionary Russia*, 26, no. 2 (2013): 97–127.

Kantemir, A. D. *Sobranie stikhotvorenii*. Leningrad: Sovetskii pisatel', 1956.

Karamzin, N. M. "Pis'ma russkogo puteshestvennika." In *Izbrannye sochineniia v 2-kh tomakh* by idem. Vol. 1, 79–600. Moscow-Leningrad: Khudozhestvennaia literatura, 1964.

Kareev, N. I. *Pis'ma k uchashcheisia molodezhi o samoobrazovanii*. St. Petersburg, 1894.

———. "Samoobrazovanie." In *Entsiklopedicheskii slovar'*. Vol. 28a, edited by K. K. Arsen'ev and F. F. Petrushevskii, 220–223. St. Petersburg: Brokgauz-Efron, 1900.

———. "Otnoshenie Istorikov k Sotsiologii." *Rubezh: Al'manakh Sotsial'nykh Issledovanii* 3 (1992): 4–36.

Kartsov, Iu. S. *Sergei Spiridonovich Tatishchev: Stranitsa Vospominanii*. Petrograd, Tip. Tovarishchestva gazety "Svet," 1916.

Kassow, Samuel D. *Students, Professors, and the State in Tsarist Russia*. Berkeley and Los Angeles: University of California Press, 1989.

Katsev, Allison Y. "In the Forge of Criticism: M. T. Kachenovskii and Professional Autonomy in Pre-Reform Russia." In *Historiography of Imperial Russia: The Profession and Writing of History in a Multinational State*, edited by Thomas Sanders, 45–68. Armonk, New York: M.E. Sharpe, 1999.

Kavelin, Leonid (Arkhimandrit). *Istoricheskoe Opisanie Borisovskoi Pustyni, Sostavlennoe po Monastyrskim Dokumentam i Zapisiam*. N. p., 1884.

Kazakova-Apkarimova, E. Iu. *Formirovanie Grazhdanskogo Obshchestva: Gorodskie Soslovnye Korporatsii i Obshchestvennye Organizatsii na Srednem Urale*. Ekaterinburg: RAN, Ural'skoe otdelenie, Institut istorii i arkheologii, 2008.

Keenan, Paul. *St. Petersburg and the Russian Court, 1703–1761*. Basingstoke, UK: Palgrave Macmillan, 2013.

Kelly, Catriona. *Refining Russia: Advice Literature, Polite Culture, and Gender from Catherine to Yeltsin*. Oxford: Oxford University Press, 2001.

Kelly, Catriona and Vadim Volkov. "Obshchestvennost', Sobornost': Collective Identities." In *Constructing Russian Culture in the Age of Revolution, 1881–1940*, edited by Catriona Kelly and David Shepherd. Oxford: Oxford University Press, 1998.

Khartanovich, M. F. *Gumanitarnye Nauchnye Uchrezhdeniia Sankt-Peterburga XIX Veka*. St. Petersburg: Nestor-Istoriia, 2006.

Khil'dermaier, M. "Obshchestvo i Obshchestvennost' na Zakate Tsarskoi Imperii: Nekotorye Razmyshleniia o Novykh Problemakh i Metodakh." In *Stranitsy Rossiiskoi Istorii: Problemy, Sobytiia, Liudi. Sbornik Statei v Chest' B. V. Anan'icha*, edited by N. Iu. Zavarzina, 217–221. St. Petersburg: Dmitrii Bulanin, 2003.

Khlobustov, O. M. "Iz Istorii Bor'by s Terrorizmom v Rossii v XIX- Nachale XX Veka: Istoriko-kriminologicheskii aspect." *Istoriia Gosudarstva i Prava*, no. 5 (2006): 19–24.

Khokhlova, O. N. "O. M. Bodianskii i A. A. Maikov: K Voprosu o Vzaimootnosheniiakh v Universitetskoi Srede." *Vestnik Tverskogo Gosudarstvennogo Universiteta*, no. 34 (2008): 77–83.

Khodnev, A. I. *Istoriia Imperatorskogo Vol'nogo Ekonomicheskogo Obshchestva s 1765 do 1865 goda, Sostavlennaia po Porucheniiu Obshchestva Sekretarem Ego*. St. Petersburg, 1865.

Khrushchov, I. P. *Nastol'naia Kniga Dlia Naroda*. St. Petersburg: Izdatel'stvo postoiannoi komissii po ustroistvu narodnykh chtenii v St. Peterburge i ego okrestnostiakh, 1887–1891.

———. *Besedy o Drevnei Russkoi Literature*. St. Petersburg, 1900.

———. *Ob Izdatel'skoi Deiatel'nosti Postoiannoi Komissii Narodnykh Chtenii i Uchrezhdennogo pri Nei Obshchestva za Piatnadtsat' Let, 1881–1896*. St. Petersburg, 1901.

———. *Sbornik Rasskazov iz Russkoi i Chuzhezemnoi Zhizni: Chasy Dosuga*. St. Petersburg, 1905.

———. *Sbornik Chtenii po Russkoi Istorii s Drevneishikh Vremen do XIV veka*. St. Petersburg, 1907.

Kir'ianov, Iu. I. *Russkoe Sobranie, 1900–1917*, Moscow: ROSSPEN, 2003.

Kizevetter, A. A. *Istoricheskie Ocherki*. Moscow, 1912.

———. "V. I. Semevskii v Ego Uchenykh Trudakh." *Golos Minuvshego*, no. 1 (1917): 199–200.

Kliuchevskii, V. O. "Istoriia Soslovii v Rossii." In *Sochineniia v 8-mi Tomakh* by idem. Vol. 6, *Spetsial'nye kursy*, 276–466. Moscow: Izdatel'stvo sotsial'no-ekonomicheskoi literatury, 1959.

———. "Lektsii po Russkoi Istoriografii." In *Sochineniia v 8-mi tomakh* by idem. Vol. 8, *Issledovaniia, Retsenzii, Rechi (1890–1905)*, 396–452. Moscow, Izdatel'stvo sotsial'no-ekonomicheskoi literatury, 1959.

———. "Istoriograficheskie Etiudy: D. I. Ilovaiskii i I. E. Zabelin" and "Iubilei Obshchestva Istorii i Drevnostei Rossiiskikh." In *Neopublikovannye Proizvedeniia* by idem, 177 and 187–195. Moscow: Nauka, 1983.

Kliuev, I. A., and A. V. Sveshnikov. "Predstaviteli Peterburgskoi Shkoly Medievistiki v Permskom Universitete v 1916–1922." In *Sankt-Peterburgskii Universitet v XVIII–XX Vekakh: Evropeiskie Traditsii i Rossiiskii Kontekst*, edited by A. Iu. Dvornichenko and I. L. Tikhonov, 350–364. St. Petersburg: Izdatel'stvo SPbGU, 2009.

Knight, Nathaniel. "Science, Empire, and Nationality: Ethnography in the Russian Geographical Society, 1845–1855." In *Imperial Russia: New Histories for the Empire*, edited by Jane Burbank and David L. Ransel, 108–141. Bloomington: Indiana University Press, 1998.

———. "Ethnicity, Nationality and the Masses: Narodnost' and Modernity in Imperial Russia." In *Russian Modernity: Politics, Knowledge, Practices* edited by David L. Hoffmann and Yanni Kotsonis, 41–66. London: Macmillan, 2000.

———. "Was the Intelligentsia Part of the Nation? Visions of Society in Post-Emancipation Russia." *Kritika: Explorations in Russian and Eurasian History 7*, no. 4 (2006): 733–58.

Kobeko, Dmitrii. "Uchenik Vol'tera: Graf Andrei Petrovich Shuvalov (1744–1789)." *Russkii Arkhiv*, no. 2 (1881): 277–278

Kobrin, B. B., and K. A. Aver'ianov. *S. B. Veselovskii: Zhizn', Deiatel'nost', Lichnost'*. Moscow: Nauka, 1989.

Kochetkova, N. D. "Ideino-literaturnye Pozitsii Masonov 80–90-kh godov XVIII i N. M. Karamzin." In *Russkaia Literatura XVIII Veka: Epokha Klasitsizma, XVIII Vek.*, Vol. 6, edited by P. N. Berkov and I. Z. Serman, 176–196. Moscow-Leningrad: Nauka, 1964.

Kolonitskii, B. I. "Identifikatsiia Rossiiskoi Intelligentsii i Intelligentofobiia (Konets XIX-Nachalo XX Veka)." In *Intelligentsiia v Istorii: Obrazovannyi Chelovek v Predstavleniiakh i Sotsial'noi Deistvitel'nosti*, edited by D. A. Sdvizhkov, 150–170. Moscow: RAN, Institut Vseobshchei istorii, 2001.

———. *"Tragicheskaia Erotika": Obrazy Imperatorskoi Sem'i v Gody Pervoi Mirovoi Voiny*. Moscow: Novoe literaturnoe obozrenie, 2010.

Kondrashov, N. A. *Osip Maksimovich Bodianskii*. Moscow: Izdatel'stvo Moskovskogo Universiteta, 1956.

Koposov, N. E., ed. *Istoricheskie Poniatiia i Politicheskie Idei v Rossii XVI–XX Veka*. St. Petersburg: EUSP Press/Aletheia, 2006.

Kornilov, I. P. *Ocherk Istorii Russkoi Shkoly, Ee Sovremennoe Sostoianie i na Kakikh Nezyblemykh Nachalakh Ona Dolzhna Byt' Utverzhdena*. St. Petersburg, 1901.

Korol'kov, K. N. *Zhizn' i Tsarstvovanie Imperatora Aleksandra III: 1881–1894*. Kiev, 1901.

Korsakov, D. M. *Votsarenie Imperatritsy Anny Ioanovny*. Kazan': Tipografiia Imperatorskogo universiteta, 1880.

Korzun, V. P. *Obrazy Istoricheskoi Nauki na Rubezhe XIX–XX vv.: Analiz Otechestvennykh Istoriograficheskikh Kontseptsii*. Ekaterinburg-Omsk: Omskii gosudarstvennyi universitet, 2000.

Koselleck, Reinhart. *"Futures Past: On the Semantics of Historical Time*. Cambridge, MA: MIT Press, 1985.

———. *Critique and Crisis: Enlightenment and the Pathogenesis of Modern Society*. Cambridge, MA: MIT Press, 1988.

Kostylev, V. N. "Vybor L'va Tikhomirova." *Voprosy Istorii*, no. 6–7 (1992): 30–46.

Kozlov, V. P. "Polemika Vokrug 'Istoriia Gosudarstva Rossiskogo' N. M. Karamzina v Otechestvennoi Periodike (1818–1830 gg.). *Istoriia SSSR*, no. 5 (1984): 88–102.

———. *Rossiiskaia Arkheografiia Kontsa XVIII- Pervoi Chetverti XIX Veka*. Moscow: Rossiiskii gosudarstvennyi gumanitarnyi universitet, 1999.

Krasko, A. V. "Zhiznennyi Put' i Tvorcheskoe Nasledie Grafa S. D. Sheremeteva (k 150-iu so Dnia Rozhdeniia)." *Izvestiia Russkogo Genealogicheskogo Obshchestva*, no. 2 (1995): 13–19.

Krestinin, V. V. *Kratkaia Istoriia o Gorode Arkhangel'skom*. St. Petersburg: pri Imperatorskoi Akademii Nauk, 1792.

Krukovskii, A. "Pevets Bezmiatezhnykh Perezhivanii." *Filologicheskie Zapiski*, no. 4 (1915): 523–560.

Kulakova, A. P. *Universitetskoe Prostranstvo i Ego Obitateli: Moskovskii Universitet v Istoriko-Kul'turnoi Srede XVIII Veka*. Moscow: Novyi khronograf, 2006.

Kulakova, L. I. "Kheraskov." In *Istoriia Russkoi Literatury*. Vol. 4, part 2, edited by G. A. Gukovskii and V. A. Desnitskii, 320–341. Moscow-Leningrad: Izdatel'stvo Akademii Nauk, 1947.

———. "N. I. Novikov v Pis'makh M. N. Murav'eva." In *XVIII vek*. Vol. 11, *N. I. Novikov i Obshchestvenno-Literaturnoe Dvizhenie Ego Vremeni*, edited by G. P. Makagonenko, 16–23. Leningrad: Nauka, Leningradskoe otdelenie, 1976.

Kunik, A., ed., *Sbornik Materialov Dlia Istorii Imperatorskoi Akademii Nauk v XVIII v.* St. Petersburg, 1865.

Landes, Joanne. *Women and the Public Sphere in the Age of the French Revolution*. Ithaca: Cornell University Press, 1988.

LaVopa, Anthony J. "Conceiving a Public: Ideas and Society in Eighteenth-Century Europe." *Journal of Modern History* 64, no. 1 (March 1992): 79–116.

Levine, Philippa. *The Amateur and the Professional: Antiquarians, Historians and Archaeologists in Victorian England, 1838–1886*. Cambridge: Cambridge University Press, 1986.

Leckey, Colum. "Patronage and Public Culture in the Russian Free Economic Society, 1765–1796." *Slavic Review* 64, no. 2 (Summer 2005): 355–379.

Leont'ev, T. V. *Narodnye chteniia*. Petrograd: Kul'turno-prosvetitel'noe kooperativnoe tovarishchestvo "Nachatki znanii," 1919.

Lindenmeyr, Adele. "Voluntary Associations and the Russian Autocracy: The Case of Private Charity." *The Carl Beck Papers in Russian and East European Studies*, no. 807 (1990).

———. "The Rise of Voluntary Associations During the Great Reforms: The Case of Charity." In *Russia's Great Reforms, 1855–1881*, edited by Ben Eklof, John Bushnell, and Larissa Zakharova, 264–279. Bloomington: Indiana University Press, 1994.

———. *Poverty Is Not a Vice: Charity, Society and the State in Imperial Russia*. Princeton: Princeton University Press, 1996.

———. "'Primordial and Gelatinous?': Civil Society in Imperial Russia." *Kritika: Explorations in Russian and Eurasian History* 12, no. 3 (Summer 2011): 705–720.

———. "Building Civil Society One Brick at a Time: People's Houses and Worker Enlightenment in Late Imperial Russia." *Journal of Modern History* 84, no. 1 (2012): 1–39.

Lipski, Alexander. "The Foundation of the Russian Academy of Sciences." *Isis* 44, no. 4 (1953): 349–354.

———. "The Beginnings of General Secondary Education in Russia." *History of Education Journal* 6, no. 3 (1955): 201–210.

————. "Some Aspects of Russia's Westernization during the Reign of Anna Ioannovna, 1730–1740." *American Slavic and East European Review* 18, no. 1 (February 1959): 1–11.

Lilti, Antoine. "The Kingdom of *Politesse*: Salons and the Republic of Letters in Eighteenth-Century Paris." *Republics of Letters: A Journal for the Study of Knowledge, Politics, and the Arts* 1, no. 1 (May 1, 2009). http://arcade.stanford.edu /rofl/kingdom-politesse-salons-and-republic-letters-eighteenth-century-paris.

Litvinskii, B. A."K Istorii Zakaspiiskogo Kruzhka Liubitelei Arkheologii i Istorii Vostoka." *Izvestiia Akademii Nauk Tadzhikskoi SSR, Otdelenie Obshchestvennykh Nauk*, no. 14 (1957): 157–167.

Liubichankovskii, S. V. *Formation and Development of Informal Associations of the Ural's Provincial Officials at the End of the 19th Century and the Beginning of the 20th Century*. Lewiston-New-York: Edwin Mellen, 2014.

Longinov, M. N. *Novikov i Shvarts: Materialy dlia Istorii Russkoi Literatury v Kontse XIX Veka*. Moscow: V tipografii Katkova i K°, 1857.

————. *Novikov i Moskovskie Martinisty*. Moscow: Tipografiia Gracheva i Komp, 1867. .

Lotman, Iu. M. "Ocherki po Istorii Russkoi Kul'tury XVIII-Nachala XIX Veka." In *Iz Istorii Russkoi Kul'tury*. Vol. 4, *XVIII-Nachalo XIX Veka*, edited by A. D. Koshelev, 13–346. Moscow: Iazyki russkoi kul'tury, 2000.

Lotman, Iu. M., and M. G. Al'tshuller, eds. *Poeziia 1790–1810-kh godov*. Leningrad: Sovetskii pisatel,' 1971.

————. "The Poetics of Everyday Behavior in Russian Eighteenth Century Culture." In *The Semiotics of Russian Culture*, edited by Ann Shukman, 231–256. Ann Arbor: University of Michigan, 1984.

Lovell, Stephen. "From Genealogy to Generation: The Birth of Cohort Thinking in Russia." *Kritika: Explorations in Russian and Eurasian History* 9, no. 3 (Summer 2008): 567–594.

Lowood, Henry Ernst. *Patriotism, Profit, and the Promotion of Science in the German Enlightenment: The Economic and Scientific Societies, 1760–1815*. Berkeley: University of California Press, 1987.

Lukoianov, I. V. "Russkoe Sobranie." In *Rossiia v XIX–XX vv.: Sbornik Statei k 70-iu R. Sh. Ganelina*, edited by A. A. Fursenko, 165–171. St. Petersburg: Dmitrii Bulanin, 1998.

Lunin, B. V. *Iz Istorii Russkogo Vostokovedeniia i Arkheologii v Turkestane: Turkestanskii Kruzhok Liubitelei Arkheologii (1895–1917 gg.)*. Tashkent: Izdatel'stvo Akademii Nauk UzSSR, 1958.

de Madariaga, Isabelle. *Russia in the Age of Catherine the Great*. London: Weidenfeld and Nicholson, 1981.

Maikov, L. N. *Materialy dlia biografii kniazia A. D. Kantemira, Sbornik Otdeleniia Russkogo Iazyka i Slovesnosti Imperatorskoi Akademii Nauk*. Vol. 73, 1–344. St. Petersburg, 1903.

Maguire, Muireann. "The Wizard in the Tower: Iakov Brius and the Representation of Alchemists in Russian Literature." *Slavonic and East European Review* 90, no. 3 (July 2012): 401–427.

Miljan, Toivo. *Historical Dictionary of Estonia*. Lanham, Maryland and Oxford: Scarecrow, 2004.

Makarikhin, V. P. *Gubernskie Uchenye Arkhivnye Komissii Rossii.* Nizhnii Novgorod: Volgo-viatskoe knizhnoe izdatel'stvo, 1991.

Makhonina, S. Ia. *Istoriia Russkoi Zhurnalistiki Nachala XX Veka.* Moscow: Nauka-Flinta, 2002.

Maksheev, Z. A. *50-letie Pedagogicheskogo Muzeia Voenno-Uchebnykh Zavedenii: Kratkaia Istoricheskaia Zapiska.* St. Petersburg, 1914.

Makushin A. V., and P. A. Tribunskii. *Pavel Nikolaevich Miliukov: Trudy i Dni (1859–1904).* Riazan', 2001.

———. "Iz Istorii Dvizheniia za Rasprostranenie Universitetskogo Obrazovaniia v Rossii (Nizhegorodskie Lektsii V. A. Goltseva, I. I. Ivanova, P. I. Miliukova i Ikh Posledstviia)." In *Obshchestvennaia Zhizn' Tsentral'nogo Chernozem'ia Rossii v XVII- Nachale XX veka: Sbornik Nauchnykh Trudov*, edited by M. D. Karpachev, 169–191. Voronezh: Izdatel'stvo Voronezhskogo gosudarstvennogo universiteta, 2002.

———. "Dnevnikovye Zapisi M. S. Korelina o P. N. Miliukove." In *Arkheograficheskii Ezhegodnik za 2005 god*, edited by S. O. Shmidt, 411–429. Moscow: Nauka, 2007.

Malinov, A. V., and A. V. Pogodin. *Aleksandr Lappo-Danilevskii: Istorik i Filosof.* St. Petersburg: Iskusstvo-Spb, 2001.

Malinov, A. V. *Filosofiia i Ideologiia Oblastnichestva.* St. Petersburg: Intersotsis, 2012.

Malinova, O. Iu. "Obshchestvo, Publika, Obshchestvennost' v Rossii Serediny XIX-Nachala XX Veka: Otrazhenie v Poniatiiakh Praktik Publichnoi Kommunikatsii i Obshchestvennoi Samodeiatel'nosti." In *Poniatiia o Rossii: k Istoricheskoi Semantike Imperskogo Perioda*, edited by Aleksei Miller, Denis Sdvizhkov and Ingrid Shirle. Vol. 1, 428–463. Moscow: Novoe literaturnoe obozrenie, 2012.

Malysheva, S. Iu. *Osnovy Arkhivovedeniia.* Kazan': Tatarskoe Respublikanskoe Izdatel'stvo "Kheter," 2002.

Mandrik, M. V. "D. M. Petrushevskii i Ego Uchitelia: k Voprosu o Lichnykh i Nauchnykh Vzaimootnosheniiakh." In *Prizvanie—Istoriia: Sbornik Nauchnykh Statei k 55-letiiu Professora Iu. V. Krivosheeva: Trudy Istoricheskogo Fakul'teta Sankt-Peterburgskogo Gosudarstvennogo Universiteta*, edited by A. A. Meshchenina and P. A. Sokolov, 63–70. St. Petersburg: Izdatel'skii dom Sankt-Peterburgskogo Universiteta, 2010.

Markov, A. *Imperatorskoe Odesskoe Obshchestvo Istorii i Drevnostei: Obzor ego deiatel'nosti za 1839–1888 g.* St. Petersburg: St. Peterburgskii Arkheologicheskii Institut, 1888.

Marker, Gary. *Publishing, Printing and the Origins of Intellectual Life in Russia, 1700–1800.* Princeton: Princeton University Press, 1985.

Maslikov, S. "Istoriia Liubitel'skoi Astronomii v Rossii i SSSR, Chast' 1. Liubiteli-Odinochki, XVII—nachalo XX veka," *Astronomiia i Teleskopostroenie* (August 2004). http://www.astronomer.ru/library.php?action=2&sub=2&gid=66.

McArthur, Gilbert. "Freemasonry and Enlightenment in Russia: The Views of N. I. Novikov." *Canadian-American Slavic Studies* 14, no. 3 (Fall 1980): 361–375.

McClellan III, James Edward. *The International Organization of Science and Learned Societies in the Eighteenth Century.* Ann Arbor: University Microfilms International, 1982.

———. *Science Reorganized: Scientific Societies in the Eighteenth Century.* New York: Columbia University Press, 1985.

McMullin, Ernan. "The Development of Philosophy of Science, 1600–1900." In *Companion to the History of Modern Science*, edited by Cantor, G. N., J. R. R. Christie, M. J. S. Hodge, and R. C. Olby, 816–837. London and New York: Routledge, 1990.

McNeely, Ian F. "The Renaissance Academies between Science and the Humanities." *Configurations* 17, no. 3 (Fall 2009): 227–258.

Mellok, V. H. *Sotsial'noe Ravenstvo. Perevod s Angliiskogo A. Velitsyna.* Moscow: Sotsial'no-politicheskaia biblioteka, 1899.

Mel'nikov, A. V. "Neopublikovannye Otzyvy M. M. Bogoslovskogo o Kandidatskikh Sochineniiakh Vypusknikov Moskovskoi Dukhovnoi Akademii (1916–1917)." In *Arkheograficheskii Ezhegodnik za 2004 god*, edited by S. O. Shmidt, 517–526. Moscow: Nauka, 2005.

Meshchenina, A. A. *S. D. Sheremetev: Deiatel'nost' v Oblasti Organizatsii Russkoi Istoricheskoi Nauki Kontsa XIX-Nachala XX Veka.* PhD. diss., St. Petersburg State University, 2004.

Miagkov, G. P. *Nauchnoe Soobshchestvo v Istoricheskoi Nauke: Opyt "Russkoi Istoricheskoi Shkoly."* Kazan': Izdatel'stvo Kazanskogo Universiteta, 2000.

Mikhal'chenko, C. I. *Kievskaia Shkola v Rossiiskoi Istoriografii (Shkola Zapadno-Russkogo Prava).* Moscow/Briansk: Izdatel'stvo BGPU, 1996.

Milevskii, O. A. "L. A. Tikhomirov i K. Leont'ev: k Istorii Vzaimootnoshenii." *Vestnik Tomskogo Gosudarstvennogo Pedagogicheskogo Universiteta* 1 (1997): 70–74.

———. "K Istorii Ideinoi Evoliutsii L. Tikhomirova: Poslednie Gody Emigratsii (1885–1888)." In *Problemy Otechestvennoi i Vseobshchei Istorii: Sbornik Statei Posviashchennyi 70-Letiiu Prof. L. I. Bozhenko*, edited by A. M. Salagaev and F. N. Podustov, 96–111. Tomsk: Izdatel'stvo Tomskogo pedagogicheskogo universiteta, 1999.

Miliukov, P. N. "Letnii Universitet v Anglii (Iz Poezdki v Kembridzh)." *Mir Bozhii*, no. 5 (May 1894): 194–206.

———. "Russia" *The Athenaeum*, 1894, 22–24.

———. *Ocherki po Istorii Russkoi Kul'tury.* Moscow: Progress-Kul'tura, 1995.

———. "Rasprostranenie Universitetskogo Obrazovaniia v Anglii, Amerike i Rossii." *Russkoe Bogatstvo*, no. 3 (1896): 79–121.

———. "Rets. na: Chechulin N. D., Goroda Moskovskogo Gosudarstva v XVI veke, St. Petersburg, 1889." *Russkaia Mysl',* no. 12 (1889): 522–524.

———. "Retsenziia na ocherk: N. D. Chechulin, 'Russkoe Provintsial'noe Obshchestvo vo Vtoroi Polovine XVIII veka.'" *Russkaia Mysl',* no. 9 (1889): 381–387.

———. "University Extension." In *Entsiklopedicheskii Slovar'.* Vol. 34a, edited by K. K. Arsen'ev and F. F. Petrushevskii, 803–809. St. Petersburg: Brokgauz-Efron, 1902.

———. "The Chief Currents of Russian Historical Thought." In *Annual Report of the American Historical Association for the Year 1904*, 109–114. Washington: Government Printing Office, 1905.

Mironov, Boris N. with Ben Eklof. *A Social History of Imperial Russia, 1700–1917* in two volumes. Boulder: Westview, 2000.

Moiseeva, G. N. "Arkheograficheskaia deiatel'nost' N. I. Novikova." In *XVIII Vek.* Vol. 11, *N. I. Novikov i Obshchestvenno-literaturnoe Dvizhenie Ego Vremeni*, edited by G. P. Makagonenko, 24–36. Leningrad: Nauka, Leningradskoe otdelenie, 1976.

———. "'Slovo o Polku Igoreve' i Ekaterina II." In *XVIII Vek*. Vol. 18, edited by N. D. Kochetkova, 3–30. St. Petersburg: Nauka, 1993.

Moiseenkova, L. S. "Pavel Gavrilovich Vinogradov." In *Portrety Istorikov: Vremia i Sud'by*. Vol. 2. *Vseobshchaia Istoriia*, edited by G. N. Sevast'ianov, L. P. Marinovich, and L. T. Mil'skaia, 116–124. Moscow-Jerusalem: Universitetskaia kniga-Gesharim, 2000.

Morris, R. J. "Voluntary Societies and British Urban Elites, 1780–1850." *Historical Journal* 26, no. (1983): 95–119.

———. "Clubs, Societies and Associations." In *The Cambridge Social History of Britain, 1750–1950*. Vol. 3. *Social Agencies and Institutions*, edited by F. M. L. Thompson, 403–443. Cambridge: Cambridge University Press, 1990.

Morson, Gary Saul. "The Intelligentsia and Its Critics." In *A Companion to Russian History*, edited by Abbott Gleason, 261–278. Chichester, UK; Malden, MA: Wiley Blackwell, 2009.

Motley, Mark Edward. *Becoming a French Aristocrat: The Education of the Court Nobility, 1580–1715*. Princeton: Princeton University Press, 1990.

Murav'ev, M. N. "Pis'ma k Molodomu Cheloveku o Predmetakh Kasaiushchikhsia Istorii i Opisaniia Rossii." In idem, *Sochineniia v 2-kh tomakh* by idem. Vol. 1, 375–445. St. Petersburg: Izdanie Aleksandra Smirdina, 1847.

———. *Stikhotvoreniia*. Leningrad: Sovetskii pisatel,' 1967.

Murdin, Lesley. *Under Newton's Shadow: Astronomical Practices in the Seventeenth Century*. Bristol: Adam Hilger, 1985.

Nadler, V. K. *Imperator Alexander I i Ideia Sviashchennogo Soiuza*. Riga: N. Kimmel, 1886.

Nasonkina, L. I. "Bodianskii, Osip Maksimovich." In *Sovetskaia Istoricheskaia Entsiklopediia*, edited by E. M. Zhukov. Vol. 2, 515. Moscow: Sovetskaia entsiklopediia, 1962.

Nethercott, Frances. "Reevaluating Russian Historical Culture." *Kritika: Explorations in Russian and Eurasian History* 15, no. 2 (Spring 2014): 421–439.

Novick, Peter. *That Noble Dream: The "Objectivity Question" and the American Historical Profession*. Cambridge: Cambridge University Press, 1988.

Novikov, N. I. *Izbrannye sochineniia*. Moscow-Leningrad: Gosudarstvennoe izdatel'stvo khudozhestvennoi literatury, 1954.

Obolenskii, V. A. "Vospominaniia o Golodnom 1891 gode." *Sovremennye zapiski*, no. 7 (1921): 261–285.

Offord, Derek. *Journeys to a Graveyard: Perceptions of Europe in Classical Russian Travel Writing*. Dordrecht: Springer, 2005.

Ogilvie, Sheilagh . "'So That Every Subject Knows How to Behave': Social Disciplining in Early Modern Bohemia." *Comparative Studies in Society and History* 48, no. 1 (2006): 38–78.

Okenfuss, Max J. "Technical Training in Russia under Peter the Great." *History of Education Quarterly* 13, no. 4 (Winter 1973): 325–345.

Oldenburg, E. G. "Studencheskoe Nauchno-Literaturnoe Obshchestvo Pri S.-Peterburgskom Universitete." *Vestnik Leningradskogo Universiteta*, no. 2 (1947): 145–155.

Oreshkin, V. V. *Vol'noe Ekonomicheskoe Obshchestvo v Rossii (1765–1917)*. Moscow: Izdatel'stvo Akademii nauk SSSR, 1963.

Ostrovitianov, K. V., ed. *Istoriia Akademii Nauk SSSR*. Vol. 1. 1724–1803. Moscow-Leningrad: Izdatel'stvo Akademii Nauk SSSR, 1958.

Outram, Dorinda. *The Enlightenment*. Cambridge: Cambridge University Press, 1995.

Pamiatnaia knizhka Orlovskoi gubernii na 1897 g.: Izdanie Orlovskogo gubernskogo statisticheskogo komiteta. Orel: Tipografiia gubernskogo pravleniia, 1897.

Panaitescu, P. P. *Dimitrie Cantemir, His Life and Work*. Bucharest: Romanian Academy's Printing House, 1958.

Paneiakh, V. M. *Tvorchestvo i sud'ba istorika: Boris Aleksandrovich Romanov*. St. Petersburg: Dmitrii Bulanin, 2000.

Papmehl, K. A. "The Empress and 'Un Fanatique': A Review of the Circumstances Leading to the Governmental Action against Novikov in 1792." *Slavonic and East European Review* 68, no. 4 (1990): 665–691.

Parry, Albert. "Charles R. Crane, Friend of Russia." *Russian Review* 6, no. 2 (Spring 1947): 20–36.

Pashkurov, A. N., and O. V. Miasnikov. *M. N. Murav'ev: Voprosy poetiki, Mirovozzreniia i Tvorchestva*. Kazan': Kazanskii Gos. Universitet, 2004.

Pate, Alice K. "Workers and *Obshchestvnnost'*: St Petersburg, 1906–14." *Revolutionary Russia* 15, no. 2 (December 2002): 53–71.

Pekarskii, P. P. *Istoriia Imperatorskoi Akademii Nauk v Peterburge*. Vol. 1. St. Petersburg: Tipografiia Imperatorskoi Akademii Nauk, 1870.

Pertsov, P. P. "Graf A. A. Golenishchev-Kutuzov." In *Filosofskie Techeniia Russkoi Poezii* by idem, 365–378. St. Petersburg: Tip. M. Merkusheva, 1896.

Peshtich, S. L. *Russkaia Istoriografiia XVIII v.* Leningrad: Leningrad State University, 1965.

Péteri, György, ed. *Patronage, Personal Networks and the Party-State: Everyday Life in the Cultural Sphere in Communist Russia and East Central Europe*, special issue of *Contemporary European History* 11, no. 1 (February 2002).

Petrovich, Michael B. "V. I. Semevskii (1848–1916): Russian Social Historian." In *Essay in Russian and Soviet History: In Honor of Geroid Tanquary Robinson*, edited by John Shelton Curtiss, 63–84. New York: Columbia University Press, 1968.

Pinaeva, E. V. "Peterburgskii Period v Zhizni N. D. Chechulina (1881–1915): Biograficheskii Ocherk." In *Nikolai Dmitrievich Chechulin—Uchenyi, Kraeved, Bibliotekar': Materialy Nauchno-Prakticheskoi Konferentsii*, 22–31. Cherepovets: Tsentral'naia gorodskaia biblioteka im. V. V. Vereshchagina, 2002.

Pirumova, N. M. *Zemskoe Liberal'noe Dvizhenie: Sotsial'nye Korni i Evoliutsiia do Nachala XX Veka*. Moscow: Nauka, 1977.

———. "L. N. Tolstoy na Moskovskikh 'Besedakh' 90-kh godov," *Izvestiia AN SSSR, Seriia Literatury i Iazyka* 37, no. 4 (1978): 314–317.

Platonov, S. F. "Rets. na: Chechulin N. D., Goroda Moskovskogo gosudarstva v XVI Veke, St. Petersburg, 1889." *Zhurnal Ministerstva Narodnogo Prosveshcheniia*, no. 5 (1890): 140–154.

Plekhanov, G. V. *Istoriia Russkoi Obshchestvennoi Mysli*. Vol. 2. Moscow: Izdanie Tovarishchestva "Mir," 1925.

———. *History of Russian Social Thought*. New York: Howard Fertig, 1967.

Pogodin, S. N. *Russkaia Shkola Istorikov: N. I. Kareev, I. V. Luchitskii, M. M. Kovalevskii*. St. Petersburg: SPbGTU, 1997.

Pohoață, Gabriela. "Dimitrie Cantemir and G. W. Leibniz: Encyclopedists with European Vocation," *Cogito: Multidisciplinary Research Journal* II, no. 4 (December 2010). Accessed August 24, 2015. http://cogito.ucdc.ro/n4e/DIMITRIE -CANTEMIR-AND-GWLEIBNIZ-ENCYCLOPEDISTS-WITH-EUROPEAN -VOCATION.pdf.

Pokrovskii, V., ed. *Antiokh Dmitrievich Kantemir, Ego Zhizn' i Tvorchestvo: Sbornik Istoriko-Literaturnykh Statei*. Moscow: V. Spiridonov and A. Mikhailov, 1910.

Poliakova, U. M. "V. V. Krestinin i Obshchestvennaia Bor'ba v Arkhangel'skom Posade v 60-kh–90-kh gg. XVIII v." *Istoriia SSSR*, no. 2 (1958): 78–102.

Popov, N. A. *Tatishchev i ego vremia*. Moscow, 1861.

———. *Istoriia Imperatoskogo Moskovskogo Obshchestva Istorii i Drevnostei Rossiiskikh, Part I (1804–1812)*. Moscow: Imperatorskoe Obshchestvo Istorii i Drevnostei Rossiiskikh, 1884.

———. *Uchenye i Literaturnye Trudy V. N. Tatishcheva*. St. Petersburg, 1886.

Porciani, Ilaria and Tollebeek, Jo, eds. *Setting the Standards: Institutions, Networks, and Communities of National Historiography*. Basingstoke, UK: Palgrave Macmillan, 2012.

Pratt, Joan Klobe. "The Free Economic Society and the Battle Against Smallpox: A 'Public Sphere' in Action." *Russian Review* 61, no. 4 (October 2002): 560–578.

Preobrazhenskii, A. A. *Istorik ob Istorikah Rossii XX Stoletiia*. Moscow: Russkoe slovo, 2000.

Prescott, James Arthur. "The Russian Free Economic Society: Foundation Years," *Agricultural History* 51, no. 3 (July 1977): 503–512.

Presniakov, A. E. "Reforma Arkhivnogo Dela," *Russkii Istoricheskii Zhurnal*, no. 5 (1918): 205–222.

Priima, F. Ia. "Antiokh Dmitrievich Kantemir: Vstupitel'naia Stat'ia." Intorduction to *Sobranie Stikhotvorenii* by Antiokh Kantemir, 5–56. Leningrad: Sovetskii pisatel,' 1956.

———. "Timkovskii kak Issledovatel' 'Slova o Polku Igoreve.'" In *Trudy Otdela Drevne-Russkoi Literatury, Akademiia Nauk SSSR, Institut Russkoi literatury (Pushkinskii Dom)*. Vol. 14, edited by V. I. Malyshev, 89–95. Moscow-Leningrad: Izdatel'stvo Akademii Nauk SSSR, 1958.

Prokopovich, Feofan. *Sochineniia*. Moscow-Leningrad: Izdatel'stvo Akademii Nauk SSSR, 1961.

Radovskii, M. I. *Kantemir i Peterburgskaia Akademiia Nauk*. Moscow-Leningrad: Izdatel'stvo AN SSSR, 1959.

Raeff, Marc. *Origins of the Russian Intelligentsia: The Eighteenth-Century Nobility*. New York: Harcourt, Brace & World, 1966.

———. *Plans for Political Reform in Imperial Russia, 1730–1905*. Englewood Cliffs, New Jersey: Prentice-Hall, 1966.

———. "The Enlightenment in Russia and Russian Thought in the Enlightenment." In *The Eighteenth Century in Russia*, edited by J. G. Garrard, 25–47. Oxford: Clarendon, 1973.

———. "The Well-Ordered Police State and the Development of Modernity in Seventeenth- and Eighteenth-Century Europe: An Attempt at a Comparative Approach." *American Historical Review* 80, no. 5 (December 1975): 1221–1243.

———. *The Well-Ordered Police State: Social and Institutional Change through Law in the Germanies and Russia, 1600–1800.* New Haven: Yale University Press, 1983.

———. *Understanding Imperial Russia.* New York: Columbia University Press, 1984.

———. "At the Origins of a Russian National Consciousness: Eighteenth Century Roots and Napoleonic Wars." *The History Teacher* 25, 1 (1991): 7–18.

———. "Transfiguration and Modernization: The Paradoxes of Social Disciplining, Pedagogical Leadership, and the Enlightenment in Eighteenth-Century Russia." In *Political Ideas and Institutions in Imperial Russia* by idem, 334–347. Boulder: Westview, 1994.

Raikov, B. E. *Ocherki Istorii Geliotsentricheskogo Mirovozzreniia v Rossii.* Moscow and Leningrad: Izdatel'stvo Akademii Nauk SSSR, 1947.

Ramati, Ayval. "Harmony at a Distance: Leibniz's Scientific Academies." *Isis* 87, no. 3 (September 1996): 430–452.

Ransel, David L. "Character and Style of Patron-Client Relations in Russia." In *Klientelsysteme im Europa der Frühen Neuzeit*, edited by Antoni Maczak and Elisabeth Mueller-Leuckner, 214–224. Munich: R. Oldenbourg Verlag, 1988.

———. "The Government Crisis of 1730." In *Reform in Russia and U.S.S.R.: Past and Prospects*, edited by Robert O. Crummey, 45–71. Urbana: University of Illinois Press, 1989.

Repina, L. P., ed. *Soobshchestvo Istorikov Vysshei Shkoly Rossii: Nauchnaia Praktika i Obrazovatel'naia Missiia.* Moscow: IVI RAN, 2009.

———. ed. *Istoricheskaia Nauka i Obrazovanie v Rossii i na Zapade: Sud'by Istorikov i Nauchnykh Shkol.* Moscow: IVI RAN, 2012.

Repnikov, A. V. "Lev Tikhomirov—Ot Revoliutsii k Apokalipsisu." *Rossiia i Sovremennyi Mir*, 3 (1998): 189–198.

Repnikov, A. V., and O. A. Milevskii. *Dve zhizni L'va Tikhomirova.* Moscow: Academia, 2011.

Reutskaia, R. I., and V. G. Sidorov, eds., *Deiateli Knizhnoi Kul'tury Orlovskogo Kraia.* Orel: Izdatel'skii dom "Orlik," 2003.

Riazonovsky, Nicholas. *A Parting of Ways: Government and the Educated Public in Russia, 1801–1855.* Oxford: Oxford University Press, 1977.

Riber, Alfred J. "The Sedimentary Society." In *Between Tsar and People: Educated Society and the Quest for Public Identity*, edited by Edit W. Clowes, Samuel D. Kassow and James L. West, 343–366. Princeton: Princeton University Press, 1991.

Rice, James L. "The Bolotov Papers and Andrei Timofeevich Bolotov, Himself." *Russian Review* 35, no. 2 (April 1976): 125–144.

Richter, Eugene. *Pictures of the Socialistic Future (Freely Adapted from Bebel).* London, Swan Sonnenschhein & Co., 1907.

Richter, Melvin. "Reconstructing the History of Political Languages: Pocock, Skinner, and the *Geschichtliche Grundbegriffe.*" *History and Theory* 29, no. 1 (February 1990): 38–70.

Riha, Thomas, ed., *Readings in Russian Civilization.* Vol. 2, *Imperial Russia, 1700–1917,* 2nd rev. ed. Chicago: University of Chicago Press, 1969.

Robbins, Richard G. *Famine in Russia, 1891–1892: The Imperial Government Responds to a Crisis.* NY: Columbia University Press, 1975.

Rose, Arnold. *Theory and Method in the Social Sciences.* Minneapolis, University of Minnesota Press, 1954.

Rostovtsev, E. A. "N. I. Kareev i A. S. Lappo-Danilevskii: Iz Istorii Vzaimootnoshenii v Srede Peterburgskikh Uchenykh na Rubezhe XIX–XX vv." *Zhurnal Sotsiologii i Sotsial'noi Antropologii* 3, no. 4 (2000): 105–121.

———. *A. S. Lappo-Danilevskii i Peterburgskaia Istoricheskaia Shkola*. Riazan': NRIID, 2004.

Rozental', I. S. "*I Vot Obshchestvennoe Mnenie!*" *Kluby v Istorii Rossiiskoi Obshchestvennosti, Konets XVIII-Nachalo XX vv.* Moscow: Novyi khronograf, 2007.

Ruane, Christine, and Ben Eklof. "Cultural Pioneers and Professionals: The Teachers in Society." In *Between Tsar and People: Educated Society and the Quest for Public Identity*, edited by Edit W. Clowes, Samuel D. Kassow and James L. West, 199–211. Princeton: Princeton University Press, 1991.

Rubakin, A. N. *N. A. Rubakin: Lotsman Knizhnogo Moria*. Moscow: Molodaia gvardiia, 1967.

Rubinshtein, N. L. *Russkaia Istoriografiia*. Moscow: OGIZ Gospolitizdat, 1941.

Rudakov, V. "Krestinin Vasilii Vasil'evich (Po povodu stoletiia so dnia smerti)," *Zhurnal Ministerstva Narodnogo Prosveshcheniia* 299, no. 5 (May 1895): 219–225.

Rukovodstvo k Poznaniiu Drevnostei g. Al. Millenia, Izdannoe s Pribavleniiami i Zamechaniiami v Pol'zu Uchashchikhsia v Imp. Mosk. Un-te Nik. Koshanskim, Iziashchnykh Nauk Magistrom i Filosofii Doktorom. Moscow, 1807.

Rychkov, A. L., ed., *Utrennii svet Nikolaia Novikova*. Moscow: Tsentr knigi Rudomino, 2012.

Ryu, In-Ho L. "Moscow Freemasons and the Rosicrucian Order." In *The Eighteenth Century in Russia*, edited by J. G. Garrard, 198–232. Oxford: Clarendon, 1973.

Safronov, B. G. *N. I. Kareev o structure istoricheskogo znaniia*. Moscow: Izdatel'stvo moskovskogo universiteta, 1995.

Sagalakova, G. A. *Samosoznanie Soobshchestva Rossiiskikh Martinistov i Rozenkreitserov v Otechestvennoi Kul'ture Poslednei Chetverti XVIII veka*. PhD. diss., Altai State University, Barnaul, 2004.

Sakharov, A. N., ed., *Istoriki Rossii XVIII-nachalo XX veka*. Moscow: Institut istorii RAN/Skriptorii, 1996.

Samokvasov, D. Ia. *Arkhivnoe Delo v Rossii*. Moscow: Tovarishchestvo tip. A. I. Mamontova, 1902.

Sanders, Thomas. "The Third Opponent: Dissertation Defense and the Public Profile of Academic History in Late Imperial Russia." In *Historiography of Imperial Russia: The Profession and Writing of History in a Multinational State*, edited by idem, 69–97. Armonk, NY: M.E. Sharp, 1999.

———. "The Chechulin Affair or Politics and *nauka* in the History Profession of Late Imperial Russia." *Jahrbücher für Geschichte Osteuropas* 49, no. 1 (2001): 1–23.

Sapchenko, L. A. ed. *Karamzin: Pro et Contra*. St. Petersburg: RKhGA, 2006.

Sapogov, A. I. "Khrushchov Ivan Petrovich." In *Tambovskaia Entsiklopediia*, edited by L. G. Protasov, 650. Tambov: Iulis, 2004.

Schimmelpenninck van der Oye, David. *Toward the Rising Sun: Russian Ideologies of Empire and the Path to War with Japan*. Dekalb: Northern Illinois University Press, 2001.

Schumacher, Ryan. "The Wisconsin Magazine of History: A Case Study in Scholarly and Popular Approaches to American State Historical Society Publishing, 1917–2000." *Journal of Scholarly Publishing* 44, no. 2 (2013): 114–141.

Sdvizhkov, D. A. "Ot Obshchestva k Intelligentsii: Istoriia Poniatii kak Istoriia Samosoznaniia." In *Poniatiia o Rossii: k Istoricheskoi Semantike Imperskogo Perioda*, edited by Aleksei Miller, idem and Ingrid Shirle. Vol. 1, 382–427. Moscow: Novoe literaturnoe obozrenie, 2012.

Seeley, John Robert. *Life and Times of Stein, Or Germany and Prussia in the Napoleonic Age*. London: Cambridge University Press, 1879.

Senn, Alfred Erich. *Nicholas Rubakin: A Life for Books*. Newtonville, MA: Oriental Research Partners, 1977.

Serman, I. Z. "Prosvetitel'stvo i Russkaia Literatura Pervoi Poloviny XVIII veka." In *Problema Russkogo Prosveshcheniia v Literature XVIII veka*, edited by P. N. Berkov, 28–44. Moscow: Akademiia Nauk, 1961.

Serykh, A. A. *Pokolencheskaia Identichnost' Istorikov Rossii v Kontse XIX-Nachale XX vv.* PhD diss., Omsk State Pedagogical University, 2010.

Shakhanov, A. N. *Russkaia istoricheskaia nauka vtoroi poloviny XIX- nachala XX veka: Moskovskii i Peterburgskii Universitety*. Moscow: Nauka, 2003.

Shapin, Steven. "The House of Experiment in Seventeenth-Century England." *Isis* 79, no. 3, A Special Issue on *Artifact and Experiment* (September 1988): 373–404.

Shchapov, A. P. *Sochineniia*. Vols. 1–3. St. Petersburg: Izdatel'stvo M. V. Pirozhkova, 1906–1908.

Shelokhaev, V. V. "Dmitrii Ivanovich Shakhovskoi." *Otechestvennaia istoriia*, no. 5 (2001): 107–120.

Shevtsov, V. V. "Sergei Spiridonovich Tatishchev: Istorik i Diplomat Na Strazhe Ofitsial'noi Pechati, Ili Kak Tsarskoe Pravitel'stvo Proigralo Informatsionnuiu Voinu." In *Chelovek-Tekst-Epokha: Sbornik Nauchnykh Statei i Materialov*, vyp. 2: *Sovremennye Problemy Istochnikovedeniia*, edited by V. P. Zinov'ev and E. E. Dutchak, 302–313. Tomsk: Izdatel'stvo Tomskogo Universiteta, 2006.

Shevyrev, S. P. *Istoriia Imperatorskogo Moskovskogo Universiteta, Napisannaia K Stoletnemu Ego Iubileiu*. Moscow: Izdatel'stvo MGU, 1998.

Shmidt, S. O. "Sergei Fedorovich Platonov." In *Portrety Istorikov: Vremia i Sud'by*. Vol. 1. *Otechestvennaia Istoriia*, edited by G. N. Sevast'ianova and L. T. Mil'skaia, 100–135. Moscow-Jerusalem: Universitetskaia kniga/Gesharim, 2000.

Shokhin, L. I. "Neopublikovannaia Rabota S. D. Sheremeteva o Smutnom Vremeni: Lev Sapega i Fedor Sheremetev." In *Arkheograficheskii Ezhegodnik za 1994*, edited by S. O. Shmidt, 185–191. Moscow: Nauka, 1996.

———. "S. D. Sheremetev-istorik v Svoikh Dnevnikovykh Zapisiakh." In *Arkheograficheskii Ezhegodnik za 1994*, edited by S. O. Shmidt, 191–222. Moscow: Nauka, 1996.

Shtorm, G. P. "Novoe o Pushkine i Karamzine." *Izvestiia AN SSSR, Otdel Literatury i Iazyka* 19, no. 2 (1960): 144–150.

Shvarts, I. G. *Lektsii*. Donetsk: Izdatel'stvo "Veber," Donetskoe otdelenie, 2008.

Sills, David L. "Voluntary Associations: Sociological Aspects." In *International Encyclopedia of the Social Sciences*, edited by David L. Sills and Robert K. Merton. Vol. 16, 363–379. New York, Macmillan and Free Press, 1968.

Simmel, Georg. "The Sociology of Sociability." *American Journal of Sociology* 55, no. 3 (November 1949): 254–261.

Simms, James Y. "The Crop Failure of 1891: Soil Exhaustion, Technological Backwardness, and Russia's 'Agrarian Crisis.'" *Slavic Review* 41, no. 2 (Summer 1982): 236–250.

Sinenko, A. A. "Mezhpokolencheskie Kommunikatsii i Formirovanie Obraza Uchitelia Russkimi Istorikami Kontsa XIX v." In *Mir Istorika: Istoriographicheskii Sbornik*. Vol. 5, edited by V. P. Korzun and A. V. Iakub, 140–151. Omsk: OmGU, 2009.

Skvortsova, L. A. "Mir Bozhii." In *Literaturnyi Protsess i Russkaia Zhurnalistika Kontsa XIX - Nachala XX Veka*, edited by B. A. Bialik, 136–197. Moscow: Nauka, 1981.

Slanevskii, V. U. "K Istorii Tverskoi Uchitel'skoi Shkoly P. P. Maksimovicha." *Sovetskaia pedagogika*, no. 4–5 (1946): 75–83.

———. "Fedor Fedorovich Oldenburg." In *Rossiiskaia Pedagogicheskaia Entsiklopediia v 2-kh Tomakh*, edited by V. V. Davydov. Vol. 2, 83. Moscow: Bol'shaia Rossiiskaia Entsiklopediia, 1999.

Slonimskii, A. G. "Semevskii, Vasilii Ivanovich." In *Sovetskaia Istoricheskaia Entsiklopediia*, edited by E. M. Zhukov. Vol. 12, 726–727. Moscow: Sovetskaia Entsiklopediia, 1969.

Slovar' Akademii Rossiiskoi. St. Petersburg, pri Imperatorskoi Akademii Nauk, 1793.

Smirnov, Ia. E. "S. F. Platonov i Iaroslavskoe Kraevedenie." In *Arkheograficheskii Ezhegodnik za 2009–2010 gg.*, edited by S. O. Shmidt, 227–286. Moscow: Nauka, 2012.

Smith, Constance and Freedman, Anne. *Voluntary Associations: Perspective on the Literature*. Cambridge, MA: Harvard University Press, 1972.

Smith, Alison K. *For the Common Good and Their Own Well-Being: Social Estates in Imperial Russia*. Oxford : Oxford University Press, 2014.

Smith, Douglas. "Freemasonry and the Public in Eighteenth-Century Russia." In *Imperial Russia: New Histories for the Empire*, edited by Jane Burbank and David L. Ransel, 281–304. Bloomington: Indiana University Press, 1998.

———. *Former People: The Final Days of the Russian Aristocracy*. Farrar, Straus and Giroux, 2012.

———. *Working the Rough Stone: Freemasonry and Society in Eighteenth-Century Russia*. DeKalb: Northern Illinois University Press, 1999.

Solov'ev, K. A. *Kruzhok "Beseda": v Poiskakh Novoi Politicheskoi Real'nosti 1899–1905*. Moscow: ROSSPEN, 2009.

Solov'ev, S. M. *Istoriia Rossii s Drevneishikh Vremen*. Book 10. Vol. 20. Moscow: Izdatel'stvo sotsial'no-ekonomicheskoi literatury, 1963.

Steeves, H. R. *Learned Societies and English Literary Scholarship in Great Britain and the United States*. New York: Columbia University Press, 1913.

Stepanskii, A. D. "K Istorii Nauchno-Istoricheskikh Obshchestv v Dorevoliutsionnoi Rossii." In *Arkheographicheskii Ezhegodnik za 1974 g.*, edited by S. O. Shmidt, 38–55. Moscow: Nauka, 1975.

———. *Obshchestvennye Organizatsii v Rossii na Rubezhe XIX–XX vv.* Moskovskii gosudarstvennyi istoriko-arkhivnyi institut, 1982.

Stockdale, Melissa Kirshke. *Pavel Miliukov and the Quest for Liberal Russia, 1880–1918*. Ithaca: Cornell University Press, 1996.

Stogov, D. I. *Pravomonarkhicheskie Salony Peterburga-Petrograda (Konets XIX- Nachalo XX Veka)*. St. Petersburg: Dmitrii Bulanin, 2007.

Strakhov, P. I. *Kratkaia Istoriia Akademicheskoi Gimnazii Byvshei pri Imperatorskom Moskovskom Universitete*. Moscow: Izdatel'stvo Moskovskogo Universiteta, 2000.

Stuart, Mary. "'The Ennobling Illusion': The Public Library Movement in Late Imperial Russia." *Slavonic and East European Review* 76, no. 3 (July 1998): 401–440.

Sukhomlinov, M. I. *Istoriia Rossiiskoi Akademii*. St. Petersburg: Tipografiia Imperatorskoi Akademii Nauk, 1874.

Sushkov, N. V. *Moskovskii Universitetskii Blagorodnyi Pansion i Vospitanniki Moskovskogo Universiteta, Gimnazii Ego, Universitetskogo Blagorodnogo Pansiona i Druzheskogo Obshchestva*. Moscow: Universitetskaia tipografiia, 1858.

Sutton, Geoffrey V. *Science for a Polite Society: Gender, Culture, and the Demonstration of Enlightenment*. Boulder: Westview, 1995.

Sverdlov, M. B. *Vasilii Nikitich Tatishchev—Avtor i Redaktor "Istorii Rossiiskoi."* St. Petersburg: Evropeiskii dom, 2009.

Sveshnikov, A. V. "'Vot Vam Istoriia Nashei Istorii': k Probleme Tipologii Nauchnykh Skandalov Vtoroi Poloviny XIX-Nachala XX Veka." In *Mir Istorika: Istoriograficheskii Sbornik*. Vol. 1, edited by V. P. Korzun and G. K. Sadretdinova, 231–262. Omsk: Izd-vo OmGU, 2005.

———. "Kak Possorilsia Lev Platonovich s Ivanom Mikhailovichem: Istoriia Odnogo Professorskogo Konflikta." *Novoe Literaturnoe Obozrenie* no. 96 (2009): 42–72.

———. *Peterburgskaia Shkola Medievistov Nachala XX Veka: Popytka Antropologicheskogo Analiza Nauchnogo Soobshchestva*. Omsk: Omskii gosudarstvennyi universitet, 2010.

Tatishchev, S. S. *Pamiati Imperatora Aleksandra III*. St. Petersburg, Tip. Tovarishchestva Obshchestvennaia pol'za, 1894.

———. *Imperator Aleksandr II, Ego Zhizn' i Tsarstvovanie*. Vols. 1–2. St. Petersburg, A.S. Suvorin, 1903.

Tatishchev, V. N. "Proizvol'noe i Soglasnoe Rassuzhdenie i Mnenie Sobravshegosia Shliakhetstva Russkogo o Pravlenii Gosudarstva." In *Utro: Literaturnyi sbornik*, edited by M. P. Pogodin, 359–369. Moscow, 1859.

Terrall, Marry. "The Culture of Science in Frederick the Great's Berlin." *History of Sciences* 28, no. 4 (December 1990): 333–365.

Thaden, Edward C. "Tatishchev, German Historians, and the Academy of Sciences." In *Interpreting History: Collective Essays on Russia's Relations with Europe* by idem, with the collaboration of Marianna Forster Thaden, 21–52. Boulder: Social Science Monographs/New York: Columbia University Press, 1990.

———. *The Rise of Historicism in Russia*. New York: Peter Lang, 1999.

Tikhomirova, E. M. "Obrazovannoe serdtse: kniaginia Aleksandra Alekseevna Obolenskaia." In *Rossiiskie Zhenshchiny i Evropeiskaia Kul'tura: Materialy Konferentsii, Posviashchennoi Teorii i Istorii Zhenskogo Dvizheniia*, edited by G. A. Tishkin, 127–131. St. Petersburg: St. Peterburgskoe Filosofskoe Obshchestvo, 2001.

Timofeev, N. V. *Izdaniia Grafa S. D. Sheremeteva*. St. Petersburg: Tipografiia M. N. Aleksandrova, 1913.

Tiurikov, A. D. "Podvizhnik Russkoi Kul'tury: I. G. Shvarts—Filosof, Pedagog, Obshchestvennyi Deiatel' XVIII Veka." In *Lektsii* by I. G. Shvarts, 112–170. Donetsk: Izdatel'stvo "Veber," Donetskoe otdelenie, 2008.

Tikhomirov M. N. "Russkaia Istoriografiia XVIII Veka: v Poriadke Obsuzhdeniia." *Voprosy istorii*, no. 2 (1948): 95–97.

———. 1955. *Ocherki Istorii Istoricheskoi Nauki v SSSR*. Vol. 1. Moscow: AN SSSR Institut Istorii, 1955.

Tikhonravov, N. S. *Sochineniia*. Vol. 3. *Russkaia Literatura XVIII i XIX Vekov*. Moscow: Izdanie M. and S. Sabashnikovykh, 1898.

Tikhonov, V. V. *Moskovskaia Istoricheskaia Shkola v Pervoi Polovine Dvadtsatogo Veka: Nauchnoe Tvorchestvo Iu. V. Got'e, S. B. Veselovskogo, A. I. Iakovleva, S. V. Bakhrushina.* Moscow-St. Petersburg: Nestor-Istoriia, 2012.

Todd III, William Mills. *Fiction and Society in the Age of Pushkin.* Cambridge, MA: Harvard University Press, 1986.

Tolochko, Aleksei. *"Istoriia Rossiiskaia" Vasiliia Tatishcheva: Istochniki i Izvestiia.* Moscow: Novoe literaturnoe obozrenie; Kiev: Kritika, 2005.

Tolz, Vera. "European, National and (Anti-) Imperial: The Formation of Academic Oriental Studies in Late Tsarist and Early Soviet Russia." *Kritika: Explorations in Russian and Eurasian History* 9, no. 1 (Winter 2008): 53–81.

———. *"Sobstvennyi Vostok Rossii": Politika Identichnosti i Vostokovedenie v Posdneimperskii i Rannesovetskii Period.* Moscow: Novoe literaturnoe obozrenie, 2013.

Townsend, Robert B. *History's Babel: Scholarship, Professionalization, and the Historical Enterprise in the United States, 1880–1940.* Chicago: University of Chicago Press, 2013.

Trakhtenberg, L. A. "Sumasbrodneishii, Vseshuteishii i Vsep'ianeishii sobor." In *Odissei: Chelovek v Istorii. Vremia i Prostranstvo Prazdnika,* edited by A. Ia. Gurevich, 89–118. Moscow: Nauka, 2005.

Trentmann, Frank, ed. *Paradoxes of Civil Society: New Perspectives on Modern German and British History.* New York: Berghahn, 2000.

Troitskii, N. A. *Russkoe Revoliutsionnoe Narodnichestvo 1870-kh Godov: Istoriia Temy.* Saratov: Izdatel'stvo Saratovskogo universiteta, 2003.

Trokhina, O. M. "Iz Istorii Narodnogo Obrazovaniia v Orlovskoi Gubernii." *Obrazovanie i Obshchestvo,* no. 1 (1999). Accessed August 10, 2015. http://www.jeducation.ru/1_1999/44.html.

Trubetskoi, S. N. *Sobranie Sochinenii.* Vol. 1. *Publitsisticheskie Stat'i, Napechatannye s 1896 g. po 1905 g. Vkliuchitel'no.* Moscow: Tipografiia G. Lissnera i D. Sobko, 1907.

Tsvirkun, Viktor. "Nauchnye Sviazi Antiokha Kantemira s Sankt-Peterburgskoi Akademiei Nauk." *Rossiiskaia Istoriia,* no. 2 (March-April 2013): 97–101.

Tsygankov, D. A. "Issledovatel'skie Traditsii Moskovskoi i Peterburgskoi Shkol Istorikov." In *Istoriia Mysli: Russkaia Myslitel'naia Traditsiia,* edited by I. P. Smirnov, 66–77. Moscow: Vuzovskaia kniga, 2005.

———. *Professor V. I. Ger'e i Ego Ucheniki.* Moscow: ROSSPEN, 2010.

Tsyganov, A. V. "Rossiiskii Tsenzor Nikitenko: po Materialam Dnevnika." *Molodoi Uchenyi* 2, no. 4 (2011): 51–54.

Tukalevskii, V. N. "N. I. Novikov i I. G. Schwarz." *Istoriia Masonstva: Velikie Tseli, Misticheskie Iskaniia, Tainstva Obriadov,* edited by M. Ianovskaia, 254–318. Moscow: EKSMO-Press, 2002.

Tumanova, A. S. *Obshchestvennye Organizatsii g. Tambova na Rubezhe XIX–XX Vekov (1900–1917 gg.).* Tambov: Tambovskii gosudarstvennyi universitet imeni G. R. Derzhavina, 1999.

———. *Samoderzhavie i Obshchestvennye Organizatsii v Rossii: 1905–1917.* Tambov: Tambovskii gosudarstvennyi universitet imeni G. R. Derzhavina, 2002.

Tumanova, A. S., ed. *Samoorganizatsiia Rossiiskoi Obshchestvennosti v Poslednei Treti XVIII- Nachale XX vv.* Moscow: ROSSPEN, 2011.

Usova, S. E. *N. I. Novikov, Ego Zhizn' i Obshchestvennaia Deiatel'nost'*. St. Petersburg: Tipografiia tovarishchestva Obshchestvennaia pol'za, 1892.

Uspenskii, B. A. *Tsar' i Imperator: Pomazanie na Tsarstvo i Semantika Monarshikh Titulov*. Moscow: Iazyki russkoi kul'tury, 2000.

Vakhterov, V. P. *Vneshkol'noe Obrazovanie Naroda*. Moscow: Tipografiia tovarishchestva Sytina, 1896.

Vakhtina, P. L., and Ostroi, O. S. "Nikolai Dmitrievich Chechulin i Ego Kniga." In *Russkaia Provintsiia vo Vtoroi Polovine XVIII Veka* by N. D. Chechulin, 5–20. St. Petersburg: Rossiiskaia natsional'naia biblioteka, 2010.

Valk, S. N. "Sud'by 'Arkheografii.'" In *Arkheograficheskii Ezhegodnik za 1961 God*, edited by M. N. Tikhomirov, 453–465. Moscow: Nauka, 1962.

———. "V. N. Tatishchev i Nachalo Novoi Russkoi Istoricheskoi Literatury." In *Rol' i Znachenie Literatury XVIII Veka v Istorii Russkoi Kul'tury: k 70-iu so Dnia Rozhdeniia P. N. Berkova*, edited by D. S. Likhachev, G. P. Makogonenko, and I. Z. Serman, 66–73. Moscow-Leningrad: Nauka, 1966.

Valkina, I. V. "K Voprosu Ob Istochnikakh Tatishcheva." In *Rol' i Znachenie Literatury XVIII Veka v Istorii Russkoi Kul'tury: k 70-iu so Dnia Rozhdeniia P. N. Berkova*, edited by D. S. Likhachev, G. P. Makogonenko, and I. Z. Serman, 74–85. Moscow-Leningrad: Nauka, 1966.

Van Horn Melton, James. "The Emergence of 'Society' in Eighteenth- and Nineteenth-Century Germany." In *Language, History and Class*, edited by Penelope J. Corfield, 132–149. Cambridge, MA: Basil Blackwell, 1991.

Vengerov, S. A. *Russkaia Poeziia*. Vol. 1. St. Petersburg, 1897.

Veselago, F. *Ocherk Istorii Morskogo Kadetskogo Korpusa s Prilozheniem Spiska Vospitannikov za 100 let*. St. Petersburg: Tipografiia Morskogo Kadetckogo Korpusa, 1852.

Viatkin, V. V. "Aleksei Ivanovich Musin-Pushkin." *Voprosy Istorii*, no. 9 (2013): 20–32.

Volkov, Vadim. "Obshchestvennost': Russia's Lost Concept of Civil Society." In *Civil Society in the Baltic Sea Region*, edited by Norbert Götz and Vörg Hackmann, 63–82. Aldershot: Ashgate, 2003.

Vorontsov-Vel'iaminov, B. A. *Ocherki Istorii Astronomii v Rossii*. Moscow: Fizmatgiz, 1956.

Voskresenskii, G. A. "Akademik A. F. Bychkov, Pochetnyi Chlen Moskovskoi Dukhovnoi Akademii." *Bogoslovskii Vestnik*, no. 5 (1899): 114–126.

Vucinich, Alexander. *Science in Russian Culture: A History to 1860*. Stanford: Stanford University Press, 1963.

Vysotskii, I. I. *Poeziia grafa A. A. Golenishcheva-Kutuzova*. Riga, Tip. A. Nitavskogo, 1913.

Wakefield, Andre. *The Disordered Police State: German Cameralism as Science and Practice*. University of Chicago Press, 2009.

Wartenweiler, David. *Civil Society and Academic Debate in Russia, 1905–1914*. Oxford: Clarendon, 1999.

Wirtschafter, Elise Kimerling. *Structures of Society: Imperial Russia's "People of Various Ranks."* Dekalb: Northern Illinois University Press, 1994.

———. *Social Identity in Imperial Russia*. Dekalb: Northern Illinois University Press, 1997.

———. "The Groups between: Raznochintsy, Intelligentsia, Professionals." In *The Cambridge History of Russia*. Vol. 2, *Imperial Russia, 1689–1917*, edited by Dominic Lieven, 245–263. Cambridge: Cambridge University Press, 2006.

———. "Social Categories in Russian Imperial History." *Cahiers du Monde russe* 50, no. 1 (2009): 231–250.

Walker, Barbara. "Kruzhok Culture: The Meaning of Patronage in the Early Soviet Literary World." *Contemporary European History* 11, no. 1 (2002): 107–123.

Wortman, Richard. *Scenarios of Power: Myth and Ceremony in Russian Monarchy from Peter the Great to the Abdication of Nicholas II*. Princeton: Princeton University Press, 2006.

Yates, Frances. *The French Academies of the Sixteenth Century*. London: Warburg Institute, 1947.

Zapadov, A. V. "Tvorchestvo Kheraskova." In *Izbrannye proizvedeniia* by M. M. Kheraskov, 5–56. Moscow-Leningrad: Biblioteka poeta, 1961.

———. *Poety XVIII veka: A. Kantemir, A. Sumarokov, V. Maikov, M. Kheraskov*. Moscow: Izdatel'stvo Moskovskogo universiteta, 1984.

Zapadov, V. A. "M. N. Murav'ev." In *Slovar' Russkikh Pisatelei XVIII veka*. Vol. 2, edited by A. M. Panchenko, 308–309. St. Petersburg: Nauka, 1999.

Zav'ialov, D. A. *Studencheskie Nauchnye Obshchestva Sankt-Peterburgskogo Universiteta v Kontse XIX-Nachale XX v.* PhD diss., St. Petersburg State University, 2006.

Zdravomyslov, K. Ia. *Svedeniia o Sushchestvuiushchikh v Eparkhiiakh Tserkovno-Arkheologicheskikh Uchrezhdeniiakh i Konsistorskikh Arkhivakh*. Petrograd, 1917.

Zitser, Ernest. *The Transfigured Kingdom: Sacred Parody and Charismatic Authority at the Court of Peter the Great*. Ithaca: Cornell University Press, 2004.

Zlatopol'skaia, A. A. "D. I. Shakhovskoi—Istorik Russkoi Filosofii i Obshchestvennoi Mysli." In *Filosofskii Vek: Almanakh*, no. 26, *Istoriia Idei v Rossii: Issledovaniia i Materialy*, edited by T. V. Artem'eva and T. V. Mikeshin, 111–117. St. Petersburg: Sankt-Peterburgskii Tsentr Istorii Idei, 2004.

Zolotarev, V. P. *Istoricheskaia Kontseptsiia N. I. Kareeva: Soderzhanie i Evoliutsiia*. Leningrad: Izdatel'stvo Leningradskogo Universiteta, 1988.

———. "Nikolai Ivanovich Kareev (1850–1931)." In *Portrety Istorikov: Vremia i Sud'by*. Vol. 2, *Vseobshchaia Istoriia*, edited by G. N. Sevast'ianova and L. T. Mil'skaiia, 276–293. Moscow-Jerusalem: Universitetskaia kniga/Gesharim, 2000.

Zonova, N. S. *Rossiiskie Istoriki na Mezhdunarodnykh Kongressakh Istoricheskikh Nauk Nachala XX Veka*. PhD diss., Nizhnii Novgorod State University for Architecture and Civil Engineering, 2004.

Zorin, Andrei. *Kormia Dvuglavogo Orla . . . : Literatura i Gosudarstvennaia Ideologiia v Rossii v Poslednei Treti XVIII-Pervoi Treti XIX Veka*. Moscow: Novoe literaturnoe obozrenie, 2004.

———. "The Perception of Emotional Coldness in Andrei Turgenev's Diaries." *Slavic Review* 68, no. 2 (Summer 2009): 238–258.

Zotov, V. P. "Liberal'nyi Tsenzor i Professor-Pessimist (Biograficheskii Ocherk)." *Istoricheskii Vestnik* 54, no. 10 (1893): 194–210.

Index

Page numbers in italics refer to illustrations

Friendly Learned Society (*Druzheskoe uchenoe obshchestvo*), 9, 53-63, 83; Typographical Company (*Tipograficheskaia kompaniia*) of, 59, 60. *See also* Novikov

Ger'e, Vladimir Ivanovich, 15n4 (Intr), 121, 124, 125, 127, 133-136, 150n204 (chap2), 151n214 (chap2), 152n236 (chap2), 175
Golenishchev-Kutuzov (Kutuzov), Arsenii Arkad'evich, 1, 183-188, 192-194, 196-199, 204, 209-210, 214, 215, 217-219, 243, 256n13 (chap4)
Golenishchev-Kutuzov, Pavel Ivanovich, 85-87, 140n32 (chap2)
Grevs, Ivan Mikhailovich, 120, 126, 130, 156-161, 166, 177n8 (chap3)
Gringmut, Vladimir Andreevich, 203, 206, 215, 216-218
Grot, Konstantin Iakovlevich, 230-232
Grot, Iakov Karlovich, 101, 235
gubernia scholarly archival commissions, 93-97, 97, 107, 175, 202, 222, 227, 269, 270-271, 272

historical assembly (*istoricheskoe sobranie*): of the Academy of Sciences, 34-35; of Catherine II, 42-43, 263
historical societies, 2, 3, 7, 11-13, 80, 90, 99, 124, 136-138, 175-176, 182-183, 197, 201-202, 206, 225, 249n56 (chap4), 256n194 (chap4), 262-264, 268-271, 273; local American, 265-268, 287; local Russian, 90-91, 93. *See also* American Historical Association; Free Historical Assembly for the City of Arkhangel'sk's Antiquities (*Vol'noe istoricheskoe dlia arkhangelogorodskikh drevnostei sobranie*); Historical Society at Moscow University; Historical Society at St. Petersburg University; Historical Society of Nestor the Chronicler (*Istoricheskoe Obshchestvo Nestora-Letopitsa*); Russian Historical Society (*Russkoe Istoricheskoe Obshchestvo* [RIO]); Society for Russian History and Antiquities (*Obshchestvo Istorii i Drevnostei Rossiiskikh* [OIDR]); Society of Zealots of History (*Obshchestvo Revnitelei Istorii*); Society of Zealots of Russian Historical Education in Memory of Alexander III (*Obshchestvo Revnitelei Russkogo Istoricheskogo Prosveshcheniia v Pamiat' Imperatora Aleksandra III*)
Historical Society at Moscow University, 133-137
Historical Society at St. Petersburg University, 124-132; 137

Historical Society of Nestor the Chronicler (*Istoricheskoe Obshchestvo Nestora-Letopitsa*), 93, 228
history: as a discipline, 2, 30, 33-35, 42, 54, 60-63, 70n82 (chap1), 81, 84, 87, 91-93, 95-96, 110, 123-128, 137, 151n231 (chap2), 229, 233, 239, 263, 265-266, 270, 271; as a profession, 13, 14n4 (int), 104-105, 107, 126, 131-132, 137-138, 162, 175, 202, 236, 264-268, 275n18 (con); politicization of, 96, 98, 103, 131-132, 176, 182, 189, 192, 243, 245; popularization of, 224-232, 256n194 (chap4), 264, 270; textbook on, 239-241

Ianzhul, Ivan Ivanovich, 165-166
Ilovaiskii, Dmitrii Ivanovich, 162, 163, 164, 178n41 (chap3), 200, 203, 228
Ikonnikov, Vladimir Stepanovich, 92, 96, 98, 103, 105, 269
Imperial Archeographic Commission, 92, 99
Imperial Public Library, 99, 201, 208, 270
intelligentsia, 6, 10, 12, 19n25 (int), 62, 95, 122-123, 154, 160-161, 164, 171, 174-176, 191-193, 273
Iuzefovich, Boris Mikhailovich, 203, 217-218, 240

Kachenovskii, Mikhail Trofimovich, 84, 86
Kalmykova, Alexandra Mikhailovna, 158
Kantemir, Antioch Dmitrievich, 26-28, 30, 31
Kantemir, Dmitrii Konstantinovich, 31, 69n65 (chap1)
Karamzin, Nikolai Mikhailovich, 8-9, 56, 59, 62, 83, 99, 140n32 (chap2), 162, 221
Kareev, Nikolai Ivanovich, 124-132, 135, 137, 160, 161, 165, 166, 169, 266
Kheraskov, Mikhail Matveevich, 46-48, 51, 55, 57, 58, 81
Khrushchov, Ivan Petrovich, 93, 200, 207, 208, 212, 227-230, 241
Kizevetter, Alexander Alexandrovich, 121, 132-133, 134-135, 154, 159, 164, 166-170, 174, 175, 176, 186, 188, 214, 229, 269
Kliuchevskii, Vasilii Osipovich, 41, 42, 62, 90, 109, 117, 121, 125, 132, 134, 162, 172, 173, 197-198, 226, 228, 269, 270
Krestinin, Vasilii Vasil'evich, 35, 39

Lappo-Danilevskii, Alexander Sergeevich, 89, 108, 114-115, 124, 126-132, 137, 156, 160, 271-272
Leibniz, Gottfried Wilhelm, 28-29
Liaskovskii, Valerii Nikolaevich, 220, 226, 234, 238
Likhachev, Nikolai Petrovich, 240-241, 270

VERA KAPLAN is Senior Lecturer at the Department of History and director of the Cummings Center for Russian and East European Studies, Tel Aviv University. Her research interests lie in the areas of cultural and social history and history of education in Russia, focusing especially on the history of voluntary associations, which she argues constituted the "building blocks" of modern Russian society. Her new research project, tentatively titled "Weathering the Revolution," seeks to explore the life of the professional community of Russian historians across 1917.

CPSIA information can be obtained
at www.ICGtesting.com
Printed in the USA
BVOW06*1256220217

476891BV00007B/41/P